Handbook of Research Methods in
Human Memory and Cognition

This is a volume in

ACADEMIC PRESS
SERIES IN COGNITION AND PERCEPTION

A Series of Monographs and Treatises

A complete list of titles in this series appears at the end of this volume.

Handbook of Research Methods in Human Memory and Cognition

Edited by

C. Richard Puff

Department of Psychology
Whitely Psychology Laboratories
Franklin and Marshall College
Lancaster, Pennsylvania

1982

ACADEMIC PRESS

A Subsidiary of Harcourt Brace Jovanovich, Publishers
New York   London
Paris   San Diego   San Francisco   São Paulo   Sydney   Tokyo   Toronto

ACADEMIC PRESS, INC.
111 Fifth Avenue, New York, New York 10003

United Kingdom Edition published by
ACADEMIC PRESS, INC. (LONDON) LTD.
24/28 Oval Road, London NW1 7DX

Library of Congress Cataloging in Publication Data
Main entry under title:

Handbook of research methods in human memory and
cognition.

   (Academic Press series in cognition and perception)
   Includes index.
   1. Memory--Research--Methodology. 2. Cognition--
Research--Methodology. I. Puff, C. Richard. II. Series.
[DNLM: 1. Cognition. 2. Memory. 3. Psychology,
Experimental--Methods. BF 371 H236]
BF371.H36   153'.072   81-17661
ISBN 0-12-566760-4   AACR2

PRINTED IN THE UNITED STATES OF AMERICA

82 83 84 85   9 8 7 6 5 4 3 2 1

Contents

LIST OF CONTRIBUTORS xi

PREFACE xiii

1 Recognition Memory

BENNET B. MURDOCK, JR.

Definitions	2
Accuracy	6
Latency	14
Covariation of Accuracy and Latency	18
Guidelines	20
Notes on the Guidelines	21
Reference Notes	24
References	24

2 Visual Search

PATRICK RABBITT

Relationship of Visual Search Tasks to Categorization Tasks	28
What Constitutes a "Class" or "Category" of Visual Stimuli?	35

Positional Effects and Order of Scanning of Items on Displays   47
Temporal and Spatial Sequential Effects in Visual Search   52
Redundancy in the Structure of Displays: The Word-Superiority Effect 55
Active Control of Visual Search   56
Practice Effects in Visual Search   58
Conclusions   58
Reference Notes   59
References   59

3 Short-Term Memory

MURRAY GLANZER

Introduction   63
Recall Paradigms   64
Recognition Paradigms   77
Rehearsal and Repetition   80
Modality Effects   85
Preload and Concurrent Task Load   87
Measures of the Amount Held in Short-Term Storage   89
Concluding Remarks   92
Reference Note   93
References   93

4 Free Recall: Basic Methodology and Analyses

MARTIN D. MURPHY AND C. RICHARD PUFF

Introduction   99
Manipulation and Control of Task Parameters   101
Scoring and Measures   112
Some Variations   123
Reference Notes   125
References   125

5 The Analysis of Organization and Structure in Free Recall

JAMES W. PELLEGRINO AND LAWRENCE J. HUBERT

Introduction   129
Analysis of Single-Item Information   133
Analysis of Item-Pair Information   144
Analysis of Item-Group Information   159
Comparison of Alternative Hypotheses   161

Exploratory Analysis   163
Generalization and Extension of Analytic Procedures   166
Reference Notes   169
References   170

6 Cued Recall

MICHAEL J. WATKINS AND JOHN M. GARDINER

Introduction   173
Reference Experiments   174
Experimental Parameters   179
Measurement of Performance   184
Relation to Other Paradigms   191
References   194

7 Incidental Learning and Orienting Tasks

MICHAEL W. EYSENCK

Introduction   197
Incidental versus Intentional Learning   198
Orienting Tasks and Processing Activities   206
Conclusions   223
References   225

8 Cognitive Strategies

ROBERT V. KAIL, JR. AND JEFFREY BISANZ

Introduction   229
Methods from the Memory Literature   231
Methods from the Problem-Solving and Reasoning Literature   237
Concluding Remarks   251
Reference Note   253
References   253

9 Picture Memory Methodology

GEOFFREY R. LOFTUS

Current Theoretical Issues   258
Experimental Paradigms   260

Stimulus Presentation 261
The Choice of a Test 270
Counterbalancing Measures 274
An Example: Yes-No Counterbalancing 274
Eye-Movement Methodologies 275
A Complete Experiment 280
Reference Note 283
References 283

10 Semantic and Lexical Decisions

EDWARD SHOBEN

Basic Empirical Findings 288
Materials 291
Data Collection 300
Data Analysis 302
Statistics 305
Experimental Logics 306
Concluding Remarks 310
Reference Notes 311
References 311

11 Imagery

STEPHEN M. KOSSLYN AND KEITH J. HOLYOAK

Introduction 315
Specific Paradigms 319
Conclusions 342
Reference Note 343
References 343

12 Prose Comprehension and Memory

JAMES VOSS, SHERMAN W. TYLER, AND GAY L. BISANZ

Introduction 349
Methods Related to the Study of Text Structure 351
Methods Related to Variables Studied in the Task Situation 363
Methods Focused on the Higher-Level Knowledge Structures 367
Summary and Evaluation: Methods and Measures 371
Concluding Comments 382
Reference Notes 383
References 383

13 The Activation and Utilization of Knowledge

JEFFERY J. FRANKS, JOHN D. BRANSFORD, AND PAMELA M. AUBLE

Prerequisites to Comprehension 396
Studies of Elaboration 407
Effects of Context on Significance 410
Reorganization and Changes in Significance 415
Summary and Conclusions 423
References 424

14 Long-Term Ecological Memory

HARRY P. BAHRICK AND DEMETRIOS KARIS

Historical Aspects 427
Major Parameters of Ecological Memory Content 428
Criteria for the Evaluation of Ecological Methods 430
Methods of Investigating Shared-Semantic Memory 431
Methods of Investigating Individual-Semantic Memories 445
Methods of Investigating Shared-Episodic Memory 446
Methods of Investigating Individual-Episodic Memories 449
Concluding Comments 460
Reference Notes 462
References 462

SUBJECT INDEX 467

List of Contributors

Numbers in parentheses indicate the pages on which the authors' contributions begin.

PAMELA M. AUBLE (395), Department of Psychology, Vanderbilt University, Nashville, Tennessee 37240

HARRY P. BAHRICK (427), Department of Psychology, Ohio Wesleyan University, Delaware, Ohio 43015

GAY L. BISANZ (349), Department of Psychology, University of Alberta, Edmonton, Alberta T6G 2E9, Canada

JEFFREY BISANZ (229), Department of Psychology, University of Alberta, Edmonton, Alberta T6G 2E9, Canada

JOHN D. BRANSFORD (395), Department of Psychology, Vanderbilt University, Nashville, Tennessee 37240

MICHAEL W. EYSENCK (197), Department of Psychology, Birkbeck College, University of London, London WC1E 7HX England

JEFFERY J. FRANKS (395), Department of Psychology, Vanderbilt University, Nashville, Tennessee 37240

JOHN M. GARDINER (173), Department of Social Science and Humanities, The City University, London EC1V OHV, England

MURRAY GLANZER (63), Psychology Department, New York University, New York, New York 10003

KEITH J. HOLYOAK (315), Department of Psychology, University of Michigan, Ann Arbor, Michigan 48104

LAWRENCE J. HUBERT (129), Graduate School of Education, University of California, Santa Barbara, Santa Barbara, California 93106

ROBERT V. KAIL, JR. (229), Department of Psychological Sciences, Stanley Coulter Annex, Purdue University, West Lafayette, Indiana 47907

DEMETRIOS KARIS (427), Department of Psychology, University of Illinois at Urbana-Champaign, Champaign, Illinois 61820

STEPHEN M. KOSSLYN (315), Program in Linguistics and Cognitive Science, Brandeis University, Waltham, Massachusetts 02154

GEOFFREY R. LOFTUS (257), Department of Psychology, University of Washington, Seattle, Washington 98195

BENNET B. MURDOCK, JR. (1), Department of Psychology, University of Toronto, Toronto, Ontario, Canada M5S 1A1

MARTIN D. MURPHY (99), Department of Psychology, The University of Akron, Akron, Ohio 44325

JAMES W. PELLEGRINO (129), Graduate School of Education, University of California, Santa Barbara, Santa Barbara, California 93106

C. RICHARD PUFF (99), Department of Psychology, Franklin and Marshall College, Lancaster, Pennsylvania 17604

PATRICK RABBITT (27), Department of Experimental Psychology, University of Oxford, South Parks Road, Oxford, England

EDWARD SHOBEN (287), Department of Psychology, University of Illinois-Champaign, Champaign, Illinois 61820

SHERMAN TYLER (349), Learning Research and Development, University of Illinois-Champaign, Champaign, Illinois 61820

JAMES VOSS (349), Department of Psychology and Learning Research and Development Center, University of Pittsburgh, Pittsburgh, Pennsylvania 15260

MICHAEL J. WATKINS (173), Department of Psychology, Rice University, Houston, Texas 77001

Preface

This volume is intended to be a reference tool for those interested in research in the area of human memory and cognition. Its purpose is to help people be aware of important methodological issues in planning investigations and evaluating existing literature. Toward this end, a group of senior investigators provide a critical examination of the major contemporary research methods.

The need for such a book stems from the methodological challenge created by the rapid evolution in the kinds of problems of interest and the progressive refinement in methodology within specific problem areas. It is increasingly difficult for anyone to pursue competently or to evaluate research in more than a few subareas in which he or she can develop and maintain a high level of expertise. The hope is that the existence of a single, authoritative source will introduce newcomers to the range of methodologies in the area, and will enable established investigators to be more flexible in the choice of problems and methods by which to attack them.

The specific topics covered in the book represent areas of substantial current interest and research activity. To minimize overlap, most of the topics were defined in terms of experimental tasks and materials rather than theoretical constructs. There are chapters on recognition memory, free-recall, and prose memory, but not on encoding, storage, or retrieval, because of the overlapping methodological approaches the latter notions involve.

So that the book can function effectively as a reference tool or handbook, each chapter is designed to stand on its own, and the chapters can thus be read in any order. To achieve the most complete coverage of methods and issues relevant to a particular type of investigation, the chapters can be read in pairs or clusters. Thus, for example, if someone is interested in the effects of various orienting tasks in incidental learning on recognition test performance, he or she would want to read the chapter by Eysenck and the one by Murdock. A number of these cross-references are included in the chapters.

There is considerable diversity in organization and approach within the chapters. However, each chapter covers some reference experiments that serve as prototypes for research in the particular area, some treatment of the important parameters of the materials and presentation conditions, and some consideration of how performance is evaluated. Beyond this, the chapters differ in how heavily the discussion of methodology is tied to theoretical issues, and whether the balance of the weight is given to the details of how to carry out specific procedures, or to the consideration of conceptual issues involved in designing the research. These alternative emphases, no doubt, partly reflect the nature of the subareas and partly the inclinations of the different contributors who were given the freedom to emphasize what they thought most appropriate.

The book begins with a chapter on the methodology in the study of recognition memory by Murdock. He describes the types of recognition memory tests and measures, including the application of signal-detection theory and concludes with a set of guidelines for designing experiments on recognition memory.

In Chapter 2, Rabbitt examines the methodology in visual search experiments, stimulus categorization paradigms, the Sternberg search paradigm, and binary classification tasks. He emphasizes the variables affecting performance in these tasks and the common logical structure of the decisions made.

The variety of tasks used in studying short-term memory is reviewed in Chapter 3 by Glanzer. He concentrates on a set of representative studies ranging across distractor, probe, PI release, and other paradigms, along with consideration of the role of rehearsal, modality, pre– and concurrent–task loads.

Murphy and Puff (Chapter 4) review the methodology in the free recall paradigm. They discuss the manipulation and control of task parameters and the measurement of recall performance. This chapter is essentially prefatory to Chapter 5.

Pellegrino and Hubert (Chapter 5) present a systematic approach to the analysis of organization and structure in free recall protocols. Their analytic procedures, developed within an explicit conceptual framework, are applicable to testing the well-known, list-learning hypotheses of clustering, subjective organization, seriation, etc. as well as original structural hypotheses in list learning, prose memory, sorting, and other paradigms.

Chapter 6, by Watkins and Gardiner, analyzes cued recall performance in terms of types of designs for studying it, important task parameters, and measures for evaluating it. The relation between the conventional cued recall procedure and other experimental paradigms is also considered.

In Chapter 7, Eysenck critically evaluates paradigms for comparing intentional and incidental learning. He also considers the relationship between orienting tasks and processing activities, including the interaction of orienting tasks with other variables such as the type of retention test employed.

Kail and Bisanz (Chapter 8) focus on conceptual issues to be considered in determining the appropriateness of methods for assessing strategic activity. They examine the use of inferential, direct, and correlative measures in memory tasks, along with the use of task analysis, latencies, and verbal reports in problem solving tasks.

The methods used in the study of the encoding of pictures are described by Loftus in Chapter 9. He discusses the role of eye movements and fixation patterns, characteristics of the presentation such as luminance and masking, and the implementation of different types of retention tests.

In Chapter 10, Shoben discusses semantic and lexical decision tasks as they are used to investigate the structure and processing of semantic knowledge. He emphasizes, in particular, the issues involved in the use of natural language materials, the treatment of reaction time data, and the application of the additive, subtractive, and order types of logic used in such studies.

The issues and paradigms in the study of imagery are examined in Chapter 11 by Kosslyn and Holyoak. They cover basic methodological problems, such as how to avoid biasing the subjects in imagery studies, and they emphasize the importance of an appropriate match-up between a particular kind of question about imagery and the nature of the paradigm used to investigate it.

Voss, Tyler, and Bisanz (Chapter 12) review the methodology that has developed in the study of prose comprehension and memory. They consider the methodological contributions of lines of prose research involving models of text structure, investigation of parameters of the task situation, and the study of how higher-level knowledge structures influence text processing.

Franks, Bransford and Auble (Chapter 13) discuss procedures for exploring the relationship between retention and the learner's previously acquired knowledge. These procedures are designed explicitly to manipulate available knowledge and its usefulness in the retention situation by considering the nature of the target information, contextual information, the sequencing of these, and the nature of the criterion task.

In the final chapter (Chapter 14), Bahrick and Karis describe the methods used to study memory for real life experiences as viewed within a framework for classifying memory content. They provide an evaluation of the methods in this area, stressing the advantage of ecological validity and the problem of verification.

Handbook of Research Methods in
Human Memory and Cognition

CHAPTER **1**   BENNET B. MURDOCK, JR.

Recognition Memory

The term *recognition memory* can have at least two quite different meanings. In one sense, it refers to the act of recognizing someone or something: a familiar face, a familiar piece of music, a familiar scene. (See Mandler, 1980, for a discussion of this meaning.) In the second sense, it refers to a method of testing memory that presents one or more alternatives and asks for a judgment of familiarity. I shall concentrate on the second meaning, though at times I must consider the first as well. Recognition is one of the oldest and best established techniques of testing memory. Much is known about recognition memory. By now we have standard techniques and, as a result of their use, much data and theory. The techniques are popular today, and will likely continue to be widely used.

Designing experiments in recognition memory can sometimes get tricky. As an example, see the rather elaborate precautions necessary to guard against confoundings in some tests of a scanning model (Murdock, Hockley, & Muter, 1977). In this chapter, I will not go into such detail; rather, I shall indicate only general principles.

It has long been known that retention is a function of the method of measurement. In one of the early classic studies Luh (1922; see also Postman & Rau, 1957) compared recognition, relearning, reconstruction, written reproduction, and anticipation. The recognition scores were the

1

HANDBOOK OF RESEARCH METHODS IN
HUMAN MEMORY AND COGNITION

highest. This finding agrees with our intuitions; we have all had situations in which we could not recall something but could recognize it. It is appropriate that a book on research methods in memory and cognition start with recognition.

It is generally thought that the distinction between recall and recognition involves whether or not the alternatives are presented to the subject. If I ask, *What is the capital of X?* I am testing recall, but if I ask, *What is the capital of X: A, B, C, D?* then I am testing recognition. This distinction may be too simple. Another distinction (Murdock, 1970; Tulving, 1976) might be in terms of the availability of the alternatives. If the subject can readily generate all possible alternatives or if they are present, then the method would be recognition; otherwise, it would be recall. Thus, the question *What is the fifteenth letter of the alphabet?* would be testing recognition, not recall, even though the form of the question implies recall. Actually, even such a basic distinction as this is probably a theoretical issue, and cannot be decided arbitrarily.

DEFINITIONS

Basic Processes

The three basic processes of memory are *encoding, storage,* and *retrieval.* Encoding refers to the process by which information presented to a person is transformed from some physical form (light waves or sound waves impinging on the receptors) into a memorial representation (memory trace or engram). Storage refers to the persistence of this information over time. Forgetting is generally considered to be a storage phenomenon, since the information does not persist with adequate fidelity to support remembering. Retrieval is the utilization of this stored information at the time of test, whatever the test: recall, recognition, or some other. Failure to retrieve information does not necessarily imply forgetting; the difficulty could be in accessing the information or in the initial encoding. Encoding, storage, and retrieval are sequential processes— encoding first and retrieval last. Successful performance on a memory test means that all three processes are above some minimum required level. However, failure on a memory test is not sufficient, by itself, to localize which process may be at fault.

Stages

Utilization of stored information, or retrieval, involves two stages: *memory* and *decision.* This point is illustrated in the simple flow chart

Figure 1.1. A flow chart showing the role of memory and decision.

of Figure 1.1. The output from the memory system is input into the decision system, and, speaking metaphorically, the decision system decides whether to output a response or query the memory system again. Suppose a short list of items is presented to a person and is followed by a single item about which a "yes" or "no" decision is required: ("yes," the item had been in the list, or "no," the item had not been in the list). Somehow the person makes a comparison between the encoded version of the probe item and the memory trace(s) comprising the list. If a clear match or nonmatch occurs, the person has enough information to give a "yes" or "no" response. In the event of uncertainty, the person might quiz the memory system again. Decision factors certainly affect performance on many tests of recognition memory. Failure to take these two stages of information processing into account may lead to erroneous conclusions on the part of the experimenter. The section on accuracy will deal with this problem in detail.

Types of Information

By now it seems quite clear that there are at least three different types of information in human memory. These are *item information, associative information,* and *serial-order information.* Item information is information that some item, object, or event has occurred in the past. Item information may be tied to some context—have you seen the word *decision* in this chapter? Associative information relates two items, objects, or events. Common examples are names and faces, words and their meanings, and artists and their works. The discussion of the association of ideas and the role of contiguity and similarity has been part of Western culture since the time of the early Greek philosophers. Serial-order information is sequence information, information about the order in which items or events occur. We all know the days of the week, the letters of the alphabet, and, in spelling, that "i" comes before "e" except after "c." In a more naturalistic vein, we could put many events of our past life in chronological order if we were told the events and asked to arrange them in the order in which they occurred. How item, associative, and serial-order information is encoded, stored, and retrieved is far from a settled matter, but there is abundant experimental evidence to support these distinctions (Murdock, 1974).

The distinction between recall and recognition is orthogonal to the distinction between item, associative, and serial-order information. To name the first five presidents of the United States requires recall of serial-order information, whereas a subject asked to arrange pictures of items in the order in which they were just presented requires recognition. Thus, one can use recall or recognition with serial-order information. Likewise with associative information: If I present the pairs A–B and C–D, I can test for recall with A–? or C–?, or I can test for recognition by asking whether A–B or A–D was a correct pairing. Whether one can have recall of item information is a moot point; one could argue that the experimental paradigm of free recall would be an example. On the other hand, it could be that free recall involves associative or serial-order information. In any case, it is important to appreciate that recognition is not just for item information. One can test for recognition of item, associative, or serial-order information.

Types of Tests

There are three main types of tests that are used in the study of recognition memory: *yes–no tests, forced-choice tests,* and *batch testing.* Yes–no (or true–false) tests simply require a binary response to a question. *Was item X in the list,* or *Is Brasilia the capitol of Brazil?* In forced-choice tests, m alternatives are presented, of which $m - 1$ are incorrect and one is correct. The multiple-choice test, so popular in large undergraduate classes, is a well-known example. The guessing, or chance, level is lower in forced-choice than in yes–no, though by how much depends on the value of m. In signal-detection theory there is a standard way of relating performance on yes–no tests to performance on m-alternative forced-choice tests, and forced-choice tests are often considered to bypass the criterion (or guessing) problem. Both these matters will be discussed in the section on accuracy. Finally, in batch testing all alternatives (correct and incorrect) are simultaneously presented to the subject, who must then work through the items, indicating in some fashion the old and new items. This procedure is less popular than the first two, and with good reason. For one thing, the experimenter loses control of the pacing of the test session. Also lost is the opportunity to measure the latency of each response. Finally, continual adjustment of the subject's own criterion (generally considered to be undesirable) is quite easy because the subject can always review the answer sheet.

Types of Procedures

There are two main types of procedures used in the study of recognition memory: the *study–test procedure* and the *continuous-task procedure*. The study–test procedure was (to my knowledge) first used by Strong (1912, 1913), and it has not changed greatly since then. A list of items (words, pictures, sentences, advertisements) is shown to the subject, followed by a test list. Whereas forced-choice or yes–no can be used, assume the test is yes–no. Old and new items are shown, generally in randomized order, and the subject must respond to each as it occurs. One trial, then, consists of a single study–test sequence. Generally a number of trials are given in a single experimental session. The continuous-task procedure was introduced by Shepard and Teghtsoonian (1961). Here, study and test items are randomly intermingled so there is no clear separation of the study and test phase. The subject responds to each item as it appears. On the first presentation of an item, the correct response is "no" (*I have not seen this item before in this list*) and on subsequent presentations the correct response is "yes" (*I have seen this item before in this list*). Thus, the subject responds to each item each time it appears from the beginning of the list to the end, so there is no clear separation of the study and the test phase of the experiment.

The single-item probe technique is a popular variant of the study–test procedure. A short list of items is presented, followed by a single-item probe. The one item constitutes the test phase. This procedure has become popular through the work of Sternberg (1966, 1969, 1975), who has used this method to obtain latency data under conditions of relatively error-free performance. Whereas one could consider this method a special type of procedure, it seems more logical to view it as a special case of the study–test procedure. (Parenthetically, it might be noted that there is an "inertia" effect in switching over from the study phase to the test phase in a study–test procedure. The first few response latencies are abnormally high, so this might pose problems in comparing study–test data with single-item probe data. Evidence for this inertia effect may be found in Murdock and Anderson [1975].)

Experimental Measures

The three main measures in the study of recognition memory are *accuracy, latency,* and *confidence.* Accuracy is generally determined by the proportion of correct responses, either summed over old and new items in a yes–no procedure or given separately for each. (The d' of signal detection theory is a derived measure and will be described in the section on accuracy.) Latency is the length of time elapsing between presentation of the test item and initiation of the response. (Visual rather than auditory presentation obviates the problem of determining precisely the onset of a spoken word, and key presses rather than spoken responses do likewise on the response side.) Confidence judgments are the subject's assessment of his own accuracy, and they can be integrated with yes–no responses or given separately. If given separately, the subject first makes the yes–no response and then evaluates it on a separate confidence-judgment scale. If integrated, a 6-point scale—"sure no" (–––), "probably no" (––), "maybe no" (–), "maybe yes" (+), "probably yes" (+ +), and "sure yes" (+ + +)—is popular. The data seem quite comparable for these two procedures (Mandler & Boeck, 1974). Finally, latency and confidence can be combined by simply recording the length of time to make each confidence judgment.

ACCURACY

One cannot discuss accuracy of recognition memory in any depth without recourse to signal–detection theory. Consequently, this section on accuracy will be devoted to an account of signal–detection theory and its application to recognition memory.

Signal–detection theory has been widely used in the study of recognition memory. This application stems from a technical report by Egan (Note 1), who not only spelled out in considerable detail the nature of the application, but also provided some relevant data. Other early references are Murdock (1965) and Norman and Wickelgren (1965). There are probably two main advantages in using a signal-detection analysis of recognition memory. First, it provides an economical summary statistic (d') to characterize overall accuracy. Otherwise, there are two separate measures, one for performance on old items, and one for performance on new items. The d' measure combines them both. One measure is much easier to handle than two. Second, signal-detection theory provides a clean way of separating memory and decision (see Figure 1.1). Thus, even though both memorial and decision factors affect performance, the theory allows separation of the two effects in the data.

Standard Signal-Detection Analysis

The basic idea of signal-detection analysis is that there are two underlying distributions: a noise (or new-item) distribution and a signal (or old-item) distribution. As far as recognition memory is concerned, it does no great harm to think of these as "strength" distributions. The concept of memory-trace strength is old and venerable and, though no one quite knows what it means, many feel comfortable in using it. The general idea is that new items (items not presented in the study list) have some variability. This variability is the starting point for the theoretical development. Old items (items presented in the study list) have comparable, and in some cases, equal, variability, but their mean strength is higher. It is conventional to represent this state of affairs with overlapping normal distributions—see Figure 1.2.

Not only are there two distributions, but there is also a criterion, or cutoff, as well. The recognition process is assumed to go as follows. The subject is presented with the probe item and must interrogate memory to determine whether the probe item is an old item or a new item. The probe is compared to the contents of memory and the result of this comparison process must be assessed. The assessment is the decision process and is logically equivalent to the statistical problem of inferring the origin of a single observation drawn at random from one of two possible distributions. The criterion is the cutoff for the decision. If the observation falls below the criterion, the subject says "no," but if the observation falls above, the subject says "yes." The criterion thus constitutes the line dividing "yes" and "no."

A few comments are now in order. First, on a single trial (i.e., a single probe test) the assessment of the probe has a fixed value. The variability is the variability of many such samples pooled over trials. If the distributions did not overlap, there would be no problem. Observations falling in the range of the lower distribution would always be called new, whereas observations falling in the range of the upper distribution would always be called old, and the subject would be 100% accurate. Since in practice this does not occur (conditions where it might occur are not very informative, so the experimenter makes sure it does

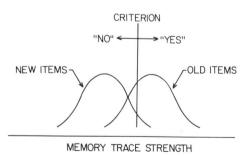

Figure 1.2. The underlying old- and new-items distributions as suggested by an application of signal-detection theory to recognition memory.

not occur), the criterion is necessary to partition the responses in the case of uncertainty. Second, there may be some variability in the placement of the criterion. Criterion variability has the effect of lowering d' (making the distributions seem closer together; see, for example, McNicol, 1972), but trying to separate criterion variability from other sources of variability is not an easy undertaking. Third, an extension to latency data has been made by Norman and Wickelgren (1969), who suggested that latency was an inverse function of distance from the criterion. Thus, extreme observations, both "yes" and "no," are made quickly, but intermediate observations take longer. Whereas this suggestion has considerable intuitive appeal, some experimental problems have been pointed out by Murdock and Dufty (1972).

Definitions

A number of standard definitions from signal-detection theory will be given next. There are four types of responses: *hits, false alarms, correct rejections,* and *misses.* Hits are "yes" responses to old items. False alarms are "yes" responses to new items. Correct rejections are "no" responses to new items. Misses are "no" responses to old items. Hits and correct rejections are correct responses, misses and false alarms are errors. These four types of responses can be reported as frequencies, but they are more commonly reported as conditional probabilities. The hit rate would then be the proportion of old items given a "yes" response, and the false alarm rate would be the proportion of new items given a "yes" response. These are not the only two conditional probabilities that could describe the data, but are commonly used. This terminology is illustrated in Figure 1.3.

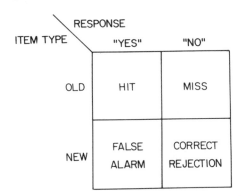

Figure 1.3. The terminology for "yes" and "no" responses to old and new items.

The two basic dependent variables are d' and β. A simple formula for d' is

$$d' = z(\text{FA}) - z(\text{H}) \qquad (1)$$

where $z(\text{FA})$ is the standard (or z) score corresponding to the given false alarm rate and $z(\text{H})$ is the standard score corresponding to the given hit rate (see, e.g., McNicol, 1972). As an example, suppose, out of 120 old items, the subject said "yes" 102 times; the hit rate would be .850. Suppose, out of 120 new items, the subject said "yes" nine times; the false alarm rate would be .050. From tables of the normal distribution, $z(\text{H}) = -1.04$ and $z(\text{FA}) = 1.64$. Consequently, $d' = 1.64 - (-1.04) = 2.68$.

One can think of d' itself as a simple standard score; It is the mean of the old-item distribution expressed in units of the standard deviation of the new-item distribution. (The assumption is always that the mean of the new-item distribution is zero.) As a dependent variable, d' is generally regarded as a measure of the average strength of the old items.

The second measure, β, is a measure of the location or placement of the criterion on the strength axis. Technically, it is the ratio of the ordinates of the two distributions (old to new) at the criterion. It can easily be computed from any table of the unit normal curve given, for example, the hit rate and the false alarm rate. If $\beta = 1.0$, then the criterion is located at the point of intersection of the old- and new-item distributions. Other measures of the criterion are possible and sometimes preferable (see, e.g., Donaldson & Glathe, 1970). One such measure is the location of the criterion as a standard score relative to the mean of the new-item distribution.

The a priori probability is the probability that a probe item will be an old item. This probability is fixed by the experimenter, and generally is told to the subjects so they can set their criterions appropriately. The a posteriori probability is the probability that a probe item was old, given a "yes" response. This probability is not fixed by the experimenter; rather, it depends upon the subject's performance. It is quite useful in confidence-judgment experiments, since it gives an indication of how accurate the subject is at different points along the strength dimension. Costs and payoffs refer to the values associated with errors and correct responses. Costs are negative values and payoffs are positive values. A full payoff matrix specifies the cost for both types of error and the payoff for both types of correct responses. From this and the a priori probability, one can derive the optimum criterion placement.

The optimum criterion placement is that placement of the criterion which maximizes the "net profit" (in a monetary sense, what is won from being correct minus what is lost from being incorrect). In fact, this is why β is used in signal-detection theory. According to a maximum-likelihood principle, β should equal $p/(1 - p)$ where p is the a priori probability. If $p = .5$, and the payoff matrix is symmetric, then, by this principle, β should equal 1.0. That is, the criterion should be located at the point of intersection of the two distributions. This analysis is based on a rational analysis of the subject's performance in a recognition-memory task. Whether the subjects actually behave in this fashion (and at times they clearly do not) is an open question.

Experimental Manipulations

One can always obtain a value of d' from a single 2 × 2 contingency table. This table can be either pooled over subjects or applied on a subject-by-subject basis. Unfortunately, such an analysis does not give any indication of whether the theory is appropriate for the given application. Given the many applications of the theory, this question should not be ignored. There are two standard manipulations that can be used to shed light on the matter. One is to vary the a priori probability, so that there are as many 2 × 2 tables as levels of the probability manipulation. Then one can construct a receiver operating characteristic, as described in the next section. Generally, the probability manipulation is a between-sessions (or between-lists) manipulation, and the subject is informed as to what the probability setting is under each condition.

This procedure necessitates collecting a lot of data. An alternative is to use a confidence-judgment procedure. Only a single a priori probability value need be used, but on each test the subject gives a confidence judgment (either incorporated into a yes–no judgment or kept separate). To do so, the subject is assumed to set up multiple criteria (one less than the number of scale values), and each judgment locates that observation within a region of the strength (decision) axis. Suppose a 6-point scale is used. The confidence-judgment matrix would then be 2

Table 1.1
Frequencies of Six Confidence Judgments to Old and New Items (Illustrative Data)

	Confidence judgments					
	− − −	− −	−	+	+ +	+ + +
Old items	25	35	40	40	28	32
New items	90	50	28	18	10	4

× 6; the rows would indicate probe type (old or new); and the columns, the six confidence judgments. Cell entries would be frequencies. An example is given in Table 1.1.

Extracting Signal-Detection Measures from Data

Given that one has several 2 × 2 tables from varying the probability, or given that one has a confidence-judgment matrix, how can d' and β be obtained? One method is to construct a *receiver operating characteristic,* or ROC curve. An ROC curve is a plot of hit rate as a function of false alarm rate.

An example is shown in Figure 1.4 of an ROC curve for the data shown in Table 1.1. To obtain the hits and false alarms, compute cumulative proportions for old and new items separately. That is, start with the strictest criterion (here, + + +); the hit rate is 32/200 = .16 and the false alarm rate is 4/200 = .02. For the next strictest criterion (+ +), the hit rate is (32 + 28)/200 = .30, and the false alarm rate is (4 + 10)/200 = .07. The five pairs of values for the six confidence judgments are shown in Table 1.2.

Given an ROC curve, how is the value of d' obtained? One method is to take the intersection of the ROC curve with the negative diagonal, as illustrated in Figure 1.4. [Determine the hit rate and the false alarm

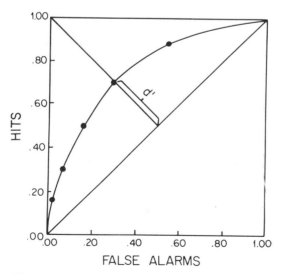

Figure 1.4. An ROC curve for the data of Table 1.1.

Table 1.2
Hits and False Alarms for the Data of Table 1.1

Criterion	Hits	False alarms
+ + +	.16	.02
+ +	.30	.07
+	.50	.16
−	.70	.30
− −	.88	.55

rate at the point of intersection; then use Eq. (1).] This is simple, but it is not the best estimation procedure.[1]

Actually, the value of the ROC curve is that it provides a way of seeing whether the underlying assumptions of the theory are violated by the data. If they are not, the ROC curve should be linear when plotted on double-normal probability paper. Also, the slope of the ROC curve gives the variance ratio of the two distributions; see, for example, Donaldson and Murdock (1968). As for β, it is the slope of the ROC curve for any given hit and false alarm rate. However, investigators of memory have not made much use of this measure in this context.

Justification for Signal-Detection Analysis

There are two justifications for a signal-detection analysis of recognition-memory data, one empirical and one theoretical. The empirical justification is that, in many cases, the underlying assumptions of the model are met. In particular, the assumption of this version of the theory is that the underlying distributions are normal. Egan found this to be the case in his early study. We have conducted many recognition-memory experiments in our lab, and normality seems to be the rule. The other justification is theoretical. Signal-detection theory provides a conceptual way of thinking about recognition memory that is quite congruent with the information-processing viewpoint so dominant in cognitive psychology today. More specifically, strength theory is a particular version of signal-detection theory and, despite its problems (see Anderson & Bower, 1972), it remains an important and influential theory.

[1] Ogilvie and Creelman (1968) have developed a maximum-likelihood estimation procedure based on the logistic as an approximation to the normal distribution. EPCROC, a FORTRAN coding of this procedure, is very easy to use, and I will be glad to provide a listing on request.

Alternatives

If a signal-detection analysis is not used, what is used? One possibility is to report just the hit rate. This practice would be hard to condone, since the hit rate describes only a portion of the data (accuracy of responses to old items). If one places any credence at all in the view that performance on a memory task involves a decision component, failure to report accuracy of responses to new items could make it possible to overlook large criterion effects. To report both hit (or miss) rate and false alarm (or correct rejection) rate is certainly acceptable, for then any reader has enough information to compute d' directly from the data. I think the conceptual advantages of working (and thinking) in d' terms are important, but not everyone shares my bias.

Sometimes a "corrected" percentage correct score is given, for example, hits minus false alarms or hits minus some function of false alarms. This practice makes me uneasy. In some cases, this correction is a "high-threshold" correction; that is, one based on the assumption of all-or-none memory. There is much data showing that an all-or-none view of recognition of item information is wrong, though there may be exceptions. Before an investigator resorts to such a correction, he or she should be very sure that the data are the exception and not the norm.

The previous discussion applies to a yes–no procedure. In a forced-choice procedure, percentage correct is generally an adequate measure. According to the traditional view, in m-alternative forced-choice, the subject is choosing the strongest one of m alternatives. Since criterion effects are absent, percentage correct is an acceptable measure. If one wishes to convert to a d' measure, tables (Hacker & Ratcliff, 1979) are available.

Precautions

This discussion has emphasized the positive benefits of using a signal-detection analysis in the study of recognition memory. However, there are a number of precautions to be observed. The first deals with the distributional assumptions. One can simply take the model as given and apply it directly to the recognition-memory situation. Whereas this may be justified empirically, conceptually it may be questionable. The model was originally developed to account for the detection of a weak signal against the background of Gaussian noise. The analysis of the noise process, so important in the basic theory, is a direct consequence of using white noise and a fixed observation interval, and the derivation

is quite straightforward (see Green & Swe...
(Norman & Wickelgren, 1969; Wickelgr...
over these assumptions, part and pa...
reason for their application. In...
reassuring to have a firm...
about how the mem...
application.

Another...
in Lockh...
dete...

In
dep...
lieve
ables.
quite ge...
to turn fi
analysis an...

Subspan Lists

Sternberg (197...
involving short lists...
method is the probe v...
a short (1–6) list of ite...
a single-item probe. The...
been in the list, otherwise,...
span is 5 ± 2 items (Drew...
range tends to insure virtually...
terest then shifts to latency.

BENNET B. MURDOCK, JR.

further. If one does, however, accept the scanning model, then the slope of the reaction-time function is a measure of scanning rate in the comparison stage, and the intercept would be a measure of the other stages. By the additive-factors logic, one might reasonably expect differences in the intercept of the scanning function if the experimental manipulation affected the encoding or the response-selection stage, whereas variables that affected the comparison stage would show up as slope differences. Again, it should be emphasized that such an interpretation is model-dependent. But data do not speak for themselves. They must be interpreted within a given framework, explicit or implicit. (As an example, see Townsend, 1974.)

Supraspan Lists

If one uses lists that exceed memory span, the surprising resu... that the reaction-time functions are still linear, but the slopes are a... an order of magnitude less (typically something of the order of 5... per item; Murdock, 1980). Here the independent variable is eit... (number of items intervening between study and test) or output... (position of the item in the test series). New items, of course,... lag, so for them output position must be the basis of classifica... linear lag-latency function for supraspan lists is specific to the... method of testing recognition memory. It occurs in a stud... cedure. When a continuous recognition memory task is us... latency function is probably best characterized as being... celerated, possibly logarithmic (Hockley, Note 2).

The contrast between subspan lists and supraspan list... in data reported by Burrows and Okada (1975). Using th... lists paradigm developed by Atkinson and Juola (197... steep linear function in the subspan range; the break rather clearly com... in the supraspan range; the break rather clearly com... number seven" (Miller, 1956). (In the prememorized... jects learn the list before testing begins, so suprasp... with low error rates.) Does all this mean that sc... memory span as well as below memory span, but fa... are theoretical more than methodological; so the... here. For discussion of these matters, see Murdo... next chapter by Rabbitt for further applications...

The main reason for introducing these to... reaction-time data can be collected under con... is far from perfect. For lists of, say, 15–30 it...

cedure, accuracy ranges from .99+ at the shortest lags, to perhaps .80 at the longest lags. One can use longer lists and the accuracy goes down still further. Clearly this is very far from error-free performance, but virtue can be made of necessity. It can be argued that one should be above the floor but below the ceiling for both accuracy and latency data. The interpretive problem is to explain both the accuracy and the latency data with the same model, and success in this enterprise is a very impressive accomplishment (see Ratcliff, 1978). Actually, error-free performance could be a liability, because then speed–accuracy tradeoffs might go unnoticed (Pachella, 1974).

One important development that has come out of work with supraspan lists is that the empirical reaction-time distributions are generally well fit by a theoretical distribution. The theoretical distribution that works best is the convolution of an exponential (or waiting-time) distribution and a normal distribution (Ratcliff & Murdock, 1976). This is a three-parameter model and the parameters are μ, the mean of the normal distribution, σ, the standard deviation of the normal distribution, and τ, the rate constant of the exponential distribution. Fitting a theoretical distribution to data is much more informative than simply working with mean reaction times. In the case of the convolution model, an analysis of how the three parameters change with lag raises some very serious problems for a scanning interpretation—yet these same data, using only mean reaction times, suggested the idea for scanning of supraspan lists in the first place. As another example, dual-process models, such as those suggested by Atkinson and Juola (1973) and Mandler (1980), would seem to require bimodality in reaction-time distributions, but we don't find bimodality in the data (Ratcliff & Murdock, 1976).

Obtaining reliable estimates of the parameter values can require rather substantial amounts of data. However, as small computers become more available in the memory laboratory, large data-collection enterprises will become more feasible. Also, it turns out to be quite possible to fit reaction-time distributions to group data with only a small number of observations per subject. This method is essentially a variation of an old technique in the verbal-learning laboratory (Vincentized learning curves; see, e.g., Hilgard, 1951). The reaction-time method, which works well for the convolution model, has been developed by Ratcliff (1979).

Judgments of Recency

Much of the work using latency in recognition memory has focused on the recognition of item information using subspan or supraspan lists. Another potentially fruitful approach is to study judgments of recency.

A list of items is presented, followed by a two-item probe. The subject indicates which of the two items in the probe had been more recently presented in the study list. This method can provide a powerful means of testing theories of storage and retrieval processes (Hacker, 1980; Muter, 1979).

COVARIATION OF ACCURACY AND LATENCY

I have considered accuracy and latency separately, and now it is time to consider their interrelationship. It is sometimes the case that accuracy and latency are positively correlated; long latencies are associated with high accuracy, whereas short latencies are associated with low accuracy. This relationship goes under the name of *speed–accuracy tradeoff,* and is illustrated in Figure 1.5. At point A on the curve, responses are fast but accuracy is low; at point C on the curve, responses are slow but accuracy is high; at point B, both are intermediate.

The speed–accuracy tradeoff function is generally considered to be an *iso-performance* curve. Just as different points on the ROC curve indicate equal discriminability (d'), so different points on a speed–accuracy tradeoff function are taken to indicate equal performance. This view has important implications for interpreting experimental data. The fact that accuracy is higher, or that responses are faster in one condition than in another condition, cannot insure that performance is superior in the more accurate, or in the faster, condition. It could be that there are compensating differences in the other measure so that performance is equivalent (conceivably even reversed) in the two conditions.

This tradeoff relationship makes it desirable (some would say mandatory) to collect both accuracy and latency data in studies of recognition memory. If one has accuracy differences but no latency measures, what

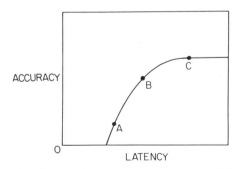

Figure 1.5. A hypothetical speed–accuracy tradeoff function.

guarantee is there that compensating differences in reaction time do not exist? A strong position on this issue might claim that accuracy data in the absence of latency data are uninterpretable. A less adamant position would be that accuracy is only a partial measure of performance, and for a complete picture both accuracy and latency measures are needed.

Even if one does collect both accuracy and latency data, the interpretive problem remains. Accuracy differences among conditions may be compared, and latency differences among conditions may be compared, but how are the differences of the differences compared? When working with an explicit theory that deals with these matters (for example, random-walk models), then perhaps the only problem is to estimate parameters of the model and draw conclusions accordingly. The alternative (or at least one alternative) is to obtain empirical speed–accuracy curves for each condition. Then the comparison among conditions is a comparison of the tradeoff functions, not of the separate accuracies and latencies.

How is a speed–accuracy tradeoff function obtained, assuming it really is necessary? Until recently, the only option available was to force the subject to operate at various points on the function during each and every condition in the experiment. Two methods would be the deadline method (Snodgrass, Luce, & Galanter, 1967) or the response-signal method (Reed, 1973; Schouten & Bekker, 1967). Varying the deadline or the response signal would be analogous to obtaining an ROC curve by varying the a priori probability. In the ROC case, the a priori probability manipulation would move the subject's location on the function around, and there would have to be a separate point on the ROC curve for each experimental condition. In the speed–accuracy case, the comparable manipulation would do the same thing, and again there would have to be a separate point for each condition. Pachella (1974), Wickelgren (1977), and Wickelgren, Corbett, and Dosher (1980) have proposed some alternatives. One possibility is to obtain on-line recording of the progress of the response as it develops, and the "growth" of the response would inform as to speed–accuracy characteristics. The particular techniques for observing the growth of a response are still very new, and will not be detailed here. However, continued progress in this area is to be expected.

Having said all this, let me hasten to add that the picture is not quite so one-sided. There would seem to be a simple solution for the investigator who chooses not to record latency data. If subjects were instructed to stress accuracy at the expense of speed, then perhaps it could be argued that subjects were at an asymptotic level of performance, and latency differences were no longer germane. That is, the speed–accuracy tradeoff function is an iso-performance curve over whatever range is possible for a given task or condition. So, even if subjects take longer than necessary to make their responses, their accuracy level still indicates all the necessary information about performance under that condition. (Notice that the curve in Figure 1.5 levels off well under perfect accuracy.)

Furthermore, there will be many conditions in which accuracy and latency will be negatively correlated. For instance, in a study–test procedure, over the course of the test phase, accuracy will decrease and latency will increase. So again, accuracy and latency are interrelated, but in the opposite direction. Obviously, one should distinguish these two situations. Under a steady-state condition, performance may well vary over the iso-performance curve. Under conditions in which the performance level is changing, it is more likely that accuracy and latency will be negatively correlated, not positively correlated.

Finally, I can think of a very good reason not to try to obtain a speed–accuracy tradeoff function. A very general principle of measurement is that the act of measuring affects that which is being measured. Suppose a deadline or a response-signal method is used. The subject must then do two things: process the information for the response, and monitor his own processing to terminate it at the desired time. It is difficult to believe that the latter would not affect the former.

GUIDELINES

Let me close by suggesting 10 guidelines to keep in mind when designing an experiment on recognition memory. These guidelines are merely suggestions to be followed if there is no reason not to follow them. That is, many times the research under investigation must violate one or more of these suggestions because of the nature of the problem under investigation. I am certainly not trying to discourage such research. All I intend to do is point out some principles that might be useful if they do not conflict with the purpose of the experiment.

1. The stimulus material presented to the subject should be a random sample from some specified population.
2. Each subject should have a different random sample.
3. Present an equal amount of unfamiliar (new) and familiar (old) material in the test phase.
4. Tell the subject that this is being done.
5. Make sure there is no basis for discriminating old and new

material other than the fact that the old material (but not the new material) was presented in the study phase.

6. Use as independent variables those variables which you yourself manipulate or control. Do not rely on the subject's previous life history to manipulate the variables.
7. Record and report both accuracy and latency data.
8. Set the overall difficulty level of the task so as to avoid "floor effects" (too hard) or "ceiling effects" (too easy).
9. Remember that performance on recognition tests involves both memory and decision. Try to have some way of separating them.
10. Remember that all that is really being measured is the overt performance of the subject on some test material. Attributing any obtained results to encoding, storage, or retrieval requires a theoretical commitment, explicit experimental manipulations, and careful controls.

NOTES ON THE GUIDELINES

1. Why should the stimulus material be a random sample from some specified population? Because then it is clear to what extent results can be generalized. This is simply a basic principle of experimental design; if the sample (subjects, stimuli, and so forth) is a random sample from some population then results can be generalized to that population. Otherwise, the results are specific to the particular material used and the statistical analysis will be greatly complicated. If the stimulus material cannot be considered a random treatment variable it may have to be considered a fixed effect (in the ANOVA sense) and quasi-F ratios (Clark, 1973) may have to be computed.

2. Why should each subject have a different random sample? If subjects all have the same lists, even though these lists were originally random samples from a population, then the results may be specific to this sample from this population. Actually, I am not sure how serious a problem this is, but my own preference is to use different random samples when possible. Then I know I do not have to worry about quasi-F's, and so on and the whole problem of generality is much simpler.

If the stimulus material is randomly sampled, and if each subject has a different random sample, will this solve the troublesome problem of possible subject–item interactions? *Subject–item interactions* refer to the fact that, over and above subject and item differences, specific items may be easier or harder for specific subjects. This will vary from subject to subject and item to item (hence the term subject–item interactions) and, at the least, will be an added source of noise in the data. This would seem to be impossible to pin down.

In fact, there is a way of at least assessing the magnitude of these interactions, if only after the fact. As described in Murdock and Ogilvie (1968), the data should be saved in binary form and then formed in macroblocks before doing the ANOVA. In a factorial design, the magnitude of the expected mean-squares value of the higher-order interactions is inversely related to macroblock size. If the expected and obtained values are close, the interactions should not be a major factor in the results.

3. Why should the test list contain an equal number of old and new items? Simply because this makes the a priori probability .5, and the subjects are being tested in the most sensitive region of the curve.

4. Why should the subject be told? For one thing, if the subjects are to behave optimally, then this is information they need to have. For another, subjects learn, and if they get repeated tests under constant conditions, they will gradually realize that old and new items are about equally likely. If they do not know this early in the experiment, but they do know it later in the experiment, then an extra factor in the design will have been introduced. Furthermore, there is no way of knowing when the change occurred, so it cannot be traced later.

5. It seems obvious that the subjects should have no basis for differentiating old and new test items other than the fact that old items were presented in the study list and new items were not. Otherwise, it is not a memory test but something else. Suppose there were subtle differences between old and new items. Naive subjects might fail the obvious test (discriminating the material prior to seeing the input list), yet sophisticated experimental subjects could pick up clues to aid their performance. Performance on a recognition test probably is an additive combination of a number of factors. Make sure that systematic differences between old and new items is not one of them.

6. If the experimenter does not personally manipulate or vary the independent variable, there is the risk of unsuspected confoundings. As an example, suppose one wants to find out the effect of word frequency on recognition memory. Recognition memory for high-frequency words is compared with recognition memory for low-frequency words—there may be a confounding of word-frequency effects with age of acquisition. That is, high-frequency words are acquired earlier in life than low-frequency words; so is it word frequency per se, or age of acquisition? Suppose age of acquisition is under study, then age of acquisition may

be confounded with word frequency. There are other documented examples of confounding (e.g., Kintsch, 1972; McCloskey, 1980), and these complicate the interpretation. On the other hand, to avoid confoundings completely is probably almost impossible, but at least the experimenter should be aware of the problems.

7. By now it should be clear why both accuracy and latency data are desirable. If both data are not obtained there is the possibility of a speed–accuracy tradeoff. Admittedly, having both types of data does not guarantee being able to exclude that possibility, but with the latency data at least there is some hope of finding an acceptable answer.

8. Generally, experimenters are looking for differences, not trying to accept the null hypothesis. So, it makes sense to peg the difficulty level in a sensitive region of the curve. Also, if one is "close to the floor" or "close to the ceiling," null effects are probably uninterpretable. If no differences are obtained among conditions, is it because there aren't any, or is it because, at the extremes, the resolving power of the test is low?

9. Much has already been said about memory and decision. The role of decision factors in memory tests generally, and recognition tests in particular, has gained quite wide acceptance. Yet, at times it seems that we accept the principle and fail to apply it in our analysis. It is not uncommon to find psychologists interpreting their results in "memory" terms when they have not ruled out the possibility of criterion effects— and there are cases where criterion effects are a very likely possibility. Since the techniques for separating memory and decision are well known, well established, and easy to use, it seems rather foolhardy not to use them.

10. Relatively speaking, memory–decision and speed–accuracy distinctions are newcomers on the scene compared to the encoding–storage–retrieval distinction. So, respect tradition and exert due care in interpretations. Each of us may have a favorite way of making the experimental separation. Make it any way that seems best, but don't overlook the three traditional phases of memory: encoding, storage, and retrieval.

ACKNOWLEDGMENTS

Preparation of this chapter was supported by Research Grant 146 from the Natural Sciences and Engineering Research Council of Canada. I would like to thank Dave Burrows, Bill Hockley, Paul Muter, and Roger Ratcliff for critical comments on the manuscript; also, Pat Franklin for technical assistance in the preparation of the paper.

REFERENCE NOTES

1. Egan, J. P. *Recognition memory and the operating characteristic.* (Technical Note AFCRC-TN-58-51). Indiana: Indiana University, Hearing and Communication Laboratory, 1958.
2. Hockley, W. E. *Recognition performance under steady-state conditions.* Unpublished doctoral dissertation, University of Toronto, 1980.

REFERENCES

Anderson, J. R., & Bower, G. H. Recognition and retrieval processes in free recall. *Psychological Review,* 1972, *79,* 97–123.
Atkinson, R. C., & Juola, J. F. Factors influencing speed and accuracy of word recognition. In S. Kornblum (Ed.), *Attention and Performance IV.* New York: Academic Press, 1973. Pp. 583–612.
Burrows, D., & Okada, R. Memory retrieval from long and short lists. *Science,* 1975, *188,* 1031–1033.
Clark, H. H. The language-as-fixed-effect fallacy: A critique of language statistics in psychological research. *Journal of Verbal Learning and Verbal Behavior,* 1973, *12,* 335–359.
Donaldson, W., & Glathe, H. Signal-detection analysis of recall and recognition memory. *Canadian Journal of Psychology,* 1970, *24,* 42–56.
Donaldson, W., & Murdock, B. B., Jr. Criterion change in continuous recognition memory. *Journal of Experimental Psychology,* 1968, *76, 325–330.*
Drewnowski, A., & Murdock, B. B., Jr. The role of auditory features in memory span for words. *Journal of Experimental Psychology: Human Learning and Memory,* 1980, *6,* 319–332.
Green, D. M., & Swets, J. A. *Signal detection theory and psychophysics.* New York: Wiley, 1966.
Hacker, M. J. Speed and accuracy of recency judgments for events in short-term memory. *Journal of Experimental Psychology: Human Learning and Memory,* 1980, *6,* 651–675.
Hacker, M. J., & Ratcliff, R. A revised table of d' for M-alternative forced choice. *Perception & Psychophysics,* 1979, *26,* 168–170.
Hilgard, E. R. Methods and procedures in the study of learning. In S. S. Stevens (Ed.), *Handbook of Experimental Psychology.* New York: Wiley, 1951. Pp. 517–567.
Kintsch, W. Abstract nouns: Imagery versus lexical complexity. *Journal of Verbal Learning and Verbal Behavior,* 1972, *11,* 59–65.
Lockhart, R. S., & Murdock, B. B., Jr. Memory and the theory of signal detection. *Psychological Bulletin,* 1970, *74,* 100–109.
Luh, C. W. The conditions of retention. *Psychological Monographs,* 1922, *31,* No. 142.
McClelland, J. L. On the time relations of mental processes: An examination of systems of processes in cascade. *Psychological Review,* 1979, *86,* 287–330.
McCloskey, M. The stimulus familiarity problem in semantic memory research. *Journal of Verbal Learning and Verbal Behavior,* 1980, *19,* 485–502.
McNicol, D. *A primer of signal detection theory.* London: Allen and Unwin, 1972.
Mandler, G. Recognizing: The judgment of previous occurrence. *Psychological Review,* 1980, *87,* 252–271.

Mandler, G., & Boeck, W. J. Retrieval processes in recognition. *Memory & Cognition*, 1974, *2*, 613–615.

Miller, G. A. The magical number seven, plus or minus two: Some limits on our capacity for processing information. *Psychological Review*, 1956, *63*, 81–96.

Murdock, B. B., Jr. Signal-detection theory and short-term memory. *Journal of Experimental Psychology*, 1965, *70*, 443–447.

Murdock, B. B., Jr. Short-term memory for associations. In D. A. Norman (Ed.), *Models of human memory*. New York: Academic Press, 1970. Pp. 285–304.

Murdock, B. B., Jr. *Human memory: Theory and data*. Potomac, Md.: Lawrence Erlbaum Associates, 1974.

Murdock, B. B., Jr. Short-term recognition memory. In R. S. Nickerson (Ed.), *Attention and performance VIII*. Hillsdale, N.J.: Lawrence Erlbaum Associates, 1980. Pp. 497–519.

Murdock, B. B., Jr., & Anderson, R. E. Encoding, storage and retrieval of item information. In R. L. Solso (Ed.), *Information processing and cognition: The Loyola symposium*. Hillsdale, N.J.: Lawrence Erlbaum Associates, 1975. Pp. 145–194.

Murdock, B. B., Jr., & Dufty, P. O. Strength theory and recognition memory. *Journal of Experimental Psychology*, 1972, *94*, 284–290.

Murdock, B. B., Jr., Hockley, W. E., & Muter, P. Two tests of the conveyor-belt model for item recognition. *Canadian Journal of Psychology*, 1977, *31*, 71–89.

Murdock, B. B., Jr., & Ogilvie, J. C. Binomial variability in short-term memory. *Psychological Bulletin*, 1968, *70*, 256–260.

Muter, P. Response latencies in discrimination of recency. *Journal of Experimental Psychology: Human Learning and Memory*, 1979, *5*, 160–169.

Norman, D. A., & Wickelgren, W. A. Short-term recognition memory for single digits and pairs of digits. *Journal of Experimental Psychology*, 1965, *70*, 479–489.

Norman, D. A., & Wickelgren, W. A. Strength theory of decision rules and latency in short-term memory. *Journal of Mathematical Psychology*, 1969, *6*, 192–208.

Ogilvie, J. C., & Creelman, C. D. Maximum likelihood estimations of receiver operating characteristic curve parameters. *Journal of Mathematical Psychology*, 1968, *5*, 377–391.

Pachella, R. G. The interpretation of reaction time in information-processing research. In B. H. Kantowitz (Ed.), *Human information processing: Tutorials in performance and cognition*. Hillsdale, N.J.: Lawrence Erlbaum Associates, 1974. Pp. 41–82.

Postman, L., & Rau, L. Retention as a function of the method of measurement. *University of California Publications in Psychology*, 1957, *8*, 217–270.

Ratcliff, R. A theory of memory retrieval. *Psychological Review*, 1978, *85*, 59–108.

Ratcliff, R. Group reaction time distributions and an analysis of distribution statistics. *Psychological Bulletin*, 1979, *86*, 446–461.

Ratcliff, R., & Murdock, B. B., Jr. Retrieval processes in recognition memory. *Psychological Review*, 1976, *83*, 190–214.

Reed, A. V. Speed–accuracy tradeoff in recognition memory. *Science*, 1973, *181*, 574–576.

Reed, A. V. List length and the time-course of recognition in immediate memory. *Memory & Cognition*, 1976, *4*, 16–30.

Schouten, J. F., & Bekker, J. A. M. Reaction time and accuracy. *Acta Psychologica*, 1967, *27*, 143–153.

Shepard, R. N., & Teghtsoonian, M. Retention of information under conditions approaching a steady state. *Journal of Experimental Psychology*, 1961, *62*, 302–309.

Snodgrass, J. G., Luce, R. D., & Galanter, E. Some experiments on simple and choice reaction time. *Journal of Experimental Psychology*, 1967, *75*, 1–17.

Sternberg, S. High-speed scanning in human memory. *Science*, 1966, *153*, 652–654.

Sternberg, S. The discovery of processing stages: Extensions of Donders' method. *Acta Psychologica*, 1969, *30*, 276–315.

Sternberg, S. Memory scanning: New findings and current controversies. *Quarterly Journal of Experimental Psychology*, 1975, *27*, 1–32.

Strong, E. K., Jr. The effect of length of series upon recognition memory. *Psychological Review*, 1912, *19*, 447–462.

Strong, E. K., Jr. The effect of time-interval upon recognition memory. *Psychological Review*, 1913, *20*, 339–372.

Taylor, D. A. Stage analysis of reaction time. *Psychological Bulletin*, 1976, *83*, 161–191.

Townsend, J. T. Issues and models concerning the processing of a finite number of inputs. In B. H. Kantowitz (Ed.), *Human information processing: Tutorials in performance and cognition*. Hillsdale, N.J.: Lawrence Erlbaum Associates, 1974. Pp. 133–185.

Tulving, E. Ecphoric processes in recall and recognition. In J. Brown (Ed.), *Recall and recognition*. London: Wiley, 1976. Pp. 37–73.

Wickelgren, W. A. Speed–accuracy tradeoff and information processing dynamics. *Acta Psychologica*, 1977, *41*, 67–85.

Wickelgren, W. A., Corbett, A. T., & Dosher, B. A. Priming and retrieval from short-term memory: A speed–accuracy trade-off analysis. *Journal of Verbal Learning and Verbal Behavior*, 1980, *19*, 387–404.

Wickelgren, W. A., & Norman, D. A. Strength models and serial position in short-term recognition memory. *Journal of Mathematical Psychology*, 1966, *3*, 316–347.

CHAPTER **2**   PATRICK RABBITT

Visual Search

Experiments on visual search may be defined as experiments in which subjects have to make decisions about the states of displays which contain more than one symbol, word, or picture of an object, or which are too complex to be processed all at once. Thus, a review of methodology used in visual search experiments might be considered barely adequate if it touched on the precautions necessary when measuring tachistoscopic recognition thresholds in studying metacontrast or backward and forward masking, pre- and post-cuing, rapid serial visual presentation of successive displays, forced-choice judgments among sets of stimuli, head and eye-movement recording techniques, the computer generation and presentation of complex displays, and (at some length!) the many precautions that are necessary to prevent subjects from cheating or making unnecessary blunders while sorting packs of cards or scanning printed lists and pages of text. This chapter cannot be so ambitious. It deals only with experiments in which subjects search static displays for as long as they need to locate a target object, word, or symbol.

Science has been called "the art of the possible." The current state of methodology determines what is possible. But methodological solutions are not produced in a vacuum; they are forced and shaped by the theoretical questions that investigators find urgent at any time in the growth of their science.

27

HANDBOOK OF RESEARCH METHODS IN
HUMAN MEMORY AND COGNITION

This chapter attempts to show how methodological solutions have been developed to breach theoretical *impasses* in a very limited area of research. In doing so, it points to some attractive questions that seem on the verge of solution, and that might repay investigation. In passing, it offers comment on what has been called "Rabbitt's Law of Experimentation": "The subject does what he or she damn well pleases." There are ways, though they are few, to curtail even this freedom.

One general methodological point about visual search has been persistently missed. People carrying out visual search scan their environment to detect any or all objects in at least one arbitrary set (*target items*) and ignore all objects not in this set (*background items*). Thus, a person carrying out visual search must, logically, classify each object in his or her visual field as belonging to one of at least two classes. For this reason, we would expect data from visual search experiments to closely resemble data from many other paradigms in which similar, many-to-one classifications are made. Examples are stimulus categorization paradigms (Pollack, 1963; Rabbitt, 1959); the "Sternberg memory search paradigm" (Sternberg, 1966; 1967, 1969, 1975); and binary classification tasks in which subjects have to say whether two symbols, presented together or in succession, are members of the same arbitrary class or not (Posner 1979; Posner & Mitchell, 1967). In fact, each of these paradigms has spawned an intricate and isolated literature, and results obtained from them have seldom been compared. It is the thesis of this chapter that, only by understanding the common logical structure of the decisions which subjects make in all these paradigms and thinking about the agreements and apparent disagreements between the data that these decisions yield, can we begin to have useful models for the cognitive systems that underlie any of them.

RELATIONSHIP OF VISUAL SEARCH TASKS TO CATEGORIZATION TASKS

Rabbitt (1959) investigated a simple, two choice, many-to-one categorization task in which subjects inspected one symbol (letter or digit) at a time, and made one response if it was a member of one arbitrary set and another if it was a member of another, similar set. Each symbol was printed on a different playing card. Subjects sorted packs of 50 such cards, holding them face-down so that they could not overlap sorting of one card with inspection of the next. They were timed with a stopwatch. Even this crude technique made some interesting relationships apparent. Sorting times increased as the number of symbols in each set increased from one to two. But, even for relatively unpracticed subjects, sorting times remained constant, though the number of different symbols in each set increased from 2 to 16 or 17. Later work showed that this was partly due to the fact that sets of symbols were "nested" so that subjects received most practice on members of the smallest symbol sets because they recurred during all sortings as members of the larger sets.

Pollack (1963) used a different technique, more similar to those used in visual search tasks. His subjects scanned down columns of nouns that were names of particular exemplars of semantic categories (e.g. *rose, lily* or *daisy,* all of which were flowers, or *cat, dog,* or *pig,* all of which were animals). Subjects responded to each word in turn by saying aloud the name of its superordinate class (e.g., *Animal–Animal–Flower–Animal*). Times to work through columns of standard length were measured with a stopwatch. Pollack's ingenious technique allowed him easily to vary both the numbers of different semantic categories that his subjects had to use and the number of particular exemplars of each category that might appear. In his two-choice tasks he found that his fastest subjects, like Rabbitt's practiced subjects, showed a sharp increase on reaction time (RT) when class size increased from 1 to 2, but little increase as class size thereafter increased from 2 to 20 or more.

Both Rabbitt (1959) and Pollack (1963) also examined the effects of independently varying the number of classes into which symbols were divided (*response entropy*) and the overall number of symbols sorted into classes (*signal entropy*). They both found that RT varied multiplicatively with signal and response entropy. That is, subjects took the same time to sort 32 symbols into 4 classes of 8 and 16 symbols into 4 classes of 4, but they took much longer to sort 32 symbols into 8 classes of 4 than 16 symbols into 8 classes of 2. Let us see how this may explain differences in the results obtained in various visual search paradigms.

The best-known visual search experiments are those carried out by Neisser (1963) and Neisser, Novick, and Lazar (1963). In these studies, subjects searched computer-generated lists of 100 random letters, usually printed as columns of 20 lines of 5 symbols, that became visible to a waiting subject only when a light was switched on. As the light was switched on, a timer started. Each subject was instructed to scan the column of letters, from top to bottom, searching for any and all members of a set of 1 to 10 different targets. As soon as any target was located, the subject pressed a button that switched off the illuminating light and stopped the timer. He or she also placed his or her finger on the screen above the point where the target had appeared. Targets appeared at positions systematically varied between lists so that the number of background items that a subject had to scan before finding a target also varied among trials. Thus, Neisser was able to plot total scanning time against number of background items scanned. Note that this only allowed him to compare the rates at which subjects scanned *background* items when they were searching for 1 to 10 targets. After 14 days of practice, his subjects scanned background items at the same rates whether they were looking for 1 or for 10 targets.

At about the same time, Rabbitt (Note 1, 1964) also carried out visual search experiments in which subjects sorted cards, each of which carried a display including a single target letter (e.g., A or B). In addition to this target letter, cards in different packs carried zero, one, four, or eight irrelevant background letters. Thus, by comparing the sorting times for these packs, Rabbitt estimated the time taken to scan and reject each background letter. These experiments were extended so that subjects had to distinguish among two, four, or eight different target letters, *placing cards marked with each on to a separate pile.* In Rabbitt's experiments, even highly practiced subjects took longer to scan and reject background items when searching for four or eight targets than when searching for only two.

At the time when these experiments were done, the difference between Neisser's and Rabbitt's results was embarrassing—at least to myself. It need not have been so, because, as is always the case, honest differences in the results of careful experiments show that differences in method which have been thought to be trivial, in fact, reflect critical features of the process studied. Because we have had to consider these apparently slight methodological differences more carefully, we have emerged with a much better understanding of the processes underlying visual search and their general logical relationships to all other categorization tasks.

We have seen that Rabbitt (1959) and Pollack (1963) found that when there are more sets of symbols among which a subject has to distinguish, his or her decision time will be affected more strongly by variations in the size of one or more of these sets. Thus, a first, crucial difference between these visual search experiments was that, whereas Neisser's subjects had to distinguish between only two classes of symbols, making the same response (button press) to all targets and a different response (carry on scanning) to all background items, Rabbitt's subjects had to make a different response to each target. Thus, when they were searching for A and B, they divided the symbol set into three classes (A, B, and all background symbols) but when they were searching for light symbols they had, in effect, to divide the symbol set into nine classes (A/B/C/D/ E/F/G/H and all background symbols). Rabbitt's (1959) and Pollack's (1963) data would lead us to expect that discriminations between target and background classes would take much longer in the second case than in the first.

Rabbitt (Note 2) compared two tasks in card sorting experiments, in one of which subjects made the same response to all targets, and in the other, made a different response to each target. In the first case, his results approximated those obtained by Neisser (1963), and in the second they showed increases in search time with target set size.

Other differences between Neisser's and Rabbitt's experiments have proved to be equally critical and illuminating. In Neisser's experiments, the ratio of target to background items was always very low (usually 1 : 100), whereas in Rabbitt's experiments, this ratio varied between packs. (Retrospectively, this was a serious inadequacy of Rabbitt's [Note 1, 1964] technique, which confounded target probability with differences in the number of background letters scanned and displayed. This particular methodological issue will certainty repay careful investigation, but has been neglected in every experiment in the literature known to the author.) In Rabbitt's experiments, target : background ratios were always quite high (1 : 0, 1 : 1, 1 : 2, 1 : 4, 1 : 8). Rabbitt (Note 2) later confirmed that target probability affects both the number of errors and search times. When ratios are low, search times are as fast and errors are as frequent as in Neisser's experiments. When ratios are high, search times are slower and errors are much more rare. But work still needs to be done on the tradeoff between target probability, decision time, and detection accuracy.

In Rabbitt's experiments, subjects were instructed to be accurate, and averaged only .9% errors. All errors that subjects made could easily be checked. In Neisser's experiments, errors were more difficult to check and, perhaps for this reason, high error rates were tolerated. Subjects were instructed to scan as fast as possible, and made 10–20% errors. Since then, Wattenbarger (Note 3) has elegantly shown that subjects instructed for accuracy show increases in search time with target set size whereas subjects instructed for speed do not. Tradeoff between speed and accuracy of visual search also requires much more detailed investigation. For example, do subjects make errors because they systematically neglect to scan for some members of the target set? Or does speed stress lower detection probability by the same amount for all targets?

A final point is that subjects made different *kinds* of errors in Rabbitt's and Neisser's experiments. In Neisser's experiments, subjects could either miss a target (*omission*—most errors were of this kind) or they might mistake some background letter as a target (*false positive*). Rabbitt, Cumming, and Vyas (1978) have shown that, whereas people can detect many of their false positive errors they cannot detect most of their omissions. Thus, subjects may be unaware of large drifts from accurate performance unless experimenters provide accurate and continuous feedback. In contrast, in Rabbitt's (Note 1, 1964) experiments there was *always* a target symbol on each display, so that subjects could not make omissions, and all their errors were false positives. Such errors were very rare, probably because, as Rabbitt *et al.* (1978) discovered subsequently, subjects nearly always detect and correct them and can easily countermand impulsive responses during a sorting task.

This unsatisfactory story can be used to point out a moral for practical research. There is little cause for excitement when we get identical results from different paradigms that make identical demands on our subjects. Replications may be reassuring but are never provocative. But we may have a key to interesting and fruitful discoveries if we find that two paradigms that *seem* to us to make identical demands produce very different results. When such a fortunate event occurs, it is a waste of an opportunity to struggle to discover, by trial and error, all possible factors that affect variance in the results we obtain from each paradigm. The ambition of getting "really tight data" in order to fit a "really rigorous model" to each possible variant of a particular paradigm is usually chimerical. We may, indeed, master paradigms one at a time, but this will leave us with independent models for each related paradigm rather than with a common model for the cognitive processes that underlie performance in all of them.

A better plan may be to give up restless experimentation for a while in order to consider precisely *how* the task demands made by the two paradigms differ (for differ they must). Critical differences, which may reflect differences in underlying processes, *must* be reflected in differences among task demands. We must continually determine what our measurements of performance actually mean in terms of these task demands. Our results may differ simply because we are measuring different things in each task.

It is easy to show that we have not yet clearly thought through what our measurements in performance in visual search tasks actually tell us. All of us, so far, have discussed our experimental results as if we knew, or could safely assume, that the time taken to decide that a given symbol on a display is a target is precisely the same as the time taken to decide that it is a background item. But every single visual search experiment that has yet been published *has measured only the time taken to inspect and reject background items*. Furthermore, there are two good reasons why we cannot assume that times to recognize targets and background items are identical, or are even necessarily symmetrical. First, in all published experiments, the numbers of symbols in target and background sets have been very different. Most experiments have used displays of letters in which target sets have varied from 1 to 10 items and background sets have, correspondingly, varied from 25 to 16 items. Second, a very large literature on binary classification tasks tells us that people can usually decide that two items are members of the same class faster than they can decide that two items are members of different classes. In both cases, decision times are related to class size (see an undeservedly neglected Figure 2 on page 404 of Posner and Mitchell, 1967, for an early illustration of this point).

Vyas and I developed an experimental technique that illustrates this problem of measurement in visual search tasks. The technique rests on the fact that, for at least some types of display, we can show that subjects inspect symbols serially and independently, one at a time, in order to decide whether each is a target (Rabbitt and Anderson's technique, to be described, is one way to demonstrate this for any given display). Consider an experiment in which all displays are of the kind just described, and in which each display bears N symbols. On half of the displays one of these N symbols is a target. On the rest no target is present. Subjects choose between two timed responses to each display in turn, signaling whether a target is present. On average, latencies for responses signaling detections of targets will be shorter than those signaling that no target is present. This is because, when a target is present, a subject will only have to scan, on average $(N + 1)/2$ symbols in order to detect it, whereas a subject must always scan all N symbols on a display in order to be sure that none of them is a target.

This makes it possible to carry out separate experiments in which we can compare scanning times for the same N symbols between cases in which one of them is a target (and is detected) and cases in which no target is present. For example, if $N = 3$ or $N = 5$ "no target" decisions will require scanning of 3 or 5 symbols, and can be compared to cases in which $N = 5$ or $N = 9$, and mean RTs for "target present" decisions will, also, be the average times for scanning 3 or 5 symbols, respectively. The point is that measured RTs for no-target displays will include only times for inspecting and rejecting background letters, whereas measured RTs for equivalent target displays will also include the times for inspecting and recognizing one target. As Figure 2.1 shows, it is thus possible to obtain plots of a series of equivalent target and no-target decision times. If data points for displays including targets fall above data points for displays without targets we must conclude that subjects take longer to recognize that a symbol is a target than to recognize that it is a background symbol. The converse is true if positions of data points are reversed. Only overlapping functions would suggest

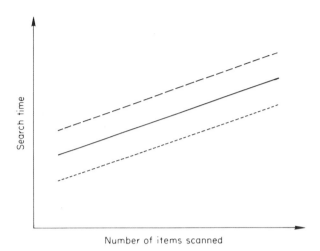

Figure 2.1. Total N on display, for display without targets. Average N scanned = (N + 1)/2 for targets with displays. (——): Nontarget Displays (– – –): Target displays if target detection is slower than background identification. (------): Target displays if target detection is faster than background identification.

that times taken to recognize targets and to reject background items are indeed identical—as has been tacitly assumed in the literature to date.

Vyas and I have found that this technique is workable in practice, though it is very tedious, since it requires data from single, highly practiced subjects. Variance between individual subjects makes pooled data useless. Even with single subjects, variance due to order effects among conditions makes the technique imprecise. In general, for most individual subjects, we find that times taken to recognize targets seem to be longer than times taken to scan and reject background items. We had hoped to use the technique to answer an undecided question in visual search: Under what circumstances (if any) can we decide that a symbol we inspect is some member of a target set, though we do not yet know *which particular* member of the target set it is? We supposed that subjects searching for large sets of targets might be able to make two successive decisions about each symbol they scanned: the first to decide whether or not it was a target and the second, conditionally, to decide which target it was. We had supposed that since the first decision was categorial, the time taken to make it might not vary with the number of symbols in the target set (as Neisser's [1963]; Pollack's [1963]; and Rabbitt's [1959] results would suggest). We furthermore supposed that once a target symbol had been located, the time taken to decide which target it was might well increase with the size of the target set. However, we were unable to show any systematic changes in target recognition RT in relation to target set size. We offer these comments only to illustrate a neglected methodological shortcoming in all visual search experiments reported to date, and in the hope of stimulating other investigators to find a better way to measure and compare identification times for targets and background items.

WHAT CONSTITUTES A "CLASS" OR "CATEGORY" OF VISUAL STIMULI?

It is impressive that, in everyday life, people scan their visual fields to detect any one of an enormous variety of different objects. A person scanning a crowd can very rapidly pick out any one of several hundred different acquaintances who could possibly be present. How is this done? What can the faces of several hundred friends have in common that allows them to be recognized so rapidly in this way? What perceptual commonalities can be used to detect that complex objects, such as *Mammals, Articles of furniture* or *Birds,* are members of the same "class"?

Possession of Single Critical Features

These questions become trivial in cases in which it can be shown that all, and only all, members of a class of stimuli share a single discriminating characteristic. Neisser (1963) and Rabbit (Note 1, 1967) illustrated this by showing that subjects who searched for target letters made up of straight lines (such as H, A, W or X) found them much faster when they were embedded in displays of other letters made up entirely of curved lines (such as C, O, or Q) than when they were in displays of other straight-line letters (e.g., F, V, K, T). Rabbitt (1967) showed that subjects learn to detect and use the minimum number of critical discriminating features that can be used to distinguish target from background letters. Separate groups of subjects searched for either straight-line letters or curved-line letters embedded among a set of straight-line letters (e.g., W, M, H, K, L, and E). As might be expected, subjects who had to search for curved-line targets, such as C and O, found them more quickly than subjects who had to search for straight-line targets, such as A and Z.

Both groups were then transferred to a new task in which they searched for the same target letters (i.e., C and O, or A and Z) among a different set of straight-line background letters (e.g., N, V, Y, F, Z, and I). Subjects who had searched for Z and A were considerably slowed by the transfer, showing that part of their previous improvement with practice had been due to their learning to use a small set of critical cues optimal for discriminations between a particular target and a particular background set. But subjects who continued to search for rounded target letters were not slowed by the transfer. This suggested that the perceptual features that they had used to discriminate between the first target and background sets (probably any curved line) remained optimal for use with the new background set.

A very elegant experiment by Corcoran and Jackson (1979) neatly uses the transfer paradigm. Subjects were trained to search for the composite pseudoletter ∅ among all rounded or among all straight-line background symbols. Then the subjects transferred to *mixed* (rounded *plus* straight-line) background sets. Whereas there was perfect transfer between pure sets (e.g., rounded to straight-line or vice versa), there was negative transfer from pure set to the mixed set and vice versa. Thus, subjects detect and use one of two different single factors (in this case, straight line or curve) to discriminate the same symbol as the context of background letters demands, but they are disturbed when each cue alone is not sufficient and they have to use a wider range of stimulus properties to make the discrimination.

Categories Defined by Constellations of Features

In everyday life it is very unlikely that all objects that are, fortuitously, members of a common semantic category will also possess a single common physical feature that is not shared by any object in any other category. Usually, each member of a target set may be identified by one or more of a set of different critical features, but no single feature, and perhaps no subset of features, will be common to all. In such a case we might assume that, on average, the number of features critical for discriminations between a given target and a background set will be directly proportional to the number of items in both sets—or at least proportional to the number of items in the target set. Rabbitt (1967) used the training-and-transfer paradigm to show that this was the case, finding that subjects showed considerably greater negative transfer when they were trained to find eight target symbols than when they were trained to find only two. This paradigm can also be used to reveal individual differences. Comparing old and young subjects, Rabbitt (1968) showed that elderly people suffer more when they are transferred from one to another set of background symbols than do the young. This seems to mean that elderly people base their discriminations between target and background sets on a larger, and therefore more redundant, set of critical cues than do the young. Thus they are more perturbed when transfer occurs.

Experiments by Prinz (1979) illustrate some limitations to the use of these training–transfer paradigms and, incidentally make a similar theoretical point about the recognition of very familiar sets of symbols. The precise details of Prinz's (1979) experimental design are difficult to discover from the text of his paper but his main innovation seems to have been to train subjects to search for particular target letters among particular background letters and then to transfer them to various tasks in which the target set alone was changed; the background set alone was changed; both sets were changed; the target and background sets were reversed; or the target set became a background set for new targets. Prinz's (1979) main finding seems to be that disruption of performance on transfer is greatest when a learned target set becomes a background set in the transfer task. Prinz is certainly correct in his view that this must imply that target letters are, in some sense, completely identified as individual symbols rather than merely detected by the presence of some critical common feature. But his further conclusion that perceptual categorization always, and solely, depends on total identification and *never* depends on discovery and use of critical discriminating features goes beyond his data.

Critical Discriminating Features versus Perceptual Dimensions

Methodological control in visual search experiments requires that we should know what our subjects are looking for when they scan a display. So far we have used the phrase *critical discriminating feature* with a deliberate ambiguity that suggests that any perceptible difference among visual stimuli—whether it is the shape or orientation of a line or a difference in color, relative size, or brightness—may indifferently be used for discrimination. This is indeed true, but not all *pairs* or *combinations* of these characteristics are equivalent in terms of the categorization strategies apparently possible for the human visual system.

An important methodological innovation by Felfoldy and Garner (1971) and Garner and Felfoldy (1970) has clarified this. In one instance, their subjects sorted packs of cards to which Munsell color chips were attached. All chips were of the same color, but some differed in saturation or brightness. In one control pack all chips were of the same brightness, but half were of one level of saturation and half of another. In the other control pack, saturation was constant, and brightness was varied. Sorts of these packs yielded baseline latencies for brightness and saturation discriminations. It is part of the logic of the experiment that one of these discriminations (it does not matter which) should be easier (and so faster) than the other.

In the third and fourth packs, both the brightness and the saturation of chips were simultaneously varied. In one of these packs they covaried so that all chips at each brightness level were the same saturation level— and vice versa. In this case, if subjects had been able to consider brightness and saturation independently of each other, we might suppose that whether they were asked to sort for saturation or for brightness they would be able, prudently, to use whichever dimension was easier for themselves, and so to sort faster. Thus, in this case, their sorting times would be either the same as for the control packs, or as fast as for the faster of the control packs. In the last pack, brightness and saturation did not covary so that the value of one dimension could never be used to infer the other. Here, it was assumed that subjects would at best sort for each dimension as fast as they did on the relevant control pack, but that they might perhaps be slower because of distraction from variation in a (momentarily) irrelevant dimension.

In fact, sorts for the pack in which brightness and saturation covaried were faster than for any other pack. Combinations of brightness and saturation evidently provided greater stimulus discriminability than independent changes in these dimensions. Felfoldy and Garner (1971) speak of this as a case in which two perceptual dimensions of difference among stimuli may be integrated with each other and so be processed simultaneously. This would be trite if it were not for the fact that other perceptual dimensions (such as color and shape) seem difficult to integrate and subjects process them separately even when they covary.

This makes for a strong methodological distinction between visual search experiments in which stimuli differ from each other only in terms of a single critical dimension (e.g., brightness, shape, color, size) and visual search experiments in which stimuli differ from each other in terms of two or more such dimensions. It also implies a methodological distinction between cases in which two critical dimensions of difference are "integral" or "separable," in Garner and Felfoldy's (1970) useful terminology. As we shall see, these distinctions greatly affect experimental results. We are liable to misinterpret our results if we neglect them.

When dimensions of difference among stimuli are separable, it seems that people can scan displays very efficiently after making two successive decisions, first on the basis of one decision and then, subsequently and independently, on the basis of the other. Green and Anderson (1956) showed that, when all symbols on a display differ in both color and shape, subjects can reduce the number of symbols they inspect by considering only symbols of the critical color. Search time is then affected by the range of *shapes* in the *critical color* but not at all by the *range of shapes* in the *irrelevant colors*.

Although it was not designed to make this point, a clever experiment by Farmer and Taylor (1980) shows that such efficient, successive–conditional scanning is not possible when symbols differ in terms of integral dimensions such as brightness and hue. As Farmer and Taylor point out, another important methodological issue needs to be borne in mind in such experiments. Even when symbols differ in terms of separable dimensions, such as color and shape, search time will increase with the variation among background stimuli in terms of one or both of these dimensions. Gordon (1968) and Gordon, Dulewitz and Winwood (1971) were the first to show that when stimuli only differ in shape detection, times for targets increase with the variability of background items. In a different version of the Green and Anderson (1956) experiment, Cahill and Carter (1976) have shown that any increase in the diversity of colors in which background stimuli are printed slows search time. We shall discuss this finding further.

Perceptual Dimensions and Patterning of Displays

A neglected methodological point is that when stimuli vary in terms of two or more separable dimensions, physical proximity (grouping) of stimuli that share a common value on any one dimension will greatly speed search. Consider an imaginary extension of Cahill and Carter's (1976) experiment, in which all symbols on a display are arranged in columns of different colors. Obviously, in this case, to find *Red X*, a subject need only locate and scan the red column. Thus, scanning time would be little affected by the number of other symbols printed in other colors or by the number of different colors used.

It is also evident that location and scanning of monochromatic stimuli will be greatly facilitated if they are arranged in some easily recognizable outline, such as a square, circle, or rectangle. Banks and Prinzmetal (1976) and Prinzmetal and Banks (1977) have shown that when groups of symbols are clustered together in correspondence with Gestalt principles of organization, such as "good figure" and "continuity," targets are very rapidly recognized if they are spatially offset from such defined background clusters. Targets are found more slowly if they fall within a cluster because, to find them, the subject has to work through all members of a cluster as quickly as possible. But symbols can be scanned faster when they are arranged in regular lines rather than distributed at random. An experiment that has yet to be tried is one in which symbols are patterned on a display in the form of two overlapping outlines, such as stylized "tree" or "house" shapes. It is likely that normal young subjects would be able to separate shapes and use them to guide and speed search, since Neisser and Becklen (1975) report a very striking experiment in which two continuously moving scenarios were videotaped and superimposed on the same display and subjects could efficiently follow *either* of them as instructed, with little or no distraction from the other. Meaningfulness of objects and cues of joint movement of outlines (cf. Gestalt law of "common fate") were apparently adequate to allow subjects to do this.

The application of weak, descriptive "Gestalt principles," such as "pattern," "meaningfulness," or "common fate," is not really helpful in discussing these results. More pertinent are the clever experiments by Julesz (1975), discussed and extended by Frisby and Mayhew (1979), that study detector systems in the human visual system (including spatial-frequency-detector systems) by examining conditions under which subjects detect boundaries and configurations in displays on which clusters of adjacent symbols either have or lack particular features and characteristics.

Can Categorization of Symbols in Visual Search Be Based on Other Factors Than Identification of Perceptual Attributes?

The logical issues underlying this question are simple, but methodological problems have proved intractible. Experiments have been dictated by the convenience of using familiar stimulus material, such as letters or digits. This is because we still know so little about how people actually discriminate between complex symbols (i.e., if in terms of critical features alone, what constitutes a feature, and what does not? If in terms of overall Gestalt characteristics what constitutes such characteristics?). Thus, it is extremely difficult to find a rationale for the invention of novel symbol sets that would control their mutual discriminability in any tightly specifiable way. Further, it is extremely difficult to persuade groups of people to practice discriminations among unfamiliar nonsense symbols until one can be sure that their performance has reached a limiting level of efficiency.

Let us consider cases in which subjects have to discriminate between symbols in a target set T and a background set B. Suppose that each T item has a set of physical characteristics, $T_1^B, T_2^B, \ldots, T_N^B$ which discriminates it from all B items. Suppose also that it has a set of characteristics $T_1^T, T_2^T, \ldots, T_N^T$ which discriminates it from all other T items.

We may now consider limiting cases: first the case in which all T^T characteristics are quite distinct from all T^B characteristics. Evidently, in this case we could recognize that a symbol was a member of the T set rather than of the B set without necessarily also recognizing *which* T symbol it was. To make the former judgment, we need consider only T^B characteristics, but to make the latter judgment, we would have to consider the different set of T^T characteristics as well. Note that in this limiting case, we could not discriminate T from B items by considering T^T characteristics, since these have been specified as being different from all T^B characteristics, and so are necessarily invalid for discriminations between the T and B sets.

The other limiting case is where the sets of T^T and T^B characteristics overlap completely. In this case, subjects would have to use precisely the same cues to distinguish targets from background items as they would to decide which target they were viewing. Here, categorization and identification of targets would be identical processes.

All other cases are intermediate situations in which there is partial, but not total, overlap between T^B and T^T characteristics. In those situations, the cues that identify a symbol as a *particular* member of the target set might also, sometimes, be those that are necessary to discriminate the symbol from all background set items. This might not be true for all target symbols. Thus, for *some* symbols, categorization would not necessarily entail identification, whereas for other symbols, categorization and identification would be equivalent processes.

Apart from the question of the degree to which the sets of T^T and T^B characteristics overlap, there is the issue of their relative sizes in any given task. We must also consider that there must be some upper limit to the total number of stimulus characteristics for which a human being can simultaneously test when making discriminations among symbols. When both T^T and T^B sets are very small, a subject may be able to simultaneously consider both, so that simultaneous categorization and identification may be possible. But if the *joint* size of the sets exceeds some unknown upper limit, then subjects may have to consider characteristics successively, or even piecemeal, so that they may be unable to simultaneously establish the category and identity of T symbols.

Ideal experiments would require symbol sets for which complete lists of T^T and T^B characteristics were known, or could be determined unambiguously and varied. Unfortunately, at present, we must make such inferences as we can from experiments on discriminations between letters and digits—very familiar symbols that have been learned as separate sets. Early studies showed that people can find letters among digits or digits among letters faster than they find letters among letters or digits among digits (Ingling, 1971; Rabbitt, Note 1). A particularly clever experiment by Brand (1971) showed that subjects can search among digits as fast and accurately under instructions to find "any letter" as they can when asked to search for only a single, specified letter.

The debate over the interpretation of such results illustrates the shortcomings of our methodology. On the one hand, it can be argued that there are distinctive perceptual features that are common to all letters and absent from all digits, and vice versa. This view is often supported by somewhat anecdotal points, such that more digits than letters have left-facing concavities or that the two classes of symbols must have different configurational properties since digits are derived from Arabic symbols designed to be drawn with a brush whereas letters were derived from Latin symbols designed to be incised with stylus or chisel. But these are unsatisfactory arguments.

Experiments by Gleitman and Jonides (1976) and Jonides and Gleitman (1976) suggest that subjects may be able to locate members of a target set of symbols (letters or digits) on a display before identifying them. This envisages a two-stage process in which symbols are first rapidly scanned to decide whether they are target set members or not and that only symbols established as target set members are, then, conditionally, further analyzed to decide to which target set they may belong.

In view of our earlier discussion, the use of a two-stage process is a very plausible hypothesis since the number of characteristics that must be considered in order to discriminate both between the T and B sets *and* to discriminate within the T set (i.e., T^B and T^T characteristics) must usually be greater than the number of characteristics that must be considered in order to discriminate between the sets (i.e., than the number of T^B characteristics alone). At worst, when T^T and T^B characteristics are identical, $T^B + T^T \equiv T^B$ and categorization + identification is no harder than categorization alone. But such claims can be directly tested only when the precise characteristics of T^T and T^B sets are known. To learn more we need very painstaking studies that will derive perceptual confusion matrices based on the latencies and accuracies of discriminations between all possible pairs of symbols within and between two sets of letters and digits. A major obstacle is that there are many highly idiosyncratic styles and typefaces, each of which, very plausibly, may produce a different, highly idiosyncratic confusion matrix. Useful studies, such as that by Townsend (1971), are only the first step in this direction.

Meanwhile, questions based on assumptions of the relative discriminability of the physical features of letters and digits may be beside the point. Jonides and Gleitman (1972) report a neat experiment in which they found that subjects searching for the symbol "O" found it faster among letters when they were instructed to look for "zero" and faster among digits when instructed to look for "Oh." As Deutsch (1977) points out, this would imply that subjects can identify completely and name all symbols on a display, and that they can use differences between symbol–name categories in order to facilitate choices between them. Although White (1977) now reports partial failures to replicate Jonides and Gleitman's (1972) experiment, there is accumulating evidence from studies of other kinds that the speed of discriminations between target and background symbols on displays may vary with arbitrary properties of the names assigned to them, or even with their respective semantic associations.

Facilitation and Interference Between Detections of Physical Features, Detections of Names, and Detections of Semantic Associations

As we have seen, at least in theory, a person can use one set of physical characteristics, $T_1^B, T_2^B, T_3^B, \ldots, T_N^B$ *to discriminate between* target and background symbols but can use quite a different set of characteristics, $T_1^T, T_2^T, T_3^T, \ldots, T_N^T$ *in order to distinguish among* target symbols and so, inferentially, to name them.

The question that immediately arises is whether these decisions are mutually exclusive, so that they can only be made independently and at best successively, or whether they can be made simultaneously and in parallel. Can we simultaneously and independently name symbols and discriminate them from background items *using different sets of cues to make each of these decisions*? (As we have seen, the *same* cues may be both necessary and sufficient for both decisions, but then the decisions are identical.) If so, two consequences might follow. When a decision about the name of a symbol, and a decision as to its category (T or B) lead to compatible conclusions, recognition of names may facilitate perceptual discriminations. But when they lead to conflicting conclusions perceptual discriminations may be made more difficult. Discussion of concrete evidence for both kinds of effect may clarify this point.

A classic experiment by Conrad (1964) neatly illustrates the distinction between the visual properties of symbols and the properties of the names that we assign to them. People recalling *visually* presented letters systematically confuse pairs of letters with acoustically similar names but not pairs with acoustically distinct names. Krueger (1970b) required subjects to search for target letters among background letters with acoustically similar and with acoustically distinct names. He found they searched slower when names were confusible, and he inferred that subjects named both target and background letters, and that interference between similar letter names caused this effect. Davy-Smith, working in my laboratory, has pointed out that Krueger's (1970b) results do not necessarily mean that his subjects *only* categorized target and background letters by naming them individually. They might have simultaneously, and in parallel, detected critical distinctive features between target and background sets and so named symbols by making decisions on the basis of both processes simultaneously. Davy-Smith argued that these two hypothetical, parallel processes may be independent but may have different latencies for completion, or may actually not be independent, and may compete for information processing capacity. On the first model, if subjects are forced to make decisions as fast as possible, they may base these decisions only on the outcome of the first of the two processes to terminate. On the second model, they may be able to use one, but not both, processes. In either case, we might expect a speed–accuracy tradeoff such that subjects would have to base all their judgments on the outcome of a single process when they are required to search very fast, but base them on the outcome of both processes when they are allowed to scan slowly with emphasis on accuracy. Like Wattenbarger (1969), Davy-Smith indeed found that the nature as well as the number of errors varied with the speed stress under which subjects worked. But in no condition of his experiments was he able to replicate Krueger's results. Further work is necessary to explain this discrepancy.

Krueger (1970b) himself points to the key methodological problem by acknowledging that since we do not have any really trustworthy visual confusibility matrix for the letters he used, we cannot be sure that his subsets of acoustically confusible letters were not also visually alike. As we have pointed out, the best way out of this difficulty would seem to be the most laborious. We need to invent artificial vocabularies of symbols, establish confusion matrices for them, assign to them sets of names of known and orthogonal acoustic confusibility, and train our subjects with these symbols until practice ceases to affect the speed with which they name them or discriminate among them. Tversky (1969) went to some trouble to study the effects of visual and name confusibility on binary discriminations among members of a small set of schematic faces. But other experimenters have been deterred by the labor involved, and by the fact that, after all the necessary trouble has been taken, only a positive demonstration of effects of acoustic confusibility would be interesting, since a failure to show interference might merely mean that subjects had still not been sufficiently practiced to name symbols as rapidly as they could discriminate them into categories in terms of their physical features.

Practice effects bring about other acute methodological difficulties. When subjects in experiments such as Krueger's are instructed to search for some letters among others, they are told the target set by name. Since the set is arbitrary, early in practice there is no way in which subjects can remember which symbols they are looking for unless they name them and then decide, by memory search, whether or not they are target set members. Thus, unless subjects are very highly practiced, it makes no sense to ask whether or not they name target set members. Their inexperience with the task gives them no option but to name symbols first and, subsequently, categorize them on that basis.

Though the evidence that naming interferes with visual search is still weak, the evidence that naming can facilitate visual search is quite substantial. Corcoran and Weening (1968) found that subjects searching pages of text for the letter *p* located it more often in words like *pathology,* in which it is pronounced, than in words like *psychology,* in which it is silent. Recent studies by Healy (1976) confirm and extend a similar finding.

Recently, however, experimenters have preferred to avoid some of the problems of uncertain relative visual confusibility among symbol sets by examining the ways in which the semantic attributes of words affect the latencies of discriminations among them.

Semantic Factors in Visual Search

Whereas words that look alike will generally be pronounced alike, words with similar meanings like "rock" and "stone" may be visually very different. Karlin and Bower (1976) found that target words are located faster on tachistoscopically presented displays when all background words belong to a different, common semantic class. Henderson and Chard (1978) obtained the same result in one experiment in which subjects linearly scanned columns of printed words. Both these experiments have a common methodological limitation. As we shall see later, decisions about symbols or words are facilitated if they involve similar decisions about similar stimuli. Thus, these results may merely mean that subjects scan background words faster when the words all come from the same category, because a decision about each word facilitates (*primes*) a decision about the next (see Meyer, Schvaneveldt, & Ruddy,

that are processed during a single fixation varies inversely with the informational redundancy of the decisions that people have to make. Eye-movement recording techniques are still technically difficult, and analysis of eye-movement records is still laborious. Nevertheless, they have been extensively and fruitfully used in studies of reading (cf. the particularly sophisticated techniques described by Rayner (1975), and Rayner & McConkie, Note 5). It is regrettable that they have not also been exploited in simpler search tasks. We might expect them to directly answer three outstanding questions: First, when subjects search for 8 or 10 targets simultaneously, is the number of fixations per standard display greater (making the number of symbols processed at each fixation inferentially smaller) than when subjects search for only one? And what is the result in this respect when subjects have to make a different response to each possible target rather than the same response to all? Second, eye-movement recordings coupled with simultaneous, msec recordings of decision times to each of a series of displays would directly tell us whether recognition latencies for targets are longer, shorter, or equal to scanning latencies for background items, and if differences of decision times for background items and for targets are affected by changes in the number of different stimuli for which subjects simultaneously search. Finally, eye-movement recordings would tell us how all these factors change with increasing practice. Pending such direct investigations, we only have a little evidence from cruder, inferential techniques.

For example, Rabbitt (Note 1) reported that when subjects sorted cards on which letters were arranged in horizontal lines, detection times for targets increased discontinuously as the number of symbols on a display were increased. When subjects searched for only two letters there was little or no increase in sorting time until a total of five letters were present. But when they simultaneously searched for four letters, sorting time discontinuously increased as the number of letters present increased from three to four. This might be taken to mean that subjects process letters simultaneously, in batches, but that the number of letters that can be simultaneously processed in each batch systematically reduces as the size of the target set (information load of the task) increases.

Unfortunately, many attempts to replicate this result with msec timing of decisions made to individual displays presented on computer VDUs have given very ambiguous results. Further discussion of the many variables affecting scanning time will show why this is not a good technique for this particular purpose.

There is no difficulty in answering the much simpler question as to how long, on average, a person takes to process each letter on a display.

Neisser (1963) trained his subjects to scan columns of letters systematically from top to bottom. Targets occurred at various locations, and scanning times increased linearly with depth of column scanned. Since subjects apparently scanned at a constant rate, the slopes for scanning time against numbers of symbols scanned allowed Neisser to estimate 100 msec as the average time which subjects took to reject each background item on a display. Rabbitt *et al.* (1978) were able to make more precise estimates in a task in which subjects searched single displays of five or nine letters to decide whether a target was present or not. Individual decision times per display were recorded to within 1 msec. When no target was present, decision times represented times to scan five or nine letters; but when a target was present decision times represented, on average, times to scan three letters in one case and five letters in the other. Thus, four separate estimates for decision times per target scanned could be obtained and cross-checked within the same experiment. For each individual subject, there was close agreement among these four independent estimates, and across subjects times clustered closely in the range 80–110 msec—satisfactorily close to Neisser's early estimate.

An extension of this technique allowed Rabbitt and Anderson (unpublished) to ask the further question of whether subjects actually make decisions about each individual letter on a display one at a time or whether they may rather "batch process" letters in groups of two or more. Note that the average estimates obtained by Neisser (1963) and by Rabbitt *et al.* (1978) do not answer this question, since they were obtained simply by dividing search times by the estimated number of letters scanned. Rabbitt and Anderson used displays of two, five, or nine letters which subjects searched, one at a time, in order to decide whether either of the targets, A or B, were present. There was an equal probability that each display did or did not contain a target. Target displays contained a single target (A or B) or two identical targets (two As or two Bs) or two different targets (an A and a B). Targets occurred equally often in all display locations. The idea was that, if subjects could make simultaneous decisions about blocks of two or more adjacent letters, they might be able to respond faster when two adjacent targets fell within the same perceptual sample—particularly if the targets were identical. Actually, even when only two letters were displayed, there was no facilitation when targets were adjacent and identical, and estimates for scanning time were closely consistent with the model that subjects made successive, independent decisions about each letter they scanned. Doubling the targets on a display appeared to merely reduce the average number of letters that subjects had to scan before encountering a target.

Note that these results do not necessarily tell us that subjects *fixate* letters on a display one at a time. They may fixate batches of 1–N adjacent letters. But we do know that within each such sample, fixated letters seem to be processed, or identified, separately and serially. It follows from all this that people must have considerable choice as to the temporal, and so spatial, order in which they process letters on a display. They can control their scanning strategy. We shall discuss this further when we consider techniques that we can use to investigate the active control of visual search. Ultimately, only direct eye-movement recording techniques, such as those pioneered by Yarbus (1956) and developed by Gippenreiter (1978), will give adequate answers to these questions.

However, there are some lessons to be learned from simple studies of latencies for detections of targets among strings of letters arranged with normal typographical spacing across the center of a display, so that, in effect, they form nonsense words of varying lengths.

Very early tachistoscopic recognition studies, such as those by Mishkin and Forgays (1952), among others, have shown that, for most people, the preferred order of scan for such letter strings is from left to right (with possible reversals for practiced readers of Hebrew and other scripts that are read from right to left). This has the effect that targets are detected most rapidly if they occur on the left side of the display and that detection times rise as target positions shift to the right. However, another factor is introduced by the fact that letters embedded in a display are partially masked by those adjacent to them. In simple experiments in which all letters appear on a display simultaneously, lateral masking effects are apparent because unmasked letters at the ends of strings (extreme left and right positions) are detected more rapidly than others. Thus RTs for target detection times usually give an inverted U function across display positions.

We must always be aware of these systematic differences in detection latencies since they demand, at the very least, the simple and obvious control of ensuring that targets fall equally often at all display positions. But if we wish to fit very stringent and specific models to our data, this control is not enough and it may be necessary to carry out a post hoc analysis of detection latencies and accuracies across individual left-to-right target locations. Those interested in the intracacies of formal mathematical models that may be used to interpret effects of target position on detection efficiency when displays are continuous from left to right or have interpolated gaps in them can do no better than study the excellent discussions by Harris, Shaw, and Bates (1979).

We must add a caveat that, during continuous experiments, we can only assume that, *on average,* subjects scan from left to right, but we cannot say that they do so on any specific display presented during a series. This is because the position of a target on one display is likely to be the first display position that the subject will inspect on the next. This is particularly evident when displays are successively presented on a computer-driven VDU so that each display is present only until the subject makes a response to it and then disappears to be replaced by the next in a long series. In such tasks, Rabbitt, Cumming, and Vyas (1977) found that when a target was detected at any particular display location, the target on the *next* display was detected most rapidly if it fell on the same spatial location and more slowly as its location changed, falling progressively to the left or right of its former position. This effect was most marked when the interval between each response and the onset of the next display lasted less than 200 msec (i.e., less than the average interval between successive fixations made while reading). The effect was reduced when intervals of 2000 msec and above were allowed between the disappearance of one display and the onset of the next. No doubt subjects use such long intervals to refixate, probably in accordance with their left–right scanning habits.

Obviously, effects of this kind may not be serious sources of error if we only intend to fit models to gross averaged results. But even then we must take the precaution of balancing target locations across displays so that targets not only occur equally often at all display locations but, also, so that all transitions between successive target locations are equally frequent and occur in random order. For more precise model fitting it is obligatory to take this precaution and to consider only target detections that occurred when a display containing a target followed a display containing no target. This is because on "no target" displays we can be reasonably sure that subjects were always fixating the same point on the display when they finished their scan, so that their scans of all sequent displays would usually begin in the same way. This technique has disadvantages, since it means that we only partially analyze our data. Loss of observations is not just a trivial inconvenience. Partial selection of subsets of data for analysis may entail the very dubious assumption that the variance within the sample of data that is analyzed is representative of the variance in the experiment as a whole. The best method is, therefore, to compute mean detection latencies not only for each display position independently but also for all possible transitions between display positions and all transitions in which displays containing targets follow displays without targets.

These sequential effects can be more than inconvenient sources of experimental error. They may be fruitful objects of investigation in their own right, and may allow us insights into the mechanisms of perceptual information processing.

TEMPORAL AND SPATIAL SEQUENTIAL EFFECTS IN VISUAL SEARCH

We have seen that targets are very rapidly recognized when they are located in identical positions on displays that rapidly follow each other. Evidence for this is available only from experiments in which single displays were successively presented. But we might expect similar effects when subjects scan, at their own pace, columns of blocks of letters in any of which targets may appear at any location. No work has yet been done on this point.

Effects of this kind are most marked when successive targets are identical, but also occur when subjects have to detect any of several different possible targets (e.g., any of the letters A, B, C, or D), and when one target is followed by another, physically different one (e.g., an A on one display followed by a C on the next). Distinctions between these two situations are interesting because it seems that when two displays, or objects, are scanned in immediate succession, people carry out a very rapid scan of the second in order to discover whether it is identical to, or different from, the first. If successive displays or symbols are identified as identical, subjects can very rapidly repeat a response they made to the first in order to signal detection on the second. But when successive displays are discovered to be dissimilar, a subject has to initiate a slower and more complex mode of perceptual analysis in order to decide which of several possible new stimuli have occurred (Fletcher & Rabbitt, 1978; Rabbitt, Cumming, & Vyas, 1977).

These effects are modified in interesting ways when subjects are given extensive practice. Bertelson (1965) and Rabbitt (1968) first noted this in tasks in which people responded to individual digits and letters. Subjects made the same response to either of one pair of symbols (e.g., the digit 2 or the digit 4) and a different response to either of another pair (e.g., the digit 1 or the digit 3). Early in practice repeated responses to repeated identical symbols (e.g., 3 after 3) were much faster than repeated responses to physically different, but categorically related, symbols (e.g., 1 after 3). But late in practice RTs for transitions between identical symbols became as fast as RTs for transitions between physically different, but categorically related, symbols.

This facilitation of perceptual recognition and of response production to categorically equivalent symbols is of direct relevance in visual search tasks. Rabbitt *et al.* (1977) studied a task in which subjects scanned sheets of random letters of the alphabet, printed on both upper and lower case versions, in order to detect and cross out target letters that also occurred in either upper or lower case. It turned out that if a person had successfully detected a particular target letter in one format (e.g., E) he or she was, for a short time, more likely to detect it again if it soon recurred, even in the alternative format (e.g., in this case e). This facilitation seemed to persist even over scans of three to eight intervening background letters. The converse proposition is, of course, that subjects were slightly *less* likely to detect one target letter immediately after they had detected another, different target. This possibility of negative, as well as positive sequential effects in serial scanning of a display could not be substantiated by Rabbitt *et al.* (1977) but remains a topic for better experiments. If such effects exist, they must certainly be a potent source of experimental error. It is certain that similar effects have been neglected in analysis of data from otherwise trustworthy experiments. For example, when an experimenter *sets* subjects to find any of up to 10 different targets on a list (as did Neisser, 1963, and Neisser, Novik, & Lazar, 1963) it is necessary to examine the results carefully in order to make sure that subjects were actually detecting all targets equally often. A high error rate may conceal the fact that a subject has systematically neglected to search for some part of the target set. He or she may, in fact, only actively search for 5 out of 10 possible targets. Even if such neglect is only partial it may seriously alter the subject's perception of the task and so change the meaning of the results he or she provides. For example, if a subject detects 100% of occurrences of the letter A, but only 75% of occurrences of letter B, 50% of occurrences of letter C, and just 10% of occurrences of letter D, he or she might actually come to believe that the actual probabilities of occurrence of the various targets differ in this way.

This opens up a considerable field of research—as far as I know, still unexplored—as to how *real* variations in the *relative* probabilities of targets may affect the *relative* efficiency with which they are detected. Note that the relative probabilities with which targets occur will also determine the relative probabilities with which they follow each other on sequent displays or are repeated in close juxtaposition during scans of large complex displays. These questions of target repetition and of the absolute and conditional probabilities of successive target occurrence have been raised together, since they will always be confounded in practice unless steps are taken to study them separately.

Repetitions of background symbols on successive displays and, inferentially, also on successively scanned parts of the same display, also affect efficiency of search. Rabbitt, Cumming, and Vyas (1979a) showed that subjects detected targets faster when successive displays contained the same background letters in the same left to right positions. They also responded faster when successive displays without targets had the same background letters in the same positions. But it seems that when one display contains no target and the next does, the recurrence of the same arrangement of background letters in both slows responses and may cause extra errors. In this case, it seems possible that subjects make wholistic comparisons between successive, small displays (e.g., of five letters or less), producing rapid responses if they are judged to be identical. Where all letters but one (i.e., the target) are repeated, this test for identity may be imprecise and fail, leading to errors or, at least, to slow "double-takes."

Once again, it must be stressed that if such effects are merely seen as undesirable sources of "noise" in data, balancing of transitions between successive displays must include balancing for transitions between sets of background symbols. A better course is balancing followed by post hoc analysis of all transition classes.

Recent work shows that sequential effects occur not only between immediately successive displays, but may also affect displays separated by time and intervening events. Rabbitt and Fleming (in press) required subjects to classify successively presented words, either responding to each in a letter-search task (to detect whether the letter E or the letter A was present) or classifying each according to its semantic category (i.e., living creatures versus inanimate objects). Facilitation of letter-detection was observed when an identical word recurred after one or two intervening decisions about other words. But in the semantic classification task, facilitation occurred when occurrences of identical words were separated by as many as three or four intervening decisions about other words. Thus, the duration of facilitation due to repetitions of entire displays or parts of displays may be quite considerable. Moreover, the duration of facilitation, as distinct from its magnitude, seems to depend on the complexity of the analysis required to reach a decision about each successive display. In all tasks involving visual search for some words among others—and very many tasks in everyday life are precisely of this kind—such factors will be a potent source of variation and their existence must be acknowledged by careful balancing of the order in which stimuli occur and of the intervals that are allowed to elapse between their successive occurrences. When this is done, investigation by post hoc analysis may enrich the interpretation of the data.

REDUNDANCY IN THE STRUCTURE OF DISPLAYS: THE WORD-SUPERIORITY EFFECT

Reicher (1969) and Wheeler (1970) were the first to show that subjects can locate target letters that are embedded in words faster than those that are embedded in random strings of background letters. A large literature has grown up around the methodology of such experiments (for applications to visual search, see Krueger, 1970a; Krueger & Weiss, 1976; Reicher, Snyder & Richards, 1976; Schindler, 1978; and Staller & Lappin, 1979). This literature, however, deals with debates about the processes underlying word recognition. Although the existence of such effects has obvious methodological implications for visual search experiments, little or no attempt has been made to follow these up.

An obvious caveat is that results of visual search experiments in which displays of target and background letters may inadvertently form words or parts of words may well be atypical. It seems that "top down" processing, from recognition of a word to recognition of some of its constituent letters, is sometimes possible. A number of factors, including the relative orthographical regularity of random letter-strings (i.e., the extent to which the left–right transitions between letters within letter-strings correspond to digram and trigram probabilities of English) and their relative pronounceability (cf., Rubenstein, Richter, & Kay, 1975) are known to affect the speed with which words can be distinguished from nonwords. It would not be surprising if targets could be located faster on displays in which the left-to-right order of letters approximates to high probability digram and trigram sequences in a language familiar to a subject, or in which letter strings form easily pronounceable sequences. But for some puzzling preliminary results see McClelland and Johnstone (1977).

Besides the more abstract relationships that subjects evidently detect when they distinguish between familiar and unfamiliar lettersequences there are concrete relationships evident in the real visual world that we have to scan in order to manage our everyday lives. Real world scenes are scanned systematically and economically in order to detect salient features necessary for particular decisions. Again, the development of a truly convenient and accurate eye-movement recording system that does not interfere with subjects' freedom of movement, and that simultaneously registers, not only the details of the scene subjects are examining, but also their precise, changing, point of fixation within it, will allow really important discoveries to be made. A head-mounted video-camera system developed by Mackworth (1968) has already allowed much useful work. Many important discoveries have been made using systems in which subjects' heads are fixed in position. Those interested in a discussion of techniques might begin with recent symposium proceedings edited by Monty and Senders (1976) and by Senders, Fisher, and Monty (1978). An excellent introduction to the main methodological points is given by Loftus in his chapter in this book. It is also possible to do useful work without eye-movement recording. Biederman (1972) and Biederman, Glass, and Stacey (1973) showed that subjects scan faster and better remember photographs or drawings of real-life scenarios than they do random montages of disassembled fragments of the same pictures. The visual world is highly structured, and recognition of this structure is a prerequisite for active, efficient control of visual search (see Meyers & Rhoades, 1978).

ACTIVE CONTROL OF VISUAL SEARCH

Visual search is always actively controlled. This is apparent from the simple fact that subjects can search a display in any order they are told. Neisser's (1963) analysis of his results hinged on the assumption that when he asked his subjects to scan columns of letters from top to bottom they indeed did so. The consistency of his results justified the assumption he had made. But search in the everyday world could not be as efficient as it is if it always proceeded in the same way—perhaps a smooth, uninterrupted, scan from left to right and top to bottom like the progress of a TV raster across a screen. Our gaze leaps from one salient point to the next, and we seem to be guided to what to look for next by what we have found already.

An early experiment by Neisser and Stoper (1965) illustrates a clever technique for studying this control. Subjects were told to scan columns of letters from top to bottom in order to locate targets. But during the course of the scan they might also encounter other symbols which informed them that no target would occur for at least 5 lines (5/6 in., "hop" instruction) or for at least 15 lines (2.5 in., "jump" instruction). The results were not clear-cut because Neisser and Stoper (1965) could only measure differences in target location times within columns of letters in which such instructions had, or had not, been embedded. They thus found advantages to inclusion of "jump" but not of "skip" instructions. This is an unexploited field of research and the use of computer-controlled VDUs and msec timing of responses would tell us much more about what kinds of instructions subjects can profitably use to tell them where to look next on a display.

It is much easier for people to control their visual search when all displays have common characteristics that can be learned. For example, Rabbitt and Vyas (described in Rabbitt, 1979) made an experiment in which targets occurred more frequently at some locations on displays than at others. Young, but not elderly, subjects could rapidly learn this and optimize their search by systematically scanning display locations in order of target probability. It is of great interest to know the precise ways in which people can optimize their interrogations of display locations. This, like so many other important problems, awaits the improvement of eye-movement recording systems. But Senders (1973) has made a useful start by using displays of lights on each of which brief signals may be flashed with unequal probability. The lights were placed so far apart that subjects had to move their heads in order to fixate one after another. Head-movements could easily be videotaped in lieu of eye-movements to give a complete record of the sequences and durations of display interrogations. Moray (1978) very insightfully reviews this work, pointing out that the necessary mathematics for description of optimal scanning strategies under various conditions of signal probability bias have been worked out by Sheridan and Johanssen (1977) and that the behavior of humans can be shown to approximate to those strategies after relatively little experience of a particular situation.

Objects in the everyday world tend to occur in clusters. For example, in a living room, a chair is more likely to be found adjacent to a table than to a bathtub. A simple technique for studying how subjects learn and use conditional probabilities of juxtaposition of objects on artificial displays is to systematically bias the probability that particular target letters will occur among, or adjacent to, particular background letters (Rabbitt and Vyas, in Rabbitt, 1981, in press). The ability of subjects to use such information is an interesting topic for research as well as a factor to be taken into consideration when preparing displays for use in experiments to investigate other issues.

As we have seen, people very flexibly and efficiently control the order in which they inspect objects in the everyday world and inspect symbols on displays that they have to search during laboratory experiments on visual search. This is, once again, an important and neglected topic for further investigation. It may also be a source of loss of experimental control for cases in which we wish to obtain accurate estimates of the minimum times necessary to locate and identify words, symbols, or objects on structured displays. One extreme recourse is to order the successive presentation of displays so that subjects have no option as to what to look at next and are obliged to simply look at whatever the experimenter decides to show them. The technique of rapid, serial, visual presentation (RSVP) is the ultimate control that experimenters can exercise to achieve this end (cf. Hoffman, 1978; Krueger & Shapiro, 1979; Lawrence, 1971).

PRACTICE EFFECTS IN VISUAL SEARCH

There is no single factor so neglected in experimental psychology as practice effects. In visual search we know that everything changes with practice. Practice reduces the number of cues necessary to make discriminations (Rabbitt, 1967). Such specific practice effects may last as long as four weeks (Rabbitt, Cumming, & Vyas, 1979b). Early in practice, search-time increases with the number of targets sought, but late in practice, search time remains constant over a wide range of target set sizes (Rabbitt *et al.*, 1979b). This improvement is not solely due to learned specific cue-systems that distinguish target from background stimuli. A number of recent studies reviewed by Rabbitt (1981) show that practice shapes and guides the active control of visual search. Prinz (1979) neatly points up the effects of specific practice on recognition of individual items from familiar target and background sets. Practice establishes perceptual categories in ways not yet clearly understood. For example it may be claimed that the entire literature on discriminations between and among letters and digits only represents the use of lifetime practice to obtain stability of categorical decisions.

Since, so far as we know, no single experimental result in the visual search literature is stable with practice, it is impossible to recommend any specific level of practice to which subjects should be brought in any particular task. However, it cannot be too often repeated that the presentation of results obtained only at *one* level of practice, or the presentation of results obtained only with 50 to 100 trials on each condition compared is quite pointless if we wish to advance this field of research.

CONCLUSIONS

As in other areas of science, methodology in visual search is not a profitable topic for investigation *in vacuo*. We encounter methodological difficulties when we are vexed by a theoretical question, and become concerned to find a good way to bring it to a test. Thus, methodology is not merely the folk-wisdom of elderly experimenters, nor the sum of the contents of statistics cook books and catalogues of available equipment. It is common sense, sharpened by recognition of the traps into which my colleagues and I have already fallen. We hope that the brief list of such traps given in this chapter may be of use to others with the same theoretical obsessions.

REFERENCE NOTES

1. Rabbitt, P. M. A. *Perceptual discrimination and the choice of responses.* Unpublished doctoral dissertation, University of Cambridge, 1962.
2. Rabbitt, P. M. A. In O. S. Vinozradova, & V. V. Noroselova Proceedings of XVIII International Congress of Psychology, Moscow, 1966.
3. Wattenbarger, B. L. *Speed and accuracy set in visual search performance.* Unpublished doctoral dissertation, University of Michigan, 1969.
4. Fletcher, C. Unpublished doctoral dissertation, University of Oxford, 1982.
5. Rayner, K., & McConkie, E. W. *A computer technique for indentifying the perceptual span in reading.* Paper presented at the meeting of the Eastern Psychological Association, Washington, D. C., 1973.

REFERENCES

Banks, W. P., & Prinzmetal, W. Configurational effects in visual information processing. *Perception and Psychophysics,* 1976, *19,* 361–367.

Bertelson, P. Serial choice reaction-time as a function of response versus signal-and-response repetition. *Nature, Land,* 1965, *206,* 217–218.

Biederman, I. Perceiving real-world scenes. *Science,* 1972, *177,* 77–80.

Biederman, I., Glass, A. L., & Stacey, E. W. Searching for objects in real-world scenes. *Journal of Experimental Psychology,* 1973, *97,* 22–27.

Brand, J. Classification without identification in visual search. *Quarterly Journal of Experimental Psychology,* 1971 *23,* 178–186.

Cahill, M. C., & Carter, R. C. Color code size for searching displays of different density. *Human Factors,* 1976, *18,* 273–280.

Conrad, R. Acoustic confusions in immediate memory. *British Journal of Psychology,* 1964, *55,* 75–83.

Corcoran, D. W., & Jackson, A. Flexibility in the choice of distinctive features in visual work with random cue blocked designs. *Perception,* 1979, *6,* 629–633.

Corcoran, D. W. J., & Weening, D. L. Acoustic factors in visual search. *Quarterly Journal of Experimental Psychology,* 1968, *20,* 83–85.

Deutsch, J. A. On the category effect in visual search. *Perception and Psychophysics,* 1977, *21,* 590.

Farmer, E. W., & Taylor, R. M. Visual search through color displays: Effects of target–background similarity and background uniformity. *Perception and Psychophysics,* 1980, *27,* 267–272.

Felfoldy, G. L., & Garner, W. R. The effects on speeded classification of implicit and explicit instructions regarding stimulus dimensions. *Perception and Psychophysics,* 1971, *9,* 289–292.

Fletcher, C. E., & Rabbitt, P. M. A. The changing pattern of perceptual analytic strategies and response selection with practice in a two-choice reaction time task. *Quaterly Journal of Experimental Psychology,* 1978, *30,* 417–427.

Frisby, J., & Mayhew, J. In J. Frisby (Ed.), *Seeing: Illusion, brain and mind.* Oxford: Oxford University Press, 1979. Pp. 114–115.

Garner, W. R., & Felfoldy, G. L. Integrality of stimulus dimensions in various types of information processing. *Cognitive Psychology,* 1970, *1,* 225–241.

Gippenreiter, I. B. *Dbizheniya chelovecheskovo glaza.* Moscow: Moscow University Press, 1978.

Gleitman, H., & Jonides, J. The cost of categorization in visual search: Incomplete processing of targets and field items. *Perception and Psychophysics,* 1976, *20,* 281–288.

Gordon, I. E. Interaction between items in visual search. *Journal of Experimental Psychology,* 1968, *76,* 348–355.

Gordon, I. E., Dulewicz, V., & Winwood, M. Irrelevant item variety and visual search. *Journal of Experimental Psychology,* 1971, *88,* 295–296.

Green, B. F., & Anderson, L. K. Color coding in a visual search task. *Journal of Experimental Psychology,* 1956, *51,* 19–24.

Harris, J. R., Shaw, M. L., & Bates, M. Visual search in multicharacter arrays with and without gaps. *Perception and Psychophysics,* 1979, *26,* 69–84.

Healey, A. Detection errors on the word "the"; evidence for reading units larger than letters. *Journal of Experimental Psychology: Human Perception and Performance,* 1976, *2,* 235–242.

Henderson, L., & Chard, J. Semantic effects in visual work detection with visual similarity controlled. *Perception and Psychophysics,* 1978, *23,* 290–298.

Hoffman, J. E. Search through a sequentially presented visual display. *Perception and Psychophysics,* 1978, *23,* 1–11.

Ingling, N. W. Categorization: A mechanism for rapid information processing. *Journal of Experimental Psychology,* 1971, *94,* 239–243.

Jonides, J., & Gleitman, H. A conceptual category effect in visual search: O as letter or as digit. *Perception and Psychophysics,* 1972, *1,* 172–174.

Jonides, J., & Gleitman, H. The benefit of categorization in visual search: Target localization without identification. *Perception and Psychophysics,* 1976, *20,* 289–298.

Julesz, B. Experiments in the visual perception of texture. *Scientific American,* 1975, *232,* 34–43.

Karlin, M. B., & Bower, G. H. Semantic category effects in visual search. *Perception and Psychophysics,* 1976, *19,* 417–424.

Krueger, L. E. Search time in a redundant visual display. *Journal of Experimental Psychology,* 1970a, *83,* 391–399.

Krueger, L. E. The effect of acoustic confusibility on visual search. *American Journal of Psychology,* 1970b, *83,* 399–400.

Krueger, L. E., & Shapiro, R. G. Letter detection with rapid, serial visual presentation: Evidence against word superiority at feature extraction. *Journal of Experimental Psychology: Human Perception and Performance,* 1979, *5,* 657–673.

Krueger, L. E., & Weiss, M. E. Letter search through words and nonwords: The effect of fixed, absent, or mutilated targets. *Memory and Cognition,* 1976, *4,* 200–206.

Lawrence, D. H. Two studies of visual search for word targets with controlled rates of presentation. *Perception and Psychophysics,* 1971, *10,* 85–89.

Mackworth, N. H. The wide-angle reflection eye camera for visual choice and pupil size. *Perception and Psychophysics,* 1968, *2,* 547–552.

McClelland, J. L., & Johnstone, J. C. The role of familiar units in perception of words and nonwords. *Perception and Psychophysics,* 1977, *22,* 249–261.

Meyer, D., Schvaneveldt, R. W., & Ruddy, M. G. Loci of contextual effects on word recognition. In P. M. A. Rabbitt & S. Dornic (Eds.), *Attention and performance V.* London: Academic Press, 1975. Pp. 98–118.

Meyers, L. S., & Rhoades, R. W. Visual search of common scenes. *Quarterly Journal of Experimental Psychology*, 1978, *30*, 297–310.

Mishkin, M., & Forgays, D. G. Word recognition as a function of retinal locus. *Journal of Experimental Psychology*, 1952, *43*, 43–48.

Monty, R. A., & Senders, J. W. *Eye movements and psychological processes*. Hillsdale, N.J.: Lawrence Erlbaum Associates, 1976.

Moray, N. The strategic control of information processing. In G. Underwood (Ed.), *Strategies of information processing*. New York: Academic Press, 1978. Pp. 265–294.

Morton, J. The effects of context upon speed of reading, eye movements, and eye–voice span. *Quarterly Journal of Experimental Psychology*, 1964, *16*, 340–354.

Neely, J. H. Semantic priming and retrieval from lexical memory: Evidence for facilitatory and inhibitory processes. *Memory and Cognition*, 1976, *4*, 648–654.

Neely, J. H. Semantic priming and retrieval from lexical memory: Roles of inhibitionless spreading activation and limited capacity attention. *Journal of Experimental Psychology*, 1977, *106*, 226–254.

Neisser, U. Decision time without reaction time: Experiments in visual scanning. *American Journal of Psychology*, 1963, *76*, 376–385.

Neisser, U., & Becklen, R. Attending to visually specified events. *Cognitive Psychology*, 1975, *7*, 450–494.

Neisser, U., & Beller, H. K. Searching through word lists. *British Journal of Psychology*, 1965, *56*, 349–358.

Neisser, U., Novick, R., & Lazar, R. Searching for ten targets simultaneously. *Perceptual and Motor Skills*, 1963, *17*, 955–961.

Neisser, U., & Stoper, A. Redirecting the search process. *British Journal of Psychology*, 1965, *56*, 359–368.

Pollack, I. Speed of classification of words into superordinate categories. *Journal of Verbal Learning and Verbal Behaviour*, 1963, *2*, 159–165.

Posner, M. I. *The chronometric analysis of mind*. Potomac, Md.: Lawrence Erlbaum Associates, 1979.

Posner, M. I., & Mitchell, R. A chronometric analysis of classification. *Psychological Review*, 1967, *74*, 394–409.

Prinz, W. Locus of the effect of specific practice in continuous visual search. *Perception and Psychophysics*, 1979, *25*, 137–142.

Prinzmetal, W., & Banks, W. P. Good continuation affects visual detection. *Perception and Psychophysics*, 1977, *21*, 389–395.

Rabbitt, P. M. A. Effects of independent variations in stimulus and response probability. *Nature*, 1959, *183*, 1212.

Rabbitt, P. M. A. Ignoring irrelevant information. *British Journal of Psychology*, 1964, *55*, 403–414.

Rabbitt, P. M. A. Learning to ignore irrelevant information. *American Journal of Experimental Psychology*, 1967, *80*, 1–13.

Rabbitt, P. M. A. Age and the use of structure in transmitted information. In G. Talland (Ed.), *Human aging and behaviour*. New York: Academic Press, 1968.

Rabbitt, P. M. A. Some experiments and a model for changes in attentional selectivity with old age. In Huffmeister and Muller (Eds.), *Bayer symposium VII: Brain function in old Age*. Bonn: Springer–Verlag, 1979.

Rabbitt, P. M. A. Cognitive psychology needs models for changes in performance with old age. In A. D. Baddeley and J. Long, (Eds.), *Attention and performance IX*. Potomac, Md.: Lawrence Erlbaum Associates, in press.

Rabbitt, P. M. A., Cumming, G., & Vyas, S. M. An analysis of visual search: Entropy and sequential effects. In S. Dornic (Ed.), *Attention and performance VI*. Potomac, Md.: Lawrence Erlbaum Associates, 1977.

Rabbitt, P. M. A., Cumming, G., & Vyas, S. M. Some errors of perceptual analysis in visual search can be detected and corrected. *Quarterly Journal of Experimental Psychology*, 1978, *30*, 319–322.

Rabbitt, P. M. A., Cumming, G., & Vyas, S. M. Modulation of selective attention by sequential effects in visual search tasks. *Quarterly Journal of Experimental Psychology*, 1979a, *31*, 305–317.

Rabbitt, P. M. A., Cumming, G., & Vyas, S. M. Improvement, learning, and retention of skill at visual search. *Quarterly Journal of Experimental Psychology*, 1979b, *31*, 441–459.

Rabbitt, P. M. A. & Fleming, M. J. Priming effects and levels-of-processing effects in the elderly. *Memory and Cognition*, 1982, *10*, in press.

Rayner, K. The perceptual span and peripheral cues in reading. *Cognitive Psychology*, 1975, *7*, 65–81.

Reicher, G. M. Perceptual recognition as a function of the meaningfulness of the material. *Journal of Experimental Psychology*, 1969, *81*, 275–280.

Reicher, G. M., Snyder, C. R. R., & Richards, J. T. Familiarity of background letters in visual scanning. *Journal of Experimental Psychology: Human Perception and Performance*, 1976, *2*, 522–530.

Rubenstein, H., Richter, M. L., & Kay, E. J. Pronounceability and the visual recognition of nonsense words. *Journal of Verbal Learning and Verbal Behaviour*, 1975, *14*, 651–657.

Schindler, R. M. The effect of prose context on visual search for letters. *Memory and Cognition*, 1978, *6*, 124–130.

Senders, J. W. *Visual scanning behaviour in visual search*. Washington, D.C.: New York Academy of Sciences, 1973.

Senders, J. W., Fisher, D. F., & Monty, R. A. *Eye movements and the higher psychological functions*. Hillsdale, N.J.: Lawrence Erlbaum Associates, 1978.

Sheridan, T., & Johannsen, G. (Eds.), *Monitoring Behavior and Supervising Control*. New York: Plenum Press, 1977.

Staller, J. D., & Lappin, J. S. Word and nonword superiority effects in a letter detection task. *Perception and Psychophysics*, 1979, *25*, 47–54.

Sternberg, S. High speed scanning in human memory. *Science*, 1966, *153*, 652–654.

Sternberg, S. Two operations in character recognition: Some evidence from reaction time measurements. *Perception and Psychophysics*, 1967, *2*, 45–53.

Sternberg, S. The discovery of processing stages: Extensions of Donders' method. *Acta Psychologica*, 1969, *30*, 276–315.

Sternberg, S. Memory scanning: New findings and current controversies. *Quarterly Journal of Experimental Psychology*, 1975, *27*, 1–32.

Townsend, J. T. Theoretical analysis of an alphabetic confusion matrix. *Perception and Psychophysics*, 1971, *9*, 40–50.

Tversky, B. Pictorial and verbal encoding in a short-term memory task. *Perception and Psychophysics*, 1969, *6*, 225–233.

Wheeler, D. D. Processes in word recognition. *Cognitive Psychology*, 1970, *1*, 59–85.

White, M. J. Identification and categorization in visual search. *Memory and Cognition*, 1977, *5*, 648–657.

Yarbus, A. L. Dvizhenie glaz v protsesse zrennie: Tochek fixsatsii. *Biofizika*, 1956, *1*, 1–15.

CHAPTER **3**   MURRAY GLANZER

Short-Term Memory

INTRODUCTION

The study of short-term memory involves a broad range of techniques organized on the basis of theoretical issues concerning the nature of memory. Such a broad range makes it difficult to set up general prescriptions concerning the research methods in this area. Certain general cautionary rules do hold, particularly those concerning the handling of delay periods. Many of the rules will, however, be specific to particular paradigms.

Given the range of different techniques used in the field, the best procedure is to use a case method approach. A set of representative experiments covering much, but not all, of the relevant range will be described. (For example, work on the continuous distractor task, signal-detection methods, and division of attention could not be included.) The special problems that have appeared with each of the included techniques, and the solution of those problems will be described. The full theoretical background for the experiments described will be found in the work of Atkinson and Shiffrin (1968, 1971) and Waugh and Norman (1965) on stage or dual-store models. The reader is also referred to extensions and revisions of the stage model (Atkinson & Juola, 1973; Baddeley & Hitch, 1974) and alternative models employing the concept

HANDBOOK OF RESEARCH METHODS IN
HUMAN MEMORY AND COGNITION

of "levels of processing" (Craik & Lockhart, 1972). Although the dual-store conceptualization has undergone extensive attack and extensive proposed alteration, it remains a key reference point in memory work and in work on cognition generally (e.g., work on reading comprehension).

RECALL PARADIGMS

The major source of information about short-term memory is a set of recall tasks: distractor tasks, probe recall, free recall, and serial recall.

Distractor Tasks

These tasks are also called Brown–Peterson tasks, after the investigators who introduced them (Brown, 1958; Peterson & Peterson, 1959). In these tasks, the subject is presented with a sequence of items to be recalled, followed by a rehearsal-blocking or distractor task which is continued for varying periods of time. In the usual experiment each sequence of items is presented once. The subject is tested with a large number of such sequences. In the Peterson and Peterson (1959) experiment, the subject heard a sequence of three consonants, then heard a three-digit number and was required to count backward by threes or fours from that number, to the beat of a metronome for 3, 6, 9, 12, 15, or 18 sec. A light at the end of the delay period signaled the start of the ordered recall. In addition to accuracy of the response, the length of time between the recall signal onset and the subject's response was recorded. The curve presented by Peterson and Peterson for proportion of correct recalls as a function of delay shows a regular decline to near zero. The Petersons checked on the role of proactive interference by comparing performance on successive blocks of 12 presentations and found no evidence for such effects. As will be seen, this check was not adequate. The effects probably occur within the first 12 trials.

The Petersons' study sparked extensive experimentation. Some of the work explored the parameters of the forgetting function presented. Other work was aimed at challenging the implication that a new short-term memory system was involved.

Before continuing with the discussion of this task, a critical point should be made. Families of curves are obtained in distractor task experiments in which variables, such as number of presentations, are imposed. For an analysis of the underlying process, it is important to know whether the family of curves being considered consists of several curves going to the same asymptote at different rates; to different asymptotes at the same rate; or some condition between those two. Families of curves useful for resolving theoretical issues may be found in studies such as Hellyer's (1962). Hellyer systematically varied the presentation of the consonants, presenting them to the subject either one, two, four, or eight times. He demonstrated a family of declining curves of proportion correct as a function of length of the delay period. The curves level off at higher values as the number of presentations increases. Other variables demonstrated to have systematic effect on the curves generated by the distractor task over delay are the following: number of consonants to be recalled (Melton, 1963); with words instead of consonants, number of words to be recalled (Murdock, 1961); difficulty of delay task (Posner & Konick, 1966; Posner & Rossman, 1965); confusability of the elements of the consonant sequence to be recalled (Posner & Konick, 1966); and meaningfulness of the trigram to be recalled (Lindley, 1963).

Most of the work on short-term memory involves the use of delay tasks. These tasks produce special method problems. Posner and Rossman (1965) faced a method problem that is characteristic of attempts to manipulate the delay task. The tasks that they inserted in the delay period differed in difficulty and, therefore, also differed in the amount of time each unit of the task took. The demonstration of an effect of interpolated task difficulty could also be interpreted as an effect of length of delay.

Posner and Rossman solved the problem by running two kinds of trials. In one, the number of task units was varied by the experimenter while the subject determined the length of the total delay period. In the other, the time was varied by the experimenter while the total number of task units completed was determined by the subject. Since, for a fixed time interval, task difficulty still shows a systematic effect, that variable cannot be reduced to length of delay.

The challenge to a separate short-term system, was started with work of Keppel and Underwood (1962). They argued that the Petersons' delay curve was produced by the pileup of proactive inhibition from the successive trials presented to the subjects in this task. The delay period served, according to their analysis, to allow the proactive inhibition to work on the most recently learned sequence. The implication of this assertion was, of course, that the delay effects should not appear in the early trials of a session. Experiments carried out by Keppel and Underwood showed just that. On the first trial there was no decline in the proportion of correct recalls over a delay period. The decline appeared more and more fully as the number of trials increased from two to six. The same observation had been made earlier by Murdock (1961). Keppel and Underwood argued for the continuity of proactive interference effects in short-term and long-term memory tasks. Melton (1963) used those data to make a stronger argument that short-term and long-term effects did not involve distinct systems.

The attempt to reduce the two conceptual structures to a single system on the basis of proactive interference effects poses special problems, for example, the very rapid buildup of those effects in the short-term memory tasks as opposed to their slow buildup in long-term memory tasks. A more general issue stems from the interpretation of delay functions. For a proponent of a dual system, short-term and long-term, that delay function reflects two components, with one component, the short-term, playing a major role in the declining portion of the delay curve. The other component, the long-term, plays a major role in the flat portion of the curve, the asymptote. The importance of this distinction between segments of curves will come up again in the other situations that will be discussed, for example, probe recall and free recall. It will be brought home in another set of analyses by Craik and Birtwhistle (1971) considered later.

Probe Tasks

In the probe-recall task, the experimenter requires the subjects to recall particular elements in a sequence of elements. There are three forms of this task: *sequential, position,* and *paired-associates* probe. In a sequential probe, the subject, after being presented with a sequence, is given a list item and asked to give its successor in the list. A preceding item can also be asked for. The succeeding probe arrangement is found in the work of Waugh and Norman (1965). In their influential paper, "Primary memory," they report an experiment in which the subjects heard a sequence of 16 digits at either the rate of 1 per sec or 4 per sec. The last digit was a repetition of one of the preceding digits. When subjects heard that digit they were to recall the digit that followed it in the list. The subjects in this experiment were also requested to rehearse only the digit that had just been presented and no others. The absence of a difference between the two rate conditions is interpreted by Waugh and Norman as evidence that interference rather than decay determines the loss of items from short-term storage. If decay were an important factor, then the fast presentation rate, with less opportunity for decay to occur, should, they argued, have produced a superior performance.

A second type of probe recall is a position probe. This can be carried out by presenting subjects with a sequence of items and then asking them to recall a particular position, for example, the first, the third, and so on. It can also be carried out by the use of spatial position probes. Atkinson and Shiffrin (1968) report the following procedure. A series of color cards was shown at a 2-sec rate to the subject, who named the color of each card. After being shown, the card was turned over so that the color was hidden. The reversed cards were placed sequentially with the first card on the subject's left. When the last reversed card had been placed, the experimenter pointed to one. The subject had to recall the hidden color. The subjects were also asked for a confidence rating of the recall. Confidence ratings are useful secondary data to strengthen and elaborate a theoretical analysis. Atkinson and Shiffrin use them in that way.

The third type of probe task, paired-associates probe, is very widely used both for issues specific to short-term memory and as a general technique for the study of memory. In it, subjects are presented with several paired associates and are then given the cue item as the probe for the response item of the pair. The similarity of this procedure to the preceding probe types is obvious.

An example of paired-associates procedure is found in a study by Murdock (1963b). Subjects saw a sequence of six pairs of English words presented at a 1-, 2-, or 3-sec rate. This sequence was followed by a cue word from one of the six pairs. When that appeared the subject was to give the paired response word. Each subject was repeatedly tested under all the experimental conditions. The results for that experiment show a serial position curve with an end peak much like that of Waugh and Norman (1965). The general pattern of a set of curves with a common high point that separates out to different asymptotes is characteristic of several sets of results in this study. These include the following: the number of presentations per pair (Experiment III) and the length of the list (Experiment II). The results for number of presentations are homologous to the Hellyer (1962) results for the distractor task. The results for length of list are similar to the Atkinson–Shriffrin (1968) results using a spatial position probe, except for the absence of a primacy effect in the Murdock data. Another experiment (Murdock, 1964) examines the change in the serial position function over successive trials. This parallels the procedure, but not the results, of Keppel and Underwood (1962) on proactive interference in the distractor task. The findings for the paired-associates probe show a slight change that is restricted to a systematic depression of the primacy effect. This is a different finding than the one established for the distractor task.

A finding of considerable importance is the demonstration (Murdock, 1963a) that in the paired-associates probe task, a filled, postlist delay resulted in the elimination of that end peak. The filled delay in this case resulted from the testing of other pairs in the six-pair sequence.

Much of the paired-associates probe work consists of a single probe after each list. When, however, several items are probed, the early probes may be viewed as producing a filled delay for the later probes. Tulving and Arbuckle (1963) carried out such a multiple-probe experiment. When the serial position curves are separated into early versus late probe data, the reduction of the end peak is again seen. This finding is important because it parallels the finding in free recall that is used in the analysis of short-term storage components, namely, the loss of items from the end peak with the imposition of filled delay. This multiple–probe technique has the advantage of producing more information in an experimental session. It does so at the cost of complicating the analysis and interpretation of the data.

Free Recall

The third and most widely used technique for the examination of short-term memory is free recall. In this technique, a sequence of words is presented to the subject, who is then asked to recall as many of the words as possible. A sample experiment is the following, conducted by Glanzer and Cunitz (1966). Subjects heard a sequence of 20 words presented at a 3-, 6-, or 9-sec interval. After each list, they wrote down the words they recalled. The serial position curves, that is, the plot of proportion of correct recalls as a function of presentation position, clearly show a pattern found repeatedly in other experiments. The serial position curves are systematically separated by the experimental variables at all but the last four or five positions. The pattern is similar to that seen in Murdock (1963b) for paired-associates probes at different presentation rates.

Other experimental variables that produce the same pattern are the following: word frequency (Raymond, 1969; Sumby, 1963); imageability of list words (Richardson, 1974); list length (Murdock, 1962; Postman & Phillips, 1965; Tulving & Colotla, 1970), paralleling the Atkinson and Shiffrin (1968) results for probe recall; mnemonic or associative structure (Glanzer & Schwartz, 1971); imposition of a concurrent task—either card sorting (Baddeley, Scott, Drynan, & Smith, 1969; Bartz & Salehi, 1970; Murdock, 1965), or arithmetic (Silverstein & Glanzer, 1971); encoding (Glanzer & Koppenaal, 1977); repetition of the entire word list under spaced, as opposed to massed, conditions (Roediger & Crowder, 1975); presentation rate (Glanzer & Cunitz, 1966; Murdock, 1962; Raymond,

1969); and phonemic and semantic relations among list words (Craik & Levy, 1970; Glanzer, Koppenaal, & Nelson, 1972; Watkins, Watkins, & Crowder, 1974) with the presence of such relations improving performance. In addition to these experimenter-controlled variables, there are a number of subject variables that produce the same pattern: age changes in young children (Thurm & Glanzer, 1971); age changes in the old (Craik, 1968a); and mnemonic skill (Raymond, 1968).

The interpretation given to these findings was that the early portions of the serial position curve reflected primarily or wholly output from long-term storage, whereas the late portions of the serial positions curve reflected primarily, but not wholly, output from short-term storage. Before going on with that interpretation, it should be noted that some of the findings presented difficulties of one type or another. The finding of the depressing effect of concurrent tasks on the long-term storage component raises a question as to whether the concurrent task should not also affect short-term storage. The data on the facilitating effect of phonemic similarity on the long-term component of free recall raises a question about the relation of those data to the results for ordered recall; in that paradigm phonemic similarity reduces the amount recalled.

In order to strengthen the dual-store interpretation it is necessary to find variables that will affect the end peak but not the earlier portions of the serial position curve. The most important of these is a filled or rehearsal-blocking delay. The effect of filled delay was shown in an experiment by Glanzer and Cunitz (1966). The procedure was basically the same as that described for free recall, except that the subjects were presented with one of several signals at the end of each list. If a ''#'' appeared, the subject started to recall immediately. If any digit from 0–9 appeared, the subject started counting from that digit and continued until told to recall by the experimenter. This arrangement permitted the random assignment of delays of 0, 10, or 30 sec across the lists.

The results of that experiment showed that the delay affected only the end peaks, in other words, output from short-term storage. With this experimental separation of output from short-term and long-term storage, detailed examination of the characteristics of both kinds of storage is possible.

One investigation (Glanzer, Gianutsos, & Dubin, 1969) concerned the relative role of passage of time and number of intervening items during delay as factors in eliminating the short-term storage component. To determine this, free-recall lists were presented, followed by either a 2- or 6-sec delay, during which the subject read either a 2-word or 6-word additional list. This factorial combination of conditions clearly shows that the effective variable is the number of words read, not the amount of time elapsed. This experiment is parallel to the Waugh and Norman (1965) experiment described earlier and gives the same message. Subsequent experiments involving the distractor task will be described that will rescue decay or passage of time as a factor.

Another experiment in the same study (Glanzer *et al.,* 1969) was concerned with the role of information load or task difficulty in the loss of short-term storage material during a delay. Delays of 1, 5, or 10 sec were imposed after lists, and during those delays subjects added by 1s, 4s or 7s from a 2-digit number presented at the start of the delay. The difficulty of the addition task was demonstrated to be related to the size of the addend. In one experiment on this topic, the number of additions within each delay period was controlled by the subject. In another experiment, the number of additions was controlled at 1 per sec by having the subject pace his additions to the beat of a metronome. This was the solution to the same problem faced by Posner and Rossman (1965) which was described earlier. The results of both experiments indicated regular effects of the number of additions but no differential effect of delay task difficulty. The latter results do not correspond to the distractor task results of Posner and Rossman (see Glanzer, 1972, for an explanation).

The content of the delay task plays a critical role in both theory and method in the area of short-term memory. Several experiments were carried out (Glanzer, Koppenaal, & Nelson, 1972) to determine if the similarity of delay list words to main list words have a specific effect on the short-term component in free recall. The experiments involved presenting the subjects with lists to read during the delay, in which the words had either a phonemic relation (e.g., *chick* is in the main list, *check* in the delay list) or, in another experiment, a semantic relation (e.g., *doctor* in the main list, *dentist* in the delay list). The results in free recall are unequivocal. Just as in the case of either semantic or phonemic relations within the list, such relations between list and delay task have no effect on short-term storage. Again, as in the case of intralist relations, these relations do facilitate the retrieval of words from long-term storage. The findings are not congruent with those to be discussed for fixed-order recall which show detrimental phonemic similarity effects.

Another question addressed concerned the size of the unit in short-term storage. Craik (1968a) tried to determine whether the number of syllables in a word had any effect on the amount held in short-term storage. To do this, he presented subjects with word lists composed of either one-, two-, three-, or four-syllable words. He found no effect of number of syllables on either short-term or long-term storage. In analyzing his data, he used both the Murdock and Waugh–Norman estimates described later (see pages 89–92). The question about word length was asked again in a study by Glanzer and Razel (1974). Lists composed of one- and two-syllable words were used. Moreover, the two-syllable words in some lists were single morpheme words, for example, *fiber,* and in some lists were two morphemes, for example *earthquake.* Again, no difference in the amount held in short-term storage was found. In terms of the size of the unit held in short-term storage, the data indicated that the unit was a word or something larger. These findings contradict an earlier development in which the tendency was to view short-term storage as restricted to the processing of fairly simple and "early" units, in other words, phonemic as opposed to semantic information. Data in support of such a view is found in reports by Craik (1968b) and Shallice (1974). They found that phonemic intrusions characterize the early rather than the late output of the subjects and come from the later input serial positions.

The question of units was pursued further by Glanzer and Razel (1974) in a series of experiments in which the list items were familiar sentences, proverbs, or new sentences. The findings were that sentences taken as units produce serial position curves much like those produced by words, with an end peak that is vulnerable to filled delay. The delay task was a paced series of four simple additions. The study also examined the free recall of lists of new sentences. For new sentences, as compared to familiar sentences, there was a marked reduction in the number held in long-term storage and a somewhat lesser reduction in the amount held in short-term storage. The argument is presented that the familiar sentences function as a unit in short-term storage very much the way single, unrelated words do in the usual recall experiment.

The picture developed out of the free-recall work is of a very robust storage mechanism unaffected by a large variety of variables—rate of presentation, semantic and phonemic similarities, and so on. There are, however, at least two variables that have a strong effect on the end peak. One is grouping, and the other is presentation modality, specifically, auditory, as opposed to visual, presentation.

Grouping has been demonstrated to have a strong effect on ordered recall (Wickelgren, 1964; Ryan, 1969a, 1969b). Its role in free recall was determined in a series of experiments by Gianutsos (1972). In those experiments, subjects recalled lists of words that were (a) grouped temporally with an additional time period between successive groups of three words; (b) grouped visually by coloring the background differently for successive groups of three words, or (c) not grouped.

The serial position curve for grouped presentation shows a marked elevation of the end peak. Instead of the usual end peak, a steplike function appears on the last two groups. These groups also show a different order of recall than in ordinary free recall, being recalled in forward order. End-peak words are usually recalled in backward order.

In a subsequent study (Glanzer, 1976), it was shown that the effect of grouping, here imposed by intonation, can be extended to the earlier, long-term positions of the list if the intonation grouping is coordinated with semantic relations embedded in the list. On the basis of the findings, the effects of grouping were related to speech processing. It was argued that intonation grouping sets up initial processing units. If those processing units are meaningful, they are selected, and are registered strongly in long-term storage.

Another effect that is specific to the end peak is the modality effect. Auditory presentation produces an elevated end peak as compared with visual presentation (Murdock & Walker, 1969). This modality effect is quite general, being reported for both the distractor task (Grant & McCormack, 1969) and paired-associates probe (Murdock, 1966, 1967a). A considerable body of work has been directed at determining if this effect can be ascribed to the precategorical acoustic store of Crowder and Morton (1969) (see Crowder, 1976).

An extension of the free-recall technique introduced by Craik (1970) has been widely used and has raised certain theoretical problems of interpretation. The technique is that of final recall. In this technique, the subject is given a number of different free-recall trials, each followed by immediate recall. After the recall of the last list, the subject is asked to recall as much as he can from all the lists. The striking characteristic of the final free-recall curve is the negative recency effect—the downturn at the end of the serial position curve. Craik interprets the effect as consistent with the idea that the final items in a list are normally held in short-term storage for a short period of time, giving them less time for transfer to long-term storage. Another explanation or phrasing in terms of depth of processing and strategy was later presented by Watkins and Watkins (1974). They predicted that only if subjects knew the length of the list would they shift from deep to shallow processing and thus produce a negative recency effect in final free-recall. If, however, they were unsure of the length of the list, they would continue deep processing to the end of the list. Since the final list words would have been deeply processed, there should be no negative recency in that condition. Their results support the theoretical prediction.

Serial Recall

Serial recall also is called ordered recall or immediate recall. It is an old experimental short-term memory technique. It has also continued to be widely used as part of intelligence testing.

The procedure is simple. The experimenter presents a sequence of items, such as numerals, letters, or words, and has the subject repeat them, ordinarily in the same order. In the framework of mental testing, the concern is with the amount that the individual subject can retain. This led to the procedure of giving subjects sequences of increasing length with the individual's span defined as the length of the sequence that he reports correctly 50% of the time.

The number of digits that the average adult can retain is six plus or minus one (Spitz, 1972). The number increases from early childhood to age 16 and then levels off. The span can be increased by training (Martin & Fernberger, 1929).

Extensive work has been carried out on the effect of different types of materials. Data by Crannell and Parrish (1957) show significant differences in the spans of three types—digits (7), letters (6), and words (5). The numbers in parentheses indicate the average spans. A more extensive survey of types of materials was carried out by Brener (1940), who presented data not only on the span for digits, letters, and words, with an ordering like Crannel and Parrish's, but also for a variety of other material, such as nonsense syllables, paired associates, and simple sentences. The most recent study of differences in span is by Cavanagh (1972), who summarized data from a large number of studies. The order found, going from the largest to the smallest span, is as follows: digits, colors, letters, words, geometric shapes, random shapes, and nonsense syllables.

Serial recall entered into an important role in modern work on short-term memory with Miller's (1956) argument that memory span was determined, not by the amount of information in the sequence, but by the number of chunks. That assertion is not correct. Span is determined in part by the information content. If that were not so then there should be no difference between the memory span for digits and the memory span for words (see Cavanagh, 1972). A more direct refutation is found in work showing that vocabulary size has a clear effect on immediate recall of consonant–vowel–consonant (CVC) syllables, this effect specific to item rather than order information (Drewnowski, 1980).

Serial-recall was used in another influential study by Conrad (1964). In that study subjects saw six-letter sequences chosen from the set B, C, P, T, V, F, M, N, S, and X. The subjects wrote the sequence in order after each had been shown. Conrad also recorded, in another experiment, the confusions generated by the same letters when subjects heard them against white noise. He then showed that recall confusions generated by visual presentation, and the auditory confusions were significantly and highly correlated; $\rho = .64$. This study resulted in a major role being assigned to acoustic aspects in short-term memory. The effect was replicated and analyzed extensively by Conrad, his associates (Conrad, Freeman, & Hull, 1965; Conrad & Hull, 1964) and other investigators (Baddeley, 1966; Baddeley, Thomson, & Buchanan, 1975; Hintzman, 1967; Wickelgren, 1965, 1969). Baddeley (1966) had subjects listen to and recall sequences of five acoustically similar words (*cap, cad, cat,* etc.) or five semantically similar words (*big, long, broad,* etc.) and control sequences of unrelated words. The data show a very large adverse effect for acoustic similarity and a small but statistically significant effect, also adverse, for semantic similarity.

In subsequent work using paired associates, Baddeley has argued that acoustic similarity has an effect only on short-term storage whereas semantic similarity has an effect only on long-term storage (Baddeley, 1970; Baddeley & Levy, 1971). The issue of semantic confusions in short-term storage is closely related to the issue of whether semantic information is represented in short-term storage. A different point of view, by Shulman, will be described.

There is an important point to be noted about immediate recall experiments. In general, they use a limited vocabulary over a series of trials, for example, Conrad's (1964) set of 10 letters. This means that the subjects know the items that will appear on a list and have the order as their main problem. In some cases, the experimenter makes available to the subject a list of all the items being presented.

Parametric work on the serial-recall task by Jahnke (1963, 1965, 1968a, 1968b) has established a number of characteristics of performance on this task. Those characteristics show many parallels to the characteristics of free-recall performance. It should be noted, however, that Jahnke has always used lists constructed of different items. In all his studies but one, nonrepeated words were used. In the one study that used consonants, the subjects were tested on only one list (Jahnke, 1963). They were not faced with the usual arrangement in immediate memory studies of the same items reappearing in different permutations in one sequence after another.

The results of the series of studies show that ordered recall produces a bowed serial position function that differs from that of free recall in that the end peak is lower than the primary peak (Jahnke, 1963, 1965). Imposing a filled delay after list presentation eliminates that end peak as it does in free recall. Increasing list length lowers the performance (Jahnke, 1965) as it does in all the other paradigms. Increasing rate of presentation also lowers performance in much the same way as it does in free recall. This effect, however, is one about which the memory literature is unclear (Aaronson, 1967). In the previously cited study by

Ryan (1969b), rate of presentation varied for sequences of nine consonants. The fast presentation was 1 letter every .55 sec, and the slow was
1 every 1.1 sec. There was no difference in accuracy of recall.

Another factor of importance in serial recall is grouping. It was
noted early that grouping played an important role in improving ordered
recall (Adams, 1915; Martin & Fernberger, 1929). Two investigators have
explored the effects of varying the grouping by various techniques.
Wickelgren (1964) imposed rehearsal grouping on subjects, with instructions to rehearse nonoverlapping groups of various sizes ranging from
groups of one to groups of five. The sequences of digits he presented
varied from 6 to 10 digits. He found that groups of three or four digits
were most efficient and relates that to a theory of serial positions within
groups as cues. Ryan (1969a, 1969b) used three methods to induce grouping—instructions, visual marking, and temporal spacing between items.
She found the temporal spacing most helpful to subjects. The other types
of grouping in her experiment produce a clear, but by her analysis, not
a statistically significant effect. The result of all types of grouping is to
take the usual bowed serial position curve and turn it into several successive bowed serial position curves at a higher accuracy level. Ryan
systematically varied the group sizes for sequences of 9 digits, using all
28 possible groupings. The data clearly show that the grouping has its
effect by permitting the subject to use positions within groups for order
information. The results for grouping correspond to the results for grouping found in free recall (see page 71). There, however, the favorable
effects of grouping are restricted to the end peak.

Comments

This survey of the various techniques used in measuring short-term
storage has noted certain similarities that run across the set. All produce
vulnerable end peaks or their equivalent. All show the effect of list
length. On the other hand, there are effects that are different for the
several techniques. Acoustic similarity has a strong adverse effect for
ordered recall, probe recall (Bruce & Murdock, 1968) and distractor
tasks (Posner & Konick, 1966). It has the opposite effect in free recall.
The first suggestion to rationalize that difference is to point out that in
all the techniques except free recall, order information is called for from
the subject. This, however, is probably only part of the answer. Not
only is order information important in the distractor task, probe recall,
and ordered recall, but ordinarily, the same vocabulary—digits or letters—is used repeatedly from trial to trial. The two aspects, required

order information and limited vocabulary, generally go together. The role of each in making the order information tasks sensitive to similarity effects has not been analyzed.

Release from Proactive Inhibition

As noted, Keppel and Underwood (1962) demonstrated the development of proactive inhibition (PI) over a series of distractor test trials. This effect was used by Wickens as the basis for another memory technique, labeled the "release from PI task." It involves, in general, a series of distractor task trials at a fixed delay with one class of materials, for example, consonants, followed by a trial with another type of material, for example, digits. The trials with the same class of materials result, as shown by Keppel and Underwood (1962), in a decline in the amount recalled. The trial with the new materials often results in an improvement. This is described or analyzed as a "release from PI." The technique is of interest in its own right. It is also the basis for a further analysis of the issues involved in the Keppel and Underwood (1962) paper. An early experiment by Wickens, Born, and Allen (1963) is a good example of the technique.

This technique has been used extensively by Wickens and other investigators to determine the psychological differences among various classes of material. The amount of the release was taken as an index of the difference. Wickens (1970) summarized much of this work, citing 14 different pairs of materials, from those that produce large PI release, for example, a shift from one semantic category to another, such as birds to trees, to those pairs of materials that produce little or no recovery at all, for example, a shift from one- to two-syllable words.

The evidence of both proactive inhibition and its release were used in the argument that short-term storage showed the same regularities as long-term storage, and that theories involving two storage mechanisms were, therefore, unnecessary. Craik and Birtwhistle (1971), however, used the phenomena of inhibition and release to clarify the separate effects of the two stores. They report two experiments—one analyzing the inhibition effect, the other the release effect. In the first experiment, they gave subjects a series of eight free-recall lists. The subjects' responses were divided into output from short-term and from long-term storage on the basis of the Tulving–Colotla (1970) scoring procedure (see page 91). The plot of the amount recalled from short-term storage remains constant across the successive lists. The plot for the amount from long-term storage shows a marked decline. In other words, proactive inhibition is restricted to long-term storage. In a second experiment, the subjects were given four lists, all drawn from a single semantic category, for example, *trees,* followed by a fifth list that used words from either the same category or another category, for example, *animals.* The same analysis of the responses into short-term and long-term storage output shows the following. The group that had all five lists from the same category showed the same pattern as in the first experiment. The group with the shift in category showed a constant output from short-term storage across all lists including the fifth. The output ascribed to long-term storage showed a decline, however, only over the first four lists. On the fifth list, with the new category, the long-term storage component rises sharply. In other words, release from proactive inhibition occurs but only for long-term storage. The fact, therefore, that proactive inhibition effects appear in short-term memory tasks does not mean that there is only one memory system. It means that output from both long-term and short-term storage appear in short-term memory tasks.

In both of the experiments just described, the subjects were asked to recall the final list items first on each recall. The reason for the instruction to recall from the end of the list is probably that subjects, over a series of free-recall trials, learn that the end list items are vulnerable to output interference. They will, therefore, learn to report those items first. If Craik and Birtwhistle had allowed that to happen, there would have been an increase in the short-term storage component over trials that would have complicated their analysis.

RECOGNITION PARADIGMS

Two recognition paradigms are used to study particular aspects of short-term storage. One is the *Sternberg scanning paradigm,* which focuses on search processes. The other is a *differential probe paradigm,* which analyzes the contents of short-term storage.

Scanning Task

This paradigm, developed by Sternberg (1969), has generated a large body of work. The task is a simple one. In the first study reported by Sternberg, a set of 1 to 6 digits is presented sequentially to the subject at the rate of a digit every 1.2 sec. A test item is presented 2 sec later. The test item either is one of the previously displayed digits—the positive set—or is not. The subject's task is to indicate whether or not the test

response was measured. All three conditions give similar bow-shaped serial position curves for accuracy with a pronounced end peak. The *S* condition does, however, give responses that are lower in accuracy and slower than the other two. On the basis of these serial position curves, Shulman argues that semantic encoding can occur in short-term storage, depending on the task, very much the same way as phonemic encoding. He views it as a slower process on the basis of the fact that reducing presentation rate improves performance in the *S* condition but not in the *H* or *I* conditions.

Another experiment of the same form as the preceding experiment, again, aimed at determining the contents of memory, uses more complex material. Sachs (1967) presented subjects with stories. Zero, 80, or 160 syllables after they heard a given sentence, they heard a bell followed by a test sentence. They were required to indicate whether the test sentence was the same as or changed from the previously heard sentence. Three main classes of test sentences were used—identical, changed in meaning, and changed in form but not meaning, for example, an active text sentence tested with its passive form. The forgetting curves based on the responses to these classes show that subjects initially have both the syntactic details and the meaning in memory but that the former are lost more rapidly. The Sachs technique has recently been adapted to the study of the role of speech recoding in reading. (See Levy, 1977.)

REHEARSAL AND REPETITION

A major concern of any experimenter or theorist is what the subject is doing while the material to be remembered is being presented. The subject may report doing nothing, being passive. He or she may report repeating either the item just presented or earlier items. Or he or she may report doing some more elaborate cognitive or associative processing of items such as using mnemonic devices. Rehearsal usually refers to the covert repetition of list items. It may also mean the more complex mnemonic work. Concern with keeping the experimental situation simple has led to instructions to think only of the currently presented item (Waugh & Norman, 1965). Concern with what the subject is actually doing has led to the use of techniques in which subjects are required to say out loud what they are rehearsing (Rundus & Atkinson, 1970). A variety of theoretical concerns have led experimenters to specify the amount or character of rehearsal either directly (Bower & Winzenz, 1970) or indirectly (Craik & Watkins, 1973), as will be described. Although the Atkinson–Shiffrin (1968) model did assume that there were a variety of processes active while an item was held in short-term storage, length of stay in the rehearsal buffer was given a major role. Work by Rundus further emphasized this role (Rundus, 1971; Rundus & Atkinson, 1970). Rundus developed the technique of making the subject's rehearsal overt, recording that rehearsal and relating it to other characteristics of recall. In one study (Rundus & Atkinson, 1970), subjects were given 20-word free-recall lists at a 5-sec rate. They were instructed to repeat the list word items out loud during the list presentation. The subjects could choose any list words and say them at any rate. They were required, however, to keep talking. The spoken rehearsals were recorded and a variety of scores derived from them—the number of rehearsal sets in which an item appeared; the number of rehearsals in a rehearsal set; and the mean number of rehearsals given to a word. Rehearsal set of a word was the set of all words spoken during 5 sec that that word was being shown. A key finding is the relation between the probability of recall of a word and the mean number of rehearsals of that word. The long-term components of the serial position curve show the effect of the number of rehearsals. The end peak does not. The end peak can be explained as a result of reading out items that are still present in the last rehearsal set. Further parametric work with this technique (Rundus, 1971) showed that, indeed, probability of recall was strongly determined by serial position of the last rehearsal set in which a word appeared. That is, if a word last appeared in the twentieth rehearsal set it was much more likely to be recalled than if it last appeared in the fifteenth. The several experiments reported in this study replicated the findings of the first study and showed a number of additional relations of interest: that output order was related to rehearsal pattern; and that distinctive items affected the pattern of rehearsal in a way that predicts their advantage in recall (the Von Restorff effect). Other correspondences shown between effects on rehearsal and effects on recall were for lag of repetitions and the presence of category-related words in the lists.

The technique gave results that support the Atkinson–Shiffrin view of the role of the rehearsal buffer. Two aspects about the technique should, however, be noted. First, it yields correlational data. It is possible that something else goes on during the presentation of a list that produces both the number of rehearsals and the proportion of recalls of a particular word. Second, the experimenter has constrained the subject to repetition rehearsal. Although subjects very often do that when left on their own, they also do many other things. And in the Rundus situation, they could well be doing those other things while they followed the instructions by just saying the list words aloud. For further discussion of this technique, see Chapter 8 by Kail and Bisanz.

A challenge to the view that amount of time spent in repetitive rehearsal is of major importance came from Craik and Lockhart (1972). They asserted that repetitive rehearsal, which they called *maintenance rehearsal,* did nothing but hold an item in short-term storage. This challenge was followed by a demonstration by Craik and Watkins (1973) that maintenance of an item in memory when the subject does not intend to learn has no effect on recall. They gave subjects lists of 21 words with the instruction that they were to retain the last list word that started with a specified letter. For example they could be given G as the critical letter and then hear the list that started as follows: *daughter, oil, rifle, garden, grain, table, football, anchor, giraffe. . . .* If *giraffe* was the last word in the list starting with the letter G, the subject would report just that word at the end of the list. With this arrangement the subject held the word *garden* in memory for 1 unit of time, *grain* for 4 units and *giraffe* over the remaining 12 list words for 13 units of time. The time intervals obtained this way were systematically varied across the lists. After 27 lists had been presented and responded to in this way, the subjects were given a final free recall. Those data show that rate of presentation and whether the word had been recalled in the immediate-recall test had a significant effect. The amount of time that a word was held in memory during list presentation had no effect.

A second experiment made the same point about the absence of effect of the simple length of time an item was in short-term storage. Craik and Watkins (1973) gave subjects 12-word free-recall lists with either immediate recall or recall after an unfilled delay. The subjects were asked to do overt rehearsal and also to concentrate on the last four list items. The effect of the unfilled delay was to produce many more overt rehearsals of the last four items. The final free recall showed no difference, however, between the two conditions.

The same point was made by Woodward, Bjork, and Jongeward (1973). They used a technique similar to that in Craik and Watkins' (1973) first experiment, instructed forgetting. They showed subjects lists of 36 words. Each word was followed by a period of 0–12 sec unfilled delay and then a green dot indicating that the word was to be remembered or a red dot indicating that it was to be forgotten. Each list was followed by immediate recall. After four such lists, the subjects were given final free recall, both classes of words being requested. There is no effect of the length of the rehearsal period either on the immediate recall of the to-be-remembered words or on the final recall of either class of words. This is further support for the Craik–Lockhart proposal. Woodward, Bjork, and Jongeward (1973) also report a result that goes counter to that proposal. They report in a subsequent experiment the results of a final recognition test for this same procedure. The results show a statistically significant effect of length of rehearsal for both the to-be-remembered and the to-be-forgotten words.

This finding received further support in a study by Glenberg, Smith, and Green (1977). They used a procedure in which they reversed the focus of the distractor task. They gave subjects four-digit numbers followed by varying intervals in which a word repetition task was carried out as an ostensible distractor task. A final recall test showed no effect of the length of the rehearsal but a final recognition test did.

Further limitations on the generality of the original Craik–Lockhart proposal may be found in a recent study by Rundus (1980) using the same procedure as Glenberg, Smith, and Green (1977), but extending the period of rehearsal time into the range of 6–60 sec. The preceding study used a maximum of 18 sec of rehearsal. After 20 distractor test trials, final free recall was given. The results show a clear and statistically significant effect of length of rehearsal.

In the studies discussed previously, the length of time an item is held in short-term storage has been examined. The closely related topic of the role of repetition was studied by Nelson (1977). After subjecting the Craik–Lockhart proposal to a critical analysis, Nelson demonstrated that, contrary to that proposal, repetition that involved the same level of encoding increased both recall and recognition. In the first experiment of the study, he showed subjects a list of 20 words with the instruction to classify each word for the presence of a given phoneme, for example, /r/. Some subjects saw each list word only once. Others saw the list a second time. In the single presentation condition, either a 4-sec or 8-sec rate was used. The 2-presentation condition was run at a 4-sec rate. The 2 single presentation rates permitted unambiguous interpretation of any effect found for 2 presentations, since 2 presentations meant that each individual word was seen by the subject for 8-sec. After classification of the list words was completed, subjects were given an unexpected free-recall trial. The results show a clear effect of repetition. A subsequent study shows that that effect is not restricted to the spaced repetitions used in the first experiment. Massed repetition also has a clear effect.

Rehearsal plays a critical role in the evaluation of the basic nature of forgetting from short-term storage. The question of whether forgetting is due to decay, displacement, or some other factor has been repeatedly addressed, as previously noted. One attempt to evaluate the role of decay in forgetting shows the problems involved in trying to control rehearsal.

Reitman (1971) tried to determine whether decay, in other words, forgetting in the absence of interference, occurred. To obtain a delay without interference she used the distractor task with three words to be recalled. The 15-sec delay period was occupied with a difficult signal detection task—listening for a faint tone against white noise. The tone was set so that each subject could detect it only 50% of the time. To check if the subjects were indeed paying full attention to the detection task, she also measured their performance when they did not have the memory task. She found no difference.

With tone detection during the delay she found no evidence of forgetting. When, however, the subjects had a syllable detection task during the delay interval there was a loss. These findings, replicated and extended by Atkinson and Shiffrin (1971), are contrary to the idea of decay.

A further and fuller investigation by Reitman (1974), however, showed that the original set of results was misleading. First, there was a problem of ceiling effects. If the memory task is too easy, subjects may forget some of the material and still show no loss on the experimental measures. To make ceiling effects less likely, Reitman increased the sequence to be recalled from three to five words. Second, there was the problem of subjects rehearsing covertly. She devised a set of stricter tests for the presence of rehearsal. Accuracy (d's) and latency on the tone distractor task and tradeoffs were examined for each trial. The performance across the trials was determined for both the experimental and control condition. The performance across the trials was also determined for both the experimental and control condition. The pattern obtained when the subjects were instructed to rehearse covertly was determined. The subjects were also, in one of the two experiments reported, interrogated as to whether they had done any rehearsal on the experimental trials. Their responses were related to the results of the detailed analysis of their detection task performance.

In one experiment, Reitman shows that with the five-word task to eliminate ceiling effects, there is a decline in recall over the delay period with tone detection. This decline becomes more pronounced if the original group of 29 subjects is reduced to 6 who showed clear positive evidence of following instructions. In a second experiment, Reitman divided the group of 23 subjects into those who confessed to rehearsing despite the instructions and those who did not. Only the second group shows a drop in recall of the words. Reitman further examined the ways in which the detailed data just described can be used to partition subjects into covert rehearsers and nonrehearsers.

The results of the series of experiments underline the difficulty of maintaining experimental control over covert rehearsal. They also leave decay—loss of material from memory—as a function of time without rehearsal, a viable factor in theories of memory.

MODALITY EFFECTS

A simple and pretheoretical question about memory tasks is whether the modality of presentation makes a difference. The answer to this question is clearly "yes" (see page 72). That answer leads to a complex question with major theoretical implications—whether there are different types of codes in memory, for example, visual and auditory.

Early work had emphasized the dominant role of acoustic factors in short-term memory. Visual information was considered to require translation into a verbal code in order to be held in short-term storage and in order to be processed further. Semantic information was considered to be the result of processing the primitive acoustic information in short-term storage, and to be restricted to long-term storage. More extensive consideration led to the demonstration that auditory, visual, and other sense modality information was encoded distinctively in short-term storage and that the distinctive information could be found carried through, and stored, in long-term storage. Evidence of long-term retention of visual information is found in Kolers (1975), and evidence of auditory information in Nelson and Rothbart (1972). The idea that semantic information was represented only in long-term storage was countered by the previously cited work of Shulman (1970).

A variety of different techniques have been used to establish the special sensory characteristic of memory. One is to show that the material from one modality has a differential effect on memory. An example of this is the demonstration by Murdock and Walker (1969) that auditory presentation produces better recall of free-recall lists than visual presentation does. This advantage of auditory presentation is concentrated in the end peak. Another technique is to show that some specific characteristic of the material to be learned, such as acoustic similarity, has an effect on performance. Baddeley and Dale (1966) used this technique. A third technique is to show that the specific character of the distractor or delay task, for example, whether it is auditory or not, is important in determining the loss of items from short-term storage. Watkins and Watkins (1980) used this to show that the end peak in ordered recall of a list presented auditorally was depressed more by an auditory delay task than a visual delay task. A fourth technique, which is closely related to the second, involves the examination of the characteristics of errors in recall. If these errors can be shown to be acoustic confusions of list items, then support is found for auditory encoding. Conrad (1964) used this technique, as previously noted, for ordered recall. Craik (1968b) carried out a similar analysis for free recall, showing that the errors could be related to items from the end of the list.

The same techniques have been used to establish the presence of special visual encoding. An influential example of the use of the structure of the task material to support a claim of visual encoding is found in a study by Posner, Boies, Eichelman, and Taylor (1969). The basic paradigm involves presenting two letters visually. The subject was required to indicate, by pressing a key, whether the letters were the same or not. There were two pairings to which the subject was supposed to respond "same." One was called a physical match, A and A or a and a. The other was called a name match, A and a or a and A. Posner *et al.* showed that physical matches are faster than name matches and that this advantage declines systematically over a 2-sec period. The explanation of the effect is that the visual encoding of the stimuli used for the physical matches, follows a faster and different course than the verbal encoding needed for the name matches. Presenting a random visual mask in the interval between the first and second letter does not eliminate this effect. Therefore, it can be argued that the effect is not in iconic memory, which would be affected by such a mask (Sperling, 1963).

The technique just described is somewhat indirect, depending on a difference between two measures. A more direct demonstration of a different time course is found in a study by Kroll, Parks, Parkinson, Bieber, and Johnson (1970). Letters that were to be recalled were presented either visually or aurally while the subjects shadowed other letters that were presented aurally. The aural presentation of letters to be recalled was in a male voice, whereas that for the letters to be shadowed was in a female voice, to distinguish the two. The retention over delay periods was higher for the visual presentation.

Murray and Newman (1973) varied the characteristics of the delay task in order to show visual encoding in a variant of the distractor task. Their subjects were shown a matrix containing a circle, a square, and a triangle. They were required to reproduce the positions of the three in a blank matrix after a delay interval of 0–20 sec. During the delay the subjects carried out a variety of tasks, including counting and drawing. The verbal task, counting, produced no decline in recall. The visual task, drawing, did.

The Watkins and Watkins (1980) study cited earlier in this section includes an experiment in which performance on an orally presented ordered-recall task is lowered more by an auditory than a visual delay task. In the same experiment, a visually presented ordered-recall task is lowered more by a visual than an auditory delay task.

The studies discussed above do not always analyze the effects into long-term and short-term components. It can be argued, however, that the analysis is less important here than in other areas. If specific modality information is reflected in long-term storage, it presumably was also present in short-term storage. The system is ordinarily viewed as a serial system with information going first to short-term storage and then to long-term storage. (See, however, Warrington & Shallice, 1969.)

PRELOAD AND CONCURRENT TASK LOAD

In the earlier section, "Rehearsal and Repetition," examples were given of the imposition of various tasks during a delay period (Reitman, 1971, 1974). These may be viewed as examples of dual tasks. One task was the maintenance of information in memory, and the other was the detection task, designed to prevent rehearsal.

There are two other ways in which the experimenter can impose a second task during a memory task. One, called concurrent load, is imposed during the presentation of the material to be remembered. The other, preload, is imposed before the presentation. In the case of preload, the expectation is that the subject will have to carry out some activity, for example, rehearsal, on the basis of that imposed task. The purpose of imposing a concurrent task or preload is to analyze some aspect of the process of memory. At a general level, this may be to determine how much loss occurs in order to determine how a reduction of capacity affects the memory task. An example of this is the work showing an effect of concurrent card sorting (Murdock, 1965; Baddeley, Scott, Drynan, & Smith, 1969), arithmetic (Silverstein & Glanzer, 1971), tracking (Martin, 1970), and reaction time tasks (Johnston, Wagstaff, & Griffith, 1972). The work also can be used to determine a general effect on the system or an effect that is specific to some part of the system. Thus, since the card sorting and arithmetic tasks have an effect on the early part of the serial position curve, the assertion is made that those tasks affect some aspect of long-term storage, for example, transfer of information into it. Other specific uses of concurrent load may be found in experiments in which the form of a concurrent task is varied to determine the nature of the processing or the form of information, for example, articulatory or acoustic, in primary memory. Some examples of the use of concurrent task and preload by Levy and Baddeley will be described briefly.

Levy (1971) carried out experiments to examine the role of articulation in short-term memory. She showed subjects sequences of eight letters which were tested by sequential probe. In one condition of the experiment, the subjects read the letters aloud as they were presented. In the other, an articulation suppression task adopted from Murray (1967) was carried out. They said "hi-ya" as each letter appeared. The results show a strong effect of the articulation suppression task. Other conditions were included in the experiment in order to analyze the role of articulation, for example, simultaneous auditory presentation of the letters. A second experiment using words gave the same results both for probe recall and recognition. The serial position curves reported indicate an effect on both short-term storage and long-term storage of the suppression. Levy (1975) has subsequently extended this approach to memory for sentences.

Baddeley and Hitch (1974) have carried out a number of experiments using both concurrent loads and preloads to analyze the role of working memory in a variety of tasks—reasoning, comprehension, and recall. In one experiment, they gave subjects 16-word lists for free recall. In the control condition, the lists were given without any other task. In the preload condition, the subject was given a three-digit or six-digit sequence before the word list, with the instruction to retain that sequence for recall. The subject then received the word list, recalled the words, and then recalled the digits. The preload has a systematic effect on the long-term storage component, as can be seen in the serial position curves for the three conditions. There does not seem to be an effect on the short-term storage component. The authors do not report the accuracy of recall of the digits. Since, for the digits, this experimental arrangement is the equivalent of a distractor task, those data are relevant. The word lists were spoken at a 2-sec rate. This means that 22 sec plus the free-recall response time elapsed between the digit presentation and recall. If the recall of the digits was without error then the interpretation would be that they had entered long-term storage. The effects on the long-term component of the free recall might be considered equivalent to the effects found in lengthening a list.

In another experiment, the subjects saw either three- or six-digit sequences, which they wrote during blank intervals between sequences. While they carried out this task, they heard 16-word lists, which they were required to recall. There was also a control condition in which the subjects wrote the digit sequences as they saw them, not waiting for blank periods. This was to produce a minimal memory load. The results show an effect on the long-term storage component of the serial position curve, produced by the six-digit condition. The performance on the digit task is not reported. This task is, of course, similar both in design and results to the other concurrent load tasks previously reported.

MEASURES OF THE AMOUNT HELD IN SHORT-TERM STORAGE

In the preceding sections, a rough separation of output from short-term and long-term storage was made on the basis of the serial position curve in free recall or probe recall. A similar rough separation was made on the basis of the declining and the asymptotic sections of the forgetting function obtained with the distractor technique.

Up to this point, the discussion of material held in short-term storage has not touched on the measures of the amounts held. This amount is, of course, of considerable interest. It is apparent, however, that if it is assumed that the subject's output consists of commingled response from long-term and short-term storage, the estimation of amounts is not simple.

In cases in which there is a detailed theory, such as that of Atkinson and Shiffrin (1968), there may be a parameter that designates either the size of the buffer or the average amount of material held in the buffer. In that theory, as applied to a set of probe recall data, the parameter that designated buffer size was estimated at five in the course of obtaining a minimum χ^2 fit to the data. The same kind of estimation appears in other theories, for example, Kintsch and van Dijk's (1978) model of text comprehension.

A number of estimation procedures have also been devised that are not embedded in extensive, formal theories. They can be used to analyze serial position curves into short-term and long-term components and assign quantities to those components. Each is based on a number of assumptions about short-term and long-term storage. They do not involve the routines of curve fitting and have been used in a large number of studies. Three main procedures will be described. They and some others have been reviewed in detail by Watkins (1974).

Waugh–Norman Estimates

Working from their presentation of a two-store model, Waugh and Norman (1965) set up the following equation

$$R_i = PM_i + SM_i - PM_iSM_i \tag{1}$$

where R_i is the probability that item i is recalled, PM_i is the probability that it is in primary memory, or short-term storage, and SM_i that it is in secondary memory, or long-term storage. Since Waugh and Norman assume that the probability that an item is in one store is independent of the probability that it is in the other, the probability of an item being in both is equal to the product of PM_i and SM_i, as indicated in Eq. (1). Eq. (1) can then be rewritten as:

$$PM_i = \frac{R_i - SM_i}{1 - SM_i} \tag{2}$$

Since R_i is an observed value, if SM_i can be estimated it is simple to estimate PM_i. Waugh and Norman use the middle section of serial position curve, excluding the primary peak and the end peak, to estimate this value. A second assumption is, therefore, made that the long-term components stay at the same level for the final list positions, that is, the $SM_i = SM$, a constant.

An example of an estimation using this equation is the following. If the proportion correct at position 19, R_{19}, in a 20-item list is .51 and the mean of the middle positions 7–15, used to estimate SM, is .29 then

$$PM_{19} = \frac{.51 - .29}{1 - .29} = \frac{.22}{.71} = .31$$

A third assumption often made in using this estimate is that the probability of retrieving an item from short-term storage is unaffected by previous retrievals, that is, that there is no output interference. (This assumption was not made by Waugh and Norman. They take account of both output and input in measuring the interference imposed on a list item.) A fourth assumption is that all presented elements enter short-term storage.

There are logical or empirical bases to question each of these assumptions. Watkins (1974) details some of them. He suggests that the problem of items not entering short-term storage can be handled by rewriting Eqs. (1) and (2) as follows:

$$R_i = PM_i + SM_i - (PM_i SM_i / R_j) \tag{3}$$

where R_j is the probability of recall of the last list item, used as an estimate of the probability that items are entering short term storage.

If the proportion recalled from the last serial position in a 20-item list, R_j, were equal to .80, the estimate for position 19 would be revised as follows:

$$PM_{19} = \frac{.80\,(.51 - .29)}{.80 - .29} = \frac{.176}{.51} = .35$$

This correction, however, has not been used in the literature.

The assumption that the long-term storage component remains constant through the final list positions may be questioned on the basis of negative recency effects. A procedure used by Raymond (1969) may be considered a solution to handling violations of that assumption. In it, serial position curves are obtained for any experimental condition of interest under both delayed and immediate recall. The values of the delay curve are used to give each of the SM_i values in Eqs. (1) and (2).

Whatever form of the Waugh–Norman estimate is used, one aim is to obtain a single number describing the amount held in short-term storage. This is done by summing the PM_i's obtained across all serial positions i. This type of estimate remains a useful one for investigations of primary memory.

Tulving–Colotla Estimates

A second type of estimate has been presented by Tulving and Colotla (1970). The estimate is based on the count of all items that are recalled with no more than seven input or output items intervening since presentation. For example, suppose a subject has received a 12-word list symbolized by the letters A, B, C, D, E, F, G, H, I, J, K, and then recalls words K, J, C, A, I, B, D, and H, in that order. The entire input and output list is then A, B, C, D, E, F, G, H, I, J, K, / K, J, C, A, I, B, D, H. There are three words assigned to short-term storage in this estimate—K (zero intervening between input and output), J (two intervening), and I (six intervening). This estimate assumes that short-term storage suffers equal interference amounting to the loss of one item from any input or output item. It also assumes that no word further than eight items from the end of the list can be held in short-term storage. The selection of seven as the number of intervening items is based on the extent of the recency effect. Other investigators have chosen five (Roberts, 1969) or six (Craik, 1970).

Murdock Estimates

A third procedure is one devised by Murdock (1967b). It is based on the observation that the number of items recalled in free recall is a linear function of the total presentation time.

$$R = kT + m \qquad (4)$$

where R is number recalled and T the total time for list presentation.

The terms k and m are slope and intercept constants. The m may be viewed as a measure of the amount held in short-term storage.

In order to use this estimate, it is necessary to carry out an experiment that varies total time per list. This can be done using either lists of fixed length with variation of the amount of time per list or lists that vary in length with fixed time per item. To obtain Murdock estimates, a special experimental design is, therefore, needed. This technique, moreover, runs into difficulties when list lengths are near m.

Watkins (1974) compared the Waugh–Norman and Tulving–Colotla estimates on the basis of two statistical tests, using 18 sets of data from Tulving and Colotla (1970). One test involves determining the variance of the estimates over these sets of data. The other test involves a more complex comparison to determine the sensitivity of the estimators to differential effects on long-term and short-term storage. In both tests, the Tulving–Colotla procedure turns out to be better.

At this point, it seems premature to select one or the other of these estimation procedures. The three characteristics, convenience, stability, and logical relation to the theory being used, should determine the choice. The two popular methods, moreover, the Waugh–Norman and the Tulving–Colotla, give similar estimates as can be seen by examining them for the 18 data sets listed by Watkins (1974). The mean for Waugh–Norman in those data sets is 2.93. For Tulving–Colotla it is 3.18. In a study by Glanzer and Koppenaal (1977) the Waugh–Norman estimates of short-term storage for two different experimental conditions were 2.54 and 2.55. The Tulving–Colotla estimates were 2.83 and 2.88. It is not likely that the choice of one or the other of these procedures will lead to any markedly different interpretation of any set of data.

CONCLUDING REMARKS

In the preceding sections, some of the key experiments in the area of short-term memory have been described. They have been given in detail so that they can be used as guides for further experimental work. The theoretical questions that gave rise to the experiments have also been presented briefly since the techniques do not make sense except as devices to answer those questions. The last sentence understates the relation between theory and technique. Methods used to set delay periods must be determined by theories about the processing carried out during delay. Methods used to block or control rehearsal are determined by theories about the role and effect of rehearsal. Techniques not only address theoretical questions, they are determined by those theoretical questions.

ACKNOWLEDGMENTS

Preparation of this chapter was supported by Grant 1R01MH32779 from the National Institute of Mental Health. The author thanks Doris Aaronson for comments on an earlier draft.

REFERENCE NOTE

1. Raymond, B. *Factors affecting long-term and short-term storage in free recall.* Unpublished doctoral dissertation, New York University, 1968.

REFERENCES

Aaronson, D. Temporal factors in perception and short-term memory. *Psychological Bulletin,* 1967, *67,* 130–144.

Adams, H. F. A note on the effect of rhythm on memory. *Psychological Review,* 1915, *22,* 289–299.

Anders, T. R., Fozard, J. L., & Lillyquist, T. D. Effects of age upon retrieval from short-term memory. *Developmental Psychology,* 1972, *6,* 214–217.

Atkinson, R. C., Holmgren, J. E., & Juola, J. F. Processing time as influenced by the number of elements in a visual display. *Perception & Psychophysics,* 1969, *6,* 321–327.

Atkinson, R. C., & Juola, J. F. Factors influencing speed and accuracy of word recognition. In S. Kornblum (Ed.), *Attention and performance IV.* New York: Academic Press, 1973. Pp. 583–612.

Atkinson, R. C., & Shiffrin, R. M. Human memory: A proposed system and its control processes. In K. W. Spence & J. T. Spence (Eds.), *The psychology of learning and motivation: Advances in research and theory* (Vol. 2). New York: Academic Press, 1968. Pp. 89–195.

Atkinson, R. C., & Shiffrin, R. M. The control of short-term memory. *Scientific American,* 1971, *August,* 82–90.

Baddeley, A. D. Short-term memory for word sequences as a function of acoustic, semantic, and formal similarity. *Quarterly Journal of Experimental Psychology,* 1966, *18,* 362–365.

Baddeley, A. D. Effects of acoustic and semantic similarity on short-term paired-associate learning. *British Journal of Psychology,* 1970, *61,* 335–343.

Baddeley, A. D., & Dale, H. C. A. The effect of semantic similarity on retroactive interference in long- and short-term memory. *Journal of Verbal Learning and Verbal Behavior,* 1966, *5,* 417–420.

Baddeley, A. D., & Hitch, G. Working memory. In G. H. Bower (Ed.), *The psychology of learning and motivation: Advances in research and theory.* (Vol. 8). New York: Academic Press, 1974. Pp. 47–89.

Baddeley, A. D., & Levy, B. A. Semantic coding and memory. *Journal of Experimental Psychology,* 1971, *89,* 132–136.

Baddeley, A. D., Scott, D., Drynan, R., & Smith, J. C. Short-term memory and the limited capacity hypothesis. *British Journal of Psychology,* 1969, *60,* 51–55.

Baddeley, A. D., Thomson, N., & Buchanan, M. Word length and the structure of short-term memory. *Journal of Verbal Learning and Verbal Behavior,* 1975, *14,* 575–589.

Bartz, W. H., & Salehi, M. Interference in short- and long-term memory. *Journal of Experimental Psychology*, 1970, *84*, 380–382.

Biederman, I., & Stacy, E. W., Jr. Stimulus probability and stimulus set size in memory scanning. *Journal of Experimental Psychology*, 1974, *102*, 1100–1117.

Bower, G. H., & Winzenz, D. Comparison of associative learning strategies. *Psychonomic Science*, 1970, *20*, 119–120.

Bracey, G. W. Two operations in character recognition: A partial replication. *Perception and Psychophysics*, 1969, *6*, 357–360.

Bregman, A. S. Forgetting curves with semantic, phonetic, graphic, and contiguity cues. *Journal of Experimental Psychology*, 1968, *78*, 539–546.

Brener, R. An experimental investigation of memory span. *Journal of Experimental Psychology*, 1940, *26*, 467–482.

Brown, H. L., & Kirsner, K. A within-subjects analyses of the relationship between memory span and processing rate in short-term memory. *Cognitive Psychology*, 1980, *12*, 177–187.

Brown, J. Some tests of the decay theory of immediate memory. *Quarterly Journal of Experimental Psychology*, 1958, *10*, 12–21.

Bruce, D., & Murdock, B. B., Jr. Acoustic similarity effects on memory for paired associates. *Journal of Verbal Learning and Verbal Behavior*, 1968, *7*, 627–631.

Burrows, D., & Okada, R. Serial position effects in high-speed memory search. *Perception & Psychophysics*, 1971, *10*, 305–308.

Cavanagh, J. P. Relation between the immediate memory span and the memory search rate. *Psychological Review*, 1972, *79*, 525–530.

Conrad, R. Acoustic confusions in immediate memory. *British Journal of Psychology*, 1964, *55*, 75–84.

Conrad, R., Freeman, P. R., & Hull, A. J. Acoustic factors versus language factors in short-term memory. *Psychonomic Science*, 1965, *3*, 57–58.

Conrad, R., & Hull, A. J. Information, acoustic confusion, and memory span. *British Journal of Psychology*, 1964, *55*, 429–432.

Craik, F. I. M. Two components in free recall. *Journal of Verbal Learning and Verbal Behavior*, 1968a, *7*, 996–1004.

Craik, F. I. M. Types of error in free recall. *Psychonomic Science*, 1968b, *10*, 353–354.

Craik, F. I. M. The fate of primary memory items in free recall. *Journal of Verbal Learning and Verbal Behavior*, 1970, *9*, 143–148.

Craik, F. I. M., & Birtwhistle, J. Proactive inhibition in free recall. *Journal of Experimental Psychology*, 1971, *91*, 120–123.

Craik, F. I. M., & Levy, B. A. Semantic and acoustic information in primary memory. *Journal of Experimental Psychology*, 1970, *86*, 77–82.

Craik, F. I. M., & Lockhart, R. S. Levels of processing: A framework for memory research. *Journal of Verbal Learning and Verbal Behavior*, 1972, *11*, 671–684.

Craik, F. I. M., & Watkins, M. J. The role of rehearsal in short-term memory. *Journal of Verbal Learning and Verbal Behavior*, 1973, *12*, 599–607.

Crannell, C. W., & Parrish, J. M. A comparison of immediate memory span for digits, letters, and words. *The Journal of Psychology*, 1957, *44*, 319–327.

Crowder, R. G. *Principles of learning and memory*, 1976, Hillsdale, N.J.: Lawrence Erlbaum Associates.

Crowder, R. G., & Morton, J. Precategorical acoustic storage (PAS). *Perception & Psychophysics*, 1969, *5*, 365–373.

Cruse, D., & Clifton, C., Jr. Recoding strategies and the retrieval of information from memory. *Cognitive Psychology*, 1973, *4*, 157–193.

Drewnowski, A. Attributes and priorities in short-term recall: A new model of memory span. *Journal of Experimental Psychology: General*, 1980, *109*, 208–250.

Gianutsos, R. Free Recall of grouped words. *Journal of Experimental Psychology*, 1972, *95*, 419–428.

Glanzer, M. Storage mechanisms in recall. In G. H. Bower (Ed.), *The psychology of learning and motivation: Advances in research and theory* (Vol. 5). New York: Academic Press, 1972. Pp. 129–193.

Glanzer, M. Intonation grouping and related words in free recall. *Journal of Verbal Learning and Verbal Behavior*, 1976, *15*, 85–92.

Glanzer, M., & Cunitz, A. R. Two storage mechanisms in free recall. *Journal of Verbal Learning and Verbal Behavior*, 1966, *5*, 351–360.

Glanzer, M., Gianutsos, R., & Dubin, S. The removal of items from short-term storage. *Journal of Verbal Learning and Verbal Behavior*, 1969, *8*, 435–447.

Glanzer, M., & Koppenaal, L. The effect of encoding tasks on free recall: Stages and levels. *Journal of Verbal Behavior*, 1977, *16*, 21–28.

Glanzer, M., Koppenaal, L., & Nelson R. Effects of relations between words on short-term storage and long-term storage. *Journal of Verbal Learning and Verbal Behavior*, 1972, *11*, 403–416.

Glanzer, M., & Razel, M. The size of the unit in short-term storage. *Journal of Verbal Learning and Verbal Behavior*, 1974, *13*, 114–131.

Glanzer, M., & Schwartz, A. Mnemonic structure in free recall: Differential effects on STS and LTS. *Journal of Verbal Learning and Verbal Behavior*, 1971, *10*, 194–198.

Glenberg, A., Smith, S. M., & Green, C. Type I rehearsal: Maintenance and more. *Journal of Verbal Learning and Verbal Behavior*, 1977, *16*, 339–352.

Grant, K. W., and McCormack, P. D. Auditory and visual short-term memory with successive syllable presentation in both modalities. *Psychonomic Science*, 1969, *17*, 341–342.

Hellyer, S. Supplementary report: Frequency of stimulus presentation and short-term decrement in recall. *Journal of Experimental Psychology*, 1962, *64*, 650.

Hintzman, D. L. Articulatory coding in short-term memory. *Journal of Verbal Learning and Verbal Behavior*, 1967, *6*, 312–319.

Hoving, K. L., Morin, R. E., & Konick, D. S. Recognition reaction time and size of the memory set: A developmental study. *Psychonomic Science*, 1970, *21*, 247–248.

Jahnke, J. C. Serial position effects in immediate serial recall. *Journal of Verbal Learning and Verbal Behavior*, 1963, *2*, 284–287.

Jahnke, J. C. Supplementary report: Primacy and recency effects in serial-position curves of immediate recall. *Journal of Experimental Psychology*, 1965, *70*, 130–132.

Jahnke, J. C. Delayed recall and the serial-position effect of short-term memory. *Journal of Experimental Psychology*, 1968a, *76*, 618–622.

Jahnke, J. C. Presentation rate and the serial-position effect of short-term memory. *Journal of Verbal Learning and Verbal Behavior*, 1968b, *7*, 608–612.

Johnston, W. A., Wagstaff, R. R., & Griffith, D. Information processing analysis of verbal learning. *Journal of Experimental Psychology*, 1972, *96*, 307–314.

Keppel, G., & Underwood, B. J. Proactive inhibition in short-term retention of single items. *Journal of Verbal Learning and Verbal Behavior*, 1962, *1*, 153–161.

Kintsch, W., & van Dijk, T. A. Toward a model of text comprehension and production. *Psychological Review*, 1978, *85*, 363–394.

Kolers, P. A. Specificity of operations in sentence recognition. *Cognitive Psychology*, 1975, *7*, 289–306.

Kroll, N. E. A., Parks, T., Parkinson, S. R., Bieber, S. L., & Johnson, A. L. Short-term memory while shadowing: Recall of visually and orally presented letters. *Journal of Experimental Psychology,* 1970, *85,* 220–224.

Levy, B. A. The role of articulation in auditory and visual short-term memory. *Journal of Verbal Learning and Verbal Behavior,* 1971, *10,* 123–132.

Levy, B. A. Vocalization and suppression effects in sentence memory. *Journal of Verbal Learning and Verbal Behavior,* 1975, *14,* 304–316.

Levy, B. A. Reading: Speech and meaning processes. *Journal of Verbal Learning and Verbal Behavior,* 1977, *16,* 623–638.

Lindley, R. H. Effects of controlled coding cues in short-term memory. *Journal of Experimental Psychology,* 1963, *66,* 580–587.

Martin, D. W. Residual processing capacity during verbal organization in memory. *Journal of Verbal Learning and Verbal Behavior,* 1970, *9,* 391–397.

Martin, P. R., & Fernberger, S. W. Improvement in memory span. *American Journal of Psychology,* 1929, *41,* 91–94.

Melton, A. W. Implications of short-term memory for a general theory of memory. *Journal of Verbal Learning and Verbal Behavior,* 1963, *2,* 1–21.

Miller, G. A. The magical number seven, plus or minus two: Some limits on our capacity for processing information. *Psychological Review,* 1956, *63,* 81–97.

Murdock, B. B., Jr. The retention of individual items. *Journal of Experimental Psychology,* 1961, *62,* 618–625.

Murdock, B. B., Jr. The serial position effect of free recall. *Journal of Experimental Psychology,* 1962, *64,* 482–488.

Murdock, B. B., Jr. Interpolated recall in short-term memory. *Journal of Experimental Psychology,* 1963a, *66,* 525–532.

Murdock, B. B., Jr. Short-term memory and paired–associate learning *Journal of Verbal Learning and Verbal Behavior,* 1963b, *2,* 320–328.

Murdock, B. B., Jr. Proactive inhibition in short-term memory. *Journal of Experimental Psychology,* 1964, *68,* 184–189.

Murdock, B. B., Jr. Effects of a subsidiary task on short-term memory. *British Journal of Psychology,* 1965, *56,* 413–419.

Murdock, B. B., Jr. Visual and auditory stores in short-term memory. *Quarterly Journal of Experimental Psychology,* 1966, *18,* 206–211.

Murdock, B. B., Jr. Auditory and visual stores in short-term memory. *Acta Psychologica,* 1967a, *27,* 316–324.

Murdock, B. B., Jr. Recent developments in short-term memory. *British Journal of Psychology,* 1967b, *58,* 421–433.

Murdock, B. B., Jr., & Walker, K. D. Modality effects in free recall. *Journal of Verbal Learning and Verbal Behavior,* 1969, *8,* 665–676.

Murray, D. J. The role of speech responses in short-term memory. *Canadian Journal of Psychology,* 1967, *21,* 263–276.

Murray, D. J., & Newman, F. M. Visual and verbal coding in short-term memory. *Journal of Experimental Psychology,* 1973, *100,* 58–62.

Nelson, T. O. Repetition and depth of processing. *Journal of Verbal Learning and Verbal Behavior,* 1977, *16,* 151–171.

Nelson, T. O., & Rothbart, R. Acoustic savings for items forgotten from long-term memory. *Journal of Experimental Psychology,* 1972, *93,* 357–360.

Peterson, L. R., & Peterson, M. J. Short-term retention of individual verbal items. *Journal of Experimental Psychology,* 1959, *58,* 193–198

Posner, M. I., Boies, S. J., Eichelman, W. H., & Taylor, R. L. Retention of visual and name codes of single letters. *Journal of Experimental Psychology Monograph* 1969, *79,* (1, Part 2). Pp. 1–16.

Posner, M. I., & Konick, A. F. On the role of interference in short-term retention. *Journal of Experimental Psychology*, 1966, *72*, 221–231.

Posner, M. I., & Rossman, E. Effect of size and location of informational transforms upon short-term retention. *Journal of Experimental Psychology*, 1965, *70*, 496–505.

Postman, L., & Phillips, L. W. Short-term temporal changes in free recall. *Quarterly Journal of Experimental Psychology*, 1965, *17*, 132–138.

Raymond, B. Short-term storage and long-term storage in free recall. *Journal of Verbal Learning and Verbal Behavior*, 1969, *8*, 567–574.

Reitman, J. S. Mechanisms of forgetting in short-term memory. *Cognitive Psychology*, 1971, *2*, 185–195.

Reitman, J. S. Without surreptitious rehearsal, information in short-term memory decays. *Journal of Verbal Learning and Verbal Behavior*, 1974, *13*, 365–377.

Richardson, J. T. E. Imagery and free recall. *Journal of Verbal Learning and Verbal Behavior*, 1974, *13*, 709–713.

Roberts, W. A. The priority of recall of new items in transfer from part-list learning to whole-list learning. *Journal of Verbal Learning and Verbal Behavior*, 1969, *9*, 645–652.

Roediger, H. L., III, & Crowder, R. G. The spacing of lists in free recall. *Journal of Verbal Learning and Verbal Behavior*, 1975, *14*, 590–602.

Rundus, D. Analysis of rehearsal processes in free recall. *Journal of Experimental Psychology*, 1971, *89*, 63–77.

Rundus, D. Maintenance rehearsal and long-term recency. *Memory & Cognition*, 1980, *8*, 226–230.

Rundus, D., & Atkinson, R. C. Rehearsal processes in free recall: A procedure for direct observation. *Journal of Verbal Learning and Verbal Behavior*, 1970, *9*, 99–105.

Ryan, J. Grouping and short-term memory: Different means and patterns of grouping. *Quarterly Journal of Experimental Psychology*, 1969a, *21*, 137–147.

Ryan, J. Temporal groupings, rehearsal, and short-term memory. *Quarterly Journal of Experimental Psychology*, 1969b, *21*, 148–155.

Sachs, J. S. Recognition memory for syntactic and semantic aspects of connected discourse. *Perception & Psychophysics*, 1967, *2*, 437–442.

Shallice, T. On the contents of primary memory. In P. M. A. Rabbit & S. Dornic (Eds.), *Attention and performance V*. Amsterdam: North-Holland, 1974. Pp. 269–280.

Shulman, H. G. Encoding and retention of semantic and phonemic information in short-term memory. *Journal of Verbal Learning and Verbal Behavior*, 1970, *9*, 499–508.

Silverstein, C., & Glanzer, M. Difficulty of a concurrent task in free recall: Differential effects on STS and LTS. *Psychonomic Science*, 1971, *22*, 367–368.

Sperling, G. A model for visual memory tasks. *Human Factors*, 1963, *5*, 19–31.

Spitz, H. H. Note on immediate memory for digits: Invariance over the years. *Psychological Bulletin*, 1972, *78*, 183–185.

Sternberg, S. Memory-scanning: Mental processes revealed by reaction time experiments. *American Scientist*, 1969, *57*, 421–457.

Sternberg, S. Memory-scanning: New findings and current controversies. *Quarterly Journal of Experimental Psychology*, 1975, *27*, 1–32.

Sumby, W. H. Word frequency and serial position effects. *Journal of Verbal Learning and Verbal Behavior*, 1963, *1*, 443–450.

Thurm, A. T., & Glanzer, M. Free recall in children: Long-term store versus short-term store. *Psychonomic Science*, 1971, *23*, 175–176.

Townsend, J. T. A note on the identifiability of parallel and serial processes. *Perception and Psychophysics*, 1971, *10*, 161–163.

Tulving, E., & Arbuckle, T. Y. Sources of intratrial interference in immediate recall of paired associates. *Journal of Verbal Learning and Verbal Behavior*, 1963, *1*, 321–334.

Tulving, E., & Colotla, V. Free recall of trilingual lists. *Cognitive Psychology*, 1970, *1*, 86–98.

Warrington, E. K., & Shallice, T. The selective impairment of auditory verbal short-term memory. *Brain*, 1969, *92*, 885–896.

Watkins, M. J. The concept and measurement of primary memory. *Psychological Bulletin*, 1974, *81*, 695–711.

Watkins, M. J., & Watkins, O. C. Processing of recency items for free recall. *Journal of Experimental Psychology*, 1974, *102*, 488–493.

Watkins, M. J., Watkins, O. C., & Crowder, R. G. The modality effect in free and serial recall as a function of phonological similarity. *Journal of Verbal Learning and Verbal Behavior*, 1974, *13*, 430–447.

Watkins, O. C., & Watkins, M. J. The modality effect and echoic persistence. *Journal of Experimental Psychology: General*, 1980, *109*, 251–278.

Waugh, N, C., & Norman, D. A. Primary memory. *Psychological Review*, 1965, *72*, 89–104.

Wickelgren, W. Size of rehearsal group and short-term memory. *Journal of Experimental Psychology*, 1964, *68*, 413–419.

Wickelgren, W. A. Acoustic similarity and intrusion errors in short-term memory. *Journal of Experimental Psychology*, 1965, *70*, 102–108.

Wickelgren, W. A. Auditory or articulatory coding in verbal short-term memory. *Psychological Review*, 1969, *76*, 232–235.

Wickens, D. D. Encoding categories of words: An empirical approach to meaning. *Psychological Review*, 1970, *77*, 1–15.

Wickens, D. D., Born, D. G., & Allen, C. K. Proactive inhibition and item similarity in short-term memory. *Journal of Verbal Learning and Verbal Behavior*, 1963, *2*, 440–445.

Woodward, A. E., Jr., Bjork, R. A., & Jongeward, R. H., Jr. Recall and recognition as a function of primary rehearsal. *Journal of Verbal Learning and Verbal Behavior*, 1973, *12*, 608–617.

CHAPTER **4**

MARTIN D. MURPHY
C. RICHARD PUFF

Free Recall: Basic Methodology and Analyses

INTRODUCTION

The basic procedure of the typical free-recall experiment is probably easier to grasp than that of any other task normally used in the study of human memory and cognition. In its prototypical form, a list of words is presented to subjects who are instructed that, following the presentation, they will be asked to reproduce the items in any order that they choose.

One appeal of the method stems from the ability to perform analyses of input–output discrepancies, using the evidence of transformations imposed by the subject as a basis for making inferences about the nature of intervening mental processes. To increase our understanding of the nature of the intervening transformational, or organizational, processes, the influence of a great variety of input manipulations on the output has been studied. Furthermore, several types of output analyses have been developed in order to specify the nature of mental transformations.

Two of the major organizational phenomena investigated in free-recall studies are referred to as *clustering* and *subjective organization*. Taken together, these two phenomena have been the object of the great preponderance of free-recall research over the past 25 years. A brief introduction to the defining operations for these phenomena is necessary for understanding much of the methodological effort in this area.

99

HANDBOOK OF RESEARCH METHODS IN
HUMAN MEMORY AND COGNITION

The standard operations for the study of clustering follow from the work of Bousfield (1953). The typical study of clustering begins with the investigator selecting stimulus materials that comprise items from a number of different taxonomic categories, such as *animals, vegetables, pieces of furniture,* or *occupations*. Items from the different categories are scrambled into a randomized sequence for presentation to the subjects who are given the usual instructions that they can recall the items in any order. The sequence of items recalled by each subject is then scored to determine the extent to which he or she has recalled items from the same categories together in runs, or clusters. The discrepancy between the haphazardly arranged input and the categorically organized output is taken as strong evidence that the organizing process of clustering has intervened.

The basic defining operations for the phenomenon of subjective organization follow primarily from Tulving's (1962) study. In this case, the experimenter usually begins by selecting a list of items that are operationally unrelated in the sense that they do not come from the same categories and do not elicit each other in free association. Multiple randomizations of the list are prepared for presentation over a series of free-recall trials. The subject's recall protocols are scored in successive pairs (i.e., Trials 1 and 2, 2 and 3, etc.) to determine the extent to which items recalled in adjacent positions on one trial are again recalled in adjacent positions on the next trial. The inference of an intervening organizing process is made when the subject draws together items that were presented in haphazardly varying positions over trials in the input list and repeatedly recalls them in adjacent positions in the output list. The repeated adjacency of the items in recall allows the inference that they reflect an organized, or integrated, unit. The phenomenon is referred to as subjective organization because the experimenter, having created a list of operationally unrelated items, is normally quite unaware of the basis on which the subject has formed the unit; all the experimenter may know is that the subject has organized consistently on some basis.

Because of great interest in subjective organization and clustering, much of the methodology in the free-recall area has involved (*a*) the selection of materials to be explicitly related or unrelated, (*b*) the manipulation of parameters of the situation to influence the opportunity for the subject to detect and use the structure built into the list or to impose his or her own structure, and (*c*) the exploration of alternative techniques for assessing and specifying the extent to which the output reflects the operation of several different organizing and strategic activities.

In the remainder of this chapter, we will review some of the important methodological considerations involved in the collection of free-recall data, as well as a few of the more traditional ways of measuring the characteristics of the output. We will pay special attention to some of the particular problems associated with life-span developmental research in free recall, because there are a number of those, and because this is one of the most active areas of free-recall research today. This chapter is prefatory to the next one by Pellegrino and Hubert. Their chapter picks up where this one leaves off, in the sense that it presents a new systematic approach to the analysis of many facets of organization and structure.

MANIPULATION AND CONTROL OF TASK PARAMETERS

Many of the potentially important task parameters that need to be taken into account in free-recall research are discussed in this section in order to help with the kinds of decisions just mentioned. This brief analysis cannot cover all of the relevant variables or their interactions. A few explicit suggestions will be offered, but the major goal of this section is to provide some background for thinking about what levels of what variables are appropriate for what purposes in free-recall studies. This kind of framework should presumably generalize to other variables and combinations of variables.

Input Parameters

LIST LENGTH

Because secondary organizational processes, such as clustering or subjective organization, are frequently of interest, list length is usually chosen to be well above the immediate memory span of approximately seven items. Otherwise, perfect recall in the order of presentation may result, leaving no room for such organizational effects.

The finding that recall level dramatically increases with age in children (Cole, Frankel, & Sharp, 1971) has led to some concern in developmental studies that the presentation of the same number of items may represent subjectively different tasks for subjects of different ages. One solution has been to present more items to the older children (e.g., Moely, Olson, Halwes, & Flavell, 1969). However, whereas the concern about subjective difficulty is reasonable, the problem is probably most severe with the short lists commonly used in serial-recall studies. Generally, free-recall studies employing the same number of items across ages have replicated those in which number of items and age covary (Neimark, Slotnick, & Ulrich, 1971).

ITEM CHARACTERISTICS

Selection of items for free-recall studies involves decisions about a number of normative characteristics, including intraitem properties such as frequency, meaningfulness, and imagery values, as well as interitem association, or relatedness.

The major principle in selecting items for studies of subjective organization is to avoid interitem associations and categorical relationships (Tulving, 1962; Bousfield, Puff, & Cowan, 1964). The items are selected to be operationally unrelated, so that the subjects can impose their own organizational schemes rather than adopting some salient structure built into the list by the experimenter.

For studies of clustering, on the other hand, some basis for organization is intentionally built into the list by choosing groups of two or more items that are related in some way. Both the type and the strength of the relatedness are important factors. Most often, the items are chosen to represent conceptual, or taxonomic, categories such as *animals, pieces of furniture,* or *occupations* (e.g., Bousfield, 1953). However, interitem relatedness can also be defined on the basis of direct association strength (Jenkins, Mink, & Russell, 1958), physical characteristics, such as shape (Frost, 1971), or functional relationships, such as *foot–sock* (Denney & Ziobrowski, 1972). In addition, the relatedness, or categorization, can be induced situationally on the basis of spatial locations (Stukuls, 1975).

The strength with which the instances represent the categories is also an important parameter of recall and clustering, as demonstrated, for example, by Bousfield, Cohen, and Whitmarsh (1958). With taxonomic categories, the extent to which the instances represent the category can be readily specified through the use of a set of category norms such as those constructed by Battig and Montague (1969) for college students, Posnansky (1978) for children of different ages, and Howard (1980) for adults of different ages. Work on exemplar typicality can also serve as a basis for item selection.

Clearly, if one is interested in getting a good look at the operation of organizing processes, it makes little sense to select items that are only weakly representative of the categories. However, there are also problems associated with picking the items that are the highest in strength or typicality. Such items can be guessed by simply remembering the category name, and they are often directly associated with each other. Such problems have led Lange (1978) to argue that clustering of such highly related items might not reflect categorical organization at all, especially with young children. Differences in the normative properties of the materials may thus be responsible for discrepant findings about the age of occurrence of significant clustering in young children. A reasonable solution in many situations is to choose items that are moderately related to the category name and minimally associated with each other. If high strength items need to be used, some from each category can be included in the list and other high strength exemplars omitted. Guessing rates can then be estimated from the frequency of intrusion in recall of the items that were not in the list.

An item selection issue of increasing concern in developmental and cross-cultural studies involves possible differences among subject populations in both the preferred bases for organizing and the within-category organization of exemplars. For example, investigators such as Nelson (1977) have discussed the possibility that young children may prefer functional rather than taxonomic organizations. Chi (1978) has strongly argued for the importance of semantic knowledge in accounting for developmental differences. Furthermore, Myers and Perlmutter (1978) have found developmental differences in knowledge structures among preschool children. An outcome of this work should be a better description of developing category knowledge and more useful theoretical accounts of the development of knowledge and how it may interact with episodic free recall.

NUMBER OF CATEGORIES AND ITEMS PER CATEGORY

The impact of variations in the number of categories and the number of items per category has not been the subject of much systematic investigation. Some investigators have shown that recall and clustering vary as an inverted-U function of the number of categories (or number of items per category) with list length held constant (e.g., Murphy, 1979). With a small number of large categories, little can be learned about differential category accessibility; with many small categories, a high proportion of the categories may not appear in recall without explicit cuing. Unless there is a specific reason to do otherwise, the best procedure is probably to follow previous work that has generally used 3–12 categories of 3–5 items with children and up to 10 items per category with adults.

PRESENTATION ORDER

Once the items have been selected, they have to be ordered for presentation. In the study of clustering, the degree of contiguity among the members of the same category in the presentation order must be decided upon. The most common types of presentation orders are *random, explicitly unblocked,* and *blocked.* A randomized sequence allows the chance occurrence of runs of items from the same category, though a restriction is usually added to limit the length of such runs to no more than two or three consecutive words from a category. The explicitly unblocked presentation order is constructed with the restriction that an item from a given category cannot be followed by another item from the same category. In the blocked, or completely organized presentation, all items from the same category are presented contiguously. Some studies have included still other degrees of stimulus list organization. See Puff (1974) for a review of much of the earlier list organization research and Batchelder and Riefer (1980) for an extensive recent investigation.

The explicitly unblocked presentation has often been used to insure that subjects recalling in serial order do not show clustering that could be confused with that produced by the operation of an organizing process. However, with clustering measures for which a chance value can be computed, perfect serial recall of unblocked lists would lead to below-chance values. Since below-chance values of many of these measures are difficult to interpret, the random (or random with restrictions) ordering would seem to be preferable. Blocked presentation almost invariably leads to greater clustering and frequently to greater recall (Puff, 1974), especially with children. These effects of blocked presentation may follow from a number of factors, including the optimal opportunity for same-category items to be rehearsed together and the increased salience of the structure of the list. These possibilities make blocked presentation a particularly good procedure for promoting organization when the category structure is otherwise fairly weak. However, if the list includes more than a few categories, blocked presentation may result in fewer of the categories being represented in recall.

Regardless of the type of stimulus list organization that is chosen, the use of multiple input orders for presentation to different subjects is desirable. This controls for any effects due to the particular item adjacencies as well as for effects arising from which categories are represented (and by which items) in the primacy and recency portions of the input sequence. If the situation will allow it, a separate input sequence should be used for every subject.

When unrelated lists are used, as in studies of subjective organization, some of the same considerations are relevant. Since each subject receives multiple trials, a series of presentation sequences is required. The major issue in this case is whether to randomize the orders on each trial, thereby allowing a chance number of items to appear contiguously on successive trials, or to order the items so that no two items appear together on consecutive lists. Since the latter would lead to below-chance organization scores if recall is serial, the randomization alternative seems preferable. However, as suggested for categorized lists, the same items should not be allowed to appear consistently in the primacy or recency portions of the sequences across trials. Furthermore, if every subject does not receive a unique set of presentation orders, then the fixed set of orders should be presented in different sequences to different subjects.

PRESENTATION MANNER AND MODALITY

Decisions about whether to present the materials serially or simultaneously, visually or auditorially, and as words or pictures in the visual modality are most often based on convenience or convention in a particular line of research unless these variables are of direct interest to the investigator. A serial, or successive, presentation helps to insure that the subjects are exposed to every item and equates the nominal amount of study time for all of the items. The simultaneous presentation of all items, on the other hand, allows the subject more flexibility in making interitem comparisons, rehearsing same category items together, and so on. Simultaneous presentation should, therefore, be expected to facilitate organization and recall of unrelated or weakly categorized materials, especially by subjects who may not be highly efficient in holding previously presented items in memory while implementing rehearsal strategies. Finally, it should be noted that the potential advantage of the simultaneous presentation might be augmented by combining it with the opportunity for the subjects to move items into groups (e.g., Mandler, 1967).

Several factors are relevant to the choice of the modality of presentation. First, it is well known that auditory presentation of words leads to a slightly increased recency effect on an immediate test (Cole *et al.*, 1971; Murdock & Walker, 1969). Second, the visual presentation of printed words may introduce a decoding (reading) problem that is obvious with prereading children but may also be a factor with elderly subjects, low socioeconomic class, or low IQ groups. The auditory presentation of words reduces this concern, although the investigator has to be careful about unintentionally including items that have homonyms. The visual presentation of pictures also circumvents the reading problem, but a picture may often have several possible labels. Therefore, with pictorial presentation, subjects are usually asked to label the items as they are presented. Labels that differ from those of the researcher are then either corrected at presentation or counted as correct at recall.

RATE OF PRESENTATION

In general, a slower rate leads to better performance, but the main consideration about the rate of presentation (or the total study time with a simultaneous presentation) is that there be sufficient time for the subjects to do whatever the experimenter expects them to be able to do during the input phase of the task. For example, a rate as fast as one item per sec does not afford much opportunity to engage in rehearsal or organization at input. Furthermore, a rapid rate of input might put younger or older subjects at a disadvantage in comparison with college students, even if memory ability per se does not differ. If precise control of the rate by the experimenter is not essential, some of these concerns can be overcome by allowing the subjects to control their own presentation rates. The distribution of times during study can then become an informative component of the results (Belmont & Butterfield, 1971).

INSTRUCTIONS

There are several elements that can be considered for inclusion in the instructions given to the subjects. If the task is intentional, the subjects are asked to study the items and informed that a memory test will follow. Also, subjects are generally told that they may recall the items in any order. In the case of categorized lists, if there is any concern about whether or when different subjects may detect the categorical structure, the structure can be described in the instructions. Finally, if written recall is to be obtained, it is helpful to use a lined data sheet and to instruct the subjects neither to skip lines as they are writing nor to insert any items between previously filled lines so that the experimenter has an unambiguous record of the order of recall.

The Retention Interval

The recall test usually begins immediately after the presentation is finished. The use of an immediate test can be expected to result in a high probability of recall of items presented at the end of the list. These items are generally recalled early and may preclude the occurrence of much organization until somewhat later in recall. If the experimenter is interested in minimizing the primary organizational components in the output, longer retention intervals can be used that are filled with some rehearsal inhibiting activity such as arithmetic problems (Puff, Murphy,

& Ferrara, 1977) or backward counting (Glanzer & Cunitz, 1966). Distractor tasks are normally chosen for the specific population under study so that young children might be asked to count forward by ones, older children to count backward by ones, and college students to count backward by threes or sevens. Distractor tasks are normally seen as reducing, but not completely eliminating, the possibility for rehearsal. In general, effective distractor tasks tend to decrease the recency effect, but they may thereby lead to increased clustering or subjective organization. Finally, the effects of rehearsal activities between presentation and recall can be assessed by comparing performance following filled and unfilled intervals.

Output Parameters

OUTPUT MODE

Whether the subjects are asked for written or spoken recall is usually not much of an issue. Spoken recall sequences have to be transcribed and cannot be obtained in group testing situations. However, written recall is slower and may lead to decreased recency effects. In addition, with written recall the subjects can (unless a mask is used) look back at previously remembered items. Looking back may provide retrieval cues for the recall of additional items and might well facilitate the editing process so that fewer items are recalled a second time. Of course, in comparing different subject populations capable of different writing speeds (i.e., college students versus just about anyone else), spoken recall would be the preferred mode of output.

OUTPUT DURATION

A fixed period of between 1 and 5 min is usually allowed for recall, with the exact length depending upon the number of items in the list. Population differences may be important here, also. It has been argued that older adults' recall performance may be disproportionately hampered if they are pushed for speed at recall (Botwinick, 1978). On the other hand, if young children are given too long, they tend to get bored with the task. The use of a dual criterion is a possible solution to some of these problems. The maximum recall period is set, but if the subject recalls no items in a given time period (about 15 sec), the experimenter asks "Can you remember some more?" If not, recall is terminated.

CUED RECALL

Since there is a separate chapter on cued recall by Watkins and Gardiner, our discussion will be brief. The extra cues used in a free-recall study are most often category names and are at an intermediate level of specificity since they point to subsets of the list rather than to the whole list or to individual items. Such cuing, based on the a priori categories in a clustering study, provides a retrieval analogy to blocking at input. In some sense, the organization is done for the subject at retrieval so that the effect of organizational differences can be observed by comparing cued and uncued conditions. However, subjects cued by category may also have more information available during retrieval than uncued subjects. Especially when the number of categories in the list is large, participants may fail to remember whole categories on their own. Thus, cued subjects have more organized recall but also more information about the list as well. Cuing by category is probably best viewed as a method to determine how many items could be accessed if there were no loss of category existence information with recall constrained to be very orderly. Because of the constraint on recall order imposed by the usual cuing procedure, the increase in clustering that is produced is usually seen as trivial.

Counterbalancing

OPTIONS

In addition to the specific suggestions presented above, there are several general issues concerning the selection of materials, the ordering of items, the assignment of subjects to conditions, and, in some cases, the ordering of multiple conditions for the same subjects. In most of these cases there are three general alternatives. Such variables can be held constant, randomized, or randomized with systematic constraints (counterbalanced).

An advantage associated with keeping stimulus items and order the same across people is that variation due to materials cannot contribute to differences among subjects or conditions. Error variance should be reduced and more sensitive statistical tests are therefore possible. A disadvantage of holding stimulus variables constant is that the generality of the findings may be badly compromised. Results may hold only for the particular items or item order used in the study. As discussed more fully in Shoben's chapter, Clark (1973) has forcefully argued that generality across stimuli may be an important problem in several areas of memory research. If the particular items or item orders chosen from a population are interchangeable, then varying these across subjects should increase error variance very little and provide a real increase in the generality of the findings.

Here, as in other areas, however, the purposes of the research are critically important. Varying stimulus material is usually appropriate in an experimental study for which a group is the basic unit of analysis. But, if individual differences are the object of interest, varying stimulus material or orders across subjects is a crucial mistake. When the individual is the unit for analysis, we want any differences between subjects to be due to subject variables not stimulus material variation.

If different items and/or item orders are to be given to different participants, the next question is how to choose the items or orders. Random selection is reasonable with a very large number of samples. However, most often in memory research, considerations of economy lead researchers to choose relatively few samples. In the small sample case, random selection can be very unbalanced. For example, if 4 items are chosen from each of 4 categories using the first 20 exemplars listed in category norms such as Battig and Montague's (1969), we might randomly pick one set of category exemplars to have a mean ranking of 15, while another has a mean rank of 5. Since such large differences might be expected to have a large effect on the results, a better alternative might be to choose items randomly with the restriction that the mean category ranking must fall between 8 and 12 for each category.

Such counterbalancing is also an appropriate alternative in dealing with item or condition ordering. If the just mentioned list of 16 items was ordered randomly and presented several times to the participants in a study, some items might appear disproportionately often in some serial positions. If these items happen to be appreciably easier or harder than the other items, the shape of the serial position function could be badly distorted. A solution to this difficulty is to assign items to positions randomly with the restrictions that an item can appear no more than once at a given serial position, and also that each item appears proportionally often in the primacy, middle, and recency sections of the list.

Counterbalancing, then, does not remove differences due to item characteristics or effects of order. It does assure that, across serial positions, lists, or participants in a group, these effects are distributed relatively evenly. The degree of restrictiveness imposed can be quite variable. The least restrictive extreme may be almost completely random: 16 items might be assigned to 2 list orders such that an item appears in a serial position no more than once. Each order would then be given to half of the participants in each group of the study. On the other hand, the degree of restriction can be much greater. The same 16 items could be assigned to 16 list orders so that each item appears in each serial position exactly once to completely unconfound item and position. The extra work and stimulus preparation required by this latter alternative may or may not be justified depending on the researcher's interest in serial position and the variability of the items in the stimulus pool.

LATIN SQUARES

An extremely handy tool for the construction of restrictive counterbalancing schemes is the Latin square. If n elements are to be assigned to a matrix with n rows and columns, a Latin square arrangement has each element appearing in each row and each column once and only once. For example, if we wish to present each of four stimulus conditions to four subjects in a counterbalanced order, the Latin square that follows might be used. This arrangement insures that each participant receives each condition and that, over the set of four participants, condition is unconfounded with presentation position so that practice or fatigue effects do not influence the results. A similar (but larger) Latin square could be used to assign 16 items to 16 serial positions.

Subject	Position				
	1st	2nd	3rd	4th	
1	1	2	3	4	
2	2	4	1	3	*condition*
3	3	1	4	2	←
4	4	3	2	1	

The 4 × 4 Latin square shown here has an additional property. Across the rows, each number follows and is followed by every other number exactly once. If the researcher is concerned about carryover effects (as is almost always the case for within-subject designs), the use of such a Latin square can assure that direct carryover effects from one condition to the next are evenly distributed. For instance, if Condition 1 is taxing and causes poorer performance on any condition following it, with the Latin square we can know that the detrimental effect of Condition 1 is equally spread across the other three conditions.

Latin squares like that just shown can be constructed only if the number of positions (columns) and subjects (rows) is one less than a prime number. An easy algorithm to find the condition associated with any cell is to first multiply its row number by its column number and then to subtract from the row × column product the highest multiple of the prime that will leave a positive integer (designating one of the conditions) as a remainder. The following are examples of the calculation of some of the cells in the matrix just shown.

Cell	Row × Column	Multiple of prime	Condition
2,2	2 × 2 = 4	0 × 5 = 0	4
2,3	2 × 3 = 6	1 × 5 = 5	1
3,4	3 × 4 = 12	2 × 5 = 10	2
4,4	4 × 4 = 16	3 × 5 = 15	1

If carryover effects from one condition to another are expected to be large and important, of course the researcher should not simply rely on counterbalancing; other action, such as giving the conditions to different subjects, must be taken. If, however, carryover effects are likely to be small and unimportant, careful counterbalancing can provide an elegant solution.

ADDITIONAL CONSIDERATIONS

In a typical experiment, a fairly large number of events and event orders must be handled. Factors that are candidates for counterbalancing, depending on the specifics of the study, include item selection, assignment of items to lists, assignment of items or positions within a list to conditions, assignment of whole lists to conditions, ordering of items within lists, arrangement of categories in a list, selection of lists and conditions for each participant, and ordering of the conditions to be given to each participant. Whereas counterbalancing a large study can obviously be rather complex, decisions about what to control are usually not difficult in specific situations. The researcher simply works out what stimulus variables might confound the interpretation of the interesting variables in the study and then acts to avoid the possible confoundings.

Situations are often encountered that involve the need to impose several different restrictions at the same time. If, for instance, a researcher wants to follow Pellegrino and Battig's (1974) suggestion to compare multiple output measures on the same data, a study might be designed to look at clustering, subjective organization, and serial position as possible bases for recall organization across successive presentations of the same set of items. After initial item selection, items might be

ordered fairly randomly for the first presentation, with a possible restriction that two items from a category should appear contiguously no
more often than would be expected by chance. The order of items for
lists after the first presentation, however, might be subject to several
different restrictions to insure that (a) items are evenly distributed across
serial positions, (b) items that were presented contiguously on an earlier
trial appear together with no more than chance frequency on later trials,
(c) same category items appear together no more often than predicted
by chance, (d) categories, irrespective of specific exemplars, are equally
represented in primacy and recency positions across lists, and so on.

As pointed out by Bray and Murphy (1973), it is not at all difficult
to choose enough restrictions so as to eliminate all possible counterbalancing solutions. Whereas a perfect counterbalancing solution can be
truly elegant (and provide a dedicated graduate student with many hours
of labor), it is often necessary to settle for approximate perfection! That
is, instead of requiring each item to appear next to every other item
exactly two times in a study, we might set the restriction to be at least
once and no more than three times.

SCORING AND MEASURES

After the study is designed and the data are collected, a number of
new problems arise. Subjects perversely recall some list items more than
once while also producing items not present in the list at all. These recall
errors must be dealt with in scoring the recall protocols. Once the data
are scored, measures must be chosen to reflect the processes of interest.
Whereas a number of different measures, especially for clustering and
subjective organization, have been proposed and used, the literature on
the measures is replete with conflicting statements on underlying assumptions, criteria for evaluation of the measures recommendations as
to which measure is best, and just about everything else.

First, some common data scoring problems and suggested solutions
are described, and then we will briefly discuss several issues related to
choice of measures.

Scoring

Two types of decisions are required in scoring recall protocols. First,
we must determine which items are correct recalls and which are not,
and then we must decide what to do with incorrectly produced items.

Correct recalls are usually defined as the first mention of any item in the to-be-remembered list, with minor pronunciation or spelling errors (for oral or written recall, respectively) ignored. Minor errors in word form, such as singular–plural substitutions, are usually ignored as well. Synonym substitutions, on the other hand, are usually not considered to be correct recalls because it is difficult to know where to draw the line on these. However, with pictorial stimuli, alternative labels are usually considered correct. Often the researcher will ask child participants to name the items during study and then use the child-generated label as the correct one.

Recall errors include repeated mentions of a list item, called *double recalls,* and the production of items not in the list, called *intrusions.* Depending on the nature of the study, intrusions can be subdivided as from a previous list, from the same category as one used in the list, as being an associate or synonym of a list item, and so on. Some of the classification decisions can be quite difficult as some items may fit into one of several categories. For example, is *piano* a musical instrument or an article of furniture? Furthermore, almost any intrusion might be an associate of a list item if the list is sufficiently long and varied.

Nevertheless, recall errors can be interesting in their own right. The relationships between intrusions and list items provide clues as to the nature of organized memory just as clustering and subjective organization do. Most intrusions are semantically related to list items and/or categories, implying a semantically based memory system. Specific types of intrusions can, under some circumstances, provide important information about memory process and structure (Cofer, Bruce, & Reicher, 1966). The usefulness of recall errors as data is related to their frequency. If errors occur only rarely, as is the usual case, a study must be very large for stable patterns of data to emerge. With higher error rates, even moderately sized experiments may show systematic error patterns.

Double recalls have almost always been ignored. However, they provide inferential leverage on the fascinating issue of how subjects remember that they have remembered an item so as not to recall it again. That few double recalls are produced normally is evidence that this editing process is quite effective. In fact, the memory involved in editing may be a good deal more accurate than that for the episodic sets of items that we usually study. Systematic research on double recalls and editing might well be warranted.

A review of the published literature on free recall provides little help in answering the question of what to do with the errors inasmuch as most researchers include little or no information about how errors are dealt with. There are several possibilities.

The first and simplest method is to completely ignore all recall errors. The recall protocols are edited so that they include only correctly recalled list items, and appropriate dependent measures of recall, clustering, subjective organization, and so on, are then computed. A difficulty with this solution is that recall errors carry information that is lost if they are ignored. Further, errors may systematically affect measured organization. Consider the following recall output:

fox	(Animal)
telephone	(Noncategory intrusion)
dog	(Animal)
wolf	(Intrusion, Animal category)
potato	Vegetable)
bean	(Vegetable)
pig	(Animal)
dog	(Double recall, Animal category)
cat	(Animal)

For virtually all measures of clustering, the number of category repetitions—adjacent mentions of two items from the same category—provides the key index of organization. With recall errors deleted, the number of repetitions in the example protocol is three (*fox–dog, potato–bean,* and *pig–cat*); with errors included, two repetitions are lost (*fox–dog* and *pig–cat*), but three are gained (*dog–wolf, pig–dog,* and *dog–cat*). While there is no a priori correct answer here, it is apparent that how recall errors are dealt with is important.

If errors are not to be ignored, an alternative possibility is to score them as correct recalls for the purpose of organizational analyses. In scoring clustering with this method, repeated recalls are all scored as correct, category intrusions are viewed as category exemplars, and noncategory intrusions are scored as examples of new categories. Including such errors instead of ignoring them may well lead to rather different results. This type of scoring along with Bousfield and Rosner's (1970) instructions to produce all items as they are thought of (uninhibited free recall) certainly seems capable of capturing more of the available information than does the practice of ignoring recall errors.

However, several problems exist here, aside from the extra work in scoring and the already mentioned difficulties in assigning category membership. First, some of the measures of both clustering and subjective organization (e.g., the Ratio of Repetition measure to be discussed) assume a baseline or random model, with the expected number of category repetitions or intertrial repetitions being a function of the input list parameters, such as the total number of items and number of items in each category. The possibility of having more than two intertrial repetitions in computing measures of subjective organization with an item (due to double recalls) or more category repetitions for a category than there are category members (due to category intrusions and double recalls) means that the functional input list is no longer known. Estimates of random recall for measures like the Ratio of Repetition, then, cannot be used if errors are counted as correct. Second, if errors are scored as correct, the subject, not the researcher, controls the number of possible categories, the number of exemplars in each category, and total possible correct recall. To the degree that the measures of clustering are sensitive to these variables, artifacts in measures of organization may be introduced. See Murphy (1979) for a discussion of the effects of number of categories on the measures.

Another way of dealing with recall errors is a compromise between ignoring them and scoring them as correct. With this method, category intrusions are counted as correctly recalled items from the appropriate category, but all other recall errors are ignored except when they detract from observed organization. For example, the recall of *fox* (a correct item), *telephone* (a noncategory intrusion), followed by *dog* (a correct item) would be counted as two items recalled with no category repetitions. Several other such compromise solutions could be constructed with the goal of each being to take the effect of recall errors into account while disturbing the recall output as little as possible.

None of the preceding procedures is without disadvantages, and there appears to be no single best answer to the problem of recall errors. A sequential analysis procedure may provide the most information with the least effort. The data are first transcribed, with double recalls and intrusions of various types coded separately. The procedure in scoring the data is to count the various errors but to delete them prior to computation of the measures of organization. Parallel analyses are then done on recall, organization, and each of the error types. If errors are few and unrelated to group and condition variables, they can probably be safely ignored. However, if errors are frequent or if they are related to the experimental variables, the next step would be to recompute the organizational measures with errors included. The influence of the recall errors could then be seen by comparing the analyses with errors included and excluded. This sequential procedure seems to be an adequate, if not elegant, solution to the problems raised by recall errors as long as the errors are not an important focus of the research.

Measures of Recall and Organization

Free-recall protocols provide a rich array of information that can be useful in inferring mental processes and structures. To capture this information requires a correspondingly rich array of measures. The measures are divided into three main classes: recall accuracy measures, measures of organization not based on item meaning, and measures of organization that are based on meaning. These latter two were referred to as measures of primary and secondary organization, respectively, by Tulving (1968). Our discussion covers some of the more traditional approaches within each of these classes. Pellegrino and Hubert's chapter in this book extends the discussion of the measurement of these kinds of information by illustrating important similarities across measure domains and by presenting an integrated approach to their measurement.

RECALL

Number, or proportion, correctly recalled is the single most basic measure of memory performance in free-recall studies. With categorized lists, total recall can be broken into two components: the number of categories recalled and the number of items per category. Together, total recall, number of categories recalled, and number of items per category can serve as a fairly complete description of memory performance and are useful in comparing memory accuracy in different populations of subjects and under different instructions or stimulus conditions. Total recall is also a criterion against which different measures of organization can be evaluated. Organizational measures that are not related to mnemonic effectiveness are usually regarded with less interest than those that are highly related to the efficiency of memory performance.

Researchers, such as Tulving and Pearlstone (1966), have been interested in the components of recall as measures of memory processes. Number of categories recalled is seen as an index of the accessibility of higher order memory units or categories; items per category is an index of item accessibility within categories. Whereas the recall components may provide useful information, the usual practice of assessing a measure's importance by correlating it with recall level is dangerous with the components. A positive correlation with total recall is built into the components by virtue of their mathematical definition, since, if total recall increases, so must one or both of its components. Care must be taken, therefore, not to infer that effects that may be caused by the mathematical properties of the measures are due to subjects' mental operations.

PRIMARY ORGANIZATION

Primary organization is generally defined by exclusion. It involves nonrandom aspects of recall that are not due to the meanings of the list items. Included are primacy and recency effects, seriation, priority of recall for newly remembered items (PRNI), and so on. Since these measures are not dependent on item meaning, they can be investigated in studies using both categorized and uncategorized lists.

Serial position effects. The observation of elevated accuracy of recall for items presented at the beginning of the list (called the *primacy effect*) and items presented at the end of the list (called the *recency effect*) has received more attention than all the other types of primary organization combined. More specifically, primacy and recency effects are defined by demonstrating a significantly greater level of recall for the first and last groups of items presented than is observed for the items presented in the middle of the list.

The question of how many items from each end of the list to test against the middle can be answered in several ways. The investigator can define the blocks of positions to be examined a priori in order to test for the replication of the findings in previous similar research or to test an explicit model. This might lead one, for example, to test the first two and the final five to seven items against the remaining middle items. Theoretical interpretations of primacy and recency effects and some of the previous findings are discussed in Glanzer's chapter in this volume. Alternatively, one might look at the data first and then conduct several tests designed to establish the extent to which both types of effects are, or are not, observed under the specific conditions of the particular study.

Seriation. Especially when a list is presented several times in the same order, another organizational phenomenon appears, reflecting the serial positions of the items in the input sequence. This phenomenon, known as seriation, appears when items that are presented together are also recalled together. Seriation can be computed unidirectionally, requiring items at recall to be in the same order as at input (Item 2 must follow Item 1), or bidirectionally, allowing two items to be counted on the basis of adjacency regardless of order. Following Pellegrino and Battig (1974), a reasonable way to compute seriation is to use the ARC' measure of subjective organization (as discussed later) treating the input list as if it were an output sequence. Specifically, the input is viewed as Trial t and the output as Trial $t + 1$. This input–output analysis provides a measure of seriation that has a chance value of zero and a maximum value of 1.0. The measure thus provides a scaled estimate of the degree to which an output protocol is organized according to the order of the input list.

Mandler (1969) has argued that seriation represents a legitimate alternative strategy to those usually studied, such as clustering and subjective organization. The usefulness of this strategy is probably reduced by changing input order on repeated trials of the same list and not allowing two items from the same category to appear together. Nevertheless, if unblocked presentation is used, seriation can be assessed with minimal experimental effort. Since seriation may be an important basis for organization if the study's design allows for it, the extra information provided by this measure is well worth the trouble.

Priority of recall. A measure of priority of recall for newly remembered items (PRNI) was first developed by Battig, Allen, and Jensen (1965) and is based on the output position of the items recalled for the first time on a given trial in a multitrial experiment. Flores and Brown (1974) developed the procedure shown in Table 4.1 that scales the average output ranks of new items so that chance priority is given a score of zero and maximum priority (all of the new items are recalled before any old ones) receives a score of 1.0.

As with seriation, the importance of PRNI probably varies with experimental condition, stimulus materials, and instructions. The measure is easy to compute with computer programs designed to score free-recall data. It is also worth noting that the recall priority index used as PRNI can be extended to assess priority of recall for any predefined set of items. For instance, priority of recall for primacy or recency items might be investigated. The average priority for a single list is chance, so that if above-chance priority were found for some items (they are output early), then other items would necessarily have a below-chance priority (and be recalled late).

Output stages. In some instances, the investigator may be interested in performance at various stages of the recall sequence. Investigators have studied where in the output sequence one observes the highest

Table 4.1
Priority Index Computational Chart

Terms

T = Total number of items recalled

N = Number of new items recalled

$\sum_{i=1}^{N} R_i$ = Observed priority—sum of the ranks of new items
(the first item output is given a rank of 1, the second 2, and so on)

NP = Chance expectation if no priority is given

Max = Maximum positive priority

Definitions

Max = $N(N + 1)/2$

NP = $N(T + 1)/2$

Measure

RIP = $(\Sigma R_i - NP)/(\text{Max} - NP)$ (conceptual)

RIP = $[N(T + 1) - 2\Sigma R_i]/N(T - N)$ (computational)

---

probability of recall of items from the end of the list (Deese, 1957), the greatest interword recall latency (Puff, 1972), and the greatest density of clustering (Bousfield & Cohen, 1953). The complication that arises in studying such phenomena is that different subjects recall different numbers of items. *Vincentizing* is a handy technique for specifying performance at comparable stages of recall sequences differing in length. With this method, each sequence is divided into successive halves, thirds, quarters, or other proportions, according to specific rules (e.g., see Hilgard, 1938).

SECONDARY ORGANIZATION

Both of the traditional types of secondary organization reflect the meaning of the items and their relationships. For clustering, the basis for inference about organization is the correspondence between output order and the specific categorical relationships defined, a priori, as existing in the materials; for subjective organization, the basis for inferring organization is the consistency of the output ordering of the same items across trials.

Clustering. The unit of measurement of the clustering observed in a recall protocol is the number of times two items from the same category are recalled adjacently, called category repetitions. The observed number of category repetitions is not itself a common final index of clustering, however, since it is artifactually correlated with the amount recalled. With more items recalled, more category repetitions are expected on the basis of chance. There appear to be two reasonable solutions to this problem.

The first and simplest solution is to divide the observed number of repetitions (r) by a number related to total recall (n). The most common of these ratio scores is the *Ratio of Repetition* (RR) measure defined in Table 4.2 (Cohen, Sakoda, & Bousfield, Note 1). The maximum possible value of RR is generally slightly less than 1.0 since each separate category recalled leads to a loss of one possible repetition. The term $n - 1$ takes into account only one category.

A closely related score, the *Modified Ratio of Repetition* (MRR) is also defined in Table 4.2 (Wallace & Underwood, 1964). The MRR score takes into account all of the lost repetitions due to the categories recalled and yields a maximum score of 1.0. Both measures have minimum values of zero. Of particular concern in studies where very low levels of recall sometimes occur, RR is undefined only when less than two items are recalled; MRR is undefined when every item recalled is from a different category. The expected value of RR $[(E - 1)/(N - 1)$ where E is the

Table 4.2
Clustering Measures Computational Chart

Terms

n = Number of items recalled
r = Number of category repetitions
c = Number of different categories represented in recall
n_i = Number recalled in the ith category
Max = Maximum value of r for an output
$E(r)$ = Expected value of r for an output

Definitions

Max = $n - c$

$$E(r) = \frac{\sum_{i=1}^{c} n_i^2}{n} - 1$$

Measures

RR = $r/(n - 1)$
MRR = r/Max
DS = $r - E(r)$
ARC = $[r - E(r)]/[\text{Max} - E(r)]$

number of exemplars per category and N is the number of items presented] is independent of recall when it is unorganized and both RR and MRR have been shown to be relatively statistically independent of the level of total recall (e.g., see Murphy, 1979).

Another solution has been to construct a more elaborate ratio score, called the *Adjusted Ratio of Clustering* (ARC) (Gerjuoy & Spitz, 1966; Roenker, Thompson, & Brown, 1971), that has a maximum value of 1.0 and a chance value of zero corresponding to the measures of seriation and priority already described. The ARC score (described in Table 4.2) is undefined when all of the items recalled are from the same category (when $c = 1$) or where only a single item is recalled from each category (when $n = c$) so it is less useful than the ratio measures with low levels of recall. Furthermore, negative ARC scores are a cause for some concern because of the uncertain comparability of positive and negative values with this measure.

The RR and MRR scores differ importantly from the ARC score in terms of the chance model being assumed. As pointed out by Pellegrino (1975) ARC's baseline model is a random ordering of the items actually recalled. The baseline model for RR and MRR, on the other hand, assumes random selection from the input list and then random ordering as well.

Subjective organization. The basic unit of measurement for subjective organization is the adjacent co-occurrence of items on successive output sequences. Like seriation, subjective organization can be scored unidirectionally or bidirectionally. Subjective organization can also be extended to more than two element comparisons (Pellegrino, 1971) and over more than two lists at a time (Tulving, 1962). Table 4.3 shows the computational formulas of the measures for what we believe to be the most useful conditions: pair-wise units, scored bidirectionally, for adjacent pairs of recall outputs.

Although they are computationally somewhat different, the measures of subjective organization are conceptually similar to the clustering measures. Probably the two best measures are Tulving's (1962) Subjective Organization measure (SO), which is the number of intertrial repetitions divided by the maximum possible number, similar to MRR, and Pellegrino's (1971) ARC', which is on the same scale as the ARC clustering measure. Just as an accurate assessment of clustering depends on having a reasonably large number of items recalled from several categories, reliable assessment of subjective organization requires a fairly large overlap between the items recalled on successive trials so that intertrial repetitions are possible.

Evaluation. In the preceding two sections only the best (in our opinion, of course) of the traditional secondary organization measures were described. A great many others were omitted. Murphy (1979) provides a fuller exposition of the traditional measures, and Pellegrino and

Table 4.3
Subjective Organization Measures Computational Chart

Terms

M = Number of items recalled on Trial t

N = Number of items recalled on Trial $t + 1$

C = Number of common items recalled on Trials t and $t + 1$

$O(ITR)$ = Number of observed pairwise bidirectional repetitions

R = Number of units from trial t that have one or more items not recalled on trial $t + 1$

Max = Maximum number of bidirectional repetitions

$E(ITR)$ = Expected number of bidirectional repetitions

Definitions

Max = $M - 1 - R$

$E(ITR)$ = 2 Max/N

Measures

SO = $O(ITR)/(C + 1)^a$

DS' = $O(ITR) - E(ITR)^b$

ARC' = $[O(ITR) - E(ITR)]/[\text{Max} - E(ITR)]$

---

[a] Repetitions with imaginary items at the beginning and end of the list are added to the usual $O(ITR)$ score here—see Sternberg and Tulving (1977).

[b] In computing DS' the more commonly used (but less adequate) formula for $E(ITR)$ is $[2C(C - 1)]/MN$.

Hubert's chapter in this volume describes a more recent and integrated approach to the measurement of many secondary organization phenomena along with a consideration of the criteria for choosing a measure.

The decisions among the measures discussed here are based mainly on the extent to which the measures are statistically independent of the number of items recalled. If, because of its mathematical properties, a measure of organization has a built-in relation to the amount of recall, then a test of the true correlation between organization and recall performance is impossible. Thus, for example, if a measure that is artifactually related to, or confounded with, recall is used to compare organization in young children (or older adults) with college age subjects, the group that recalls fewer items will very likely also show less organization.

The extent to which a measure is artifactually related to level of recall can, in some cases, be deduced mathematically. However, a clear demonstration of the confounding inherent in different measures, and the consequences of that confounding in the use of the measures, is provided in the simulation work by Murphy (1979) and Murphy, Sanders, and Puff (Note 2). This work examined the relation between a variety of clustering and subjective organization scores and the level of recall by comparing computer generated strings of different lengths. Both random and nonrandom recall strings were investigated. Whereas all of the measures were sensitive to differences in true organization (between random and nonrandom recall strings for example), many were also affected by length of the output sequence even though organization was held constant over sequence length. Most notably, the difference score measures (Bousfield & Bousfield, 1966) of clustering (DS in Table 4.2) and subjective organization (DS' in Table 4.3), computed by subtracting expected from observed repetitions, were strongly correlated with recall under nonrandom conditions. With organized recall sequences, these measures always showed a correlation between organization and recall, whether or not such a relation really existed in the data. The Z-score (Frankel & Cole, 1971) and Item Clustering Index (ICI) (Robinson, 1966) measures did not fare well in these analyses either. Regarding the measures of subjective organization, it should be noted that the conclusions derived from these analyses contrast with those of Sternberg and Tulving (1977). A factor involved in this discrepancy is that, though concerned about the confounding of measures and recall level, Sternberg and Tulving did not consider the possibility of such confounding with organized recall strings.

In summary, then, the RR and ARC measures seem to be the most preferable of the traditional clustering measures, whereas the ARC' and

SO measures seem best for subjective organization. The choice of measures is especially important for developmental studies and others in which recall levels are likely to vary widely.

SOME VARIATIONS

A number of variations in method, measurement, and theory have the potential to greatly advance our understanding of the phenomena of free recall. A difficulty has arisen in research on organization in making inferences about memory processes from the measures described so far in this chapter. A fairly large number of different mental processes, including encoding, rehearsal, and retrieval operations, are probably involved in the production of organized recall. Therefore, measures of secondary organization are properly viewed as summary measures of the outcome of organizational processes rather than as direct measures of some unitary organizational process. Carrying this argument somewhat further, we can see that even the primary–secondary distinction can be questioned. Nonmeaning related factors, such as the closeness of items in early presentations of a list, probably are involved in producing "meaning based" subjective organization. Conversely, "nonmeaning based" seriation is likely produced by processes that capitalize on weak, meaningful relations between adjacent items. We are left with a large and rather important gap between the processes that we are interested in and the outcome measures of organization. Several relatively new methodological variations and measures allow different and, in some cases, more direct inferences about the processes underlying organization. We will but mention some of these variations.

Virtually all of the measures discussed here can be used to investigate organization during study. For example, the rehearsal data generated using the Rundus thinking aloud technique (Rundus & Atkinson, 1970) can be analyzed for clustering, subjective organization, seriation, and so on. Similar kinds of input organizational analyses can be performed when the subjects are allowed to sort items or freely arrange pictures or objects during study (Moely *et al.*, 1969). Thus, with both sorting and overt rehearsal data, the same measures can be used to compare organization at study and at recall. Research with college students (Weist, 1972), children (Ornstein & Naus, 1978), and older adults (Sanders, Murphy, Schmitt, & Walsh, 1980) has demonstrated clear relationships between rehearsal organization and recall efficiency and structure.

The time between the recall of successive items can be recorded with little change in the standard recall procedure. These interitem latencies provide another source of data that can be used to define organization or to corroborate the organization specified by other measures (Puff, 1972; Reitman & Rueter, 1980).

Several recent techniques have been developed to better portray the contents of the units of organization rather than just assessing the degree of such organization that is present. For example, in his 2D procedure, Buschke (1977) has subjects record their recall on a two dimensional grid with items that are subjectively grouped being written together on the same line. Friendly's (1979) graphic representation of the results of the hierarchical clustering analyses of proximity data is another approach that provides a rich description of the structure of organization in free-recall and other paradigms. Ornstein and Corsale (1979) have applied the hierarchical clustering technique to children's recall.

As Colle (1972) has pointed out, the lack of an adequate theory has seriously hampered research on free recall. Such a theory has been difficult to develop, in part because of the many findings and phenomena that need to be explained. Recently, however, there have been a number of attempts to provide explicit models of some of the processes involved in free recall. Anderson's (1972) Free Recall in an Associative Net (FRAN) model, based on associative search of tagged lexical items, provides a simulation of a number of important phenomena (and its failures are also instructive). Metcalfe and Murdock (1981) present a model of single-trial free recall based on the complimentary processes of convolution and correlation. Batchelder and Riefer (1980) have developed a Markov model that separates storage and retrieval factors in the free recall of clusterable pairs. These are just some of the available examples that have the virtue of being sufficiently explicit to provide the context for meaningful empirical work. They do not, however, provide a general account of the range of phenomena in the free-recall area and cannot as yet serve as a basis for validating the various organizational measures.

The number of published free-recall studies declined in the decade of the 1970s. Some of the factors involved were arguments against list learning experiments and for more ecologically valid prose learning studies; the emergence of depth of processing (Craik & Lockhart, 1972) as a major framework for memory research; and an emphasis on cued recall. In the 1980s free-recall research seems to be making a comeback. Work on prose recall has led, if anything, to more methodological complexities than present in the list learning studies and, furthermore, many have realized that the fundamental nature of the memorizer does not change greatly with changes in type of stimulus material. Depth of processing researchers have run into difficulties in defining depth independent of recall level, which depth is supposed to explain. We have also seen that, whereas the one-item-at-a-time encoding used in the incidental paradigm associated with depth hinders the operation of cognitive organization, depth certainly does not explain organizational processes (Battig & Bellezza, 1979). Cued-recall paradigms, though providing useful information, cannot tell us much about the subject generated retrieval plans that are so strongly implicated in free recall. In addition, the rather indirect manipulations and inferential procedures associated with free recall have been complimented by a number of newer and more direct methods. These methodological and theoretical advances appear to be leading to a renewal of interest in the use of free-recall methodology.

REFERENCE NOTES

1. Cohen, B. H., Sakoda, J. M., & Bousfield, W. A. *The statistical analysis of the incidence of clustering in the recall of randomly arranged associates.* (Tech. Rep. No. 10). Connecticut: University of Connecticut, Contract NONR631(00), Office of Naval Research, July 1954. (NTIS No. PB-117 628)
2. Murphy, M. D., Sanders, R. E., & Puff, C. R. *The measurement of subjective organization: A reply to Sternberg and Tulving.* Unpublished manuscript, University of Akron, 1978.

REFERENCES

Anderson, J. R. FRAN: A simulation model of free recall. In G. H. Bower (Ed.), *The psychology of learning and motivation* (Vol. 5). New York: Academic Press, 1972.

Batchelder, W. H., & Riefer, D. M. Separation of storage and retrieval factors in free recall of clusterable pairs. *Psychological Review,* 1980, *87,* 375–397.

Battig, W. F., Allen, M. M., & Jensen, A. R. Priority of free recall of newly learned items. *Journal of Verbal Learning and Verbal Behavior,* 1965, *4,* 175–179.

Battig, W. F., & Bellezza, F. S. Organization and levels of processing. In C. R. Puff (Ed.), *Memory organization and structure.* New York: Academic Press, 1979.

Battig, W. F., & Montague, W. E. Category norms for verbal items in 56 categories: A replication and extension of the Connecticut Category Norms. *Journal of Experimental Psychology Monographs,* 1969, *80,* 1–46.

Belmont, J. M., & Butterfield, E. C. Learning strategies as determinants of memory deficiencies. *Cognitive Psychology,* 1971, *2,* 411–420.

Botwinick, J. *Aging and behavior.* New York: Springer-Verlag, 1978.

Bousfield, A. K., & Bousfield, W. A. Measurement of clustering and of sequential constancies in repeated free recall. *Psychological Reports,* 1966, *19,* 935–942.

Bousfield, W. A. The occurrence of clustering in the recall of randomly arranged associates. *Journal of General Psychology,* 1953, *49,* 229–240.

Bousfield, W. A., & Cohen, B. H. The effects of reinforcement on the occurrence of clustering in the recall of randomly arranged associates. *Journal of Psychology*, 1953, *36*, 67–81.

Bousfield, W. A., Cohen, B. H., & Whitmarsh, G. A. Associative clustering in the recall of words of different taxonomic frequencies of occurrence. *Psychological Reports*, 1958, *4*, 39–44.

Bousfield, W. A., Puff, C. R., & Cowan, T. M. The development of constancies in sequential organization during free recall. *Journal of Verbal Learning and Verbal Behavior*, 1964, *3*, 489–495.

Bousfield, W. A., & Rosner, S. R. Free vs uninhibited recall. *Psychonomic Science*, 1970, *20*, 75–76.

Bray, N. W., & Murphy, M. D. Description of a restricted randomization program (RRP). *Behavior Research Methods and Instrumentation*, 1973, *5*, 490–496.

Buschke, H. Two-dimensional recall: Immediate identification of clusters in episodic and semantic memory. *Journal of Verbal Learning and Verbal Behavior*, 1977, *16*, 201–216.

Chi, M. T. H. Knowledge structures and memory development. In R. S. Siegler (Ed.), *Children's thinking: What develops?* Hillsdale, N.J.: Lawrence Erlbaum Associates, 1978.

Clark, H. H. The language-as-fixed-effect fallacy: A critique of language statistics in psychological research. *Journal of Verbal Learning and Verbal Behavior*, 1973, *12*, 335–359.

Cofer, C. N., Bruce, D. R., & Reicher, G. M. Clustering in recall as a function of certain methodological variations. *Journal of Experimental Psychology*, 1966, *71*, 858–866.

Cole, M., Frankel, F., & Sharp, D. Development of free-recall learning in children. *Developmental Psychology*, 1971, *4*, 109–123.

Colle, H. A. The reification of clustering. *Journal of Verbal Learning and Verbal Behavior*, 1972, *11*, 624–633.

Craik, F. I. M., & Lockhart, R. S. Levels of processing: A framework for memory research. *Journal of Verbal Learning and Verbal Behavior*, 1972, *11*, 671–684.

Deese, J. Serial organization in the recall of disconnected items. *Psychological Reports*, 1957, *3*, 577–582.

Denney, N. W., & Ziobrowski, M. Developmental changes in clustering criteria. *Journal of Experimental Child Psychology*, 1972, *13*, 275–282.

Flores, L. M., Jr., & Brown, S. C. Comparison of output order in free recall. *Behavior Research Methods and Instrumentation*, 1974, *6*, 385–388.

Frankel, F., & Cole, M. Measures of category clustering in free recall. *Psychological Bulletin*, 1971, *76*, 39–44.

Friendly, M. Methods for finding graphic representations of associative memory structures. In C. R. Puff (Ed.), *Memory organization and structure*. New York: Academic Press, 1979.

Frost, N. Clustering by visual shape in the free recall of pictorial stimuli. *Journal of Experimental Psychology*, 1971, *88*, 409–413.

Gerjuoy, I. R., & Spitz, H. H. Associative clustering in free recall: Intellectual and developmental variables. *American Journal of Mental Deficiency*, 1966, *70*, 918–927.

Glanzer, M., & Cunitz, A. R. Two storage mechanisms in free recall. *Journal of Verbal Learning and Verbal Behavior*, 1966, *5*, 351–360.

Hilgard, E. R. A summary and evaluation of alternative procedures for the construction of Vincent curves. *Psychological Bulletin*, 1938, *35*, 282–297.

Howard, D. V. Category norms: A comparison of the Battig and Montague (1969) norms with the responses of adults between the ages of 20 and 80. *Journal of Gerontology,* 1980, *35,* 225–231.

Jenkins, J. J., Mink, W. D., & Russell, W. A. Associative clustering as a function of verbal association strength. *Psychological Reports,* 1958, *4,* 127–136.

Lange, G. Organization-related processes in children's recall. In P. A. Ornstein (Ed.), *Memory development in children.* Hillsdale, N.J.: Lawrence Erlbaum Associates, 1978.

Mandler, G. Organization and memory. In K. W. Spence and J. T. Spence (Eds.), *The psychology of learning and motivation* (Vol. 1). New York: Academic Press, 1967.

Mandler, G. Input variables and output strategies in free recall of categorized lists. *American Journal of Psychology,* 1969, *82,* 531–539.

Metcalfe, J., & Murdock, B. B. An encoding and retrieval model of single-trial free recall. *Journal of Verbal Learning and Verbal Behavior,* 1981, *20,* 161–189.

Moely, B. E., Olson, F. A., Halwes, T. G., & Flavell, J. H. Production deficiency in young children's clustered recall. *Developmental Psychology,* 1969, *1,* 26–34.

Murdock, B. B., Jr., & Walker, K. D. Modality effects in free recall. *Journal of Verbal Learning and Verbal Behavior,* 1969, *8,* 665–676.

Murphy, M. D. Measurement of category clustering in free recall. In C. R. Puff (Ed.), *Memory organization and structure.* New York: Academic Press, 1979.

Myers, N. A., & Perlmutter, M. Memory in the years from two to five. In P. A. Ornstein (Ed.), *Memory development in children.* Hillsdale, N.J.: Lawrence Erlbaum Associates, 1978.

Neimark, E., Slotnick, N. S., & Ulrich, T. Development of memorization strategies. *Developmental Psychology,* 1971, *5,* 427–432.

Nelson, K. The syntagmatic–paradigmatic shift revisited: A review of research and theory. *Psychological Bulletin,* 1977, *84,* 93–116.

Ornstein, P. A., & Corsale, K. Organizational factors in children's memory. In C. R. Puff (Ed.), *Memory organization and structure.* New York: Academic Press, 1979.

Ornstein, P. A., & Naus, M. J. Rehearsal processes in children's memory. In P. A. Ornstein (Ed.), *Memory development in children.* Hillsdale, N.J.: Lawrence Erlbaum Associates, 1978.

Pellegrino, J. W. A general measure of organization in free recall for variable unit size and internal sequential consistency. *Behavior Research Methods and Instrumentation,* 1971, *3,* 241–246.

Pellegrino, J. W. A reply to Frender and Doubilet on the measurement of clustering. *Psychological Bulletin,* 1975, *82,* 66–67.

Pellegrino, J. W., & Battig, W. F. Relationships among higher order organizational measures and free recall. *Journal of Experimental Psychology,* 1974, *102,* 463–472.

Posnansky, C. J. Category norms for verbal items in 25 categories for children in grades 2–6. *Behavior Research Methods and Instrumentation,* 1978, *10,* 819–832.

Puff, C. R. Temporal properties of organization in recall of unrelated words. *Journal of Experimental Psychology,* 1972, *92,* 225–231.

Puff, C. R. A consolidated theoretical view of stimulus-list organization effects in free recall. *Psychological Reports,* 1974, *34,* 275–288.

Puff, C. R., Murphy, M. D., & Ferrara, R. A. Further evidence about the role of clustering in free recall. *Journal of Experimental Psychology: Human Learning and Memory,* 1977, *3,* 742–753.

Reitman, J. S., & Rueter, H. H. Organization revealed by recall orders and confirmed by pauses. *Cognitive Psychology,* 1980, *12,* 554–581.

Robinson, J. A. Category clustering in free recall. *Journal of Psychology,* 1966, *62,* 279–285.

Roenker, D. L., Thompson, C. P., & Brown, S. C. Comparison of measures for the estimation of clustering in free recall. *Psychological Bulletin,* 1971, *76,* 45–48.

Rundus, D., & Atkinson, R. C. Rehearsal processes in free recall: A procedure for direct observation. *Journal of Verbal Learning and Verbal Behavior,* 1970, *9,* 99–105.

Sanders, R. E., Murphy, M. D., Schmitt, F. A., & Walsh, K. K. Age differences in free-recall rehearsal strategies. *Journal of Gerontology,* 1980, *35,* 550–558.

Sternberg, R. J., & Tulving, E. The measurement of subjective organization in free recall. *Psychological Bulletin,* 1977, *84,* 539–556.

Stukuls, H. I. Clustering as determined by exposure time and spatial arrangement of objects. *Psychological Reports,* 1975, *37,* 159–166.

Tulving, E. Subjective organization in free recall of "unrelated" words. *Psychological Review,* 1962, *69,* 344–354.

Tulving, E. Theoretical issues in free recall. In T. R. Dixon & D. L. Horton (Eds.), *Verbal behavior and general behavior theory.* Englewood Cliffs, N.J.: Prentice–Hall, 1968.

Tulving, E., & Pearlstone, Z. Availability versus accessibility of information in memory for words. *Journal of Verbal Learning and Verbal Behavior,* 1966, *5,* 381–391.

Wallace, W. P., & Underwood, B. J. Implicit responses and the role of intralist similarity in verbal learning by normal and retarded subjects. *Journal of Educational Psychology,* 1964, *55,* 362–370.

Weist, R. M. The role of rehearsal: Recopy or reconstruct. *Journal of Verbal Learning and Verbal Behavior,* 1972, *11,* 440–450.

JAMES W. PELLEGRINO
CHAPTER **5**   LAWRENCE J. HUBERT

The Analysis of Organization and Structure in Free Recall

INTRODUCTION

Overview

A survey of the human learning and memory literature from the past 20 years would show free–recall as the primary paradigm and method for studying verbal recall. This emphasis reflects the increased importance of free–recall as a list learning paradigm and as a method or means for studying memory organization and structure. Interest in free-recall data has transcended concerns associated with the study of word lists per se and has moved in the direction of general issues associated with the organization, structure, and processing of information in memory.

It is not our purpose in this chapter to review the empirical and theoretical literature on organization, storage and retrieval in free recall. A number of such reviews are available for those interested in the myriad issues studied within the context of free-recall learning (e.g., Bower, 1970, 1972; Pellegrino & Ingram, 1979; Postman, 1972; Puff, 1979; Shuell, 1969; Tulving, 1968). What is, perhaps, most significant about the free-recall paradigm is that it has substantially influenced current thought relative to the active nature of information processing. A key assumption is that the free–recall of a list of words, sentences, and so on, is not

129

HANDBOOK OF RESEARCH METHODS IN
HUMAN MEMORY AND COGNITION

random, but that it is organized and structured in ways that reflect systematic temporal, spatial, and/or semantic properties of list items. All *organizational phenomena,* such as category clustering, priority in the recall of newly learned items, and seriation refer to the structuring of free-recall output in terms of some a priori structural characteristic or distinction among the set of items to be recalled. Thus, an important question that is frequently asked is whether characteristics of the input have influenced the structure of the output. This chapter is concerned with the analysis of free-recall data given the goal of testing or generating an explicit hypothesis about systematic properties of recall protocols. The systematic properties can focus on individual items or groups and their position, and probability of recall.

To provide a general context, it may be useful to review briefly the prototypic free-recall situation (treated more fully in the preceding chapter by Murphy and Puff) and some of the major variants that might exist. As the name implies, free–recall generally involves an unpaced attempt by an individual to remember as much of some content as possible, with the output being written or spoken. Prior to the recall attempt, there is usually an input or "study" phase. In typical episodic memory situations, the input is controlled by the experimenter and occurs in a "laboratory" setting. Free-recall in a semantic memory study, however, may have no explicit input or study phase, since the information to be recalled is presumed to reside in the individual's permanent memory store. In any event, the material to be recalled can be individual words, clauses, sentences, propositions, and so on. There may also be a single recall attempt or multiple recall episodes preceded by separate presentation or input phases. These are all variations on one or more themes, and their occurrence depends on the type of question that the researcher is attempting to ask. In all cases, however, the critical data in the recall protocol are the individual items and their unique temporal and/or spatial position. Those instances in which the researcher may be only interested in whether an item or set of items was recalled are straightforward and only of secondary importance in this chapter. What is of primary concern here is the analysis of protocol structure.

The remainder of the chapter is organized around several specific goals. First, we focus on general methods for analyzing the properties of recall protocols. The methods are independent of the units or type of information recalled. The experimenter defines the unit of analysis, which can be a word, phrase, proposition, sentence, paragraph, and so on. Since much of the literature on the analysis of organization has dealt with very limited problems and confounded sets of issues, our second goal is to develop a general scheme for laying out a set of higher order issues applicable to all cases of organization and structural analysis. Third, we develop and illustrate a set of analytic procedures that includes all of the many variations as special cases. Finally, we suggest how other data sources can be approached with the same set of analytic procedures.

Conceptual and Analytic Issues: A General Discussion

CONFIRMATORY VERSUS EXPLORATORY ANALYSIS

There are two basic strategies of analysis that can be involved in any recall study. The first strategy has the goal of testing some explicit hypothesis about recall structure. Thus, the analysis is designed to assess the match between protocol structure and some preexisting structural "hypothesis." The classic example of the confirmatory mode of analysis in free recall is category clustering. Here, the hypothesis being tested is that the structure of the recall protocol matches the semantic category structure of the list. The null conjecture is that nothing more than a random match exists and the analytic procedures are designed to determine if such a baseline assumption can be rejected.

The alternative mode of analysis is exploratory and the goal is to determine empirically the nature of the protocol structure. Since it is assumed that some structure exists and recall is not random, the procedures of analysis are now very different. In general, an attempt is made to fit the given recall data by a specific representation chosen from some broad class; for example, by a particular partition hierarchy, a Euclidean multidimensional scale, and so on.

LEVELS OF STRUCTURAL ANALYSIS

A recall protocol can be analyzed for different structural characteristics reflecting information available for an individual item or sets of items. A distinction will be drawn among single-item information, item-pair information, and, more generally, item–group information. In the simplest form of analysis, we focus on information that is assigned to single items. The list is divided into individual elements, and information is sought about each element's position (or presence) in the recall protocol. This is in contrast to the analysis of information defined by specific pairs of items. The information being analyzed is unique to the pair and is based on some specific relationship between the members of the pair. Thus, in the analysis of single-item information, the absolute position of an item would be of concern. In the analysis of item-pair information, the absolute position of an item is important only insofar as it enters into the calculation of the proximity of that item relative to some other item. Finally, in the analysis of item–group information the emphasis is on information uniquely defined by groups of three or more objects.

DESCRIPTION VERSUS INFERENCE

In attempting to analyze single-item through item–group information, the initial step is to develop an index or descriptive statistic that numerically represents the match between the hypothesized structure and an actual protocol. Unfortunately, a raw measure by itself cannot be interpreted as to its relative size unless some baseline is established against which the measure can be compared. Baselines are typically determined by finding the distribution of the measure under some null conjecture of randomness for the match between the hypothesized structure and the given protocol. Given that the obtained value can be related to a known distribution of values generated from some null conjecture, it may be desirable for inferential purposes to express the index as a normalized value or Z-score that can be interpreted with respect to statistical significance.

The issue of hypothesis testing is distinct from the somewhat thorny problem of scaling a raw measure to provide a final descriptive index. The need to develop a final descriptive index that can be related to some scale of measurement is critical when one wishes to make comparisons between index values obtained from two different recall protocols.

CONDITIONAL VERSUS UNCONDITIONAL INFERENCE

The process of deriving a descriptive statistic for the correspondence between actual and hypothesized structure and then evaluating the level of significance can be done under two general models. In most recall situations, the content of the recall protocol is less than or equal to the total number of elements that could have been produced. The raw descriptive index that is calculated can therefore be compared to one of two different probability distributions. In the conditional inference model, the baseline distribution is restricted to the particular set of elements actually recalled, in other words, the calculation is conditional for the set of elements produced. As an example, consider the recall of a list containing common category members. If the list contains 12 items representing 4 categories and 3 instances per category, and the subject recalls all 12 items, then the baseline distribution is constructed by assuming all 12! possible protocols are equally likely, that is, the subject merely picks one at random. If the subject recalled only eight items, then conditional inference requires a redefinition of the input list to be exactly the same. Thus, for whatever number of categories and instances per category that actually turn out for the reduced list of 8, the baseline distribution is generated by assuming the subject merely chooses at random one of the 8! possible protocols of the reduced list. The four unrecalled items play no direct role in the construction of the baseline distribution in conditional inference.

Alternatively, in unconditional inference, and even though the subject only recalls 8 items, the baseline distribution depends on all 12 items. It is assumed that the subject first picks one of the $\binom{12}{8}$ possible subsets of size 8 for recall and then within this particular subset, one of the 8! possible orderings. Clearly, the baseline distributions will generally be different, since in unconditional inference the salience of the eight items actually picked is confounded with the order information in the protocol. Conditional inference is based on the subject picking one of 8! possible protocols at random; alternatively, unconditional inference is based on the subject picking one of $\binom{12}{8}$ 8! possible protocols at random. The unconditional inference case attempts to take both the content and structure of the protocol into account whereas the conditional inference case deals only with the structure of what was produced.

The problem with the baseline distribution under the unconditional inference model is that it reflects two sources of information; thus, a hypothesis about structure cannot be evaluated apart from the content of the items chosen. The same type of problem exists in the case of multiple recalls as in a multitrial free-recall situation. The analysis of organization on any given trial can be made conditional on what was recalled or unconditional on total list content and structure.

ANALYSIS OF SINGLE-ITEM INFORMATION

Illustration and Quantification

The analysis of single-item information is involved if the question to be answered can be phrased in the following generic form: *Is there a relationship between **an item's** recall position and its* ————?'' Potential completions include: *printed frequency; serial position; prior recall history; occurrence in the recency portion of the list,* and so on. To answer this type of question, the variable of interest, that is, the hypothesis, and the actual recall data must be in the form of two numerical sequences $x_1, x_2, \ldots, x_n$ and $y_1, y_2, \ldots, y_n$, where the values of x_i and

y_i both refer to information about the same ith object or unit o_i. If the objects are words, then x_i typically denotes some prior characteristic of o_i based on either (a) extraexperimental information (e.g., meaningfulness, concreteness, familiarity, frequency, or some other individual item characteristic defined by a scaled value or a zero–one dichotomy), or (b) intraexperimental information (e.g., input structure specifying presentation order or previous recall history). The corresponding value in the second sequence y_i will usually characterize output position or another numerical variable defined by recall. As a frame of reference, the reader may assume for now that the sequence $y_1, y_2, \ldots, y_n$ refers to the results obtained from a single subject on a single trial.

A hypothesis about recall structure can be phrased in the following way: differences among items expressed as x_i values in the x sequence will covary with differences among items in recall position (or probability) expressed as y_i values in the y sequence. Various specific hypotheses can be entertained, and all such cases will be expressed as a particular set of values for the sequence $x_1, x_2, \ldots, x_n$. Table 5.1 illustrates several ways in which hypotheses about recall structure can be expressed using an example list of twenty objects—in this instance, words. The numerical sequence labeled *seriation* represents a "hypothesis" that the recall order will be related to presentation order; the second "hypothesis" is that the recall order will be related to an alphabetical sequence. These two cases involve the use of rank data for representing a hypothesis about the recall sequence and all list items are represented by a different value. The third and fourth hypotheses are based upon the concreteness of the words in the list with the aim of relating recall order to word concreteness. Hypothesis 3 treats the concreteness difference among items as rank data, whereas Hypothesis 4 expresses it in terms of actual normative concreteness values (Toglia & Battig, 1978). As in the case of Hypotheses 1 and 2, all members of the list contribute to defining the values in the x sequence.

Continuing with the illustrations in Table 5.1, Cases 5–8 represent hypotheses about a differential order of recall for parts of the list. Hypothesis 5 is a representation, using dichotomous values, of the assumption that items occupying the recency portion (final five positions) of the list will have different recall positions than other items. Thus, the list has been partitioned and, rather than assigning ranks to members of the recency set, the entire set is given the same value of 1 to differentiate these words from the other list members. Hypothesis 6 is a similar representation but for items occupying the primacy portion (first five positions) of the list. Hypothesis 7 is simply a composite conjecture in which differential recall position is assumed for both primacy and recency

Table 5.1
Sequence Representation of "Hypothetical" and Actual Recall Structures

List members (o_i)	(1) Seriation	(2) Alphabetization	(3) Concreteness rank	(4) Concreteness scaled	(5) Recency	(6) Primacy	(7) Primacy + Recency	(8) New vs. old item	(9) Recall rank
				Recall structure "hypotheses" (x_i)					Recall representation (y_i)
car (o_1)	1	3	1	6.35	0	1	1	0	3
fuel (o_2)	2	6	11	5.55	0	1	1	0	4
open (o_3)	3	15	17	3.77	0	1	1	0	7
star (o_4)	4	19	10	5.67	0	1	1	1	1
job (o_5)	5	10	15	4.28	0	1	1	0	6
girl (o_6)	6	7	4	6.05	0	0	0	1	2
leg (o_7)	7	12	2	6.22	0	0	0	1	5
rule (o_8)	8	18	19	2.82	0	0	0	0	8
nest (o_9)	9	14	12	5.53	0	0	0	1	10
book (o_{10})	10	2	3	6.09	0	0	0	0	11
train (o_{11})	11	20	6.5	5.88	0	0	0	0	9
egg (o_{12})	12	5	6.5	5.88	0	0	0	0	13
army (o_{13})	13	1	13	5.24	0	0	0	1	15
kill (o_{14})	14	11	16	3.82	0	0	0	0	12
pin (o_{15})	15	16	9	5.81	0	0	0	0	14
hat (o_{16})	16	8	5	5.97	0	0	0	0	18
queen (o_{17})	17	17	14	5.05	1	0	1	0	20
more (o_{18})	18	13	20	2.80	1	0	1	0	17
dog (o_{19})	19	4	8	5.84	1	0	1	0	16
idea (o_{20})	20	9	18	2.87	1	0	1	0	19

items relative to all remaining items. The final illustration is a dichotomization of list members based upon prior response or recall history.
Assume that the items *girl, leg, nest,* and *star* were not recalled on a
previous trial. All the remaining items thus represent "old" or previously
recalled items. Hypothesis 8 reflects the assumption that newly recalled
items will be given different positions in recall output, for example, they
may be recalled earlier or later than the other "old" items.

The representation of one or more hypotheses about factors related
to recall order as numerical sequences is half of the initial stage of
conceptual and empirical analysis. The second half is to represent numerically the actual protocol to be compared against the sequence representing the hypothesized effect of some variable. The rightmost portion
of Table 5.1 shows the typical representation of recall structure with the
sequence representing actual recall rank. An alternative is to divide the
recall protocol into fourths, thirds, halves, and so on, and then assign
values based upon the portion of the recall protocol into which an object
falls.

Thus far, the x sequences derived from hypotheses about factors
governing recall order and the representation of actual recall order all
deal with the structure of the protocol, given that items o_1 to o_n have
all been recalled. The representation is conditional on the items actually
contained in the protocol. However, it is often the case that the objects
recalled are a subset of the larger set of objects that could have been
recalled. Imagine that for our original set of 20 words only 17 were recalled on the trial we wish to analyze, and we are faced with the problem
of how to represent hypotheses about protocol structure. In the conditional inference case, there is a simple solution. The nonrecalled items
are treated as nonexistent and the x sequences are expressed in the
slightly modified form shown in Table 5.2. If the items *army, dog,* and
hat were not recalled, the recall sequence would be as shown in the
ninth column of Table 5.2. The sequence representing a hypothesis about
serial presentation order governing recall order is now made conditional
on what was recalled; that is, it is adjusted for serial presentation order
of the recalled items and ignores those items that were not present in
the protocol. Similar modifications have been made for the sequences
representing hypothesized relationships between recall order and alphabetical ordering, concreteness, recency, primacy, old–new item differences, and so on. Any hypothesis about a factor governing recall structure is now expressed in a form conditional on what was recalled, not
on what could have been recalled.

Given that the x and y sequences have been specified, the next step
is to define some quantitative index of their correspondence and specify

Table 5.2
Sequence Representation of "Hypothetical" and Actual Recall Structures

List members (o_i)	Recall structure "hypotheses" (x_i)								Recall representation (y_i)
	(1) Seriation	(2) Alphabet-ization	(3) Concreteness rank	(4) Concreteness scaled	(5) Recency	(6) Primacy	(7) Primacy + Recency	(8) New vs. old item	(9) Recall rank
car (o_1)	1	2	1	6.35	0	1	1	0	3
fuel (o_2)	2	4	9	5.55	0	1	1	0	4
open (o_3)	3	12	14	3.77	0	1	1	0	7
star (o_4)	4	16	8	5.67	0	1	1	1	1
job (o_5)	5	7	12	4.28	0	1	1	0	6
girl (o_6)	6	5	4	6.05	0	0	0	1	2
leg (o_7)	7	9	2	6.22	0	0	0	1	5
rule (o_8)	8	15	16	2.82	0	0	0	1	8
nest (o_9)	9	11	10	5.53	0	0	0	1	10
book (o_{10})	10	1	3	6.09	0	0	0	0	11
train (o_{11})	11	17	5.5	5.88	0	0	0	0	9
egg (o_{12})	12	3	5.5	5.88	0	0	0	0	13
*army									
kill (o_{13})	13	8	13	3.82	0	0	0	0	12
pin (o_{14})	14	13	7	5.81	0	0	0	0	14
*hat									
queen (o_{15})	15	14	11	5.05	1	1	1	0	17
more (o_{16})	16	10	17	2.80	1	0	1	0	15
*dog									
idea (o_{17})	17	6	15	2.87	1	0	1	0	16

* Nonrecalled items

the basis for evaluating its statistical significance. Instead of proceeding inductively through a discussion of special cases, we will present the general inference problem first and then show its applications. At this initial level our first task is to measure the correspondence between x_1, $x_2, \ldots, x_n$ and $y_1, y_2, \ldots, y_n$ through a raw index defined by

$$\Gamma = \sum_{i=1}^{n} f(x_i, y_i).$$

Whereas the function $f(x_i, y_i)$ can be chosen by the experimenter to suit a particular application, we will only consider the simple multiplicative form $x_i y_i$. In addition, various normalizations and scaling of the raw index can be suggested that define final descriptive indexes of the correspondence between the two sequences. To simplify matters, we will primarily consider the normalization and scaling based upon the logic of correlation. As always, these normalized indexes could simply be considered as dependent measures in traditional statistical analyses. Our emphasis, however, will be much more basic to begin with and will focus on an inference model that permits significance testing of a single index derived from a single subject or protocol.

The raw index Γ is presented in a very general form and includes a host of measures that may be of interest in comparing two sequences. In all cases, however, the same general statistical inference model can be used. Under the null assumption that the two sequences bear no systematic relation to one another, the n values of $x_1, x_2, \ldots, x_n$ can be considered matched at random to $y_1, y_2, \ldots, y_n$ (or the converse). Based on this notion of independence

$$E(\Gamma) = (\frac{1}{n}) \sum_{j=1}^{n} \sum_{i=1}^{n} f(x_i, y_j), \tag{1}$$

and

$$\text{Var}(\Gamma) = \{1/[n(n-1)]\}\{(1/n)A_1 - (A_2 + A_3) + nA_4\},$$

where

$$A_1 = \left[\sum_{j=1}^{n} \sum_{i=1}^{n} f(x_i, y_j) \right]^2;$$

$$A_2 = \sum_{j=1}^{n} \left[\sum_{i=1}^{n} f(x_i, y_j) \right]^2;$$

$$A_3 = \sum_{i=1}^{n} \left[\sum_{j=1}^{n} f(x_i, y_j) \right]^2;$$

$$A_4 = \sum_{j=1}^{n} \sum_{i=1}^{n} f(x_i, y_j)^2.$$

When n is reasonably large (>20) and using the simple multiplicative function to define Γ, the distribution of Γ can be assumed normal, with mean and variance given by the above formulas. Thus, the Z statistic, $[\Gamma - E(\Gamma)]/[\text{Var}(\Gamma)]^{1/2}$, can be referred to the standard normal distribution to obtain an appropriate significance level for the raw index Γ.

In many applications, the adequacy of a normal approximation may be poor, given the sizes of the protocols that we typically would wish to analyze. As a preferable alternative in general, a random sample (e.g., $100+$) of matchings of the actual x and y sequences could be constructed by computer, and the size of the obtained Γ index evaluated against the generated distribution of indexes. In particular, the proportion of indexes with values equal to or greater than the obtained index is reported directly as the significance level (assuming that the obtained index is also considered part of the random sample). A complete discussion of this Monte Carlo significance testing strategy is given by Edgington (1980) in the context of evaluating experimentally obtained data through a variety of nonparametric procedures.

Seriation

One very familiar measure that will serve as our first specific illustration involves the situation where the hypothesis about recall structure is that it will be related to input or presentation order. Thus, x_i denotes the input position of object o_i and y_i denotes output position; that is, both sequences consist of the integers $1-n$. Then, if $f(x_i, y_i)$ is defined multiplicatively as $x_i y_i$, Γ is merely the sum of the cross products of input and output ranks. Moreover, since the multiplicative form is assumed, the mean and variance formulas for the raw index simplify considerably, as shown in the top row of Table 5.3 (also, see Hubert & Levin, 1978).

Given the calculation of Γ, $E(\Gamma)$ and $\text{Var}(\Gamma)$, a Z-score can be constructed to evaluate the significance of the match between the x and y sequences. We can use the sequence information in Table 5.1 to illustrate the computational steps involved in evaluating a seriation hypothesis. Column 1 in Table 5.1 represents the x sequence, whereas Column 9 in Table 5.1 represents the y sequence. The raw index Γ equals 2823. The expected value $E(\Gamma)$ equals 2205 and the standard deviation $[\text{Var}(\Gamma)]^{1/2}$ equals 152.6. Thus, the Z-score for the match between list order and recall order is equal to 4.05. By referring to tables for the standard normal distribution we find that the probability of obtaining such a Z-score is less than .01. We can reject the hypothesis of a chance correspondence and state that seriation has occurred; that is, recall order is significantly related to input or presentation order.

Table 5.3
Summary of Representative Single-Item Analyses

x Sequence	y Sequence	Γ	$E(\Gamma)$	$\text{Var}(\Gamma)$	Final normalized index
Multivalued	Multivalued				
Multivalued	Dichotomous	$\displaystyle\sum_{i=1}^{n}(xy_i)$	$\dfrac{1}{n}(\Sigma x_i)(\Sigma y_i)$	$\dfrac{1}{n-1}\,[\Sigma(x_i - \bar{x})^2][\Sigma(y_i - \bar{y})^2]$, where $\bar{x}$ any $\bar{y}$ are sequence means	$\dfrac{\Gamma - E(\Gamma)}{(n-1)^{1/2}[\text{Var}(\Gamma)]^{1/2}}$ (Pearson r_{xy})
Dichotomous	Multivalued				
Dichotomous	Dichotomous				
Special Cases Dichotomous	Recall rank	$\displaystyle\sum_{i=1}^{n}(xy_i)$	$I(n+1)/2$ where I = the number of x_i items with a value of 1	$\dfrac{(n+1)(n-I)I}{12}$	$\dfrac{\Gamma - E(\Gamma)}{(n-1)^{1/2}[\text{Var}(\Gamma)]^{1/2}}$ (Pearson r_{xy})
(Old versus new items) (Recency) (Primacy)					

While it is simple to construct a Z-score to evaluate a seriation hypothesis for a given recall protocol, the Z-score is an inappropriate final descriptive statistic. It is inappropriate because it is unbounded and can vary as a function of the size of the numerical sequences being compared. This is problematic for comparing seriation on two trials where the amount of recall differs greatly or for two subjects who recall different numbers of items. It is possible, however, to normalize and scale Z-scores by simply dividing by $(n - 1)^{1/2}$. When this is done, the Z-score based upon Γ, $E(\Gamma)$ and $\text{Var}(\Gamma)$ is converted into the Pearson product–moment correlation. Thus, we can go from a raw index Γ to a normalized final descriptive index $r(xy)$. The equivalences are as follows:

$$r_{(xy)} = \frac{\sum_{i=1}^{n} x_i y_i - (1/n) \sum_{i=1}^{n} x_i \sum_{i=1}^{n} y_i}{\left[\sum_{i=1}^{n} (x_i - \bar{x})^2 \sum_{i=1}^{n} (y_i - \bar{y})^2 \right]^{1/2}}$$

$$= \frac{\Gamma - E(\Gamma)}{(n - 1)^{1/2} [\text{Var}(\Gamma)]^{1/2}} = \frac{Z}{(n - 1)^{1/2}}$$

If we directly calculate $r(xy)$ for our example case, the value is .93.

When Γ is defined by the function $x_i y_i$, then Γ is set in the familiar statistical context of product–moment correlation. With in that context it is possible to illustrate the complete cycle of description–inference–scaling. The correlation coefficient provides an ideal final descriptive index since it has a chance value of 0 and is bounded by -1 and $+1$. For the seriation case it can be evaluated for significance using the original Z-statistic and r values obtained for different protocols or subjects can be contrasted. The experimenter can simplify computation by immediately calculating $r(xy)$ or deriving it from Γ, $E(\Gamma)$, $\text{Var}(\Gamma)$, and n.

Primacy, Recency and Priority

Our second general illustration of single-item information applies to those cases where the list is dichotomized on the basis of some item characteristic. The most common illustrations are the separation of subsets of the list on the basis of occurrence in the primacy and/or recency portions of the list or from an old versus a newly recalled contrast. However, any such dichotomization is possible. In Table 5.1 we illustrated how the x_i values for such situations would be represented. For our present purposes, we will consider the analysis of new item priority, since substantial effort has gone into defining measures for this particular situation (e.g., Battig, Allen, & Jensen, 1965; Flores & Brown, 1974; Postman & Keppel, 1968; Shuell & Keppel, 1968).

Given that x_i equals 0, if o_i is old, and 1, if it is new, and that y_i is actual recall position, then the index Γ with $f(x_i, y_i) = x_i y_i$ is equal to the sum of the recall position ranks for the "new" items. Thus, Γ defines the basis for a measure of the priority effect in free recall introduced by Battig *et al.* (1965). The expected value, $E(\Gamma)$, equals $I(n + 1)/2$ and the variance, $\text{Var}(\Gamma)$, equals $I(n + 1)(n - I)/12$, where I is the number of new items. The examples in Table 5.1 provide the basis for a computational illustration. Column 8 in Table 5.1 represents the x sequence and Column 9 again represents the y sequence. The value of Γ is 18, $E(\Gamma) = 42$ and $\text{Var}(\Gamma) = 112$. The Z-score value is -2.27, which is significant. The final descriptive index $r(xy)$ can be obtained by dividing Z by $(n - 1)^{\frac{1}{2}}$, or it can be computed directly. For the present example the value is $-.52$. The $r(xy)$ value should be used as the final descriptive index in any subsequent statistical analyses (e.g., ANOVA) or comparison across protocols or subjects.

Summary of General Principles and Procedures

Certain key points can be summarized that should be of use in establishing practical guidelines in any analysis of single-item information. Because of its very simple form, the multiplicative index Γ is preferred and it should always be related to its baseline distribution, and in particular, to a chance expected value $E(\Gamma)$ and a variance $\text{Var}(\Gamma)$. These parameters can then be used to define a Z-score that can be interpreted for statistical significance using the standard normal distribution, if n is reasonably large, or a Monte Carlo significance testing strategy otherwise. The raw index Γ can and should be converted into scaled normalized values representing the Pearson product–moment correlation coefficient. Such scaled values avoid the obvious problems encountered when comparing scores obtained from two different subjects who recall different amounts of material or from two protocols from the same subject based upon differing amounts recalled, for example, the first and last trials of a multitrial situation.

In those cases where recall structure is to be related to some multivalued scaled variable, such as serial position, frequency, concreteness, and so on, one can proceed directly to the computation of the Pearson product–moment correlation r between the recall rank of an item and its corresponding value on the multivalued dimension. Significant positive and negative r values are readily interpreted relative to the scaled variable of interest, be it serial position, concreteness, and so on. Other analysis situations typically represent the dichotomization of the list into subsets that differ in some important characteristic. The question of interest is whether the division is associated with differentiation of recall order in the actual protocol, for example, early or late recall. A summary of various single-item information analyses is provided in Table 5.3.

Conditional versus Unconditional Inference

Our discussion thus far has focused on the analysis of a correspondence between x and y sequences given a conditional inference model. Thus, the x sequence represents sequence information about what was recalled. Suppose that now, however, we let the x sequence represent information about all the members of the list, irrespective of recall. If a simple 0–1 dichotomy is defined for the y sequence depending on recall (1 for recall and 0 for nonrecall) then the multiplicative function $f(x_i, y_i) = x_i y_i$ turns the index Γ into the sum of values in the x sequence that are actually assigned to recalled objects. Furthermore, a test based on the usual mean and variance terms can be given for the hypothesis that recall is random with respect to the variable defining the x sequence. For example, if $x_1, x_2, \ldots, x_n$ denote frequency values, the randomness conjecture states that the subset recalled is no greater or less in average frequency than what would be expected if m (the number of recalled objects) were picked at random from the total pool of n available.

Although this application is a straightforward way to evaluate whether total recall represents differential salience as characterized by the numerical sequence $x_1, x_2, \ldots, x_n$, an ambiguous inference problem exists if we try to extend the paradigm in a natural way. For instance, suppose $x_1, x_2, \ldots, x_n$ denote input positions for the n objects, and we define the values in the y sequence as 0, if the object was not recalled, and equal to the recall position otherwise. If Γ is defined by the multiplicative function, the index Γ is a raw correlational index between input and output ranks. Unfortunately, the unconditional distribution of Γ is confounded by total recall in addition to providing information on position correspondence.

There are two facets of recall that need to be distinguished—what is recalled per se, and then, within this subset, how the objects are arranged. These are two distinct questions and should be dealt with separately. Total recall can be evaluated by defining y_i through a 1–0 dichotomy based on recall or failure to recall, respectively. Alternatively, order of recall can be evaluated conditionally by considering only that part of the input sequence which actually corresponds to the generated protocol. These issues of conditional and unconditional inference are discussed in detail by Hubert and Levin (1977), where it is argued that an unconditional inference model that confounds amount of recall with its structure should, in general, be avoided.

ANALYSIS OF ITEM-PAIR INFORMATION

Illustration and Quantification

The single-item analyses just described all deal with the evaluation of data defined by numerical values attached to single objects. Item-pair assessments, on the other hand, are based on numerical relationships between object pairs, for example, preexisting norms of associative relatedness, measures of similarity for input position, categorical membership, and output position. Item-pair information must be analyzed whenever the question being asked has the following generic form: "*Are items ——— being recalled in close temporal or spatial proximity?*" Potential completions include: "*from the same conceptual category, presented contiguously, previously recalled together,*" etc. Again, the comparison task can be phrased in terms of two object sequences, but now the information among the n objects is coded by matrices. Thus, for n objects, $o_1, o_2, \ldots, o_n$, an $n \times n$ matrix A is defined with an arbitrary element a_{ij} in the ith row and jth column. Similarly, the simple numerical y sequence is replaced by a second $n \times n$ matrix B with an arbitrary entry of b_{ij}. In both instances, the main diagonal is considered irrelevant and set equal to 0, that is, $a_{ii} = b_{ii} = 0$ for $1 \leq i \leq n$.

The matrix representation can be illustrated for the classic case of testing a hypothesis about the existence of category clustering in the recall protocol. Consider the situation in which a list contains 12 items, representing 3 instances in each of 4 categories. The representation of the categorical structure of the list is given by the A matrix shown in Table 5.4. A 1 is entered in each cell that labels two items from the same conceptual category. An alternative A matrix for this set of words can be generated by ignoring categorical structure and focusing instead on alphabetical groupings. If we assign 1 to any cell representing two words with the same initial letter and 0 to all other cells, then the A matrix has the form shown in Table 5.5.

The two preceding A matrices represent hypotheses about structural relationships among pairs of list members that may be reflected in the

Table 5.4
Representation of the A Matrix for Categorical Structure

	bomb	cannon	pistol	banana	cherry	plum	book	catalog	paperback	beaver	camel	panther
bomb	—	1	1	0	0	0	0	0	0	0	0	0
cannon	1	—	1	0	0	0	0	0	0	0	0	0
pistol	1	1	—	0	0	0	0	0	0	0	0	0
banana	0	0	0	—	1	1	0	0	0	0	0	0
cherry	0	0	0	1	—	1	0	0	0	0	0	0
plum	0	0	0	1	1	—	0	0	0	0	0	0
book	0	0	0	0	0	0	—	1	1	0	0	0
catalog	0	0	0	0	0	0	1	—	1	0	0	0
paperback	0	0	0	0	0	0	1	1	—	0	0	0
beaver	0	0	0	0	0	0	0	0	0	—	1	1
camel	0	0	0	0	0	0	0	0	0	1	—	1
panther	0	0	0	0	0	0	0	0	0	1	1	—

Table 5.5
Representation of the A Matrix for Alphabetical Structure

	bomb	cannon	pistol	banana	cherry	plum	book	catalog	paperback	beaver	camel	panther
bomb	—	0	0	1	0	0	1	0	0	1	0	0
cannon	0	—	0	0	1	0	0	1	0	0	1	0
pistol	0	0	—	0	0	1	0	0	1	0	0	1
banana	1	0	0	—	0	0	1	0	0	1	0	0
cherry	0	1	0	0	—	0	0	1	0	0	1	0
plum	0	0	1	0	0	—	0	0	1	0	0	1
book	1	0	0	1	0	0	—	0	0	1	0	0
catalog	0	1	0	0	1	0	0	—	0	0	1	0
paperback	0	0	1	0	0	1	0	0	—	0	0	1
beaver	1	0	0	1	0	0	1	0	0	—	0	0
camel	0	1	0	0	1	0	0	1	0	0	—	0
panther	0	0	1	0	0	1	0	0	1	0	0	—

actual recall protocol. Assume now that the actual recall sequence is as follows: *beaver, camel, cherry, catalog, paperback, panther, plum, banana, book, bomb, cannon, pistol*. This information must now be converted into one or more **B** matrices reflecting relationships between pairs of items in the actual protocol. For example, the typical clustering case would involve assigning a value of 1 to a cell if those two words occur in immediately adjacent recall positions and 0 otherwise. Thus, the **B** matrix for the assessment of category or alphabetic clustering would be as shown in Table 5.6.

The example we have chosen to illustrate produces **A** and **B** matrices that are symmetric; that is, the same information is represented above and below the main diagonal. As mentioned later, however, this will not always be the case. In any event, given that **A** and **B** matrices have been defined for a given protocol, the next step involves computation of a general index of correspondence.

Considering the general inference task first without specific examples, the matrices **A** and **B** are compared through a raw cross-product measure

$$\Lambda = \sum_{j=1}^{n} \sum_{i=1}^{n} a_{ij} b_{ij} \qquad (2)$$

that has the same type of multiplicative structure used for the earlier raw index Γ.

We restrict ourselves to this cross-product form in Eq. (2), even though it is possible to develop a more general analogue that includes Λ as a special case (see Hubert, 1979). The inference model for Λ follows directly from the one used for the single-item statistic Γ that assumes that one of the object sequences is fixed and the second is randomly matched with it. In the matrix context, this is equivalent to holding **A** fixed, and simultaneously permuting the rows and columns of **B** at random (or equivalently, fixing **B** and permuting the rows and columns of **A**). Based on this mechanism of random matching

$$E(\Lambda) = \frac{1}{[n(n-1)]} \left[\sum_{j=1}^{n} \sum_{i=1}^{n} a_{ij} \right] \left[\sum_{j=1}^{n} \sum_{i=1}^{n} b_{ij} \right].$$

The actual variance of Λ is available in Hubert (1979) for the multiplicative index given in Eq. (2). However, instead of giving these very complicated general formulas here, we will subsequently provide the simplified formulas for several special cases of particular importance.

If a normalized version of Λ is desired, the simple Pearson product–moment correlation $r(\mathbf{AB})$ between the corresponding off-diagonal matrix entries in **A** and **B** is one natural alternative. Even though $r(\mathbf{AB})$

Table 5.6
Representation of the B Matrix for Recall

	bomb	cannon	pistol	banana	cherry	plum	book	catalog	paperback	beaver	camel	panther
bomb	—	1	0	0	0	0	1	0	0	0	0	0
cannon	1	—	1	0	0	0	0	0	0	0	0	0
pistol	0	1	—	0	0	0	0	0	0	0	0	0
banana	0	0	0	—	0	1	1	0	0	0	0	0
cherry	0	0	0	0	—	0	0	1	0	0	1	0
plum	0	0	0	1	0	—	0	0	0	0	0	1
book	1	0	0	1	1	0	—	0	0	0	0	0
catalog	0	0	0	0	0	0	0	—	1	0	0	0
paperback	0	0	0	0	0	0	0	1	—	1	0	1
beaver	0	0	0	0	0	0	0	0	1	—	1	0
camel	0	0	0	0	1	0	0	0	0	1	—	0
panther	0	0	0	0	0	1	0	0	1	0	0	—

has not been discussed in the free-recall literature as such, probably since the matrix structure of the inference problem has been clarified relatively recently, this index has many of the properties that are desirable for a final descriptive measure. Besides being easy to understand, it is corrected for chance (the expectation of $r(\mathbf{AB})$ is 0), bounded by -1 and $+1$, controls for the size of object sequences, and relates directly to the obvious single-item multiplicative measure of correspondence between two numerical sequences.

Although the significance level of the Z and r statistics for single-item information could be determined by reference to the normal distribution, the same cavalier comparison for Λ could lead to problems, since for some definitions of $\mathbf{A}$ and $\mathbf{B}$, asymptotic normality is not appropriate even when n is large (see Mielke, 1978). The most judicious alternative may be to estimate the significance level of an index by taking a random sample of the n possible permutations of the $\mathbf{B}$ matrix against a fixed $\mathbf{A}$ matrix, and then calculating the proportion of such indexes that give values as large or larger than the obtained index (or as small or smaller, depending on the way the measure is keyed). As mentioned earlier, a complete discussion of this procedure is given by Edgington (1980).

A statistic based on single-item information is somewhat restricted in the type of information that is compared across two sequences, since the measure is limited to data defined on single objects. An index based on item-pair information, however, can be tailored to an enormous variety of evaluation tasks. Our purpose here is to mention a number of special $\mathbf{A}$ matrices that relate to the structure of the presented list of items and a number of $\mathbf{B}$ matrices that extract various types of information from the output sequence. Since it is not appropriate to pair up all examples of our $\mathbf{A}$ and $\mathbf{B}$ matrices in generating specific instances of Λ, the cases that we consider specifically are hypotheses about the influence of (a) categorical or group structure on recall, (b) presentation order or what has been termed input–output organization, and (c) prior recall order or what has been termed output–output or subjective organization.

Category Structure Analysis

In the preceding section, an example of categorical structure was used to represent the $\mathbf{A}$ matrix, and immediate adjacency of items in the recall protocol was used to define $\mathbf{B}$. Here, the multiplicative index Λ is simply twice the number of category repetitions in the recall protocol, where a category repetition is defined as the immediate sequential co-occurrence of two items from the same category or group defined a priori. The number of category repetitions forms the basis for every major index of clustering that has been proposed since the original work of Bousfield (1953). For the previously illustrated **A** matrices representing categorical and alphabetical grouping, the index Λ would be *10* and *12,* respectively, when applied to the protocol illustrated earlier as **B**. Thus, clustering as traditionally defined and assessed involves the comparison of two matrices, both of which contain dichotomous data. This simple case has the following expected value and variance:

$$E(\Lambda) = 2\left[\frac{1}{n}\left(\sum_{i=1}^{k} n_i^2\right) - 1\right];$$

$$\text{Var}(\Lambda) = 4\left\{\left[\frac{1}{n^2(n-1)}\right]\left(\sum_{i=1}^{k} n_i^2\right)^2 - \left[\frac{2}{n(n-1)}\right]\left(\sum_{i=1}^{k} n_i^3\right) \right.$$
$$\left. + \left[\frac{n+1}{n(n-1)}\right]\left(\sum_{i=1}^{k} n_i^2\right) - \frac{n}{n-1}\right\},$$

where n_i is equal to the number of items recalled from the ith category and k categories are represented in the entire protocol. A Z-statistic can be constructed to help evaluate the significance of the value of Λ, since asymptotic normality holds in this situation if n is reasonably large (>20). If we determine $E(\Lambda)$, $\text{Var}(\Lambda)$ and then a Z-score for the match between the **B** and **A** matrix based on categorical structure, the resultant values are: $E(\Lambda) = 2$, $\text{Var}(\Lambda) = 6.55$, and $Z = 3.13$, $p < .01$. Thus, there is evidence of significant category clustering in this recall protocol. We can similarly determine $E(\Lambda)$, $\text{Var}(\Lambda)$, and then a Z-score for the match between the **B** and the **A** matrix based on alphabetical structure. The resultant values are: $E(\Lambda) = 3$, $\text{Var}(\Lambda) = 8.73$, and $Z = 3.05$, $p < .01$. Thus, there is also evidence of significant alphabetic clustering in this recall protocol.

There has been considerable controversy about "best" measures and defining a suitable scale for the clustering index (e.g., Hubert & Levin, 1976; Shuell, 1975; Roenker, Thompson, & Brown, 1971; Colle, 1972; Murphy, 1979). The majority of the proposed solutions begin with $\Lambda - E(\Lambda)$ and then attempt a secondary scaling. The simplest approach may be the Z-statistic (e.g., Frankel & Cole, 1971; Hudson & Dunn, 1969), but this is inadequate for several reasons (see Murphy, 1979). The Z-statistic varies as a direct function of n and is not bounded, which confounds any comparison between groups or subjects (e.g., different age groups) recalling different amounts of material or recalling different length lists. The $r(\mathbf{AB})$ measure is one scaling that avoids this problem but it may be somewhat cumbersome to calculate given that it is defined by correlating two matrices. Additionally, it should be noted that even in cases of "perfect" clustering, an r value of 1 will generally be unobtainable. As an alternative then, an Adjusted Ratio of Clustering measure (ARC) can be used. The ARC measure represents a scaling with 0 representing chance correspondence and with an upper bound of 1 representing perfect correspondence. The ARC measure is defined as $[\Lambda - E(\Lambda)]/[\max(\Lambda) - E(\Lambda)]$, with $\max(\Lambda)$ equal to two times the number of items recalled (n) minus k, the number of groups (categories) represented in the protocol, in other words, $2(n - k)$. Since $\max(\Lambda)$ is twice the maximum number of category repetitions that could have been obtained, the final measure is the ratio of the observed deviation from chance over the maximum possible deviation. As in all scaling problems, there is no universally acceptable solution, and the choice between r and ARC is arbitrary. (See Murphy, 1979, for a more detailed discussion of the ARC measure and others that have been suggested in the literature.)

The relationship between category, or group structure, and recall has traditionally been assessed by a scoring procedure that essentially treats the $\mathbf{A}$ and $\mathbf{B}$ matrices as if they contained dichotomous data. It should be obvious, however, that the recall protocol contains more than simple zero–one information about relationships between pairs of items. One can define the $\mathbf{B}$ matrix by letting b_{ij} equal the absolute value of the difference in recall ranks for the pair of terms defining that cell. The multiplicatively defined index now assesses more generally the relationship between category structure and recall order, and the category repetition measure becomes a special case. The expected value $E(\Lambda)$ can be obtained from the general formula given earlier and the final descriptive index $r(\mathbf{AB})$ can be determined and interpreted for statistical significance, preferably by the Monte Carlo strategy since asymptotic normality may be an unjustified assumption (see Ascher, Note 1).

It should be apparent to the reader that the $\mathbf{A}$ matrix also need not be restricted to a representation of structure that is only dichotomous in form. The members of a category or group may have differing degrees of relatedness or distance in some semantic space (e.g., Henley, 1969) that could be included as additional information defining entries in the $\mathbf{A}$ matrix. This latter matrix could then be compared with a $\mathbf{B}$ matrix where the entries are again defined on the basis of absolute differences in recall rank. The expected value $E(\Lambda)$ and final index $r(\mathbf{AB})$ can be obtained, with the latter interpreted for statistical significance, and compared to values obtained for other trials, lists, and/or subjects.

Input–Output Analysis

In our discussion of single-item information, we used the example of analyzing the correspondence between input order and recall order. It is also possible to conduct a more sophisticated analysis of input–output correspondence using the item-pair type of analysis. To illustrate the application, assume that a six item list containing the words *pot, walk, paper, bone, ink, money,* is presented in the order given. We can define an **A** matrix for the input structure by assigning 1 to any a_{ij} cell that represents two items immediately contiguous in the input sequence. For our example, the **A** matrix would be as follows:

	pot	walk	paper	bone	ink	money
pot	—	1	0	0	0	0
walk	1	—	1	0	0	0
paper	0	1	—	1	0	0
bone	0	0	1	—	1	0
ink	0	0	0	1	—	1
money	0	0	0	0	1	—

This is a symmetric matrix but an asymmetric one could have been defined if we wish to deal only with a unidirectional definition of input structure—a 1 is assigned for cell a_{ij} if and only if $i = j - 1$. The earlier matrix, on the other hand, treats the input pair structure as being bidirectional, that is, a 1 is assigned for cell a_{ij} if $i = j + 1$ or $j - 1$. The actual recall sequence based on a bidirectional scoring system can also be represented in a **B** matrix by assigning 1 to cell b_{ij} if the recall position of item i equals the recall position of item j plus or minus one. Thus, if the actual recall protocol was *bone, paper, pot, money, ink, walk,* the **B** matrix under bidirectional scoring has the form:

	pot	walk	paper	bone	ink	money
pot	—	0	1	0	0	1
walk	0	—	0	0	1	0
paper	1	0	—	1	0	0
bone	0	0	1	—	0	0
ink	0	1	0	0	—	1
money	1	0	0	0	1	—

Obviously, **B** matrices could also be defined using a forward or backward unidirectional rule for assigning the values of 1 or 0. The multiplicatively defined index Λ reduces to twice the number of protocol adjacencies that represent input sequence adjacencies, which in our example equals 4. In general, the expected value formula for bidirectional scoring is

$$E(\Lambda) = [4(n - 1)]/n$$

If either **A** or **B** is defined unidirectionally, the expected value formula is

$$E(\Lambda) = [2(n - 1)]/n$$

and if both are defined unidirectionally, $E(\Lambda)$ is $(n - 1)/n$. The same general inference paradigm can be applied and a final index $r(\mathbf{AB})$ obtained. An alternative scaling can be generated by using the same logic as the ARC measure for category organization, defining the final scaled measure as $[\Lambda - E(\Lambda)]/[\max(\Lambda) - E(\Lambda)]$ where $\max(\Lambda)$ equals $2(n - 1)$ for bidirectional scoring and $n - 1$ for unidirectional definition of **A** and/or **B**.

At this point it should be apparent that the **B** matrix could be constructed differently by using the absolute value of the differences in the recall ranks and comparing it with the **A** matrix as we have defined it. Additionally, the **A** matrix could be based on the absolute value of the differences in input ranks and compared with the bidirectionally or unidirectionally defined **B** matrix or the one just proposed based upon recall rank differences. A Λ index and $E(\Lambda)$ can be determined in each case and $r(\mathbf{AB})$ can always serve as the final descriptive index. A final point to be noted here is that a test of input–output correspondence will be most sensitive when the **A** and **B** matrices represent some multivalued scores for individual pairs rather than the simple dichotomy illustrated earlier as the traditional form of analysis.

Subjective Organization

The analysis of subjective organization is traditionally interpreted to mean the assessment of the correspondence between two structures defined by recall order on a pair of trials (Bousfield & Bousfield, 1966; Bousfield, Puff, & Cowan, 1964; Tulving, 1962, 1968). This is an interesting and problematic case of item-pair data analysis since it often confounds sequence and content information in the same analysis; that is, the descriptive index typically used is interpreted as if it involved conditional inference when, in fact, it involves unconditional inference. To illustrate the general problems that arise when a correspondence measure is to be derived for two recall trials, we begin with a prototypic analysis situation.

On Trial t an individual recalls the following words in sequence: a, b, c, d, e, f, g, h; on Trial $t + 1$ the sequence recall is, f, h, i, j, a, c, d, k, e, l. Thus, we have six items in common to both recall protocols, two unique to t and four unique to $t + 1$, a situation not uncommon in multitrial tasks. The typical assessment of subjective organization begins by determining the number of bidirectional pairwise intertrial repetitions from trial t to $t + 1$, where an intertrial repetition (ITR) is defined as the occurrence in the $t + 1$ protocol of a pairwise adjacency from the t protocol. In our simple example, there are seven pairwise adjacencies in t but only three could be present in $t + 1$. This is due to the nonrecall of b and g, thereby eliminating the ab, bc, fg and gh adjacencies. Of the three remaining possibilities, one actually appears in $t + 1$, the cd adjacency. The number of actual or observed pairwise adjacencies corresponds to one half the multiplicatively defined index Λ (we will illustrate how, shortly). The expected value formula for bidirectional pairwise repetitions ($E(\Lambda)$) has been determined (Pellegrino, 1971) and can be given as

$$E(\Lambda) = 4p/n,$$

where n equals the number of items recalled on Trial $t + 1$ and p equals the number of pairwise adjacencies from Trial t that could be present on Trial $t + 1$. The variance formula for this case has also been derived (see Hubert & Levin, 1977). The situation we have described, however, is a case of unconditional inference when the interpretation of Λ is made relative to $E(\Lambda)$ and $\mathrm{Var}(\Lambda)$.

The unconditional inference nature of the situation becomes clear only when we consider the expression of subjective organization analysis in terms of the general matrix comparison model. The items recalled on t but not on $t + 1$ are not a serious problem, since they are treated as if they did not exist. However, the items recalled on $t + 1$ that are not recalled on t pose a problem, since our matrix structure is defined relative to the items in $t + 1$. Consider first our **B** matrix, which is the bidirectional representation of recall order adjacencies on $t + 1$:

	f	h	i	j	a	c	d	k	e	l
f	—	1	0	0	0	0	0	0	0	0
h	1	—	1	0	0	0	0	0	0	0
i	0	1	—	1	0	0	0	0	0	0
j	0	0	1	—	1	0	0	0	0	0
a	0	0	0	1	—	1	0	0	0	0
c	0	0	0	0	1	—	1	0	0	0
d	0	0	0	0	0	1	—	1	0	0
k	0	0	0	0	0	0	1	0	1	0
e	0	0	0	0	0	0	0	1	—	1
l	0	0	0	0	0	0	0	0	1	—

All 10 items from $t + 1$ define this matrix. Similarly, the **A** matrix is implicitly constructed in terms of these same 10 items even though 4 were not recalled on t. The only cells in **A** that are assigned a value of 1 are those that represent a pairwise adjacency from t that could have occurred on $t + 1$. All cells in **A** involving items unique to $t + 1$ are restricted to 0. Thus, the **A** and **B** matrices contain both pairwise co-occurrence and order information. The raw index Λ based on the **A** by **B** multiplication is not affected but the $E(\Lambda)$ value relates to a distribution that reflects more complex sampling assumptions. Up to now, it has generally been assumed that the assessment of subjective organization using Λ and $E(\Lambda)$, that is, pairwise ITRs, was an unconfounded inference case which obviously it is not.

The problem that we have just described is one of comparability in the contents of two recall protocols, both of which represent subsets of a larger set. Fortunately, this difficulty does not exist in every other case we have considered and in this context there is a simple solution. In particular, the **A** and **B** matrices can be defined only for those items common to both t and $t + 1$. A value of 1 is assigned to the cell b_{ij} if the two items defining that cell are adjacent to the $t + 1$ recall protocol, otherwise the cell is defined as 0. For the **A** matrix, a value of 1 is assigned to the cell a_{ij} if the two items defining that cell are adjacent in the t protocol. (Alternative rules for defining the 1 and 0 values for both the **A** and **B** matrices can also be used and the reader should consult Pellegrino, 1971, for these possibilities.)

The multiplicatively defined index Λ for these two matrices is still twice the number of ITRs that occur in the $t + 1$ protocol. The expected value and variance, however, are now made conditional on information about the items common to both trials. The expected value formula for the bidirectional scoring case is:

$$E(\Lambda) = 4p/n_c,$$

where n_c is equal to the number of items in common on trials t and $t + 1$ and p again equals the number of pairwise adjacencies from trial t that could be present on trial $t + 1$. The Z-statistic or the final descriptive index $r(\mathbf{AB})$ can be interpreted for significance as before or, alternatively, an ARC measure can be used as a substitute for $r(\mathbf{AB})$ based on a maximum of $2p$ for bidirectional scoring. However, the simple deviation index $\Lambda - E(\Lambda)$ [typically shown as $O(\text{ITR}) - E(\text{ITR})$] or the Z-statistic itself should not be used in any comparison across different pairs of trials, subjects, conditions, and so on, contrary to the conclusion of Sternberg and Tulving (1977). Their conclusions were based on faulty logic and their empirical validation capitalized on an artifactual correlation between a deviation score (or its Z-score normalization) and total amount recalled given that the null conjecture does not hold. A more detailed treatment of this problem can be found in Murphy, Sanders, and Puff (Note 2).

The **A** and **B** matrices and the analysis of correspondence through the multiplicatively defined Λ index can be varied so that multivalued rather than dichotomous values are represented in one or both matrices. This is the same type of extension that was proposed for category structure and input–output organization analysis. Traditional subjective organization analysis need not impose restrictions on the analysis of correspondence between the structure of two protocols. The major caution, however, is to avoid an ambiguous unconditional inference situation which demands some care in defining the **A** and **B** matrices so that only items common to both protocols dictate the row and column structure. In addition, final **A** and **B** matrices with a small n should be avoided since, if there is little in common that is recalled on trials t and $t + 1$, an analysis of structural correspondence is generally weak from an inference standpoint and can border on logical absurdity.

Text Analysis Applications

Our three examples of item-pair measures have been generally derived from common types of analyses that have been attempted in the list-learning–memory-organization literature. The situations that have been outlined, however, can be extended to the recall of text where the text unit is typically specified at the propositional or idea unit level (e.g., Kintsch, 1974). (See also the chapter in this volume by Voss, Tyler, & Bisanz.) It may be of interest to test one or more hypotheses about the relationship between a theoretical analysis defining a text base and the structure of a recall protocol for the same text. In both cases, the unit would be the proposition or sentence rather than the single word. Each of the three cases that we have illustrated for item-pair data analysis (as well as single-item type data) can be shown to have an analogue in the literature on text structure and processing.

There have been several attempts to specify categories of information that typically occur as units in stories (e.g., Mandler & Johnson, 1977; Stein & Glenn, 1979; Rumelhart, 1977; Spilich, Vesonder, Chiesi, & Voss, 1979). Each unit comprises some number of presented propositions that can be dealt with in the same way as categories in word lists. Propositions from the text can be grouped to define a hypothetical structure represented as a 0–1 dichotomous **A** matrix. Similarly, the recall generated by a subject can be used to generate a second 0–1 dichotomous **B** matrix based on adjacencies of the propositions recalled. The multiplicatively defined index Λ is based on the number of immediately adjacent propositions in the protocol that come from the same "conceptual" story category. Thus, a clustering index can be generated for recall organization with respect to some hypothesis about the propositional structure of the text. See Mandler (1978) and Mandler and DeForest (1979) for actual illustrations of such an analysis.

Similar analogues can be generated for the analysis of story recall relative to the input or presentation order of the text propositions or relative to some prior recall order for the text propositions. Either dichotomous or multivalued **A** and **B** matrices can be generated in these two cases, and all the inference procedures and rules that have been described so far are applicable. In general, the power of such item-pair (and single-item) analyses of structure is the ability to make inferences about a single protocol generated by a single subject.

Summary of General Principles and Procedures

The analysis of item-pair information follows the same general rules as described for analyses of single-item information. The type of information that can be represented in matrix format for pairs of objects is richer and more varied than in the single-item case. The traditional cases of category clustering, input–output and output–output organization essentially define simple types of item-pair structural analysis. The computation of the index Λ and the expected value $E(\Lambda)$ for these cases is readily generated from simple formulas. Variance formulas are also available but are usually more complicated. The major cautions that must be observed involve general problems of small n; care in determining the $E(\Lambda)$ value so that it is conditionally defined; and use of a final index that represents a suitable scaling. The $r(\mathbf{AB})$ or ARC measures serve as reasonable alternatives. Straight Z-statistics can be used (with caution) for inferences about significance (preferably through the Monte Carlo strategy) but they, along with simple deviation scores $\Lambda - E(\Lambda)$ should never be used to compare different protocols. Past errors in the literature on analysis of item-pair information have involved ignorance of the description–inference–scaling problems inherent in item-pair analysis as well as lack of awareness of the conditional versus unconditional inference problem. A summary of various specific applications of item-pair analysis is provided in Table 5.7.

The item-pair type of analysis, when conceptualized as a matrix structure problem, opens up the possibility of using many different schemes for specifying the structural hypothesis, for example, using

Table 5.7
Summary of Representative Item-Pair Analyses

Problem type	Λ	E(Λ)	Final normalized index	
			Correlation	ARC
Categorical structure	$\sum_{i=1}^{n}\sum_{j=1}^{n} a_{ij}b_{ij} =$ $2 \times (\Sigma$ category repetitions)	$2[\frac{1}{n}(\sum_{i=1}^{k} n_i^2) - 1]$ where n_i equals the number of items in the kth group and k equals the number of groups (categories) in the recall protocol	Pearson r(**AB**) (*Note:* The upper bound of +1 will not necessarily be reached under "perfect" clustering)	$\dfrac{\Lambda - E(\Lambda)}{\max(\Lambda) - E(\Lambda)}$ where max(Λ) equals $2(n - k)$
Input–output correspondence	$\sum_{i=1}^{n}\sum_{j=1}^{n} a_{ij}b_{ij} =$ $2 \times (\Sigma$ITRs) where an ITR is an input sequence pairwise adjacency that also occurs in recall	$4p/n$ (for bidirectional ITRs) $2p/n$ (for unidirectional ITRs) where n equals the number of items recalled and p equals the number of input sequence pairwise adjacencies that could occur in recall. If all presented items are recalled, the expected values are $4(n - 1)/n$ and $2(n - 1)/n$	Pearson r(**AB**) (*Note:* The upper bound of +1 can be attained for such problems)	$\dfrac{\Lambda - E(\Lambda)}{\max(\Lambda) - E(\Lambda)}$ where max (Λ) equals $2p$ for bidirectional scoring and p for unidirectional scoring)
Output–output correspondence ("Subjective Organization")	$\sum_{i=1}^{n}\sum_{j=1}^{n} a_{ij}b_{ij} =$ $2 \times (\Sigma$ITRs) where an ITR is a pairwise adjacency from Trial t that also occurs on Trial $t + 1$	$4p/n_t$ (for bidirectional ITRs) $2p/n_t$ (for unidirectional ITRs) where n_t equals the number of items common to t and $t + 1$ and p equals the number of pairwise adjacencies from Trial t that could occur in Trial $t + 1$. If all the t items are recalled in $t + 1$, then the expected values are $4(n_t - 1)/n_t$, and $2(n_t - 1)/n_t$	Pearson r(**AB**) (*Note:* The upper bound of +1 can be attained for such problems)	$\dfrac{\Lambda - E(\Lambda)}{\max(\Lambda) - E(\Lambda)}$ where max(Λ) equals $2p$ for bidirectional scoring and p for unidirectional scoring)

spatial distance data (Moar, 1977), as well as for specifying the information derivable from the actual protocol. Recall procedures that do not
confine the subject to a linear ordering, but which allow two-dimensional
recall structuring for example, Buschke (1977), can be analyzed using
these procedures. We have also offered the possibility that item–pair
data analysis may be of use in testing hypotheses about the structure
of protocols based upon recall of simple and complex discourse.

ANALYSIS OF ITEM–GROUP INFORMATION

Given the previous discussion of single-item and item–pair indexes,
an obvious next step would be to develop item–triplet, –quadruplet, and
in general, group-k measures. Exactly the same format can be followed.
Instead of two place functions, k-place functions would be defined and
a new cross product statistic Θ obtained. For example, in the item–triplet
case, Θ would be represented as:

$$\Theta = \sum_{i=1}^{n} \sum_{j=1}^{n} \sum_{k=1}^{n} a_{ijk} b_{ijk}.$$

In this context, the **A** and **B** matrices are actually three-dimensional,
with each cell, a_{ijk}, and b_{ijk}, representing information about a triad of
items. As an example, three items may come from the same conceptual
category or story structure unit. The cells representing this triad would
be assigned a value of 1 in the **A** matrix. Similarly, in **B** the cells representing this triad could be assigned a value of 1 if the three items occur
together in a recall protocol. We will not present a more extended illustration because of the complexities of the k-dimensional matrix representation and some other general reservations that will be mentioned
shortly. The inference model for Θ remains as before, but the moments
are in general very complex. If it is assumed that all cells in **A** and **B**
that are not defined by distinct indexes are zero, a general expected
value formula can be presented. For example, in the item–triplet framework, we would obtain

$$E(\Theta) = \frac{1}{n(n-1)(n-2)} \left(\sum_{i=1}^{n} \sum_{j=1}^{n} \sum_{k=1}^{n} a_{ijk} \right) \left(\sum_{i=1}^{n} \sum_{j=1}^{n} \sum_{k=1}^{n} b_{ijk} \right).$$

(For the more general representation, the reader is referred to Hubert
and Levin, 1980.) Given the complexity of the moments and the lack of
good information on the adequacy of a normal approximation, it may
be best to estimate the significance level of Θ, as mentioned earlier, by
taking a random sample of permutations. Even this, however, is not a

trivial computational chore given the size of the matrices involved. Everything that has been discussed relative to normalization, inference, and scaling is again applicable to the item–group generalization including a final descriptive index $r(\mathbf{AB})$ or ARC measure (see Pellegrino, 1971, for calculation of the latter).

We are generally skeptical about the value and utility of conducting an analysis of item–triplet and higher order units, in part because of the computational complexities involved. For instance, given a list of 10 items, the analysis of units of Size 3 involves $\mathbf{A}$ and $\mathbf{B}$ matrices that contain a thousand cells each. When the typical dichotomous coding scheme is used there is a remarkable paucity of information represented. For 10 items, 8 possible triads can be formed; consequently, if a 1 is assigned to each a_{ijk} cell representing one of the triads, then only 48 of the 1000 cells contain a nonzero entry. Given the Monte Carlo approach, the repeated calculation of index values for a given pair of $\mathbf{A}$ and $\mathbf{B}$ matrices is obviously very costly if it has to be done over a reasonably large number of subjects. The most obvious use of an item–group analysis is where the individual is concerned with whether the items defining the unit are recalled together in some wholistic fashion. Given that the individual knows the contents of the unit, the majority of information about the adjacent or proximal recall of items from the same higher order group can be obtained through simpler item-pair analyses. It is possible, however, to quickly obtain the value of the multiplicatively defined Θ index for higher order units by simply counting their occurrence in the recall protocol. The major attempt at applying item–group type analyses has been in the subjective organization area (Pellegrino, 1971, 1972; Pellegrino & Battig, 1974). Procedures for assessing the occurrence of higher order units in two sequences, along with expected value formulas, can be found in Pellegrino (1971, 1972).

The value of doing analyses of information beyond item-pairs is probably quite limited. Most situations of interest typically involve sets of materials that are not extremely lengthy or where the higher-order structure is known in advance. Item–pair analyses that make use of $\mathbf{B}$ matrices defined in terms of absolute values of the distances between pairs of items will lead to a Λ index that captures most of the information about the relationship between recall structure and the hypothesized group or category structure. In the case where the higher order units are not known, in other words, the typical subjective organization case, quantification on the basis of such units does not provide much information beyond what can be obtained from item-pair units. Moreover, since the values obtained for individual subjects tend not to be reliable (Sternberg & Tulving, 1977), it could be argued that the analysis of higher order organizational units in a multi-trial subjective organization situation is really best done from an exploratory rather than confirmatory perspective.

COMPARISON OF ALTERNATIVE HYPOTHESES

For all of the indexes that we have discussed, whether they are single-item, item-pair, or the more general item–group, the emphasis has been on evaluating single hypotheses in isolation. Obviously, if more than one hypothesis is to be tested, one simple approach would be to carry out separate tests of each. Besides being very ad hoc, this sequential process does not permit any rigorous assessment as to which hypothesis is most consistent with the observed data. When multiple subjects are available, one immediate solution that, essentially, avoids the problem altogether involves using the various normalized indexes in a repeated measures analysis of variance paradigm. Unfortunately, this strategy is not appropriate for a single subject and deviates from the general approach that we have advocated which permits evaluations even at the individual subject level.

Suppose, for a single subject's data, that two hypotheses are of interest, H_1 and H_2, and that both are represented either by sequences (single-item), two-dimensional matrices (item-pairs), or k-dimensional matrices (item–groups). The information that is to be analyzed in a subject's protocol is similarly specified and we will denote this as D. In all cases, the final normalized correlations between the data and each of the two hypotheses can be generated—these are denoted by r_{DH_1} and r_{DH_2}. Our basic task is to evaluate the size of the observed difference $r_{DH_1} - r_{DH_2}$ and to determine whether this value is sufficiently extreme to assert that H_1 is closer to the data D than H_2 (or the converse) in terms of the final scaled indexes based on the correlation normalization.

Our illustration of the comparison between alternative hypotheses is based upon the single-item information examples presented in Table 5.1. (A similar contrast can be done for item-pair information.) For the 20-item recall protocol, we are interested in comparing 2 hypotheses, both of which turned out to be significant with respect to observed recall rank. The first is the seriation hypothesis that has a value of 2553 for the multiplicatively defined index Γ and an r value of .93. The second hypothesis is based on the old–new item dichotomy that has a value of 18 for the multiplicatively defined index Γ and an r value of $-.52$. Our concern, then, is whether there is a significant difference between H_2, the old–new item hypothesis, and H_1, the seriation hypothesis, in the fit to the obtained recall protocol.

Before proceeding further it is important to recognize that the hypothesis based on an old–new item split was represented dichotomously. The r value of $-.52$ results when 1 is assigned to new items and 0 to old items, whereas an r value of .52 results when the opposite assignment rule is used. Since our concern is with the general fit of the old–new item split to the data and not the direction, we want to compare the value of .52 for the hypothesis based on an old–new item split against the .93 value for the seriation hypothesis. A comparison of the r of $-.52$ against the r of .93 would probably be significant but would not address the basic question of whether one hypothesis generates a better fit in an absolute sense.

The two hypotheses and the actual recall data are reproduced in Table 5.8. (The representation of the hypothesis based on old versus new is the one yielding an r of .52.) Our first step is to normalize the representation of each hypothesis to create H_1^* and H_2^*. These two new representations are also shown in Table 5.8. Thus, we are now in the position to define our new hypothesis $H_1^* - H_2^*$ shown as the third column of Table 5.8. This difference hypothesis can then be related to the actual recall rank shown in the last column producing an $r_{D(H_1^* - H_2^*)}$ of

Table 5.8
Normalized Sequence Representation for Comparison of Fit of Alternative Hypotheses

	H_1^* Seriation	H_2^* Old versus new item	$H_1^* - H_2^*$	Recall rank
army	.44	.58	$-.14$	15
book	$-.08$	.58	$-.66$	11
car	-1.62	.58	-2.20	3
dog	1.46	.58	.88	16
egg	.27	.58	$-.31$	13
fun	-1.45	.58	-2.03	4
girl	$-.76$	-1.74	.98	2
hat	.95	.58	.37	18
ice	1.64	.58	1.06	19
jar	$-.93$	.58	-1.51	6
kite	.61	.58	.03	12
leg	$-.59$	-1.74	1.15	5
man	1.29	.58	.71	17
nest	$-.25$	-1.74	1.49	10
open	-1.28	.58	-1.86	7
pin	.78	.58	.20	14
queen	1.12	.58	.64	20
rope	$-.42$	.58	-1.00	8
star	-1.10	-1.74	.64	1
train	.09	.58	$-.49$	9

.40. Given the reasonably large value of n, this value is significant, assuming a normal approximation to the baseline distribution, and thus, the hypothesis that recall order is related to serial presentation order is a significantly better fit to the data than the hypothesis based on an old–new item split. This statement can be made even though the latter, when examined in isolation, produces a significant index. Part of the reason for this set of outcomes is that H_1 and H_2 are not completely independent, and in fact, the absolute value of the correlation between H_1 and H_2 is .35. The example we have illustrated emphasizes the point that care must be taken in interpreting the results from a comparison of several alternative hypotheses against the same data. The alternative hypotheses may contain redundant information (i.e., when $r_{H_1H_2} > 0$), so it may be necessary to directly compare the separately determined correlation values to find the most appropriate interpretation of the data. If $r_{H_1H_2}$ is very large then it may be very difficult to determine whether one hypothesis provides a better representation than a second.

EXPLORATORY ANALYSIS

Often, the researcher may wish to determine how a given set of materials is being organized or structured by an individual over multiple recalls or by a group of individuals recalling the same set of materials. All the major procedures for seeking and representing the structure of a given set of data require an initial definition of a data matrix which can then be submitted to analytic techniques designed to seek some representation within a specific class of structures. As noted by Friendly (1979), exploratory analysis is a two-step operation in which there is an initial translation of the raw protocol data into one or more data matrices representing relationships among the n objects defining the rows and columns of the matrix. The second step uses the matrix in an analysis strategy that fits some type of structure, for example, a serial, hierarchical, or multidimensional representation.

The protocol data defining the individual entries in the matrix are provided by either (a) multiple recalls from a single subject or (b) single or multiple recalls from multiple subjects, and a variety of multivalued data types can be used to construct the matrix. The following set of recall protocols provides an illustration of the initial translation process.

Trial 1	a,c,e,f
Trial 2	b,a,c,d,g,e,f
Trial 3	h,c,a,b,d,i,f,e,g
Trial 4	$e,f,g,h,d,c,b,a,i,j.$

Across these four protocols, there are 10 distinct objects or items. Thus, we can define a 10×10 matrix that represents each possible pair of objects (the main left-to-right diagonal of the matrix is ignored). The next step is to define the entries to the matrix. One way to do so is in terms of the frequency with which o_i and o_j occur in immediately adjacent recall positions.

An alternative procedure, suggested by Friendly (1977, 1979), which makes use of more of the information contained in the recall protocols, is based on average recall proximity for each possible item pairing. Proximity on any given trial can be defined as n (list length) minus the difference in recall rank for the given pair of items. On Trial 1 the ac pair has a proximity value of 3, and on Trials 2, 3, and 4 the values are 6, 8, and 8, respectively, yielding an average proximity of 6.25. The ab pair, which only occurs on Trials 2–4, has proximities of 6, 8, and 9, respectively, for an average of 7.67. The proximity matrix for our four-trial example would then be:

	a	b	c	d	e	f	g	h	i	j
a	—	7.67	6.25	6.33	3.00	3.00	4.00	6.50	7.50	8.00
b		—	7.00	6.67	3.67	4.00	4.33	6.50	7.50	7.00
c			—	7.00	3.75	3.75	4.67	8.00	6.00	6.00
d				—	5.67	6.00	6.33	7.00	7.00	5.00
e					—	7.67	7.33	4.50	7.50	1.00
f						—	5.00	5.50	5.50	2.00
g							—	5.00	5.00	3.00
h								—	4.50	4.00
i									—	9.00
j										—

The entries in a proximity matrix can be viewed as measures of item relatedness or similarity and can be analyzed using a variety of different procedures. Figure 5.1 and Table 5.9, adapted from Friendly (1979), illustrate some of the possibilities. A treatment of these different forms of representational analysis cannot be done here. However, Table 5.9 provides references that can be used to describe the assumptions, procedures, and computer programs that conduct the various types of analyses.

Proximity analysis, as we have described it, represents one way of transforming multitrial or multisubject data into a form where further analyses of structure can then be performed. The matrix of proximities, without any form of structural analysis, can be used as a hypothesis about recall structure that can be compared against a new data matrix derived from another subject or group of subjects. Thus, in our item-pair confirmatory analysis procedures, the proximity matrix would serve

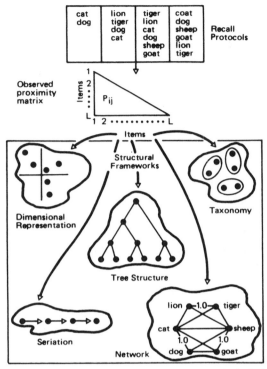

Figure 5.1. Illustrative types of exploratory structural analysis (Friendly, 1979).

Table 5.9
Summarization of Exploratory Analyses

Memory model	Structural framework	Representative scaling methods
Serial Chain	Seriation	Guttman scale (Hubert & Baker, 1978)
		Hamiltonian path (Hubert & Baker, 1978)
Dimensions	Euclidean space	Multidimensional scaling (Carroll & Arabie,
	Overlapping	1980; Kruskal & Wish, 1978)
	attributes	ADCLUS (Shepard & Arabie, 1979)
		MAPCLUS (Arabie & Carroll, 1980)
Tree Structure	Strict hierarchy	Complete link clustering (Johnson, 1967)
	Overlapping clusters	Jardine and Sibson (1971)
	Free trees	Cunningham (1978); Sattath and Tversky (1977)
Network	Undirected graph	Minimum spanning tree (Hubert, 1974b)
		Maximal connected subgraphs (Hubert, 1974a)

165

as the **A** matrix, while a new set of proximities derived from a different data source could serve as one of several possible **B** matrices.

Friendly (1979) has also described other algorithmic procedures that are designed to identify recurrent groups or clusters in recall protocols (e.g., Buschke, 1977; Monk, 1976; Reuter, Note 3; Zangen, Ziegelbaum, & Buschke, 1976). The techniques vary, and a description and critique is beyond the scope of this chapter. The reader is referred to Friendly (1977, 1979) for a more complete treatment of proximity analysis and other methods of exploratory structural analysis.

One final point must be made about interpreting the results obtained from different exploratory analysis procedures. It is possible to submit the same data matrix to a variety of different structural analyses. Consequently, since the results of such separate analyses can always be transformed back into matrix representations, it is then possible to compare two alternative structural representations with respect to their goodness of fit to the actual data matrix using the procedures described earlier, that is, those procedures for comparing the fit of two hypotheses to the same data. In the present situation, the structure resulting from one type of analysis represents H_1, while the structure resulting from a second analysis represents H_2. The two matrices corresponding to these two hypothesized structures can then be normalized and used to derive a difference hypothesis that is compared against the original data. A word of caution, however: This is not a confirmatory type of analysis in the usual sense, but is simply a method to discriminate between two different fits to the same data, both of which represent "best" structures under a given set of assumptions.

GENERALIZATION AND EXTENSION OF ANALYTIC PROCEDURES

Our discussion of confirmatory and exploratory analysis procedures has focused on data obtained from a free-recall situation. However, the procedures are not restricted in their applicability and can be used to analyze a variety of different types of data. In all cases, the goal is to test or generate some hypothesis about structural relationships that exist among the objects (items) of interest. There is, however, one important extension that is applicable to free recall. In its typical form, free recall produces unidimensional spatial data, and thus, relationships among items in the recall protocol are constrained to some form of temporal or spatial proximity. A two-dimensional recall procedure can also be used, however, to provide a potentially richer set of data for an analysis of structure (see Buschke, 1977). The actual spatial distances between the objects in the two-dimensional recall protocol could be used to define an item-pair **B** matrix that could then be compared against alternative **A** matrices.

The major extensions of the analytic procedures are, to sources of data, other than recall. One obvious source of data is the sorting paradigm that has been used extensively for exploratory structural analyses. In a sorting task, the individual is given a set of objects (e.g., words, pictures, sentences) and then allowed to sort into as many groups as desired (*free sort*) or, alternatively, into a given number and type (*constrained sort*). In either case, the sorting data can be transformed into a matrix where the cells represent the frequency (or probability) with which two objects o_i and o_j occur in the same group. This can be done for multiple sorts produced by a single individual or for multiple sorts representing data from a group of subjects. The sorting paradigm has also been used extensively by Mandler (1967) for assessments of organization prior to free recall and could be used to specify an a priori hypothesis.

A second source of data is a rating task where objects are compared to each other or to some standard. Similarity judgments can be obtained by a number of procedures, including the use of ranking data and absolute rating data. Such data are immediately representable as a similarity (or dissimilarity) matrix that can be evaluated from either an exploratory or confirmatory perspective. Although seldom done, it is also possible to use absolute latency data to define a similarity matrix. An example is a semantic memory experiment where members of a category are presented as pairs and the data are the latencies used to verify common category membership. Since each item pair has a latency that can be used to define a matrix entry, a "similarity" matrix is formed that could be compared against one derived from rating data (e.g., Rosch, 1975). The "similarity" matrix defined on the basis of verification latency could also be analyzed by an exploratory analysis strategy.

Rehearsal protocols constitute yet another source of data that can be analyzed for structure. In a typical unconstrained rehearsal situation (e.g., Rundus, 1971), there is a rehearsal sequence that can be transformed into an adjacency or proximity matrix and matched against some preexisting structural hypothesis, for example, one based on presentation order (Einstein, Pellegrino, Mondani, & Battig, 1974). The data matrix could also be analyzed from an exploratory perspective, in addition to serving as a structural hypothesis to be compared against a matrix derived from recall data or other rehearsal data.

As an example of the applicability of the confirmatory analysis procedures to other sources of data, we focus on a recent study by Pollard-Gott, McCloskey, and Todres (1979). College students read a series of simple and complex stories and passages, and for each story or passage the individual sentences were then free-sorted into groups on the basis of coherence relative to the story as a whole. The resultant group data was used to define a matrix where the cells represented the number of times that sentences i and j were sorted into the same group. This matrix could obviously be analyzed from an exploratory perspective using a hierarchical clustering procedure (e.g., Johnson, 1967), and in fact, such an analysis was done by Pollard-Gott et $al.$ However, their use of exploratory analysis procedures did not lead to a direct test of the real hypothesis of interest.

Table 5.10 illustrates two such cases in the Pollard-Gott et $al.$ study.

Table 5.10
Example Story Structure Analyses

Story Grammar Categories (Glenn, 1978)	Story sentences
Setting	1–3
Event	4–11
Internal Response	12–19
Attempt	20–27
Consequence	28–35
Reaction	36–42

Story Grammar Representation (Mandler & Johnson, 1977)	Sentence number
	1
	2
	3
	4
	5
	6
	7
	8
	9
	10
	11
	12
	13
	14
	15
	16

The first case in Table 5.10 shows the correspondence between individual sentences in a specific story and a theoretical analysis based on a simple-story grammar model (Glenn, 1978). The story structure representation involves categories of information, and individual sentences contain information pertaining to only one of the categories. This story grammar representation could easily be converted into a matrix representation that could be matched against the data matrix resulting from the sorting task. A direct test of correspondence could then be carried out.

The second example in Table 5.10 shows a more complex hierarchical representation of a story containing 16 sentences constructed from the Mandler and Johnson (1977) story grammar. This theory-based representation could also be converted into a matrix and matched against the corresponding data matrix derived from the sentence sorting. In both of the cases illustrated in Table 5.10, an a priori hypothesis was available and its fit to the data could have been tested directly. Instead, the data matrices were submitted to an exploratory analysis that was visually compared for correspondence with the theoretically defined structure. Finally, it would have also been possible in the Pollard-Gott *et al.* study to determine if the theoretical structure and that derived from cluster analysis differed significantly in their fit to the actual data.

There are, no doubt, a variety of other procedures and data sources that can be analyzed for structure. The major interest is usually an item-pair type of analysis rather than the simpler and less informative single-item type of analysis. So long as data can be transformed into a matrix where each cell represents information about the pair of objects on the basis of real or psychological space, time, or similarity, then a confirmatory or exploratory structural analysis may be pursued. Large group designs are not always needed for statistical significance statements since inference procedures have been presented that allow tests of significance for a single subject (single matrix).

REFERENCE NOTES

1. Ascher, S. *Moments of the Mantel Valand Statistic.* Paper presented at the annual meeting of the American Statistical Association, Houston, Texas, August 1980.
2. Murphy, M. D., Sanders, R. E., & Puff, C. R. *The measurement of subjective organization: A reply to Sternberg and Tulving.* Unpublished manuscript, University of Akron, 1978.
3. Reuter, H. *Hierarchical memory structures from systematic aspects of free-recall output orders.* Unpublished manuscript, University of Michigan, 1976.

REFERENCES

Arabie, P., & Carroll, J. D. MAPCLUS: A mathematical programming approach to fitting the ADCLUS model. *Psychometrika*, 1980, *45*, 211–235.

Battig, W. F., Allen, M., & Jensen, A. R. Priority of free recall of newly learned items. *Journal of Verbal Learning and Verbal Behavior*, 1965, *4*, 175–179.

Bousfield, A. K., & Bousfield, W. A. Measurement of clustering and of sequential constancies in repeated free recall. *Psychological Reports*, 1966, *19*, 935–942.

Bousfield, W. A. The occurrence of clustering in the recall of randomly arranged associates. *Journal of General Psychology*, 1953, *49*, 229–240.

Bousfield, W. A., Puff, C. R., & Cowan, T. M. The development of constancies in sequential organization during free recall. *Journal of Verbal Learning and Verbal Behavior*, 1964, *3*, 489–495.

Bower, G. H. Organizational factors in memory. *Cognitive Psychology*, 1970, *1*, 18–46.

Bower, G. H. A selective review of organizational factors in memory. In E. Tulving & W. Donaldson (Eds.), *Organization of memory*. New York: Academic Press, 1972.

Buschke, H. Two dimensional recall: Immediate identification of clusters in episodic and semantic memory. *Journal of Verbal Learning and Verbal Behavior*, 1977, *16*, 201–216.

Carroll, J. D., & Arabie, P. Multidimensional scaling. In M. R. Rosenzweig & L. W. Porter (Eds.), *Annual review of psychology*. Palo Alto, Ca.: Annual Reviews, 1980.

Colle, H. A. The reification of clustering. *Journal of Verbal Learning and Verbal Behavior*, 1972, *11*, 624–633.

Cunningham, J. P. Free trees and bidirectional trees as representations of psychological distances. *Journal of Mathematical Psychology*, 1978, *17*, 165–188.

Edgington, E. J. *Randomization tests*. New York: Marcel Dekker, 1980.

Einstein, G. O., Pellegrino, J. W., Mondani, M. S., & Battig, W. F. Free recall performance as a function of overt rehearsal frequency. *Journal of Experimental Psychology*, 1974, *103*, 440–449.

Flores, L. M., Jr., & Brown, S. C. Comparison of output order in free recall. *Behavior Research Methods and Instrumentation*, 1974, *6*, 385–388.

Frankel, F., & Cole, M. Measures of category clustering in free recall. *Psychological Bulletin*, 1971, *76*, 39–44.

Friendly, M. L. In search of the M-Gram: The structure of organization in free recall. *Cognitive Psychology*, 1977, *9*, 188–249.

Friendly, M. Methods for finding graphic representations of associative memory structures. In C. R. Puff (Ed.), *Memory organization and structure*. New York: Academic Press, 1979.

Glenn, C. G. The role of episodic structure and story length in children's recall of simple stories. *Journal of Verbal Learning and Verbal Behavior*, 1978, *17*, 229–247.

Henley, N. M. A psychological study of the semantics of animal terms. *Journal of Verbal Learning and Verbal Behavior*, 1969, *8*, 176–184.

Hubert, L. J. Some applications of graph theory to clustering. *Psychometrika*, 1974, *39*, 283–309.(a)

Hubert, L. J. Spanning trees and aspects of clustering. *British Journal of Mathematical and Statistical Psychology*, 1974, *27*, 14–28.(b)

Hubert, L. J. Matching models in the analysis of cross-classifications. *Psychometrika*, 1979, *44*, 21–41.

Hubert, L. J., & Baker, F. B. Applications of combinatorial programming to data analysis: The traveling salesman and related problems. *Psychometrika*, 1978, *43*, 81–91.

Hubert, L. J., & Levin, J. R. A general statistical framework for assessing categorical clustering in free recall. *Psychological Bulletin*, 1976, *83*, 1072–1080.

Hubert, L. J., & Levin, J. R. Inference models for categorical clustering. *Psychological Bulletin*, 1977, *84*, 878–887.

Hubert, L. J., & Levin, J. R. Evaluating priority effects in free recall. *British Journal of Mathematical and Statistical Psychology*, 1978, *31*, 11–18.

Hubert, L. J., & Levin, J. R. Measuring clustering in free recall. *Psychological Bulletin*, 1980, *87*, 59–62.

Hudson, R. L., & Dunn, J. E. A major modification of the Bousfield (1966) measure of category clustering. *Behavior Research Methods and Instrumentation*, 1969, *1*, 110–111.

Jardine, N., & Sibson, R. *Mathematical taxonomy*. New York: John Wiley and Sons, 1971.

Johnson, S. C. Hierarchical clustering schemes. *Psychometrika*, 1967, *32*, 241–254.

Kintsch, W. *The representation of meaning in memory*. Hillsdale, N.J.: Lawrence Erlbaum Associates, 1974.

Kruskal, J. B., & Wish, M. *Multidimensional scaling*. Beverly Hills, Ca.: Sage, 1978.

Mandler, G. Organization and memory. In K. W. Spence & J. T. Spence (Eds.), *The psychology of learning and motivation* (Vol. 1). New York: Academic Press, 1967.

Mandler, J. M. A code in the node: The use of a story schema in retrieval. *Discourse Processes*, 1978, *1*, 14–35.

Mandler, J. M., & DeForest, M. Is there more than one way to recall a story? *Child Development*, 1979, *50*, 886–889.

Mandler, J. M., & Johnson, N. S. Remembrance of things parsed: Story structure and recall. *Cognitive Psychology*, 1977, *9*, 111–151.

Mielke, P. W. Clarification and appropriate inferences for Mantel and Valand nonparametric multivariate analysis technique. *Biometrics*, 1978, *34*, 277–280.

Moar, I. Spatial organization in the free recall of pictorial stimuli. *Quarterly Journal of Experimental Psychology*, 1977, *29*, 699–708.

Monk, A. F. A new approach to the characterization of sequential structure in multi-trial free recall using hierarchical grouping analysis. *British Journal of Mathematical and Statistical Psychology*, 1976, *29*, 1–18.

Murphy, M. D. Measurement of category clustering in free recall. In C. R. Puff (Ed.), *Memory organization and structure*. New York: Academic Press, 1979.

Pellegrino, J. W. A general measure of organization in free recall for variable unit size and internal sequential consistency. *Behavior Research Methods & Instrumentation*, 1971, *3*, 241–246.

Pellegrino, J. W. A Fortran IV program for analyzing higher order subjective organization units in free-recall learning. *Behavior Research Methods and Instrumentation*, 1972, *4*, 215–217.

Pellegrino, J. W., & Battig, W. F. Relationships among higher order organizational measures and free recall. *Journal of Experimental Psychology*, 1974, *102*, 463–472.

Pellegrino, J. W., & Ingram, A. L. Processes, products, and measures of memory organization. In C. R. Puff (Ed.), *Memory organization and structure*. New York: Academic Press, 1979.

Pollard-Gott, L., McCloskey, M., & Todres, A. K. Subjective story structure. *Discourse Processes*, 1979, *2*, 251–281.

Postman, L. A pragmatic view of organization theory. In E. Tulving & W. Donaldson (Eds.), *Organization of memory*. New York: Academic Press, 1972.

Postman, L., & Keppel, G. Conditions determining the priority of new items in free recall.

Journal of Verbal Learning and Verbal Behavior, 1968, *7*, 260–263.

Puff, C. R. (Ed.), *Memory organization and structure*. New York: Academic Press, 1979.

Roenker, D. L., Thompson, C. P., & Brown, S. C. A comparison of measures for the estimation of clustering in free recall. *Psychological Bulletin*, 1971, *76*, 45–48.

Rosch, E. Cognitive representations of semantic categories. *Journal of Experimental Psychology: General*, 1975, *104*, 192–233.

Rumelhart, D. E. Understanding and summarizing stories. In D. Laberge & S. J. Samuels (Eds.), *Basic processes in reading: Perception and comprehension*. Hillsdale, N.J.: Lawrence Erlbaum Associates, 1977.

Rundus, D. Analysis of rehearsal processes in free recall. *Journal of Experimental Psychology*, 1971, *89*, 63–77.

Sattath, S., & Tversky, A. Additive similarity trees. *Psychometrika*, 1977, *42*, 319–345.

Shepard, R. N., & Arabie, P. Additive clustering: Representation of similarities as combinations of discrete overlapping properties. *Psychological Review*, 1979, *86*, 87–123.

Shuell, T. J. Clustering and organization in free recall. *Psychological Bulletin*, 1969, *72*, 353–374.

Shuell, T. J. On sense and nonsense in measuring organization in free recall—oops, pardon me, my assumptions are showing. *Psychological Bulletin*, 1975, *82*, 720–724.

Shuell, T. J., & Keppel, G. Item priority in free recall. *Journal of Verbal Learning and Verbal Behavior*, 1968, *7*, 969–971.

Spillich, G. J., Vesonder, G. T., Chiesi, H. L., & Voss, J. F. Text processing of domain-related information for individuals with high and low domain knowledge. *Journal of Verbal Learning and Verbal Behavior*, 1979, *18*, 275–290.

Stein, N. L., & Glenn, C. G. An analysis of story comprehension in elementary school children. In R. O. Freedle (Ed.), *New directions in discourse processing: Advances in discourse processes* (Vol. 2). Norwood, N.J.: Ablex Publishing Corporation, 1979.

Sternberg, R. J., & Tulving, E. The measurement of subjective organization in free recall. *Psychological Bulletin*, 1977, *84*, 539–556.

Toglia, M., & Battig, W. F. *Handbook of semantic word norms*. Hillsdale, N.J.: Lawrence Erlbaum Associates, 1978.

Tulving, E. Subject organization in free recall of "unrelated words." *Psychological Review*, 1962, *69*, 344–354.

Tulving, E. Theoretical issues in free recall. In T. R. Dixon & D. L. Horton (Eds.), *Verbal behavior and general behavior theory*. Englewood Cliffs, N.J.: Prentice–Hall, 1968.

Zangen, M., Ziegelbaum, P., & Buschke, H. CLUSTER: A program for identifying recurrent clusters. *Behavior Research Methods and Instrumentation*, 1976, *8*, 388.

MICHAEL J. WATKINS
JOHN M. GARDINER

CHAPTER **6**

Cued Recall

INTRODUCTION

In essence, the cued–recall procedure is a form of memory testing that incorporates particular cues for the recall of specific information. In a typical cued–recall experiment the to–be–recalled information consists of words in a study list, or, more precisely, of the presentation or occurrence of words in a study list. The cues are prompts or reminders that have been carefully selected as having some special relation to the to–be–recalled words. They are nearly always other words. In most cases one cue is given for each "target" word, although sometimes one cue is given for more than one target word, and sometimes more than one cue is given for the same target word.

We do not think it would be helpful to attempt a more formal definition of the cued–recall procedure, especially one that tried to distinguish sharply between cued recall and other experimental procedures. Indeed, it would perhaps be easier to define the procedure so as to include *all* memory experiments. And, as we shall suggest toward the end of the chapter, thinking of all recall as cued recall may have advantages. But for the most part, this chapter is about the conventionally accepted cued–recall procedure that we have just described.

The chapter is divided into four main sections. The first describes

HANDBOOK OF RESEARCH METHODS IN
HUMAN MEMORY AND COGNITION

some prototypical cued–recall experiments; the second notes major experimental variables affecting cued–recall performance; the third section is about measurement and evaluation of performance; and the final section concerns more theoretical matters, mainly the relation between the conventional cued–recall procedure and other experimental paradigms.

REFERENCE EXPERIMENTS

In this part of the chapter we describe five experiments that were culled from the literature with a view to illustrating the cued–recall procedure.

Cued Recall and Free Recall

A particularly clear and simple illustration of a cued–recall experiment is provided by two conditions from a study by Wood (1967). Subjects in these conditions listened to the experimenter read out a list of 40 words at the rate of one word every 3 sec. Each word was an instance of a different taxonomic category. For example, the list might have included RAT, CANNON, SPINACH, and BLUE as instances of the categories *Four-footed animals, Weapons, Vegetables,* and *Colors.* After list presentation the subjects were given one of two types of recall tests. Half the subjects were given standard free-recall instructions and wrote their responses on a blank sheet. The other half were category-cued and wrote their responses on a sheet containing the names of the 40 categories represented in the study list. The average number of words produced was 11.69 in the free-recall condition and 16.16 in the category-cued condition, an appreciable and statistically reliable difference in favor of the cued condition.

To conclude from such an experiment that cues facilitate recall, it is essential that the conditions differ only with respect to the cuing variable. In particular, it is essential that the state of memory be equivalent across conditions at the time of the recall test. Of course, this equivalence will not be exact, but the inexactness should be due to an inevitable sampling variability and not to some systematic effect. Thus, the subjects should be assigned to condition at random (or at least in a way that can be assumed to be at random with respect to performance in the memory test), and the experimental treatment should be constant across conditions until the time of test. This identity of treatment should extend not only to such obvious factors as type of materials presented and study time allowed, but also to the subjects' test expectations. If the subjects know during the study phase precisely how they will be tested, any between-condition difference in recall could conceivably be due, in part if not entirely, to this knowledge and its effect on the way the subjects studied the to–be–remembered items, rather than to a direct effect of cuing. Since in Wood's experiments all of these conditions were met, we may conclude with the confidence indicated by his statistical analysis ($p < .001$) that the difference in recall was indeed the result of cuing. At a more theoretical level, we might conclude that the difference in recall represents a failure of retrieval in the free-recall condition; or, to use Tulving and Pearlstone's (1966) distinction, a reduced accessibility, as opposed to availability, of information in memory.

Cuing Recall with Qualitatively Different Cues

In the experiment we describe next several types of cues were used and these cues may be thought of as differing in a qualitative fashion— they seem to be cues of rather different sorts. The experiment, a rather elaborate one, was reported by Bregman (1968). It involved four different sorts of memory cuing crossed with eight different retention intervals. The experiment had a completely within-subject design. The subjects were presented with a long list of several hundred words, one word to each page of a booklet which they were required to work through at the rate of one page every 3 sec. Test pages with a particular cue for the recall of a word presented earlier in the booklet were scattered between presentation pages. Specifically, test pages occurred at intervals of 1, 2, 3, 6, 12, 24, 48, and 96 pages after the word had been presented. The four types of cues were: a semantic cue (*is a chemical element*); a phonemic cue (*rhymes with "thread"*); a graphic cue (*is spelled le—*); and a contiguity cue, which was the immediately preceding list word (*came after "cousin"*). The target words were randomly reassigned to different delays for each successive group of subjects. Cue type was rotated such that, for any particular target word cued at a given delay, each type of cue was used equally often across subjects. Also, subjects could neither anticipate when a test page might occur nor predict which type of cue would be used for any particular list word, thus ensuring that the state of memory was statistically equivalent across cuing conditions.

Bregman found that the effectiveness of all four cues declined sharply with increasing delay; most forgetting occurred within an interval of six items. This outcome was interpreted as evidence for a distinction between short-term and long-term memory. However, Bregman's data also indicated that the effect of delay did vary with type of cue. The decline was sharpest for the graphic cues and gentlest for the semantic cues. In addition, the contiguity cues were weaker than the other three at all delays.

Cuing Recall with Quantitatively Different Cues

In the following experiment it seems more reasonable to think of the cues as differing in a quantitative rather than in a qualitative fashion. The different kinds of cues seem to represent different points along some continuum. The experiment is from a study by Bahrick (1969). The cues (Bahrick called them prompters) were associatively related to the target words. They varied, however, in the strength of this association. To estimate this strength of associative relation, a group of people, who did not take part in the experiment but belonged to the same subject population, were given a free-association test. They were asked to produce a single free associate for each of a list of stimulus words. Working from the collective responses, the experimenter selected for use as target words in the experiment a set of 20 stimulus words that evoked a response in each of five probability ranges. These responses formed the cues of the experiment. For example, the successively more powerful cues for the target word CHAIR were *leg, cushion, upholstery, furniture,* and *table.* The mean associative strengths of the successive levels of cuing are shown in Table 6.1.

In the experiment, all the subjects learned a paired-associate list of 20 A–B pairs chosen so that there was no associative relation between the A and B items (e.g., *top*–CHAIR). The subjects studied this list until they achieved a specified level of performance. Following a delay they were given another test, again of a conventional paired-associate kind. Then the subjects were given a cued–recall test for those targets not

Table 6.1
Associative Strength and Probability of Recall for Each Cue Level in Bahrick's (1969) Experiment

	Cue level				
	1	2	3	4	5
Mean associative strength	.04	.14	.30	.52	.74
Mean probability of recall	.15	.40	.53	.69	.79

produced in the preceding paired-associate test. For this test, subjects were randomly assigned to one of five groups, each group corresponding to one of the five levels of cue–target relation, and the appropriate A items were re-presented together with a particular cue (e.g., Upholstery: *Top*–?).

Table 6.1 also shows the mean level of recall in the final test. It is clear that the effectiveness of the cues varied systematically with the mean associative strength of the cue–target relation as indexed by the results of the free-association test. From this result Bahrick argued that the "mechanism" underlying free-association responding is also involved in cued recall. More specifically, the relation has been used to support the theory that memory for the occurrence of a word, as in its presentation as a member of a study list, is represented in the form of a modification or tagging of a permanent representation of that word (or rather of the concept corresponding to that word) which is assumed to exist within the rememberer's storehouse of general knowledge. This storehouse is frequently conceptualized as an associative network and the representation of the word as a node within the network. It is assumed that whether a word is presented as a stimulus in a free-association task or as a cue in the cued-recall procedure, it initiates a search from its underlying node, with the nature of the search reflecting the associative structure of the network. We might add that, in the hands of Bahrick and others (e.g., Anderson & Bower, 1972; Kintsch, 1970), this general mode of theorizing has, in turn, provided the basis of the generate–recognize theory of recall (see Watkins & Gardiner, 1979, for a review).

Compatibility Between Recall Cue and Study Context

Unlike the three experiments we have described so far, the two experiments that follow are concerned with interactions between cuing and study conditions. In the first experiment, reported by Fisher and Craik (1977), there were two kinds of study contexts and two kinds of cues. All subjects studied a list of 56 A–B pairs in the expectation of a conventional paired-associate test. Within any one list, half the A items rhymed with their B items (e.g., *Hat*–CAT) and half were associatively related to their B items (e.g., *Dog*–CAT). Study condition was combined factorially with cuing condition, which was defined in terms of type of cue. In one case the cues were the A items from the study list and in the other they were the alternative A items. Each cue was identified as being of the rhyme or of the associate type.

The results of this experiment are summarized in Table 6.2. They

Table 6.2
Probability of Recall as a Function of Study and Test Conditions in Fisher and Craik's
(1977) Experiment

| | Test condition | | |
Study condition	Rhyming cue	Associative cue	Mean
Rhyme	.26	.17	.21
Associative	.17	.44	.30
Mean	.21	.30	

showed that an associative study context led to higher recall levels than did a rhyming study context and that associative cues were more effective than were rhyme cues. These main effects, however, are qualified by a clear interaction: For each type of cue, recall was substantially more likely when the cue matched the study context. As Fisher and Craik concluded, this pattern of results underscores the importance of the compatibility of encoding context and recall cue. The findings were interpreted to mean that both the principle of encoding specificity (Tulving & Thomson, 1973) and depth of processing ideas (Craik & Lockhart, 1972) are necessary for a complete description of memory.

Our last illustrative experiment is taken from the study by Thomson and Tulving (1970). This experiment is not unlike the previous one, though this time there are three types of study contexts and three types of cues, and the relation among the latter is ordinal or systematic rather than merely categorical. Using published norms, Thomson and Tulving constructed two types of A–B study pairs, one in which the association between the A and B items was weak (a mean of less than 1%) and one in which it was strong (a mean of 42%); examples are *Hand*–MAN and *Woman*–MAN. There were three study conditions: The 24 B items of a list were studied in a strong associative context, a weak associative context, or in the absence of any explicit associative context. Subjects in the first two conditions were told that A items should be studied as possible aids to recalling the B items. The three study conditions were factorially combined with three test conditions to yield nine experimental conditions, each of which involved an independent group of subjects. The three test conditions were free recall, cuing with the weak associates, and cuing with the strong associates. Since subjects could not anticipate test condition, any differences in recall performance within a study condition can be attributed to the cuing manipulation.

The results of this experiment, summarized in Table 6.3, show an-

Table 6.3

Probability of Recall as a Function of Study and Test Conditions in Thomson and Tulving's (1970) Experiment

	Test condition		
Study condition	No cue	Weak associative cue	Strong associative cue
No associate	14.1	11.1	19.0
Weak associate	10.7	15.7	13.9
Strong associate	12.2	9.2	20.2

other clear interaction between study and test conditions. The encoding specificity principle was formulated on the basis of just this sort of interaction. According to this principle, the effectiveness of a cue depends directly on how its encoding relates to the way the target item was encoded during the study phase of the experiment, rather than, as generate–recognize theory has it, on the preexisting cue–target relation in the subject's permanent repository of knowledge.

EXPERIMENTAL PARAMETERS

What are the parameters that determine level of performance in a cued-recall test? This question is not quite as straightforward as it at first appears. There are two major problems. The first is the paucity of direct evidence. Only in recent years has the cued-recall procedure been used on a large scale, and systematic evidence on the effects of experimental variables is still sparse. For the present purposes, however, this problem may not be too serious. Our solution is to supplement what we know directly from the cued-recall procedure with reasonable inferences made from free-recall, paired-associates, and recognition research. If a variable has a substantial effect with these procedures, then it is likely that it will also have an effect with the cued-recall procedure. Certainly this assumption is consistent with the view, presented later in the chapter, that the distinction between the cued-recall and other procedures is not a fundamental one.

The second problem is that the precise effects of a variable will depend on the levels of a host of other variables. For this reason we restrict consideration to variables whose effects are likely to be substantial over a wide range of experimental conditions, and even for these variables our comments should be regarded merely as a somewhat rough and incomplete guide.

List Materials

As with virtually all experimental procedures for studying memory and cognition, the materials used in most cued-recall research have been verbal. The reason for this is that verbal materials are enormously convenient to work with. They are not only easily obtained, but their preparation and presentation could hardly be simpler. Similarly, subjects can easily demonstrate their recollections of verbal items by writing them down or reporting them aloud. And in the case of individual words, which are by far the most popular type of verbal item, recall comes as close as it ever does to being all or none, which means that there is relatively little arbitrariness or uncertainty in scoring.

Another convenient property of verbal materials is that they can be readily organized into various categories that differ in ease of recall. For example, the more meaningful or familiar an item, the more likely it is to be recalled. Thus, other things being equal, words show a higher level of recall than do pseudowords or nonsense syllables, and relatively common words (run, toy, man) are usually recalled at a higher level than are relatively uncommon words (plod, nib, mole). No less important is the concreteness of the to-be-recalled words. Concrete words (trombone, brick, rocket) have a greater probability of being recalled than do abstract words (patience, justice, future).

Of the many such forms of categorization of the to-be-remembered items, which, if any, should be incorporated within an experimental design? In some cases, of course, this decision will depend on the theory or theoretical issues that gave rise to the experiment. In other cases a type-of-item variable will be included as a means of gauging the generality of the effects of a variable of more focal interest. In this case the type-of-item variable should be one that, like familiarity or concreteness, is likely to affect level of recall to an appreciable degree.

In preparing presentation materials, reference is often made to published information. For example, if an experimenter needs a number of instances of several different conceptual categories he will as likely as not turn to Battig and Montague's (1969) category norms. These norms provide instances generated by students to each of 56 taxonomic category names, such as professions, musical instruments, and vegetables. The instances are ordered according to the number of subjects producing them; the actual production frequencies are also listed. From these norms, the experimenter might select, say, the 12 most frequently produced instances, or perhaps those instances having a frequency rank between 11 and 20, for each of, say, 16 categories. Clearly, using such materials may obviate the need for pilot research. Moreover, to the extent that the same materials are used in different studies, cross-study comparisons are facilitated.

Although the relevant information about potential verbal study materials is scattered throughout the literature, many useful sources are described in a catalog prepared by Brown (1976). This catalog summarizes and indexes in a variety of ways a total of 172 publications that together provide all manner of useful information on words, letters, numbers, consonant–vowel–consonant trigrams, and other kinds of verbal stimuli.

We might add that, although it is not difficult to understand why verbal materials are so popular in memory research, this very popularity produces uncertainty about how well the conclusions drawn from verbal memory experiments generalize to memory for encounters with other sorts of items. Research with nonverbal items is often difficult and expensive, but a complete understanding of cued recall will have to wait until a great deal more nonverbal research has been done.

List Length and Number of Items per Cue

Level of recall depends on the number as well as the type of items presented. Although increasing the number of items in the study list generally results in an increase in the number of items recalled, it causes a reduction in the *proportion* of items recalled. In other words, the probability of recalling any given item from a list declines as the number of other list items is increased. The detrimental effect of additional items arises not only when such items are members of the same study list, but also when they are presented (whether in the form of other lists, distractor material, or something else) before the target study list (cf. Greenberg & Underwood, 1950) or, more especially, at some point between presentation of the list and the cue (e.g., Müller & Pilzecker, 1900).

As a rule, the list length effect is considerably less pronounced in cued recall than in free or serial recall. An exception, however, occurs when each cue serves for more than one item, in which case the effect reveals itself as a number-of-items-per-cue effect. For example, with a categorized list the effectiveness of a category-name cue with respect to any category instance varies inversely with the number of category instances presented (Patterson, 1972; Tulving & Pearlstone, 1966); in the extreme case where every word in a list is drawn from the same category, cuing subjects with the category name would presumably be no more effective than giving free-recall instructions. And again, the relation holds if, instead of being members of the target study list, the additional items are presented before the list (cf. Watkins & Watkins, 1975), or after the list and together with the cue (Watkins, 1975).

The range of list lengths actually used in cued-recall research is huge. Experiments with as few as 10 or 20 items in a study list are not uncommon, whereas for others as many as a hundred or even several hundred items make up a single list. Care should be taken to avoid using lists that are so short that all or nearly all of the items are recalled, or so long that only a small fraction are recalled, for in either case the average information gained from the fate of each presented item will be small and the experiment as a whole inefficient. In most cases the experimenter is in a position to be flexible about list length and can divide the total number of items he or she wishes to present to a subject into lists of a length likely to result in a desirable level of recall. Occasionally it is necessary to use a single long list, as, for example, when the experimenter does not wish the subject to know until after the presentation phase that a memory test will be given. In such cases an adequate level of performance can be obtained by using relatively powerful cues, or by using a categorized list and testing category by category.

Presentation Rate

Level of recall also varies inversely with the rate at which the list items are presented. That is, the more slowly the items are presented, and the more time available between successive items, the greater the proportion of items recalled (Glanzer & Cunitz, 1966; Murdock, 1962). The rate of presentation in many experiments is one item every 2–3 sec; it is rarely faster than one every half sec and rarely slower than one every 10 sec.

Mode of Study

Although it is still the case that in most cued-recall experiments subjects are not given precise instructions as to how they should study the list items, the last several years have produced a great deal of research demonstrating mode of study to be an important factor (Craik & Tulving, 1975; Hyde & Jenkins, 1969, 1973). This research has typically involved holding constant such variables as type of item and presentation rate, while varying the instructions on how the list words should be studied. For example, subjects might be told that, as each word is presented, their task is to count the number of letters it contains, or to supply a rhyming word, or to decide whether it fits within a given sentence frame (see Chapter 7). By and large, performance in a subsequent recall test has been found to be higher when such orienting tasks entail thinking about the meaning of the word, rather than about its graphemic or phonemic properties. Recall performance also depends on whether the subject studies the items with the intention of remembering them or whether the recall test comes as a surprise, although the effect of this variable is not usually so pronounced as is that of orienting task.

Nature of Cue

The nature of the cue is as potent as any variable in controlling level of recall. This point is illustrated by an experiment reported by Tulving and Watkins (1973), in which a given set of 5-letter words were cued by a variable number of letter cues (e.g., GRAPH was cued by *gr, gra, grap,* or *graph*). Probability of recall was shown to vary sharply and systematically with the number of letters in the cue. The point is also made by Bahrick's (1969) experiment, described earlier, involving cues of varying associative strengths. In each of these experiments the relation among the types of cues involved is in an obvious sense quantitative. The effectiveness of cues that vary in a qualitative way can differ just as strongly, though such differences are usually less predictable and may have to be determined empirically. The choice of cue for an experiment will sometimes be dictated by theoretical issues, and will sometimes be arbitrary. In the latter case, cues can be selected with an eye toward an optimal level of recall.

Relation Between Study and Test Context

Study and test contexts can be manipulated both in a general way and in a way that is specific to each to-be-remembered item. One general way of manipulating context is to vary study and test environments, as between different rooms (e.g., Smith, Glenberg, & Bjork, 1978), or between underwater and dry land (Godden & Baddeley, 1975). Another general way of manipulating context is through the use of different drug states (Eich, 1980). Specific manipulations of context often involve providing a context word for each to-be-recalled word, as in the experiments by Fisher and Craik (1977) and by Thomson and Tulving (1970) described earlier. Matched study–test environments, either the general or the specific sort, typically lead to superior recall performance. Note that specific test context is merely another way of referring to a cue, so that claims of differences in the effectiveness of various types of cues need to be qualified by reference to the study context of the target items, and more particularly to the relation between the study context and the cues.

MEASUREMENT OF PERFORMANCE

In this part of the chapter we consider certain details of how recall performance is assessed. We begin with the problem of deciding whether a given response should be counted as a correct production of the target item. There follows a discussion of guessing, specifically of the problem of estimating how much guessing has occurred and of how to correct for it. Next, the benefits of and procedures for applying more than one cue to one and the same target item are considered. Finally, we note that cue effectiveness can be assessed in terms, not only of probability of recall, but also of the time the subject takes to respond.

Criteria of Recall

When is recall achieved? We have already mentioned that as a rule criteria for recall are more easily applied to verbal items than to nonverbal items. But even with verbal material, including word lists, the matter is not completely clear-cut. To be sure, if the subject produces a word that seems entirely unrelated to the target word most experimenters would score the response as incorrect. And if the subject makes a slight spelling error that leaves little doubt that the word intended was the target word, then most experimenters would score the response as correct. But between these two extremes there is a gray area where arbitrariness prevails, where the experimenter has to set some criteria in deciding where to draw the line between correct and incorrect responses. The only rule here is that the criteria must not be confounded with condition. Perhaps the best precaution against this danger is to score blind with respect to condition. The same rule applies for material that is inherently more difficult to score than random words, such as verbal passages or drawings. Whenever the form of the response is such that the experimenter cannot be blind to condition during scoring and there is a nontrivial chance that he or she will unwittingly adopt different scoring criteria for different conditions, then a copy of the responses should be prepared in a form that can be scored blind with respect to condition by one or more other persons.

Another problem is whether a response has to be aligned with its intended cue in order to be scored as correct, for it sometimes happens that a response sought with one cue is elicited by another. Here one can score with a strict criterion that accepts the response as correct only if paired with its intended cue, or a lenient criterion that accepts all target responses as correct regardless of which cues elicited them. One argument against the strict criterion is that the probability of a cue being effective might change if the response was recalled to a previous cue. However, in most cases there will be arguments in favor of both criteria, and the choice between them may be somewhat arbitrary.

Choice of scoring criteria will not usually affect the essential conclusions of the experiment. If there is any doubt about this, then data should be scored two or more times, each time using a different set of criteria.

Problem of Guessing

In the free-recall procedure the chances of the subject successfully guessing a target item seem in most cases quite remote, and so the problem is often ignored. With cued recall, as with recognition (see Chapter 1), the chances of an item being guessed can be substantial, and so the problem usually needs addressing. The first step here is to try to estimate the extent of guessing. This estimate can then be used to adjust the observed level of performance. But before we discuss how the extent of guessing should be estimated, we need to be clear about what is meant by guessing.

In what sense are subjects' erroneous responses guesses? The subjects' erroneous responses in a word-list experiment are never anything but words, and moreover they are often words that seem not altogether unrelated to the list words. Therefore, even erroneous responses indicate recall, if only of the fact that the to-be-recalled items were words. If this is true of erroneous responses, then it is certainly true of any lucky guesses that happen to be target words. So correct guesses should not be defined merely as list items produced in the absence of any recall. Rather, they should be defined as list items produced in the absence of any recall beyond that of the characteristics of the population from which the target items were sampled. It follows that in order to estimate the extent of guessing we need to know the likelihood of a target item being produced when the subject does not recall the presentation of the word but does know the population from which it came.

One seemingly straightforward way that is sometimes used to estimate the likelihood of producing a target item to a cue solely by knowing the population of items to which the target item belongs, is to inform a control group—subjects who have never seen the study list—about the general nature of the list words, and to ask them to guess from the cues given what those words are. There are at least two serious weaknesses with this procedure. First, it is unlikely that control subjects would know as much about the target population as would experimental subjects who have carefully studied the target words, in which case the experimental subjects would have a greater chance of guessing correctly. The second and perhaps more serious weakness of the procedure lies in its failure to distinguish between the probability that subjects *can* guess and the probability that they *do* guess. It is the latter that is required in estimating how much guessing has occurred, but it is the former that is estimated from the control group. Although these two weaknesses of the control group procedure lead to biases in opposite directions, it does not, of course, follow that they cancel each other out.

For such reasons, it is preferable to estimate guessing from the number of erroneous responses made in the very same conditions in which correct responses are made. The most direct way to do this is to include in the test, cues for words that were not presented in the study list. The proportion of such cues is not critical. What is important is that cue–target pairs for targets that are included in the study list be sampled from the same population as those for targets that were not. In effect, this procedure amounts to deleting part of the study list. If for a given subject only a small number of words are deleted then, to ensure that they are adequately representative of the target population, it is best to vary the choice of these words systematically across subjects or subject-groups. In any event, the probability of a target word not presented in the study list being produced at test provides a measure of the extent of guessing and can be used to correct the raw recall scores.

This brings us to the issue of correcting for guessing, and specifically to the question of how the measure of guessing just discussed can be used to adjust the proportion of target words actually reported in order to obtain a measure of "true" recall uncontaminated by guessing. Assume that the probability of a list word being recalled (R) is the sum of the probability of its being truly recalled (T) and the probability that it was not truly recalled but was guessed. Hence,

$$R = T + (1 - T)g, \tag{1}$$

where g is the probability of the target word being guessed, as estimated by the probability of its being produced when it did not occur in the study list. The terms of Eq. (1) can be rearranged to give the probability of true recall:

$$T = (R - g)/(1 - g). \tag{2}$$

With this equation, it is a simple matter to obtain an estimate of recall corrected for guessing merely by knowing the probabilities of presented and unpresented words being produced in the recall test.

The correction for guessing described by Eq. (2) conforms to what is known as the high-threshold model of responding, and it assumes that the subject produces two quite distinct types of correct responses, genuine recalls and guesses, and that from the subject's point of view erroneous responses and correct guesses are completely equivalent. It seems unlikely, however, that these assumptions are entirely valid. A prediction of the model is that the proportion of items truly recalled is independent of the guessing rate (g). This prediction could be tested by inducing subjects to exercise varying degrees of caution in responding, thereby obtaining sets of responses that vary in degree of guessing. If sufficient data were collected, the prediction would probably be found to be somewhat inaccurate.

Supposing that the high-threshold model is not in fact quite valid, how then should corrections for guessing be made? This question will require a great deal of research, but it seems likely that a wholly satisfactory solution will never be found, if only because the premise that the observed proportion correct is the product of a true recall rate contaminated by guessing may be an oversimplification. Be that as it may, the derivation of a corrected measure of recall, whether by the high-threshold model or some other model, may be of considerable convenience in practice. But if corrections for guessing are made, it is desirable that, in reporting the experiment, the description of the experimental results include the raw recall rate and the guessing rate for each condition. Readers are then free to reject the model used for correcting the scores, and to perhaps apply a model of their choice.

Multiple Cuing

It is sometimes convenient to use more than one cue for each target item. For example, comparatively detailed information about the recallability of a target word can be obtained by cuing with successively increasing numbers of letters contained by the word. For a list of 5-letter words, each word might be cued first with one letter (–h–––); then, if the subject fails to produce the word after, say 5 sec, a 2-letter cue that includes the letter of the 1-letter cue would be presented (–h––e); then after 5 more sec a 3-letter cue (–h–le); then a 4-letter cue (–hale); and if the target is still not produced all of the letters would be given (*whale*). The number of such cues required to effect recall provides a more sensitive measure of recallability than does the all-or-none effect of a single cue.

Implicit in this procedure is the assumption that the useful information in each successive cue subsumes that in the previous cue, that a word recallable to one cue in the series will necessarily be recallable to the next. This assumption seems intuitively reasonable, but it does not follow that the same relation holds among all pairs of cue types. Suppose we know that under some particular set of conditions the target word WHALE has a probability of .60 of being recalled in response to the semantic cue *aquatic animal,* and a probability of .45 to the phonemic cue *rhymes with trail*—these probabilities being obtained from two statistically equivalent groups of subjects. Consider the state of the subjects' memories immediately prior to the presentation of these cues. Since the semantic cue is more potent than the phonemic cue, there must be some subjects for whom the semantic cue would be effective and the phonemic cue ineffective. What is not clear, however, is whether there would be subjects for whom the phonemic cue is effective and the semantic cue ineffective.

At issue here is the contingency relation between two types of cues. Perhaps the most obvious way to determine this relation is to include both cues in a single test. Assume that when the semantic cue is given first, the probability of the target being recalled is, as before, .60. If the useful information in the weaker phonemic cue, given at some later point in the test, is totally subsumed by that in the semantic cue, then the phonemic cue will never succeed in effecting recall of words for which the semantic cue was not successful. Thus, the proportion of target words produced in response to at least one of the two cues will remain at the proportion for the semantic cue, namely .60, and the contingency relation between the cues will be as shown in Panel (a) of Table 6.4. If, on the other hand, the useful information in the phonemic cue is entirely independent of that in the semantic cue, then the probability of a phonemic cue effecting recall of a target word not produced in response to the prior semantic cue should be the same as that for the target words as a whole, namely .45. Hence, in this case the probability of recalling a target word to at least one of the two cues would be .60 + (1 − .60).45, or .78, and the contingency relation would be as shown in Panel (b) of Table 6.4. More likely than not, however, the relation between the two cues will be neither one of total inclusion nor one of total independence, but rather one of intermediate value, as in the example given in Panel (c) of Table 6.4.

Table 6.4
Possible Contingency Relations between Semantic and Phonemic Cues as Determined by the Reduction Method

		Phonemic cue (a)		
		+	−	
Semantic cue	+	.45	.15	.60
	−	.00	.40	.40
		.45	.55	

		Phonemic cue (b)		
		+	−	
Semantic cue	+	.27	.33	.60
	−	.18	.22	.40
		.45	.55	

		Phonemic cue (c)		
		+	−	
Semantic cue	+	.35	.25	.60
	−	.10	.30	.40
		.45	.55	

The procedure for deriving such contingency relations is referred to as the reduction method, and it has been discussed at length elsewhere (Tulving & Watkins, 1975; Watkins, 1979). It is sufficient for the present purposes to stress the need to determine the probability of each type of cue effecting recall when it is the first cue to be presented. Besides these two probabilities, one needs to know the probability of failing to recall in response to one of these cue types and yet subsequently recalling in response to the other. The object of the procedure is to avoid using previously recalled items when estimating cue effectiveness, since a prior act of recalling an item may well affect the probability of recalling the item again. The importance of the procedure is that the contingency relation it yields could reveal that experimental variables have effects that might never have been suspected from their effects on the two cues taken separately.

Response Time

Throughout this chapter we have concerned ourselves with research in which performance is measured in terms of the proportion of target words correctly recalled. Performance can also be measured in terms of the time taken to recall. Individual researchers tend to concentrate on one or the other of these measures, and indeed within this volume discussion of experimental procedures involving response-time measures is to be found in other chapters (Chapters 1, 2, and 10). On the other hand, the distinction between these two approaches to measuring performance is not quite as clear cut as might be imagined.

The distinction is sharp only to the extent that when response time is being measured there are no errors, and when proportion recalled is being measured the time allowed for response is of no consequence. In practice, just as errors do occur with response time procedures, so time allowed for responding is a factor when measuring proportion recalled. It is instructive to plot the temporal course of recall, and often this can be done simply and unobtrusively. In free recall, for example, subjects can be instructed to write their responses in a column, and after successive intervals of say, one minute, to draw a line under the last word written. By counting the total number of words recalled before each successive line, a cumulative record of recall can be obtained. Such a record allows estimation of the effects experimental variables have on the rate at which the asymptote is approached, as well as of the asymptotic levels themselves. In free recall, these two measures of performance are often related in that the higher the level of recall, the slower the rate at which the asymptote is approached (Bousfield & Sedgewick, 1944). But even with free recall it may sometimes be useful to have both measures (Roediger, Stellon, & Tulving, 1977); and with procedures involving conventional cues, about whose temporal characteristics we know virtually nothing, it may be no less useful.

RELATION TO OTHER PARADIGMS

At the beginning of the chapter we implied that it is by no means easy to give an entirely satisfactory definition of the cued-recall procedure. The difficulty arises in trying to define a recall cue. It seems that the only simple solution is to define it in very broad terms, such as, say, any stimulus that can be sufficiently specified to allow others to replicate the research in which it is used and whose effectiveness in triggering recall of some specific event (or events) one would like to know about. A disadvantage of this definition is that it means applying cued recall to procedures not conventionally characterized as such. Indeed, since with this definition it is possible to identify recall cues in most, if not all of the procedures used in memory research, cued recall ceases to be an informative description. On the other hand, this broad definition does have certain advantages. Chief among these is that it brings out a relation among—and so provides a common conceptual framework for—experimental paradigms in all their variety. And of particular relevance to the present purposes, an appreciation of how procedures conventionally described as cued recall relate to other procedures with which the experimenter may be more familiar could well be helpful in deciding upon methodological details.

To be sure, some common paradigms fit very obviously within a cuing framework. For example, in what is sometimes called the probed-recall procedure, in which recall of a particular list item is solicited by indicating its position in the sequence, it is natural to think of recall as being cued. No less obvious is the cuing that occurs in the paired-associate learning paradigm.

It is somewhat less easy to see how a cuing framework might be applied to certain other paradigms, most notably free recall and recognition. Indeed, these are the two procedures that are, perhaps, most frequently contrasted with cued recall. From a conventional standpoint, free recall is often thought of as "uncued recall" and so is used to provide a baseline for evaluating the effectiveness of cued recall. Conversely, the recognition procedure is often viewed as providing an upper limit against which the effectiveness of conventional cues can be compared, on the assumption that recognition provides an infallible measure of what is "in" memory. So what are the free-recall and recognition cues in terms of our broad definition of a cue? In free recall the cue is the instruction, given at least implicitly, specifying the set of to-be-recalled items—for example, *recall in any order as many words as you can from the list just presented*. In recognition the cue is the literal copy of the list item presented as a target in the recognition test.

Just how far thinking of free recall and recognition in this way brings out the relation of these procedures to other and more obviously cued-recall procedures has been discussed at length elsewhere (Watkins, 1979). But it is perhaps appropriate here to point out why the free-recall and recognition procedures may not be so special as they might appear.

Although the cues of most other procedures are more effective than is the free-recall cue, there are exceptions. For example, cuing by initial letter can be less effective than instructing for free recall (Earhard, 1967). Another example is to be found in Slamecka's (1968) part-set cuing procedure, in which a random subset of items from the study list are presented at test as cues for the remaining items. The proportion of these remaining items recalled is slightly lower than that under standard free-recall conditions. It would seem, then, that it is not altogether appropriate to single out free recall as being qualitatively different from other paradigms by virtue of its being minimally effective.

Another way in which free recall differs from most other paradigms lies in its use of a single cue for all of the to-be-recalled items. But even this distinction loses its sharpness under scrutiny. Thus, when the study list comprises words drawn from several distinct semantic categories and the names of these categories are given at test, we characterize the procedure as one of cued recall. Yet it can be shaded into free recall simply by reducing the number of categories, and hence cues, to say four or two or one. Just where cued recall ends and free recall takes over seems arbitrary.

Characterizing the recognition paradigm as one of cued recall brings out the abbreviated and potentially misleading nature of the usual way of describing the recognition task. When a test item is said to be recognized, what is really meant is that the test item caused recall of the occurrence of a literal copy of the item as a member of the study list. This description of recognition memory calls into question any assumption that the recognition test provides an accurate indication of the information available in memory. Instead, it suggests that whether the recognition cue is effective in eliciting recall of an item's occurrence in the study list will depend on how well the perception of the occurrence is reinstated by the cue. It seems reasonable to suppose that the representation of an item in a recognition test will be perceived similarly to the item's presentation in the study list, but just how similarly will depend on a number of factors. And indeed, there is much evidence to this effect. For example, recognition is more probable if the typescript or voice of presentation of the item is the same at study as at test (Craik & Kirsner, 1974; Hintzman & Summers, 1973). Also, recognition performance is higher when context—at least when given by adjacent items—is preserved from study to test (e.g., DaPolito, Barker, & Wiant, 1972; Tulving & Thomson, 1971). Such recognition context effects are clearly contrary to the notion that recognition is qualitatively different from other procedures by virtue of maximal sensitivity, of providing an upper bound on what is potentially recallable. The point is made dramatically by the finding that under certain conditions the recognition test item is substantially less likely to effect recall than is a cue that reinstates merely the item's study context (e.g., Tulving & Thomson, 1973). Note that when recognition is viewed as a form of cued recall, none of these findings is in any way problematic.

And so it seems that not only can free recall and recognition be readily described within a cued-recall framework, but also that the usual grounds for distinguishing these procedures from others are less than compelling. In a more theoretical vein, conceiving of all memory paradigms as involving cued recall may have the advantage not only of underscoring the relations among these paradigms, but also of providing a foundation for potentially useful lines of research. It suggests, for example, the need for distinguishing between nominal and functional cues, nominal cue meaning the stimulus whose cuing properties the experiment is designed to determine, and functional cue meaning a more hypothetical entity that can be thought of as mediating the effect of a nominal cue. For instance, though initial-letter cues are effective to some degree, the finding that they are no more effective than is the free-recall instruction (Earhard, 1967) leaves open the possibility that the functional cue corresponding to the nominal initial-letter cue is the same as that for free recall. Research designed to explore this and a vast number of other such questions could prove to be of considerable interest.

Throughout this entire discussion consideration has been restricted to cuing of what Tulving (1972) has called episodic memory—that is, of specific, personally experienced episodes, such as the appearance of words in a study list. As our final comment, we note that just as it is useful to consider extending the definition of cued recall to include free recall, recognition, and perhaps all other episodic memory paradigms, it may also be useful to consider extending the definition of a to-be-recalled item to include memory in a broader sense, including general knowledge. Much of our discussion would survive such an extension.

ACKNOWLEDGMENTS

Preparation of this chapter was supported by Grant MH35873 from the National Institute of Mental Health and by a grant from the Social Science Research Council, England.

REFERENCES

Anderson, J. R., & Bower, G. H. Recognition and retrieval processes in free recall. *Psychological Review*, 1972, *79*, 97–123.

Bahrick, H. P. Measurement of memory by prompted recall. *Journal of Experimental Psychology*, 1969, *79*, 213–219.

Battig, W. G., & Montague, W. E. Category norms for verbal items in 56 categories: A replication and extension of the Connecticut category norms. *Journal of Experimental Psychology Monograph*, 1969, *80*, 1–46.

Bousfield, W. A., & Sedgewick, C. H. An analysis of sequences of restricted associative responses. *Journal of General Psychology*, 1944, *30*, 149–165.

Bregman, A. S. Forgetting curves with semantic, phonetic, graphic, and contiguity cues. *Journal of Experimental Psychology*, 1968, *78*, 539–546.

Brown, A. S. Catalog of scaled verbal material. *Memory & Cognition*. 1976, *4*, 1S–45S.

Craik, F. I. M., & Kirsner, K. The effect of speaker's voice on word recognition. *Quarterly Journal of Experimental Psychology*, 1974, *26*, 274–284.

Craik, F. I. M., & Lockhart, R. S. Levels of processing: A framework for memory research. *Journal of Verbal Learning and Verbal Behavior*, 1972, *11*, 671–684.

Craik, F. I. M., & Tulving, E. Depth of processing and the retention of words in episodic memory. *Journal of Experimental Psychology: General*, 1975, *104*, 268–294.

DaPolito, F., Barker, D., & Wiant, J. The effects of contextual change on component recognition. *American Journal of Psychology*, 1972, *85*, 431–440.

Earhard, M. Cued recall and free recall as a function of the number of items per cue. *Journal of Verbal Learning and Verbal Behavior*, 1967, *6*, 257–263.

Eich, J. E. The cue-dependent nature of state-dependent retrieval. *Memory & Cognition*, 1980, *8*, 157–173.

Fisher, R. P., & Craik, F. I. M. The interaction between encoding and retrieval operations in cued recall. *Journal of Experimental Psychology: Human Learning and Memory*, 1977, *3*, 701–711.

Glanzer, M., & Cunitz, A. R. Two storage mechanisms in free recall. *Journal of Verbal Learning and Verbal Behavior*, 1966, *5*, 351–360.

Godden, D. R., & Baddeley, A. D. Context-dependent memory in two natural environments. *British Journal of Psychology*, 1975, *66*, 325–332.

Greenberg, R., & Underwood, B. J. Retention as a function of stage of practice. *Journal of Experimental Psychology*, 1950, *40*, 452–457.

Hintzman, D. L., & Summers, J. S. Long-term visual traces of visually presented words. *Bulletin of the Psychonomic Society*, 1973, *1*, 325–327.

Hyde, T. S., & Jenkins, J. J. Differential effects of incidental tasks on the organization of recall of a list of highly associated words. *Journal of Experimental Psychology*, 1969, *82*, 472–481.

Hyde, T. S., & Jenkins, J. J. Recall of words as a function of semantic, graphic, and syntactic orienting tasks. *Journal of Verbal Learning and Verbal Behavior*, 1973, *12*, 471–480.

Kintsch, W. Models for free recall and recognition. In D. A. Norman (Ed.), *Models of human memory*. New York: Academic Press, 1970.

Müller, G. E., & Pilzecker, A. Experimentalle Beitrage zur Lehre vom Gedächtnis. *Zeitschrift für Psychologie*, 1900, *1*, 1–300.

Murdock, J. J., Jr. The serial position effect of free recall. *Journal of Experimental Psychology*, 1962, *64*, 482–488.

Patterson, K. E. Some characteristics of retrieval limitation in human memory. *Journal of Verbal Learning and Verbal behavior*, 1972, *11*, 685–691.

Roediger, H. L., Stellon, C. C., & Tulving, E. Inhibition from part-list cues and rate of recall. *Journal of Experimental Psychology: Human Learning and Memory*, 1977, *3*, 174–188.

Slamecka, N. J. An examination of trace storage in free recall. *Journal of Experimental Psychology*, 1968, *76*, 504–513.

Smith, S. M., Glenberg, A., & Bjork, R. A. Environmental context and human memory. *Memory & Cognition*, 1978, *6*, 342–353.

Thomson, D. M., & Tulving, E. Associative encoding and retrieval: Weak and strong cues. *Journal of Experimental Psychology*, 1970, *86*, 255–262.

Tulving, E. Episodic and semantic memory. In E. Tulving & W. Donaldson (Eds.), *Organization of memory*. New York: Academic Press, 1972.

Tulving, E., & Pearlstone, Z. Availability versus accessibility of information in memory for words. *Journal of Verbal Learning and Verbal Behavior*, 1966, *5*, 381–391.

Tulving, E., & Thomson, D. M. Retrieval processes in recognition memory: Effects of associative context. *Journal of Experimental Psychology*, 1971, *87*, 116–124.

Tulving, E., & Thomson, D. M. Encoding specificity and retrieval processes in episodic memory. *Psychological Review*, 1973, *80*, 352–373.

Tulving, E., & Watkins, M. J. Continuity between recall and recognition. *American Journal of Psychology*, 1973, *86*, 739–748.

Tulving, E., & Watkins, M. J. Structure of memory traces. *Psychological Review*, 1975, *82*, 261–275.

Watkins, M. J. Inhibition in recall with extralist "cues." *Journal of Verbal Learning and Verbal Behavior*, 1975, *14*, 294–303.

Watkins, M. J. Engrams as cuegrams and forgetting as cue overload: A cueing approach to the structure of memory. In C. R. Puff (Ed.), *Memory organization and structure*. New York: Academic Press, 1979.

Watkins, M. J., & Gardiner, J. M. An appreciation of generate–recognize theory of recall. *Journal of Verbal Learning and Verbal Behavior*, 1979, *18*, 687–704.

Watkins, O. C., & Watkins, M. J. Buildup of proactive inhibition as a cue-overload effect. *Journal of Experimental Psychology: Human Learning and Memory*, 1975, *1*, 442–452.

Wood, G. Mnemonic systems in recall. *Journal of Educational Psychology Monographs*, 1967, *58* (6, Pt. 2).

Incidental Learning and Orienting Tasks

INTRODUCTION

Throughout almost the entire history of memory research, the primary emphasis has been on intentional rather than incidental learning. In some respects, this seems rather puzzling, since most human learning can reasonably be regarded as incidental, in the sense that no formal test of what has been learned is anticipated. Thus, considerations of ecological validity suggest quite strongly that the incidental-learning paradigm should be the source of especially important and realistic data concerning the normal functioning of memory processes.

One complicating factor is that a simple dichotomy between incidental and intentional learning is difficult to justify. Certainly the notion that incidental learning, in the laboratory or elsewhere, occurs with the total absence of an intention to acquire information is erroneous. McGeoch (1942) made the point in the following way: "Much of the learning which goes on with no overt instructions is, nonetheless, influenced by implicit instructions and sets. . . . It cannot be said with any conclusiveness that there are experiments in which implicit sets have not operated; but, more than this, the probability is on the side of the hypothesis that all of the results [in incidental learning] have been determined by set [p.304]."

197

HANDBOOK OF RESEARCH METHODS IN
HUMAN MEMORY AND COGNITION

One of the reasons for the relative neglect of incidental-learning paradigms, then, may be the problem of establishing whether the observed learning is truly incidental. At a fairly superficial level, there also appears to be the problem of ensuring that subjects pay close attention to stimulus materials that they have not been asked to remember. Finally, during the "Dark Ages" of memory research (i.e., until about 20 years ago), investigators devoted their energies to a remarkably circumscribed set of paradigms and theoretical notions, and incidental learning did not come within their purview.

From a historical perspective, two great eras of research on incidental learning can be identified. In the first era, which culminated with the work of Postman and Mechanic in the 1950s and 1960s, the emphasis was on contrasting intentional and incidental learning. It was usually assumed that intentional learning was superior to incidental learning, and that the extent of that superiority mirrored the importance of intentionality in learning.

The second era was adumbrated by Hyde and Jenkins (1969), but owes most of its continuing preeminence to the influence of the ideas of Craik and Lockhart (1972). They argued that incidental learning was of major interest because of the potential control it offered over an individual's processing activities. This contemporary era is very different from the previous era, in that incidental learning is now regarded as interesting in its own right rather than as merely a kind of control or baseline condition against which to compare intentional learning.

In the next two major sections of this chapter, the main research eras are discussed in chronological order. After that, there is a final section in which some general conclusions are presented.

INCIDENTAL VERSUS INTENTIONAL LEARNING

Experimental Paradigms

Any attempt to compare intentional and incidental learning must start by deciding how they are to be distinguished. As we have already seen, theoretical considerations suggest that no absolute distinction can be drawn between these two forms of learning. However, matters are relatively straightforward at the operational level, since intentional and incidental learning can be distinguished in terms of the use of prelearning instructions that either do, or do not, forewarn subjects about the existence of a subsequent retention test. Since subjects have a perverse tendency to see through the trickiness of experimenters, it is a good idea to question postexperimentally those who have received the incidental learning instructions in order to ensure that they did not anticipate a retention test. For some strange reason, this simple precaution has been omitted from most recent studies.

The early work on incidental learning (reviewed by McLaughlin, 1965, and Postman, 1964) was concerned primarily with two main issues: (*a*) whether the phenomenon of incidental learning could be demonstrated; and (*b*) the demonstration that incidental learning (if it could be shown to exist) was inferior to intentional learning. Considerable evidence was found in favor of the notion that incidental learning is typically inferior to intentional learning through the use of two somewhat different paradigms. In the *Type I* paradigm, the subjects perform an orienting task on the stimulus materials, but there are no learning instructions for subjects in the incidental-learning condition. In the *Type II* paradigm, all subjects are given instructions to learn some of the stimuli that are presented to them; additional stimuli, which the subjects are not told to learn, are presented at the same time. These additional stimuli may be either intrinsic (e.g., colors in which the to-be-remembered stimuli are printed) or extrinsic (e.g., extra stimuli) to the experimenter-defined learning task; such intrinsic or extrinsic stimuli form the basis for assessment of incidental learning.

From the methodological point of view, there appear to be some advantages with the Type I paradigm. If an appropriate orienting task is used, one can be fairly certain that the subjects have at least perceived the incidental stimuli; such certainty is lacking in the case of Type II incidental learning, especially when the incidental stimuli are extrinsic to the learning task.

An unresolved issue that was once the focus of some experimental interest is whether the Type I or Type II situation is more favorable to incidental learning. As is usually the case with such issues, no definite answer is possible, since the results depend on a number of factors. It was often claimed that the Type II situation produces considerable incidental learning when the learning processes occurring in intentional learning generalize to the incidental stimuli. On the other hand, the processing of relevant stimuli preempts most of the available time and resources, especially when the presentation rate is fast, thus greatly restricting incidental learning in the Type II situation.

Experiments using both types of paradigm have (at least until the 1970s) usually indicated that intentional learning is better than incidental learning; in virtually all cases where this was not the case, there was no effect of intentionality upon learning. However, several of these early studies were extremely suspect methodologically. What often happened in Type I studies was that the memory performance of subjects who were simply instructed to learn the presented items was compared with that of subjects who were given an orienting task to perform on the items and who were not informed of the subsequent retention test. These two groups of subjects differ with respect both to the intentionality of learning and of the presence versus absence of an orienting task; accordingly, any performance differences between these two groups cannot be interpreted unequivocally.

The most common methodological problem with Type II studies is that the intentional and incidental stimuli are often very different from each other (e.g., words versus colors or words versus geometrical figures). In this case, it is the confounding between intentionality and type of stimulus item that bedevils interpretation.

Early Theorizing

Postman (1964) attempted to account for the apparent inconsistencies in the literature by suggesting that the effects of intent to learn on memory are minimal or nonexistent when the stimulus materials are either very easy or very difficult to learn. There is a grain of truth to this suggestion, perhaps because of floor and ceiling effects; however, it is obviously lacking in real explanatory power.

Postman (1964) also provided a more promising lead. He argued that the effects of intentionality on learning depend critically on the responses that the subject makes in the learning situation: "Intent per se has no significant effects on learning. All its effects are indirect, i.e., instructions to learn activate *responses to the materials* which are favorable to acquisition. The same results can be achieved by appropriate orienting tasks without instructions to learn [p. 189]." Whereas there may be many kinds of responses, Postman considered only naming or labeling responses, responses elicited by stimulus generalization, and responses establishing associative links among the stimulus items.

The response-based theory sometimes works quite well, especially when subjects only engage in simple processing operations. For example, Mechanic (1964) argued that the learning of pronounceable trigrams depends largely on the number of pronouncing responses made to the trigrams. There was the usual superiority of intentional over incidental learning when the incidental learners merely guessed at a number that was supposed to be associated with each item; however, when they were instructed to repeat each item over and over again, the performance level of incidental learners improved up to that of intentional learners.

In other words, the frequency of pronouncing responses rather than intention per se is the prime determinant of the amount of learning that occurs in this particular task.

The greatest problem with Postman's response theory is that it is often extremely difficult to identify the hypothetical responses produced by a given orienting task. For example, Hyde and Jenkins (1973) discovered that estimating the frequency with which words are used in the English language produced a high level of incidental learning, but response theory can only interpret this finding in an entirely ad hoc way.

Recent Research

A major breakthrough in thinking and research in this area was initiated by Hyde and Jenkins (1969). In their study, incidental learners performed an orienting task, and intentional learners either performed the same orienting task or did not carry out an orienting task at all (these subjects were *pure intentional learners*). Various orienting tasks were used, including rating pleasantness, detecting the presence of the letter "e" in list words, and estimating the number of letters in each word.

Subsequent free recall was better after the performance of relatively semantic orienting tasks (e.g., pleasantness ratings) than after nonsemantic tasks (e.g., "e"-checking) for both intentional and incidental learners. Indeed, the recall performance of intentional and incidental learners who had performed the same orienting task was very similar, although the intentional learners sometimes obtained modestly higher recall scores. These results suggest that retention is determined mainly by the processing activities associated with the performance of each orienting task. In contrast, the intent to learn per se was only marginally related to subsequent free recall.

A comparison of the performance of those intentional learners who did not perform an orienting task with those who did revealed that some of the orienting tasks acted as sources of interference. In general terms, intentional learners who did not carry out an orienting task recalled as much as intentional learners given a semantic orienting task, and considerably more than intentional learners who received a nonsemantic orienting task.

Broadly similar findings were subsequently reported in a number of other studies (e.g., Craik & Tulving, 1975; Hyde & Jenkins, 1973; Till & Jenkins, 1973). Most of the available evidence indicates that retention (or at least free recall) is determined by the kinds of processing activities engaged in by the subject while performing the orienting task. However, this still leaves one perplexing question: Why do intentional learners given a nonsemantic orienting task process the stimulus items in a non-optimal way such that their recall performance is markedly lower than that achieved by intentional learners not receiving an orienting task or incidental learners given a semantic task?

The most obvious answer is that the use of a fairly rapid presentation rate (usually 5 sec or fewer per item) does not permit intentional learners to do any more than complete the orienting task. The time factor was investigated by McDaniel and Masson (1977), who discovered that in-tentionality affected recall at a 24-hour retention interval when a 10-sec presentation rate was used, but not when a 5-sec rate was used. However, it is possible that the intentional learners may simply have rehearsed the words during the retention interval. That seems especially likely in view of the fact that McDaniel and Masson were unable to replicate these findings in a second, methodologically sounder experiment.

An alternative possibility was explored by Postman and Kruesi (1977). They pointed out that the instructions typically used placed major emphasis on the orienting task, with only a brief mention of the fact that recall would be required for intentional subjects. As a consequence, intentional learners are likely to regard the recall task as being of sec-ondary importance, and so devote little effort to preparing for it. Postman and Kruesi compared the recall performance of various groups of subjects who had all performed the nonsemantic orienting task of rating the pleas-antness of sound of the list words. Intentional subjects whose instructions did not emphasize the subsequent recall test recalled no more words than the incidental learners, but a second group of intentional learners whose instructions did stress the importance of learning the words out-performed the incidental learners.

The most intriguing possibility is that subjects in learning experi-ments are simply unaware of the potential enhancement of memory that can occur as a result of semantic processing. Although this notion may seem rather far-fetched, there is some empirical support for it. Cutting (1975) asked incidental learners to rate the pleasantness of words or to decide whether each word contained the letter "e." After the orienting task had been completed, subjects were asked to judge how well they might do if asked for recall. Finally, they were given a recall test. Pleas-antness raters actually recalled an average of 5.5 words more than "e"-checkers, but both groups rated themselves approximately the same in their ability to recall the words.

In a second, very similar, experiment, Cutting (1975) asked subjects to estimate the precise number of words they might be able to recall. Pleasantness raters recalled 4.9 words more on average than "e"-checkers, but the former group underestimated their ability to recall whereas the latter group overestimated. There was a difference between the two groups of 21% in actual recall, against a difference of only 10% in the recall estimates.

Cutting's findings clearly suggest that subjects have little insight into the relationships between encoding operations and retention. The same issue was investigated by Chow, Currie, and Craik (1978). They discovered that a very slow rate of presentation (12 sec per word) did not enhance retention to any great extent among intentional learners performing a nonsemantic orienting task. Such learners only produced high levels of recall and recognition when they were explicitly instructed to engage in semantic processing after they had completed the nonsemantic orienting task on each word. It is hard to disagree with the following conclusion drawn by Chow et al. (1978): "Subjects are rather poorly aware of the mental processes necessary to support good retention [p. 111]."

Thus far we have seen that there is a characteristic pattern of results in research that compares intentional and incidental learning. There is usually no difference in retention between incidental and intentional learners when both groups are required to perform the same orienting task. Possible reasons for this include insufficient processing time for the intentional learners to do more than perform the orienting task, the use of instructions that do not stress sufficiently the importance of learning the presented material thoroughly, and a lack of awareness on the part of intentional learners of the advantages of semantic processing. Even when conditions are set up in such a way that intentional learners show a memorial advantage over incidental learners, the size of the advantage is usually very much smaller than that gained with the use of semantic orienting tasks over nonsemantic orienting tasks. The conclusion is fairly compelling that memory performance is determined far more by the nature of the processing activities engaged in by the learner than it is by the intention to learn per se.

The further comparison of intentional learners who have to perform an orienting task with those who do not, also produces a fairly clear pattern of results. The typical finding is that intentional learners not performing an orienting task recall at least as well as intentional learners who are given a semantic orienting task, and much better than intentional learners who carry out a nonsemantic orienting task. An implication of these findings is that nonsemantic orienting tasks are a source of interference that reduces the efficiency of memory. It is worth noting that orienting tasks cannot be directly classified as facilitative or interfering when incidental learning is considered, due to the lack of a baseline condition in which there are no instructions to learn the material and no orienting task.

Will intentional learners unhindered by an orienting task always display good retention test performance? Probably not, in spite of the fact that most of the available evidence points to a positive answer. As a result of many years of practice, intentional learners are likely to process the meaning of the stimulus words, and this is typically advantageous with respect to the kinds of retention test normally used. However, if one were to surprise the intentional learner by giving him or her a retention test necessitating recollection of nonsemantic information, then rather poor levels of retention would be anticipated.

Recall versus Recognition

There has been continuing interest over the years in comparing the effects of intention to learn on recall and recognition. Mandler (1979) has identified some of the salient differences between the two kinds of retention test. He argued that intraitem processing, which makes the representation of items in memory more distinguishable from other encoded events, is especially important for recognition memory. In contrast, interitem processing serves an elaborative function by producing interconnections between the target item and other information, and is of greatest value for recall.

Mandler argued that the two types of processing represent different dimensions of organization, but it seems plausible to regard them as different types of rehearsal. In this connection, the findings of Schwartz and Humphreys (1974) are of special interest. They discovered that reducing interitem processing by requiring subjects to rehearse only the item currently being presented reduced recall by over 20%, but had no effect at all on recognition memory.

In general terms, it seems plausible to assume that intentional learners will be more likely than incidental learners to rehearse different list words together. This increased interitem processing should facilitate recall but have little or no effect on recognition memory. Whereas there are several studies that we have already discussed in which there was no effect of intentionality on free recall, it is possible that the orienting tasks used in those studies inhibited rehearsal processes. A typical orienting task requires treating each word as a separate entity, and the performance of an orienting task may tend to displace previous words from working memory, and thus restrict concurrent rehearsal of different list words.

An implication of this position is that intentional learners might recall more than incidental learners if conditions were favorable for interitem processing. Hyde and Jenkins (1973) found that intentional learners recalled more than incidental learners when the list contained associatively related words, but not when the words were unrelated; perhaps intentional learners were more likely to rehearse different list words together when there was a discernible structure to the list.

The first systematic attempt to compare the effects of intentionality on recall and recognition was by Postman, Adams, and Phillips (1955). An incidental learner spelled each nonsense syllable as it was presented on a memory drum, and an intentional learner pronounced the syllable as soon as it had been spelled out by the incidental learner. Intentionality did not affect either free recall or recognition; however, intention to learn tended to increase recall of low associative-value syllables but to reduce recall of high associative-value syllables.

Eagle and Leiter (1964) found that the free-recall performance of unhindered intentional learners was better than that of incidental learners and of intentional learners who also had to perform the orienting task (writing down the part of speech of each word). In recognition memory, however, these latter two groups performed better than the former group. This study has often been cited as revealing different effects of intention to learn on recall and recognition; in fact, intentionality per se had no effect on either recall or recognition, as indicated by the comparison between incidental and intentional learners, all of whom had performed the orienting task. Intentional learners not doing an orienting task may have performed relatively well on the recall test and poorly on the recognition test because their initial instructions led them to anticipate only a recall test.

From a methodological point of view, the study by Dornbush and Winnick (1967) compares favorably with most of the others. All of the subjects were given the orienting task of pronouncing each word as it appeared. Intention to learn had no effect on recognition memory but did enhance free recall when a relatively slow rate of presentation (4 sec per word) was used.

The most thorough study in this area was carried out by Estes and DaPolito (1967). They presented paired associates consisting of numbers and nonsense syllables, and asked incidental learners to abstract the rule or principle by which each specific number was paired with each nonsense syllable; intentional learners were simply told to learn each pair for a subsequent test. Subjects were presented with two recall tests followed by a recognition test, or with two recognition tests followed by a recall test. On the first test, intentional subjects recalled more than incidental subjects, but there was no effect of intention to learn on recognition memory. On the third test, prior recognition tests enhanced recall only for incidental learners, perhaps because the recognition tests provided an opportunity for them to rehearse appropriate responses. In contrast, prior recall tests impaired recognition memory only for incidental subjects, perhaps because they formed incorrect associations during unsuccessful attempts at recall.

Studies of picture memory have tended to support the generalization that intention to learn affects recall but not recognition. Cohen (1973) presented words and pictures together and discovered that recall was much better for the intentionally learned stimuli (whether words or pictures). Incidental learning was better for pictures than for words, possibly because rehearsal is less necessary for picture recall than for word recall. In contrast, Bird (1976) found that recognition memory for black-and-white line drawings was unaffected by intentionality, and Bower and Karlin (1974) observed that recognition memory for pictures of faces was influenced by the type of orienting task (judgments of sex, likableness, or honesty), but not by intentionality. Bower and Karlin (1974) concluded as follows: "The mode of processing the input is critically important, whereas the intention to learn or the expectation of a retention test appears to be of lesser importance [p. 754]."

What are we to make of these various findings? The first point that needs to be made is that some of the findings (e.g., those of Estes and DaPolito, 1967, and the significant ones of Eagle and Leiter, 1964) involve a confounding between the nature of the orienting task and intentionality, and are thus, strictly speaking, uninterpretable. As a consequence, the notion that intention to learn per se enhances recall but not recognition has only been demonstrated unequivocally within the confines of a single experiment by Dornbush and Winnick (1967). The most appropriate generalization is probably that intention to learn has little or no effect on recognition memory, whereas its effects on recall are more variable. Different effects of intentionality on recall and recognition may mean that interitem processing is more important to recall memory than to recognition memory, but the data are suggestive rather than compelling.

ORIENTING TASKS AND PROCESSING ACTIVITIES

Introduction

Memory theorists in recent years have increasingly focused on the processes involved in human memory rather than on the structure of the memory system. This shift in theoretical emphasis has been reflected at the experimental level by attempts to devise paradigms permitting systematic investigation of the memorial consequences of different processing activities. It has seemed to many researchers that the most appropriate paradigm is one involving incidental learning, with processing of the stimulus material being systematically manipulated by the use of a variety of orienting tasks. Why have incidental learning paradigms been regarded as preferable to intentional learning paradigms? A very influential answer was provided by Craik and Lockhart (1972:677): "Under incidental conditions, the experimenter has a control over the processing the subject applies to the material that he does not have when the subject is merely instructed to learn and uses an unknown coding strategy."

Processing in the incidental learning paradigm is controlled by means of an orienting task which must be performed on each stimulus item. Since there is an infinite number of orienting tasks that can be used, it is obvious that, for purposes of prediction, some kind of theoretically-based classification system for orienting tasks is indispensable. Craik and Lockhart (1972) argued that a key characteristic of any orienting task was the depth of processing that it involved. Depth is determined by the semanticity of processing, that is, the extent to which meaningfulness is extracted from the stimulus. While depth of processing has usually been considered to depend solely on the nature of the orienting task, it is clear that the nature of the stimulus material (e.g., its intrinsic meaningfulness) must also play a part in determining processing depth.

Craik and Lockhart were primarily interested in qualitative differences in the nature of the processing activities that occurred across a range of orienting tasks. However, it seems equally sensible to focus on quantitative differences in the demands imposed by orienting tasks, and a number of theorists have favored this approach (e.g., Craik & Tulving, 1975; Johnson-Laird, Gibbs, & de Mowbray, 1978). It is, of course, entirely possible that both qualitative and quantitative differences in processing play a part in determining retention, and the experimental evidence is broadly consistent with this viewpoint.

Depth of Processing

BASIC FINDINGS

The crucial theoretical assumption that has motivated interest in the effects of depth of processing on incidental learning was put forward by Craik and Lockhart (1972) They argued that there was something intrinsically superior about semantic processing; in their own words,

"Trace persistence is a function of depth of analysis, with deeper levels of analysis associated with more elaborate, longer lasting, and stronger traces [p. 675]."

This prediction has most often been tested in a paradigm in which various groups of subjects each perform a different orienting task on a list of words under incidental learning conditions, followed by an unexpected test of free recall. All groups of subjects receive the same list of words so that any group differences in recall can be attributed to the influence of the orienting tasks themselves rather than to uncontrolled stimulus differences. In practice, most researchers have used a gallimaufry of semantic and nonsemantic orienting tasks, and it has typically been found that tasks of the former type produce much better recall than tasks of the latter type.

A concrete example will clarify the nature of the experimental situation and highlight the importance of certain methodological questions. Hyde and Jenkins (1973) used lists of words that were either associatively related or unrelated, and a different group of subjects carried out each of these five orienting tasks: (a) rating the words for pleasantness (b) estimating the frequency with which each word is used in the English language; (c) detecting the occurrence of the letters "e" and "g" in the list words; (d) deciding the part of speech appropriate to each word; and (e) deciding whether the list words fit into sentence frames. They regarded the first two tasks as semantic tasks and the remainder as nonsemantic tasks. On an unexpected test of free recall given shortly after the completion of the orienting task, retention was 51% higher after the semantic tasks than the nonsemantic tasks on the unrelated list; with the related list, there was an 83% advantage for the semantic tasks.

At first glance, these data provide strong support for the hypothesis that retention is strongly determined by the depth or semanticity of processing. However, the astute reader will find himself or herself asking a series of questions about this study (and the many others like it): How do we know which tasks should be regarded as semantic tasks? Did the orienting tasks really control the subjects' processing activities? Was depth of processing confounded with other variables? Would semantic tasks still lead to superior memory performance if other kinds of retention tests were used (e.g., cued recall or recognition)? These and other methodological issues will now be explored in some detail.

MEASURING PROCESSING DEPTH

If one is attempting to test the assumption that event retention is a direct function of the depth to which events have been processed at input, then a necessary prerequisite is an independent index of depth. Some of the problems associated with the typical failure to provide a measure of processing depth were spelled out by Eysenck (1978a): "In view of the vagueness with which depth is defined, there is the danger of using retention-test performance to provide information about the depth of processing, and then using the putative depth of processing to 'explain' the retention-test performance, a self-defeating exercise in circularity [p. 159]."

It could, of course, be argued that the depth of processing necessitated by the performance of an orienting task is usually fairly obvious. However, there are some anomalies in the literature. For example, Craik (1973) argued that the task of deciding whether or not a word fit into a sentence frame involved semantic processing, whereas Hyde and Jenkins (1973) claimed that their sentence-frame task did not involve semantic processing. In similar fashion, there has been some disagreement in the literature as to whether the orienting task of deciding the part of speech to which a word belongs is a shallow or a deep processing task. Even for those tasks whose depth can apparently be estimated fairly easily, the emphasis has been on a simple dichotomy into semantic versus nonsemantic tasks, rather than on an ordinal scale for different kinds of processing.

In their original formulation, Craik and Lockhart (1972) suggested that the depth of processing involved in carrying out an orienting task might be indexed by processing time. The argument was that processing typically proceeds from the more obvious physical characteristics to the semantic attributes, so that deep levels of processing take longer than shallow levels. In order to test this notion empirically, it has usually been assumed that the time taken for the products of processing to be available to consciousness represents an adequate estimate of processing time, an assumption that may well be erroneous.

Some of the early studies (e.g., Craik, 1973) indicated that processing time was positively related to processing depth. However, this finding raises the methodological problem of processing time and depth being confounded. This particular problem was then resolved in later work (e.g., Craik & Tulving, 1975; Gardiner, 1974), in which it was discovered that stimulus processing time is not necessarily positively related to the putative depth of processing. Indeed, Gardiner found that his subjects performed a semantic task (deciding whether words belonged to a semantic category) *faster* than a shallow or nonsemantic task (deciding whether words contained a particular sound or particular sounds).

It is now clear at an empirical level that processing time does not provide an adequate measure of processing depth. At the theoretical level, the view that processing proceeds in an orderly and rigid manner from shallow to deep levels of analysis has been superseded by the notion that the order in which processing occurs in different processing "domains" is relatively flexible (Lockhart, Craik, & Jacoby, 1976).

It has increasingly been assumed that the search for an adequate measure of processing depth is doomed to failure. However, total pessimism is probably unwarranted in view of recent developments. Parkin (1979) has advocated use of a paradigm in which two words are presented in rapid succession, the second being printed in a certain color of ink. An orienting task is performed on the first word, and the color of the ink in which the second word is printed is named as quickly as possible. Previous work had indicated the existence of an associative interference effect, in which the speed of color naming was inversely related to the strength of the semantic associative link between the two words.

Parkin (1979) argued that this associative interference effect would only occur when the first word was semantically or deeply processed. He found that there was an associative interference effect when a semantic task (deciding whether the word referred to part or all of a living thing) was performed on the first word, but this effect disappeared when a nonsemantic task (deciding whether the word had one or two syllables) was used. These findings validate the allocation of the two tasks to different processing depths, and the subsequent unexpected test of free recall produced the usual memorial superiority of semantic over nonsemantic encodings.

CONTROL OF PROCESSING

Perhaps the most important single assumption that is made by those who compare the effects of various orienting tasks on subsequent retention is that the subject's processing activities are controlled effectively by the orienting tasks used. This assumption may be erroneous for two reasons: the subject may fail to perform all of the processing activities required by a particular orienting task, or the subject may engage in extraneous processing which is not strictly necessitated by the orienting task. In practice, it is relatively easy to be sure that adequate processing has occurred; all that is necessary is that the subject provide a separate response (vocal or written) for each stimulus item. These responses can then be evaluated to see whether they are in line with task demands.

The problem of additional or extraneous processing is more vexatious. Nelson (1979) argued in favor of what he referred to as the "focal" code assumption. According to this, an orienting task focuses the encoding operations on particular features, but other attributes are also processed and incorporated into the memorial representation. As an example, Hyde and Jenkins (1973) found that incidental learners who checked for the occurrence of "e"'s and "g"'s in a set of unrelated words recalled almost seven words on average. It seems improbable that this level of recall performance was mediated solely by encoding two letters of the alphabet!

Even more conclusive and devastating data were reported by Stein (1978). A series of words was presented, with each word having one letter capitalized. Subjects had to either decide whether each word fitted appropriately into a sentence frame (semantic task) or determine whether each word had a particular letter capitalized (case task). On the subsequent recognition test, some of the subjects had to select the list word from distractors consisting of nonlist words with the same letter capitalized in a similar lexical configuration. If subjects in the case encoding condition had really limited their processing to the capitalized letter itself, then their performance on this recognition test would have been at chance level. In fact, they recognized 75% of the list words (chance expectation = 25%).

Stein's data provide conclusive proof that subjects in an incidental learning situation sometimes engage in processing which is extraneous to the demands of the orienting task. The methodological import of these findings is that the alleged control over processing activities provided by using an orienting task under incidental learning conditions is illusory.

This somewhat pessimistic conclusion may prove to be premature, however. One feature of Stein's study is that subjects made a mixture of case and semantic decisions within the word list. Perhaps extraneous processing is more prevalent under these conditions than when each subject performs only one orienting task. This possibility was explored by Coltheart (1977). In one experiment, subjects performed the semantic task of deciding, for some of the list words, whether a word fit into an incomplete sentence and, for the rest of the list words, the phonemic task of judging whether or not a word rhymed with a list word. On the subsequent recognition test, it was expected that errors for semantically processed words would consist mainly of selecting semantically related distractors, and for phonemically processed words the erroneously chosen distractors would tend to be acoustically similar to the original list words. This expectation was based on the assumption that there was no extraneous processing. In fact, the pattern of errors was the same for both types of orienting task, with more semantically related than acoustically related distractor words being selected. This led Coltheart (1977) to the following reasonable conclusion: "Although more items are remembered after the semantic orienting task than the acoustic one, the qualitative nature of the memory trace does not differ for the two tasks [p. 440]."

Coltheart (1977) repeated this experiment with each subject performing only one of the two tasks. Under these circumstances, the phonemic orienting task led predominantly to acoustic distractor errors, whereas the semantic orienting task produced mainly semantic distractor errors. These findings correspond closely to those of Elias and Perfetti (1973). They exposed their subjects to only one orienting task, and discovered that significant acoustic false recognitions occurred only after a phonemic orienting task, whereas semantic false recognitions occurred only after a semantic orienting task. It is intuitively reasonable, and in line with the available evidence, to conclude that relatively more control over a subject's processing activities can be achieved when he or she performs only one orienting task than when two or more different tasks have to be carried out within the list.

CONFOUNDING OF FACTORS

A cursory examination of the extensive literature on depth of processing reveals many cases in which two orienting tasks (e.g., ratings of the pleasantness of words versus detecting the occurrence of the letters "e" and "g" in the spelling of words) are so dissimilar that it is difficult to believe that the only salient difference between them is the presence versus absence of semantic processing. In this particular example, a further obvious difference is that the pleasantness-rating task necessitates treating the word as a whole, whereas the letter-detection task does not. There are several other nonsemantic tasks (e.g., deciding whether words are printed in upper or lower case) of which the same is true. Tasks not requiring analysis of the whole word are most unlikely to mediate high levels of retention, and it may well be that part of what is usually referred to as the depth effect is attributable to this fact.

However, it would probably be unwise to attach too much importance to the confounding discussed in the previous paragraph. Hyde and Jenkins (1973) used the e–g letter-detection task as well as two other nonsemantic orienting tasks that presumably required encoding of the entire word; these were deciding which part of speech a word belonged to, and deciding whether a word fit either of two sentence frames. These allegedly nonsemantic tasks led to low levels of recall that were comparable to recall in the letter-detection task, thus indicating the existence of a depth effect over and above any other effects.

In some studies, the depth of processing has been confounded with the nature of the decision required by the orienting task. When the orienting task involves rating all of the stimulus words on a single subjective scale (e.g., pleasantness), the subject may compare new words with previously presented ones in order to form a consistent scale of judgment, thus producing what Postman and Kruesi (1977) referred to as *displaced rehearsal*. Such rehearsal may facilitate recall by increasing the number of associative connections among the stimulus words.

Other orienting tasks may produce much less displaced rehearsal. For example, the task of estimating the frequency of usage in the language of certain words may be accomplished by relying on nonlist words of widely varying frequencies. Some nonsemantic orienting tasks (e.g., detecting the number of occurrences of a specified letter) involve attributes which are objective and distinguishable directly; such tasks should virtually eliminate displaced rehearsal.

There does not appear to have been any direct examination of the crucial role assigned theoretically to displaced rehearsal. However, it is clear that the rating process per se can be an important factor. When the dimension of rating was held constant by using ratings of the pleasantness of the meaning of words as the semantic orienting task and ratings of the pleasantness of the sounds of words as the nonsemantic task, there was very little effect of processing depth on either recall or recognition (Eagle & Mulliken, 1974).

A more complete examination of the relative importance of dimension of rating and depth of processing was undertaken by Postman and Kruesi (1977). Two of their four orienting tasks involved pleasantness ratings (pleasantness of meaning or of sound), and the other two involved frequency ratings (frequency of usage of the words in the language or average frequency of occurrence in the language of the component syllables of the words). Subsequent recall was higher under the semantic conditions (i.e., word pleasantness and frequency-of-usage conditions) than the nonsemantic conditions; it was also higher after pleasantness ratings than after frequency ratings. The effect of dimension of rating was so large that there was no difference in recall between the semantic frequency and nonsemantic pleasantness conditions.

Another potentially important source of confounding is between depth of processing and difficulty of processing. There are a priori reasons for arguing that semantic orienting tasks are more difficult than nonsemantic orienting tasks, because the former typically require a greater transformation of the presented stimulus than the latter. However, it could also be argued that most people have had more practice at semantic than at most forms of nonsemantic processing, with the result that semantic processing can be performed relatively effortlessly.

There are also two possible schools of thought with respect to the likely memorial consequences of variations in processing difficulty. On the one hand, relatively difficult orienting tasks may ensure that considerable attention is devoted to the stimulus words, thus enhancing subsequent retention. On the other hand, if the orienting task is very difficult or demanding, it may disrupt the processing activities that produce increased storage, and thus retention performance might be inversely related to processing difficulty.

Most of the evidence suggests that semantic processing is more demanding than nonsemantic processing. Eysenck and Eysenck (1979) assessed expended processing capacity (an approximate measure of task difficulty) by recording the amount of slowing down of simple reaction time during the concurrent performance of an orienting task. Expended processing capacity was greater when subjects were engaged in a concurrent semantic orienting task than when they performed a physical orienting task, suggesting that semantic tasks are, in some sense, more difficult than physical tasks. However, there are some fairly obvious qualifications that need to be borne in mind. For example, it is likely that, as a result of protracted practice, semantic decisions can be made automatically with minimal expenditure of processing capacity.

To what extent is incidental learning affected by the difficulty of the orienting task? Eysenck and Eysenck (1979) considered all of the conditions in their experiment, and obtained an overall correlation of .48 between expended processing capacity and free recall. While this is a significant correlation, some of the findings argued against the notion that retention is generally higher after more demanding processing. Words associated with positive decisions on the orienting task tended to be better recalled than those associated with negative responses, but expended processing capacity was *greater* on negative trials than on positive trials.

Walsh and Jenkins (1973) compared recall obtained after a semantic orienting task with that obtained after performing two orienting tasks (one semantic and one nonsemantic). The level of recall was similar whether one or two tasks were performed, despite the apparently greater difficulty of carrying out two tasks in the limited time available. However, recall was in fact higher in the single semantic task condition than in any of the ten different combined task conditions, and the average superiority of the former task in free recall was approximately 21%. This provides suggestive evidence that retention is inversely related to the difficulty of the orienting task.

Hyde (1973) compared free recall of subjects performing two orienting tasks (both either semantic or nonsemantic) with that of subjects performing only a single task. Task difficulty had no effect on amount recalled or the extent to which recall was semantically organized. However, it should be noted that Klein and Saltz (1976) did a similar experiment, and found that free recall was significantly better when two semantic tasks were performed rather than one. The most obvious reason for these apparently inconsistent findings is that Klein and Saltz's subjects were self-paced, whereas those of Hyde were experimenter-paced and usually had insufficient time to complete both tasks.

Walsh and Jenkins (1973) and Hyde (1973) adopted the approach of manipulating task difficulty while holding depth of processing constant. Treisman and Tuxworth (1974) followed the opposite procedure of equating orienting tasks in terms of difficulty while varying the level of processing. The orienting task involved listening either for a particular initial phoneme or for a semantically anomalous phrase in sentential material, and both tasks were of equal difficulty in the sense that they gave comparable detection frequencies. In spite of this control over difficulty, sentences were better recalled after the semantic task than after the phonemic task, especially when the retention interval was 20 sec rather than an extremely short length of time.

Of the various possible confounding variables we have considered, the evidence appears to be weakest that task difficulty per se is of major consequence in determining retention. There are other factors unmentioned so far that may be of far greater significance. For example, Anderson and Reder (1979) argued that depth of processing was frequently confounded with the amount of elaboration of the stimulus material, with deeper levels of analysis being associated with richer and more elaborate memory traces. The reason given for this is that, as a result of accumulated experience, most people are better able to generate semantic elaborations of the presented stimuli than nonsemantic elaborations.

There is a further possible confounding between depth of processing and distinctiveness of processing. Jacoby (1974) found that phonemic encodings were much less affected by context than semantic encodings, suggesting that different phonemic encodings of the same word would be very similar or nondistinctive. Eysenck and Eysenck (1980) gave subjects the phonemic orienting task of pronouncing nouns with irregular grapheme–phoneme correspondence as if they had regular grapheme–phoneme correspondence (e.g., pronouncing *glove* to rhyme with *cove*). This presumably produced distinctive encodings that were, in fact, recognized as well as semantic encodings and much better than normal phonemic encodings.

In sum, no straightforward interpretation of the effects of depth on retention is possible. Orienting tasks that differ in depth often differ also with respect to the type of decision required, whether the word must be treated as a whole, difficulty of processing, ease of elaboration, and distinctiveness of processing. As a result, identification of the causal factor or factors responsible for retention is difficult.

RETRIEVAL CONDITIONS

As has been pointed out a number of times (e.g., Eysenck, 1978a, 1978b, 1979), the most crucial problem with the Craik and Lockhart (1972) formulation and the paradigm associated with it is the relative (or even absolute!) neglect of retrieval factors. It is only valid to extrapolate from the results of free-recall studies provided that the ordering of different orienting tasks with respect to memory performance remains invariant, irrespective of the nature of the retention test. In other words, the existence of significant interactions between orienting tasks and retention tests would indicate that the effects of different orienting tasks on memory can only be understood by taking into account the ways in which memory is assessed.

Tulving (1979) has argued that it should be routine to include at least two encoding conditions as well as two retrieval conditions in memory experiments, so that interactions between storage and retrieval can be detected. According to Tulving, these interactions can be understood within the context of his notion of "encoding specificity." The encoding specificity hypothesis proposed that, "retrieval of event information can only be effected by retrieval cues corresponding to a part of the total encoding pattern representing the perceptual cognitive registration of the occurrence of that event [Thomson & Tulving, 1970:261]." This hypothesis was followed by Tulving and Thomson's (1973) encoding specificity principle, according to which, "only that can be retrieved that has been stored, and how it can be retrieved depends on how it was stored [p. 359]."

A somewhat more precise statement was offered by Tulving (1979): "The probability of successful retrieval of the target item is a monotonically increasing function of informational overlap between the information present at retrieval and the information stored in memory [p. 408]." These theoretical statements (especially the more recent ones) suffer from a lack of testability (e.g., there is no adequate measure of "informational overlap"). Nevertheless, the notion that memory operates on a lock-and-key basis (with the lock corresponding to the stored information and the key representing retrieval information) has proved fruitful.

Tulving's views have two major implications for studies of incidental learning: (a) the apparent memorial consequences of different orienting tasks will be greatly affected by the retrieval information available on the retention test; and (b) if there is minimal informational overlap between a semantically encoded item and the information present at retrieval, then the normal "depth" effect could be reversed.

Both of these predictions were convincingly supported in an instructive study by Stein (1978), which was discussed at some length in the section, "Control of Processing." In essence, semantic and case orienting tasks were followed by a recognition test that required retrieval of either semantic or case information. On the semantically-based recognition test, semantic encodings were better recognized than case encodings (93% correct versus 76%, respectively); more importantly, case encodings were significantly better recognized than semantic encodings on the case-based test (45% correct versus 29%, respectively). The latter finding, of course, disproves the hypothesis that deep encodings are invariably stronger and longer lasting than shallow encodings. In addition, since the results from the two recognition tests were diametrically opposed, it is clear that the use of only one form of retention test would have considerably distorted the interpretation of the findings.

Interactions between encoding and retrieval conditions have also been obtained in several other studies of incidental learning (e.g., Davies & Cubbage, 1976; Morris, Bransford, & Franks, 1977). In spite of these interaction effects, it could still be argued that there is a main effect of processing depth in addition to any interaction, a position that was adopted by Fisher and Craik (1977). However, if Stein's (1978) data are pooled across the two recognition tests, then there is no overall effect of depth on recognition performance.

Fisher and Craik (1977) measured the retention of semantically and phonemically encoded words in a cued recall test in which the cues were identical, similar, or different from the study cues. There was a mean effect of depth, and the recall superiority of the semantically encoded words over the phonemically encoded words increased as the compatibility between encoding and test conditions was increased from different through similar to identical cues (6% through 18% to 30%).

Fisher and Craik (1977) concluded that, "the beneficial effects of similarity between encoding context and cue are greatest with deep, semantic encodings [p. 709]." In other words, depth of processing and compatibility between trace and retrieval environment information are both of importance. However, on the basis of their data, it would be just as persuasive to argue that some encoding conditions are better than others.

While it is clear in a general sense that a thorough investigation of incidental learning requires the consideration of various retrieval conditions, so far we have not discussed the relative merits of different techniques. One popular approach is the method of false recognitions, which has been used in several studies (e.g., Coltheart, 1977; Davies & Cubbage, 1976; Elias & Perfetti, 1973). The recognition test includes a number of different kinds of words: words that were presented during acquisition, unrelated control words, and words sharing particular features with acquisition words (e.g., phonemic or semantic). The argument is that if, say, phonemic distractors are selected more often than unrelated distractors, then phonemic processing must have occurred.

This method poses some problems of interpretation. For example, it may be reasonable to say that a tendency to select distractors that are semantically related to list words demonstrates that the subject has processed the list words semantically. However, since these distractors are not identical semantically to their corresponding list words, they would not be selected if really thorough semantic processing had occurred. They would also not be selected if complete orthographic or phonemic information were available. Thus, this method represents a rather indirect and imprecise method of assessing what has been stored.

A more direct method which produces data that are easier to interpret is cued recall. The major assumption is that if a cue (which may be phonemically, semantically, orthographically, or otherwise related to a list word) produces recall, then the memory trace of that word must have contained the appropriate attribute or feature. This is a preferable method to that based on false recognitions; it is discussed more thoroughly in the chapter by Watkins and Gardiner (Chapter 6 of this volume).

ADDITIONAL FACTORS

In many of the studies of incidental learning, the orienting tasks have involved asking the subject questions of a semantic or nonsemantic nature (e.g., *Does* ———— belong to the category of four-footed animals? Does ———— rhyme with hare?). Words associated with positive responses are better recalled than words associated with negative responses (e.g., Craik, 1973). Since positive and negative items are presumably processed to the same depth, some additional explanatory construct is required; in this connection, the importance of "congruity" between question and word has been stressed. Craik (1977) suggested that there is greater trace integration on positive trials; this serves to facilitate reconstructive retrieval.

One potential problem with some of the studies is that the number of words associated with any particular orienting-task question has not remained constant across each processing depth. For example, the non-semantic case orienting task has usually involved a single question (e.g., *Is the word printed in capital letters?*), whereas semantic orienting tasks often involve several different questions. Moscovitch and Craik (1976) associated either one or ten words with each encoding question in each of three orienting tasks (rhyme, category, and sentence). Cued recall was better when there was a unique encoding question, but the advantage of uniqueness was much greater with semantic tasks than with the non-semantic rhyme task. Phonemic encodings may suffer little from the cue-sharing manipulation because they are intrinsically nondistinctive due to the limited pool of phonemes from which all words are formed. At a more general level, the type of processing that an item receives is by no means the only major determinant of retention; the retrievability of any item depends on the way in which other list items are encoded, and intralist interference and other characteristics of the list need to be considered.

Repetition, Rehearsal, and Elaboration

INTRODUCTION

Craik and Lockhart (1972), in their original formulation, argued that memory could be facilitated by deeper processing, but not by repeated processing at any given depth. This aspect of their theorizing led them to distinguish between two major types of processing: "Type I processing, that is, repetition of analyses which have already been carried out, may be contrasted with Type II processing which involves deeper analysis of the stimulus. Only this second type of rehearsal should lead to improved memory performance [p. 276]."

This theoretical stance is in vivid contrast to the prevalent assumption that repeated processing usually does enhance subsequent retention. For example, Atkinson and Shiffrin (1968) argued that repeated processing of an item by means of rehearsal in the short-term store led to increased transfer of information about that item into long-term memory.

As a prelude to the subsequent discussion of the effects on memory of repeated processing at any particular level of analysis, it is important to distinguish three rather different ways in which such processing can occur:

1. The duration of time for which an orienting task is performed on each once-presented word is increased.
2. Some stimulus items are presented more than once, but exactly

the same orienting task is used on each presentation. This approach considers repetition of processing.

3. Some stimulus items are presented more than once, but different orienting tasks requiring a constant level or depth of processing are used on each presentation. This approach considers elaboration of processing.

DURATION AND REPETITION OF PROCESSING

In spite of Craik and Lockhart's (1972) claim that repeated processing at any one depth of analysis would not enhance retention, it has usually been found that repeated processing of an item (even with an identical orienting task on each repetition) leads to a fairly substantial improvement in memory. In one of the methodologically sounder studies, Nelson (1977) presented words once or twice; the same phonemic or semantic question was asked on each presentation of the twice-presented words. After the list had been presented, Nelson gave his subjects three retention tests in the order free recall, cued recall, and recognition. Repetition led to a substantial improvement in memory performance irrespective of the nature of the retention test. As often happens with this type of experiment, the beneficial effect of repetition was comparable for the two different kinds of orienting task (phonemic and semantic). Repeating the phonemic task did not appear to enhance free recall merely by producing greater depth of processing, since recall was not semantically organized in this condition.

Nelson (1977) noted that several previous studies had failed to detect any effects of repetition on memory. Some of these failures may have been due to "floor" effects, that is, the level of retention-test performance was so low in all conditions that the effects of repetition were masked. In other studies, subjects were not required to make overt responses, so that one cannot be sure that repeated processing actually occurred. However, the most important reason is that repeated processing produced by re-presenting each stimulus item is more likely to enhance memory than is repeated processing produced by lengthening the processing duration of a once-presented item.

This last factor was investigated by Rundus (1977). He devised an ingenious technique in which the subjects were told that their main task was to remember some numbers for a few seconds and were also told that they had to rehearse a single word repeatedly during the retention interval to prevent them from thinking about the numbers. However, at the end of the experiment the subjects were unexpectedly asked to recall all of the words. Recall performance was essentially unrelated to the length of time for which repeated rehearsal was required; this remained the case in modified versions of the basic paradigm in which the orienting task involved generating rhymes of each word or supplying several different words belonging to the same semantic category as the presented word. On the other hand, and in line with the findings of Nelson (1977), the probability of recall increased considerably when a word was presented for rehearsal on more than one trial. If one compares recall for a once-presented word rehearsed for 12 sec with a thrice-presented word rehearsed for 4 sec on each of its presentations, the total rehearsal time was the same, but recall was 21% in the former case and 40% in the latter. The beneficial effect of repeated presentations on memory may be due to the establishment of additional temporal–contextual access routes to an item.

Glenberg, Smith, and Green (1977) independently devised the same paradigm as Rundus (1977). They manipulated the duration of rehearsal, and discovered that a ninefold increase in rehearsal time produced a negligible 1.5% increase in recall. In contrast, increased rehearsal time produced a definite improvement in recognition memory. Glenberg and Adams (1978) replicated that finding, and also demonstrated that it is the phonemic components of the memory trace which are strengthened by prolonged rote rehearsal.

In sum, increasing the length of time for which an item is processed repeatedly in the same way facilitates recognition but not recall. This may be because the repeated processing does not promote the increased interitem processing that would enhance recall, but does lead to intraitem processing. When items are presented more than once but processed in the same fashion on each occasion, there is a distinct repetition effect on both recall and recognition.

ELABORATION OF PROCESSING

In a number of studies of incidental learning, experimenters have presented some of the items more than once and asked subjects to perform two somewhat different orienting tasks, or answer questions of the same type (e.g., phonemic, semantic) on each presentation. It has usually been assumed that this will produce greater spread, breadth, or elaboration of encoding than occurs for once-presented words.

Craik and Tulving (1975) discovered that the effects of repetition on recall depended on the level of processing: there were greater effects of repetition when the repeated items were processed semantically than when they were processed nonsemantically. Did each presentation of an item result in an independent memory trace being formed? Apparently not, because that would imply that the probability of recall after two presentations would be less than twice as high as that after a single presentation, whereas Craik and Tulving actually found that repetition more than doubled the probability of recall.

Rather similar results were reported by Goldman and Pellegrino ` (1977). In addition, they discovered that there was a smaller effect of elaboration on recognition than on recall, and multiple encodings enhanced recognition memory *less* at the semantic level than at the orthographic and acoustic levels. However, this was probably due to a ceiling effect.

Since people usually possess far more semantic than nonsemantic information about words, there is much more scope for elaboration of processing at the semantic level. While elaboration at the semantic level has usually led to enhanced retention, there are difficulties of interpretation with several of the studies. In particular, since elaboration is often produced by requiring subjects to answer two different questions about an item, it is possible that the beneficial effects of elaboration are attributable solely to an increase in the number of potential retrieval cues based on recollection of the original questions.

A study that avoided these methodological problems was reported by Johnson-Laird, Gibbs, and de Mowbray (1978). Subjects had to decide whether each word referred to something belonging to the category of substances that are consumable, solid, and natural. The individual words possessed zero, one, two, or all three components of the category. Elaboration or amount of processing was defined as the number of decisions about an item that yielded information relevant to the task in hand; on average, the more components of the category possessed by a word, the more such decisions are necessary. Recall was substantially affected by the number of shared components, ranging from 32% when no components were possessed, through 45% when two components were possessed, to 57% when all three components were possessed.

It has often been assumed, whether explicitly or implicitly, that retention is progressively enhanced by the sheer quantity or number of elaborations that are produced by the orienting tasks used in an experiment. However, it is likely that the nature of any elaborations must be taken into account as well as their numerosity. Bransford, Franks, Morris, and Stein (1979) provided their subjects with minimally elaborated similes (e.g., *A mosquito is like a doctor because they both draw blood*) or with multiply elaborated similes (e.g., *A mosquito is like a raccoon because they both have head, legs, jaws*). Recall with the first noun given as a cue (e.g., *mosquito*) was inversely related to degree of elaboration, with the minimal-elaboration condition producing almost perfect performance, whereas the multiple-elaboration condition led to relatively poor recall. In other words, the nature and precision of semantic elaborations need to be considered when predicting the effects of elaboration on retention. An obvious methodological problem is that the subjects may have made many uncontrolled semantic elaborations, in spite of the use of a rapid rate of presentation.

While semantic elaboration refers in a general way to increased semantic analysis, it is possible to distinguish between elaboration that involves additional processing of any given list item (intraitem processing), and elaboration that involves associating or organizing the list items together in some way (interitem processing). The emphasis in the literature on incidental learning has been very much on semantic elaboration of the former type, but there is evidence that elaboration involving interitem relationships is also important.

The two types of elaboration were compared by Bellezza, Cheesman, and Reddy (1977). Intraitem semantic elaboration was manipulated by varying the length of the sentences that subjects were asked to construct of the different list words. Interitem semantic elaboration was produced by asking the subjects to produce sentences forming part of a story for some of the words. Intraitem elaboration had no effect on subsequent free recall of the words, but interitem elaboration produced an increase of approximately 60% in recall. Bellezza *et al.* concluded as follows: "After a certain amount of semantic processing has taken place, further semantic processing or semantic elaboration of a word will not increase its probability of recall. Organization of the word must then occur if the probability of recall is to increase [p. 548]."

It is clear that different kinds of semantic elaborations have different effects on retention. One plausible way of interpreting these data is to subdivide deep or semantic processing into a number of more specific processing levels. For example, Perfetti (1979) has identified several semantic levels of sentence processing, including the referential, the thematic, and the functional (which is concerned with intentions and motivations). One of my students (Jackie Laws) has had some success in applying Perfetti's conceptualization to memory data.

CONCLUSIONS

The major inadequacy of experimentation on incidental learning is the relatively narrow range of factors that has been researched systematically. As Jenkins (1979) pertinently reminded us, human learning and memory depend upon at least four major classes of factors: the nature of the task given to the subject; the stimulus materials presented to the subject; characteristics of the subjects (e.g., their skills and past experience); and the nature of the retention test or other measure of acquisition.

While it may seem trite to emphasize the wide range of factors that jointly determine memory performance, it is obvious that most workers on incidental learning have paid little heed to most of these factors. All too frequently, investigators have focused on the memorial consequences of a variety of orienting tasks on a single retention test; they have typically only used one kind of stimulus material (usually unrelated words), and only one type of subject is used (i.e., college students).

Does this narrowness matter? Is it not better to study one or two factors in detail than many factors sketchily? The fact of the matter is that such narrowness is inappropriate because there are substantial interactions among the factors discussed above. What these interactions mean is that it is a hazardous business to extrapolate from the findings obtained under limited conditions; nevertheless, such extrapolation has been common in the incidental learning literature.

Let us now attempt to flesh out this argument. At the level of first-order interactions, there are three kinds of possible interactions involving orienting tasks. First, there are interactions between orienting tasks and stimulus materials. Jenkins (1979) reported a study in which the words that were subsequently tested for recall were presented embedded in sentences. Under those circumstances the usual retention differences between semantic and nonsemantic orienting tasks failed to occur, presumably because the sentential context led subjects to process the words semantically in all conditions. Jacoby, Bartz, and Evans (1978) compared recall for trigrams varying in meaningfulness that were processed either by a semantic or nonsemantic orienting task. The usual depth effect was obtained when the trigrams were high in meaningfulness, but not when they were low in meaningfulness. The implication is that stimulus materials must be fairly meaningful in order to permit semantic analysis. These findings also intriguingly suggest that an accurate assessment of depth of processing requires joint consideration of the orienting task and the stimulus material, rather than the orienting task alone, as has nearly always been the case.

Second, there are interactions between orienting tasks and subjects. Without actually doing the experiment, we know that there would be no memorial advantage of semantic over nonsemantic orienting tasks if the tasks were those commonly used and the subjects did not know any English! In less extreme form, individual differences in specific skills must have a major impact on the processing that occurs when an orienting task is given. For example, de Groot (1965) found that chess masters were able to reconstruct a chess position almost perfectly after viewing it for only 5 sec or so, whereas less able players showed markedly poorer memory. As a result of enormous experience, the masters were able to organize the pieces in terms of familiar or meaningful constellations, a type of processing that was not available to the less skilled players.

Third, there are interactions between orienting tasks and retention tests. We have documented several examples of such interactions in this chapter (e.g., Coltheart, 1977; Davies & Cubbage, 1976; Morris, Bransford, & Franks, 1977; Stein, 1978). In all cases, the typical superiority in memory of semantic over nonsemantic tasks was either greatly attenuated or even reversed under certain conditions of retrieval.

What does the future hold in store? Let us hope that the recent emphasis on orienting tasks as the only consequential determinant of memory performance in incidental learning studies will be replaced by a more balanced and wide-ranging perspective. We know now that memory is very sensitive to context of all kinds, and our future efforts should be addressed to theoretical explanations of the plethora of interaction effects that occur as a direct result of that sensitivity.

REFERENCES

Anderson, J. R., & Reder, L. An elaborative processing explanation of depth of processing. In L. S. Cermak & F. I. M. Craik (Eds.), *Levels of processing in human memory*. Hillsdale, N. J.: Lawrence Erlbaum Associates, 1979. Pp. 385–403.

Atkinson, R. C., & Shiffrin, R. M. Human memory: A proposed system and its control processes. In K. W. Spence & J. T. Spence (Eds.), *The psychology of learning and motivation*, (Vol. 2). New York: Academic Press, 1968. Pp. 89–195.

Bellezza, F. S., Cheesman, F. C., II, & Reddy, B. G. Organization and semantic elaboration in free recall. *Journal of Experimental Psychology: Human Learning and Memory*, 1977, *3*, 539–550.

Bird, J. E. Effects of intentional and incidental instructions on picture recognition. *Perceptual and Motor Skills*, 1976, *42*, 555–561.

Bower, G. H., & Karling, M. B. Depth of processing pictures of faces and recognition memory. *Journal of Experimental Psychology*, 1974, *103*, 751–757.

Bransford, J. D., Franks, J. J., Morris, C. D., & Stein, B. S. Some general constraints on learning and memory research. In L. S. Cermak and F. I. M. Craik (Eds.), *Levels of processing in human memory*. Hillsdale, N.J.: Lawrence Erlbaum Associates, 1979. Pp. 331–354.

Chow, P. C. P., Currie, J. L., & Craik, F. I. M. Intentional learning and retention of words following various orienting tasks. *Bulletin of the Psychonomic Society*, 1978, *12*, 109–112.

Cohen, G. How are pictures registered in memory? *Quarterly Journal of Experimental Psychology*, 1973, *25*, 557–564.

Coltheart, V. Recognition errors after incidental learning as a function of different levels of processing. *Journal of Experimental Psychology: Human Learning and Memory,* 1977, *3,* 437–444.

Craik, F. I. M. A "levels of analysis" view of memory. In P. Pliner, L. Krames, & T. M. Alloway (Eds.), *Communication and affect: Language and thought.* London: Academic Press, 1973. Pp. 45–65.

Craik, F. I. M. Depth of processing in recall and recognition. In S. Dornic & P. M. A. Rabbitt (Eds.), *Attention and performance,* (Vol. VI). New York: Academic Press, 1977. Pp. 679–697.

Craik, F. I. M., & Lockhart, R. S. Levels of processing: A framework for memory research. *Journal of Verbal Learning and Verbal Behavior,* 1972, *11,* 671–684.

Craik, F. I. M., & Tulving, E. Depth of processing and the retention of words in episodic memory. *Journal of Experimental Psychology: General,* 1975, *104,* 268–294.

Cutting, J. E. Orienting tasks affect recall performance more than subjective impressions of ability to recall. *Psychological Reports,* 1975, *36,* 155–158.

Davies, G., & Cubbage, A. Attribute coding at different levels of processing. *Quarterly Journal of Experimental Psychology,* 1976, *28,* 653–660.

de Groot, A. *Thought and choice in chess.* The Hague: Mouton, 1965.

Dornbush, R. L., & Winnick, W. A. Short-term intentional and incidental learning. *Journal of Experimental Psychology,* 1967, *73,* 608–611.

Eagle, M., & Leiter, E. Recall and recognition in intentional and incidental learning. *Journal of Experimental Psychology,* 1964, *68,* 58–63.

Eagle, M., & Mulliken, S. The role of affective ratings in intentional and incidental learning. *American Journal of Psychology,* 1974, *87,* 409–423.

Elias, C. S., & Perfetti, C. A. Encoding task and recognition memory: The importance of semantic encoding. *Journal of Experimental Psychology,* 1973, *99,* 151–156.

Estes, W. K., & DaPolito, F. Independent variation of information storage and retrieval processes in paired-associate learning. *Journal of Experimental Psychology,* 1967, *75,* 18–26.

Eysenck, M. W. Levels of processing: A critique. *British Journal of Psychology,* 1978, *69,* 157–169. (a)

Eysenck, M. W. Levels of processing: A reply to Craik and Lockhart. *British Journal of Psychology,* 1978, *69,* 177–178. (b)

Eysenck, M. W. Depth, elaboration, and distinctiveness. In L. S. Cermak & F. I. M. Craik (Eds.), *Levels of processing in human memory.* Hillsdale, N.J.: Lawrence Erlbaum Associates, 1979. Pp. 89–118.

Eysenck, M. W., & Eysenck, M. C. Processing depth, elaboration of encoding, memory stores, and expended processing capacity. *Journal of Experimental Psychology: Human Learning and Memory,* 1979, *5,* 472–484.

Eysenck, M. W., & Eysenck, M. C. Effects of processing depth, distinctiveness, and word frequency on retention. *British Journal of Psychology,* 1980, *71,* 263–274.

Fisher, R. P., & Craik, F. I. M. Interaction between encoding and retrieval operations in cued recall. *Journal of Experimental Psychology: Human Learning and Memory,* 1977, *3,* 701–711.

Gardiner, J. M. Levels of processing in word recognition and subsequent free recall. *Journal of Experimental Psychology,* 1974, *102,* 101–105.

Glenberg, A., & Adams, F. Type I rehearsal and recognition. *Journal of Verbal Learning and Verbal Behavior,* 1978, *17,* 455–463.

Glenberg, A., Smith, S. M., & Green, C. Type I rehearsal: Maintenance and more. *Journal of Verbal Learning and Verbal Behavior,* 1977, *16,* 339–352.

Goldman, S. R., & Pellegrino, J. W. Processing domain, encoding elaboration, and memory trace strength. *Journal of Verbal Learning and Verbal Behavior,* 1977, *16,* 29–43.

Hyde, T. S. Differential effects of effort and type of orienting task on recall and organization of highly associated words. *Journal of Experimental Psychology,* 1973, *79,* 111–113.

Hyde, T. S., & Jenkins, J. J. The differential effects of incidental tasks on the organization of recall of a list of highly associated words. *Journal of Experimental Psychology,* 1969, *82,* 472–481.

Hyde, T. S., & Jenkins, J. J. Recall for words as a function of semantic, graphic, and syntactic orienting tasks. *Journal of Verbal Learning and Verbal Behavior,* 1973, *12,* 471–480.

Jacoby, L. L. The role of mental contiguity in memory: Registration and retrieval effects. *Journal of Verbal Learning and Verbal Behavior,* 1974, *13,* 483–496.

Jacoby, L. L., Bartz, W. H., & Evans, J. D. A functional approach to levels of processing. *Journal of Experimental Psychology: Human Learning and Memory,* 1978, *4,* 331–346.

Jenkins, J. J. Four points to remember: A tetrahedral model of memory experiments. In L. S. Cermak & F. I. M. Craik (Eds.), *Levels of processing in human memory.* Hillsdale, N.J.: Lawrence Erlbaum Associates, 1979. Pp. 429–446.

Johnson Laird, P. N., Gibbs, G., & de Mowbray, J. Meaning, amount of processing, and memory for words. *Memory & Cognition,* 1978, *6,* 372–375.

Klein, K. & Saltz, E. Specifying the mechanisms in a levels-of-processing approach to memory. *Journal of Experimental Psychology: Human Learning and Memory,* 1976, *2,* 67 –679.

Lockhart, R. S., Craik, F. I. M., & Jacoby, L. L. Depth of processing, recognition, and recall. In J. Brown (Ed.), *Recall and recognition.* London: John Wiley & Sons, 1976. Pp. 75–102.

Mandler, G. Organization and repetition: Organizational principles with special reference to rote learning. In L.-G. Nilsson (Ed.), *Perspectives on memory research: Essays in honor of Uppsala University's 500th anniversary.* Hillsdale, N.J.: Lawrence Erlbaum Associates, 1979. Pp. 293–327.

McDaniel, M. A., & Masson, M. E. Long-term retention: When incidental semantic processing fails. *Journal of Experimental Psychology: Human Learning and Memory,* 1977, *3,* 270–281.

McGeoch, J. A. *The psychology of human learning.* New York: Longmans, Green, 1942.

McLaughlin, B. "Intentional" and "incidental" learning in human subjects: The role of instructions to learn and motivation. *Psychological Bulletin,* 1965, *63,* 359–376.

Mechanic, A. The responses involved in the rote learning of verbal materials. *Journal of Verbal Learning and Verbal Behavior,* 1964, *3,* 30–36.

Morris, C. D., Bransford, J. D., & Franks, J. J. Levels of processing versus transfer appropriate processing. *Journal of Verbal Learning and Verbal Behavior,* 1977, *16,* 519–533.

Moscovitch, M., & Craik, F. I. M. Depth of processing, retrieval cues, and uniqueness of encoding as factors in free recall. *Journal of Verbal Learning and Verbal Behavior,* 1976, *15,* 447–458.

Nelson, D. L. Remembering pictures and words: Appearance, significance, and name. In L. S. Cermak & F. I. M. Craik (Eds.), *Levels of processing in human memory.* Hillsdale, N.J.: Lawrence Erlbaum Associates, 1979. Pp. 45–76.

Nelson, T. O. Repetition and depth of processing. *Journal of Verbal Learning and Verbal Behavior,* 1977, *16,* 151–172.

Parkin, A. J. Specifying levels of processing. *Quarterly Journal of Experimental Psychology*, 1979, *31*, 175–195.

Perfetti, C. A. Levels of language and levels of process. In L. S. Cermak & F. I. M. Craik (Eds.), *Levels of processing in human memory*. Hillsdale, N.J.: Lawrence Erlbaum Associates, 1979. Pp. 159–181.

Postman, L. Short-term memory and incidental learning. In A. W. Melton (Ed.), *Categories of human learning*. New York: Academic Press, 1964. Pp. 145–201.

Postman, L., Adams, P. A., & Phillips, L. W. Studies in incidental learning: II. The effects of association value and of the method of testing. *Journal of Experimental Psychology*, 1955, *49*, 1–10.

Postman, L., & Kruesi, E. The influence of orienting tasks on the encoding and recall of words. *Journal of Verbal Learning and Verbal Behavior*, 1977, *16*, 353–369.

Rundus, D. Maintenance rehearsal and single-cued processing. *Journal of Verbal Learning and Verbal Behavior*, 1977, *16*, 665–681.

Schwartz, R. M., & Humphreys, M. S. Recognition and recall as a function of instructional manipulations of organization. *Journal of Experimental Psychology*, 1974, *102*, 517–519.

Stein, B. S. Depth of processing re-examined: The effects of the precision of encoding and test appropriateness. *Journal of Verbal Learning and Verbal Behavior*, 1978, *17*, 165–174.

Thomson, D. M., & Tulving, E. Associative encoding and retrieval: Weak and strong cues. *Journal of Experimental Psychology*, 1970, *86*, 255–262.

Till, R. E., & Jenkins, J. J. The effects of cued orienting tasks on the free recall of words. *Journal of Verbal Learning and Verbal Behavior*, 1973, *12*, 489–498.

Treisman, A. M., & Tuxworth, J. Immediate and delayed recall of sentences after perceptual processing at different levels. *Journal of Verbal Learning and Verbal Behavior*, 1974, *13*, 38–44.

Tulving, E. Relation between encoding specificity and levels of processing. In L. S. Cermak & F. I. M. Craik (Eds.), *Levels of processing in human memory*. Hillsdale, N.J.: Lawrence Erlbaum Associates, 1979. Pp. 405–428.

Tulving, E., & Thomson, D. M. Encoding specificity and retrieval processes in episodic memory. *Psychological Review*, 1973, *80*, 352–373.

Walsh, D. A., & Jenkins, J. J. Effects of orienting tasks on free recall in incidental learning: "Difficulty," "effort," and "process" explanations. *Journal of Verbal Learning and Verbal Behavior*, 1973, *12*, 481–488.

CHAPTER **8**

ROBERT V. KAIL, JR.
JEFFREY BISANZ

Cognitive Strategies

INTRODUCTION

Cognitive psychology has expanded well beyond the description of simple mediators between stimulus and response, and consequently the concept of *strategy* has become increasingly important. In contemporary research, identification of strategies is essential for a diverse set of scientific goals, including (*a*) discovery of how complex cognitive tasks are performed, and how simple operations are combined into more complex sequences of activity; (*b*) isolating strategies so that nonstrategic aspects of information processing can be studied; and (*c*) designing instructional procedures that optimize cognitive performance. All of these are important and active areas of research.

As the concept of strategy has become more prevalent, it has also become increasingly ambiguous. Strategy is such a common word that investigators rarely define it explicitly. When use of the term is examined across investigators, a variety of different connotations emerge. All would agree that strategy refers to processes or rules that underlie performance on cognitive tasks, but there are many variations on this theme. Strategy is often defined as planning or manipulation of goals (e.g., Greeno, 1978a) and the term is sometimes used interchangeably with "plan" (e.g., Day, 1975). Gagné and Beard (1978), however, reserve the

229

HANDBOOK OF RESEARCH METHODS IN
HUMAN MEMORY AND COGNITION

term "strategy" to refer to "executive control processes" that monitor and modify other cognitive operations; an algorithm for solving a problem would be considered an "intellectual skill," not a strategy. Most investigators usually use "strategy" to refer to sequences of processing that are relatively long, but the term is sometimes used in connection with rapid decision-making activities as well (e.g., Hunt, 1978). Finally, strategies are frequently considered to be "conscious" and "deliberate" (e.g., Brown, 1975), but the value of these descriptors is dubious since independent measures of consciousness and deliberation are rarely provided.

Disagreement over the exact definition of strategy may be a healthy sign, for it indicates that psychologists have learned enough about human cognition to make distinctions that were formerly unnecessary. Two prototypic features of strategic activity do emerge from the variety of definitions and connotations found in the literature. First, a strategy is a sequence of activities rather than a unitary event. Consequently, a strategy may be characterized both by its component processes and by the organization of these processes into a coherent whole. Second, strategies are considered to be more modifiable and flexible than "reflexive" in nature. The distinction between controlled and automatic processing is useful in this regard (e.g., Shiffrin & Schneider, 1977). Controlled processes are relatively slow and require attentional resources that are limited in supply, but these processes can be modified readily. Automatic processes are more rapid and are not limited by availability of attentional resources, but they are inflexible. Certain components of a strategy may be automatic, but the overall procedure is presumed to be flexible and, at least in principle, can be modified to become more adaptive.

For present purposes, then, strategy refers to a set of internal cognitive procedures, a set that can be modified and is presumed to account for observed patterns of behavior. Having stated a definition, it is important nonetheless to recognize that the term "strategy" may be defined in different ways in particular research contexts.

Identification of strategies has been of special interest to researchers in the areas of memory and problem solving. Yet despite the common concern, different methods for studying strategic activity have evolved in these two areas. In the problem-solving literature several methods are available that can readily be applied to study strategy use on quite different problems. Verbal reports, for example, have been analyzed to study strategies used in chess, geometry, and physics. In the memory literature, methods are more likely to be linked to specific strategies. Separate procedures exist, for example, to assess such mnemonic strategies as rehearsal, organization, and imagery. In this chapter we review methods from both the memory and problem-solving areas of research.

In so doing it is often necessary to choose between *describing* existing methods in great detail and *prescribing* the questions and conceptual issues that should be addressed when attempting to study strategies. We have tried to reach a satisfactory compromise between these two goals, and the reader is encouraged to consult the articles cited in cases where our compromise falls short.

METHODS FROM THE MEMORY LITERATURE

The number of mnemonic strategies that have been studied is so large that it precludes a review of all relevant methods. Consequently, rather than attempting to provide a "cookbook" of paradigms for studying mnemonic strategies, we will discuss how an investigator can determine the procedures that are best suited for assessing a person's strategic activity. We will focus on *rehearsal,* a class of mnemonic strategies defined by repetitive naming of stimuli. Naming may be overt or covert; it may consist of simply repeating the name of the stimulus just presented or naming that stimulus plus stimuli presented previously. We choose rehearsal not because it is an especially powerful mnemonic, but rather on the pragmatic grounds that rehearsal has been investigated extensively in an abundance of paradigms.[1]

Inferential Measurement

Inferential measurement (Belmont & Butterfield, 1977) refers to assessment that is temporally and/or logically separated from ongoing strategic activity. Perhaps the most common inferential measure of rehearsal is the "primacy effect" in recall. The "primacy effect" refers to the phenomenon that stimuli presented early in a relatively long list of stimuli are generally recalled quite accurately, particularly in comparison to stimuli presented in the middle portion of the list. This effect is typically attributed to rehearsal, with the following logic:

1. A common mode of rehearsal is to name the current item plus a sample of previous items.

---

[1] For researchers interested in the "nuts and bolts" of investigating other mnemonic strategies, there are several useful sources. Murdock (1974) reviews most of the major paradigms that have been used to study human memory. Included in several chapters of Kail and Hagen (1977) are discussions of procedures used to study different strategies. Finally, other chapters included in this volume are useful, notably those by Glanzer, Murphy and Puff, Pellegrino and Hubert, and Kosslyn and Holyoak.

2. Such a scheme results in more frequent rehearsal of items presented initially in a list, since they have more opportunities to be included in the sample of items rehearsed (i.e., the *rehearsal set*).
3. Assuming that frequency of rehearsal is correlated positively with the likelihood of recall, if recall of items presented early in a list exceeds recall of subsequent items (e.g., the *primacy effect*), then this suggests that subjects were rehearsing according to the scheme suggested in Assumption 1.

A study by Hagen and Kail (1973) demonstrates the use of this approach. Seven stimuli were shown individually to 7- and 11-year-olds. Each was shown for 2 sec, then turned face down. After all seven simuli had been presented, a duplicate of one stimulus was presented and the child was asked to point to the matching stimulus in the array of face-down stimuli.

Before turning to the results, several methodological features of this study should be noted. First, the instructions simply explained that children should remember the positions of the stimuli. No mention was made regarding the use of rehearsal (or any other mnemonic device). Consequently, any instances of rehearsal would reflect spontaneous strategic activity by the children. Second, only one input position was probed per trial, which means that seven trials were needed to test all seven input positions. This technique yields less data per trial than does free recall, in which an individual simply recalls all stimuli presented on a trial. The probe technique has the advantage, however, that input order is not confounded with output order. Third, the stimuli were presented at a sufficiently slow pace so that rehearsal was feasible. At least 1 sec per stimulus is necessary, and presentation rates of one stimulus every 5 sec are not uncommon.

As can be seen in Figure 8.1, recall by the older children was most accurate for the first stimulus presented and declined consistently over the next few stimuli, a pattern indicative of rehearsal Younger children's recall of all seven stimuli, in contrast, was much poorer, and was essentially constant across the first five input positions, a pattern suggesting that the younger children were not rehearsing. From these data Hagen and Kail (1973) concluded "that children in the 7-year age range do not yet characteristically engage in rehearsal to improve recall, but by age 11 children are proficient in using this strategy [p. 835]."

There are, however, several weak links in the inferential chain between the presence (or absence) of a primacy effect and conclusions regarding rehearsal. First, the distinction between "early" and "sub-

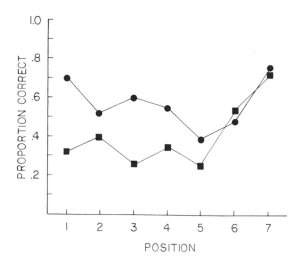

Figure 8.1.[a] Proportion of Correct Responses as a Function of Input Position for 11-Year-Olds (Circles) and 7-Year-Olds (Squares).

[a] From Hagen, J. W., & Kail, R. V. Facilitation and distraction in short-term memory. *Child Development,* 1973, *44,* 833, Figure 1. Copyright 1973 by the Society for Research in Child Development, Inc.

sequent" items is woefully imprecise. Some investigators (Wagner, 1978) use "primacy effect" to refer exclusively to accurate recall of the first item in a list; others (Kail, 1979) have used the term to refer to recall of the first half of the list. Second, recall of the first item in a list can be quite accurate but can reflect processes other than rehearsal. The first item, for example, is less prone to interference from previously presented items, and that may enhance its recall (Rosner, 1972). Third, several rational plans for rehearsal can be constructed in which all items would be rehearsed equally, or approximately so. Recall might then be unrelated to the position of an item in the list and we might erroneously infer that individuals had not rehearsed. Fourth, implicit in the usual interpretation of Assumption 3 is a linear relation between frequency of rehearsal and likelihood of recall. To the extent that this relation is nonlinear, inferences about rehearsal from recall data become increasingly hazardous.

The combined thrust of these criticisms, then, should lead one to be wary of drawing conclusions about rehearsal solely from the presence or absence of primacy effects in recall. More generally, using the primacy effect to assess rehearsal demonstrates problems associated with most inferential measures of strategic activity, including strategies other than rehearsal. Several inferential steps are involved between collecting the data and making conclusions about rehearsal. To the extent that these assumptions are not met, inferences become problematic. Further, verifying these assumptions is no small endeavor. Indeed, mapping relations between strategic activity and retention is the goal of much research in experimental and cognitive psychology.

We suggest, then, the following guidelines for an investigator proposing to use an inferential measure of strategic activity. First, do not assume any simple or direct relation between strategic activity and a measure of retention. Second, use a measure and paradigm for which the inferential sequence has been evaluated in previous work (not just assumed by others as well). Third, collect additional data that can corroborate the inferential measure.

Direct Measurement

Direct measurement refers to concurrent, "on-line" assessment of strategic activity, usually through measurement of some overt behavior. In a direct measurement analog of the Hagen and Kail (1973) study, Flavell, Beach, and Chinsky (1966) asked 5-, 7-, and 10-year-olds to recall several pictures in order. Rehearsal was assessed by observing a child's spontaneous verbalizations. This procedure was feasible for several reasons. First, pretesting suggested that children of this age would probably rehearse overtly rather than covertly. Second, pictures were selected whose names were quite discriminable from one another. Third, the observer had considerable practice reading lips, so that he could reliably record children's verbalizations. Fourth, during the period between presentation of the stimuli and recall, an opaque visor prevented the child from viewing the stimuli but allowed the observer to carefully watch the child's mouth and lips.

Only 5% of the 5-year-olds verbalized on most of the recall trials. Among the 7-year-olds, 60% rehearsed the stimuli, but only 25% did so regularly. Up to and including age 10, 85% rehearsed, and 65% did so routinely. Thus, these data, like those of Hagen and Kail (1973), suggested that not until 9 or 10 years of age do children typically rely upon rehearsal as a method of remembering.

This study represents direct measurement at its best. The strategy of interest was simple, with a clear behavioral manifestation; the tricky inferential steps discussed earlier were bypassed. If all strategies could be tapped in this straightforward manner, direct measurement might be the only approach needed. But the fact of the matter is that not all strategies can be easily studied in this way. Many mnemonic strategies have no obvious behavioral indicants. Visual imagery, for example, is a powerful mnemonic, but we know of no suitable direct measure (see Reese, 1977, and Kosslyn & Holyoak, this volume, for further commentary).

A related problem is that behavioral indexes of strategic activity may not be equally appropriate for all persons. Had Flavell *et al.* (1966) tested adolescents and adults they would probably have noted a decline in verbalization, a finding that certainly reflects the subvocalization of, rather than the disappearance of rehearsal. In this case, one approach has been to "externalize" the strategy so that it can be measured directly. Rundus and Atkinson (1970), for example, presented 20 words, one every 5 sec. Subjects were told "to study by repeating aloud items from the current list during the 5-second study intervals. There were no restrictions placed on the choice of items to be rehearsed or the rate of rehearsal as long as S's rehearsal filled the interval [Rundus & Atkinson, 1970, p. 100]." Subjects' rehearsal was tape recorded and could thus be analyzed directly.

This procedure is not without its shortcomings, however. First, requiring adults to rehearse overtly may change their rehearsal. Unfortunately, this problem cannot be addressed directly. One could compare individuals tested using the Rundus and Atkinson procedure with individuals allowed to rehearse covertly. However, such comparisons can only involve measures of retention, not strategic activity, since difficulties in measuring adults' overt rehearsal led to the Rundus–Atkinson procedure in the first place. This comparison is fraught with interpretive problems, for comparable recall need not imply comparable strategic activity.

A second issue concerns the spontaneity of the rehearsal observed in this procedure. The instructions given by Rundus and Atkinson were probably sufficiently vague so that they did not constrain subjects' selection of strategies. However, this could be a problem in other settings. For example, in some developmental research the general instruction "to study by repeating aloud items from the current list" would certainly prompt young children to behave in ways they would not have otherwise.

Correlative Measurement

Correlative measure is a compromise between direct and inferential measurement in that an investigator directly observes a close correlate of the strategy of interest. Belmont and Butterfield (1971), for example, devised a measure of rehearsal that was based on a person's allocation of study time.[2] Adolescents were asked to remember sets of six letters. Each letter was presented individually for approximately .5 sec, but subjects controlled the length of time between presentation of letters. Specifically, the apparatus consisted of several adjacent windows in which a letter could be displayed. By pushing a button, a subject could view each letter once, beginning with the letter in the left-hand window and moving serially to the last window on the right. The amount of time between offset of one letter and onset of the next was totally under the subject's control and was recorded automatically.

Previous experimentation, in which subjects were told specifically to rehearse, had revealed a distinctive pattern of "pauses" associated with rehearsal: Pauses gradually increase in length as each successive stimulus is presented, presumably reflecting the ever greater amount of time needed to rehearse the growing set of letters. In contrast, individuals who do not rehearse tend to present each letter for a relatively constant period of time. By recording the time that subjects allocate for study of each letter and examining these pause-time profiles, one can decide if subjects are indeed rehearsing.

Thus, in the correlative aproach, as in the inferential approach, the strategy is not observed directly, but instead a byproduct of the strategy is measured. However, unlike the inferential approach and in common with the direct approach, measurement is concurrent with the strategic activity of interest, rather than separated temporally from it.

One limiting factor for all correlative measures is the evidence indicating that the behavior measured and the strategy of interest are indeed closely correlated. In the case of Belmont and Butterfield's (1971) pause-time technique, the correlation is well established, since requiring subjects to rehearse produces a clear, distinct profile of pauses that can be used to decide if a subject is rehearsing spontaneously. A second limiting factor is that, as with direct measurement, correlative measures are not available for all mnemonic strategies of interest.

Recommendations

Which approach is the preferred method for studying people's use of mnemonic strategies? This depends, to a very large extent, upon the

---

[2] Belmont and Butterfield (1977) consider this technique a form of direct measurement. Exact placement of the technique along a continuum from direct to inferential measurement is not critical, as the framework is intended for heuristic rather than theoretical purposes. We agree that their procedure is a form of direct measurement if one is interested in allocation of time per se; if one makes inferences from study time to rehearsal, classification as a correlative measure seems more appropriate.

specific aims of an experiment. The inferential approach provides a completely unobtrusive means of measuring strategies, and thus may be the best way of tapping truly spontaneous strategic activity. Yet the same characteristics that make inferential measurement unobtrusive make it difficult for an investigator to have complete confidence that the strategy of interest is actually being measured. Direct measurement reduces the problem of accuracy of measurement, and thus is the best approach when one is interested in the specific contents or components of strategic activity. Direct measurement is, however, limited in applicability. Also it may prompt behaviors, and so it must be used carefully when the focus is spontaneous strategic activity. Correlative measurement takes the middle ground, combining the strengths and limitations of the other two approaches. No single approach is entirely satisfactory because each has drawbacks that preclude its being the sole source of a data base regarding strategic activity (cf. Belmont & Butterfield, 1977). Wherever possible, complementary methods (e.g., inferential and direct measures) should be used to provide converging data.

METHODS FROM THE PROBLEM-SOLVING AND REASONING LITERATURE

People often need several seconds to solve an analogy, minutes to decide on the optimal move in chess, and even longer to solve a problem in electronic circuitry or computer programming. The lengthy interval between presentation of a problem and its ultimate solution is filled with cognitive activity, making a complete description of a person's strategies a difficult task. To obtain more information about strategies, researchers have sought to develop methods that increase the *density of observations* during the interval between presentation and solution of a problem. These methods are now numerous and diverse, so it is no longer feasible to characterize the entire range of existing techniques (see Coates, Alluisi, & Morgan, 1971; Ray, 1955). Instead, we shall discuss a few prototypic methods that have been adapted for a variety of research purposes.

Task Analysis

Most investigations of problem solving and reasoning begin with *task analysis,* a procedure for arriving at an initial description of the strategies and processes underlying performance on a task. Task analysis is not a formal and standard set of procedures; the type of analysis will vary depending on the theoretical framework of the investigator (Resnick,

1976) as well as the extent and sophistication of available research and theory. Nevertheless, the outcome of these analyses is always an explicit statement of all cognitive activity that occurs between initial presentation and final solution of a problem.

In analyzing a task, an investigator might gain insights from existing cognitive theories, from the results of previous experiments with related tasks, from work in artificial intelligence, or from introspections of individuals who solve the task. Literally *any* relevant information can be used, for the objective of task analysis is to provide an explicit, testable model of the activities involved in solving the problem. Whether the initial model describes what humans actually do is a matter for subsequent experimentation.

Task analyses vary greatly in complexity and detail (see Case, 1978; Hunt, 1974), but for present purposes a simple example is most useful. Suppose we are interested in adults' addition of single-digit integers. Based on existing theory and data, as well as rational analyses, we might postulate three general processes:

1. An individual represents the written problem internally; that is, the person encodes the problem in working memory.
2. From years of drill on such problems, the addends and sum are stored together in long-term memory, and an individual next searches long-term memory for the pair of addends matching those in working memory.
3. When the matching addends are found, the sum stored with them is also retrieved and spoken aloud by the subject.

Note that, as yet, no claims have been made that people actually use this collection of processes to answer $4 + 3 = ?$ and similar problems. What matters is that we have produced a relatively precise description of what people might do, a description that can be evaluated empirically. This is typically done by varying certain characteristics of the problem and then analyzing response accuracy, response latency, and/or subjects' verbal reports, as described in the following sections. The initial task analysis is then modified in light of these results.

Analysis of Response Patterns

A prevalent method for evaluating a model derived from task analysis is to first, vary the structure of the task systematically along hypothetically important dimensions to create a set of related problems; second, generate the pattern of responses expected on these problems based on the task analysis; and, third, compare this predicted pattern with actual responses.

A straightforward example of this approach is the method of *rule assessment* used by Siegler (1976). The goal of this research was to discover how children and adolescents solve balance scale problems. Subjects were shown a balance scale in which differing numbers of weights were placed at various distances to either side of a fulcrum. Subjects were to decide which side of the scale would go down when supports were removed.

Based on an analysis of the task and previous research, Siegler (1976) proposed four strategies or rules that could be used to solve this problem (Figure 8.2). A child using Rule 1 considers only weight in predicting the actions of the scale. Children using Rule 2 consider weight, but also examine the distance from the fulcrum if the weights on the two sides are equal in number. According to Rule 3, both weight and distance are considered on all problems. However, if information about weight leads to a different prediction than does information about distance (e.g., if one side has more weight but the other has greater distance between weights and fulcrum), the child responds inconsistently because she or he has no means of resolving such a conflict. A person using Rule 4 overcomes this difficulty by computing torque for each side of the scale and comparing these two values.

To evaluate the adequacy of these strategies, Siegler (1976) created six different types of problems, three of which are shown in Figure 8.3. Since the rules differ primarily in their processing of distance and weight, the problems vary along these dimensions as well. On *distance* problems, equal numbers of weights were placed on the two sides of the fulcrum, but at different distances. On *conflict–weight* problems, the two sides differed both in weight and distance, and the side with the greater number of weights would go down when the supporting blocks were removed. On *conflict–distance* problems, the two sides again differed in both weight and distance, but now the side with the greater distance would go down.

The responses of a child using Rule 1 are easily derived from Figure 8.2. Since this child only considers weight, the child should always predict correctly on conflict–weight problems and always err on the distance and conflict–distance problems. An individual using Rule 3 provides a different profile of responses: This person solves the distance problem correctly. On the two conflict problems, chance levels of performance are expected; lacking a precise rule for computing torque, the individual simply guesses. Equally precise predictions can be made for the remaining rules and for the other types of problems.

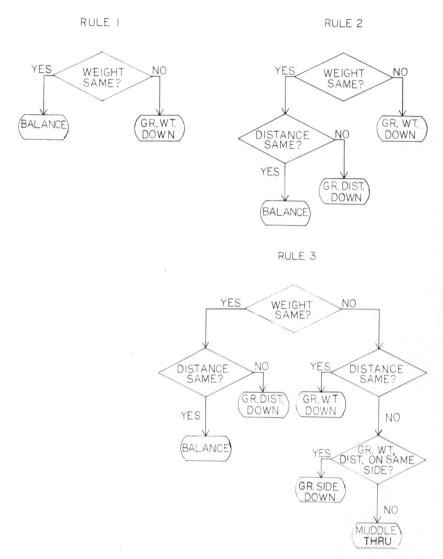

Figure 8.2. Flow Diagrams Representing Four Rules for Solving the Balance Scale Problem. Gr = greater, wt = weight, dist = distance, prod = product. (From Siegler, 1976.)

Siegler (1976) tested 120 individuals, ranging in age from 5 to 17 years, on 30 problems. Each individual's responses were compared to those predicted by each of the rules; use of a rule was attributed to an individual only when the rule correctly predicted at least 26 of the child's correct responses. Even with this stringent criterion, 107 of the 120 individuals fit a pattern corresponding to one of the 4 rules.

RULE 4

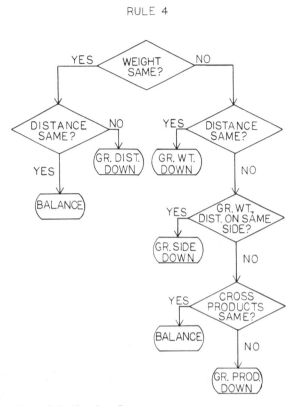

Figure 8.2. (Continued)

This research illustrates how effectively response patterns can be used to identify problem-solving strategies. Further, Siegler's findings illustrate that rule assessment is especially valuable when it is used to characterize the performance of individuals. When analysis is limited to data aggregated across individuals, an investigator may be attempting to model data that reflect a mix of strategies and do not represent a strategy actually used by any individual.

Several limitations on this type of analysis need to be considered. First, many problems usually are needed to demonstrate conclusively that a pattern of responses is truly consistent with one rule but not others, and to ascertain that the pattern differs significantly from that produced by random responses. This situation is manageable when problems are solved quickly and when only a few alternative models are tested, but becomes less practical when problems are more complex and solutions more lengthy or when a large number of models must be tested simultaneously.

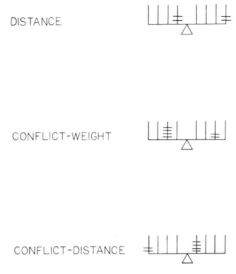

Figure 8.3. Three Types of Problems Like Those Used by Siegler (1976).

Second, if response patterns are to be analyzed effectively, individuals must respond according to one strategy on nearly all problems. If people alter their strategies as testing proceeds, this greatly complicates use of rule-assessment procedures. In some cases, rule-assessment techniques can be used to detect changes in individuals' strategies across a set of trials (e.g., Gholson & Beilin, 1979; Levine, 1975), but typically the data from a subset of trials will be insufficient to evaluate strategies of any complexity.

Finally, rule assessment cannot distinguish strategies that are "functionally equivalent" with respect to patterns of responding. Rule 4, for example, does not distinguish between a model in which weight is processed before distance from a model in which that order is reversed. Rule assessment cannot detect such a difference because no observations are made between stimulus and response. In this case, the difference between strategies is minor. In some instances, however, radically different strategies can result in identical patterns of response (Simon, 1975). Here, more sensitive methods, including analysis of response latencies, are needed.

Analysis of Response Latencies

Measurement of response latencies has become increasingly important for identifying strategies used to solve a variety of tasks. The underlying assumption is that cognitive processes operate in real time and that such times are additive. Total response time can therefore be decomposed to discover the duration and organization of processes. The general approach is to (a) analyze the task; (b) construct conditions that require slightly different processes or different frequencies of a given process, as specified in the task analysis; (c) write equations to express the latency of each condition as a function of the processes involved; (d) measure response latencies in each condition; and (e) compare latencies across conditions to determine the duration of each process. This last step can often be accomplished by subtracting one latency from another or, for cases involving many variables and conditions, by using multiple regression to estimate particular parameters (for details, see Pachella, 1974, and Sternberg, 1977). These parameters can then be put back into the original equations to produce "predicted" latencies for each condition. The degree of relation between predicted and observed latencies provides a measure of the extent to which the proposed strategy (or set of strategies) accounts for differences in latency across conditions of the experiment.

Research by Mumaw, Pellegrino and Glaser (Note 1) provides an elegant demonstration of the power of this method of analysis. Mumaw *et al.* were interested in adults' solution of problems like those on the Minnesota Paper Form Board test, a common measure of spatial aptitude (Fig. 8.4). The individual is asked to determine which of the five squares labeled A–E could be constructed from the pieces in the upper left-hand corner. To simplify their analyses, Mumaw *et al.* modified the problem so that pieces were presented with only one assembled square; subjects judged if that square could be constructed from the pieces.

Mumaw *et al.* suggested that people solving these problems first *encode* one of the pieces; next they *search* for a potentially matching piece in the assembled square; the pieces are then *rotated* mentally to the orientation of the corresponding piece and *compared* to determine if they match. If not, a person decides that the assembled square is different from the pieces (i.e., cannot be constructed from them). If they match, this sequence of encode–search–rotate–compare is repeated until all pieces have been checked, at which point an individual *answers* that the square and pieces are the same.

For simplicity we consider only predictions for pieces that can be assembled to form the square. According to the model, overall response time (RT) on a problem is defined by

$$RT = N(e + s + r + c) + k$$

where N is the number of pieces; e denotes encoding time; s, search time; r, rotation time; c, comparison time; and k, a constant to represent

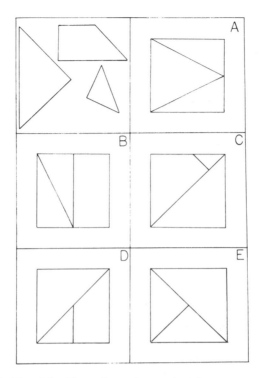

Figure 8.4. A Problem Like Those Appearing on the Minnesota Paper Form Board.

processes presumed to be the same for all problems, such as the time needed to make an overt response. To evaluate the model, Mumaw *et al.* created different types of problems that varied along dimensions relevant to the model. For example, the number of pieces in the problems varied from two to six. According to the model, RT should increase linearly as the number of pieces increases. Other variations resulted in 25 different types of problems. Several instances were created for each type of problem, resulting in a total of 300 problems.

From adults' latencies to solve these problems, parameter values for the general latency equation were derived that minimized, across all 25 types of problems, the discrepancy between observed mean latency for each problem and the latency predicted by the model. For analyses based on group data, the correspondence between predicted and observed latencies was quite good, with $R^2 = .965$. Comparable results emerged when analyses were done separately for each individual's latencies: Most adults had R^2 values greater than .90 and only 3 (of 34) were poorly fit by the model. Thus, the pattern of latency data across the different problems conforms closely to the predictions of the Mumaw *et al.* model.

Procedures like these have been applied to a wide variety of tasks with much success (see Sternberg, in press). In using this approach, however, several potential problems must be recognized. One problem concerns the evaluation and selection of models. The proportion of total variance accounted for across problems (R^2) is useful because it indicates how the model accounts for the data as a whole. But reliance on R^2 as a criterion for evaluating and selecting the "best" model has some shortcomings. One concerns deciding what constitutes a good fit between "predicted" and obtained latencies. Values of R^2 may appear to be *less* impressive than they really should be, because the reliability of data constitutes an upper limit to the goodness-of-fit that can be obtained by any model.[3] Procedures for identifying systematic variance that is *not* accounted for by a model (e.g., Sternberg & Rifkin, 1979) are useful in deciding if any model *could* have accounted for a greater proportion of variance for a given set of data.

More often, however, R^2 values will appear to be *more* impressive than they really are. An R^2 of .70 may be statistically significant and appear quite substantial, but a model that yields this result may simply be capitalizing on variability in the data in a way that is psychologically uninteresting. For example, suppose that solution latencies for multiple-choice analogy problems are substantially smaller with few than with many alternatives. This would hardly be surprising, and *any* model predicting such a result would account for a large portion of the total variance across problems, even if the model were completely inaccurate otherwise. Consequently, when the amount of information to be processed varies considerably across problems, or when only a single model is being tested, investigators must consider the possibility of spuriously high R^2 values. The problem can be alleviated to a certain extent by comparing the R^2 values of theoretically insubstantial models to those of more serious and interesting models.

Difficulties can also arise in comparing competing models, especially when two or more models consistently yield substantial R^2 values, a common situation (Sternberg, 1977). If two models are related hierarchically, the obtained fits can be compared statistically to determine if the additional parameters of the more complex model contribute significantly to the regression equation. When models are not related in this fashion, there is no good basis for purely statistical comparisons. Several

[3] Violations are possible in practice, because techniques for estimating parameters tend to capitalize on error.

guidelines for comparing models in these cases have been proposed (Sternberg & Rifkin, 1979), including the notion of consistency with existing cognitive theory and general psychological plausibility (Pellegrino & Lyon, 1979).

Other problems need to be mentioned briefly. First, models are sometimes tested by analyzing group means, whereas the preferred procedure is to test models for individuals (for reasons noted earlier). Second, sometimes little psychological interpretation is given to components of a model. For example, the search component of Mumaw *et al.'s* model represented a substantial percentage of the solution time on an average problem, yet the model provides no indication of the actual operation of this component. For latency analyses to elucidate processes and strategies involved in problem solving, the operation of such opaque components needs to be clarified. Third, these analyses rarely address the question of how a person constructs, selects, and initiates a model or strategy. Finally, interpretation of response time in the manner outlined here hinges on a number of important assumptions concerning error rates, comparability of processing across problems, and comparability of processing across different instances of the same type of problem, to name a few. Violation of any of these assumptions may seriously compromise latency analyses. [For a detailed discussion of these points, see Pachella (1974) and Kail and Bisanz (1982).]

Analysis of Verbal Reports

To increase density of observations, researchers sometimes ask people to introspect about the process of solving problems. Verbal reports can be quite useful for identifying subjects' strategies, especially on problems that require a lengthy solution interval. The resulting reports are called *concurrent verbalizations* when they are elicited during the solution process and *retrospective verbalizations* when elicited afterward.

The verbal reporting procedure typically used in contemporary research is known as "thinking aloud." After being presented with a problem, individuals describe aloud what they are thinking, doing, attending to, or planning in the course of solving a problem. Verbal reports may be elicited with a general instruction ("Tell me what you are thinking as you solve this problem") and/or specific probes that typically are prepared in advance ("What are you looking at now?" "Why did you do that?" "What will you do next?"). Verbalizations are recorded, along with notes about nonverbal behaviors and available stimuli, to form a *protocol*. According to Newell and Simon (1972),

The protocol is a record of the subject's ongoing behavior, and an utterance at time t is taken to indicate knowledge or operation at time t. Retrospective accounts leave much more opportunity for the subject to mix current knowledge with past knowledge, making reliable inference from the protocol difficult. Nor, in the thinking aloud protocol, is the subject asked to theorize about his own behavior—only to report the information and intentions that are within his current sphere of conscious awareness. All theorizing about the causes and consequences of the subject's knowledge state is carried out and validated by the experimenters, not by the subject [p. 184].

The use of thinking-aloud protocols is illustrated in a study of individual differences in problem solving by Simon and Simon (1978). Relatively simple kinematics problems were presented to an "expert" who was skilled in mathematics and physics but who had not worked on problems of this type for some time. The same problems were also presented to a "novice" who was reasonably skilled in algebra but unfamiliar with kinematics. These individuals first read the relevant sections of a physics text and then were asked to think aloud as they solved problems.

On one of the problems they were asked to compute (a) the average speed of a bullet in a gun barrel and (b) how long the bullet was in the barrel. The length of the barrel and the velocity of the bullet as it left the barrel were given. In solving this problem the novice talked more, took longer to solve the problem, was more likely to mention equations and variables found in the text, and referred to the text more often for information (see Table 8.1). However, these differences might reflect different styles of verbalizing rather than more fundamental differences in strategy. To probe the data more deeply, Simon and Simon identified the sequence of equations used by each individual to solve the problem. Comparison of these sequences, or "solution paths", revealed similarities and differences in strategy. For example, both persons followed a general pattern of (a) selecting an equation (e.g., Table 8.1, lines N22–23), (b) instantiating that equation with known variables (e.g., lines N24–25), and (c) solving the equation for the unknown variable (e.g., line N27). For the expert, these separate steps were sometimes condensed into a single report (e.g., line E5), perhaps indicating greater automaticity of the sequence.

Thinking aloud is a flexible procedure that has been implemented differently in a variety of studies and the range of application can be illustrated by several examples. Klahr and Siegler (1978) used protocols in conjunction with rule assessment of response patterns to clarify strategies used on the balance scale problem described earlier. Klahr and Robinson (1981) studied the development of planning in preschool children by asking them to report how they intended to solve a variant of the Tower-of-Hanoi problem. Verbal reports were treated as responses, and different planning strategies were detected by using rule-assessment methods to identify patterns of verbal responses across problems. Other researchers (e.g., Bisanz, in press; Goldman, in press) have classified verbal reports according to theoretically relevant categories and then have examined the distribution of responses across categories for different groups of persons.

Details of verbal report methods vary too widely to be cataloged fully in this chapter, but several commonalities can be noted. Careful,

Table 8.1
Two Thinking-Aloud Protocols[a]

Protocol for novice

N1. *A bullet leaves the muzzle of a gun at a speed of 40 meters per second.*
N2. *V-zero equals 40, no, 400 meters per second.*
N3. *The length of the gun barrel was uniformly accelerated,*
N5. *what is its average speed inside the barrel?*
N6. *Its average speed inside the barrel was from zero plus . . . to 400 . . .*
N7. *um . . . average velocity times the time it was there,*
N8. *time divided by two.*
N9. *Its average velocity was 200 meters per second.*
N10. *Assuming that the bullet was uniformly accelerated, what is the average speed inside the barrel?*
N11. *Its average speed was 200 meters per second.*
N12. *That's got to be right.*
N13. *The average speed is speed, is the speed, is the v-zero, which was zero,*
N14. *plus v, which was the other, divided by 2 . . .*
N15. *Why divided by two?*
N16. *The average of the two speeds, right?*
N17. *Or 200 meters per second.*
N18. *There's something wrong with that; maybe that's what I did something wrong with on the other one. Maybe I should have taken a square or something. I'll go back and look at it in a minute.*
N19. *How long was the bullet in the gun after it was fired?*
N20. *How long was the bullet in the gun?*
N21. *All right. The time.*
N22. *If s equals vt,*
N23. *t equals the distance divided by the average speed,*
N24. *equals 200 meters . . .*
N25. *No, point 5 divided by 200 meters.*
N26. *So let's worry about that.*
N27. *Point 5 by 200 is 002.5.*
N28. *Time equals .002.25 seconds.*
N29. *Clearly, something is wrong with Problem 18. Let's go back and do that again based on one of the sample problems.* **(continued)**

Protocol for expert

E1. *A bullet leaves the muzzle of a gun at a speed of 400 meters per second.*
E2. *The length of the gun barrel is half a meter.*
E3. *Assuming that the bullet is uniformly accelerated,*
E4. *what is the average speed within the barrel?*
E5. *Well, obviously one half of 400 is 200 meters per second.*
E6. *Ah . . . How long was the bullet in the gun after it was fired?*
E7. *If the average speed was 200 meters per second,*
E8. *and the barrel is half of a meter,*
E9. *then it would be 100 . . . one . . . wait a while . . .*
E10. *The average velocity is 200 meters per second,*
E11. *and the length is half a meter . . .*
E12. *Yeah, then . . . ah . . . it's a half meter,*
E13. *and it's 200 meters per second,*
E14. *then it would have to be one four-hundreth of a second.*

detailed recording of all problem-solving behaviors, verbal and nonverbal, is essential. Thinking-aloud verbalizations are usually recorded on audiotape, and an observer typically makes detailed notes of the proceedings that can be used later to clarify ambiguities arising from the recording. Videotaping is often preferable, especially when there is a motoric aspect to the solution process (e.g., pointing to or manipulating certain stimuli). The reasons for such extensive and detailed recording are twofold. First, subtle and unanticipated features of a person's behavior can provide important clues for identifying solution strategies. Second, contextual factors, such as the positions of relevant stimuli and the timing of probe questions by the experimenter, are often critical for accurate and reliable interpretation of verbal reports.

The result of such comprehensive recording is an enormous amount of data that must be reduced systematically for purposes of analysis. Data reduction typically involves two steps. First, data from audiotapes, videotapes, and handwritten notes are usually transcribed, especially when analysis requires repeated perusals of the protocols. It is simply much easier and more efficient to read through transcripts than to listen to tapes. Transcription might appear to be a simple and straightforward process, but in practice it may be quite difficult to generate transcripts that represent important aspects of the recordings with perfect accuracy. Garbled speech as well as ambiguous gestures and phrases can make transcription difficult, and it is often necessary at this stage of analysis to make interpretive decisions as to the nature of the actual behaviors.

Next, the data must be interpreted and categorized. Much of the material in the protocols will be irrelevant for analysis, so decisions must be made about which aspects are relevant and what the units of analysis will be. The content of a unit will depend upon the nature of the investigation; a unit may consist of goals that are stated explicitly, of particular sequences of actions, or of certain propositions expressed by the problem solver. For Simon and Simon (1978) the units of analysis were, ultimately, equations inferred from the subjects' statements. Criteria for identifying units of analysis must be described very explicitly to enable independent observers to analyze the data and to facilitate replication. Reliability of scoring is usually assessed by computing the proportion of cases in which the raters agree (see Cohen, 1960, for relevant procedures). If reliability is low, the decision criteria must be defined more explicitly and the data rescored.[4] Disagreements will arise even when reliabilities are high; such disagreements are usually resolved by invoking the decision of a third rater.

Thinking aloud is sometimes used in conjunction with computer simulation techniques to identify and represent problem-solving processes (e.g., Greeno, 1978b). Of particular interest is the possibility that computer simulations may be used to code and analyze verbal protocols, a task that is normally tedious and time consuming. An interesting glimpse in this direction is provided by Bhaskar and Simon (1977), who used a semi-automatic computer program to code protocol data and to identify qualitative differences in strategy between human performance and predicted behavior on thermodynamics problems. It is possible that formal, computer-based methods for analyzing verbal protocols will soon be developed and that the present state of the art is similar to that which existed for numerical data prior to the development of analysis of variance and related statistical procedures.

Despite the successful use of verbal report techniques in numerous studies of problem solving, two general sets of issues continue to arise (Bower, 1978; Ericsson & Simon, 1980; Newell & Simon, 1972; Nisbett & Wilson, 1977; Simon, 1978; White, 1980). The first concerns *method,* and especially the problem of how verbal reports should be obtained, analyzed, and evaluated. In the existing literature methods vary enormously, and they are often described poorly or supplemented with unconventional analyses. The second set of issues concerns *validity.* Do verbal reports accurately reflect thought processes? Do questions or instructions to verbalize alter these processes substantially? Are verbal reports complete, and are they consistent with nonverbal behaviors?

---

[4] No formal criteria exist for determining if reliability is "too" low. In practice, reliabilities above .90 are desirable, and those below .80 are often considered unacceptable.

These two issues were linked by Ericsson and Simon (1980), who argued that the validity of verbal reports depends greatly upon the methods used. They proposed that all methods should be guided by an information-processing theory of cognition that specifies the conditions under which verbal reports will be more or less valid. For example, verbal reports of information immediately available in short-term or activated memory (e.g., *What are you looking at?* when an individual is examining objects that are easily labeled) will be highly accurate and will have virtually no effect on cognitive processing. Because active memory is highly labile, reports obtained retrospectively will be less reliable than those obtained concurrently. Furthermore, verbal reports will be less accurate and will have a greater impact on processing when people are required to make inferences in order to answer questions (e.g., *Why did you answer that way?*). Thus the degree of inference required and the amount of time between strategy and report are two important methodological variables that influence the validity of verbal reports.

Ericsson and Simon (1980) contend that "verbal reports, elicited with care and interpreted with full understanding of the circumstances under which they were obtained, are a valuable and thoroughly reliable source of information about cognitive processes [p. 247]." One difficulty with this conclusion concerns the phrase "interpreted with full understanding of the circumstances under which they were obtained." Despite Ericsson and Simon's efforts to define the specific conditions for the use of verbal reports, their theory is still quite rudimentary and much of the evidence they cite is less than compelling. The boundary conditions for valid verbal reports described by Ericsson and Simon (including degree of inference and time between strategy and report) correspond roughly to those provided by Nisbett and Wilson (1977) and by White (1980), and are useful for designing verbal report procedures. But current conceptualizations do not entirely eliminate questions of method and validity that accompany the use of verbal reports.

At this point, it seems best to conclude that researchers should not hesitate to use verbal reports when such methods appear appropriate and when conditions are favorable for valid reports. Verbal protocols appear to be particularly valuable for identifying processes used to solve complex problems. However, it would be advisable to supplement these methods with other forms of data (latencies, response patterns, eye movements) whenever possible.

CONCLUDING REMARKS

Our review indicates a number of general issues that must be considered in selecting a method to study strategic activity.

1. *Individual differences.* Methods should be powerful and sensitive enough to identify strategies and processes for individuals. Reliance on group data can be misleading. Furthermore, individuals vary along important dimensions, including age, expertise, style, and psychometrically-measured ability, that often relate to remembering and problem solving.

2. *Adaptation.* Humans are extraordinarily adaptive information processors. Research methods should be sensitive not only to differences in strategies *among* individuals, but also to differences *within* individuals that may occur over the course of several recall trials or after solving several problems.

3. *Model testing.* Traditional statistical methods, such as analysis of variance, are sometimes inappropriate for testing hypotheses about strategic behavior. This is especially true for the study of problem solving. Many of the methods used to study problem solving, especially verbal report, require more rigorous evaluative procedures. Even the array of quantitative procedures used to analyze response latencies can be insufficient for discriminating among models. Without more rigorous techniques, studies of strategic activity will often be in the position of proposing models, treating these models as null hypotheses, and then accepting them on the basis of data that are only moderately consistent with the expectations of the model.

4. *Functional equivalence.* When two or more strategies produce the same response characteristics by a given criterion (e.g., pattern of responses), they are functionally equivalent. However, strategies can be functionally equivalent, but so dissimilar structurally that they entail very different cognitive demands (Simon, 1975). This being the case, methods must be capable of distinguishing among models that are functionally equivalent at a superficial level.

5. *Unique identification.* The problem of unique identification is closely related to that of functional equivalence. Many researchers seem to have as their goal identification of the single "true" model or strategy that underlies behavior in a given setting. To the contrary, cognitive theory is capable of producing a diverse set of models, several of which may account for human behavior equally well (Anderson, 1976). Given this state of affairs, it is important to select criteria by which certain theories are to be preferred over others. One such criterion might be parsimony, and another might be utility of application.

6. *Converging operations.* A recurrent theme in this chapter is that no single approach is sufficient for unambiguous and comprehensive identification of a person's cognitive strategies. This conclusion amounts to yet another affirmation of the principle of "converging operations" (Garner, Hake, & Eriksen, 1956): Hypotheses about cognitive functions

need to be tested with multiple methods that independently converge on an answer.

REFERENCE NOTE

1. Mumaw, R. J., Pellegrino, J. W., & Glaser, R. *Some puzzling aspects of spatial ability.* Paper presented at the annual meeting of the Psychonomic Society, St. Louis, 1980.

REFERENCES

Anderson, J. R. *Language, memory, and thought.* Hillsdale, N.J.: Lawrence Erlbaum Associates, 1976.

Belmont, J. M., & Butterfield, E. C. Learning strategies as determinants of memory deficiencies. *Cognitive Psychology,* 1971, *2,* 411–420.

Belmont, J. M., & Butterfield, E. C. The instructional approach to developmental cognitive research. In R. V. Kail & J. W. Hagen (Eds.), *Perspectives on the development of memory and cognition.* Hillsdale, N.J.: Lawrence Erlbaum Associates, 1977.

Bhaskar, R., & Simon, H. A. Problem solving in semantically rich domains: An example from engineering thermodynamics. *Cognitive Science,* 1977, *1,* 193–215.

Bisanz, G. L. Knowledge of persuasion and story comprehension: Developmental changes in expectations. *Discourse Processes,* in press.

Bower, G. H. Representing knowledge development. In R. S. Siegler (Ed.), *Children's thinking: What develops?* Hillsdale, N.J.: Lawrence Erlbaum Associates, 1978.

Brown, A. L. The development of memory: Knowing, knowing about knowing, knowing how to know. In H. W. Reese (Ed.), *Advances in child development and behavior* (Vol. 10). New York: Academic Press, 1975.

Case, R. Intellectual development from birth to adulthood: A neo-Piagetian perspective. In R. Siegler (Ed.), *Children's thinking: What develops?* Hillsdale, N.J.: Lawrence Erlbaum Associates, 1978.

Coates, G. D., Alluisi, E. A., & Morgan, B. B. Trends in problem-solving research: Twelve recently described tasks. *Perceptual and Motor Skills,* 1971, *33,* 495–505.

Cohen, J. A. A coefficient of agreement for nominal scales. *Educational and Psychological Measurement,* 1960, *20,* 37–46.

Day, M. C. Developmental trends in visual scanning. In H. W. Reese (Ed.), *Advances in child development and behavior* (Vol. 10). New York: Academic Press, 1975.

Ericsson, K. A., & Simon, H. A. Verbal reports as data. *Psychological Review,* 1980, *87,* 215–251.

Flavell, J. H., Beach, D. R., & Chinsky, J. M. Spontaneous verbal rehearsal in a memory task as a function of age. *Child Development,* 1966, *37,* 283–299.

Gagné, R. M., & Beard, J. G. Assessment of learning outcomes. In R. Glaser (Ed.), *Advances in instructional psychology* (Vol. 1). Hillsdale, N.J.: Lawrence Erlbaum Associates, 1978.

Garner, W. R., Hake, H. W., & Eriksen, C. W. Operationism and the concept of perception. *Psychological Review,* 1956, *63,* 149–159.

Gholsen, B., & Beilin, H. A developmental model of human learning. In H. W. Reese & L. P. Lipsitt (Eds.), *Advances in child and development and behavior* (Vol. 13). New York: Academic Press, 1979.

Goldman, S. R. Semantic knowledge systems for realistic goals. *Discourse Processes,* in press.

Greeno, J. G. Natures of problem-solving abilities. In W. K. Estes (Ed.), *Handbook of learning and cognitive processes: Human information processing* (Vol. 5). Hillsdale, N.J.: Lawrence Erlbaum Associates, 1978. (a)

Greeno, J. G. A study of problem solving. In R. Glaser (Ed.), *Advances in instructional psychology* (Vol. 1). Hillsdale, N.J.: Lawrence Erlbaum Associates, 1978. (b)

Hagen, J. W., & Kail, R. V. Facilitation and distraction in short-term memory. *Child Development,* 1973, *44,* 831–836.

Hunt, E. Quote the raven? Nevermore! In L. W. Gregg (Ed.), *Knowledge and cognition.* Hillsdale, N.J.: Lawrence Erlbaum Associates, 1974.

Hunt, E. Mechanics of verbal ability. *Psychological Review,* 1978, *85,* 109–130.

Kail, R. Use of strategies and individual differences in children's memory. *Developmental Psychology,* 1979, *15,* 251–255.

Kail, R., & Bisanz, J. Cognitive development: An information-processing perspective. In R. Vasta (Ed.), *Strategies and techniques of child study.* New York: Academic Press, 1982.

Kail, R. V., & Hagen, J. W. (Eds.), *Perspectives on the development of memory and cognition.* Hillsdale, N.J.: Lawrence Erlbaum Associates, 1977.

Klahr, D., & Robinson, M. Formal assessment of problem-solving and planning processes in preschool children. *Cognitive Psychology,* 1981, *13,* 113–148.

Klahr, D., & Siegler, R. S. The representation of children's knowledge. In H. W. Reese & L. P. Lipsitt (Eds.), *Advances in child development and behavior* (Vol. 12). New York: Academic Press, 1978.

Levine, M. *A cognitive theory of learning: Research on hypothesis testing.* Hillsdale, N.J.: Lawrence Erlbaum Associates, 1975.

Murdock, B. B. *Human memory: Theory and data.* Hillsdale, N.J.: Lawrence Erlbaum Associates, 1974.

Newell, A., & Simon, H. A. *Human problem solving.* Englewood Cliffs, N.J.: Prentice–Hall, 1972.

Nisbett, R. E., & Wilson, T. D. Telling more than we can know: Verbal reports on mental processes. *Psychological Review,* 1977, *84,* 231–259.

Pachella, R. G. The interpretation of reaction time in information-processing research. In B. H. Kantowitz (Ed.) *Human information processing: Tutorials in performance and cognition.* Hillsdale, N.J.: Lawrence Erlbaum Associates, 1974.

Pellegrino, J. W., & Lyon, D. R. The components of componential analysis. *Intelligence,* 1979, *3,* 169–186.

Ray, W. S. Complex tasks for use in human problem-solving research. *Psychological Bulletin,* 1955, *52,* 134–149.

Reese, H. W. Imagery and associative memory. In R. V. Kail & J. W. Hagen (Eds.), *Perspectives on the development of memory and cognition.* Hillsdale, N.J.: Lawrence Erlbaum Associates, 1977.

Resnick, L. B. Task analysis in instructional design: Some cases from mathematics. In D. Klahr (Ed.), *Cognition and instruction.* Hillsdale, N.J.: Lawrence Erlbaum Associates, 1976.

Rosner, S. R. Primacy in preschoolers' short-term memory: The effects of repeated tests and shift-trials. *Journal of Experimental Child Psychology,* 1972, *13,* 220–230.

Rundus, D., & Atkinson, R. C. Rehearsal processes in free recall: A procedure for direct observation. *Journal of Verbal Learning and Verbal Behavior,* 1970, *9,* 99–105.

Shiffrin, R. M., & Schneider, W. Controlled and automatic human information processing: II. Perceptual learning, automatic attending, and a general theory. *Psychological Review*, 1977, *84*, 127–190.

Siegler, R. S. Three aspects of cognitive development. *Cognitive Psychology*, 1976, *8*, 481–520.

Simon, H. A. The functional equivalence of problem solving skills. *Cognitive Psychology*, 1975, *7*, 268–288.

Simon, H. A. Information-processing theory of human problem-solving. In W. K. Estes (Ed.), *Handbook of learning and cognitive processes: Human information processing* (Vol. 5). Hillsdale, N.J.: Lawrence Erlbaum Associates, 1978.

Simon, D. P., & Simon, H. A. Individual differences in solving physics problems. In R. S. Siegler (Ed.), *Children's thinking: What develops?* Hillsdale, N.J.: Lawrence Erlbaum Associates, 1978.

Sternberg, R. J. *Intelligence, information processing, and analogical reasoning: The componential analysis of human abilities*. Hillsdale, N.J.: Lawrence Erlbaum Associates, 1977.

Sternberg, R. J. Reasoning, problem solving, and intelligence. In R. J. Sternberg (Ed.), *Handbook of human intelligence*. New York: Cambridge University Press, in press.

Sternberg, R. J., & Rifkin, B. The development of analogical reasoning processes. *Journal of Experimental Child Psychology*, 1979, *27*, 195–232.

Wagner, D. A. Memories of Morocco: The influence of age, schooling, and environment on memory. *Cognitive Psychology*, 1978, *10*, 1–28.

White, P. Limitations on verbal report of internal events: A refutation of Nisbett and Wilson and of Bem. *Psychological Review*, 1980, *87*, 105–112.

CHAPTER 9

GEOFFREY R. LOFTUS

Picture Memory Methodology

Beginning with the work of Ebbinghaus (1885), research in memory for verbal material has occupied a central position in the field of experimental psychology. Picture memory research, in contrast, was sporadic at best until 1967 when Roger Shepard reported an experiment in which pictures were recognized with over 90% accuracy. Memory researchers, who at the time were attuned to the rather meager ability of humans to remember nonmeaningful material such as nonsense syllables and isolated digits, found this result to be surprising and a consensus rapidly emerged that picture memory is a quick and phenomenally accurate process, obeying rules quite different from those that govern the workings of verbal memory (cf. Haber, 1970).

This conclusion was soon discovered to be largely incorrect, but Shepard's experiment had, nonetheless, sparked an interest in picture memory that has resulted in a rather substantial body of data. Picture memory has been probed in a variety of different ways, and, correspondingly, a variety of picture memory methodologies has been invented. My purpose here is to describe and comment on some of these methodologies, and the remainder of this chapter is organized as follows. The first section introduces a number of issues that are currently of interest in picture memory research, and then the second section describes major paradigms used to investigate these issues. The sections

HANDBOOK OF RESEARCH METHODS IN
HUMAN MEMORY AND COGNITION

following are concerned with, respectively, methods of picture presentation, selection of a test procedure, counterbalancing considerations, and eye-movement methodology. Finally, I describe a "typical" picture memory experiment that is similar to one currently being run. This experiment will serve to exemplify various issues discussed in this chapter.

Before proceeding, a note on the domain of this chapter is in order. When I talk about "pictures" I will be referring mostly to complex, naturalistic scenes and, to a lesser extent, to complex random forms. The question of how pictures of simple objects become processed forms is, in a sense, a distinct area of research. Exclusion of it here is based primarily on space considerations. See Paivio (1971) for a comprehensive discussion of issues involved in this area.

CURRENT THEORETICAL ISSUES

Since issues of investigation serve to motivate methodologies, it seems appropriate here to briefly delineate and organize some of the theoretical questions that are currently of interest in picture memory research. Elsewhere, I have sketched a "framework for a theory of picture memory" in which I have attempted to perform this task in some detail (Loftus, 1976). Within this framework, I suggested an initial dichotomy between processes that occur at the time a picture is initially viewed (encoding processes) and processes that occur at the time that information acquired via the encoding processes is used in a test of some sort (retrieval–decision–response processes). For the purposes of this chapter, I will emphasize the investigation of encoding processes, since these processes seem to have attracted the most attention in picture memory research. It should be noted, however, that in order to test any precise theory of how information from pictures is acquired and stored, one needs a linking model of the processes that occur during whatever test of the information that is being administered. This point is often overlooked; it will be reemphasized and elaborated upon in a later section.

Eye Movements

Before embarking on a discussion of encoding processes, a digression on the topic of eye movements is necessary. When an observer views a picture (or any static scene), the eye does not sweep around continuously, but rather is relatively immobile for brief periods of time called *fixations*. The duration of a fixation is somewhat variable, but a typical fixation on a picture lasts about 300 msec. Different fixations are separated by quick jumps of the eye called *saccades*. There is strong evidence that acquisition of information from the visual scene occurs during fixations, whereas vision is essentially suppressed during saccades (Latour, 1962; Volkman, 1962). Parameters of the eye-movement pattern are being used increasingly as dependent variables to investigate the microstructure of various cognitive processes, including reading (Rayner, 1978), mental rotation (Just & Carpenter, 1976), sentence processing (Just & Carpenter, 1980), decision making (Russo & Rosen, 1975), and short-term memory scanning (Gould, 1973), as well as picture processing (Loftus, 1972; Friedman, 1979). The obervation of eye movements provides a remarkably convenient methodological tool in the sense that the location of the gaze constitutes an overt, ecologically valid measure of the locus of attention at any given instant.

Encoding Processes

Given that picture processing is seen as being embedded within a series of eye fixations over a picture, three major encoding processes may be identified. First, a decision must be made about where in the picture to fixate. Second, once the gaze has been shifted to the decided-upon area, information must be extracted during the fixation period. Third, the information acquired over a series of fixations must be integrated into one coherent, overall representation of the scene. Within this framework, a number of experimental questions arise. Some of the most compelling ones are:

1. What physical aspects of the picture and cognitive aspects of the observer cause the gaze to be drawn to a particular place in the picture?
2. What is the time course of information acquisition within a fixation?
3. What factors govern the variability in fixation duration?
4. What are the relative uses of information drawn from the periphery versus information acquired foveally?
5. How is one to characterize the representation of a picture in memory? That is, how many types of information need be hypothesized? What is the relative contribution to the memory representation of pure physical information, versus preexisting information supplied by the subject?

EXPERIMENTAL PARADIGMS

Given these general issues, a variety of experimental paradigms have evolved to address them. The principal ones are as follows.

Simple Viewing of Pictures

The simplest paradigm consists of presenting pictures to subjects and recording where subjects look in the pictures. From data collected using this paradigm we can draw inferences about such things as the influence of different goals on viewing strategies (Yarbus, 1967); the relationship between the "informativeness" of an area of a picture and the probability of fixating that area (Mackworth & Morandi, 1967; Loftus & Mackworth, 1978); and developmental trends in picture viewing (Mackworth & Bruner, 1970).

Picture Presentation with Immediate Test

A second paradigm involves presenting a picture and, immediately thereafter, testing, in one way or another, for information acquired from the picture. Such a paradigm has been used to investigate acquisition of the "gist" of a picture (Biederman, Rabinowitz, Stacy, & Glass, 1974); the influence of gist on perception and encoding of objects within the scene (Biederman, 1972; Palmer, 1975); and the emergence of details from the scene into consciousness over time (Haber & Erdelyi, 1967; Erdelyi, 1970).

Study Phase–Test Phase

In the paradigms just described, no stimuli intervene between study and test of a particular picture. They therefore enjoy the advantage that encoding processes can be studied in a relatively pure way, that is, without the complicating effects of retroactive interference. However, a picture, like a verbal stimulus, may well have long- and short-term memory representations that are quite different from one another. If this is true, then only the short-term representations are being investigated using these paradigms. Very little evidence exists in the literature bearing on this issue; however, Pellegrino, Segal, and Dhawan (1975) report data indicating substantial forgetting of simple pictures over a 15-sec interval, just as in the case with verbal material (Peterson & Peterson, 1959).

In contrast, the most common paradigm used in the investigation of picture memory tests representations of pictures that are stored in a long-term form (cf. Shepard, 1967; Standing, Conezio, & Haber, 1970 as typical examples). This paradigm involves a study phase in which a list of target pictures is initially shown, followed by a test phase in which memory for these target pictures is tested in one way or another.

STIMULUS PRESENTATION

In this section, I will focus on issues involving the physical presentation of pictures. This discussion will include the importance of certain physical parameters, descriptions of various devices that can be used for picture presentation, exposure time considerations, and masking issues.

Physical Parameters

When a picture is presented to an observer, either in the study or in the test phase of a picture-recognition experiment, there are a variety of presentation parameters that can vary. Some of the most salient of these parameters are picture size, picture luminance, picture complexity, exposure time of the picture, and the study and test serial positions of the picture. Although each of these parameters can be viewed as an interesting topic of research in its own right, it is often the case that some or all of them are regarded as "nuisance variables." As such, it is of interest to specify the effect that each one has on recognition memory so that a researcher can determine which are important to control and to report in a methods section. I shall describe effects of each of these variables in turn. Although the variables may interact in various ways, I shall restrict my discussion to main effects. There are two reasons for this simplifying strategy. First, no complete factorial design has investigated all possible interactions. Second, all interactions that I have observed—both in the literature and in my own laboratory—have been nonordinal, and hence may well be removable via nonlinear transformations of the dependent variable (cf. Loftus, 1978).

PICTURE COMPLEXITY

Pictorial stimuli vary in their nature along a dimension that might be termed *complexity* which is here defined as the amount of detail included within a given area of the picture.

There have been a number of experiments dealing with the effects of complexity on recognition memory performance. Two of them (Loftus & Bell, 1975; Green & Purohit, 1976) have concluded that increased complexity increases subsequent recognition performance. The Loftus and Bell experiment varied complexity by using as stimuli either complex photographs or simple line drawings based on the photographs. All stimuli were presented at study for exposure times of 500 msec or less. The Green and Purohit study, in contrast, used matrices of 1s and 0s as stimuli and varied complexity simply by varying the number of elements in the matrix. Initial exposure times in this study were approximately 20 sec.

A third study (Nelson, Metzler, & Reed, 1974) used the same stimuli as did Loftus and Bell (1975), but with initial exposure times of 10 sec. They found no differences between photographs and line drawings in an initial exposure test. The absolute level of performance was quite high, raising the suspicion that the lack of difference could have been due to a ceiling effect. However, there was also no difference between the two types of stimuli on 3- and 7-week delayed recognition tests at which time absolute performance level was substantially lower. In brief, the only firm conclusion regarding complexity is that higher complexity leads to higher performance only when initial exposure time has not been sufficient for the subject to acquire all the information from a target stimulus necessary to distinguish it from distractors.

SERIAL POSITION EFFECTS

A number of experiments have demonstrated that, in contrast to verbal material, picture memory is relatively unaffected by the serial input position of the to-be-remembered items. Potter and Levy (1969) and Loftus (1974) have presented visual stimuli—complex pictures in the former study and random forms in the latter—at short initial exposure times (125–1500 msec) with a zero interpicture interval. Performance, as measured by a subsequent yes–no recognition test, was independent of serial input position except that the last stimulus in the presentation sequence showed higher performance than the rest of the stimuli. This effect is probably due to the fact that the last stimulus was the only one that was not masked by a subsequent picture.

In conjunction with Jane Messo and Patricia Pattee (1981), I conducted several yes–no recognition experiments designed to examine study and test serial position effects in a situation where pictures are initially presented at a relatively leisurely pace. In these experiments, exposure time at study was either .25 or 1.5 sec, and there was an interval of approximately 5 sec between pictures. The effect of serial study position on performance in a subsequent yes–no recognition test was again nil. However, there was a strong effect of serial test position; over serial test position, hit rate decreased, and false alarm rate increased. In summary, it appears that one need not worry about study serial position as a variable that affects recognition memory performance; however, performance declines quite dramatically over test serial position.

LUMINANCE

The effect of luminance on picture memory is a difficult one to deal with because the luminance of a given set of pictures is highly dependent on the nature of the pictures themselves. For example, a set of complex photographs will, when displayed on a given projection system, be less bright than will a corresponding set of black-on-white line drawings. As we have seen, photographs tend to be recognized better than line drawings. However, this effect is likely due to the complexity of the pictures rather than to the confounded variable of luminance level. To evaluate this claim, Greg Ihli and I (1981) have run an experiment in which the luminance level of a set of target pictures was systematically attenuated over a range of two log units. The unattenuated luminance level of the projector (with no slide displayed) was 41 ftl (a typical level used in picture-memory experiments). The pictures used were typical, complex "vacation slides," and the exposure time at study was either .25 or 1.5 sec. The pictures were subsequently tested in a yes–no recognition test. Luminance at test was unattenuated. The results indicated a modest decline of recognition performance over luminance level at study.

PICTURE SIZE

The effects of picture size on picture processing appear to be somewhat complicated. In an extensive series of picture-recognition experiments using different sets of pictures and different types of recognition tests, my students and I[1] have varied the size (in degrees of visual angle) of the presented pictures. In none of these experiments have I been unable to detect any effect of picture size on recognition performance. However, it is the case that eye-movement parameters appear to vary; in particular, the smaller the picture, the longer the average fixation duration. I believe that this is a theoretically interesting finding with

[1] These students were Jane Messo, Bonnie Rozanski, Art Shimamura, Jeff Whitted, and Mandy Williams.

respect to identifying processes that occur within, and control the duration of eye fixations. From a purely methodological point of view, however, it means that experimenters should be careful to control for picture size, or at least to report it when describing their procedures.

PRESENTATION TIME

The amount of time a picture is presented at study has a dramatic effect on subsequent recognition performance (cf. for example, Loftus and Kallman, 1979). Particularly when short exposure times are being used in the experiment, a difference of 50 msec of exposure time has a substantial effect on recognition memory performance.[2] Therefore, in a picture-recognition experiment, precise control over exposure time is critical, and leads to some restrictions in terms of the apparatus that is used to display the picture. These restrictions will form part of the discussion of the next section.

Devices for Displaying Pictures

A picture can be presented, both at study and at test, by using any of a variety of different devices. The purpose of this section is to list these devices and evaluate them in terms of (a) control over timing and picture size; (b) convenience with respect to counterbalancing procedures; (c) capability of running multiple subjects simultaneously; (d) ability to run the device on-line to a computer; and (e) potential for contingent presentation of stimuli (i.e., variation of presentation condition dependent on a subject's responses as described by Loftus, Mathews, Bell, and Poltrock, 1975). Note that contingent presentation typically implies an on-line capability.

HAND PRESENTATION

The simplest method of presenting pictures is to mount them on cards or in a booklet and present them by hand. This presentation mode has little to recommend it. Timing accuracy is on the order of hundreds of milliseconds and control over picture size is similarly lacking. Simultaneous presentation to multiple subjects is awkward at best, and

[2] There is a remarkable lack of research regarding the effects of exposure time at test. Freund (1971), in the only exploration of this issue using picture recognition, found that the exposure time of test slides was irrelevant with respect to recognition performance down to a test exposure of .5 sec.

contingent presentation, to the degree that it is possible at all, is difficult. Varying the order of stimuli is difficult when the pictures are mounted on cards and impossible when stimuli are made into booklets (unless multiple booklets are constructed, in which case it is merely inconvenient). In general, hand presentation should be used only as a last resort.

SLIDE PROJECTORS

If one wishes to present a large number of complex scenes, then a slide projector is a highly convenient presentation device. Slides themselves are cheap and easy to obtain (almost everyone with a camera has untold numbers of slides with which he or she is typically willing to part). Likewise, projectors (particularly carousel projectors) are readily available and easy to use. The timing characteristics of an off-the-shelf projector are not very good; however, this problem can be solved by purchasing tachistoscopic shutters to be used in conjunction with the projectors. These shutters can be made to have rise and fall times on the order of one millisecond,[3] thereby making them suitable for presentation times that are, for all intents and purposes, indefinitely low.

With a standard projector, the difficulty of varying the slide-presentation order ranges from moderate (with a carousel projector on which the "select" button can be used to hand-rotate the tray) to extreme (with a cube-type projector where slides must be ordered by hand prior to presentation). If possible, it is highly desirable to have one or more random-access projectors. The increase in cost is substantial; a random-access projector costs about $1100 versus about $200 for a standard projector. But random-access projectors greatly simplify the implementation of counterbalancing requirements as well as lending themselves to on-line computer control.

Slide projectors are obviously ideal for use with large numbers of subjects that are run simultaneously. In line with earlier remarks about effects of picture size, it is a good idea, when subjects are in groups, to position the subjects as far from the projection screen and as close to one another as is feasible so as to minimize across-subject variation in picture size.

---

[3] Actually, a rise time of 1 msec requires an amount of power that will burn out the shutter solenoids if it remains at that level for more than a few seconds. To solve this problem, manufacturers either provide power supplies that deliver less power (and open the shutters more slowly), or they provide a switch which is used when shutter on time is to be more than a few seconds. We have solved the problem by building our own power supplies that put out an initial high-power pulse which is then attenuated shortly after it is delivered. (This solution is also cheaper than buying manufactured power supplies.)

Slide projectors—particularly random access slide projectors—allow a fair degree of flexibility with respect to contingent presentation. This is especially true if computer control is available, as the shutter timing and/or the slide selector can be put under control of the computer that is simultaneously monitoring subject responses.

TACHISTOSCOPES

A standard, multichannel tachistoscope can also be used to present pictures with excellent control over timing. However, a tachistoscope is typically not the device of choice in picture-memory experiments for a variety of reasons. First, most tachistoscopes cannot be used with slides; the pictures must be made into cards. Second, only individual subjects can be run, thereby limiting the tachistoscope's flexibility as a general picture-memory laboratory instrument. Third, randomization is difficult, and fourth, most forms of contingent presentation are virtually impossible. A major virtue of a tachistoscope in perceptual work is that it permits fine control over stimulus luminance. But, as noted, such control is typically of minor interest only in picture-memory research.

COMPUTER GRAPHICS

As laboratories increasingly use computer control, computer graphics displayed on some form of CRT are becoming viable as a means of presenting even relatively complex pictures (Loftus et al., 1975).

The timing characteristics of computer-displayed graphics depend jointly on the nature of the to-be-displayed pictures, on the power of the computer system, and on the nature of the display scope. Highly complex, color pictures require a TV monitor for display, and the 60-Hz scan time associated with such devices introduces an initial timing limitation. Beyond this, complex pictures have timing limitations due to the requirements of moving the binary information corresponding to the picture from disk or other storage device to the computer memory and, less problematically, from the memory to the CRT. As an example, an Apple II computer has the graphics capability to display highly complex color pictures, but the information corresponding to a picture requires time on the order of seconds to be transferred from diskette to core. These sorts of timing problems decrease to the degree that (a) the complexity of the picture is decreased (b) the size and speed of the computer system is increased, and (c) the display time required by the experimental design increases. The same considerations enter into the capability of a computer graphics system with respect to running multiple subjects and with respect to contingent display capability. In an ideal world—that is, with a large, powerful time-sharing computer system—multiple subjects and contingent presentation are feasible. But most picture-memory laboratories do not enjoy such ideal conditions. In general, if fast timing and/or contingent presentation is required, only one subject should be run at a time.

Assuming that timing difficulties have been surmounted, computer graphics are ideal for two situations: first, when a great deal of stimulus presentation flexibility is required (e.g., when highly complex counterbalancing measures are necessary), and second, when the experimental design requires a set of stimuli that vary from each other in systematic ways. In the latter case, algorithms can be written that will generate such stimuli to the desired specifications.

FILMS

It is possible to present pictures via a movie projector by initially filming each picture for the number of frames that will eventually correspond to the required presentation time. In general, this is not a desirable system because of the relative difficulty of shooting the film to begin with, the poor control over timing, and the extreme inflexibility with respect to stimulus presentation order. The only sort of experimental procedure in which using films serves a useful purpose is one in which a large number of pictures must be displayed in rapid-fire succession, in other words, with the onset of each picture immediately following the offset of the preceding one (e.g., Potter & Levy, 1969; Potter, 1975; Intraub, 1980). Even with these requirements, however, there are two potentially better alternative systems. First, if the exposure times are relatively long (on the order of a second), such a presentation sequence could be accomplished with two (or more) slide projectors with alternating (or rotating) shutter openings and slide advancement. Second, subject to the limitations discussed in the previous section, one might be able to accomplish the job with a computer graphics system.

Range of Exposure Times

Earlier, I described the manner in which viewing of a picture takes the form of a series of eye fixations over the picture. The fact that viewing is broken up into a series of discrete periods of not less than about 200 msec apiece has certain methodological consequences. In particular, it means that one is probably studying different processes depending on whether a picture is displayed for less than 200 msec (which allows only a single fixation on the picture) or for longer times (during which multiple fixations typically occur), I will discuss these two cases in turn.

THE SINGLE FIXATION CASE

When the exposure time is such that only a single fixation is allowed on a picture, there is an advantage with respect to experimental control in the sense that the experimenter can dictate, using a preexposure fixation point, where the fixation will be in the picture. An example of this sort of control is found in a recent set of experiments reported by Nelson and Loftus (1980). Of interest in these experiments was the size of the "functional visual field" during the viewing of a picture. To investigate this issue, the experiments utilized a two-alternative forced-choice (2AFC) test in which target and distractor differed from one another by only a single critical detail. The major independent variable in the experiment was the distance (in degrees of visual angle) of the nearest fixation on the picture at study to the critical detail. In two of the experiments, this variable was controlled by allowing only a single fixation on the picture and controlling the location of the fixation (and thus its distance to the critical detail) via a prefixation point.[4]

It should be noted that within a single fixation, enough information is acquired from the periphery of the picture that an assessment of the gist of the picture can be made (cf. Biederman, 1972; Biederman et al., 1974; Potter, 1975). In short, when one presents pictures for 200 msec or less, one is studying both acquisition of the gist of the picture and fine-detail encoding of whatever in the picture is close to (i.e., is within about two degrees of) the fixation point.

THE MULTIPLE FIXATION CASE

Obviously, many classes of picture-memory experiments involve exposure times that are sufficiently long to permit multiple fixations. In this sort of experiment, one expands what one is studying to include (a) how the subject decides where in the picture to fixate, and (b) how information is integrated over fixations. Unless eye-movement recording is included in the experiment, a good deal of information about initial

---

[4] A major result of this study is that performance was at or close to chance when the distance had been greater than about two degrees of visual angle.

picture processing is lost. This issue, as well as ways of dealing with the problem will be dealt with later (see pages 275–280).

Masking Considerations

Since the classic work of Sperling (1960), we have known that an iconic image of a visual stimulus outlasts the stimulus itself. Furthermore, it is known that visual masks of various sorts will eliminate this iconic image. The reasons for the iconic image and the mechanisms by which the masking processes operate have been subject to intensive debate and investigation (Breitmeyer & Ganz, 1976, Turvey, 1973). From the standpoint of picture-memory methodology, however, the crucial point is that a mask can be presented following the offset of a picture as a means of controlling the amount of time the subject has to process information from the picture. If one is interested in precise control over the amount of time that is available for processing, then use of a mask is important, particularly if the exposure times to be used are short in comparison with the time during which information from the iconic image is available for processing (although see Ericksen, 1980, for some potential problems involving the use of a mask). In choosing the nature and intensity of the mask, a good rule of thumb is the following. Arrange the stimulus presentation situation such that the mask and the target picture are displayed continuously and simultaneously. Then adjust the intensity of the mask such that no information can be obtained from the target picture. The resulting combination of target and mask intensity can then be used within the experiment proper.

In contrast to the exposure time of the target picture, the exposure time of the mask has little effect on picture memory as long as it is greater than some minimum value. In most situations, a 300 msec mask exposure is quite sufficient.

It should be noted that use of a mask is not always required, nor is it even always desirable. A large class of experiments involves exposure times that are arbitrary and/or not of great concern with respect to the point of the experiment. Suppose, for example, that one is interested in the processes that occur within a single eye fixation and all that is of importance is the particular place in the picture that is to be fixated (as in the Nelson and Loftus experiment described earlier). A problem that can easily arise in this kind of situation is that the subject cannot obtain enough information within the fixation to respond much above chance in the ensuing test—in other words, floor-effect problems arise.

In such a situation, it would be desirable to allow the subject to process information from the iconic image. This is because the basic experimental requirement will be met—the subject will not be able to shift his or her gaze during the time that the iconic image is being processed—but additional information from the fixated area of the picture will be obtainable from the iconic image which will boost performance and attenuate the floor-effect problem.

THE CHOICE OF A TEST

In verbal memory tasks, the two most commonly used classes of tests to measure stored information are recognition and recall tests. The literature pertaining to the relative characteristics of these two types of tests is extensive, and I will not attempt to cover it here. Instead, I will discuss the unique aspects of these tests as they apply to picture memory. In addition, I will discuss three other types of tests used in picture memory research, namely object-probe tests, detection tests, and reconstruction tests.

Recall Tests

In verbal memory experiments, the principal disadvantage of a recall test is that it simultaneously measures amount of stored information and retrieval ability. Each of these two entities is necessary for successful recall; therefore one cannot make any strong conclusions from recall failure.

VERBAL RECALL OF PICTURES

The same problem plus some additional ones occur when pictures are recalled verbally. Since recall is, by nature, a verbal act, the very process of recalling necessitates that whatever is being recalled is representable in verbal form. If it were assumed that information extracted from pictures is stored completely in verbal form, then picture recall would be a perfectly reasonable test, but such an assumption hardly seems warranted. Rather, it seems more realistic to suppose that the instructions to *recall everything you can about this picture* will elicit only that information from the picture that was extracted at study, is possible to verbalize, and for which adequate retrieval paths have been constructed.

A second problem with picture recall is that it is difficult to score performance, particularly if recall consists of a written description of a picture. Even if one can determine a means for determining how much correct information is contained in the description, one must still somehow compensate for both the complexity of the picture being described and the bias problem, that is, the problem that information can be "recalled" not because it was stored in memory but rather because it is commensurate with (i.e., is a "default" given) the rest of the picture.

Despite these difficulties, recall procedures have been used to investigate some interesting issues in picture memory. Haber and Erdelyi (1967) have tested the Freudian notion of emergence of information into consciousness by presenting a picture very briefly (100 msec) and then having subjects recall as many details as possible from the picture after varying periods of time.[5] Shiffrin (1973) used recall of complex pictures to investigate certain issues involving the short-term store–long-term store dichotomy. Shiffrin's procedure involved presenting lists of pictures, following which subjects wrote short descriptions of as many of the pictures as they could remember. In a second phase of the test, the subjects saw the original pictures in conjunction with the just-written descriptions. Each description was then rated on a scale from 0 to 5 where 0 signified no description had been written and 1–5 represented the "vividness" of the recalled picture at the time that the description was generated. One can then use both the probability of a nonzero response (i.e., the probability of writing a description to begin with) or the average vividness rating given a description as dependent variables.

DRAWINGS AS RECALL

A possible way of circumventing the verbalization problem is to have subjects draw representations of the pictures that they believe they have seen. This procedure, of course, introduces another major difficulty, namely that the recall score will be dependent on the artistic ability of the subject. One might try to circumvent this problem by using trained artists as subjects. It is also of course true, that the same scoring difficulties described above will arise when drawings are used as recall protocols.

[5] Although the number of reported details increased over time, Erdelyi (1970) later showed this effect to be due to a bias shift of the sort just described.

Recognition Tests

Picture recognition is the test most commonly used to measure stored information from pictures. A recognition test, of course, suffers from the disadvantage that performance is highly dependent on the distractors that are used. Another way of putting this is that a recognition test measures not the total amount of information that had been extracted from a picture, but rather the amount of discriminative information, where discriminative information is that information that distinguishes targets and distractors. It is probably safe to assume that discriminative information is monotonically related to total information.[6] But in the absence of stronger assumptions about this relationship and a model of the means by which discriminative information is used in the decision–response process, only qualitative conclusions can be made based on data stemming from recognition tests.

TYPES OF RECOGNITION TESTS

The most commonly used types of recognition tests are yes–no and forced-choice (typically 2AFC) tests.

The major advantage of a yes–no test is the design simplicity that results when it is used (to be discussed in more detail). The major difficulty is that bias is uncontrolled. The precise implications of this difficulty as well as ways of dealing with it are covered in another chapter of this book (Murdock).

A 2AFC test is particularly advantageous when one wishes to focus on particular types of information hypothesized to be extracted from pictures. A good example of this strategy is seen in a number of experiments that have been reported by Jean Mandler and her colleagues (e.g., Mandler & Johnson, 1976; Mandler & Stein, 1974). Mandler defines several types of information, for example, type information (the presence of an object with a particular name) and token information (the visual appearance of an object bearing a particular name). Mandler can then test, using a 2AFC test, whether these (and other) types of information have been extracted. To test for type information, for example, target and distractor might be identical except that a bookcase in the target has been replaced by a map in the distractor. Likewise, token information would be tested, for example, by replacing a woman with another woman that has a different appearance.

---

[6] Experimental situations could easily be concocted, however, in which this assumption would probably be violated.

As intimated above, a 2AFC test presents certain inconvenient design problems which will be discussed in further detail. These problems become particularly annoying when slide projectors are being used to present stimuli, because target and distractor stimuli must be either copied or judiciously scattered through several slide trays. However, if a computer graphics system is being used for stimulus presentation, much of this problem is eliminated. Furthermore, as noted, computer graphics are ideal for constructing pictures that differ from one another in particular systematic ways, and, as just described, that are the exact sorts of stimuli which one typically wishes to test in a 2AFC test. The moral is that computer graphics capability and 2AFC tests constitute a rather harmonious marriage.

Other Types of Tests

Besides standard recall and recognition tests, there is a variety of other tests that have been used to address various issues. Three of them are the following.

RECONSTRUCTION

Mandler and Parker (1976) have used a reconstruction test in which the subject is presented with a grid and a collection of cutout objects which must be arranged on the grid so as to correspond as closely as possible with the original picture. This procedure is a good one to use when spatial information is being tested. The disadvantages of the procedure are that scoring is not straightforward, and the procedure can only be used when the pictures being used are relatively simple.

DETECTION

Potter (1975) has introduced a detection paradigm that is potentially useful in a variety of situations. In Potter's experiment, complex pictures were presented via a film projector in rapid-fire succession, and the subject's task was to press a button when a picture bearing a particular gist (e.g., *a game*) appeared. The subject's ability to detect the gist under various conditions could then be assessed. It is not obvious to me that Potter's exact procedure is optimal since it is somewhat difficult to control for false alarms. But a modification in which the detection response was delayed until the end of the presentation sequence would solve this problem (cf. Egeth & Smith, 1967).

PROBE RECALL

Biederman (1972) has used a modification of a paradigm first introduced by Averbach and Coriell (1961) in which a visual stimulus is
presented and, following the offset of the stimulus, is a visual marker.
The subject's task is to name the item from the original stimulus (a letter,
in the case of the Averbach and Coriell experiment) that the marker
indicated.

In Biederman's modification, the original stimulus was a complex
picture, and the item to be reported was a single object within the picture.
Biederman's interest in this experiment was in how the gist of a picture
affected encoding of particular objects within the picture. But this is a
paradigm that could prove generally useful when initial processing of
pictorial information is at issue.

COUNTERBALANCING MEASURES

I have found in picture-memory experiments that there are substantial differences in the memorizability of individual pictures. The question of how one might investigate the aspects of the pictures that cause
these individual differences is an interesting one. But if one is not specifically concerned with this issue, then strict counterbalancing measures
are essential in picture-memory experiments. In particular, it is necessary
to design the experiment so that each picture appears equally often in
each experimental condition. In the case of a recognition test, experimental condition should include target–distractor as a factor.

AN EXAMPLE: YES–NO COUNTERBALANCING

I have developed a simple algorithm for accomplishing this goal in
the case of a yes–no recognition procedure where a slide projector is
used to present stimuli (described fully by Loftus and Kallman, 1979).
A given tray of 80 slides is initially divided randomly into two sets, Set
A and Set B. Set A slides are those in the odd-numbered slots of the
tray, whereas Set B slides are those in the even-numbered slots. At
study, one shows every other slide—even slots for half the subjects, and
odd slots for the other half of the subjects. The test then takes the form
of a random presentation of all 80 slides in the tray.[7]

[7] One might ask why slides were not arranged by putting Set A in slots 1–40 and Set
B in slots 41–80, since this would facilitate study presentation. The reason this is not done

Assume now that there are J study conditions (e.g., there might be $J = 5$ exposure times at study). Of the 40 targets in a tray, $40/J$ of them are in each condition. A particular picture is rotated through study conditions across J subjects or groups of subjects who will see that picture as a target. In addition, J groups will see the picture as a distractor. Thus, $2J$ subjects or groups constitute a basic counterbalancing module in the sense that over $2J$ subjects, each picture will have been seen equally often as target and distractor and also, when shown as a target, equally often in each of the J study conditions.[8]

Two Alternative Forced-Choice Counterbalancing

These counterbalancing measures are not quite as simple if a 2AFC test is used. The reason for this is that pictures must be counterbalanced over test position (e.g., left versus right) in addition to being counterbalanced over target–distractor in order to control for bias to respond to one test position or the other. This means that for the same number of basic conditions, twice as many subjects or groups of subjects must be run in a 2AFC as opposed to a yes–no experiment.

EYE-MOVEMENT METHODOLOGIES

As mentioned earlier, an investigator interested in studying how information is acquired from pictures will find the recording of eye fixations on a picture to be highly useful since eye-movement data provide an indication of how the observer's attention has been allocated over the picture. Much has been recently published about eye-movement methodology in the study of cognitive processes, and I will not attempt to cover this literature here (see Raynor, 1978, for an excellent review). Instead, I will briefly discuss some issues involved in the process of using eye-movement recording in the investigation of picture memory.

revolves around the just-mentioned fact that the yes–no recognition test takes the form of a random presentation of all 80 slides. Since the search time of a random-access projector is typically quite audible to the subject and varies from about a second to about four seconds, short search time would cue the subject that the correct answer to the upcoming test picture is the same as the answer to the previous one.

[8] An alternative to this scheme would be to treat "distractor" as another study condition consisting of presenting a picture for zero time. With this sort of design, $J + 1$ subjects or groups would form the basic design module. I do not recommend this design, as it raises the guessing probability for targets, thereby decreasing the range of response probability within which one can observe the effects of study variables.

Types of Eye Movements

In general, there are three classes of eye movements: smooth pursuit movements that occur only to moving stimuli; saccades and several types of movements occurring within a fixation, such as microsaccades; and small drifts that are collectively referred to as *physiological nystagmus*. For the purposes of investigating the allocation of attention over complex pictures, however, the scan pattern may be viewed simply as a series of fixations separated by saccades.

Parameters of the Fixation Pattern

Given this situation, there are several parameters of the eye-movement pattern that are typically of interest. First is the number of fixations that are made in a given period of time. In past research (Loftus, 1972), I have found number of fixations to be a critical determinant of picture recognition performance, mediating the effects on recognition of several other variables such as exposure time and incentive. The second parameter is the sequence of fixation locations within a picture. The question of which parts of a picture are fixated is particularly important if one has constructed a recognition test such that certain features of the picture constitute the discriminative information referred to earlier. A related issue in a recognition paradigm involves the degree to which the scan pattern on a picture is similar at study and at test (cf. Noton & Stark, 1971).

Choice of Equipment

Over the years, a rather substantial array of eye-movement recording equipment has become available (see Young & Sheena, 1975a, 1975b, for reviews). These types of equipment may be evaluated along the following criteria:

1. *Cost.* Eye movement recording systems vary in cost from a few hundred dollars to hundreds of thousands. The very high costs of some of the more exotic devices typically stems from some capability that is not really needed in picture-memory studies, such as extreme accuracy or the ability to permit virtually unlimited head and body movement. I will not consider these in the discussion to follow.

2. *On-line computer capability.* One of the major difficulties that arises with eye-movement recording is the immense amount of data that

must be analyzed. Having the eye-movement recorder on-line to a computer eliminates much of this difficulty.

3. *Ease of use.* Eye-movement recorders vary both in how easy it is to calibrate a subject to begin with and how much recalibration is necessary as an experimental session progresses. It should be noted that with any eye-movement recording, the amount of recalibration necessary during an experimental session is highly dependent on the sort of eye-movement data that one wishes to collect. For example, if one is interested only in observing fixation rate (as opposed to the exact locations of fixations) then frequent recalibration is unnecessary.

4. *Capability of visual output.* A desirable property of an eye-movement recorder is the capacity to provide as part of the output a continuous image of the scene being viewed by the subject along with an indication of the point of regard within the scene. Such an output makes it very simple to analyze which parts of the scene have been viewed (cf. Loftus, 1979), and is particularly useful if one is interested in determining whether or not particular areas or objects in the scene are fixated.

POINT-OF-REGARD EVALUATION

Several techniques make use of the fact that the a light source at the point of regard is reflected in the center of the pupil. The most powerful such technique employs a bright spot of light, fixed relative to the scene being viewed, whose position with respect to the center of the pupil is automatically computed. Since this position is directly related to the position of the eye, it can be used to determine the point of regard. A quite popular recorder that uses this technique is one manufactured by Gulf and Western. This device is relatively high in cost (on the order of $25,000) but evaluates quite favorably on the rest of the criteria. It allows continuous $x-y$ digital output, making it suitable for running on-line (although the output eminates from a TV camera which means that position can only be sampled at a 60-Hz rate). It can be calibrated in a matter of minutes, and a fair degree of head movement is tolerable, eliminating the need for a biteboard. Analog output (in the form of crosshairs representing eye position superimposed over a TV picture of the scene being viewed) is also available. A much less powerful reflection technique is one in which the scene itself is reflected in the pupil, and the eye is continually photographed[9] during viewing (Mackworth, 1968).

[9] If one has a choice of using a film system versus a closed-circuit television system as a recording device, a television system is far preferable, since movie film is very expensive, nonreusable, and must be processed before results can be seen.

The position of the eye is then determined from the recordings by assessing which part of the scene is reflected in the center of the pupil. Although cheap and easy to use, this latter technique does not lend itself to on-line capability. The necessary hand data analysis is extremely tedious and time-consuming.

ELECTRO-OCULOGRAPHY

This technique involves placing of skin electrodes around the eye and monitoring the corneoretinal potential, which varies with the position of the eye. Electro-oculography has a fair amount to recommend it with respect to picture memory studies. It is relatively cheap. The output consists of continuous voltages that correspond to the x- and y-positions of the eye which make it suitable for on-line monitoring. It is quite simple to use, particularly since there is no equipment required in front of the eye to impede normal vision. However, there is constant drift, which requires frequent recalibration, and the head must be held very steady. The principal disadvantage is that there is no visual output.

CORNEAL REFLECTION

This technique is one in which visible light is reflected off the eye and the reflection from the corneal reflex, which moves with the eye, is optically superimposed on an image of the scene being viewed (Mackworth, 1967; see also, Loftus, 1979, for a detailed description of a picture memory laboratory incorporating one such device). The resulting visual output—the scene, plus the superimposed spot corresponding to the point of regard—can then be recorded on videotape.[10]

This device is relatively cheap, and, like the Gulf and Western point-of-regard recorder, has the desirable property of providing a visual output. However, it does not readily lend itself to on-line capability, thereby making data analysis somewhat difficult. Additionally, it is extremely sensitive to head movements and frequent recalibration is necessary.

LIMBUS AND EYELID MONITORING

A fairly popular technique has involved bathing the eye with light and using an arrangement of photodetectors to monitor the limbus, that is, the boundary between iris and sclera (for detecting horizontal position) and the boundary between iris and eyelid (for monitoring vertical po-

---

[10] See Footnote 9, page 277.

sition). This technique is relatively cheap and provides continuous x and y electrical signals, making it suitable for on-line monitoring. However, vertical tracking is very inaccurate due to the relative instability of the eyelid, and no visual output is provided. It is therefore not well suited to picture-memory work.

Alternatives to Eye-Movement Recording

There are two major difficulties with eye-movement recording. First, as should be evident from the previous discussion, there is no way to avoid either cost, or difficulty, or both if eye movements are to be recorded. Second, since eye-movement parameters—both gaze location and fixation durations—are under control of the subject, any data involving the relationship between eye-fixation parameters and recognition data are necessarily correlational and therefore open to subject-selection and item-selection effects. Some possible solutions to these problems are the following.

RESTRICTING EXPOSURE TIME

The first solution has already been discussed. If exposure time of a picture is kept at less than about 200 msec, then only one fixation is possible; hence, both processing time and point of regard can be controlled. The problem with this procedure, of course, is that the range of theoretical and experimental questions that it can be used to address is quite limited.

TACHISTOSCOPIC MODELS OF EYE FIXATIONS

I have recently been using what I have dubbed a *multiflash paradigm,* in which a series of eye fixations is simulated by a series of masked, sequential tachistoscopic exposures of a picture (Loftus, 1981). In this paradigm, a picture is displayed at study for n exposures, each exposure of duration of d msec, and each exposure followed by a 300 msec noise mask. Here, n simulates the number of fixations on a picture, and d simulates the duration of each fixation. In the work I have performed so far using this paradigm, subjects have been free to move their eyes between sequential exposures, or not move their eyes as they wish. The result of using this manipulation in the study phase of a recognition test has been that recognition performance increases with increasing exposures only to the degree that subjects move their eyes between exposures, in other words, to the degree that they use additional exposures to fixate additional places in the picture. This paradigm could be refined in terms of experimental control by presenting a fixation point prior to each exposure, thereby allowing control over three of the critical parameters of the eye-movement pattern: number of fixations, duration of each fixation, and the locations in the picture that are fixated. So far, I have used slide projectors as a presentation mode. It could be improved through the use of computer graphics to display the pictures.

A COMPLETE EXPERIMENT

To conclude this chapter, it seems worthwhile to describe a "typical" picture memory experiment that is very similar to one that Carrie Johnson, Brian Williamson, and I are currently carrying out in my laboratory. I have selected this experiment for description because it is fairly complex and illustrates a number of methodological considerations.

The Issue

The general question under investigation is: How much information does an observer acquire from the iconic image that follows the offset of a briefly presented picture? To address this issue, the experiment involves a yes–no recognition procedure, in which target pictures are initially presented across a range of exposure times and are either followed by a noise mask or not followed by a mask. The major results of this experiment will consist of two functions relating recognition performance to initial exposure time: one function for masked pictures and one function for unmasked pictures. (Of interest will be an assessment of the horizontal difference between these two curves that is, the amount of additional exposure time necessary to raise performance level for a masked picture to that of an unmasked picture.)

What Stimuli Should Be Used in This Experiment?

We decided to use complex, naturalistic pictures. These stimuli were selected for three reasons. First, as noted, it is possible to easily obtain virtually unlimited numbers of them. Second, slides are ideal for use with our most convenient display system, namely a slide projector. And third, such pictures endow the study with some degree of ecological validity.

What Range of Exposure Times Should Be Used at Study?

A critical aspect of this experiment is a comparison of two complete functions relating performance to exposure time. Thus, a fairly wide range of exposure times was needed. Additionally, since curves were to be compared horizontally, a large number of exposure times was needed so that the shape of the curves could be determined without recourse to an outrageous degree of interpolation. Finally, we wanted to compare performance under conditions that would allow both single and multiple eye fixations. Ultimately, we chose six exposure times. Three of these—50, 100, and 250 msec—would, for the most part, permit only a single eye fixation. The other three—500, 1000, and 1500 msec— were sufficient to allow multiple fixations.

The Experimental Design

We used the procedure described earlier with 80-slot slide trays. Targets consisted of the slides in the even slots for half the subjects, and slides in the odd slots for the other half of the subjects. Note, however, that there are 6 exposure times × 2 masking conditions, for a total of 12 study conditions. We wanted to arrange the experiment so that the number of target slides was divisible by the number of study conditions. Additionally, we wanted to have equal numbers of targets and distractors. These considerations lead us to use only 72 of the 80 slides in the tray (36 targets and 36 distractors . The remaining 8 slides in the tray were used as practice during the initial instructions.[11]

[11] From a logistical standpoint, it might make sense to block study conditions (see section below on "Experimenter Sanity"). The blocking–randomization question, of course, depends on the particular experiment. (In this experiment, we randomized study conditions so as not to permit particular strategies for particular conditions.) If study conditions are to be blocked, however, it is not a good idea to do so in such a way that there will eventually be separate false alarm rates for the separate study conditions. With a single false alarm rate and multiple hit rates, the hit rates can be compared with one another directly. However, comparison of different hit rates in the presence of separate false alarm rates will probably require some response model such as a signal-detection or a correction-for-guessing model.

In my earlier discussion of counterbalancing considerations, I pointed out that $2J$ subjects were necessary for this type of design where J is the number of study conditions. Since there are here 12 study conditions, a total of 24 subjects were needed in all. Actually, we run subjects in groups of five, simply as an efficient means of collecting as much data as possible. Thus, 24 five-subject groups were actually run.

Projection Equipment

This experiment requires two slide projectors: A random-access projector to present the pictures at study and test, and a second projector to present the mask. Each projector is equipped with Gerbrands one msec rise and fall time tachistoscopic shutters. The slide tray in the second projector contained only two slides: the pattern mask and a blank opaque slide (the latter being used for the unmasked condition).

Experimenter Sanity

The experimenter has a number of tasks in this experiment. Between each study trial, he or she needs to (a) advance the random-access projector to the next target slide, (b) possibly change the masking slide in the second projector and (c) possibly change the timer to the exposure duration for the upcoming trial. Between each test trial, the experimenter needs to change the random-access projector to the next test slide and read the trial number to the subjects. Much of this work could, in principle, be accomplished by putting the slide projectors, the shutters, and the timers under computer control. Since we have not yet done this, we have prepared a design sheet for each group (via a computer program). This sheet is divided into information pertaining to the study phase and to the test phase. The study phase section lists the trial number, slot number, masking condition, and exposure time for each study trial. The test phase section lists the trial number and the slot number for each test trial. The experimenter crosses off the information corresponding to each study and test trial as that trial ends. This provides for minimal experimenter error, but does not eliminate it.

ACKNOWLEDGMENTS

The writing of this chapter was supported by a grant to the author by the National Science Foundation, Grant BNS79-06522.

REFERENCE NOTE

1. Freund, R. D. *Verbal and non-verbal processes in picture recognition.* Unpublished doctoral dissertation, Stanford University, 1971.

REFERENCES

Averbach, E., & Coriell, A. Short-term memory in vision. *Bell System Technical Journal,* 1961, *40,* 309–328.

Biederman, I. Perceiving real-world scenes. *Science,* 1972, *177,* 77–80.

Biederman, I., Rabinowitz, J. C., Glass, A. L., & Stacy, E. W. On the information extracted from the scene at a glance. *Journal of Experimental Psychology,* 1974, *103,* 597–600.

Breitmeyer, B. G., & Ganz, L. Implications of sustained and transient channels for theories of visual pattern masking, saccadic suppression, and information processing. *Psychological Review,* 1976, *83,* 1–36.

Ebbinghaus, H. *Memory* (H. Ruyer and C. E. Bussenius, trans. New York: Columbia University Press, 1913. (Originally published, 1885.)

Egeth, H., & Smith, E. E. Perceptual selectivity in a visual recognition task. *Journal of Experimental Psychology,* 1967, *74,* 543–549.

Erdelyi, M. H. Recovery of unavailable perceptual input. *Cognitive Psychology,* 1970, *1,* 99–113.

Ericksen, C. W. The use of a visual mask may seriously confound your experiment. *Perception and Psychophysics,* 1980, *28,* 89–92.

Friedman, A. Framing pictures: The role of knowledge in automatized encoding and memory for gist. *Journal of Experimental Psychology: General,* 1979, *108,* 316–355.

Gould, J. D. Eye movements during visual search and memory search. *Journal of Experimental Psychology,* 1973, *98,* 184–195.

Green, D. M., & Purohit, A. K. Visual recognition memory for large and small binary pictures. *Journal of Experimental Psychology: Human Learning and Memory,* 1976, *2,* 32–37.

Haber, R. N. How we remember what we see. *Scientific American,* May 1970, 104–112.

Haber, R. N., & Erdelyi, M. Emergence and recovery of initially unavailable perceptual material. *Journal of Verbal Learning and Verbal Behavior,* 1967, *6,* 618–628.

Intraub, H. Presentation rate and the representation of briefly-glimpsed pictures in memory. *Journal of Experimental Psychology: Human Learning and Memory,* 1980, *6,* 1–12.

Just, M., & Carpenter, P. A. Eye fixations and cognitive processes. *Cognitive Psychology,* 1976, *8,* 441–480.

Just, M., & Carpenter, P. A. A theory of reading: From eye fixations to comprehension. *Psychological Review,* 1980, *87,* 329–354.

Latour, P. Vision thresholds during eye movement. *Vision Research,* 1962, *2,* 261–262.

Loftus, G. R. Eye fixations and recognition memory for pictures. *Cognitive Psychology,* 1972, *3,* 525–551.

Loftus, G. R. A framework for a theory of picture memory. In J. W. Senders & R. Monty (Eds.), *Eye Movements and Cognitive Processes.* Hillsdale, N.J.: Lawrence Erlbaum Associates, 1976.

Loftus, G. R. On interpretation of interactions. *Memory and Cognition,* 1978, *6,* 312–319.

Loftus, G. R. On-line eye movement recorders: The good, the bad, and the ugly. *Behavior Research Methods and Instrumentation*, 1979, *11*, 188–191.

Loftus, G. R. Acquisition of information from rapidly-presented verbal and nonverbal stimuli. *Memory and Cognition*, 1974, *2*, 545–548.

Loftus, G. R. Tachistoscopic simulations of eye fixations on pictures. *Journal of Experimental Psychology: Human Learning and Memory*, 1981, *7*, 369–376.

Loftus, G. R., & Bell, S. M. Two types of information in picture memory. *Journal of Experimental Psychology: Human Learning and Memory*, 1975, *1*, 103–113.

Loftus, G. R., & Kallman, H. J. Encoding and use of detail information in picture recognition. *Journal of Experimental Psychology: Human Learning and Memory*, 1979, *5*, 197–211.

Loftus, G. R., & Mackworth, N. H. Cognitive determinants of fixation location during picture viewing. *Journal of Experimental Psychology: Human Perception and Performance*, 1978, *4*, 565–572.

Loftus, G. R., Mathews, P., Bell, S. M., & Poltrock, S. E. General software for an on-line eye movement recording system. *Behavior Research Methods and Instrumentation*, 1975, *7*, 201–204.

Mackworth, N. H. A stand camera for line of sight recording. *Perception and Psychophysics*, 1967, *2*, 119–127.

Mackworth, N. H. The wide-angle reflection eye camera for visual choice and pupil size. *Perception and Psychophysics*, 1968, *3*, 32–34.

Mackworth, N. H., & Bruner, J. S. How adults and children search and recognize pictures. *Human Development*, 1970, *13*, 149–177.

Mackworth, N. H., & Morandi, A. J. The gaze selects informative details within pictures. *Perception and Psychophysics*, 1967, *2*, 149–177.

Mandler, J. M., & Johnson, W. Some of the thousand words a picture is worth. *Journal of Experimental Psychology: Human Learning and Memory*, 1976, *2*, 529–540.

Mandler, J. M., & Parker, R. E. Memory for descriptive and spatial information in complex pictures. *Journal of Experimental Psychology: Human Learning and Memory*, 1976, *2*, 38–48.

Mandler, J. M., & Stein, N. L. Recall and recognition of pictures by children as a function of organization and distractor similarity. *Journal of Experimental Psychology*, 1974, *102*, 657–669.

Nelson, T. O., Metzler, J., & Reed, D. A. Role of details in the long-term recognition of pictures and verbal description. *Journal of Experimental Psychology*, 1974, *102*, 184–186.

Nelson, W. W., & Loftus, G. R. The functional field of view during picture viewing. *Journal of Experimental Psychology: Human Learning and Memory*, 1980, *6*, 391–399.

Noton, D., & Stark, L. Scanpaths in eye movements during pattern perception. *Science*, 1971, *171*, 308–311.

Paivio, A. M. *Imagery and verbal processes*. New York: Holt, Rinehart and Winston, 1971.

Palmer, S. E. The effect of contextual scenes on identification of objects. *Memory and Cognition*, 1975, *3*, 519–526.

Pellegrino, J., Segal, A. W., & Dhawan, M. Evidence for dual-coding systems. *Journal of Experimental Psychology: Human Learning and Memory*, 1975, *1*, 95–102.

Peterson, L. R., & Peterson, M. J. Short-term retention of individual items. *Journal of Experimental Psychology*, 1959, *58*, 193–198.

Potter, M. C. Meaning in visual search. *Science*, 1975, *187*, 965–966.

Potter, M. C., & Levy, E. I. Short-term conceptual memory for pictures. *Journal of Experimental Psychology*, 1969, *81*, 10–15.

Rayner, K. Eye movements in reading and information processing. *Psychological Bulletin*, 1978, *85*, 618–660.

Russo, J. E., & Rosen, L. D. Eye fixations of multialternative choice. *Memory and Cognition*, 1975, *3*, 267–276.

Shepard, R. N. Recognition memory of words, sentences, and pictures. *Journal of Verbal Learning and Verbal Behavior*, 1967, *6*, 156–163.

Shiffrin, R. M. Visual free recall. *Science*, 1973, *180*, 980–982.

Sperling, G. The information available in brief visual presentations. *Psychological Monographs*, 1960, *74*, 1–29.

Standing, L., Conezio, J., & Haber, R. N. Perception and memory for pictures: Single-trial learning of 2500 visual stimuli. *Psychonomic Science*, 1970, *19*, 73–76.

Turvey, M. T. On peripheral and central processes in vision: Inferences from an information-processing analysis of masking with patterned stimuli. *Psychological Review*, 1973, *80*, 1–52.

Volkmann, F. C. Vision during voluntary saccadic eye movements. *Journal of the Optical Society of America*, 1962, *52*, 571–578.

Yarbus, A. L. *Eye movements and vision*. New York: Plenum Press, 1967.

Young, L. R., & Sheena, D. Survey of eye-movement recording methods. *Behavior Research Methods and Instrumentation*, 1975, *7*, 397–429. (a)

Young, L. R., & Sheena, D. Eye-movement measurement techniques. *American Psychologist*, 1975, *30*, 315–330. (b)

Semantic and Lexical Decisions

Semantic and lexical decisions are experimental tasks in which cognitive psychologists investigate the structure and processing of semantic knowledge. In one variant of these tasks, subjects are presented with a single word. In the semantic decision task, they decide if the word is a member of a particular semantic category. In the lexical decision task, they decide if the presented string of letters is a word. Common variations of this lexical decision task call for presenting subjects with two strings and asking subjects to decide "yes" if both strings are English words and "no" otherwise. The most common semantic task involves presenting subjects with a simple English sentence such as *Rubies are gems* and asking them to decide if the sentence is true or false.

The theoretical goal of most of this research is to make inferences about the organizational structure of semantic knowledge and the processes that operate on that structure. For example, the finding that prior presentation of the word *nurse* will facilitate the decision that *doctor* is a word (Meyer & Schvaneveldt, 1971) has been taken as evidence that the two terms are stored close together in memory. Analogously, similar studies (e.g., Schvaneveldt & Meyer, 1974) have sought to determine the processes by which this organization speeds retrieval of semantically similar terms. Similar experiments have been performed with categorical decisions (Collins & Quillian, 1970), in which subjects verify, for example, that *robins are birds*.

287

HANDBOOK OF RESEARCH METHODS IN
HUMAN MEMORY AND COGNITION

From this commonality of interest, one might be tempted to conclude that these two paradigms are equivalent. One might argue that "English words" is simply a very large category, and consequently all lexical decisions are necessarily category verifications. This assumption was at least implicit in some of the early work in this area (Meyer & Ellis, Note 1). Moreover, many theories in these two areas are quite comparable [for example, Collins & Loftus's (1975) semantic memory theory and the spreading activation model of lexical decisions discussed by Meyer & Schvaneveldt (1975)]. However, it has become clear that although these two areas of inquiry share a common paradigm, they do not necessarily share a common set of experimental results. This lack of commonality has important methodological implications, primarily in the area of what variables to control.

Because there are disparate results, it is appropriate that we begin this chapter by reviewing these basic results in some detail. In the second section, we discuss the materials used in these experiments, often the most flawed aspect of the study. Within this section, we discuss the implications of the inherently correlational nature of work with natural language materials and how one can decide which variables to control. We also focus on the particular problem of the distractors (negative items), and on minimizing the possibility that the composition of items will permit experiment-specific strategies to be used. Finally, we discuss the importance of ratings and how to obtain them. In the third section, we discuss the practical consideration of data collection. Analysis is discussed in the fourth section, where we deal with reaction times (RTs), errors, and the relationship between the two. Particular attention is paid to the problem of long RTs, and the disproportionate impact they have on the mean. In the fifth section, we discuss statistics and, more specifically, the appropriate time to use the quasi-F. In the last section, we talk about some experimental logics (such as additive factors) that have been employed in research on semantic and lexical decisions, and offer some opinions on their utility.

BASIC EMPIRICAL FINDINGS

The two most robust findings in the semantic memory literature are the typicality and the relatedness effects. These two effects should be considered together, because the former influences the verification of true statements, whereas the latter has its effect on false ones. Typical exemplars are items that are good examples of their respective category (Rosch, 1973). For example, *robin* and *sparrow* are both good examples of the category *bird*. For a given category, the more typical exemplars of that category will be verified more rapidly than the less typical ones. Rosch and Mervis (1975) have suggested that these exemplars possess most of the common attributes of the category *bird*. In contrast, *penguin* and *chicken* are bad examples of this category in that they do not possess as many of the category's attributes. Smith, Shoben, and Rips (1974) have suggested that typical exemplars possess not only those attributes that are relatively defining of category membership, but also those attributes that are only incidental or characteristic of it. Thus, for example, all four birds mentioned above have wings, are animate, and have two feet, but robins and sparrows can sing, can fly high, and are about the size of a softball, whereas chickens and penguins do not possess these characteristic attributes. The importance for semantic memory verification is that typical exemplars are verified more rapidly than atypical ones (Rips, Shoben, & Smith, 1973; Smith, 1978; Shoben, 1976). There is also some indication that typicality may influence lexical decisions as well (Antos, 1979).

Relatedness refers to an analogous finding for false statements. Disconfirmations are more difficult if category and exemplar are semantically similar or related than if category and exemplar are semantically dissimilar or unrelated. For example, *Bats are birds* is more difficult than *Chairs are birds*. This effect is also robust, and has been shown in a number of studies (McCloskey & Glucksberg, 1979; Rips *et al.,* 1973; Smith *et al.,* 1974). Two exceptions to this general result (Glass, Holyoak, & O'Dell, 1974; Landauer & Meyer, 1972) will be discussed later in reference to specific methodological problems.

Analogously, the effect of context has been most ably demonstrated in lexical decisions. Many studies in the lexical decision area have demonstrated that ease of decision can be altered by context. Early studies demonstrated that even one word contexts can have an effect. Meyer and Schvaneveldt (1971), for example, showed that subjects can determine that *doctor* is a word more readily if it is preceded by *nurse* than if it is preceded by *butter*. Although the size of this effect is small (usually between 25 and 100 msec), it is found in a number of tasks, and no one in the area argues that the context effect is not real. More recent studies (Kleiman, 1980; Schuberth & Eimas, 1977) have found similar effects using sentence contexts. For semantic decisions, context effects have not been investigated very thoroughly. Although there are a number of recall studies that show an effect of context (Anderson, Pichert, Goetz, Shallert, Stevens, & Trollip, 1976; Barclay, Bransford, Franks, McCarrell, & Nitsch, 1974), there are no published studies that demonstrate such an effect in a semantic verification experiment. However, Roth

(Note 2) has recently demonstrated a context effect in a number of circumstances. In one task she presented a category in a sentence context, such as *Mary cooked the bird for Christmas dinner*. Subjects were then presented with a single exemplar which they had to determine was true or false of the context constrained category. Roth found analogues of both the typicality and relatedness effects. *Turkey* was judged true more rapidly than *goose*, and *robin* was rejected more rapidly than *hawk*. Importantly, judged typicality to the target category in the absence of explicit context did not correlate with RT in her experiment.

Word frequency has a clear influence in lexical decision tasks. As one would expect, more frequent items are more readily identified as words than infrequent items. This result is not unexpected, and has been observed in a number of circumstances (Becker & Killion, 1977; Taft & Forster, 1975). What is perhaps unexpected is that there is no clear effect of word frequency in semantic decisions. Some studies have reported near zero correlations (Rips *et al.*, 1973), whereas others have found more sizeable effects (Wilkins, 1971). In one of the largest and most carefully done regression studies, Anderson & Reder (1974) found only a slight correlation between word frequency and RT when other semantic factors were partialed out. Moreover, work by McCloskey (1980) would suggest that whatever small correlation may exist between word frequency and RT may actually be due to unfamiliarity of some terms. Such unfamiliar terms (such as *zircon*) are usually of very low frequency and may be the predominant cause of this small correlation.

Finally, it is clear that for both semantic and lexical decisions, the type of distractor items is important. This has been investigated most thoroughly in the lexical decision context, but there are clear effects in semantic verifications as well. For example, McCloskey and Glucksberg (1979) have recently shown an increase in the size of the typicality effect when the distractors (false statements) were made more related. Similarly, Rips (1975) found that the presence of related distractors led to increased RTs for true items. In the case of lexical decisions, the effects are clearer and stronger. Specifically, the use of orthographically irregular distractors (nonwords) can eliminate some of the most robust effects. For example, James (1975) found no effect of word frequency when these irregular nonwords were used. There is also some conflict as to whether the nonwords should be just orthographically regular, or whether they should be additionally constrained to be misspellings of target words. Specifically, Antos (1979) used nonwords such as *roben,* along with targets such as *robin* and found results that were somewhat, though not drastically, different from Neely's (1977) findings. In an equivalent case, Neely might use a distractor like *borin,* a regular nonword, but not a recognizable misspelling of a target word. In addition to these global problems, we will discuss some more specific issues about distractors in the next section.

MATERIALS

The selection of materials for an experiment is perhaps the most important aspect of the entire design. This importance stems, in large part, from the inherently correlational nature of natural language research. In many areas of psychology, it is possible to manipulate a variable. For example, if one is interested in the effect of spacing on the perception of consonant–vowel–consonant trigrams (CVCs), one can simply alter the distance between the letters, and be reasonably confident that the two sets of stimuli differ only on this dimension. In contrast, consider how one might vary the size of the semantic category, where size refers to the presumed number of possible exemplars. For example, most would agree that *living thing* is a larger category than *animal,* and Landauer and Freedman (1968) used just these categories to test if there was a category size effect in the verification of statements. Landauer and Freedman (1968) found that smaller categories were responded to more rapidly. Collins and Quillian (1970b) suggested that it was not the size, but the nesting relationship of the categories that was important. They argued that with categories that were not nested (*dog* and *bird*), the category size relationship expected by Landauer and Freedman did not hold. Smith *et al.,* (1974) subsequently suggested that neither category size nor nesting relationship affected RT in semantic verification. Instead, they argued that the semantic similarity between the subject (exemplar) and predicate (category) was the crucial variable, and they produced a set of materials for which the smaller category was more difficult. Evidence that this issue is of continuing interest comes from the paper by McCloskey (1980) that argues that the familiarity of the terms is an important variable. His example of the importance of this variable is the Smith *et al.* study. McCloskey argues that in the stimulus set for which the smaller category was easier, the smaller category was more familiar and in the set for which the larger category was easier, the larger category was more familiar. Thus the reverse category size effect might have resulted from variations in familiarity.

The irony of all this is that we are now back where we started. One might summarize this work by suggesting that originally the dispute was whether category size or nesting relationship was an important determiner of RT. Smith *et al.* suggested that neither was important but that semantic similarity was. McCloskey suggests that similarity may have been familiarity and thus the category size effect (or nesting effect) may be real. The serious methodological problem here is how do we know when we have reached the end? The next step in this chain might be that familiarity in McCloskey's experiment may have been confounded with some unknown Factor A which can be shown to affect categorization time. Then, if the Smith *et al.* items are not confounded with Factor A, their interpretation stands.

The problem of possible confoundings is one that is common to all main effect studies. The reason that this problem is so terribly acute in the semantic decision literature is that one cannot really control the stimuli; one must select from what is available. It is impossible to select a large category and a small one and have them be identical on all other factors. Moreover, given the virtually infinite number of dimensions on which words can vary, it is not surprising that alternative explanations, which require only one such dimension, are so prevalent. Although one may need to do these main effect studies in order to test some fundamental predictions of various theories, it is argued here that studies that seek an interaction are more informative because in them it is much more difficult to generate an alternative explanation.

One example of this interaction approach is a study by Rubin, Becker, and Freeman (1979). Rubin *et al.* were testing some predictions made earlier by Taft and Forster (1975, 1976) concerning lexical decisions. More specifically, Taft and Forster (1975) argued that prefixed words were processed by decomposing the string into a prefix and a stem. Next a check is performed to see if both stem and prefix are allowable and subsequently, the entire combination is checked. If both prefix and stem are regular, but the combination is not (as in *devade*), then the subject checks for a whole word entry in the lexicon. Rubin *et al.* compared prefixed words (*unlike*) with pseudoprefixed words, words that appeared to have a prefix (such as *uncle*). The important methodological point is that they performed this task in two different contexts. In the first, the filler items and distractors were primarily prefixed words or nonwords. In the second, the distractors were primarily nonprefixed words and nonwords. The results confirmed the Taft and Forster predictions in the first context. When nearly all of the trials were prefixed items, prefixed words were recognized more rapidly than pseudoprefixed ones. However, in the second context, in which nearly all of the other trials were nonprefixed words and nonwords, the superiority of prefixed words over pseudoprefixed ones was greatly reduced. Rubin *et al.* interpreted this condition by context interaction as suggesting that the Taft and Forster model really has the status of a strategy. In a context of primarily prefixed items, it may be helpful to separate prefix and stem; however, in a less unusual context, such a strategy may not be employed as often.

The merits of the Rubin *et al.* interpretation are not at issue here. From a methodological perspective, it is important to notice that there is no simple single factor explanation of their results. If they had run only the prefixed condition, then one might quite reasonably have tried to explain the superiority of prefixed words over pseudoprefixed ones in terms of imagability, familiarity, or some other factor. With the interaction, such simple alternative explanations are not available.

Controls

Whether or not one is able to do interaction work, one must still face the question of what variables should be controlled in these types of experiments. In one sense, the answer is the same as for psychology experiments in general; the variables to be controlled are those that might otherwise explain a difference among conditions. In another sense, however, the areas of semantic and lexical decisions have specific problems. In particular, differences in the models of these tasks are sufficiently large so that there is no agreement on what is an important factor (i.e., has an effect) and what is not.

Thus, what one chooses to control is dependent on one's theoretical perspective. Ideally, one might try to control for all possible effects, but this is usually not possible, because of the limited number of materials. Because of the correlational nature of the research, it is not possible to construct items that have the required characteristics; one must select from those that naturally occur in English. As anyone who has ever tried to come up with a set of materials for a semantic memory experiment knows, it is not possible to control a set of items on more than a couple of factors. Lastly, the issue is complicated by the fact that the variables that need to be controlled are different in semantic decision experiments and lexical decision studies.

It would seem that the only sensible solution might be to control for what one believed to be demonstrated effects. For example, if one espoused the category search model of semantic memory (Landauer & Meyer, 1972), then one would certainly want to control for word frequency and for category size. On the other hand, if one espoused the feature comparison model of semantic memory (Smith *et al.*, 1974), such control is unnecessary, according to this view, because neither variable has an effect on RT. From a practical standpoint, of course, one should control for as many variables as possible, and one should not interpret this section as a license to ignore effects claimed by other models. The most important of these effects are discussed below.

Semantic Decision Controls

For semantic decisions, it is clear that one must control for the semantic relationship between subject and predicate. For example, if one is looking for an effect on true category statements, then one should control for the typicality of the exemplar to its category. Analogously, one should control the semantic relatedness between subject and predicate on false statements. Although there is currently widespread agreement on the need to control for this variable, there is a wide diversity of opinion on how this should be done. Some early studies simply obtained ratings of how closely associated the subject and predicate were (Smith *et al.*, 1974). Others tried to measure subjective conjoint frequency, or the frequency with which two concepts co-occur (Conrad, 1972; Wilkins, 1971). Still others have used production frequency: the frequency with which a predicate is given as a completion to a sentence frame such as *A robin is a* _____ (Glass *et al.*, 1974). Still others have used the dominance ratings from the Battig and Montague (1969) norms (Rips *et al.*, 1973) or typicality norms (Rips, 1975; Rosch & Mervis, 1975), or ratings of semantic relatedness (McCloskey & Glucksberg, 1979; Shoben, 1976).

Not surprisingly, these ratings are all intercorrelated. Mervis, Catlin, and Rosch (1976) showed that typicality ratings correlated highly with the Battig and Montague norms. Shoben, Rips, and Smith (Note 3) showed that subjective estimates of conjoint frequency correlated more highly with semantic relatedness ratings than with actual co-occurrence. They also provided evidence (as did McCloskey & Glucksberg, 1979) that association ratings were not as successful as relatedness ratings in predicting RT. Moreover, production frequency has the disadvantage in that it is difficult to determine what the appropriate measure is for false statements, because most people complete sentence frames so as to make them true. More detailed arguments may be found in McCloskey and Glucksberg (1979) and in Shoben *et al.* (1978).

Thus, semantic relatedness ratings seems to be the most critical control for the semantic relationship between subject and predicate. For true category statements, one can ask about this relationship in terms of typicality: how good an example is this exemplar of this category? For detailed descriptions of ratings, see McCloskey and Glucksberg

(1979) for relatedness ratings and Rosch (1973) for typicality instructions. One should not take this problem of rating instructions lightly, as subtle differences can produce fairly large effects, as will be documented later.

The second factor that should be controlled is relatively new. McCloskey (1980) has shown that the familiarity of the individual words may influence semantic decision time. Moreover, McCloskey goes to considerable trouble to demonstrate that stimulus familiarity is not simply word frequency or word length. Instructions for obtaining these ratings are given in his article (1980, p. 494). Although familiarity has not been subjected to much empirical scrutiny, it seems appropriate to control for it. Familiarity sounds a great deal like word frequency, and thus controlling for it may eliminate urgings to control for frequency.

The last factor that merits some consideration as a control variable is word length. Most investigators have not examined this variable specifically, and those who have (McCloskey, 1980) have not really questioned whether the small correlation between word length and RT can be wholly explained by other factors in the experiment. At present, it is not mandatory to control for this variable; however, one should not allow huge variation in length among experimental conditions. If one group of words was short, such as *elk* and *rat,* whereas another group was long, *hippopotamus* and *porcupine,* then one could reasonably argue that the second required more time than the first because of length.

Lexical Decision Control

Although we have argued that word length is not a particularly important variable to control in semantic decisions, it is almost always controlled in lexical decisions. Although some investigators have matched length in terms of number of syllables (Schuberth & Eimas, 1977), it is more common to match in number of letters (Kleiman, 1980; Swinney, 1979). For the most part, this distinction does not matter as it is hard to imagine a circumstance in which these two measures would not be extremely highly correlated. Interestingly, Fredriksen and Kroll (1976) found no difference in lexical RT between four-letter words and six-letter words.

The other factor that must be controlled is word frequency. Except in very special cases (James, 1975), word frequency normally has a large effect on lexical decision and should be controlled.

Although the issue of which variables to control in these types of experiments is not always an easy one, in some ways other questions are more difficult. In particular, the questions of what kind of distractors to use is a difficult problem for both semantic and lexical decisions. The nature of the distractors can clearly influence the results one obtains from the positive trials. For example, McCloskey and Glucksberg (1979) found that the size of the typicality effect in semantic memory increased when they changed their distractors from unrelated sentences to related ones. Similarly, for lexical decisions, James (1975) found that if the distractors were not pronounceable (e.g., *bneo*), then word–nonword judgments were very easy, and common effects, such as the word frequency effect, disappeared under these circumstances. Additionally, Davalaar, Coltheart, Besner, and Jonasson (1978) found that the homophone effect disappeared when unpronounceable nonwords were used.

Thus it appears that the selection of nonwords (for lexical decisions) or false statements (for semantic decisions) can radically alter the result that one obtains from positive trials. For semantic decisions, there is no clear-cut rule to follow. If one were to generalize freely from the McCloskey and Glucksberg (1979) result, one might argue that the distractors should be as difficult as possible. For lexical decisions, one should employ nonwords that follow the orthographic constraints of English. A related problem for lexical decisions is the relationship of the nonwords to the target words. Antos (1979), for example, has argued that the nonwords should be misspellings of target words. More specifically, in a typical lexical decision experiment in which one is presented with two words and the variable of interest is how rapidly the second word is processed, subjects might make decisions on the basis of just the first few letters of the string. In the Antos study, there was a very small and predictable set of second words, such as *bird* following *robin*. In this study, if Antos had used conventional distractors, a subject would have been correct a large proportion of the time by responding positively to any string following robin that began with a "b" and negatively otherwise. Antos's (1979) use of misspellings eliminated this possible strategy, and additionally let him look at facilitation effects on nonwords.

However, it appears that there are drawbacks to choosing this method of constructing the nonwords. First, it seems that this method changes the lexical decision into a spelling test; one is not deciding if a string has meaning, but whether a string is properly spelled. Moreover, some misspellings are clearly identifiable with their target word whereas others are not. For example, *goverment* is easily recognized as a misspelling of *government,* but *froit* is unlikely, without other contextual cues, to be identified immediately as a misspelling of *fruit.*

Assuming one is not interested in interactions with distractor type, the most reasonable generality would be to use difficult distractors if one wants to maximize the chance of finding significant effects. For lexical decisions, the safest course would seem to be pronounceable nonwords that obey the orthographic rules of English rather than misspellings of target words. For semantic decisions, one should use the most related false sentences that are consistent with the constraints of the design.

Difficulty of the distractors should not lead one to use highly unfamiliar words or to employ sentences whose truth value is not universally agreed upon. As noted earlier, McCloskey (1980) has argued that use of unfamiliar terms such as *zircon* can obfuscate the results of an experiment. Conditions that contain a higher proportion of unfamiliar terms may exhibit greater difficulty for this reason alone. One way to insure against this possibility is to rate the items for familiarity; a less costly though less convincing alternative is simply to avoid the use of unfamiliar items.

A related problem is the use of sentences of indeterminate truth value. For example, is the statement *All drapes are curtains* true or false? In an experiment that purported to test the effect of subject–predicate set relation on RT, Shoben *et al.* (1978) used a number of sentences that had this problem. They found a large difference among set relation that was only marginally significant. My own subsequent attempts to replicate this finding have been unsuccessful. There may be two problems with these sentences. First, subjects may not process them in the same way that other sentences with determinate truth values are processed; subjects may, for example, search for a counterexample in an attempt to falsify them. Second, subjects may operate under a kind of deadline model in which they guess after a certain subjective amount of time has elapsed. Either of these processes would tend to result in longer times for sentences of indeterminate truth value. Finally, it seems that this problem is not soluable by relatedness ratings. People rate curtains and drapes as very similar, but they also rate hawks and eagles as very similar, yet *All eagles are hawks* is definitely false and *All drapes are curtains* is indeterminate.

Overall Considerations

Despite extreme care in the selection of individual items, one can still unnecessarily admit alternative explanations if extreme care is not taken in the overall composition of the materials. The set of stimulus items should not admit some special strategy. This problem is most likely to occur with small stimulus sets. For example, the second experiment performed by Smith *et al.* (1974) required subjects to decide if a test item was a member of a prespecified semantic category. Only four categories were used, and for any given category, all of the distractors were from a single category. For example, all of the negative instances for the category *bird* were members of the category *insect*. Glass and Hol-yoak (1975) suspected that this highly restricted set of items may have promoted the use of a special strategy and argued that subjects could choose between two methods of verifying the sentences. For example, in the sentence *A robin is a bird,* subjects could respond true either because robins are birds or because robins are not insects. These two strategies are also available for false items. Glass and Holyoak were able to show, through correlations, that RT for "trues" depended to some degree on the relatedness of the exemplar to the nontarget category.

Such alternative strategies are possible whenever the universe of test items is especially narrow. This kind of problem can occur in lexical decision experiments as well as in semantic decision studies. For ex-ample, Taft and Forster (1975, 1976) found evidence for lexical decom-position in a group of studies mentioned earlier. However, Rubin *et al.* (1979) demonstrated that these results depended on a particular context in which the vast majority of the items are prefixed words. In the absence of such a constrained context, there is no difference between prefixed and pseudoprefixed words.

In some cases, the availability of strategies can be used to make a theoretical point. For example, Fischler (1977) sought to test the hy-pothesis that the context effect in lexical decisions was due to a guessing strategy. Becker, for instance, has suggested (Becker, 1976; Becker & Killion, 1977) that subjects are faster in determining that two associated words are words than two unassociated ones because subjects use the first word to generate guesses about the second. Fischler compared two experimental sets of materials. In the first, this guessing hypothesis was made quite plausible in that associated pairs were presented on two-thirds of the trials in which both strings were words. In the second set of materials, no associated pairs were presented. On a single test trial, Fischler compared the latency for a single associated trial. He found that the amount of facilitation (the size of the context effect) was equally great in the two conditions. Thus, if one assumes that his strategy ma-nipulation was successful, it would seem that the context effect is not due solely to a guessing strategy.

Ratings

For almost any set of materials, some ratings are necessary. Al-though some experiments on lexical decisions indicate only that asso-ciated words and unassociated words were determined by the experi-menter's judgment, most studies (e.g., Kleiman, 1980) that examine a more subtle distinction do involve ratings. Although some ratings do seem trivially easy to construct, it is not always easy to distinguish among similar underlying variables. For example, there has been a considerable debate in the semantic memory literature over whether relatedness or production frequency is the better predictor of RT. Glass and Holyoak (1975) have been the principal proponents of the production frequency view, and they employed ratings to support their argument. Specifically, Holyoak and Glass (1975) constructed two sets of false items. One set contained items that had a high production frequency contradiction, which should have lead to fast disconfirmations. In the second set, the production frequency of the contradictions was lower. Most importantly, Holyoak and Glass's ratings indicated that the high production frequency group was composed of items that were higher in relatedness than those in the low production frequency group. Thus, Holyoak and Glass were able to generate contrasting predictions for the two groups. According to the Smith *et al.* (1974) model, false RT should be longer for the high production frequency group, because high relatedness leads to long RT in false statements. In contrast, according to the Glass and Holyoak model, high production frequency leads to fast disconfirmations, and consequently this group should have faster RTs than the low production frequency group. Holyoak and Glass's results supported their model's predictions.

However, the way in which Holyoak and Glass obtained their relatedness ratings may severely question their results. In their instructions to subjects they defined semantic relatedness (in part) as "the degree to which one word reminds you of the other [p. 223]." Working independently, both Shoben *et al.* (1978) and McCloskey and Glucksberg (1979) obtained ratings for the same set of items that, in contrast to Holyoak and Glass's results, indicated that the low production frequency group contained items of higher relatedness than the high production frequency group. Thus, the RT results obtained by Holyoak and Glass were consistent both with the Smith *et al.* proposal and with the Glass and Holyoak model. McCloskey and Glucksberg asked subjects to rate the semantic similarity of the subject and predicate of the test sentences, and they emphasized in their instructions that subjects were to focus on the semantic relationship between the two terms and not on the association between them. Shoben *et al.* (1978) asked subjects to estimate the number of changes in meaning required to transform the subject into the predicate. The results of these procedures gave similar results, and effectively removed the Holyoak and Glass results as evidence for the Glass and Holyoak model.

It would seem that the important lesson to be learned is that one's instructions are very important. Subtle changes in wording can lead to significant changes in performance. As much as possible, the description of the task in the instructions should mirror the theoretical construct itself. In the case of semantic relatedness, the instructions should reflect the underlying definition of the concept and should not simply rely on old operational definitions of association.

There are several other precautions that should be heeded. First, one should use a relatively broad rating scale. Seven point scales are perhaps the most common, but nine or ten point scales are reasonable. For similar reasons, subjects should be encouraged to use the full range of the scale. The goal is that the rating scale should not keep subjects from making any distinctions of which they are capable. Examples, using materials that are not among the test stimuli, are also useful in increasing the probability that subjects will follow the instructions.

DATA COLLECTION

Although the actual collection of data in this field may seem straight-forward, there are a number of precautions that can be taken to minimize the variability of the RTs collected. Some of these, such as the use of fixation points and practice trials, are general to RT experiments, but others, such as the duration of the context item in lexical decisions, are neither very general nor intuitively obvious.

Fixation points and practice trials should be used. The location of the fixation point should be such that it indicates to the subject where the test stimulus will be located. The important point is that the subject should not have to search for the stimulus. Practice trials can also min-imize variation in RT. It is generally true that RT declines quite rapidly over the first few trials and more slowly after that, eventually reaching an asymptote. If this practice effect were the only consideration, then one would simply run a large number of practice trials. Unfortunately, large numbers of practice trials have at least two costs associated with them. First, practice trials take time, and a subject's time is usually limited. Second, large amounts of practice may change the process by which the subject performs the task. Thus, we must often limit the practice trials to materials that are not among the test stimuli. In general, about 20 practice items is sufficient to eliminate a large part of the practice effect.

The test materials themselves should be presented as simply as possible. For example, in a categorization experiment in which subjects are to verify statements such as *All chairs are furniture,* one should strongly consider presenting only the exemplar and the category:

chair–furniture. This simpler procedure is preferable because it will free the subject from having to read the other words in the sentence that are constant from trial to trial. If a computer is available, then it may be advisable to follow Meyer (1970) and remind subjects of the underlying sentence by presenting *All* _____ *are* _____ before the test pair as a kind of sentence frame.

Finally, the subject's responses should be monitored. Although there is no hard evidence to support this contention, it has been my experience that it is important to inform subjects of their errors in a relatively forceful way. Because our primary dependent variable in these experiments is usually RT (though exceptions will be discussed later), I usually encourage subjects to make few errors. If subjects are not told of their errors, they tend to become increasingly careless over the course of the experiment. Usually, an experimenter's admonition to "try to be more careful" will eliminate this tendency. When multiple subjects are run at the same time under computer control, the problem is more difficult. My own limited experience under these circumstances is that a message displayed on the screen for four or five seconds is sufficient.

It is also useful to record error latencies for diagnostic purposes. Such latencies will sometimes alert an experimenter to problems with a particular item. For example, in a categorization experiment, fast errors to *bean–animal* and *bear–vegetable* suggest that subjects had difficulty distinguishing *bean* from *bear*. If such orthographic confusions are not the subject of interest, then changing one of the items or at least changing the type font may eliminate the problem. In addition, long error RTs may be an indication that subjects are unsure, or at least unfamiliar, about a particular item. Long errors to *kumquats are fruits* may indicate some uncertainty about *kumquats*.

One problem that is specific to certain lexical decision experiments is the interval between items in a pair. More specifically, some experiments present a prime word (to which no response is required) and then a test word which may or may not be associated with the prime word. The question is how long the prime word should be displayed in order to obtain maximum association effects. Although Fischler and Goodman (1978), for example, have found a context effect for stimulus onset asynchronies as small as 40 msec, other research (Neely, 1977; Antos, 1979) suggests that the maximum effect may occur with considerably larger intervals. They found maximum effects around 500–700 msec. The extent to which this context effect can be ascribed to facilitative influences (rather than inhibitory ones) is a matter of some dispute; methodologically, however, it is reasonably clear that large asynchronies produce large context effects.

One way of coping with the asynchrony problem is simultaneous presentation. Although no explicit manipulations have been performed, Kleiman (1980) compares a number of studies that suggest that maximum context effects may be obtained with simultaneous presentation. However, this procedure does have some drawbacks in that, for example, one is never certain that subjects are reading the top word first. In addition, this procedure may allow reciprocal facilitation between the two words instead of the more common relationship where the first word is a prime for the second.

DATA ANALYSIS

Reaction Times

The first question that arises in connection with the RTs collected is whether they should be transformed. Many classical statistics books will argue that one should perform a log transformation when there is a dependency between the mean and variance. Most, if not all, RT distributions have this dependency. Although such a transformation may be good statistical practice, there are a number of reasons why RT data is not usually transformed. First, transformation is antithetical to additive factors logic (Sternberg, 1969); the analysis requires real times. Secondly, RTs are often viewed as a kind of naturalistic measure. Unlike percent correct, which is determined by the experiment, one can argue that RTs truly reflect the time required to perform a particular cognitive operation. To the best of my knowledge, there have been no Monte Carlo studies with actual RT distributions. My own experience is that transformation has very little influence on the statistics one performs, provided extremely long RTs have been excluded. Current practice seems to permit raw RTs to be used, and lacking any evidence that this procedure leads to statistical errors, it seems very reasonable.

For long RTs, there is no consensus. For a start, there is no fixed definition of what constitutes a long RT. Often, an arbitrary cutoff is selected (e.g., Rubin et al., 1979). In other cases, long RTs are defined as exceeding some number of standard deviations above the mean. Still other papers have used no cutoff at all. The reason for using some cutoff is to eliminate the impact of very long RTs on the mean reported for a particular item. For example, in an experiment with 16 subjects, if there is one long time of 6 sec, and the other 15 RTs average 1 sec, then including the long time raises the mean from 1 sec to over 1.3 sec. Because 300 msec is almost always a significant difference in these studies, the question of whether to exclude long RTs is an important one. In this example, the question is whether 1.00 sec or 1.31 sec more accurately represents the mean time for this condition. If one accepts the fact that an RT that is six times as long as the average does not reflect the standard processing for that item, then it would seem that one would want to exclude it. These long RTs are often the results of a subject's inattention or unfamiliarity with the words used in the item. Although excluding long RTs seems desirable, one should not exclude too much data. If long RTs constituted more than 2% of the data, one might reasonably be suspicious that many of the items used were unfamiliar to subjects. In most studies, the excluded data constitute about 1% of the total.

   If one is willing to establish some criterion for determining long times, then the next decision is what to do with these excluded items. There have been two common procedures in the literature. First, one can treat the long times as errors. This treatment has some intuitive appeal, in that it is consistent with the idea that some kind of nonnormal processing is occurring on these trials. The undesirable effect of this procedure is that it tends to reduce the mean RT of difficult items, because the longest times are excluded before the mean is calculated. This drawback has resulted in the practice of truncating the excluded RTs to the criterion value. Thus, if long RTs are defined as those that exceed 2.5 sec, then all times over this value are entered into the analysis as 2.5 sec. Although this procedure avoids the drawback of the count-as-error method, it would seem that it has no a priori justification. If long RTs reflect erroneous processing, then it would seem that we would not include them in the mean for the same reasons that error RTs are nearly always excluded from the determination of mean RT. This procedure can also lead to misleading results. Let us assume that the cutoff time is 2500 msec and that 16 subjects are in our hypothetical experiment. In both conditions, 13 subjects have a mean of 1000 msec. In one condition there are two errors and one long time. By the truncation method, the mean time for the first condition is (13,000 + 2500)/14 or 1107 msec. In the second condition, there are no errors but three long RTs. For this condition, the mean RT is (13,000 + 7500)/16 or 1281 msec. In most experiments, the variances would be small enough that this 174-msec difference would be significant. Yet, in the cases where the material was processed in a reasonable time, the two conditions are identical. It is tenuous at best to conclude from these data that the second condition is more difficult than the first. Consequently, excessively long RTs should be counted as errors and not included in the analysis of correct RT.

Errors

Errors are usually accorded only cursory attention in semantic and lexical decision experiments. It is still relatively common to report only the overall error rate in an experiment and the correlation between errors and RT. However, many have urged that experimenters pay more attention to error rates (Pachella, 1974; Wickelgren, 1977). At a minimum, one should report error rates in tandem with RTs. After all, error rate is an indicator of processing difficulty just as RT is. Usually, these two indicators agree, and this agreement is reflected in the positive correlation between these two dependent measures. However, the issue is more complicated than just the overall correlation. For example, one will often want to compare two specific conditions in a factorial experiment. For example, Neely (1977) wished to conclude that there was no difference between a neutral condition and an inhibitory condition at short delay intervals. Looking only at RT, the two conditions differed by only 4 msec. However, as Antos (1979) noted, the errors in Neely's study suggested that the inhibitory condition was more difficult. Antos himself found an inhibitory effect (for both errors and RT) under comparable conditions.

The important issue here is to examine one's error data seriously. It is sometimes possible to analyze error data as well as RTs (Shoben, Wescourt, & Smith, 1978). However, it would be excessive to state that one must always do so, because the number of errors is often so small that one may be unable to detect any significant differences. The reason for presenting the error results is primarily to allow assessment of the possibility of a speed–accuracy tradeoff in which one condition may show shorter latencies, but more errors, than another condition. Although one can never determine with certainty if subjects have sacrificed accuracy for speed in a particular condition, presenting error rates and RTs together does allow an informed assessment of that possibility.

There has been no systematic investigation of the type of instructions for these experiments that promotes or inhibits speed–accuracy tradeoffs. Some anecdotal evidence suggests that tradeoffs can occur when the material is unfamiliar. One possible reason for this particular problem may be that subjects are more reluctant to respond when the material seems unfamiliar. Thus, with familiar material, they may try to respond rapidly and may be willing to accept a reasonably high error rate; however, with unfamiliar material, they may behave more deliberately and make fewer errors.

It is not clear whether speed–accuracy problems are more prevalent when the error rate is relatively high or when it is relatively low. Error rates were quite low in the Neely study discussed earlier, but relatively high in Holyoak's (1978) fourth experiment, which also exhibited a speed–accuracy tradeoff. As the primary dependent variable of interest is usually the RTs, subjects are ordinarily instructed to minimize errors. In the absence of empirical evidence about the relationship between overall error rate and the likelihood of a speed–accuracy tradeoff, these instructions seem reasonable.

STATISTICS

The most common analysis performed on the data from semantic and lexical decision experiments is the analysis of variance. Although the complex designs used can often lead to confusions, the primary opportunity for error here is the failure to use the quasi-F (Clark, 1973) test when it is required. This procedure treats both subjects and items as a random effect in the analysis of variance. The net effect is that the test *appears* very much more conservative than the comparable F computed when subjects are treated as the only random effect.

In fact, the quasi-F is not unduly conservative, at least judged from the two available Monte Carlo studies performed to date (Forster & Dickinson, 1976; Santa, Miller, & Shaw, 1979). Both of these studies indicated that overall the true alpha level approximated the stated alpha level very closely.

The reason that this quasi-F is required is because one wants to generalize one's results not only over subjects but also over items. Just as one takes a sample of subjects, one also takes a sample of items. Although the item sample is seldom truly random, the population of items is still functionally infinite, and, therefore, the effect of items must be treated as a random effect. This argument is discussed in much greater detail in Clark's original paper (1973). In that article, Clark also showed how serious alpha errors could occur when the quasi-F procedure was not used.

Just recently, the quasi-F has become the standard for both lexical and semantic decision experiments. However, several relatively recent studies (Becker & Killion, 1977; McKoon & Ratcliff, 1979; Neely, 1977) did not employ the quasi-F, and one therefore can only speculate if results reported as statistically significant are truly reliable when the appropriate quasi-F is performed.

There are three circumstances in which the quasi-F need not be used. Two of these were noted by Clark (1973). In the method of single cases, the materials are limited to a very small set for which one cannot reasonably analyze each item. Much of the work with stories and scripts falls into this category, where subjects are typically asked to recall a prose passage under a variety of conditions. In studies of this type (e.g., Bower, Black, & Turner, 1979) it is often not practicable to include in the study the number of items necessary to make it possible to analyze variability across items. In such cases, one is forced to argue that one's items are truly representative of stories (for example) in general, and that one would expect similar results with another set of materials. Often, this method of single cases is the only way to study particular phenomena, but it is clearly not as convincing a logic as a quasi-F analysis, which enables generalization over items. The second design in which the quasi-F should not be used is one in which items and subjects are confounded. Here, each subject gets a different set of items so that the error term in the analysis of variance reflects both item variability and subject variability. In these circumstances, therefore, the analysis of variance with only one random factor is appropriate. This design is used only rarely, probably because it requires a large pool of items. When possible, however, it is an excellent way to achieve generality across items.

The third situation is one in which the quasi-F is not really appropriate, but should still be used. In this restricted domain experiment, the implicit assumption that the population of items is infinite is clearly and grossly incorrect. For example, Cech and Shoben (1980) investigated the processing of core kin terms. Because the number of kin terms is finite, they were able to determine, for example, that for many of their conditions there were only four or six possible stimulus items. In some cells their sample corresponded to the population. As Meyers (1979) notes, there is no easy statistical solution to this problem, because there is no category between fixed and random. It would seem better to err on the side of conservatism, and, therefore, one should follow Cech and Shoben (1980) and use the quasi-F unless one believes that one's sample virtually depletes the population in most conditions.

EXPERIMENTAL LOGICS

In this last section, some specific experimental logics are examined. Some, such as additive factors, are very general, but others have seen more limited application. The methods covered here are not meant to be exhaustive; they were selected because there are certain methodological problems or pitfalls associated with them.

Additive Factors

Sternberg's (1969) additive factors logic has probably received more scrutiny than any other in the field, and it is widely used throughout cognitive psychology. Because it is discussed at some length in a number of texts (e.g., Lachman, Lachman, & Butterfield, 1979), a complete outline will not be presented here. Instead, we will focus on problems of interpretation and on possible overgeneralizations of the method. Other discussion is presented in Chapter 1 of this volume by Murdock.

One interesting experiment that employed additive factors logic was the study done by Meyer, Schvaneveldt, and Ruddy (1974). In this lexical decision experiment, subjects were presented with two orthographic strings, and they decided in sequence if each was a word. The primary dependent variable of interest was the RT to the second word. The second word was preceded, in the critical conditions, by either an unrelated word or a related one. Thus the test word *doctor* might be preceded either by *nurse* (a related word) or *butter* (an unrelated one). This context factor was crossed with stimulus quality. *Doctor* might appear either intact (that is, without any visual noise) or it might be presented with dots superimposed on it in order to make it more difficult to read. Meyer *et al.* reasoned that the stimulus quality variable would affect the encoding of the stimulus and the context variable would affect the lexical retrieval stage. Therefore, according to additive factors, these two independent variables should not interact. Contrary to these expectations, Meyer *et al.* found a significant interaction between these two factors, and were therefore forced to conclude that context and stimulus quality influenced a common stage. Because it seemed unlikely for a number of reasons that stimulus quality influenced the lexical retrieval operation, Meyer *et al.* concluded that context must have an effect on the encoding stage.

This was an important result, and it is a good example of the theoretical power of additive factors logic. However, McClelland (1979) has recently provided an alternative account of additive factors experiments in general and this study in particular. McClelland argued that if one allowed a subsequent stage to begin before a prior stage had ended, then one might find that two factors, each of which affected a different stage, might produce a statistical interaction. In terms of the Meyer *et al.* (1974) study, McClelland argued that stimulus quality might affect the rate at which information was extracted (encoding), whereas context might affect the overall level of performance in the retrieval stage.

Although McClelland's argument is quite persuasive, its implication is not that additive factors has completely lost it utility. However, it does mean that interactive results in analysis of variance designs are considerably more open to interpretation than they used to be. The cascade analysis forces us to question the assumptions underlying additive factors. In this particular case, the assumption at issue is the strict serial operation of the stages. Before applying the additive factors method, one must consider carefully the appropriateness of this assumption.

One class of models where these assumptions are clearly not satisfied is the probabilistic stage models (Atkinson & Juola, 1973; Smith *et al.*, 1974). Glass and Holyoak (1975), for example, tried to apply this logic to the Smith *et al.* model. This model of semantic memory asserts that an overall comparison of subject and predicate is made in the first stage, and this initial comparison is sufficient if the amount of semantic overlap is either very high (leading to a true response) or very low (leading to a false response). If the overlap is intermediate, then the second stage (which compares defining features) is required. Thus, the relatedness of subject and predicate determines the probability that the second stage will be executed. Glass and Holyoak asserted that the model then predicted that semantic relatedness should affect the duration of the first stage and category size should affect the duration of the second. Although their first claim is inaccurate, the important point is the misapplication of additive factors. If we assume both that the model is right and that Glass and Holyoak's prediction is appropriate, then we still should not expect additivity. To take a limiting example, when semantic relatedness is high, the second stage may never be executed; consequently, category size would have no effect. On the other hand, with low relatedness, the second stage might be needed almost all the time, giving maximum opportunity for a category size effect. Because of this probabilistic relationship between the stages, additive factors is not a diagnostic procedure at all, and it should not be used.

Subtraction Logic

One research strategy that is very appealing at first blush is *subtraction logic*. Subjects perform two related tasks. In the first, subjects perform the task of interest, and in the second, they perform the same task minus some critical stage. The assumption that causes trouble for this experimental strategy is the pure deletion assumption. More specifically, the assumption is that one can remove one whole stage without altering any other aspect of the procedure. As Sternberg (1969) and many others have noted, this assumption is often unwarranted. It is important to consider only because there are examples in other areas of cognitive psychology where subtraction logic is tacitly used to reach certain conclusions, and also because one might be able to make some theoretical strides by using it. Meyer (1970), for example, fully recognized the dangers of subtraction logic, but he employed it to generate some very interesting hypotheses about the relationship between universally and existentially quantified statements in semantic memory. Although the implications of the work did not prove to be true (Rips, 1975), the work did broaden the scope of semantic memory theorizing.

Order Logic

Particularly in the area of lexical decisions, investigators have sought to determine the order in which cognitive operations occur. Specifically, investigators have sought to determine if a phonological code must be generated before a lexical decision can be made. The strategy used by several investigators (Meyer *et al.*, 1974; Rubenstein, Lewis, & Rubenstein, 1971) has been to see if the phonological nature of the items affects lexical access. If there is an effect, then we must conclude that a phonological code precedes lexical access. The Meyer *et al.* experiment is an excellent example of this logic. They presented subjects with pairs of words that varied in their orthographic and phonological similarity to each other. In one of the two experimental conditions, rhyming words such as *bribe–tribe* and *fence–hence* were used. Meyer *et al.* found performance in this phonologically similar condition to be superior to that observed in a control condition in which the words were repaired *bribe–hence* and *fence–tribe*. In contrast, orthographic similarity coupled with phonological dissimilarity led to inhibition relative to a control. Reaction times to pairs such as *couch–touch* and *freak–break* were actually longer than to the repaired control condition. Meyer *et al.* concluded that word recognition is mediated by a phonological representation.

Although this conclusion may seem straightforward, Kleiman and Humphrey (Note 4) argued that the phonological code may have been activated as a result of lexical access. They argued that the phonological dimension may have functioned in the Meyer *et al.* study as a kind of irrelevant dimension. Subjects may use this dimension when they believe it will be helpful in making their decision but they need not (Shulman, Hornak, & Sanders, 1978). An alternative way to conceptualize the problem is in terms of congruence. If we assume that similarity will bias toward a positive response, and dissimilarity toward a negative one, then phonologically similar words should facilitate positive responses and phonologically dissimilar words should inhibit positive responses.

Kleiman and Humphrey tested this alternative explanation by examining whether semantic relations would influence judgments that required a phonological code. More specifically, subjects judged whether a pair of words had the same number of syllables; the pairs were either semantically similar or semantically dissimilar. If phonological coding precedes lexical access, then the semantic relationship should be irrelevant to the syllabic decision. On the other hand, if the phonological code arises at the same time as the semantic code, or later, then we might expect semantic similarity effects on the syllabic judgment. Under this last explanation, semantic similarity effects would be expected because of the congruence principle. The results were in accord with the congruence principle. For "yes" judgments, RTs were significantly faster when the two words were semantically similar.

The results of this study suggest not only that the conclusions reached by Meyer *et al.* were unwarranted, but they also suggest a refinement on order logic. Specifically, if one wants to show that phonological coding precedes semantic coding, then one must show two things: first, in a task that requires a semantic decision, one must demonstrate an effect of phonology; second, in a task that requires a phonological decision, one must demonstrate the absence of a semantic effect. Such a pattern of results would provide strong evidence for the conclusion that Meyer *et al.* drew.

CONCLUDING REMARKS

In working with natural language materials, it is often difficult to do exactly what one wants to do. In categorization experiments in particular, controlling for six or seven factors, such as word frequency, may reduce the population of items to zero for a particular cell. The shortcoming of most early experiments in this area was that they did not generalize over items. This failure resulted from a number of factors, such as inadequate controls (for variables such as relatedness), using the wrong statistics, or having too few items per cell. All decisions about materials involve tradeoffs, and no one has worked out any rules for optimizing these decisions. In the absence of such rules, the goal of generalizing over items would seem to be a good guiding principle in constructing the materials for an experiment in this area.

ACKNOWLEDGMENTS

I would like to thank Glenn Kleiman, Emilie Roth, and Paula Schwanenflugel for their helpful comments on an earlier draft of this chapter.

REFERENCE NOTES

1. Meyer, D. E., & Ellis, G. B. *Parallel processes in word recognition.* Paper presented at the meeting of the Psychonomic Society, San Antonio, November 1970.
2. Roth, E. M. *Context effects on the representation of meaning.* Unpublished doctoral dissertation, University of Illinois, 1980.
3. Shoben, E. J., Rips, L. J., & Smith, E. E. *Issues in semantic memory: A response to Glass and Holyoak. (Tech. Rep.) Illinois: University of Illinois, Center for the Study of Reading, 1978.*
4. Kleiman, G. M., & Humphrey, M. M. *Phonological representation in visual word recognition: The adjunct access model.* Unpublished manuscript, 1981.

REFERENCES

Anderson, J. R., & Reder, L. M. Negative judgments in and about semantic memory. *Journal of Verbal Learning and Verbal Behavior, 1974, 13,* 664–681.
Anderson, R. C., Pichert, J. W., Goetz, E. T., Shallert, D. L., Stevens, K. W., & Trollip, S. R. Instantiation of general terms. *Journal of Verbal Learning and Verbal Behavior,* 1976, *15,* 667–679.
Antos, S. J. Processing facilitation in a lexical decision task. *Journal of Experimental Psychology: Human Perception and Performance,* 1979, *5,* 527–545.
Atkinson, R. C., & Juola, J. F. Factors influencing speed and accuracy of word recognition. In S. Kornblum (Ed.), *Attention and performance* (Vol. 6), New York: Academic Press, 1973.
Barclay, J. R., Bransford, J. D., Franks, J. J., McCarrell, N. S., & Nitsch, K. Comprehension and semantic flexibility. *Journal of Verbal Learning and Verbal Behavior,* 1974, *13,* 471–481.
Battig, W. F., & Montague, W. E. Category norms for verbal items in 56 categories: a replication and extension of the Connecticut Category Norms. *Journal of Experimental Psychology Monograph,* 1969, *80,* (3, Pt. 2).
Becker, C. A. Allocation of attention during visual word recognition. *Journal of Experimental Psychology: Human Perception and Performance,* 1976, *2,* 556–566.
Becker, C. A., & Killion, T. H. Interaction of visual and cognitive effects in word recognition. *Journal of Experimental Psychology: Human Perception and Performance,* 1977, *3,* 389–401.
Bower, G. H., Black, J. B., & Turner, T. J. Scripts in memory for text. *Cognitive Psychology,* 1979, *11,* 177–220.
Cech, C. G., & Shoben, E. J. Componential reasoning in kinship. *Journal of Experimental Psychology: General,* 1980, *109,* 393–421.

Clark, H. H. The language-as-fixed-effect fallacy: A critique of language statistics in psychological research. *Journal of Verbal Learning and Verbal Behavior*, 1973, *12*, 335–359.

Collins, A. M., & Loftus, E. F. A spreading activation theory of semantic processing. *Psychological Review*, 1975, *82*, 407–428.

Collins, A. M., & Quillian, M. R. Retrieval time from semantic memory. *Journal of Verbal Learning and Verbal Behavior*, 1969, *8*, 240–248.

Collins, A. M., & Quillian, M. R. Facilitating retrieval from semantic memory: The effect of repeating part of an inference. *Acta Psychologica*, 1970, *33*, 304–314. (a)

Collins, A. M., & Quillian, M. R. Does category size affect categorization time? *Journal of Verbal Learning and Verbal Behavior*, 1970, *9*, 432–438. (b)

Collins, A. M., & Quillian, M. R. Experiments on semantic memory and language comprehension. In L. Gregg (Ed.), *Cognition in learning and memory*. New York: John Wiley and Sons, 1972.

Conrad, C. Cognitive economy in semantic memory. *Journal of Experimental Psychology*, 1972, *92*, 149–154.

Davalaar, E., Coltheart, M., Besner, D., & Jonasson, J. T. Phonological recoding and lexical access. *Memory & Cognition*, 1978, *6*, 391–402.

Fischler, I. Associative facilitation without expectancy in a lexical decision task. *Journal of Experimental Psychology: Human Perception and Performance*, 1977, *3*, 18–26.

Fischler, I., & Goodman, G. O. Latency of associative activation in memory. *Journal of Experimental Psychology: Human Perception and Performance*, 1978, *4*, 455–470.

Forster, K. I., & Dickinson, R. G. More on the language as fixed-effect fallacy: Monte Carlo estimates of error rates for F_1, F_2, F', and min F. *Journal of Verbal Learning and Verbal Behavior*, 1976, *15*, 135–142.

Frederiksen, J. R., & Kroll, J. F. Spelling and sound: Approaches to the internal lexicon. *Journal of Experimental Psychology: Human Perception and Performance*, 1976, *2*, 361–379.

Glass, A. L., & Holyoak, K. J. Alternative conceptions of semantic memory. *Cognition*, 1975, *3*, 313–339.

Glass, A. L., Holyoak, K. J., & O'Dell, C. Production frequency and the verification of quantified statements. *Journal of Verbal Learning and Verbal Behavior*, 1974, *13*, 237–254.

Holyoak, K. J. Comparative judgments with numerical reference points. *Cognitive Psychology*, 1978, *10*, 203–243.

Holyoak, K. J., & Glass, A. L. The role of contradictions and counterexamples in the rejection of false sentences. *Journal of Verbal Learning and Verbal Behavior*, 1975, *14*, 215–239.

James, C. T. The role of semantic information in lexical decisions. *Journal of Experimental Psychology: Human Perception and Performance*, 1975, *1*, 130–136.

Kleiman, G. M. Sentence frame context and lexical decisions: Sentence acceptability and word relatedness effects. *Memory & Cognition*, 1980, *8*, 336–344.

Lachman, R., Lachman, J. L., & Butterfield, E. C. *Cognitive psychology and information processing: An introduction*. Hillsdale, N.J.: Lawrence Erlbaum Associates, 1979.

Landauer, T. K., & Freedman, J. L. Information retrieval from long-term memory: Category size and recognition time. *Journal of Verbal Learning and Verbal Behavior*, 1968, *7*, 291–295.

Landauer, T. K., & Meyer, D. E. Category size and semantic memory retrieval. *Journal of Verbal Learning and Verbal Behavior*, 1972, *11*, 539–549.

McClelland, J. L. On the time relations of mental processes: An examination of systems of processes in cascade. *Psychological Review*, 1979, *86*, 287–330.

McCloskey, M. The stimulus familiarity problem in semantic memory research. *Journal of Verbal Learning and Verbal Behavior*, 1980, *19*, 485–502.

McCloskey, M., & Glucksberg, S. Decision processes in verifying category membership statements: Implications for models of semantic memory. *Cognitive Psychology*, 1979, *11*, 1–37.

McKoon, G., & Ratcliff, R. Priming in episodic and semantic memory. *Journal of Verbal Learning and Verbal Behavior*, 1979, *18*, 463–480.

Mervis, C. B., Catlin, J., & Rosch, E. Relationships among goodness-of-example, category norms, and word frequency. *Bulletin of the Psychonomic Society*, 1976, 7(3), 283–284.

Meyer, D. E. On the representation and retrieval of stored semantic information. *Cognitive Psychology*, 1970, *1*, 242–299.

Meyer, D. E., & Schvaneveldt, R. Facilitation in recognizing pairs of words: Evidence of a dependence between retrieval operations. *Journal of Experimental Psychology*, 1971, *90*, 227–234.

Meyer, D. E., & Schvaneveldt, R. W. Meaning, memory structure, and mental processes. In C. Cofer (Ed.), *The structure of human memory*. San Francisco: Freeman, 1975.

Meyer, D. E., Schvaneveldt, R. W., & Ruddy, M. G. Functions of graphemic and phonemic codes in visual word recognition. *Memory and Cognition*, 1974, *2*, 309–321.

Meyers, J. L. *Fundamentals of experimental design*. Boston: Allyn and Bacon, 1979.

Neely, J. H. Semantic priming and retrieval from lexical memory: Roles of inhibitionless spreading activation and limited-capacity attention. *Journal of Experimental Psychology: General*, 1977, *106*, 226–254.

Pachella, R. G. The interpretation of reaction-time in information processing research. In B. Kantowitz (Ed.), *Human information processing: Tutorials in performance and cognition*. Hillsdale, N.J.: Lawrence Erlbaum Associates, 1974.

Rips, L. J. Quantification and semantic memory. *Cognitive Psychology*, 1975, *7*, 307–340.

Rips, L. J., Shoben, E. J., & Smith, E. E. Semantic distance and the verification of semantic relations. *Journal of Verbal Learning and Verbal Behavior*, 1973, *12*, 1–20.

Rosch, E. On the internal structure of perceptual and semantic categories. In T. E. Moore (Ed.), *Cognitive development and the acquisition of language*. New York: Academic Press, 1973.

Rosch, E., & Mervis, C. Family resemblances: Studies in the internal structure of categories. *Cognitive Psychology*, 1975, *7*, 573–605.

Rubenstein, H., Lewis, S., & Rubenstein, M. A. Evidence for phonemic recoding in visual word recognition. *Journal of Verbal Learning and Verbal Behavior*, 1971, *10*, 645–657.

Rubin, G. S., Becker, C. A., & Freeman, R. H. Morphological structure and its effect on visual word recognition. *Journal of Verbal Learning and Verbal Behavior*, 1979, *18*, 757–767.

Santa, J. L., Miller, J. J., & Shaw, M. L. Using quasi-*F* to prevent alpha inflation due to stimulus variation. *Psychological Bulletin*, 1979, *86*, 37–46.

Schuberth, R. E., & Eimas, P. D. Effects of context on the classification of words and nonwords. *Journal of Experimental Psychology: Human Perception and Performance*, 1977, *3*, 27–36.

Schvaneveldt, R. W., & Meyer, D. E. Retrieval and comparison processes in semantic memory. In S. Kornblum (Ed.), *Attention and performance IV*. New York: Academic Press, 1974.

Shoben, E. J. The verification of semantic relations in a same–different paradigm: An asymmetry in semantic memory. *Journal of Verbal Learning and Verbal Behavior,* 1976, *15,* 365–379.

Shoben, E. J., Wescourt, K. T., & Smith, E. E. Sentence verification, sentence recognition, and the semantic–episodic distinction. *Journal of Experimental Psychology: Human Learning and Memory,* 1978, *4,* 304–317.

Shulman, H. G., Hornak, R., & Sanders, E. The effects of graphemic, phonetic, and semantic relationships on access to lexical structures. *Memory & Cognition,* 1978, *6,* 115–123.

Smith, E. E. Theories of semantic memory. In W. K. Estes (Ed.), *Handbook of learning and cognitive processes* (Vol. 6). Potomac, Md.: Lawrence Erlbaum Associates, 1978.

Smith, E. E., Shoben, E. J., & Rips, L. J. Structure and process in semantic memory: A featural model for semantic decisions. *Psychological Review,* 1974, *81,* 214–241.

Sternberg, S. The discovery of processing stages: Extensions of Donders' method. *Acta Psychologica,* 1969, *30,* 276–315.

Swinney, D. A. Lexical access during sentence comprehension: Reconsideration of context effects. *Journal of Verbal Learning and Verbal Behavior,* 1979, *18,* 645–659.

Taft, M., & Forster, K. I. Lexical storage and retrieval of prefixed words. *Journal of Verbal Learning and Verbal Behavior,* 1975, *14,* 638–647.

Taft, M., & Forster, K. I. Lexical storage and retrieval of polymorphic and polysyllabic words. *Journal of Verbal Learning and Verbal Behavior,* 1976, *15,* 607–620.

Wickelgren, W. Speed–accuracy tradeoff and information processing dynamics. *Acta Psychologica,* 1977, *41,* 67–85.

Wilkins, A. T. Conjoint frequency, category size, and categorization time. *Journal of Verbal Learning and Verbal Behavior,* 1971, *10,* 382–385.

STEPHEN M. KOSSLYN
KEITH J. HOLYOAK

CHAPTER **11**

Imagery

INTRODUCTION

General Considerations

Imagery was one of the first topics to be studied experimentally in psychology (see Boring, 1950). Given the amount of time and attention it has subsequently received, it is not surprising that there are numerous and varied methodologies for studying imagery. In this chapter we hope to accomplish two things. First, we will provide detailed descriptions of the major paradigms currently in use. Second, we will try to provide some guidelines concerning when it makes sense to use a given paradigm. This second point is especially important in the study of imagery because of the range of issues currently being studied. Specifically, questions about the structure of images require different paradigms than are required for questions about the function of imagery. As will be discussed, some fine distinctions concerning the structure of images simply cannot be addressed using some of the paradigms.

Let us begin by discussing some general points that apply to virtually all imagery experiments, and then turn to the major specific paradigms.

HANDBOOK OF RESEARCH METHODS IN
HUMAN MEMORY AND COGNITION

NONIMAGINAL EXPLANATIONS

Perhaps the most important general considerations hinge on what one is trying to demonstrate in an experiment. If one is trying to ascribe a special role to imagery in some task, care must be taken to eliminate a host of possible counterexplanations. The two most important of these are the following.

Demand characteristics. The experimenter must take care not to lead the subject to perform in particular ways. Unintended biases may be introduced either by subtle (or not so subtle) reinforcement contingencies or by allowing the subject to infer the purposes or predictions of the experiment. Particular care should be taken to ensure that the instructions do not lead the subject to expect that only one pattern of responding is acceptable in performing the task. This is a very subtle kind of demand, in which subjects are led to understand the nature of the task in a way that constrains what they take to be acceptable performance—to the point where the outcome is a foregone conclusion. There is a very fine line between ensuring that subjects actually do the requisite task and nudging them to perceive the task in a manner that will necessarily yield the expected results (see Pylyshyn, 1981, and Kosslyn, 1981, for extended discussions of this point).

Nonimagery processing. One must take care to rule out nonimagery accounts of the data. These include not only explanations based on verbal rehearsal, but also explanations based on the notion of "abstract propositional" descriptions. Given that these sorts of languagelike data structures can be made to mimic imaginal ones to some degree of accuracy, this often proves a challenging task (see Anderson, 1978; Pylyshyn, 1979; Hayes-Roth, 1979). Kosslyn (1980) provides many examples of how these kinds of alternative accounts can be eliminated, often by making use of "privileged properties" of imagery in some aspect of the task. That is, imagery, by its very nature, has properties that are not shared by propositional representations. For example, one *cannot* represent a shape using an image, without at the same time, representing some size and orientation. In a propositional representation, in contrast, any one of these parameters can be represented without the others. Hence, showing that values on one dimension (e.g., size) affect the ease of processing information on another dimension (e.g., "seeing" aspects of an object's shape, such as the presence or absence of particular parts) is suggestive evidence against the kinds of propositional counter-accounts currently popular in some circles.

GENERAL METHODOLOGICAL CONSIDERATIONS

In addition to anticipating and precluding counterexplanations that do not implicate imagery, one must also take the following methodological considerations into account.

Definitions. Some subjects do not initially know the meaning of terms such as "imagery". It helps to simply explain to the subject that images are "mental pictures before the mind's eye." It is a *very* rare subject who will not be able to understand the referent of the term when given such a definition.

Instructions. Many imagery experiments hinge on the subject's performing some mental act on an image. As noted above, a major problem is to ensure that the subject understands the task without leading the subject to produce the expected results. One way to deal with this problem is always to use written instructions that are couched in neutral terms so as to avoid task demands (e.g., the relationship between time and the variables of interest should be obscured). Following this the subject can be asked to paraphrase the instructions back to the experimenter, who should ask the subject to reread the instructions until the paraphrase is correct.

Practice trials. The use of practice trials has two purposes. First, it provides yet another check of the subject's understanding of the instructions. If the subject is asked to describe what he or she did on a given trial two or three times during practice, the experimenter can be sure the subject understands the task. Further, the use of special "catch trials" may be helpful. For example, in an "imagery detection" task, in which subjects are asked to examine images for given properties, a probe such as "zebra's tongue" might be used. If the subject is following the instructions, he or she will have to image "opening the animal's mouth and having it stick out its tongue." The second purpose of practice trials is more commonplace: to give the subject time to become familiar with the various aspects of the procedure.

Imagability. The imagery system has only a limited capacity. Hence, the complexity of a stimulus is important: if a stimulus is too complex, subjects will not be able to keep the image in mind during the task. There is no adequate way of computing complexity for all possible stimuli. This requires pilot work, perhaps in conjunction with collection of ratings.

Counterbalancing. Whenever possible, groups of subjects should be created so that every item occurs equally often in each condition over groups.

Controls. The use of nonimagery controls is often useful. These controls are of two general types. The first type is a condition identical to the imagery one except that the subjects are not told to use their images in performing the task. If imagery is not used habitually to perform the task, such a control group should yield different results than those obtained in the imagery condition. Thus, this control serves to implicate imagery per se in the original results. For example, Kosslyn, Ball, and Reiser (1978) showed that response times increased with increased distance between an initial point of focus on an image and a probed property, but only if subjects were asked to search the image. Even when subjects began by forming an image and focusing on a given location, distance did not affect times when the subjects were not required to use the image. Thus, the effects of distance on the time to scan an image reflected image processing per se. The second type of control is the pseudoexperiment. In this paradigm a group of subjects is told the method and procedure of the experimental task given to the actual subjects and asked to guess the outcome. If subjects cannot guess the actual results, one has a good argument against task–demand counteraccounts (see Kosslyn, Pinker, Smith, & Shwartz, 1979).

Rest periods. It is useful to allow the subjects 2-min breaks after 30 or so trials in many of the current reaction-time paradigms.

Debriefing. Debriefing has a number of different purposes. First, the experimenter should ask subjects to estimate the percentage of time they actually performed the task as instructed. Somewhat surprisingly, subjects are usually quite candid in informing the experimenter that they failed to use imagery—providing an unintended nonimagery control! (These data often look quite different from those obtained from subjects who claimed to have followed the instructions, as would be expected if imagery has distinctive effects when used in certain ways; for example, see Experiment 3 of Kosslyn, 1975). Second, the experimenter should ask the subject to guess the purposes and predictions of the experiment. If the subject guesses correctly, the experimenter may be suspicious of demand characteristics or the like. It may be useful, however, to probe further in this (rare) case to determine whether the subject reasoned out the purposes and predictions of the experiments simply by introspecting upon his or her performance during the task. If this proves to be the case, further questioning can often reveal the extent to which the subject was responding to implicit task demands. Finally, the subject should be told the point of the experiment and asked his or her opinion about the hypothesis. Not only does this enrich the experience for the subject, but on occasion astute subjects may pinpoint a flaw in the experiment or make interesting observations about their behavior or about imagery in general.

Individual differences. Finke (1980), Marks (1977), and others have found wide variations in subjects' abilities to perform different imagery tasks. Finke, in particular, has found it useful to administer various imagery ability tests (such as Marks' VVIQ test of image vividness), and to perform separate analyses investigating effects of individual differences. Various written tests may therefore be routinely administered in conjunction with any of the following paradigms, and used in the analysis of the obtained results.

Sample size. There are two schools of thought on how to conduct imagery experiments. On one view, it is best to obtain a small sample (on the order of five or six people) and administer hundreds of trials over a period of weeks. On the other view, it is best to test a larger number of people (16 to 24 or so) for less than 100 trials, all in a single session. The advantages of the first method are that the data tend to be much less variable. The major disadvantage is that the subject has a greater opportunity to infer the purposes of the experiment and/or to develop special-purpose strategies for performing that particular task. The advantages and disadvantages of the second method are essentially the obverse of those just noted for the first method: data are noisier, but subjects are more naive. Depending on the task, one may sometimes be forced to use the first method (e.g., if only people with exceptionally vivid imagery can even perform the task), or the second method (e.g., if only a single trial can be conducted, perhaps because the subject must not expect the final result of performing some image transformation). In most cases, however, the experimenter has the option of which approach to adopt.

SPECIFIC PARADIGMS

Memorization

OVERVIEW

Imagery has long been regarded as a critical component of various mnemonic devices, such as the method of loci. The renaissance of imagery as an explanatory construct within cognitive psychology began with empirical studies of the role of imagery in memorization. Two major types of studies have been conducted. The first of these involves the manipulation of the concreteness of the materials to be memorized (see

Bevan & Steger, 1971; Kintsch, 1972; Paivio, 1965; Paivio, Yuille & Madigan, 1968; for reviews see Paivio, 1969, 1971). Such studies are based on the assumption that more concrete materials (e.g., pictures rather than words) are more likely to arouse mental imagery. If mental imagery facilitates memorization, then memory performance should be superior with more concrete materials. Studies of the second type involve variations in the learning instructions given to subjects (see Bower, 1972; Bower & Winsenz, 1970; Keenan & Moore, 1979; Kosslyn & Alper, 1977; Neisser & Kerr, 1973; again, see Paivio, 1971, for a review). In particular, subjects may be explicitly asked to memorize a set of materials (e.g., a list of words) by forming mental images. Both types of studies typically use standard verbal learning procedures (paired-associate learning, free recall, serial recall, or a recognition test), with paired-associate procedures being the most common. Memorization paradigms are most suitable for assessing the functions of imagery as a memory aid, although we will see that instructional manipulations can also be used to address more structural questions about mental imagery.

INPUT PARAMETERS

Manipulations of materials. In these studies the choice of input materials constitutes the basic experimental manipulation. In one representative study, Bevan and Steger (1971) presented both adult and child subjects with a mixed list of actual objects, pictures of objects, and names of objects. Recall performance was best for objects, next best for pictures, and poorest for words, thus matching the intuitive ordering of the types of materials along a concreteness dimension. However, studies of this sort do not provide convergent evidence that the concreteness effect is mediated by variations in the evocation of mental imagery as opposed to some correlated factor, such as sheer quantity of detail in the input.

Concreteness can be manipulated even when the input is restricted to verbal materials. Paivio, Yuille, and Madigan (1968) assembled a set of norms that are standardly used in such experiments. They had a pool of subjects rate 925 nouns on scales of "concreteness" (c), defined in terms of how directly the word refers to sensory experience; and "imagery" (I), defined in terms of the ease or difficulty with which the word arouses a clear mental image. For example, the word *desk* has relatively high c and I values, whereas the word *justice* has relatively low values. While c and I values tend to be highly correlated, when they can be separated it seems that I is the better predictor of memory performance (Paivio, 1965, 1968).

The advantage of high-I materials in memory experiments is extremely robust. However, it should be noted that manipulations of input materials are inherently correlational in nature. The interpretation of the results hinges on the experimenter's success in controlling other factors that might covary with I values and influence memory performance. Paivio and Yuille (1967), and Smythe and Paivio (1968) have demonstrated that the effect of I cannot be attributed to variations in either word frequency or the number of verbal associates as indexed by Noble's (1952) "meaningfulness" (m), two additional measures provided for the words in the Paivio et al. (1968) norms. However, it is virtually impossible to identify and control every potentially relevant source of variation in verbal materials. For example, Kintsch (1972) observed that low-I words are often lexically complex (e.g., vanity), and demonstrated that lexical complexity can account for some of the variation in memory performance that might otherwise be attributed to I. It is therefore difficult to draw strong conclusions about the role of imagery in memory performance from experiments that manipulate properties of the materials, and research of this type has consequently waned in recent years.

Manipulations of instructions. If the subjects are explicitly asked to form mental images, it is generally desirable to use input materials that are readily imagable (e.g., pictures or concrete words).

PRESENTATION PARAMETERS

Manipulations of materials. Variations in concreteness of materials produce robust effects on memory performance under the range of standard list–learning procedures.

Manipulations of instructions. For studies involving instructional manipulations, the general guidelines for administering instructions and monitoring compliance naturally apply. Performance may depend on the precise strategy subjects are induced to use. In particular, performance in a paired-associate task is much better if subjects are told to form images of the two objects interacting in some manner, rather than to form two separate images (Bower, 1972). Subjects may be told to image a particular interaction, or they may be allowed to invent their own. Both procedures are effective mnemonics; however, it is important for the presentation rate to be slow enough that subjects have sufficient time to form the required image. As a general guideline, about 10 sec per pair should be allowed for forming each interactive image in a paired-associate task.

In evaluating the effectiveness of a mnemonic device, care should be taken in selecting an appropriate control condition. One possibility is to have a condition in which subjects are not given any specific learning instructions. However, college students often spontaneously use fairly sophisticated mnemonic strategies, which may make it difficult to detect the effect of a particular instructional set. An alternative procedure is to compare imagery instructions to instructions to use some specific nonimaginal strategy, such as rote rehearsal (Bower & Winzenz, 1970). To avoid "contamination" it is generally preferable to administer the alternative instructions to separate groups of subjects.

A theoretical difficulty with instructional manipulations is that it is difficult to be sure whether imagery per se is responsible for improved memory performance. For example, instructions to form interactive images may be effective because they lead subjects to form a proposition linking the two terms in a paired associate. Indeed, Bower and Winzenz (1970) found that instructions to form a sentence for each pair produced performance levels comparable to those resulting from instructions to form interactive images. However, although many studies involving imagery instructions are limited to a functional interpretation, others have attempted to derive evidence that distinctive properties of imaginal representations have consequences for memory performance. For example, if pictorial properties of images are important, then an object that is concealed behind another or imaged at a small size should be difficult to "see," and hence difficult to remember (Luria, 1968). Both of these possibilities have been supported experimentally (Keenan & Moore, 1979; Kosslyn & Alper, 1977). Because subjects may use extraneous mnemonic strategies if they expect a memory test, these studies usually employ incidental learning procedures. In these procedures subjects usually are asked to form the described images and rate their vividness, and later are given an unexpected cued recall task (e.g., see Keenan & Moore, 1979; Kosslyn & Alper, 1977). The Kosslyn and Alper study also illustrates the use of a variety of controls for nonimaginal explanations of the effect of image size on memory performance.

In addition, studies of pictorial properties of images illustrate the critical necessity of conveying clear and explicit instructions to subjects. Neisser and Kerr (1973) had subjects construct images corresponding to sentences describing pairs of objects. In one condition both objects were visible in the described scene; for example, *A harp is sitting on top of the Statue of Liberty*. In another condition one object was concealed; for example, *A harp is hidden inside a torch held by the Statue of Liberty*. This study found no differences in memory performance between these two conditions. However, only a minority of the subjects reported forming images in which an object was actually concealed. A subsequent study by Keenan and Moore (1979) replicated the null effect of concealment when only general instructions to image were given. However, when subjects were explicitly told to imagine the scenes exactly as described, recall was significantly poorer when one object was concealed. These two studies jointly demonstrate the importance of both providing explicit instructions and of monitoring subjects' compliance with them.

RETENTION PARAMETERS

As noted earlier, any of a variety of standard retention tests may be used to assess the effects of concreteness or imagery instructions. Most studies manipulating either materials or instructions employ a reasonably long retention interval (at least a few minutes) and/or interpolated activity, so as to ensure that retrieval is based on long-term memory. There is evidence that imagery encoding is effective only when long-term rather than working memory is tapped (Kosslyn, Holyoak, & Huffman, 1976; Smith, Barresi, & Gross, 1971).

PERFORMANCE MEASURES

Studies of the influence of imagery on memory performance typically use percent correct as the main dependent measure. Qualitative error analyses, such as scoring for synonym intrusions, are also sometimes employed (e.g., Bower, 1972).

Selective Interference

OVERVIEW

Basic elements. A major theoretical claim about the nature of imaginal representation is that it in some way resembles the products of actual perception. In particular, tasks involving mental imagery may depend on some of the same mental machinery as do perceptual or motor tasks. *Selective interference* paradigms are designed to test this possibility (see Brooks, 1967, 1968; Byrne, 1974; Kosslyn *et al.*, 1976; Segal, 1971, for a review). If imagery and like-modality perception compete for use of the same representational structures and/or a limited pool of shared processing resources, then tasks involving imagery and like-modality perception should selectively interfere with each other.

The essential elements of a selective interference paradigm can be illustrated by a study performed by Segal and Fusella (1970). Subjects were asked to form a visual or auditory image (e.g., an image of a tree or an image of the ringing of a telephone). As soon as the subject indicated that the specified image had been formed, a 5-sec detection interval ensued. During this interval a faint visual or auditory signal might or might not be presented. At the end of the interval the subject was required to report whether a visual signal, an auditory signal, or no signal had been presented. The main dependent measure was detection accuracy as indexed by d'. (See Murdock's chapter in this volume for a discussion of this measure.)

The experiment thus involved four conditions, defined by the factorial combination of visual versus auditory images and visual versus auditory signals. The results, depicted in Figure 11.1, took the form of a crossover interaction. When the subject formed a visual image, detection accuracy was greater for auditory signals; whereas, when an auditory image was formed, detection accuracy was greater for visual signals. In other words, imagery selectively interfered with like-modality perception.

The Segal and Fusella study illustrates several general points about selective interference paradigms. At a theoretical level, it is important to be clear about what such studies can potentially demonstrate. Segal

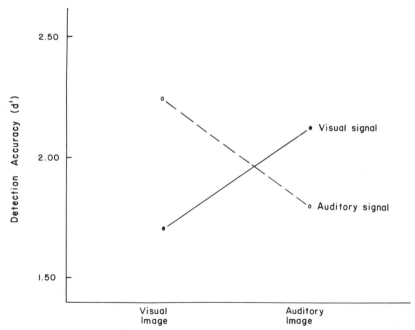

Figure 11.1. A "crossover" interaction: Selective interference between imagery and like-modality perception. (From Segal & Fusella, 1970).

and Fusella's results demonstrate that like-modality imagery and perception either make use of the same structures, and hence are confusable, or compete for common processing resources. However, the results do not tell us which hypothesis is correct (if not both), nor do they directly address the issue of the representational *format* for imagery. A propositional theorist might argue that both images and the products of perception are represented in a propositional form, and because these descriptions are similar they tend to be confused and hence interference occurs. Subtle variations of this paradigm conceivably could allow one to study the locus of the effect and the format of the representations, but no such studies have been reported to date.

The Segal and Fusella study also illustrates several critical methodological features of selective interference paradigms. Foremost of these is that such studies require a minimum of four conditions to demonstrate an interference effect that is indeed *selective*. It would not have been sufficient, for example, simply to show that it is more difficult to detect a visual than an auditory signal while maintaining a visual image, since it might be that visual signals are simply more difficult to detect in general. The critical aspect of the Segal and Fusella results is that the relative difficulty of the two detection tasks reverses across the two modalities of imagery. In the absence of such an interaction, a selective-interference interpretation would be unjustified.

A closely related point is that selective interference paradigms must involve some type of dual-task procedure. Ideally one would wish to obtain a performance measure for *both* of the concurrent tasks (Kosslyn *et al.,* 1976), since there may be a tradeoff between the processing resources allotted to each task. However, this is not always practical, as the Segal and Fusella study illustrates. Although they measured accuracy of signal detection, they did not obtain any index of the degree to which subjects successfully maintained their images during the detection interval. Since subjects formed their images prior to the detection interval and did not know what modality of signal to expect, the lack of a measure of image maintenance does not seriously affect the interpretability of the obtained results. However, suppose subjects had immediately "abandoned" their image at the onset of each detection interval, and devoted all of their processing resources to the detection task. Such a strategy might well have eliminated any detectable selective interference effect. For this and other reasons, null results in selective interference studies should be interpreted with great caution.

Interpreting interactions. Dual-task experiments are widely used in investigations of attention and performance (Kahneman, 1973; Norman & Bobrow, 1975) and some task interactions can be explained without recourse to selective interference. For example, consider the interference results obtained by Brooks (1968, Experiment VII), depicted in Figure 11.2. Brooks had subjects perform one of two tasks: (*a*) successively categorizing each word in a sentence as a noun or nonnoun; or (*b*) successively categorizing each corner of a block diagram as being located at the extreme top or bottom or in between. Subjects signalled their responses in one of two ways: (*a*) by an unmonitored movement (placing marks in a rough column on a page without looking); or (*b*) by a monitored movement (placing marks in a series of holes in a sheet of cardboard that were to be located tactually). In this experiment the overt response thus functioned as a second task. Response time was the main dependent measure, and the prediction was that monitored movements would selectively interfere with performance on the diagram task, assuming that both involved a common spatial system.

As Figure 11.2 illustrates, such an interaction was obtained. Although overall responses were slower with monitored rather than unmonitored movements, the difference was greater for the diagram than for the sentence task. However, note that the interaction depicted in

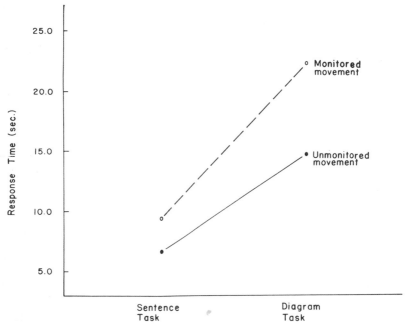

Figure 11.2. A non-crossover interaction: Possible selective interference between spatial imagery and monitored movements. (From Brooks, 1968).

Figure 11.2 is quite different in form from the Segal and Fusella (1970) results displayed in Figure 11.1. In particular, the Brooks data do not create a crossover. Such funnel-shaped interactions provide much weaker evidence for selective interference. Note that the diagram task was overall more difficult than the sentence task, whereas monitored movements produced overall slower responses than did unmonitored movements. It may be that *any* difficult response mode would be especially detrimental to performance of a relatively difficult task. The interaction in Figure 11.2 could therefore be explained without assuming that scanning a diagram and monitoring movements involve a common spatial system (Norman & Bobrow, 1975). In general, then, even a significant interaction need not unequivocally support a selective interference interpretation. We should note that Brooks was fully aware of this problem, and, in fact, suggested a type of control that can be used to overcome it (see Brooks, 1968, Experiment IV).

Since the interpretation of interactions is critical in selective interference paradigms, one more example may be useful. Kosslyn *et al.* (1976, Experiment 4) had subjects memorize 8-word lists by either a verbal-rehearsal or an imagery strategy. Immediately after each list had been presented, subjects performed one of two tasks: (*a*) a rhyme–match task (scanning a list of letters and crossing out those that rhymed with a target word); or (*b*) a visual–match task (scanning a list of letters and identifying those with a specified visual feature, such as a curve concave to the right). After performing the scanning task for 25 sec, subjects were asked to free-recall the word list. The dependent measures were number of targets identified on the scanning task and number of words correctly recalled.

Figure 11.3 presents the data for words recalled. (No interaction was apparent in the data from the scanning tasks.) A small but significant interaction was obtained, which differs in form from those depicted in Figures 11.1 and 11.2. When subjects learned the list by verbal rehearsal, recall was lower after an interpolated rhyme–match task; but when subjects learned by the imagery strategy, recall was identical after either the rhyme–match or the visual–match. This result is open to alternative interpretations. One might have expected the rhyme–match task to selectively interfere with the verbal-rehearsal condition, and the visual–match task to selectively interfere with the imagery condition. The data could be viewed as consistent with this interpretation, if it is assumed that the visual–match task was generally more difficult than the rhyme– match task (so that general and selective interference effects cancelled each other out for the imagery condition). A more direct interpretation of the data, however, is that the selective interference effect is "one-sided":

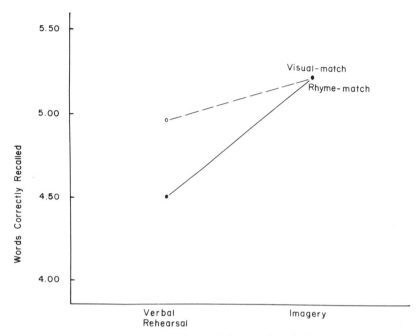

Figure 11.3. Interference pattern involving verbal versus imaginal mnemonics and acoustic versus visual search tasks. (From Kosslyn, Holyoak, & Huffman, 1976).

the rhyme–match task selectively interfered with the verbal-rehearsal condition, but neither interpolated task was especially disruptive for the imagery condition. The latter interpretation would follow from the view that the efficacy of imaginal memorization strategies is primarily due to the formation of abstract propositional codes, rather than specifically visual representations. Additional data in the Kosslyn *et al.* (1976) study support this interpretation. Across experiments the overall difficulty of the interpolated tasks was increased, but even the more difficult tasks failed to produce a differential effect for the imagery condition.

Procedural variations. The three studies just described can also serve to illustrate the range of variation in materials and procedures that can be introduced in selective interference studies. The Segal and Fusella study simply investigated the properties of the mental representations elicited by instructions to form images, whereas the Brooks study focused on the internal representations used to perform specific cognitive tasks. The Kosslyn *et al.* (1976) study dealt more directly with the nature of the memory traces produced by alternative mnemonic strategies. The Brooks study was more specifically concerned with the *spatial* aspects of imagery than were the other two studies. In general, the spatial properties of images seem to play a greater role in producing selective interference effects than do their pictorial properties (Byrne, 1974). Also, the temporal locus of the dual task can be varied. The Segal and Fusella experiment involved interference between imagery and immediate perceptual input. In the Kosslyn *et al.* study the interpolated task occurred during a retention interval, whereas in the Brooks study the interference occurred during the output of a response. Particularly for studies involving memorization, subjects can be required to perform a secondary task during input, the retention interval, or output.

A final note of caution: since certain published selective interference results have repeatedly failed to replicate, it would be wise for experimenters to replicate any new result.[1] Multiple experiments are typically necessary in any case to control for alternative interpretations of the interference pattern.

INPUT AND PRESENTATION PARAMETERS

The essential requirements for a selective interference paradigm are tasks or instructions designed to establish alternative types of mental representation (e.g., verbal versus visual), and interfering tasks that can be expected to match or mismatch the modalities of the internal representations. As noted above, the secondary task may be performed during input, retention, or response output. In some experiments, the two concurrent tasks may really be different aspects of a single task. For example, Brooks (1967) demonstrated that immediate recall of sentences describing a spatial array is poorer when the sentences are read as well as heard, rather than simply heard. The reverse was true when the sentences were nonsensical. This is a clear case of input interference, in which the visual presentation mode presumably interfered with the concurrent construction of an internal spatial representation. Brooks (1967) also found that reading as an *output* mode (i.e., use of a written response sheet) selectively interfered with subjects' ability to report the key words in a spatial message.

In order to avoid potential explanations of interference effects based on differences in overall difficulty, the overall difficulty levels of alternative tasks should be equated as closely as possible. In a signal-detection

---

[1] Personal experience makes us sensitive to this point. At an early stage in performing the Kosslyn *et al.*, (1976) study it appeared that we had obtained a difference between the two interpolated tasks for the imagery condition. Were it not for the editorial intuitions of Michael Posner, this result, which subsequently proved to be misleading, might have found its way into print.

paradigm, the ease of detecting signals can be calibrated by varying the intensity and duration of the signal. In general, interfering tasks should be sufficiently demanding that they compete for processing resources, but not so difficult as to cause performance to break down entirely. It is often useful to vary explicitly the difficulty of the interfering tasks (Brooks, 1968; Kosslyn et al., 1976). If response mode is used as a variable, it should be noted that tracking tasks create much more interference with internal spatial representations than do unmonitored movements. Interference is maximal when response output requires an overt scan that is inconsistent with a hypothesized internal scan (such as might be required to follow the contours of an imaged diagram; see Byrne, 1974).

RETENTION PARAMETERS

In studies involving a retention test, the test may be administered immediately after input, with the response mode manipulated as a variable (Brooks, 1967, 1968), or it may follow completion of an interpolated task (Kosslyn et al., 1976). Free-recall and recognition tests are among those that may be employed.

PERFORMANCE MEASURES

In signal detection tasks d' is typically the most appropriate response measure, although reaction time might also be used. Memory performance may be measured by percent correct or response time.

Perceptual Analogs

OVERVIEW

Although selective interference paradigms could be used to investigate the similarities and differences between images and percepts, they have not yet been used to do so. Two other paradigms have been so employed, however. One rests on psychophysical judgments. In these tasks, subjects make judgments about the values of imaged stimuli on intensity, size, or some other "perceived" dimension, in a manner like that required in the analogous perceptual task, where the stimuli are in fact physically present at the time of judgment (see Kerst & Howard, 1978; Moyer, Bradley, Sorensen, Whiting, & Mansfield, 1978; see Finke, 1980, and Podgorny & Shepard, 1978, for reviews). The other paradigm rests on judgments of similarity of imaged or perceived stimuli. These similarity judgments are often submitted to a multidimensional scaling analysis or the like, and the experimenter examines the similarity of the dimensions through the derived spaces for the imaged and perceived stimuli (see Shepard & Chipman, 1970; Shepard, Kilpatrick, & Cunningham, 1975; see Shepard, 1975, for a review).

INPUT PARAMETERS

Psychophysical judgments. The precise stimuli used are task-specific. Often the subject is provided with a standard (e.g., a picture of a state of the United States) and asked to assign numbers to imaged stimuli (e.g., other states) to indicate their relation to the standard along a specified dimension (e.g., area). If physical stimuli are presented in an initial learning phase of the experiment (rather than simply providing names, and hence relying on encodings previously entered into long-term memory), the elapsed time between presentation and the initiation of the judgment procedure may be varied. The stimuli should, of course, be imagable. The number of possible judgments is limited by subjects' attention span, duration of the experiment, and the like. Finally, the input parameters in the imagery and perceptual conditions, if both are included, should be comparable.

Similarity judgments. The factors previously noted are also important here. In addition, the association strengths between stimuli and other objects may affect these judgments (cf., Shepard & Cermak, 1973). The number of stimuli that should be used depends in part on the dimensionality of the expected multidimensional scaling solutions (at least 10 stimuli are required for a two-dimensional solution, increasingly more are required to obtain reasonably unique solutions with increasingly greater numbers of dimensions).

Presentation Parameters

Psychophysical judgments. The amount of time a stimulus is physically present before being removed is important, if only because more time encourages better encoding of an image. In addition, it may be that certain features of stimuli will tend to be given encoding priority in a systematic way, thereby functionally altering the structure of the stimulus-as-encoded if sufficient time is not allowed. The interstimulus interval is also important insofar as it may rush subjects; a self-paced procedure, in which subjects are given as much time as necessary to make judgments, is generally preferable to an experimenter-paced one. If stimuli are merely named in the imagery condition, the familiarity of the referents and the frequency of their prior exposures is important, as is the ability of the subject to identify the stimuli by name.

Similarity judgments. The parameters noted above are also important in this paradigm. In addition, the method whereby similarity judgments are obtained can be varied. Pair-wise ratings, rankings, and various methods of triads can be used (see Levelt, Van de Geer, & Plomp, 1966). In addition, time to compare two stimuli along the specified dimension can be measured, and these times can then be used as an index of similarity.

RETENTION PARAMETERS

In both paradigms, the amount of time elapsed between seeing a stimulus and forming an image of it seems likely to prove important, although few investigations of this have been made (cf. Kerst & Howard, 1978). It is probably best to allow subjects to make a judgment immediately after forming an image for the first time, since there is some evidence that repeatedly imaging the same object may become progressively more difficult within a relatively short period of time or, over a longer period of time, progressively more easy (these results are only preliminary, however). In addition, if both a perception and an imagery condition are used with the same subject, the order of the conditions should be counterbalanced and effects of order explicitly examined. Having seen and made judgments about the stimuli in a perceptual situation may influence performance in an imagery condition that follows shortly afterwards.

CALCULATION OF PERFORMANCE MEASURES

Psychophysical judgments. The data from the imagery condition should be of the same form as those from the analogous perceptual condition, and both should be analyzed in a parallel fashion. For example, if the task is magnitude-estimation, the data may be analyzed by computing the exponent in Stevens' Power Law (see Kerst & Howard, 1978; Moyer *et al.,* 1978). Similarly, Finke (1980) describes imagery experiments in which "perceptual" distortion was induced by images instead of by prisms worn by the subject. The analysis of the imagery data was the same as the analysis of data from the perceptual analog. As in most scientific work, the precise analysis performed depends in large part on the initial question posed and the outcomes predicted by the various hypotheses under consideration.

Similarity judgments. These data are almost always analyzed using some scaling procedure. Often KYST, MDSCAL, or some other multidimensional scaling analysis is performed. These analyses provide a geometric representation of the data, with each stimulus being represented as a point in a space such that the interpoint distances preserve the ordering of similarities in the original data (with more similar objects being represented by points closer together). The INDSCAL program allows the user to enter multiple input matrices (e.g., from separate imagery and perception conditions). It then produces a common solution with stable axes and provides weights on the axes for the different matrices. This provides a nice tool for examining the similarities and differences between imagery and perception with respect to various perceptual dimensions. Many readily available programs also allow one to specify different distance metrics, the most common being Euclidean ("as the crow flies") and City Block (not the shortest line between two points, but rather the distances along the horizontal and vertical axes that specify their coordinates—see Kruskal, 1964). Finally, various clustering programs, such as HICLUS, can be used to analyze the data, providing yet more information about how images and percepts were used in performing the judgment task. Kruskal and Wish (1978) provide an exceptionally clear description of the various scaling programs and their uses.

Mental Manipulations

OVERVIEW

There are two main paradigms that have been used to study the mental manipulations of images. The *preparation-time* task requires subjects to perform some manipulation and simply push a button when they are finished, usually in preparation for a subsequent task. The *judgment* paradigm requires subjects to manipulate an image in the course of making some evaluation of the imaged object(s). Subjects in this paradigm may or may not be explicitly told to form and manipulate images. The judgment paradigm has three main variants: either a single stimulus is presented and this stimulus is imaged and manipulated in order to make some judgment (e.g., whether it faces normally or is mirror-reversed); or two stimuli are presented one at a time, an image of the first being compared to the second; or two stimuli are presented at once and compared.

The mental manipulations most often studied are rotation, scanning (i.e., changing the point of mental focus), and scale (size) alteration. For a preparation-time task using rotation, see Cooper (1975). Judgment time tasks with single-stimulus or sequential presentation are exemplified by Cooper and Shepard (1973), and Hock and Tromley (1978) for rotation, Kosslyn *et al.* (1978) and Pinker (1980) for scanning, and Larsen and Bundesen (1978), and Sekuler and Nash (1972) for size alteration. Examples of judgment time tasks using simultaneous presentation include Shepard and Metzler (1971) for rotation, and Bundesen and Larsen (1975) for size alteration.

INPUT PARAMETERS

Preparation-time paradigms. The length of time a stimulus is studied, the time between study and the preparation cue (indicating how the image should be changed), the time between the cue and the subsequent task, and the nature of the task to follow the preparation are all important variables. If not enough time is allowed following the preparation cue, subjects may not complete the mental manipulation prior to the subsequent probe (see Experiment 1 of Cooper & Shepard, 1973). Furthermore, some preparation cues, such as orientation alone without the identity of the object to be imaged, have very little effect (Cooper & Shepard, 1973). In addition, subjects may or may not transform the entire image during preparation, depending on how much of the image is actually required to perform the subsequent task (cf. Anderson, 1978; Shwartz, Note 1). If an easy judgment follows preparation, subjects may selectively transform only portions of the image. The instructions to the subject are also critical here. Instructions can induce subjects to rotate an image clockwise or counter-clockwise (see Cooper, 1975), to vary rates, and even to alter the general strategy used in transforming the image (continuously versus in one discrete jump—see Chapter 8 of Kosslyn, 1980). Finally, the nature of the stimulus materials is critical; size, complexity and possibly other variables have some effects on how easily images can be manipulated.

One potential problem with preparation-time paradigms should be mentioned here: how does the experimenter know that the subject performed the requisite task? One way to check is to vary the relationship between the image and probe stimulus systematically. For example, if the subject should have prepared by rotating the image until it is oriented at 90 degrees from vertical, one can examine whether it is matched fastest against stimuli that are also at this orientation, and progressively slower against stimuli that are at progressively more disparate orientations. Similarly, if the image should be adjusted to some given size, variations in time to match the image against different size test probes should provide evidence that the image was in fact properly formed. A caveat is in order here, however: if the probes occur often enough at orientations, sizes, or positions other than that indicated by the original preparation cue, the motivation to manipulate the image is lost. One should, therefore, ensure that subjects will find manipulating the image as instructed useful on enough trials to motivate them to follow the instructions.

Judgment-time paradigms. If a single stimulus is presented at a nonstandard orientation, it may be imaged and mentally rotated to the standard upright orientation prior to being evaluated. Imagery is only used in this situation, however, if a relatively difficult judgment must be made about the stimulus (e.g., whether it faces normally or is mirror-reversed, or whether it is the same as or different than a similar distractor—cf., Cooper & Podgorny, 1976). When stimuli are presented sequentially, an image of the first stimulus may be used to perform a same–different "template" match with the second stimulus. Instructions to use imagery in this paradigm can affect performance (e.g., see Smith & Nielson, 1970; Nielson & Smith, 1973), in that alternative strategies can be invented. Again, imagery seems to be used spontaneously only when a relatively subtle discrimination must be performed. If the discrimination is not difficult enough, subjects may not manipulate all of the first image (if they use imagery at all) in order to match it against the percept. The nature of the discrimination required also affects how far subjects need to rotate an image (see Hock & Tromley, 1978). The complexity of the stimulus materials seems to be important, if one compares results found in different experiments (see Chapter 8, Kosslyn, 1980), but does not necessarily affect performance in a given task when the same subjects are tested over hundreds of trials (e.g., Cooper & Podgorny, 1976). In addition, the initial stimulus must be presented long enough to be encoded, and the interstimulus interval is critical (if it is long enough, the subject can prepare for the test probe in a variety of ways—see Cooper & Shepard, 1973; Smith & Nielson, 1970).

When stimuli are presented simultaneously, a number of additional parameters become important. There is evidence that subjects visually compare parts of one stimulus against parts of the other (Just & Carpenter, 1976). Effects of "landmarks"—corresponding points that allow easy judgments—are important (Hochberg & Gellman, 1977). It is not clear that mental manipulation is always required in this task, given the possibility of direct visual comparison, so explicit instructions to use imagery may be necessary. Finally, it has been found that in this paradigm rotations in the picture plane are easier than those in depth (see Pinker, 1980), and this manipulation may affect times in the other paradigms as well.

RETENTION PARAMETERS

In all of these tasks the response should be made as soon as the subject has completed the task. If properties of the manipulation itself are being studied, the judgment task should be simple enough so that variations in manipulation time are not overshadowed by variability in the time to make the judgment itself. In addition, in some experiments an initial image is maintained prior to being manipulated; in these experiments enough time should be allowed for the subject to form the image, but the manipulation should begin as soon after this as possible (images fade very rapidly). For example, in image-scanning experiments it is optimal to have subjects first respond when they have formed an image and focused on a specified location. A second stimulus (naming a possible location on the image) is then immediately presented, and the subjects scan to this location to make some judgment.

CALCULATION OF PERFORMANCE MEASURES

Times are not transformed prior to analysis (e.g., by taking logarithms) in these paradigms, since real-time performance is the measure of interest. Separate analyses of variance should be done both using subjects as a random effect and using items as a random effect. If the results do not generalize over items, this can be an important finding in its own right, leading one to examine the factors that result in some items showing an effect while others do not. The quasi-F statistic (Clark, 1973) generalizes over both subjects and items simultaneously, and is sometimes used in lieu of separate analyses of subjects and items. In the judgment tasks it is also important to examine the error rates, for two reasons. First, if error rates are too high, one cannot be certain that subjects actually imaged the stimulus (rather than some portion of it), or manipulated it in the correct way. Second, if errors increase as times decrease, the reaction time data may simply reflect an increased willingness to guess in some conditions.

Question Answering

OVERVIEW

The role of imagery in answering simple questions has mainly been explored using three types of tasks. In an *image-detection* task subjects are explicitly asked to form an image and to attempt to "detect" a named property on the image, indicating when they have either "seen" the property or examined the image and found it to be absent (see Kosslyn, 1975, 1976; Seamon, 1972; for a review see Kosslyn, 1980). In an *image-evaluation* task, subjects are asked to categorize a stimulus according to some relatively subtle distinction, such as whether a named letter of the alphabet is relatively short or tall (see Cooper, 1975; Smith & Nielson, 1970; Weber, Kelley, & Little, 1972; for a review see Kosslyn, 1980); these tasks usually require imagery in order to be performed, but subjects sometimes also are explicitly instructed to use imagery. In a *mental-comparison* task, subjects are asked to compare the relative magnitudes of two symbolic stimuli. For example, subjects may be required to decide which of two words refers to the larger object. A standard finding, termed the "symbolic distance effect," is that choice reaction-time decreases with the magnitude disparity of the items being compared (see Holyoak, Dumais, & Moyer, 1979; Moyer, 1973; Paivio, 1975, 1978; for reviews see Banks, 1977; Moyer & Dumais, 1978). Subjects in mental-comparison tasks usually do not receive explicit imagery instructions, although such instructions may be given (Holyoak, 1977). There has, in fact, been some debate as to whether imagery plays a critical role in mental comparisons (Kosslyn, Murphy, Bemesderfer & Feinstein, 1977; Paivio, 1975), or whether the comparison process is normally based on more abstract analog magnitude codes (Holyoak, 1977). The central issues in all three paradigms are how judgments can be made by "inspecting" mental images, and when imagery is used spontaneously to accomplish various sorts of judgments. Often the point of explicitly asking subjects to use imagery is to discover the "hallmarks" of imagery use, which then can be used to help the experimenter infer when other subjects use imagery without being explicitly instructed to do so (e.g., see Kosslyn *et al.,* 1977).

INPUT PARAMETERS

Image detection. In these experiments, subjects are explicitly instructed to use imagery in performing the task, although it is often possible to arrive at a correct decision without using imagery. The fact that these instructions are effective is evident in results such as those obtained in a study by Kosslyn (1976), in which very different patterns of data were obtained when imagery instructions were used than when they were not used. In that experiment, the size of a probed part determined decision times when imagery was used, whereas the association strength between the part and object determined times when imagery was not used. It is critical, then, that the instructions define the nature of the "imagery–detection" task, since time to "see" a property on an image is of central interest, rather than simply time to make a judgment using any possible strategy. The familiarity of both the object and the property is important here, as is the size and association strength of the properties. It is useful to present the stimuli auditorily, so that subjects can have their eyes closed when forming and examining images. In this case, the reaction-time clock is usually initiated by the presentation of a property name, and words have different numbers of syllables and different stress patterns. It is therefore important to counterbalance items across conditions, with different people receiving different items in the various conditions such that every item occurs equally often in each condition, and/or to demonstrate that results generalize over items. If pictures are memorized initially, the size, complexity, and familiarity of the pictured objects all are important factors to be controlled.

Image evaluation. The nature of the stimuli is absolutely critical here. Subjects appear to use imagery spontaneously when a judgment is rather subtle and not likely to have been made at the time of encoding. For example, Weber *et al.,* (1972) have found that subjects use imagery in categorizing from memory the letters of the alphabet according to height and/or width, and Cooper and Shepard (1973) found that imagery is used to evaluate whether letters are mirror-reversed or normal when the letter is presented at a nonstandard orientation. Further, Cooper (1975) found that deciding whether a nonsense form was the same as one shown initially required imagery when the form was misoriented and very similar to the original one. In these tasks the modality of stimulus presentation can also be varied, with subjects either hearing the name of some previously seen object (and imaging it), or else being presented with an object and asked to make some comparison to one previously seen.

In both of the foregoing paradigms subjects can be primed by starting off with an initial image, or they can be required to form an image only at the time of query. If an initial image is formed, the size, context, and point of focus are all important variables. If the image is too small, parts will be obscured; if it is too large, parts will "overflow"; and if the subject is focused on the wrong part, scanning may be necessary. If the image is in a complex context, it may be very degraded.

Mental comparisons. Mental comparison tasks can be performed with items that vary along any continuous magnitude dimension. Most research has involved mental size comparisons, and norms based on category ratings of object size have been published by Paivio (1975) and Holyoak *et al.*, (1979). The degree of semantic association should be controlled when constructing item pairs, since highly associated items can be compared relatively quickly (Holyoak *et al.*, 1979). The symbolic distance effect is extremely ubiquitous, as it is obtained not only with concrete dimensions such as size, but with abstract dimensions such as intelligence. The fact that distance effects are obtained with abstract dimensions has been used to argue that explicit imagery is *not* critical in performing mental comparisons (Banks & Flora, 1977; Friedman, 1978; but also see Kosslyn *et al.*, 1977 and Paivio, 1975).

Probably the strongest evidence for the use of imagery has been obtained in a task involving comparisons of "mental clocks" (Paivio, 1978). Paivio asked subjects to judge which of two digital times (e.g., 4:25 and 9:10) formed the largest angle between the hour and minute hands. The subjects were divided into groups that were low and high on imagery ability, as measured by prior tests such as *Block Visualization* (Guilford, 1967). The results were clearcut: a distance effect was obtained, as reaction time declined with increasing disparity between the two angles. Furthermore, subjects high in imagery ability responded more quickly than subjects low in imagery ability. When debriefed after performing the comparison task, most subjects reported that they formed images of clocks to answer the questions. In addition, Paivio performed a further experiment in which subjects compared the angles on visually-presented clock faces. A distance effect was obtained in this task as well, suggesting a link between the memory task based on digital times and actual perceptual comparisons. Paivio's study illustrates the use of a variety of converging evidence to argue for an imagery interpretation of the comparison process.

PRESENTATION PARAMETERS

Image inspection. The most important presentation parameters are modality and timing. If stimuli are presented visually, this may interfere with active maintenance and use of the image (Brooks, 1967; see the section on selective interference). If probes are presented too quickly, the subject may not have time to fully form the image. In general, subjects should be allowed about 5 sec between trials. If auditory presentation is used, the words should be spoken quickly but clearly, and the volume should not be too high. Furthermore, we have reason to believe that extraneous noises from the apparatus can sometimes have interesting effects on imagery (including prompting subjects to refresh their images, as well as distracting them). In addition, if pictures are shown, the time allowed to study the pictures is critical, as is the familiarity of the pictured object. Further, line drawings seem to be treated differently than photographs, with parts of line drawings generally being more discriminable in images (see Kosslyn, 1980, chapters 4 and 7).

Image evaluation. The foregoing parameters are important in these paradigms as well.

Mental comparisons. The simplest version of the comparison paradigm is to present two items simultaneously and have subjects press a response key to indicate which is greater in magnitude. However, several variants of this procedure may be employed. The two items may be presented sequentially, so that subjects are given time to comprehend the first item prior to presentation of the second. Sequential presentation is useful if subjects are instructed to form an image of the first item (Holyoak, 1977). A triplet paradigm can also be used, in which subjects are asked to judge which of two comparison items is closer in magnitude to a third reference item (Holyoak, 1978). The triplet paradigm makes it possible to perform a relative judgment task with stimuli that are inherently multidimensional. For example, Baum and Jonides (1979) had subjects judge which of two geographic locations was closer to a third. Another possible variant is a sentence verification procedure, in which subjects are asked to make true/false judgments about sentences (e.g., *Goats are larger than rabbits*).

The modality of the input can also be varied. For example, mental size comparisons can be made on the basis of pictures (Paivio, 1975), written words (Moyer, 1973), or spoken words (Kosslyn *et al.,* 1977). The evidence that reading selectively interferes with spatial imagery (Brooks, 1967) suggests that auditory presentation may be most conducive to imagery use.

An inherent property of dimensional comparisons is that the polarity of the question can be varied. For example, subjects may be asked to choose the larger or the smaller of two objects. A general finding, termed the *semantic congruity effect,* is that decisions are made more quickly if the magnitude of the items matches the pole specified by the question. That is, subjects are faster to choose the larger of two large items, but faster to choose the smaller of two small items (Jamieson & Petrusic, 1975). A semantic congruity effect can be obtained even when the question is presented after subjects have encoded the pair (Banks & Flora, 1977; Holyoak & Mah, in press). If one wishes to use choice reaction time as a measure of subjective magnitude disparity, it is desirable to amalgamate data collected using each of the two possible questions in order to obtain an unbiased estimate of "neutral" decision times.

Various procedural manipulations have been used to investigate the possible role of imagery in mental size comparisons. Paivio (1975), using pictorial stimuli, varied whether or not the relative size of the pictures matched the true relative size of the objects. He found, for example, that subjects could decide that a zebra is larger than a lamp more quickly if the zebra rather than the lamp was pictured as the larger object. This result, however, does not clearly show that the source of interference involves imagery as opposed to a semantic conflict (e.g., the fact that an object is the "smaller" picture may interfere with a decision that the actual object is the larger member of the pair). Holyoak (1977) introduced a similar size manipulation using imagery instructions. On each trial in one experiment subjects were first told the name of one of the items, and asked to image the object as large as possible, at a normal size, as small as possible, or not to form an image at all. After the subject was prepared, a second item was presented and subjects judged which item was actually the larger. In one condition, subjects were instructed to perform the comparison by normalizing and comparing images of both items, altering their image of the first item as necessary. Control subjects, while also asked to image the first item, were not asked to use any specific comparison strategy. Holyoak found that the size of the initial image had a much more pronounced effect on reaction time for those subjects who were instructed to use images to perform the comparison. These subjects also responded much more slowly than did control subjects. These results suggested that although subjects *can* use imagery to perform mental size comparisons, they do not necessarily do so. In a variation of Holyoak's experiment, Kosslyn *et al.* (1977) found that if auditory presentation of names was used (Holyoak presented his stimuli in a tachistoscope) subjects did seem to use imagery spontaneously in performing this task. In fact, only when to-be-compared items fell in different size-categories, and the categories were highly overlearned, did subjects seem *not* to use imagery in performing difficult comparisons. The variables that influence when imagery will be used in this task are not well understood at present (see Holyoak, 1977, and Kosslyn, 1980, chapter 9, for discussions).

RETENTION PARAMETERS

Image inspection. The time an image is held has remarkably little effect on inspection time, within the range of about 3 to 8 sec (Kosslyn, 1980). Because images are difficult to maintain, however, excessive retention intervals impede effective use of images. In addition, if drawings are imaged, the time between studying the drawing and imaging it is important, and subjects may be shown test drawings after the practice trials in an effort to keep their attention focused on their properties. If drawings are of common objects, it is important to realize that unless drawings are well learned subjects seem to distort images of a drawing toward the familiar rendition of the object, sometimes inserting parts that were not actually on the drawing.

Image evaluation. The foregoing considerations are important here as well. In this case the decision and response should be made as quickly as possible following presentation of the stimulus, with subjects retaining the stimulus as short a time as possible prior to responding. In addition, however, if the same stimulus is presented twice in close succession the subject may recall his or her previous response without using an image. One must therefore take care not to use the same stimuli too often, and to space replications of a stimulus throughout the presentation sequence.

Mental comparisons. The decision and response should be made as quickly as possible after stimulus presentation in this paradigm as well.

CALCULATION OF PERFORMANCE MEASURES

The same performance measures computed in image-manipulation experiments that include a judgment task are appropriate here, again with particular attention being paid to possible speed–accuracy tradeoffs and generalizability over both subjects and items.

CONCLUSIONS

The research paradigms discussed in this chapter are like any tool: they can be used in numerous different ways, in the service of accomplishing numerous different ends. However, like tools, a given paradigm is better suited for some purposes than others. In particular, most of the paradigms discussed here are difficult to use to address questions about the format of the representations underlying the experience of imagery (see Kosslyn & Pomerantz, 1977). The format is the formal structure of a representation, determined both by the nature of the representation itself and how it is interpreted (e.g., the symbol *cup* could be taken as a word or as a picture of a particular pattern, depending on how it is interpreted). The *format* must be distinguished from the *content*. The content is the information stored in a representation, which is independent of *how* it is stored (the information in this sentence could be stored using dots and dashes etched in clay, by magnetic fluxes in a computer, or using numerous other formats). The finding that imagery and perception interfere with each other demonstrates only that similar contents are represented; it does not implicate any given format. Similarly, the finding that imagery instructions improve memory says nothing about the actual form of the image representations. In order to address the issue of the format of image representations one must try to isolate some property of one format that would affect performance if image representation were in that format but not otherwise (e.g., shape, size, and orientation all must be represented together in a "depiction," but not in sets of propositions). The mental manipulation and question-answering paradigms have offered the best hope of distinguishing among different formats to date, but other paradigms can also be used if the predictions are clearly implied by the putative representation (e.g., see Kosslyn & Alper, 1977; see Kosslyn, 1980, for numerous experiments based on this logic).

ACKNOWLEDGMENTS

Preparation of this chapter was supported by NSF Grant BNS 79-12418 awarded to Stephen M. Kosslyn and NSF Grant BNS 77-01211 awarded to Keith J. Holyoak.

REFERENCE NOTE

1. Shwartz, S. P. *Studies of mental image rotation: Implications for a computer simulation of visual imagery*. Unpublished doctoral dissertation, Johns Hopkins University, 1979.

REFERENCES

Anderson, J. R. Arguments concerning representations for mental imagery. *Psychological Review*, 1978, *85*, 249–277.

Banks, W. P. Encoding and processing of symbolic information in comparative judgments. In G. H. Bower (Ed.), *The Psychology of Learning and Motivation* (Vol. 11). New York: Academic Press, 1977.

Banks, W. P., & Flora J. Semantic and perceptual processes in symbolic comparisons. *Journal of Experimental Psychology: Human Perception and Performance*, 1977, *3*, 278–290.

Baum, D. R., & Jonides, J. Cognitive maps: Analysis of comparative judgments of distance. *Memory and Cognition*, 1979, *1*, 462–468.

Bevan, W., & Steger, J. A. Free recall and abstractness of stimuli. *Science*, 1971, *172*, 597–599.

Boring, E. G. *A history of experimental psychology*, (2nd ed.). New York: Appleton–Century–Crofts, 1950.

Bower, G. H. Mental imagery and associative learning. In L. W. Gregg (Ed.), *Cognition in Learning and Memory*. New York: John Wiley and Sons, 1972.

Bower, G. H., & Winzenz, D. Comparison of associative learning strategies. *Psychonomic Science*, 1970, *20*, 119–120.

Brooks, L. R. The suppression of visualization in reading. *Quarterly Journal of Experimental Psychology*, 1967, *19*, 289–299.

Brooks, L. Spatial and verbal components of the act of recall. *Canadian Journal of Psychology*, 1968, *22*, 349–368.

Bundesen, C., & Larsen, A. Visual transformation of size. *Journal of Experimental Psychology: Human Perception and Performance*, 1975, *1*, 214–220.

Byrne, B. Item concreteness versus spatial organization as predictors of visual imagery. *Memory and Cognition*, 1974, *2*, 53–59.

Clark, H. H. The language-as-fixed-effect fallacy: A critique of language statistics in psychological research. *Journal of Verbal Learning and Verbal Behavior*, 1973, *12*, 335–359.

Cooper, L. A. Mental rotation of random two-dimensional shapes. *Cognitive Psychology*, 1975, *7*, 20–43.

Cooper, L. A., & Podgorny, P. Mental transformations and visual comparison processes: Effects of complexity and similarity. *Journal of Experimental Psychology: Human Perception and Performance*, 1976, *2*, 503–514.

Cooper, L. A., & Shepard, R. N. Chronometric studies of the rotation of mental images. In W. G. Chase (Ed.), *Visual information processing*. New York: Academic Press, 1973.

Cooper, L. A., & Shepard, R. N. Mental transformations in the identification of left and right hands. *Journal of Experimental Psychology: Human Perception and Performance*, 1975, *1*, 48–56.

Finke, R. A. Levels of equivalence in imagery and perception. *Psychological Review*, 1980, *87*, 113–132.

Friedman, A. Memorial comparisons without the "mind's eye." *Journal of Verbal Learning and Verbal Behavior*, 1978, *17*, 427–444.

Guilford, J. P. *The Nature of Human Intelligence*. New York: McGraw–Hill, 1967.

Hayes-Roth, F. Distinguishing theories of representation: A critique of Anderson's "Arguments concerning mental imagery." *Psychological Review*, 1979, *86*, 376–392.

Hochberg, J., & Gellman, L. The effect of landmark features on "mental rotation" times. *Memory and Cognition*, 1977, *5*, 23–26.

Hock, H. S., & Tromley, C. L. Mental rotation and perceptual uprightness. *Perception and Psychophysics*, 1978, *24*, 529–533.

Holyoak, K. J. The form of analog size information in memory. *Cognitive Psychology*, 1977, *9*, 31–51.

Holyoak, K. J. Comparative judgments with numerical reference points. *Cognitive Psychology*, 1978, *10*, 203–243.

Holyoak, K. J., Dumais, S. T., & Moyer, R. S. Semantic association effects in a mental comparison task. *Memory and Cognition*, 1979, *1*, 303–313.

Holyoak, K. J., & Mah, W. A. Semantic congruity in symbolic comparisons: Evidence against an expectancy hypothesis. *Memory & Cognition*, 1981, *9*, 197–204.

Jamieson, D. G., & Petrusic, W. M. Relational judgments with remembered stimuli. *Perception and Psychophysics*, 1975, *18*, 373–378.

Just, M. A., & Carpenter, P. A. Eye fixations and cognitive processes. *Cognitive Psychology*, 1976, *8*, 441–480.

Kahneman, D. *Attention and Effort*. Englewood Cliffs, N.J.: Prentice–Hall, 1973.

Keenan, J. M., & Moore, R. E. Memory for images of concealed objects: A reexamination of Neisser and Kerr. *Journal of Experimental Psychology: Human Learning and Memory*, 1979, *5*, 374–385.

Kerst, S. M., & Howard, J. H. Memory psychophysics for visual area and length. *Memory and Cognition*, 1978, *6*, 327–335.

Kintsch, W. Abstract nouns: Imagery versus lexical complexity. *Journal of Verbal Learning and Verbal Behavior*, 1972, *11*, 59–65.

Kosslyn, S. M. Information representation in visual images. *Cognitive Psychology*, 1975, *7*, 341–370.

Kosslyn, S. M. Can imagery be distinguished from other forms of internal representation? Evidence from studies of information retrieval time. *Memory and Cognition*, 1976, *4*, 291–297.

Kosslyn, S. M. *Image and Mind*. Cambridge, Ma.: Harvard University Press, 1980.

Kosslyn, S. M. The medium and the message in mental imagery: A theory. *Psychological Review*, 1981, *88*, 46–66.

Kosslyn, S. M., & Alper, S. N. On the pictorial properties of visual images: Effects of image size on memory for words. *Canadian Journal of Psychology*, 1977, *31*, 32–40.

Kosslyn, S. M., Ball, T. M., & Reiser, B. J. Visual images preserve metric spatial information: Evidence from studies of image scanning. *Journal of Experimental Psychology: Human Perception and Performance*, 1978, *4*, 47–60.

Kosslyn, S. M., Holyoak, K. J., & Huffman, C. S. A processing approach to the dual coding hypothesis. *Journal of Experimental Psychology: Human Learning and Memory*, 1976, *2*, 223–233.

Kosslyn, S. M., Murphy, G. L., Bemesderfer, M. E., & Feinstein, K. J. Category and continuum in mental comparisons. *Journal of Experimental Psychology: General*, 1977, *106*, 341–375.

Kosslyn, S. M. Pinker, S., Smith, G. E., & Shwartz, S. P. On the demystification of mental imagery. *The Behavioral and Brain Sciences*, 1979, *2*, 535–581.

Kosslyn, S. M., & Pomerantz, J. R. Imagery, propositions, and the form of internal representations. *Cognitive Psychology*, 1977, *9*, 52–76.

Kruskal, J. B. Multidimensional scaling by optimizing goodness of fit to a nonmetric hypothesis. *Psychometrika*, 1964, *29*, 1–27.

Kruskal, J. B., & Wish, W. Multidimensional scaling. In J. L. Sullivan (Ed.), *Sage University paper series on quantitative applications in the social sciences* (07-001). Beverly Hills, Ca.: Sage Publications, 1978.

Larsen, A., & Bundesen, C. Size scaling in visual pattern recognition. *Journal of Experimental Psychology: Human Perception and Performance*, 1978, *4*, 1–20.

Levelt, W. J. M., Van de Geer, J. P., & Plomp, R. Triadic comparisons of musical intervals. *British Journal of Mathematical and Statistical Psychology*, 1966, *19*, 163–179.

Luria, A. R. *The Mind of a Mnemonist*. New York: Basic Books, 1968.

Marks, D. Imagery and consciousness: A theoretical review from an individual difference perspective. *Journal of Mental Imagery*, 1977, *2*, 275–290.

Moyer, R. S. Comparing objects in memory: Evidence suggesting an internal psychophysics. *Perception and Psychophysics*, 1973, *13*, 180–184.

Moyer, R. S., Bradley, D. R., Sorensen, M. H., Whiting, J. C., & Mansfield, D. P.

Psychophysical functions for perceived and remembered size. *Science*, 1978, *200*, 330–332.

Moyer, R. S., & Dumais, S. T. Mental comparison. In G. H. Bower (Ed.), *The Psychology of Learning and Motivation* (Vol. 12). New York: Academic Press, 1978.

Neisser, U., & Kerr, N. Spatial and mnemonic properties of visual images. *Cognitive Psychology*, 1973, *5*, 138–150.

Nielson, G. D., & Smith, E. E. Imaginal and verbal representations in short-term recognition of visual forms. *Journal of Experimental Psychology*, 1973, *101*, 375–377.

Noble, C. E. Analysis of meaning. *Psychological Review*, 1952, *59*, 421–430.

Norman, D. A., & Bobrow, D. G. On data-limited and resource-limited processes. *Cognitive Psychology*, 1975, *7*, 44–64.

Paivio, A. Abstractness, imagery, and meaningfulness in paired-associate learning. *Journal of Verbal Learning and Verbal Behavior*, 1965, *4*, 32–38.

Paivio, A. A factor-analytic study of word attributes and verbal learning. *Journal of Verbal Learning and Verbal Behavior*, 1968, *7*, 41–49.

Paivio, A. Mental imagery in associative learning and memory. *Psychological Review*, 1969, *76*, 241–263.

Paivio, A. *Imagery and Verbal Processes*. N.Y.: Holt, Rinehart and Winston, Inc., 1971.

Paivio, A. Perceptual comparisons through the mind's eye. *Memory and Cognition*, 1975, *6*, 199–208.

Paivio, A. Comparisons of mental clocks. *Journal of Experimental Psychology: Human Perception and Performance*, 1978, *4*, 61–71.

Paivio, A., & Yuille, J. C. Mediation instructions and word attributes in paired-associate learning. *Psychonomic Science*, 1967, *8*, 65–66.

Paivio, A., Yuille, J. C., & Madigan, S. A. Concreteness, imagery, and meaningfulness values for 925 nouns. *Journal of Experimental Psychology Monograph Supplement*, 1968, *76*, 1–25.

Pinker, S. Mental imagery and the third dimension. *Journal of Experimental Psychology: General*, 1980, *109*, 354–371.

Podgorny, P., & Shepard, R. N. Functional representations common to visual perception and imagination. *Journal of Experimental Psychology: Human Perception and Performance*, 1978, *4*, 21–35.

Pylyshyn, Z. W. Validating computational models: A critique of Anderson's indeterminacy of representation claim. *Psychological Review*, 1979, *86*, 383–394.

Pylyshyn, Z. W. The imagery debate: Analogue media versus tacit knowledge. *Psychological Review*, 1981, *88*, 16–45.

Seamon, J. G. Imagery codes and human information retrieval. *Journal of Experimental Psychology*, 1972, *96*, 468–470.

Segal, S. J. Processing of the stimulus in imagery and perception. In S. J. Segal (Ed.), *Imagery: Current Cognitive approaches*. New York: Academic Press, 1971.

Segal, S. J., & Fusella, V. Influence of imaged pictures and sounds on detection of visual and auditory signals. *Journal of Experimental Psychology*, 1970, *83*, 458–464.

Sekular, R., & Nash, D. Speed of size scaling in human vision. *Psychonomic Science*, 1972, *27*, 93–94.

Shepard, R. W. Form, formation, and transformation of internal representations. In R. L. Solso (Ed.), *Information processing and cognition: The Loyola Symposium*. Hillsdale, N.J.: Lawrence Erlbaum Associates, 1975.

Shepard, R. N., & Cermak, G. W. Perceptual–cognitive explorations of a toroidal set of free-form stimuli. *Cognitive Psychology*, 1973, *4*, 351–377.

Shepard, R. N., & Chipman, S. Second order isomorphisms of internal representations: Shapes of states. *Cognitive Psychology*, 1970, *1*, 1–17.

Shepard, R. N., Kilpatrick, D. W., & Cunningham, J. P. The internal representation of numbers. *Cognitive Psychology*, 1975, *7*, 82–138.

Shepard, R. N., & Metzler, J. Mental rotation of three-dimensional objects. *Science*, 1971, *171*, 701–703.

Smith, E. E., Barresi, J., & Gross, A. E. Imaginal versus verbal coding and the primary–secondary memory distinction. *Journal of Verbal Learning and Verbal Behavior*, 1971, *10*, 597–603.

Smith, E. E., & Nielson, G. D. Representation and retrieval processes in short-term memory: Recognition and recall of faces. *Journal of Experimental Psychology*, 1970, *85*, 397–405.

Smythe, P. C., & Paivio, A. A comparison of the effectiveness of word imagery and meaningfulness in paired-associate learning of nouns. *Psychonomic Science*, 1968, *10*, 49–50.

Weber, R. J., Kelley, J., & Little, S. Is visual imagery sequencing under verbal control? *Journal of Experimental Psychology*, 1972, *96*, 354–362.

JAMES F. VOSS
SHERMAN W. TYLER
GAY L. BISANZ

CHAPTER **12**

Prose Comprehension and Memory

INTRODUCTION

Purpose of the Chapter

When a text is read and an individual is asked to recall its contents, recall is typically not verbatim. Instead, the individual recalls some sections of the passage while not recalling other parts, and the individual often "recalls" statements that were not in the passage. Moreover, if a recognition test containing appropriate distractor items is given, the individual often has difficulty in determining which items were or were not in the text. These results constitute the basic empirical findings in the study of prose comprehension and memory. Their explanation has been the primary goal of psychological models of text processing.

The study of prose comprehension and memory has evolved from three sources. One line of development, which has its origin primarily in linguistic theory, has focused upon the analysis of text structure. Models of text structure have been developed and the relation of the structure to performance has been studied. The second line of development, emerging from the study of human learning and memory as found in verbal learning and educational psychology, consists of studying how text is processed, especially in relation to variables of the task

349

HANDBOOK OF RESEARCH METHODS IN
HUMAN MEMORY AND COGNITION

situation. The third orientation, arising from concerns about memory structure, involves the study of how higher-level knowledge structures, such as schema, influence text processing. These three approaches, while not mutually exclusive, provide a useful organization for the purpose of this chapter, which is to review the methodology that has developed in the study of prose learning and memory. Thus, the chapter has four major sections, three related to methodological contributions associated with the respective research traditions, and a fourth which presents a summary and evaluation of these developments. Before getting into the major sections of the chapter, however, some setting information about terminology is in order.

Definitions

COMPREHENSION

In current theories of text comprehension and production (e.g., Just & Carpenter, 1980; Kintsch & van Dijk, 1978; Schank & Abelson, 1977), it is assumed that the task of understanding a text involves constructing a representation of the contents of the text. The difference between comprehending and not comprehending a given text is in the nature of the representation constructed. Although a unique representation does not exist for any text, Greeno (1977) has specified three criteria of "good comprehension": (*a*) the achievement of a coherent, that is, connected, representation; (*b*) correspondence between the internal representation and the object to be understood; and (*c*) connectedness between the concepts in the message to be comprehended and the individual's general knowledge. In this chapter, we adopt a similar notion, acknowledging that comprehension varies from person to person according to the representation that is developed.

COMPREHENSION AND MEMORY

One of the first issues that confronts any investigator of text processing is that comprehension and memory effects cannot be separated. One reason for this problem is that comprehension is usually measured by a memory task, and nonperfect performance may reflect a lack of comprehension or an inability to remember. To deal with this issue, one could argue that comprehension should be measured "immediately," that is, immediately after a passage is presented. But this argument has two problems. One is that comprehension takes place at many levels, ranging from the word, clause, sentence, or paragraph, to units such as a whole story. An "immediate" test, therefore, loses its significance because it typically would provide a test at only one level. Second, to comprehend a unit at least the size of a clause, it is usually necessary to remember information occurring earlier in the text and to integrate such information with subsequent information. Thus, comprehension necessitates maintaining information in memory on a short-term basis, in other words, comprehension of larger units has an intrinsic memory component. Thus, separating memory and comprehension is difficult, if not impossible.

PROSE

Although the term *prose* is difficult to define, it is possible to state some of its standard characteristics. These are: (*a*) It is characteristically written, although it may be either listened to or read; (*b*) it conveys meaning through use of the syntax, semantics, and pragmatics of the language in which the prose is written; (*c*) prose generally consists of sentences that are connected thematically. Finally, we note the term "discourse" is sometimes used in reference to these same characteristics. However, discourse is also used in reference to conversation, but conversation is usually not regarded as a form of prose.

PROSE TAXONOMY

Prose passages are often characterized as "expository," "narrative," "descriptive," "persuasive," and so forth. However, an accepted system of passage classification has not been developed (cf. de Beaugrande, 1980; Rockas, 1964). Most psychological research on text processing has involved the use of narrative and expository text, but there has been little attempt to differentiate processing effects associated with various types of passages.

METHODS RELATED TO THE STUDY
OF TEXT STRUCTURE

Intuitively and Empirically Derived Text Structure

APPROXIMATIONS TO ENGLISH

One of the earliest attempts to study text structure involved the concept of approximations to English (Miller & Selfridge, 1950). Text structure was defined in terms of its sequential resemblance to English.

A zero-order approximation consists of randomly selecting words from a dictionary for a passage of word length n, whereas a first-order approximation also consists of selecting words, but the words are weighted according to frequency of occurrence in the language. The remaining orders are determined by using k immediately preceding words to select the $k + 1$ word, with such selection continuing until the passage reaches length n. Miller and Selfridge (1950) studied recall as a function of level of approximation, as did Coleman (1963), Marks and Jack (1952), Richardson and Voss (1960), and Sharp (1958). In addition, Lachman and Tuttle (1965) employed texts of high-order or low-order approximation, followed by discrimination of passage and nonpassage words. The order-of-approximation procedure has received little attention in recent years, probably because there has been little interest in the statistical study of word sequences.

IDEA UNITS

The need to divide a text into a number of units arose, at least in part, from the necessity of scoring recall protocols (cf. Clark, 1940; Cofer, 1941; Henderson, 1903). One technique developed was to divide the passage into a set of "idea units," in other words, units of text that embody a single complete idea. The units were typically small, consisting of one or a few words. The investigator then determined which and how many of these units were recalled. As pointed out by Levitt (1956), the particular divisions influence the recall score, especially when comparisons are made across passages. Scoring in "idea units" permits quantification of number of units recalled, but it does not provide for qualitative distinctions.

EMPIRICALLY DERIVED UNITS

Another method of segmenting text consists of using pausal units (Johnson, 1970). Such units were established by asking subjects to indicate where pausing might occur to "catch a breath, to give emphasis to the story, or to enhance meaning" (Johnson, 1970, p. 13). In order to provide qualitative differentiation, the units were rated according to their importance in the story. This was done by deleting units until one-fourth, one-half, or three-fourths of the original words of the story remained after deletion. The structural importance of the unit was then determined by the extent to which a particular unit was maintained in the story. Johnson (1973) also related the concept of pausal units to meaningfulness, and Johnson and Scheidt (1977) used pausal units in a serial anticipation task that provided for the delineation of subjective structures similar to those obtained in serial recall (Martin & Noreen, 1974). The pausal unit method also has been used more recently to investigate developmental changes in children's metacognitive abilities and skills (e.g., Brown & Smiley, 1977; Petros & Hoving, 1980).

Similarly, in an interesting study, Rubin (1978) defined units not in pausal terms, but in terms of grammatical criteria. Each unit consisted of at least one noun, verb, adverb, or adjective. Rubin scored the data not only by determining how many units each subject recalled, but also by summing over subjects, thus determining the frequency of recall of particular units. He found that, over a number of independent variables, the relative order of recall frequency of the units was highly consistent.

Whereas empirically defined units have proved to be useful tools, the shortcoming of the method is that it lacks a conceptual rationale to suggest what makes units differentially important and why such differences influence performance. The next section describes several approaches that have been designed to provide a theoretically motivated specification of importance.

Text Structure Derived from Logic and Linguistic Theory

In recent years, a number of models have been devised for characterizing the structure of prose passages. These approaches have shared the assumption that investigators could characterize the underlying structure of a text in terms of basic units and the relations among the units.

DAWES' MODEL

One of the earliest attempts to study passage structure was that of Dawes (1964, 1966). Arguing that declarative sentences often consist of set relations, he constructed two passages based upon set inclusion principles. His structure was thus based upon logical, not linguistic, relations. His analysis of performance emphasized errors of overgeneralization and pseudodiscrimination of the relations in the passages. Incidentally, one of Dawes' (1964) passages, "Circle Island," has been used by other investigators.

CROTHERS' MODEL

Crothers (1972) developed a model designed to provide a description of the underlying structure of a text as well as a description of the text as it would be represented in memory. Crothers used graph-theoretic notation to describe relations among the text concepts, and since a particular concept could be repeated and connected to a number of other concepts, the structure was viewed as hierarchical in nature. However, especially at the higher, more general levels, Crothers found it necessary to insert inferential information, and he assumed that such inferences could be made by a knowledgeable subject. The model, however, was not successful at predicting recall.

More recently, Crothers (1979) has developed an inference theory of text structure. While the focus of the theory is on the development of a taxonomy of inferences and principles for deriving them, Crothers' analysis specifies propositional connectives, a text hierarchy, elements of propositions, and other interesting text properties. This theory has been used to represent the structure of both argumentative and narrative passages.

FREDERIKSEN'S MODEL

Frederiksen (1972, 1975a, 1975b, 1975c) developed a model of text structure that included a semantic structure and a logical structure. The former consisted primarily of sentence elements classified according to linguistic rules; the latter consisted of a structure that identified the logical relation of the concepts of the passages. The logical structure was not hierarchical. Frederiksen also found it necessary to include inferences in the model, primarily to allow for the bridging of concepts occurring in different sentences of the text. The model is somewhat cumbersome compared to other similar models, for example, Meyer (1975), and little work has been conducted in relation to the model since Frederiksen's original papers.

MEYER'S MODEL

Meyer's (1975) model of text content structure, influenced by Grimes (1972), is propositional in nature and consists of delineating a hierarchical structure of text that is based upon the classification of predicates. By selecting the major superordinate idea and relating subordinate ideas to it, the content structure is described as a tree diagram. Meyer's analysis includes the use of two types of predicates—the more standard predicate, which depicts a relation among arguments, and the rhetorical predicate, which consists of relations established between higher units of text such as sentences. Meyer (1975), as well as Meyer and McConkie (1973), demonstrated that recall of text information is related to the position of the information in the hierarchy. Moreover, in another study, Meyer

(1977) constructed two passages such that a particular paragraph was high in the structure of one passage but low in the structure of the other. It was found that recall of the target paragraph contents was superior when the target paragraph was higher in the structure (cf. Britton, Meyer, Hodge, & Glynn, 1980).

In another series of studies, capacity limitations in the processing of text were studied in relation to the text's content structure. Britton, Westbrook, and Holdridge (1978) used a secondary task technique, asking subjects when reading to press a button when a click occurred. The latency of response to the click was assumed to be a measure of the cognitive capacity devoted to the reading task; a longer latency was taken to indicate relatively more capacity being employed for reading (see also Britton, Holdridge, Curry, & Westbrook, 1979). Finally, we note that although Meyer (1975) provides a detailed description of the assumptions of the model and how text may be parsed in relation to the model, there is some question regarding the extent to which somewhat arbitrary judgments are required to perform a model-based analysis of text (cf. Ballstaedt, Schnotz, & Mandl, 1980).

KINTSCH *ET AL.* MODEL

Initially, Kintsch (1974) developed a model based upon text structure, but subsequently the model was modified in order to accommodate assumptions regarding the processing of text (Kintsch & van Dijk, 1978). The basic assumption of Kintsch's (1974) model was that a text has a deeper structure called a *text base,* which typically is different from the text's surface structure. It was also assumed that the text base consists of an ordered set of propositions that may be derived from the surface structure of the text. A manual indicating how such a propositional structure is derived is provided by Turner and Greene (1977).

Kintsch (1974) argued that coherence of the text base is provided by argument repetition, that is, the repetition of a particular argument in more than one proposition. Furthermore, it was assumed that propositions that contain a repeated argument are subordinate to the proposition that originally contained the particular argument. Kintsch and Keenan (1973) used reading time to study argument repetition effects, varying the number of propositions in the passage with total words held constant, and Kintsch, Kozminsky, Streby, McKoon, and Keenan (1975), using texts that contained few or many arguments, also used reading time as a dependent measure. Argument repetition was also studied by Manelis and Yekovich (1976), and the extent to which proposition relatedness and input order influence recall was studied by Manelis (1980).

A paper by Kintsch and Vipond (1979) detailed the means by which passage coherence could be described. The paper provided two important contributions. First, to establish a coherence graph of passage structure, a passage was divided into processing cycles. Each cycle was assumed to consist of the propositions in a simple sentence. The decision to use a sentence as a basis for delineating cycles was somewhat arbitrary and based upon the assumption that individuals processed passage information on a sentence-by-sentence basis. The second contribution was the assumption that certain propositions are carried over from one cycle to the next by the reader, and which propositions are carried over is determined by the *leading-edge strategy,* in other words, by the importance (level) and recency of the propositions within a given cycle.

The Kintsch and Vipond (1979) model was significantly advanced by taking into account the macrostructure, or global meaning, of text. Van Dijk (1977) argued that individuals use rules in generating the macrostructure of text. One rule, *generalization,* allows predicates and arguments to be generalized into a higher, more abstract form than provided in the text itself. The second rule, *deletion,* refers to dropping propositions from a text base. Such dropping may occur because a proposition is not important or because it is contained or strongly implied in another proposition. The third rule, *integration,* permits the individual to integrate a number of propositions into one or a few propositions, thus deleting some propositions. Typically, there is an initial proposition which determines the organization. The fourth rule, *construction,* is similar to integration, except that there is no initial proposition involved. Kintsch (1977) used the concept of macrostructure to consider how individuals organize story contents, and subsequently he and van Dijk published an important paper on micro- and macrostructure processes (Kintsch & van Dijk, 1978). This paper is both theoretical and methodological in scope, since it provides a statement and test of the model as well as a description of the analytic procedures employed. (The reader is urged to examine this article in special reference to the use of parameter estimation procedures in text processing.)

The primary contribution of the Kintsch and van Dijk (1978) model was to suggest that macropropositions are constructed by the reader and stored as part of the contents of the text. Furthermore, the model predicted the recall of macrostructure propositions by incorporating parameters for recall of macropropositions into a more general model. The underlying assumption is that propositional recall is a function of the number of processing cycles in which the particular proposition occurs.

Vipond (1980) further delineated micro- and macroprocesses. Using both reading time and recall measures, Vipond manipulated five variables assumed to be related to microstructure processes and five variables assumed to be related to macrostructure processes. With the use of factor analysis and multiple regression techniques, he obtained a microstructure factor and a macrostructure factor, and also found that the best data fit occurred when macroprocesses were taken into account with microprocesses, and vice-versa (cf. Spilich, Vesonder, Chiesi, & Voss, 1979). Vipond also analyzed the performance of good and poor readers and found that macroprocesses were more predictive of the performance of good readers and microstructure more predictive of the performance of poor readers.

Another paper in the evolution of the Kintsch *et al.* model is that of Miller and Kintsch (1980). While focusing on the issue of readability, especially as related to text microstructure, two modifications were made in the previously described analysis of propositional structure. The leading-edge strategy was modified in order to weight more heavily the importance of particular propositions, and the concept of chunking was introduced into the analysis. In addition, Miller and Kintsch (1980) developed three computer programs for analysis of chunking, coherence structure, and parameter estimation. In conclusion, whereas the model developed by Kintsch *et al.* has shortcomings (cf. Ballstaedt *et al.*, 1980), the model represents the most sophisticated analysis of text structure, especially with respect to text processing.

STORY GRAMMARS AND OTHER APPROACHES TO NARRATIVE

In previous sections, we discussed models of passage representation that have drawn heavily from logic and linguistic theory and that are intended to have wide applicability. However, in other models, the units and relations used to represent text are more limited in scope. Among these models are those intended to represent the structure of narrative (see also Just & Carpenter, 1980, and Vesonder, Note 1, for a similar approach to scientific expositions).

Story grammar models (Johnson & Mandler, 1980; Mandler & Johnson, 1977; Rumelhart, 1975; Stein & Glenn, 1979; Thorndyke, 1977) employ sets of rules posited to represent the individual's knowledge of story structure. This knowledge is taken to be incorporated in the form of a cognitive schema that guides expectations during comprehension, producing what has been termed "top-down" processing. The class of stories most adequately characterized by these grammars focuses on the actions of a single protagonist (see, however, Johnson & Mandler, 1980).

Rumelhart's (1975) grammar provides an example of how rewrite rules can be used to decompose a narrative. Following an original paper by Propp (1928), Rumelhart's analysis includes both syntactic and semantic components. The first syntactic rule is: *story* → *setting* + *episode*. Rule 2 defines setting as a set of stative propositions: *setting* → *state**. Rule 3 decomposes *episode* into an event and reaction by a character: *episode* → *event* + *reaction*. Another rule decomposes a reaction into an internal response and overt response. In addition to this set of syntactic rules, a number of postulated relations provide a basis for the semantic representation of the story. These include *and, cause, motivate, initiate, then, allow* (*enable*). Difficulties in applying Rumelhart's grammar to analyze the structure of stories led to many of the modifications embodied in more recent grammars.

Investigations conducted within the story grammar framework have been primarily concerned with demonstrating the existence of story grammars and showing that such grammars are used in text understanding. The procedure has consisted of delineating the major structural components of stories and showing that individuals' recall and other performance measures reflect what would be expected from processing according to such a schema (e.g., Mandler & Goodman, Note 2). Research within the story grammar context has also revealed interesting developmental differences and cross-cultural similarities in story recall (e.g., Mandler, 1978; Mandler, Scribner, Cole, & De Forest, 1980; Mandler & Johnson, 1977; Stein & Glenn, 1979). However, a number of papers have debated the adequacy of story grammars on formal and empirical grounds (e.g., Black & Bower, 1980; Black & Wilensky, 1979; Mandler & Johnson, 1980; Rumelhart, 1980).

In contrast to story grammar models, another approach is to represent narrative texts as if readers were applying knowledge of social actions or problem solving in the understanding process. Among the characterizations of passage structure emphasizing social actions are those of Bruce and Newman (1978), Omanson (in press), and Schank and Abelson (1977). Bruce and Newman present a notational system for representing *interacting plans* in stories. Omanson's analysis (Omanson, in press) is a clear attempt to develop a theory of centrality that predicts the nature of story recall. Following Rumelhart's (1977) observation that many stories seem to involve a problem solving process is Black's work (Black & Bower, 1980; Black, Note 3), which provides a description of narrative representation in terms of individuals' problem solving knowledge. As Black and Bower (1980) indicate, any process theory developed to operate on their representation "would view the story as though it were the literate 'thinking aloud' protocol of a verbose character solving an interesting problem; and the reader would be viewed as an interested observer–scientist trying to make sense of the . . . protocol [p. 244]."

The analysis of narrative text also suggests that episodes within the narrative structure may function as units within the story structure. Black and Bower (1979), using recall patterns, found that episode recall was influenced by the amount of information within the episode but not by information in other episodes. Subsequently, Haberlandt, Berian, and Sandson (1980) tested the notion by relating subject-paced reading time to episode boundaries. Via multiple regression techniques, they took out the effects of six variables and found episode boundary to be important. The significance of this work for the present context is that it points to the episode as an important unit for narrative processing.

The models of passage representation discussed so far have provided methods for specifying the organization of passage information, but all have been fairly weak in delineating the inferences a comprehender must make. Analyses by Warren, Nicholas, and Trabasso (1979), and Graesser, Robertson, and Anderson (1981), have attempted to address this concern with respect to narrative text. The latter approach is derived from work by Warren et al. (1979) and Schank's Conceptual Dependency Theory (1973, 1975c). It provides a representation of passages in terms of labelled nodes and labelled, directed arcs that include both explicitly stated passage information and inferences. Inferences are derived using Graesser's "question–answering" procedure (1978, p. 17).

Methods Derived in the Verification of Text Structure

The propositional analysis of text, the development of the concept of macrostructure, and other conceptual developments regarding text structure have led to the development of methodologies designed to study such components. We now consider some of these methods.

PROPOSITIONAL REPRESENTATION
AND A PRIMING PROCEDURE

McKoon and Ratcliff (1980) developed an interesting method to study the propositional representation of text. Following an initial study by Ratcliff and McKoon (1978) on the representation of concepts in sentences, McKoon and Ratcliff (1980) had subjects read two passages and then asked whether a particular concept (term) occurred in either passage. Furthermore, if a particular concept was related to a subsequently tested concept, then the latter concept was hypothesized to have a relatively rapid reaction time, that is, as compared to an appropriate control. Thus, representational relations are inferred by the priming effect that one concept has upon the subsequent concept. This work thus represents a technique of potential value in trying to describe how text structure influences the representation of the text.

HIERARCHICAL STRUCTURE AND GRAESSER'S "WHY" TECHNIQUE

Graesser (1978) and Graesser *et al.* (1980) used "why" questions to analyze the hierarchical nature of text structure. In the former paper, Graesser was interested in two dimensions of text that were termed *hierarchical structure* and *relational density,* both of which were defined by analysis of the answers to "why" questions. Graesser reasoned that when reading an account of procedures, such as how to catch a fish, the answers to "why" questions should provide superordinate information whereas the answers to "how" questions should provide subordinate information. By administering "why" questions to the subjects after they had read the text, Graesser was able to develop a hierarchical text structure from the answers. ("Why" questions were asked for each of the actions of the story.) In addition, relational density was measured by the frequency with which reasons given were related to each other, as measured by the use of the same concepts. (A formula for the quantification of relational density is given in the Graesser, 1978, article.) Finally, Graesser employed a control procedure that demonstrated recall was above a base-rate condition, with statement of base rate determined by a generation technique. The "why" method thus also provides a means to study the structure of representations.

MEMORY OF SURFACE STRUCTURE: TECHNIQUES USED

One of the issues that has been studied is whether individuals retain knowledge of the surface structure as well as of a deeper structure or whether the knowledge of surface structure is lost within a reasonably short period of time after the text is processed. One method used to study this issue is a false recognition procedure, in which sentences of the passage are presented along with distractor sentences, and subjects are asked to identify sentences that were in the text (e.g., Sachs, 1967). Memory for surface structure has also been studied by Kintsch and Bates (1977), who employed confidence judgments, by Bates, Kintsch, Fletcher, and Guiliani (1980), by Bates, Masling, and Kintsch (1978), and Keenan,

MacWhinney, and Mayhew (1977). One study, Keenan *et al.* (1977), involved retention of the surface structure of conversation, and the authors emphasized the role of pragmatics in the interpretation of their results. The pragmatic aspect of language, we note, has been a neglected area of study.

SCRAMBLING OF TEXT

Perhaps the most obvious way to disrupt text organization is to scramble the text. Scrambling, however, may occur on the word, clause, sentence, or multiple sentence level. At the word level, Pompi and Lachman (1967) presented a passage in regular or in scrambled order, and subsequently subjects were asked to indicate whether an individual word was in the passage. Lachman and Dooling (1968) employed both recognition and recall procedures to study scrambling effects, whereas Dooling and Lachman (1971) scrambled text at the word or at the phrase level. Research involving scrambling passages at the sentence level has also been conducted (e.g., Kintsch, Mandel, & Kozminsky, 1977).

PASSAGE SUMMARIES

One question of interest is how memory for passages is affected if summaries of the passages, rather than the total passage, are presented. In one study, McCluskey (1940) presented individuals with either an entire passage or with a summary of the passage. The summary of the passage was constructed by selection of important information. In a more extensive study, Reder and Anderson (1980) manipulated a number of parameters in studying summarization effects, using college text book chapters or summaries of the chapters.

Other Properties of Text that Influence Processing

TOPIC SIGNALLING

It has been noted (Deese & Kaufman, 1957; de Villiers, 1974) that memory of prose is marked by a primacy effect, that is, material occurring early in the text is usually recalled better than material occurring in the middle or latter portions of the text. However, initial text material usually is superordinate in nature whereas material occurring later is typically subordinate. Therefore, there is a confounding of the type of information and the position in the text. Furthermore, there is the possibility that this relation is not accidental; among writers there may be an implicit convention that information is usually placed early in a passage, providing a signal to the reader regarding what may be important in the subsequent sections of the passage. Thus, the author may use devices to "stage" the coming information. (Clements, 1979, discusses different types of staging that authors employ.)

Kieras (1978, 1980) studied the question of initial mention of a topic and whether such mention facilitates the understanding of subsequent topic-related information. After reading a brief passage, subjects were asked to state from memory the sentence that would *make the best title*. Kieras (1980) subsequently presented brief passages with the primary (topic) sentence occurring either first or embedded in the middle of the passage. Subjects were then asked to generate the main idea of the passage. Reading time was measured as well as time to generate the main idea. Finally, Kieras (1980) presented superordinate–subordinate pairs of sentences and orthogonally varied them as Sentences 1 and 2 or 4 and 5 in a 5-sentence passage. (Sentence 3 was a linking sentence.) Subjects tended to select the topic first presented as the theme, although superordinate and subordinate relations also played a role. Thus, the work does suggest that material presented early in the passage is generally regarded as important theoretically, and that this fact may be a convention of authors.

TOPIC REFERENTS

Similarly, Lesgold, Roth, and Curtis (1979) studied foregrounding and backgrounding effects. Foregrounding (Chafe, 1973) refers to the idea that a reader or listener has a particular concept in memory when a given concept of the text is being processed; if the concept of the text is not in memory, it is referred to as being backgrounded. Lesgold *et al.* manipulated the text presentation in order to provide a study of foregrounding and backgrounding in comprehension.

PARAGRAPH STRUCTURE

The legitimacy of the paragraph as a psychological unit was studied by Koen, Becker, and Young (1969). Using different types of passages that varied in length from 15 to 22 sentences, as well as passages in which nonsense paralogs were substituted for all nouns, verbs, adjectives, and adverbs, subjects placed paragraph markers where they thought new paragraphs began. The reliability of delineating the paragraph structure was obtained. The method was also employed with children.

READABILITY

The notion of readability refers to the ease with which prose material may be read and understood. Whereas readability can be measured by assessing how well subjects perform tests based upon the contents of a passage, readability has been predicted through simple counts of the frequency of various language features contained within the passage. Klare (1974) has reviewed a number of readability formulas still in use. The formulas are similar in emphasizing the roles of sentence length and word difficulty; for example, the Flesch formula (1948), one of the more popular, is computed by: Reading Ease = $206.835 - .84wl - 1.015sl$, where wl is the number of syllables per 100 words, and sl is the average number of words per sentence. In addition, there are formulas designed to apply to particular types of texts (cf., Morris, 1972, for business and government material; Caylor, Sticht, Fox, & Ford, Note 4, for U.S. army material). Generally, the formulas have been evaluated for validity according to their ability to predict performance on passages tested by a standard reading comprehension test, such as the *Standard Test Lessons in Reading* (McCall & Crabbs, 1925) or by the *cloze procedure* (Bormuth, 1969). But as Kintsch and Vipond (1979) point out, readability formulas probably ignore the major factors affecting reading ease; this becomes apparent in light of a sound reading comprehension model. It is, in fact, the interaction of reader characteristics with textual features that is of paramount importance (cf. Miller & Kintsch, 1980). For this reason, readability formulas have not played and probably will not play a major role in prose processing research.

METHODS RELATED TO VARIABLES STUDIED IN THE TASK SITUATION

Information Provided Before and During Text Processing

ADVANCED ORGANIZERS

One of the factors that has received considerable attention is how information presented prior to a particular text influences the processing of the text. One area of such research has been concerned with the effectiveness of *advanced organizers*. Ausubel (1963, 1968) defined the advance organizer as an information unit, generally a brief prose paragraph, that preceded the target passage. The preliminary passage typically contains the main concepts needed to understand the passage but at a higher level of abstraction, generality, and inclusiveness. Ausubel distinguished *expository organizers,* which simply describe concepts when these are relatively novel for the reader, and *comparative organizers,* which relate the presented concepts to concepts that the reader already possesses. Numerous investigators have pursued the study of advance organizers (e.g., Anderson, 1973; Clawson & Barnes, 1973; Grotelueschen & Sjogren, 1968; Jerrolds, 1967; Schnell, 1973). One objection to the work is that the definition of an advance organizer is vague (cf. Barnes & Clawson, 1975), although recently more theory-based constructions of the organizer have made an appearance (Mayer, 1979; Tyler, Delaney, & Kinnucan, in press). In addition, organizers in other than prose paragraph form have been tried, such as networks of technical terms (Earle, 1971), computer models (Mayer, 1976), and even games (Scandura & Wells, 1967).

LEARNING OBJECTIVES

A line of inquiry similar to advanced organizers has involved *learning objectives* (Duchastel & Merrill, 1973; Duell, 1974; Jenkins & Deno, 1971; Kaplan, 1974; Lawson, 1974; Rothkopf & Kaplan, 1972). In this work, individuals typically are told what they are expected to acquire from the text. Text recall is often divided into *intentional,* that is, information consonant with the stated objective, and *incidental,* that is, information in the text not directly related to the objectives. However, what is intentional versus what is incidental is not always easily distinguished. Other investigators have emphasized objectives by placing headings appropriately in the text (e.g., Christensen & Stordahl, 1955; Coles & Foster, 1975; Hershberger & Terry, 1956; Kozminsky, 1977; Robinson & Hall, 1941; Schallert, 1976). Finally, several studies have assessed the role of diagrams and pictures in enhancing comprehension (e.g., Davis, 1971; Dwyer, 1969; Frase, 1969; Koenke & Otto, 1969; Magne & Parknas, 1963; Peeck, 1974; and Vernon, 1953). Carroll (Note 5), in his review of prose research, mentions several other types of adjunct aids that have also received some attention.

TITLES

One of the most dramatic demonstrations of the operation of a priori factors in text processing was provided by Bransford and Johnson (1972). Basically, a text was presented without a title and was poorly recalled. Moreover, ratings of comprehensibility for the text were relatively low.

However, when a title was provided recall was much better and comprehensibility ratings were higher. A similar result occurred when a passage was presented with and without a picture. Finally, it was shown that presenting the title or picture after the presentation of the text had virtually no effect upon performance. The text used in this work was a rather extreme case, in the sense that for most nontitled texts the "contextual prerequisites" for comprehending the text are generated by the first few sentences.

QUESTION INSERTION

Research on the effects of inserting questions into text is quite extensive. Much of the early impetus for this work derived from Rothkopf (1966), who provided a theoretical rationale for question effectiveness. In addition, question position (whether placed before or after the relevant information) and the relation of test items to questions were manipulated. (Incidental items required knowledge of information not specifically requested in a question, whereas intentional items did involve such information.) Many researchers followed Rothkopf's lead (Frase, 1968; McGaw & Groetlueschen, 1972; Sanders, 1973; Snowman & Cunningham, 1975; Swenson & Kulhavy, 1974), most of whom used questions that simply required the factual information contained in a single sentence to be used in the answer. More recently, a number of individuals have looked at different types of questions, such as those requiring an inference from the content of several sentences to answer (e.g., Anderson & Biddle, 1975; Andre & Womack, 1978; Moeser, 1978; Richards & DiVesta, 1974; Rickards, 1976). In a recent review of the literature, Rickards (1979) points out some of the variables to be aware of when pursuing this line of inquiry.

Imagery

The effects of imagery instructions upon memory have been studied in the prose context (e.g., Anderson & Kulhavy, 1972; Montague & Carter, 1973). The procedure generally consisted of asking subjects to make pictures in their minds of what was happening in the text as they read or listened (e.g., Anderson & Kulhavy, 1972; Levin & Divine-Hawkins, 1974). The effect of instructions was usually assessed via short-answer or multiple-choice questions. The study of imagery is quite often concomitantly studied with the effect of pictures on prose retention (see Pressley, 1977).

Retroactive and Proactive Inhibition

Interference effects were first studied with
McGeogh and McKinney (1934a, 1934b). More re
inhibition paradigm, Bower (1974) had subject
passages about fictitious persons, with interve
highly similar or unrelated to the original pa
of the original passages were then used
Other studies have included studying r
to type of test, for example, multiple
relation to biographical and science r
and in relation to inserted question
Ausubel, Robbins, and Blake (19
Huggins (1964), Hall (1955), K
1960b, 1962), and Wong (1970
with prose materials, but no
for example, Ausubel and

Modality and Rate o

Systematic
presentation of
Most resear
entation, w
is probab
to indivi
with adults,
terials, most con
(Vipond, 1980), ten
cathode-ray tubes (Mille
subjects in these experimen
high level of reading ability in c
since experimenters are often inter
reading rate and eye movements during
is the naturally preferred choice. These prou
question of the extent to which the results of st
be compared to those conducted with adults. Argu
erality of the research are justified by assuming that the
in reading and listening are the same at some level (e.g., Kn
Dijk, 1978). In fact, studies with adults and children as youn
have shown only minor differences in performance when comparing u.

JAMES F. VOSS, SHERMAN W. TYLER, AND GAY L. BISANZ

368

and Gauld and Stephenson (1967) tested this notion using a multiple-
choice procedure.

The use of recognition procedures to test hypotheses regarding
schema was extended by Sulin and Dooling (1974). A biographical passage was presented and some subjects were told that the contents pertained to a famous man, such as Abraham Lincoln, whereas other subjects were told that the contents pertained to a fictitious person. The
greater number of false positives made by the famous man group was
used to infer the operation of knowledge about the famous man and th
integration of such a priori knowledge with that found in the text.

R. C. Anderson and his colleagues argued that text informa
should be related to one's interest and experience as well as to
orientation a person is given by instructions. To illustrate the first
an ambiguous passage that could be interpreted in relation to m
physical education was used. It was found that college students
in each of the two fields tended to interpret the passage in r
their own interest areas (Anderson, Reynolds, Schallert, & Go
To illustrate the second point, individuals were given a pa
provided a tour of a house. Instructions were given to take
either a potential buyer of the house or a burglar. What wa
reflected differences in the orientation. Moreover, after re
were provided with the orientation they did not orig
retrieval was studied (Anderson & Pichert, 1978). B
study which involved a story of a triangular situati
young woman and two young men, demonstrated
a particular character elicited attributions associate
Bower (1978) also reported a study by Snydes an
a biographical description of a woman was read,
were given a recognition test, with the subjec
things about the person. Recognition perform
story information was influenced by this i
methodological issue in this perspective-tak
sible to induce orientations for text process
knowledge of occupational function, socia
Black, 1979).

To summarize this section, two
experimenter's work involves interp
text contents and the memory perf
recall or recognition procedures. S
provided for the development of

cedures, there is a need for methodology that will provide a more precise description of schema and that will provide for the development of processing models of schema operation.

Scripts

The concept of a script (Schank & Abelson, 1977) and the related concept of frame (Minsky, 1975) were advanced by the artificial intelligence community as a means of recognizing that prototypical experiences are stored in memory and utilized in processing information. Schank (1975a) has described scripts as causal chains providing knowledge about situations which have been frequently experienced. From the point of view of text processing methodology, research on scripts has had a similar motivation to that of research on schema, namely, to demonstrate the existence of scripts and to show they operate in processing text.

The work of Schank and Abelson (1977) raised a number of interesting methodological issues, and we will briefly consider two of them. First, the work essentially adopts a strong position concerning the importance of prior knowledge with respect to the interpretation and comprehension of text. Schank (1975b, p. 16) states, "Known communication is based largely upon what is left out of discourse." In other words, the meaning we give to discourse is based upon our knowledge of the world. This position suggests that it is necessary for investigators of text processing to provide means for describing knowledge and to show how it is utilized. The second aspect of script theory we note is that in the early work, for example, Schank (1972), there was an attempt to delineate action *primitives,* in other words, to develop a set of verb-like descriptions to which most actions could be reduced. The attempt to define semantic primitives poses a challenge to investigators of text processing, because if primitives are assumed, then understanding how such primitives are utilized in comprehension is a matter of importance. (Investigators, of course, do not agree on the existence of primitives.)

A study by Bower, Black, and Turner (1979) illustrates some of the methods employed in studying script utilization. These investigators had individuals generate scripts for a number of different activities, for example, going to a restaurant, attending a lecture, and getting up in the morning. They subsequently obtained frequency counts of each event described in a given activity and found evidence for scripts; that is, there was reasonable commonality to the events of the script, although, of course, some events were found more often than others. Bower *et al.* performed a number of other manipulations designed to provide information about script utilization. First, the authors omitted particular information from scripts to determine whether such information is "recalled" in the appropriate place. Second, they presented script activities in a scrambled order. Third, they primed one activity in a script, using reading time for a measure, by presentation of the appropriate script item. Graesser, Gordon, and Sawyer (1979) also had individuals generate scripts, and then, like Bower *et al.,* used a recognition test to determine whether highly typical information was in a presented script-related passage, testing with atypical events as well as typical. Finally, we would note that, similar to the study of schema, methods to determine the precise way in which scripts are utilized in comprehension is yet to be forthcoming.

Knowledge and Text Processing: Other Methods

SCHEMA FOR CONVENTIONAL TEXTS

Relatively recent theories of text processing (e.g., Just & Carpenter, 1980; Kintsch & van Dijk, 1978) have emphasized the importance of the reader's goals in determining how processes are executed during reading. Thus, from a strategic point of view, research on comprehension should focus on those cases where readers share similar goals (Kintsch & van Dijk, 1978). One way to achieve such a situation is to examine readers' behavior while processing highly conventionalized text for which readers are likely to process information in accordance with the conventional structure. Not surprisingly then, conventionalized texts have been a major focus of investigation. Among the initial types of passages studied are psychological reports and scientific texts taken from news magazines. Excellent descriptions of how these types of schema are hypothesized to influence processing can be found in Kintsch and van Dijk (1978) and Just and Carpenter (1980).

KNOWLEDGE OF CONTENT DOMAINS

The role of domain-related knowledge in text processing was studied by Spilich, Vesonder, Chiesi, and Voss (1979). Using as text one half inning of a fictitious baseball game, individuals having high or low baseball knowledge recalled the text. (This work thus represents an extension of the expert–novice comparison approach to text processing, cf. Chase and Simon, 1973; de Groot, 1966.) The text was analyzed in terms of its propositional structure, and the propositions were classified with respect to their importance, with importance defined in terms of baseball. The authors estimated the microproposition and macroproposition processing parameters by adapting the Kintsch and van Dijk model to the recall data. Of particular note is that this work defined macrostructure not in terms of linguistic rules but in terms of the subject matter of the text, that is, baseball.

The baseball work was extended (Voss, Vesonder, & Spilich, 1980) by having high- and low-knowledge individuals generate one half inning of a fictitious baseball game. Two weeks later, the individuals recalled the text. This research thus studied recall in relation to self-generated text. Furthermore, the results suggested that low-knowledge individuals could recall information from a class of texts generated by low-knowledge individuals but had difficulty recalling information from texts generated by high-knowledge individuals. High-knowledge individuals readily recalled information from texts generated by high-knowledge individuals, but they were not better than low-knowledge individuals at recalling information from texts generated by low-knowledge individuals. These findings demonstrate that domain-related knowledge can influence text comprehension and recall, even when subjects are matched on comprehension ability, and that recall of even self-generated text is a function of knowledge.

SUMMARY AND EVALUATION:
METHODS AND MEASURES

In the previous sections, we described various methods in the context of three research traditions. In this final section, a summary of the dependent measures commonly used in these paradigms is presented, together with a discussion of the main issues surrounding each measure. Table 12.1 provides the focus for this discussion. The column labeled *Example Uses* cites concrete instances in which the given dependent measure was involved. Since virtually all of these examples can be found in prior sections of this chapter, they will not be considered in detail in this section. Instead, the purpose will be to describe the various tasks and to indicate some of their limitations. In addition, there will be discussion of some of the more novel analytic techniques that have been applied.

Table 12.1
Table of Dependent Measures Commonly Used in Prose Processing Research

Dependent Measures		Definition (scoring)	Example Uses
Task	Subtask		
Recall	Unit	Number of units in subjects' unaided retrieval corresponding to units found in target text.	Unit recall as function of unit position in text hierarchy; recall with/without text adjunct.
	Gist	Number of higher-order units recalled from text when subject is instructed to summarize text meaning within spatial or word limitations.	Comparison of summary with immediate and delayed unit recall; using as indicator of operative schema
	Inferential	Number and types of inferences found in subject's recall of text.	Occurrences of inferences derived from interpretive schema; inferences making text coherent.
	Cued	Number of units correctly recalled with aid of segment of units originally encountered in text.	Testing integration of parts of sentence into whole; to compare with unit recall in order to contrast availability with accessibility.
Recognition	Unit	Number of units correctly identified by subjects as having been in text, through either yes/no or multiple choice decision.	Accuracy for wording versus meanings; recognition of meaning-preserving units to show interpretation of ambiguous passage.
	False	Number of units incorrectly identified as having been present in text.	False recognition of script-implied items showing operation thereof; of items implied by title.
	Inferential	Number of inferences implied by text identified as having been present therein.	Effects of postreading tasks on false recognition of inferences.

Category	Technique	Description	Purpose
Organization	Similarity judgments	Ratings by subjects of similarities of group of stimuli done on pair-wise basis.	Multidimensional scaling to yield map of stimulus interrelations according to dimensions perceived by subjects.
	Grouping	Number of subjects placing given pair of stimuli in same group as being most closely related.	Hierarchical clustering analysis to reveal way subjects organize stimuli (as sentences).
Eye Monitoring	Pupil diameter	Measure of pupil diameter during the reading of segments of text by subjects.	Evaluating differing patterns of cognitive effort devoted by subjects to different text units.
	Eye movement	Measure of number of fixations, saccades, or regressions, or of total gate duration made by subjects while reading segments of text.	Testing reading process models that predict the pattern of reading.
Temporal Parameters	Reading time	Measure of time taken by subjects to read successive text segments.	As reflective of micro- and macrostructural variables; as indicative of priming by earlier information.
	Reaction time	Measure of time taken by subjects to complete a certain judgment.	Time to make recognition decisions as requiring retrieval versus inference.
Text construction and evaluation	Generative techniques	Evaluation of texts or text fragments generated by subjects according to certain constraints.	To examine similarity of "script" generations; to reveal expert–novice differences in processing.
	Verbal report	Subject gives verbal description of own subjective impression of processing that occurred while reading.	To get idea of perspective subject assumes while reading; to determine role of imagery.

Recall

UNIT RECALL

The subject in unit recall is asked to remember the contents of a prose passage without benefit of any external aids. The instructions are usually such that the subject tries to use the ordering and even the exact wording of the target passage as often as possible (Johnson, 1970). The protocols are then scored for the amount of original prose information contained therein. Generally, this is a procedure for checking whether or not the units of information determined to be in the target passage by the experimenter are present in the protocol, and paraphrasing that preserves the original intent is allowed (Frederiksen, 1977; Mandler, 1978; Stein & Nezworski, 1978). Since scoring is based on an analysis of the meaning of the original passage, the units used in scoring are basically the same as those used in decomposing that passage. Hence, these units are the same as those reviewed in the previous section on text structure, with different theoretical orientations leading to different unit choices, though the propositional form (cf. Kintsch, 1974) is emerging as the most prevalent. Therefore, the resulting dependent measure is often just a count of the number of propositions from the target passage that a recall protocol contains. In some cases, qualitative distinctions are also made, so that the position of propositions in the hierarchy of the overall structure (Bower, 1976; Clements, 1979; Meyer, 1975), or the particular story grammar role of the information in a narrative (Mandler & Johnson, 1977), is considered as a further way of looking at recall by unit type. In addition, some investigators have scored for the correctness of recall order (Johnson & Scheidt, 1977; Stein & Nezworski, 1978), and others have looked at the pattern of the number of subjects recalling individual propositions (Rubin, 1978) in relation to predictions from various theories of prose comprehension. Finally, we note that a serious problem facing investigators using unit recall is how to handle intrusions, and even more importantly, how to score generalized statements.

GIST RECALL

Another recall task requires the subject to produce a brief description of the gist of a main idea present in the prose passage (Kieras, 1978; Kintsch & Greene, 1978; Thorndyke, 1977). Generally, a limit is placed on the length of such a summary, either by requiring it to be within a certain number of words or by providing a small space for recall. Subjects are usually given ample time to revise their protocols to meet these requirements.

INFERENTIAL RECALL

Recall of inferences is another issue which the investigator can address. Inferential recall refers more to the type of items scored in recall than to the nature of the recall task. Here, the subject's protocol is examined not only for the units recalled from those explicitly in the textual material, but also for the different types of inferences contained therein (Anderson *et al.*, 1977; Frederiksen, 1975b; Goetz, 1979). The difficulty lies in deriving the inferences logically inherent in the text and determining a taxonomy of inference types for scoring purposes. There is no taxonomy that is universally accepted, although some progress has been made in this direction (Warren *et al.*, 1979). Also, the schema- and script-based views of text processing have yielded some definite techniques for deriving the inferential content from a prose passage.

CUED RECALL

In this task, subjects are given a portion of an item from a previously read text (often part of a sentence) and asked to reproduce the remainder of the item (i.e., the rest of the sentence). This measure has been employed to examine the extent to which recall may be prompted by appropriate cues, thus highlighting the difference between item accessibility and item availability. This technique has been especially helpful in research with children (Omanson, Warren, & Trabasso, 1978; Paris & Upton, 1976; Stein & Glenn, 1979).

ISSUES IN RECALL

There are a number of general concerns with recall measures. One is scoring consistency. Since division of recall protocols into segments often requires a number of subjective judgments, as does determining whether a segment is represented by a paraphrase in the protocol, there is always the worry that the method of scoring used is not a reliable one. Therefore, it is generally necessary for researchers to have at least two individuals score the protocols (or a subset thereof) to assess interrater reliability. When reliability is above 90%, there is probably no need to doubt the consistency of the scoring system. A second concern is how strict scoring should be. Dual criteria are often used, with scoring done under both strict conditions, making little allowance for paraphrase, and lenient conditions, permitting quite loose paraphrases. A third concern is the modality of recall. Subjects may be asked to recall orally, with the results tape recorded, or to recall in writing. The method therefore may determine the amount of detail subjects incorporate in their recall. This is especially a point to consider with children, where writing itself may be difficult. With writing, however, the subject has the advantage of examining his output and making additions. For this reason, children are sometimes allowed to hear the tape recording of their recall and make additions (e.g., Brown & Smiley, 1977).

There are additional concerns of significance to the developmental investigator. The first relates to the comparability of recall protocols of, for example, 6-year-olds and adults. This issue arises because the recall of an adult is typically much richer in detail. This problem may be handled at the point of materials division (by making passage units fine-grained enough to capture such differences) or in the criteria adopted at the time of scoring. The second issue relates to the validity of using free recall as the only measure of children's comprehension (see Piaget, 1926; Brown, 1975). Since young children's retention of event sequences as measured by free recall is notoriously bad compared to, say, recognition, free recall should be supplemented with other dependent measures in comprehension studies.

OTHER METHODS OF ANALYSIS

Besides typical analysis of variance techniques, several other methods have been found useful in assessing the differences among groups implied by the outcome of recall scoring. For example, it is possible, if recall level is high enough, to evaluate the correlations or conditional probabilities between propositions, that is, the extent to which recall of one proposition tends to co-occur with one or more other specific propositions (as in Frederiksen, 1977; Waters, 1978). This can aid in identifying how subjects structure propositions during prose processing; for example, does recall of subordinate propositions enhance superordinate proposition recall (Black & Bower, 1979). Another technique that may be applied, if several different recall measures are used, is factor analysis, the purpose of which is to identify the underlying variables contributing to the various recall measures (cf. Meyers & Boldrick, 1975). The chapter in this volume by Pellegrino and Hubert includes further suggestions of ways to analyze recall protocols that are based upon the methods typically employed by experimenters who use word lists as taught items.

A final technique that is used in relation to recall data and has been confined primarily to research testing one particular model of prose comprehension, is that of parameter estimation. This technique requires a model of sufficient detail to specify, in formulas using the main parameters of the model, the probability that any given proposition will be recalled. To date, only the Kintsch and van Dijk (1978) model offers such detail. The process of parameter estimation requires calculating the number of subjects recalling each proposition, then using some optimization technique to choose parameters that minimize any criterion difference between the number of subjects observed and the number predicted to recall each proposition. This also requires the use of some computer program for optimization with the choice most often being the STEPIT routine (Chandler, 1965). It is possible, after obtaining parameter estimates, to test the goodness-of-fit of the model using the chi-squared statistic, and even to test the importance of the contribution of each parameter and parameter differences between groups, by using the differences between particular chi-squared results (cf. Neyman, 1949). Thus, the technique is quite powerful as an analytic device, but has found limited use due to the lack of adequately specific models. In addition, there is sometimes a problem in knowing how to interpret goodness-of-fit measures. On the one hand, there is some freedom in choosing the criterion measure and the number of estimated parameters, and the fit is naturally better as the number of parameters increases. On the other hand, in the absence of an alternative model, a model that predicts the outcome reasonably well may be worth considering, even if the test indicates a significant lack of goodness-of-fit (as in Miller & Kintsch, 1980). Hence, some subjective judgment is often required.

Recognition

UNIT RECOGNITION

A second widely employed dependent measure is recognition. The subject is asked to determine whether or not a particular piece of information occurred in the target passage. The task may be one of saying "Yes" or "No" to individual items, or may require selecting from among a set of two or more items the one which appeared in the passage. Furthermore, included under this measure are tasks in which the subject tries to reconstruct the original information using rearranged pieces of the original. This measure can be particularly useful in developmental studies (e.g., Brown, 1975, 1976).

FALSE RECOGNITION

Recognition also constitutes an analytical tool when the foils chosen for multiple-choice recognition are carefully determined. This method is, of course, the basis of the false recognition procedure. The concern, then, is with the types of "errors" that are made.

INFERENTIAL RECOGNITION

A similar approach permits examining the inferences subjects have incorporated while reading (Thorndyke, 1976). One might wish to look at either correct or false recognition, depending on whether instructions requested subjects to say "yes" only to information explicitly contained in the text or to say "yes" to any information consistent with the text's meaning. Defining and deriving the inferences to include on the recognition test poses the same problems as seen in inferential recall.

Organizational Measures

SIMILARITY JUDGMENTS

For similarity judgments, subjects are given a series of item pairs and asked to judge on a numeric scale how similar one item of each pair is to the other item. The similarity measures are then entered into a matrix and a program is used to determine the optimal spatial arrangement of the items in an X-dimensional space, where the experimenter makes the choice of X. This is termed *multidimensional scaling* (MDS). A number of algorithms exist for analyzing the obtained results (see Green & Rao, 1972; and Shepard, Romney, & Nerlowe, 1972, for overviews). A program commonly employed for this purpose is INDSCAL, developed by Carroll and Chang (1970). (Other programs are KYST and TORSCA.) INDSCAL also produces a subject space in which each subject is mapped according to the weights given by that subject to the dimensions of the object space. In prose passages, then, one can choose the important elements of the passage and have subjects do similarity judgments for those elements after reading the passage. The resulting space shown by MDS reveals the way subjects structured those items in memory, both in terms of their proximity and in terms of the major underlying dimensions of the space. Also, the subject space can reveal whether different groups of subjects differ in those structures. Thus, for example, Bisanz, LaPorte, Vesonder, and Voss (1978) used a story passage and had subjects judge the similarity of characters from the story. They were then able to show the correspondence of the resulting space to the conceptual space used by the author in originally constructing the characters. LaPorte and Voss (1979) used a similar technique in reference to expository text.

There are many possible extensions of this technique, such as ways for interpreting the underlying dimensions and for further analyzing the groupings in the obtained space. Statistical methods are also available for choosing the spatial dimensionality that provides the best fit to the data (Kruskal & Carroll, 1969). An introduction to MDS and its extensions can be found in Kruskal and Wish (1978). The technique offers much promise and deserves further exploration.

GROUPING TASK

Subjects are asked to separate a set of items into groups, where each group contains items that "fit together" or are closely related. The number of subjects placing each pair of items in the same group can be entered into a matrix that is submitted to a hierarchical clustering analysis (such as that of Johnson, 1967). The product is a graphic indication of the hierarchy of relationships among items, where individual items are grouped together at various levels of the hierarchy until all items have been collapsed into a single cluster. Also, there are available some imprecise ways of testing goodness-of-fit of the clustering algorithm to the data (Jardine & Sibson, 1971) and testing the significance of individual clusters (Fillenbaum & Rapaport, 1971; Johnson, Note 6). Still lacking, though, are well-defined statistical criteria for evaluating these analyses and for comparing the differences between different clustering hierarchies obtained from the same material. A good general introduction to the techniques and problems of clustering analysis is provided in the book by Everitt (1974).

Eye Monitoring

PUPIL DIAMETER

An obvious source of potentially valuable information about the nature of prose processing is the behavior of the eyes during reading. Such behavior could include either the movements of the eyes or the fluctuation in pupil size. As Kahneman (1973) has argued, the latter may offer a sensitive measure of the cognitive effort variations occurring during task performance. However, the use of pupil size as a measure during reading is limited, so little can be said about it.

EYE MOVEMENT

There is a developing body of eye movement literature. In such research, the subject typically reads the prose material from a screen while the patterns of eye movements are monitored. The movements are usually recorded as spatial coordinates on a computer file (see Young & Sheena, 1975, for a survey of current eye movement equipment). Although there are some problems with interpretation of what eye movements reflect (see McConkie, Hogaboam, Wolverton, & Lucas, 1979), most research has validated the assumption that the position of the eye at any given time corresponds to what is currently being processed (Just & Carpenter, 1976, 1978, 1980). The measures obtained from eye movement data can include the number of fixations within a given text portion, the number of saccades therein, the number of regressive eye movements, or simply the total gaze duration, independent of the number of fixations. Rayner (1978) provides a good summary of these various approaches.

Just and Carpenter (1980) have shown the value of this technique. Using the gaze duration associated with particular units of text classified according to their role in that text, they have been able to derive and partially validate a general reading model. They used multiple regression, with the various text roles constituting the independent variables. Other researchers have tried other analytic techniques. Besides standard analysis of variance, McConkie, Hogaboam, Wolverton and Lucas (1979) have suggested the use of processing time profiles, that is, comparing the pattern of subjects' fixations with those predicted by various models. By and large, though the general area of eye movement research includes numerous studies (Fisher, Monty, & Senders, 1981, offer abundant examples), the number of prose processing studies involving eye monitoring has been limited, in spite of the obvious value of this technique. This situation is changing, though, as the equipment becomes more widely available and the virtues of the measure more widely recognized.

Temporal Parameters

READING TIME

Commonly, reading rate is measured by presenting subjects with a sentence or paragraph from a given passage on some type of screen and having the subject press a button to produce the next sentence or paragraph when they have finished reading the first (Black, Turner, & Bower, 1979; Cirilo & Foss, 1980; Kintsch & Keenan, 1973). Their reading times are then recorded by a simple measure of the time between button presses. The obtained measure may then be analyzed in any number of the standard ways. As an interesting example, Graesser,

Hoffman, and Clark (1980) obtained reading times for passage sentences and then did a multiple regression analysis with a number of different macro- and microstructural factors used as the independent variables.

REACTION TIME

With this metric, the time for subjects to perform some task, generally in reference to information previously encountered in a passage, is recorded. The value of reaction time measures for analyzing cognitive processes has long been apparent (Donders, 1868–1869), and this has proven equally the case in the prose processing domain. Here, at least two distinct uses of this dependent measure can be identified. First, it has been utilized to provide a more sensitive indication of the nature of the processes underlying certain standard tasks, such as recognition following prose learning (Kintsch, 1974). Second, it has been helpful in demonstrating the nature of the memorial representation following reading (Baker, 1978; Bisanz *et al.*, 1978). In both situations, standard timer equipment and/or appropriate computer facilities are employed to monitor and record the temporal characteristics of subjects' responses.

Text Construction and Evaluation

GENERATIVE TECHNIQUES

Though not a dependent measure as such, the generative technique does deserve a brief mention here as a method for obtaining protocols from which other dependent measures may be derived. For this task, subjects are asked to construct from their own knowledge a passage meeting certain requirements regarding its content domain and length. On the assumption that text production demands many of the same constituent processes as text comprehension, the resulting product may serve to indicate in new ways how subjects of different abilities or different areas of expertise vary in just those processes. Although, like several of the past dependent measures, the use of this technique has been largely unrealized in the literature, there is some indication of its fruitfulness in studies by Goldman (in press) and Voss *et al.*, (1980).

In addition to generating whole stories, a number of other interesting generative techniques have been employed recently to assess knowledge that subjects may apply to comprehend and remember texts. These range from asking subjects to anticipate particular story events to the collection of unstructured verbal protocols. Investigators interested in such techniques are referred to examples found in articles by Bisanz (in press), Mosenthal (1979), Olson, Duffy, and Mack (in press), and Poulsen, Kintsch, Kintsch, and Premack (1979).

VERBAL REPORT

Mention should be made of the few experiments in which the subject is simply asked to describe any intuitive impressions of the nature of the processes engaged in while reading. This may involve reports taken during or after the reading session. Thus, Bower (1978) had subjects fill out questionnaires after reading a story and found that the subjects were using images while reading. This questionnaire also allowed a determination of the character with whom the reader was identifying. This technique can offer more direct insight into the nature of the reading process and the perspective subjects assume while reading; yet it begs for confirmation owing to the frequent inaccuracy of intuitions.

CONCLUDING COMMENTS

In this chapter, methods employed in the study of prose learning and comprehension were reviewed. It was conceptually useful to divide the methods generally into three categories. Whereas these categories were treated separately, it is clear that they are not independent. In fact, a consideration of the interactions that occur among them, for instance, the effect of schemata on processing or of textual structure on schema formation and invocation, may provide answers to some of the most important questions in this domain. The last section was an attempt to overview the range of techniques that are presently employed to measure performance within the methodologies summarized in the previous three sections. It can be seen that there are numerous measures available to the investigator for this purpose, including free recall, recognition, organizational measures, eye monitoring, measures of temporal parameters, and techniques for text construction and evaluation. However, certain of these measures, though offering considerable promise, need to become more widely known and utilized, especially organizational and clustering measures and parameter estimation procedures. The use of parameter estimation brings us to our final comment, namely, that the study of text processing, taken as a whole, has been concerned with text structure, memory structure, and the manipulation of task variables. What is especially needed in the field, in our opinion, is the development of process models that can suggest how processing occurs in relation to such factors as text structure and memory structure.

ACKNOWLEDGMENTS

The research of this chapter was supported by the Centre for the Study of Mental Retardation, University of Alberta, Edmonton, Alberta, Canada, and the Learning Research and Development Center, supported in part as a research and development center by funds from the National Institute of Education (NIE), United States Department of Health, Education, and Welfare. The opinions expressed do not necessarily reflect the position or policy of NIE, and no official endorsement should be inferred.

REFERENCE NOTES

1. Vesonder, G. *The role of knowledge in the processing of experimental reports.* Unpublished doctoral dissertation, University of Pittsburgh, 1979.
2. Mandler, J. M., & Goodman, M. *On the psychological validity of story structure.* Paper presented at the Psychonomic Society, St. Louis, November, 1980.
3. Black, J. B. *Story memory structure.* Unpublished doctoral dissertation, Stanford University, 1978.
4. Caylor, J. S., Sticht, T. G., Fox, L. C., & Ford, J. P. *Methodologies for determining reading requirements of military occupational specialties.* (Tech. Rep. 73-5). HOMRO Western Division. Presidio of Monterey, CA: Human Resources Research Organization, March, 1973.
5. Carroll, J. B. *Learning from verbal discourse in educational media: Review of the literature.* (Final Report, Project 7-1069). Princeton, NJ: Educational Testing Service, 1971.
6. Johnson, S. C. *A simple cluster statistic.* Unpublished manuscript, 1968.

REFERENCES

Anderson, B. W. The effect of pre- versus postorganizers upon retention of economic concepts at the collegiate level. *Dissertation Abstracts International,* 1973, *34,* 3819A.
Anderson, R. C., & Biddle, W. B. On asking people questions about what they are reading. In G. H. Bower (Ed.), *The psychology of learning and motivation* (Vol. 9). New York: Academic Press, 1975.
Anderson, R. C., & Kulhavy, R. W. Imagery and prose learning. *Journal of Educational Psychology,* 1972, *63,* 242–243.
Anderson, R. C., & Pichert, J. W. Recall of previously unrecallable information following a shift in perspective. *Journal of Verbal Learning and Verbal Behavior,* 1978, *17,* 1–12.
Anderson, R. C., Reynolds, R. E., Schallert, D. L., & Goetz, E. T. Frameworks for comprehending discourse. *American Educational Research Journal,* 1977, *14,* 367–381.
Andre, T., & Womack, S. Verbatim and paraphrased adjunct questions and learning from prose. *Journal of Educational Psychology,* 1978, *70,* 796–802.
Ausubel, D. P. *The psychology of meaningful verbal learning.* New York: Grune & Stratton, 1963.
Ausubel, D. P. *Educational psychology: A cognitive view.* New York: Holt, Rinehart, & Winston, 1968.
Ausubel, D. P., & Blake, E., Jr. Proactive inhibition in the forgetting of meaningful school material. *Journal of Educational Research,* 1958, *52,* 145–149.

Ausubel, D. P., Robbins, L. C., & Blake, E., Jr. Retroactive inhibition and facilitation in the learning of school materials. *Journal of Educational Psychology*, 1957, *48*, 334–343.

Baker, L. Processing temporal relationships in simple stories: Effects of input sequence. *Journal of Verbal Learning and Verbal Behavior*, 1978, *17*, 559–572.

Ballstaedt, S. P., Schnotz, W., & Mandl, H. *Predictability of learning results on the basis of hierarchical text structures.* Tübingen, W. Germany: Deutsches Institut für Fernstudien an der Universität Tubingen, 1980.

Barnes, B. R., & Clawson, E. Do advanced organizers facilitate learning? Recommendations for further research based on an analysis of 32 studies. *Review of Educational Research*, 1975, *45*, 637–659.

Bartlett, F. C. *Remembering.* London: Cambridge University Press, 1932.

Bates, E., Kintsch, W., Fletcher, C. R., & Guiliani, V. The role of pronominalization and ellipsis in texts: Some memory experiments. *Journal of Experimental Psychology: Human Learning and Memory*, 1980, *6*, 676–691.

Bates, E., Masling, M., & Kintsch, W. Recognition memory for aspects of dialogue. *Journal of Experimental Psychology: Human Learning and Memory*, 1978, *4*, 187–197.

Bisanz, G. L. Knowledge of persuasion and story comprehension: Developmental changes in expectations. *Discourse Processes*, in press.

Bisanz, G. L., LaPorte, R. E., Vesonder, G. T., & Voss, J. F. On the representation of prose: New dimensions. *Journal of Verbal Learning and Verbal Behavior*, 1978, *17*, 337–357.

Black, J. B., & Bower, G. H. Episodes as chunks in narrative memory. *Journal of Verbal Learning and Verbal Behavior*, 1979, *18*, 309–318.

Black, J. B., & Bower, G. H. Story understanding as problem solving. *Poetics*, 1980, *9*, 223–250.

Black, J. B., Turner, T. J., & Bower, G. H. Point of view in narrative comprehension, memory, and production. *Journal of Verbal Learning and Verbal Behavior*, 1979, *18*, 187–198.

Black, J. B., & Wilensky, R. An evaluation of story grammars. *Cognitive Science*, 1979, *3*, 213–230.

Bormuth, J. R. *Development of readability analyses.* (Final Report, Project No. 7-0052). Contract No. OEC-3-7-070052-0376. Bureau of Research, U.S. Department of Health, Education, and Welfare, March 1969.

Bower, G. H. Selective facilitation and interference in the retention of prose. *Journal of Educational Psychology*, 1974, *66*, 1–8.

Bower, G. H. Experiments on story understanding and recall. *Quarterly Journal of Experimental Psychology*, 1976, *28*, 511–534.

Bower, G. H. Experiments on story comprehension and recall. *Discourse Processes*, 1978, *1*, 211–231.

Bower, G. H., Black, J. B., & Turner, T. J. Scripts in memory for text. *Cognitive Psychology*, 1979, *11*, 177–220.

Bransford, J. D., & Johnson, M. K. Contextual prerequisites for understanding: Some investigations of comprehension and recall. *Journal of Verbal Learning and Verbal Behavior*, 1972, *11*, 717–726.

Britton, B. K., Holdredge, T. S., Curry, C., & Westbrook, R. D. Use of cognitive capacity in reading identical texts with different amounts of discourse level learning. *Journal of Experimental Psychology: Human Learning and Memory*, 1979, *5*, 262–270.

Britton, B. K., Meyer, B. J., Hodge, M. H., & Glynn, S. M. Effects of the organization of text on memory: Tests of retrieval and response criterion hypotheses. *Journal of Experimental Psychology: Human Learning and Memory*, 1980, *6*, 620–629.

Britton, B. K., Westbrook, R. D., & Holdredge, T. S. Reading and cognitive capacity usage: Effects of text difficulty. *Journal of Experimental Psychology: Human Learning and Memory*, 1978, *4*, 582–591.

Brown, A. L. Recognition, reconstruction, and recall of narrative sequences by preoperational children. *Child Development*, 1975, *46*, 156–166.

Brown, A. L. Semantic integration in children's reconstruction of narrative sequences. *Cognitive Psychology*, 1976, *8*, 247–262.

Brown, A., & Smiley, S. S. Rating the importance of structural units of prose passages: A problem of metacognitive development. *Child Development*, 1977, *48*, 1–8.

Bruce, B., & Newman, D. Interacting plans. *Cognitive Science*, 1978, *2*, 195–234.

Carroll, J. B., & Chang, J. Analysis of individual differences in multidimensional scaling via an *N*-way generalization of Eckart Young decomposition. *Psychometrika*, 1970, *35*, 283–319.

Chafe, W. L. Language and memory. *Language*, 1973, *49*, 261–281.

Chandler, J. P. STEPIT Program 90PE66. *Quantum chemistry program exchange*. Bloomington, In.: Indiana University, 1965.

Chase, W. G., & Simon, H. A. Perception in chess. *Cognitive Psychology*, 1973, *4*, 55–81.

Christensen, C. M., & Stordahl, K. E. The effect of organizational aids on comprehension and retention. *Journal of Educational Psychology*, 1955, *46*, 65–74.

Cirilo, R. K., & Foss, D. J. Text structure and reading time for sentences. *Journal of Verbal Learning and Verbal Behavior*, 1980, *19*, 96–109.

Clark, K. B. Some factors influencing the remembering of prose material. *Archives of Psychology*, 1940, *253*.

Clawson, E. V., & Barnes, B. R. The effects of organizers on the learning of structured anthropology materials in elementary grades. *Journal of Educational Psychology*, 1973, *42*, 11–15.

Clements, P. The effects of staging on recall from prose. In R. O. Freedle (Ed.), *New directions in discourse processing, II*. Norwood, N.J.: Ablex Publishing Co., 1979.

Cofer, C. N. A comparison of logical and verbatim learning of prose passages of different lengths. *American Journal of Psychology*, 1941, *54*, 1–21.

Coleman, E. B. Approximations to English: Some comments on the method. *American Journal of Psychology*, 1963, *70*, 239–247.

Coles, P., & Foster, J. Typographic cuing as an aid to learning from typewritten text. *Programmed Learning and Educational Technology*, 1975, *12*, 102–108.

Crothers, E. J. Memory structure and the recall of discourse. In J. B. Carroll & R. O. Freedle (Eds.), *Language comprehension and the acquisition of knowledge*. Washington, D.C.: Winston, 1972.

Crothers, E. J. *Paragraph structure inference*. Norwood, N.J., Ablex Publishing Co., 1979.

Crouse, J. H. Transfer and retroaction in prose learning. *Journal of Educational Psychology*, 1970, *61*, 226–228.

Crouse, J. H. Retroactive interference in reading prose materials. *Journal of Educational Psychology*, 1971, *62*, 39–44.

Davis, O. L. The usefulness of a map with geographic text: A reanalysis of experimental data. *Journal of Geography*, 1971, *70*, 303–306.

Dawes, R. M. Cognitive distortion. *Psychological Reports*, 1964, *14*, 443–459.

Dawes, R. M. Memory and distortion of meaningful written material. *British Journal of Psychology*, 1966, *57*, 77–86.

de Beaugrande, R. *Text, discourse, and process.* Norwood, N.J.: Ablex Publishing Co., 1980.

Deese, J., & Kaufman, R. A. Serial effects in recall of unorganized and sequentially organized verbal material. *Journal of Experimental Psychology,* 1957, *54,* 180–187.

de Groot, A. D. Perception and memory versus thought: Some old ideas and recent findings. In B. Kleinmuntz (Ed.), *Problem solving: Research, method and theory.* New York: John Wiley and Sons, 1966.

de Villiers, P. A. Imagery and theme in recall of connected discourse. *Journal of Experimental Psychology,* 1974, *103,* 263–268.

Donders, F. C. Over de dnelheid van psychische processen. Onderzockingera gedaan in het Psyiologish Leboratorium der Utrechtsche Hoodeachool, 1868–1869. Tweede Reeks, II, 92–120.

Dooling, D. J., & Lachman, R. Effects of comprehension on retention of prose. *Journal of Experimental Psychology,* 1971, *88,* 216–222.

Duchastel, P. C., & Merrill, P. F. The effects of behavioral objectives on learning: A review of empirical studies. *Review of Educational Research,* 1973, *43,* 53–69.

Duell, O. K. Effect of type of objective, level of test questions, and the judged importance of tested materials upon posttest performance. *Journal of Experimental Psychology,* 1974, *66,* 225–232.

Dwyer, F. M. The effect of questions on visual learning. *Perceptual and Motor Skills,* 1969, *29,* 320–322.

Earle, R. A. The use of vocabulary as a structured overview in seventh-grade mathematics. *Dissertation Abstracts International,* 1971, *31,* 5929.

Entwistle, D. P., & Huggins, W. H. Interference in meaningful learning. *Journal of Educational Psychology,* 1964, *55,* 75–78.

Everitt, B. *Cluster analysis.* London, England: Heinemann Educational Books, 1974.

Fillenbaum, S., & Rapaport, A. *Structures in the subjective lexicon.* New York: Academic Press, 1971.

Fisher, D. F., Monty, R. A., & Senders, J. W. *Eye movements: Cognition and visual perception.* Hillsdale, N.J.: Lawrence Erlbaum Associates, 1981.

Flesch, R. F. A new readability yardstick. *Journal of Applied Psychology,* 1948, *32,* 221–233.

Frase, L. T. Questions as aids to reading: Some research and a theory. *American Educational Research Journal,* 1968, *5,* 319–332.

Frase, L. T. Tabular and diagrammatic presentation of verbal materials. *Perceptual and Motor Skills,* 1969, *29,* 320–322.

Frederiksen, C. H. Task-induced cognitive operations. In J. B. Carroll & R. O. Freedle (Eds.), *Language comprehension and the acquisition of knowledge.* Washington, D.C.: Winston, 1972.

Frederiksen, C. H. Acquisition of semantic information from discourse: Effects of repeated exposures. *Journal of Verbal Learning and Verbal Behavior,* 1975, *14,* 158–169.(a)

Frederiksen, C. H. Effects of context-induced processing operations on semantic information acquired from discourse. *Cognitive Psychology,* 1975, *7,* 139–166.(b)

Frederiksen, C. H. Representing logical and semantic structure of knowledge acquired from discourse. *Cognitive Psychology,* 1975, *7,* 371–458.(c)

Frederiksen, C. H. Semantic processing units in understanding text. In R. O. Freedle (Ed.), *Discourse production and comprehension,* Norwood, N.J.: Ablex Publishing Co., 1977.

Gauld, A., & Stephenson, G. M. Some experiments relating to Bartlett's theory of remembering. *British Journal of Psychology,* 1967, *58,* 39–50.

Goetz, E. T. Inferring from text: Some factors influencing which inferences will be made. *Discourse Processes*, 1979, *2*, 179–195.

Goldman, S. R. Semantic knowledge systems for realistic goals. *Discourse Processes*, in press.

Graesser, A. C. How to catch a fish: The representation and memory of common procedures. *Discourse Processes*, 1978, *1*, 72–89.

Graesser, A. C., Gordon, S. E., & Sawyer, J. D. Recognition memory for typical and atypical actions in scripted activities: Tests of a script pointer and tag hypothesis. *Journal of Verbal Learning and Verbal Behavior*, 1979, *18*, 319–332.

Graesser, A. C., Hoffman, N. L., & Clark, L. F. Structural components of reading time. *Journal of Verbal Learning and Verbal Behavior*, 1980, *19*, 135–151.

Graesser, A. C., Robertson, S. P., & Anderson P. A. Incorporating inferences in narrative representations: A study of how and why. *Cognitive Psychology*, 1981, *13*, 1–26.

Graesser, A. C., Robertson, S. P., Lovelace, E. R., & Swinehart, D. M. Answers to why-questions expose the organization of story plot and predict recall of actions. *Journal of Verbal Learning and Verbal Behavior*, 1980, *19*, 110–119.

Green, P. E., & Rao, V. R. *Applied multidimensional scaling: A comparison of approaches and algorithms*. New York: Holt, Rinehart, & Winston, 1972.

Greeno, J. G. Process of understanding in problem solving. In N. J. Castellan, D. B. Pisoni, & G. R. Potts (Eds.), *Cognitive Theory* (Vol. 2). Hillsdale, N.J.: Lawrence Erlbaum Associates, 1977.

Grimes, J. *The thread of discourse*. The Hague, Holland: Mouton Press, 1975.

Grotelueschen, A. D., & Sjogren, D. D. Effects of differentially structured introductory materials and learning tasks on learning transfer. *American Educational Research Journal*, 1968, *2*, 191–202.

Haberlandt, K., Berian, C., & Sandson, J. The episode schema in story processing. *Journal of Verbal Learning and Verbal Behavior*, 1980, *19*, 635–650.

Hall, J. F. Retroactive inhibition in meaningful material. *Journal of Educational Psychology*, 1955, *46*, 47–52.

Henderson, E. N. A study of memory for connected trains of thought. *Psychological Monographs*, 1903, *5*, 1–92.

Hershberger, W. A., & Terry, D. F. Typographical cuing in conventional and programmed texts. *Journal of Applied Psychology*, 1956, *49*, 55–60.

Hildyard, A. & Olson, D. R. Memory and inference in the comprehension of oral and written discourse. *Discourse Processes*, 1978, *1*, 91–117.

Jardine, N., & Sibson, R. *Mathematical taxonomy*, New York: John Wiley and Sons, 1971.

Jenkins, J. R., & Deno, S. L. Influence of knowledge and type of objectives on subject-matter learning. *Journal of Educational Psychology*, 1971, *62*, 67–70.

Jerrolds, B. W. The effects of advance organizers in reading for retention of specific facts. *Dissertation Abstracts International*, 1967, *28*, 4532.

Johnson, N. S., & Mandler, J. M. A tale of two structures: Underlying and surface forms in stories. *Poetics*, 1980, *9*, 51–86.

Johnson, R. E. Recall of prose as a function of the structural importance of the linguistic units. *Journal of Verbal Learning and Verbal Behavior*, 1970, *9*, 12–20.

Johnson, R. E. Meaningfulness and the recall of textual prose. *American Educational Research Journal*, 1973, *10*, 49–58.

Johnson, R. E., & Scheidt, B. J. Organizational encodings in the serial learning of prose. *Journal of Verbal Learning and Verbal Behavior*, 1977, *16*, 575–588.

Johnson, S. C. Hierarchical clustering schemes. *Psychometrika,* 1967, *32,* 241–254.

Just, M. A., & Carpenter, P. A. Eye fixations and cognitive processes. *Cognitive Psychology,* 1976, *8,* 441–480.

Just, M. A., & Carpenter, P. A. Inference processes during reading: Reflections from eye fixations. In J. W. Senders, D. F. Fisher, & R. A. Monty (Eds.), *Eye movements and the higher psychological functions.* Hillsdale, N.J.: Lawrence Erlbaum Associates, 1978.

Just, M. A., & Carpenter, P. A. A theory of reading: From eye fixations to comprehension. *Psychological Review,* 1980, *87,* 329–354.

Kahneman, D. *Attention and effort.* Englewood Cliffs, N.J.: Prentice–Hall, 1973.

Kalbaugh, G. L., & Walls, R. T. Retroactive and proactive interference in prose learning of biographical and science materials. *Journal of Educational Psychology,* 1973, *65,* 244–251.

Kaplan, R. Effects of learning with part versus whole presentations of instructional objectives. *Journal of Educational Psychology,* 1974, *66,* 448–456.

Kay, H. Learning and retaining verbal material. *British Journal of Psychology,* 1955, *46,* 81–100.

Keenan, J. M., MacWhinney, B. M., & Mayhew, D. Pragmatics in memory: A study of natural conversation. *Journal of Verbal Learning and Verbal Behavior,* 1977, *16,* 549–560.

Kieras, D. E. Good and bad structure in simple paragraphs: Effects on apparent theme, reading time, and recall. *Journal of Verbal Learning and Verbal Behavior,* 1978, *17,* 13–28.

Kieras, D. E. Initial mention as a signal to thematic content in technical passages. *Memory & Cognition,* 1980, *8,* 345–353.

King, D. J., & Cofer, C. N. Retroactive interference in meaningful material as a function of the degree of contextual constraint in the original and interpolated learning. *Journal of General Psychology,* 1960, *63,* 145–148.

Kintsch, W. *The representation of meaning in memory.* Hillsdale, N.J.: Lawrence Erlbaum Associates, 1974.

Kintsch, W. On comprehending stories. In M. A. Just & P. A. Carpenter (Eds.), *Cognitive processes in comprehension.* Hillsdale, N.J.: Lawrence Erlbaum Associates, 1977.

Kintsch, W. & Bates, E. Recognition memory for statements from a classroom lecture. *Journal of Experimental Psychology: Human Learning and Memory,* 1977, *3,* 150–159.

Kintsch, W., & Greene, E. The role of culture-specific schemata in the comprehension and recall of stories. *Discourse Processes,* 1978, *1,* 1–13.

Kintsch, W., & Keenan, J. Reading rate and retention as a function of the number of propositions in the base structure of sentences. *Cognitive Psychology,* 1973, *5,* 257–274.

Kintsch, W., & Kozminsky, E. Summarizing stories after reading and listening. *Journal of Educational Psychology,* 1977, *69,* 491–499.

Kintsch, W., Kozminsky, E., Streby, W. J., McKoon, G., & Keenan, J. M. Comprehension and recall of text as a function of content variables. *Journal of Verbal Learning and Verbal Behavior,* 1975, *14,* 196–214.

Kintsch, W., Mandel, T. S., & Kozminsky, E. Summarizing scrambled stories. *Memory & Cognition,* 1977, *5,* 547–552.

Kintsch, W., & van Dijk, T. A. Toward a model of text comprehension and production. *Psychological Review,* 1978, *85,* 363–394.

Kintsch, W., & Vipond, D. Reading comprehension and readability in educational practice and psychological theory. In L. G. Nillson (Ed.), *Perspectives on memory research.* Hillsdale, N.J.: Lawrence Erlbaum Associates, 1979.

Klare, G. R. Assessing readability. *Reading Research Quarterly,* 1974, *10,* 62–102.

Koen, F., Becker, A., & Young, R. The psychological reality of the paragraph. *Journal of Verbal Learning and Verbal Behavior,* 1969, *8,* 49–53.

Koenke, K., & Otto, W. Contribution of pictures to children's comprehension of the main idea in reading. *Psychology in the Schools,* 1969, *6,* 298–302.

Kozminsky, E. Altering comprehension: The effect of biasing titles on text comprehension. *Memory & Cognition,* 1977, *5,* 482–490.

Kruskal, J. B., & Carroll, J. D. Geometric models and badness-of-fit functions. In P. R. Krishnaiah (Ed.), *Multivariate Analysis* (Vol. 2). New York: Academic Press, 1969.

Kruskal, J. B., & Wish, M. *Multidimensional scaling.* Beverly Hills, Ca.: Sage Publications, 1978.

Lachman, R., & Dooling, D. J. Connected discourse and random strings: Effects of number of inputs on recognition and recall. *Journal of Experimental Psychology,* 1968, *77,* 517–522.

Lachman, R., & Tuttle, A. V. Approximations to English (AE) and short-term memory: Construction or storage? *Journal of Experimental Psychology,* 1965, *70,* 386–393.

LaPorte, R. E., & Voss, J. F. Prose representation: A multidimensional scaling approach. *Multivariate Behavioral Research,* 1979, *14,* 39–56.

Lawson, T. E. Effects of instructional objectives on learning and retention. *Instructional Science,* 1974, *3,* 1–21.

Lesgold, A., Roth, S., & Curtis M. B. Foregrounding effects in discourse comprehension. *Journal of Verbal Learning and Verbal Behavior,* 1979, *18,* 291–308.

Levin, J. R., & Divine-Hawkins, P. Visual imagery as a prose learning process. *Journal of Reading Behavior,* 1974, *6,* 23–30.

Levitt, E. A. A methodological study of the preparation of connected verbal discourse for quantitative memory experiments. *Journal of Experimental Psychology,* 1956, *52,* 33–38.

Lewis, F. H. Note on the doctrine of memory traces. *Psychological Review,* 1933, *40,* 90–96.

Magne, O., & Parknas, L. The learning effects of pictures. *British Journal of Psychology,* 1963, *33,* 265–275.

Mandler, J. M. A code in the node: The use of story schema in retrieval. *Discourse Processes,* 1978, *1,* 14–35.

Mandler, J. M., & Johnson, N. S. Remembrance of things parsed: Story structure and recall. *Cognitive Psychology,* 1977, *9,* 111–151.

Mandler, J. M., & Johnson, N. S. On throwing out the baby with the bathwater: A reply to Black and Wilensky's evaluation of story grammars. *Cognitive Science,* 1980, *4,* 305–312.

Mandler, J. M., Scribner, S., Cole, M., & De Forest, M. Cross-cultural invariants in story recall. *Child Development,* 1980, *51,* 19–26.

Manelis, L. Determinants of processing for a propositional structure. *Memory & Cognition,* 1980, *8,* 49–57.

Manelis, L., & Yekovich, F. R. Repetitions of propositional arguments in sentences. *Journal of Verbal Learning and Verbal Behavior,* 1976, *15,* 301–312.

Marks, M., & Jack, O. Verbal context and memory span for meaningful material. *American Journal of Psychology,* 1952, *65,* 298–300.

Martin, E., & Noreen, D. L. Serial learning: Identification of subjective sequences. *Cognitive Psychology*, 1974, *6*, 421–435.

Mayer, R. E. Some conditions of meaningful learning of computer programming: Advance organizers and subject control of frame sequencing. *Journal of Educational Psychology*, 1976, *68*, 143–150.

Mayer, R. E. Can advance organizers influence meaningful learning? *Journal of Educational Psychology*, 1979, *49*, 371–383.

McCall, W. A., & Crabbs, L. M. *Standard Test Lessons in Reading*. New York: Bureau of Publications, Teachers College, Columbia University, 1925.

McCluskey, H. Y. An experimental comparison of reading the original and digest versions of an article. *Journal of Educational Psychology*, 1940, *31*, 603–615.

McConkie, G. W., Hogaboam, T. W., Wolverton, G. S., & Lucas, P. A. Toward the use of eye movements in the study of language processing. *Discourse Processes*, 1979, *2*, 157–177.

McGaw, B., & Groetlueschen, A. Direction of the effect of questions in prose material. *Journal of Educational Psychology*, 1972, *63*, 580–588.

McGeogh, J. A., & McKinney, F. Retroactive inhibition in the learning of poetry. *American Journal of Psychology*, 1934, *46*, 19–33.(a)

McGeogh, J. A., & McKinney, F. The susceptibility of prose to retroactive inhibition. *American Journal of Psychology*, 1934, *46*, 429–436.(b)

McKoon, G., & Ratcliff, R. Priming in item recognition: The organization of propositions in memory for text. *Journal of Verbal Learning and Verbal Behavior*, 1980, *19*, 369–386.

Meyer, B. J. F. *The organization of prose and its effect upon memory*. Amsterdam: North–Holland Publishing Co., 1975.

Meyer, B. J. F. The structure of prose: Effects on learning and memory and implications for educational practice. In R. C. Anderson, R. Spiro, & W. Montague (Eds.), *Schooling and the acquisition of knowledge*. Hillsdale, N.J.: Lawrence Erlbaum Associates, 1977.

Meyer, B. J. F., & McConkie, G. W. What is recalled after hearing a passage? *Journal of Educational Psychology*, 1973, *65*, 109–117.

Meyers, L. S., & Boldrick, D. Memory for meaningful connected discourse. *Journal of Experimental Psychology: Human Learning and Memory*, 1975, *1*, 584–591.

Miller, G. A., & Selfridge, J. A. Verbal context and the recall of meaningful material. *American Journal of Psychology*, 1950, *63*, 176–185.

Miller, J. R., & Kintsch, W. Readability and recall of short prose passages: A theoretical analysis. *Journal of Experimental Psychology: Human Learning and Memory*, 1980, *6*, 335–354.

Minsky, M. A framework for representing knowledge. In P. H. Winston (Ed.), *The psychology of computer vision*. New York: McGraw–Hill, 1975.

Moeser, S. D. Effect of questions on prose unitization. *Journal of Experimental Psychology*, 1978, *4*, 290–303.

Montague, W. E., & Carter, J. F. Vividness of imagery in recalling connected discourse. *Journal of Educational Psychology*, 1973, *64*, 72–75.

Morris, J. O. *Make yourself clear!* New York: McGraw–Hill, 1972.

Mosenthal, P. Three types of schemata in children's recall of cohesive and noncohesive text. *Journal of Experimental Child Psychology*, 1979, *27*, 129–142.

Neyman, I. Contributions to the theory of the test. In J. Neyman (Ed.), *Proceedings of the Berkeley Symposium on mathematical statistics and probability*. Berkeley, Ca.: University of California Press, 1949.

Nias, A. H. W., & Kay, H. Immediate memory of a broadcast feature programme. *British Journal of Psychology*, 1954, *24*, 154–160.

Olson, G. M., Duffy, S. A., & Mack, R. L. Knowledge of writing conventions in prose comprehension. In N. J. McKeachie & K. Eble (Eds.), *New directions in learning and teaching*. San Francisco: Jossey–Bass, in press.

Omanson, R. C. An analysis of narrative: Identifying central, supportive, and distracting content. *Discourse Processes*, in press.

Omanson, R. C., Warren, W. H., & Trabasso, T. Goals, inferential comprehension, and recall of stories by children. *Discourse Processes*, 1978, *1*, 337–354.

Owens, J., Bower, G. H., & Black, J. B. The "Soap Opera" effect in story recall. *Memory & Cognition*, 1979, *7*, 185–191.

Paris, S. G., & Upton, L. R. Children's memory for inferential relationships in prose. *Child Development*, 1976, *47*, 660–668.

Paul, I. H. Studies in remembering: The reproduction of connected and extended verbal material. In G. S. Klein (Ed.), *Psychological Issues*, New York, 1959, *1*, Monograph 2.

Peeck, J. Retention of pictorial and verbal content of a text with illustrations. *Journal of Educational Psychology*, 1974, *66*, 880–888.

Petros, T., & Hoving, K. The effects of review on young children's memory for prose. *Journal of Experimental Child Psychology*, 1980, *30*, 33–43.

Piaget, J. *The language and thought of the child*. London: Routledge Kegan Paul, 1960. (Originally published, 1926.)

Pompi, K. F., & Lachman, R. Surrogate processes in the short-term retention of connected discourse. *Journal of Experimental Psychology*, 1967, *75*, 143–150.

Poulsen, D., Kintsch, E., Kintsch, W., & Premack, D. Children's comprehension and memory for stories. *Journal of Experimental Child Psychology*, 1979, *28*, 379–403.

Pressley, M. Imagery and children's learning: Putting the picture in developmental perspective. *Review of Educational Research*, 1977, *47*, 485–622.

Propp, V. *Morphology of the folktale*. Austin, Tx.: University of Texas Press, 1928.

Ratcliff, R., & McKoon, G. Priming in item recognition: Evidence for the propositional structure of sentences. *Journal of Verbal Learning and Verbal Behavior*, 1978, *17*, 403–417.

Rayner, K. Eye movements in reading and information processing. *Psychological Bulletin*, 1978, *85*, 618–660.

Reder, L. M., & Anderson, J. R. A comparison of texts and their summaries: Memorial consequences. *Journal of Verbal Learning and Verbal Behavior*, 1980, *19*, 121–134.

Richards, J. P., & DiVesta, F. J. Type and frequency of questions in processing textual material. *Journal of Educational Psychology*, 1974, *66*, 354–362.

Richardson, P., & Voss. J. F. Replication report: Verbal context and the recall of meaningful material. *Journal of Experimental Psychology*, 1960, *60*, 417–418.

Rickards, J. P. Interaction of position and conceptual level of adjunct questions on immediate and delayed retention of text. *Journal of Educational Psychology*, 1976, *68*, 210–217.

Rickards, J. P. Adjunct postquestions in text: A critical review of methods and processes. *Review of Educational Research*, 1979, *49*, 181–196.

Robinson, F. P., & Hall, P. Studies of higher-level reading abilities. *Journal of Educational Psychology*, 1941, *32*, 241–252.

Rockas, L. *Modes of Rhetoric*. New York: St. Martin's Press, 1964.

Rothkopf, E. Z. Learning from written instructional material: An exploration of the control of inspection behavior by test-like events. *American Educational Research Journal*, 1966, *3*, 241–249.

Rothkopf, E. Z., & Kaplan, R. Exploration of the effect of density and specificity of instructional objectives on learning from text. *Journal of Educational Psychology,* 1972, *63,* 295–302.

Rubin, D. C. A unit analysis of prose memory. *Journal of Verbal Learning and Verbal Behavior,* 1978, *17,* 599–620.

Rumelhart, D. E. Notes on schema for stories. In D. Bobrow and A. Collins (Eds.), *Representations and understanding: Studies in cognitive science.* New York: Academic Press, 1975.

Rumelhart, D. E. Understanding and summarizing brief stories. In D. LaBerge & J. Samuels (Eds.), *Basic processes in reading: Perception and comprehension.* Hillsdale, N.J.: Lawrence Erlbaum Associates, 1977.

Rumelhart, D. E. On evaluating story grammars. *Cognitive Science,* 1980, *4,* 313–316.

Sachs, J. S. Recognition memory for syntactic and semantic aspects of connected discourse. *Perceptual Psychology,* 1967, *2,* 437–442.

Sanders, J. R. Retention effects of adjunct question in written and aural discourse. *Journal of Educational Psychology,* 1973, *65,* 181–186.

Scandura, J. M., & Wells, J. N. Advance organizers in learning abstract mathematics. *American Educational Research Journal,* 1967, 295–301.

Schallert, D. L. Improving memory for prose: The relationship between depth of processing and context. *Journal of Verbal Learning and Verbal Behavior,* 1976, *15,* 621–632.

Schank, R. C. Conceptual dependency: A theory of natural language understanding. *Cognitive Psychology,* 1972, *3,* 552–631.

Schank, R. C. Identification of conceptualizations underlying natural language. In R. C. Schank & K. M. Colby (Eds.), *Computer models of thought and language.* San Francisco: W. H. Freeman and Co., 1973.

Schank, R. C. The role of memory in language processing. In C. Cofer (Ed.), *The structure of human memory.* San Francisco: W. H. Freeman and Co., 1975.(a)

Schank, R. C. The structure of episodes in memory. In D. G. Bobrow & A. Collins (Eds.), *Representations and understanding: Studies in cognitive science.* New York: Academic Press, 1975.(b)

Schank, R. C. *Conceptual information processing.* Amsterdam: North Holland, 1975(c)

Schank, R. C., & Abelson, R. *Scripts, plans, goals, and understanding.* Hillsdale, N. J.: Lawrence Erlbaum Associates, 1977.

Schnell, T. R. The effect of organizers on reading comprehension of community college freshmen. *Journal of Reading Behavior,* 1973, *5,* 169–176.

Sharp, H. C. Effect of contextual constraint upon recall of verbal passages. *American Journal of Psychology,* 1958, *71,* 568–572.

Shepard, R. N., Romney, A. K., & Nerlowe, S. B. *Multidimensional scaling: Theory and applications in the behavioral sciences.* New York: Seminar Press, 1972.

Slamecka, N. J. Retroactive inhibition of connected discourse as a function of similarity of topic. *Journal of Experimental Psychology,* 1960, *60,* 245–249.(a)

Slamecka, N. J. Retroactive inhibition of connected discourse as a function of practice level. *Journal of Experimental Psychology,* 1960, *59,* 104–108.(b)

Slamecka, N. J. Retention of connected discourse as a function of duration of interpolated learning. *Journal of Experimental Psychology,* 1962, *63,* 480–486.

Smiley, S., Oakley, D. D., Worthen, D., Campione, J. C., & Brown, A. L. Recall of thematically relevant material by adolescent good and poor readers as a function of written and oral presentation. *Journal of Educational Psychology,* 1977, *69,* 381–387.

Snowman, J., & Cunningham, D. J. A comparison of pictorial and written adjunct aids in learning from text. *Journal of Educational Psychology,* 1975, *67,* 307–311.

Spilich, G. J., Vesonder, G. T., Chiesi, H. L., & Voss, J. F. Text processing of domain-related information for individuals with high and low domain knowledge. *Journal of Verbal Learning and Verbal Behavior*, 1979, *18*, 275–290.

Stein, N. L., & Glenn, C. G. An analysis of story comprehension in elementary school children. In R. O. Freedle (Ed.), *New directions in discourse processing* (Vol. II). Norwood, N.J.: Ablex Publishing Co., 1979.

Stein, N. L., & Nezworski, T. The effects of organization and instructional set on story memory. *Discourse Processes*, 1978, *1*, 177–193.

Sulin, R. A., & Dooling, D. J. Intrusion of a thematic idea in retention of prose. *Journal of Experimental Psychology*, 1974, *103*, 255–262.

Swenson, I., & Kulhavy, R. W. Adjunct questions and the comprehension of prose by children. *Journal of Educational Psychology*, 1974, *66*, 212–215.

Thorndyke, P. W. The role of inferences in discourse comprehension. *Journal of Verbal Learning and Verbal Behavior*, 1976, *15*, 437–446.

Thorndyke, P. W. Cognitive structures in comprehension and memory of narrative discourse. *Cognitive Psychology*, 1977, *9*, 77–110.

Turner, A., & Green, E. The construction of a propositional text base. *JSAS Catalog of Selected Documents in Psychology*, Washington, D.C.: American Psychological Association, 1977.

Tyler, S. W., Delaney, H., & Kinnucan, M. Specifying the nature of reading differences and advance organizer effects. *Journal of Educational Psychology*, in press.

van Dijk, T. A. Semantic macrostructures and knowledge frames in discourse comprehension. In M. A. Just & P. A. Carpenter (Eds.), *Cognitive processes in comprehension*. Hillsdale, N. J.: Lawrence Erlbaum Associates, 1977.

Vernon, M. D. The value of pictorial illustration. *British Journal of Psychology*, 1953, *23*, 180–187.

Vipond, D. Micro- and macroprocesses in text comprehension. *Journal of Verbal Learning and Verbal Behavior*, 1980, *19*, 276–296.

Voss, J. F., Vesonder, G. T., & Spilich, G. J. Text generation and recall by high-knowledge and low-knowledge individuals. *Journal of Verbal Learning and Verbal Behavior*, 1980, *19*, 651–667.

Walker, B. S. Effects of inserted questions on retroactive inhibition in meaningful verbal learning. *Journal of Educational Psychology*, 1974, *66*, 486–490.

Warren, W. H., Nicholas, D. W., & Trabasso, T. Event chains and inferences in understanding narratives. In R. O. Freedle (Ed.), *New directions in discourse processing*, Norwood, N.J.: Ablex Publishing Co., 1979.

Waters, H. S. Superordinate–subordinate structure in semantic memory: The role of comprehension and retrieval processes. *Journal of Verbal Learning and Verbal Behavior*, 1978, *17*, 587–597.

Wong, M. R. Retroactive inhibition in meaningful verbal learning. *Journal of Educational Psychology*, 1970, *61*, 5.

Young L. R., & Sheena, D. Survey of eye movement recording methods. *Behavior Research Methods and Instrumentation*, 1975, *7*, 397–429.

Zangwill, O. L. Some relations between reproducing and recognizing prose materials. *British Journal of Psychology*, 1939, *30*, 370–382.

JEFFERY J. FRANKS
JOHN D. BRANSFORD
PAMELA M. AUBLE

CHAPTER **13**

The Activation and Utilization of Knowledge

The purpose of this chapter is to discuss some procedures for exploring how memory is influenced by knowledge that learners have acquired previously. As a simple example of the effects of previously acquired knowledge, imagine trying to remember a list of words composed of items such as *cat* and *boy* as opposed to a list composed of items such as *cyb* and *ota*. It seems clear that the first list will be much easier to remember than the second list because the items in the first list are more "meaningful" (cf. Underwood & Schultz, 1960). Note, however, that the items in the first list are more meaningful only by virtue of what you, the reader, have already learned (e.g., the configuration *cat* would not be meaningful to a person who understood only Japanese). All studies of memory are influenced by the previously acquired knowledge of the learners. The studies in this chapter were designed explicitly to manipulate learners' available knowledge in order to assess its influence in more detail.

This chapter is divided into four sections; each focuses on a different aspect of the relationship between retention and the learner's previously acquired knowledge. It is important to note that our goal is not to provide an exhaustive review of all the research relevant to the topic of knowledge activation and utilization. Our primary goal is to discuss methodological procedures that enable one to explore relationships between prior knowl-

395

HANDBOOK OF RESEARCH METHODS IN
HUMAN MEMORY AND COGNITION

edge and retention. Our discussion of methods will focus on four factors that appear in a wide variety of experiments. These are:

1. Nature of the target information (the information to be comprehended and remembered)
2. Nature of the contextual information (information designed to influence comprehension and retention)
3. The sequencing of target information and contextual information (whether contextual information is presented before or after the target)
4. Nature of the criterial task (whether the experiment assesses free recall, cued recall, recognition, and so forth)

These four factors will be clarified by the following discussion.

PREREQUISITES TO COMPREHENSION

The studies in this section explore relationships between comprehension and retention. We begin by discussing a prototypical experiment that focuses on this issue. This experiment will provide a basis for explaining the four methodological components that were just outlined.

A Prototypical Experiment

An effective procedure for illustrating how retention depends on the activation of relevant knowledge is to manipulate the availability of that knowledge and assess its effects on comprehension and memory. Read the following passage and imagine that you will be asked to recall it later.

> If the balloons popped, the sound would not be able to carry, since everything would be too far away from the correct floor. A closed window would also prevent the sound from carrying, since most buildings tend to be well insulated. Since the whole operation depends on a steady flow of electricity, a break in the middle of the wire would also cause problems. Of course the fellow could shout, but the human voice is not loud enough to carry that far. An additional problem is that a string could break on the instrument. Then there could be no accompaniment to the message. It is clear that the best situation would involve less distance. Then there would be fewer potential problems. With face to face contact, the least number of things could go wrong [p. 719].

Bransford and Johnson (1972) read this passage to a group of students (called the *no knowledge context* group). After hearing it, the group was asked to rate it for comprehensibility on a 7-point scale (in which 7 indicated "highly comprehensible") and then to attempt to recall it. As one might expect, people in this group rated the passage as "very incomprehensible" (the average rating was 2.3), and their recall scores were quite low (see Table 13.1).

The same passage becomes quite comprehensible if one is supplied with an appropriate context. The picture in Figure 13.1 provides such a context. Look at the picture and then read the passage again.

People who first saw the appropriate picture and then heard the passage (called the *appropriate context before* group) rated the passage as "very comprehensible" (the average rating was 6.1). Furthermore, their recall scores were over twice as high as the first group's (see Table 13.1). However, the appropriate picture had to be available while reading or hearing the passage. Bransford and Johnson presented another group with the picture *after* letting them hear the passage; this did not significantly increase their comprehension or memory scores relative to the no-context group (see Table 13.1).

Why is the balloon passage so incomprehensible when presented in isolation? How does it become comprehensible when one is first provided with the information in Figure 13.1? An answer to these questions requires an analysis of how the pictorial information provides a basis for interpreting the words and phrases that the passage contains. As an illustration, consider the first phrase, which states: *If the balloons popped, the sound would not be able to carry. . . .* What is the referent of the word *sound*? With no context, the obvious assumption is that *sound* refers to the balloons popping. Given this assumption, it is difficult to grasp the relevance of additional information in the passage. For example, what is the *correct floor* that the sound could not reach? What is the *whole operation* that depends on a steady flow of electricity? Without additional information, it is difficult to determine the referents of many of the phrases and words.

When one reads the passage in the context of the appropriate picture in Figure 13.1, it becomes clear that the theme centers around a rather unique method of communication. One therefore realizes that *sound*

Table 13.1
Comprehension and Recall Scores for the Balloon Passage

	No context	Context before	Context after	Partial context	Maximum score
Comprehension rating:	2.30	6.10	3.30	3.70	7.00
Number of idea units recalled:	3.60	8.00	3.60	4.00	14.00

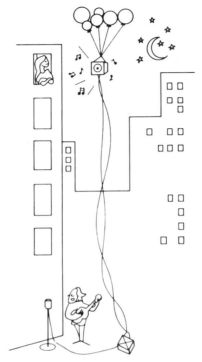

Figure 13.1. Appropriate Context for the Balloon Passage.

refers to the music from the loud speaker rather than the balloons, and that the *whole operation* refers to a particular method of communication that could break down in the ways that the passage describes. The picture in Figure 13.1 provides concrete referents for words like *balloons* and *wire,* but its most important function is to serve as a basis for specifying the goals of the "Romeo" and his unique method for solving a problem of communication. Note, for example, that the picture in Figure 13.2 contains the same concrete objects as Figure 13.1, but the method of communication is vastly different. Bransford and Johnson presented a group of students with this partial-context picture (Figure 13.2) before they heard the passage and found that it did not significantly increase comprehension and memory scores relative to the no-context group (see Table 13.1).

A Methodological Framework

The Bransford and Johnson experiment encompasses the four design components that were discussed in the introduction to this chapter. Our

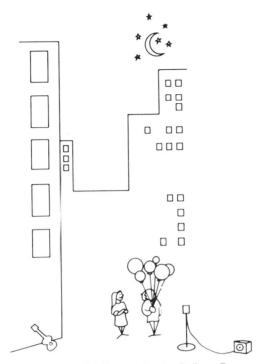

Figure 13.2. Partial Context for the Balloon Passage.

present goal is to discuss these components in more detail, using the balloon study as an illustrative example.

TARGET INFORMATION

To clarify what is involved in designing target materials we must consider the hypotheses that are being examined. Bransford and Johnson argued that to comprehend and later remember a passage one has to know what that passage is about. Phrased differently, adequate comprehension and memory for materials presupposes some preactivated knowledge about the context in which those materials can be understood. A first step in testing this hypothesis involved creation of the *balloon passage* as a target for initial comprehension and later remembering. In designing this target passage, the authors eliminated information concerning the contextual referent. Missing from the passage is information (such as that depicted in Figure 13.1) that provides concrete referents for the objects and for the spatial relations among the objects, as well as information as to the significance assumed by these objects and relations among objects in the context of a serenade. Methodologically, the balloon passage is an example of how target materials are designed. Targets are created or chosen to reduce or eliminate those aspects of the comprehension process that one wants to examine in the experiment.

CONTEXTUAL INFORMATION

Bransford and Johnson used two kinds of contexts, both of which provided additional information that was not present in the target. The first type supplied the information that was hypothesized to be important and was eliminated in the construction of the target. Figure 13.1 is an example of this kind of context. The methodological importance of this kind of context is twofold. First, the enhanced comprehension and recall performance of subjects receiving the context before hearing the target (compared to the no-context subjects who received only the target) provides a reference level for performance that demonstrates that the manipulation was, in fact, effective. If only the no-context condition was used, the data would be uninterpretable; one wouldn't know whether the comprehension ratings and level of recall were poor or not. Second, since the context is constructed to provide the information that is hypothesized to be important, the enhanced comprehension and recall is evidence that supports the particular hypothesis about an important component of the comprehension process. Bransford and Johnson constructed Figure 13.1 so that it would provide appropriate referents for the passage. They assumed that providing Figure 13.1 prior to reading the passage would facilitate comprehension (and later recall) of the passage. The enhanced performance of the context-before group thus supported their claim.

A second type of context is not concerned with providing evidence for the hypothesized process per se but rather is concerned with controlling for alternative interpretations of results. For example, in the balloon study "knowledge of appropriate contextual referent" was operationalized indirectly by what was left out of the target and directly by what was provided by the contextual picture in Figure 13.1. But what exactly was left out of the target and put in by the context? Bransford and Johnson argued that subjects needed information about the spatial relations among objects and about the general goal of "a serenade." The problem is that there can be other interpretations of what was missing from the target and supplied by the context. In general, this will always be a methodological problem that must be faced; there will often be a multitude of possible alternative interpretations. At this point pragmatics come in—the task is to deal with "reasonable" alternative explanations. The basic source of reasonable alternatives is the research literature (i.e., other psychological variables that have been found to influence the types of processes under examination). For example, when Bransford and Johnson were conducting their study, it was known that memory was affected by the concreteness, or imagery value, of verbal materials (e.g., Paivio, 1971). Thus, it could be argued that the greater recall shown by the context-before subjects was due to imagery variables rather than to "preactivated knowledge of an appropriate contextual referent." The context-before group received the picture that provided concrete referents and images for the terms in the target passage. In contrast, the no-context group did not receive concrete referents such as these.

To examine alternative interpretations regarding the effects related to targets and contexts, other control contexts must be designed. We suggest that such control conditions be set up by creating different contexts rather than by making changes in the target passage. Logically, both changes could be made; however, under most circumstances it is methodologically advantageous to adjust only contextual material. The reason is simple. Many different variables can affect memory performance, and these target materials (especially complex passages of text) can vary along a number of factors besides the major factor of interest. Given these possibilities, it is best to keep the target materials (which are the basis for comparisons of memory performance) constant across experimental conditions. In this way, any memory differences observed are more readily attributable to the variable eliminated from the target and put in the context rather than to some confounded variable due to the sources previously mentioned.

In the balloon study, Bransford and Johnson did, in fact, include a context condition to control for the alternative imagery interpretation. The imagery hypothesis suggests that the balloon passage reduced or eliminated imagery processes and that Figure 13.1 supplied the basis for reinstating these processes. One way to check this alternative is to design a different context that provides a basis for imagery but does not provide an appropriate situation as a contextual referent. This is what Bransford and Johnson did. Figure 13.2 illustrates such a context. In the partial-context condition, subjects were shown Figure 13.2 prior to reading the passage. Presumably, if the imagery alternative is correct, subjects in this condition should also show enhanced recall. Since their recall was no better than no-context subjects, the imagery alternative seems questionable. Note that the methodological impact of such control contexts is not just in ruling out possible alternative hypotheses; control contexts also make a positive contribution by refining the supported interpretation of the results. In the present case, the results of the imagery control condition has impact on what "knowledge of appropriate contextual referent'' means. The results suggest that the most important information provided in the Figure 13.1 context involves the activity (a serenade) and the significance of spatial relationships among objects with respect to the activity. This is different from assuming that the major source of difference involves information about the objects per se.

SEQUENCING OF TARGET AND CONTEXT

Besides a concern with the information contained in the target and context, an equally important concern in studies of comprehension and memory involves the sequencing of this information. Logically, the contextual information can be presented prior to, concurrent with, or after presentation of the target information (of course, the interval "prior to" or "after" can be varied in length and in terms of what occurs in the interval). Obviously, the possible variations are great. Bransford and Johnson hypothesized that "knowledge of appropriate contextual referent"must be preactivated to significantly affect comprehension and recall. Methodologically, this meant that they presented the contextual picture in Figure 13.1 immediately prior to presentation of the target passage. Roughly, their hypothesis implied that the context provided an appropriate contextual referent that was necessary for adequate initial encoding (and initial comprehension) of the target passage. By implication, the memory deficit in the no-context group was attributed to a deficit in initial encoding of the target. However, alternative interpretations are again possible. For example, it could be that the contextual material does not affect original encoding per se, but rather leads to a reorganization of some original encoding into a more comprehensible and memorable form. Another alternative is that the context affects neither original encoding nor reorganization, but rather affects the retrieval of the target information at time of recall. Alternative hypotheses such as these call for methodological variations in the sequencing of target and context information. For example, both of the alternative interpretations just mentioned suggest that presentation of the contextual picture *after* reading the target passage should be effective in enhancing later recall. Bransford and Johnson also included a control group (context-after) that was designed to examine these possibilities. Since comprehension and recall were no better in the context-after condition than in the no-context condition, the data provided further support for Bransford and Johnson's interpretation. Methodologically, manipulations of target and context sequences can be an important tool for exploring the processes involved in comprehension and memory.

The fact that the context picture had little effect on performance in the context-after condition does not mean that context-after manipulations are, in general, ineffective in altering comprehension and recall. The effects of the sequencing of targets and contexts will vary depending upon the nature of the target and context materials as well as upon the length and nature of the interval between the target and the context. This can be illustrated by a series of experiments by Auble and Franks (1978) and Auble, Franks, and Soraci (1979). Building on earlier work by Bransford and McCarrell (1974), Auble and her colleagues also manipulated the contextual information necessary for comprehension and memory. For target materials, they employed sentences such as *The haystack was important because the cloth ripped*. Like the balloon passage, these sentences were designed to be relatively incomprehensible due to the elimination of appropriate contextual referents. In this case, contexts that provided appropriate referents consisted of words rather than pictures. For example, the previous sentence is comprehensible when the word *parachute* is presented as contextual information.

Consider three of the experimental conditions used by Auble and her colleagues (Auble & Franks, 1978; Auble *et al.*, 1979). These illustrate how the relationship between comprehension and memory can vary as a function of both (*a*) the kinds of targets and contexts used and (*b*) their sequencing. In all conditions, subjects were presented with a set of target sentences, which they rated for comprehensibility. Afterward, they were asked to recall as many of the targets as possible. In a no-context condition, target sentences were presented without cues (see the previous example). In a second, context-within, condition, context cues were meaningfully incorporated into the target sentence (e.g., *The haystack was important because the parachute cloth ripped.*). For both of these conditions, presentation of the sentence was followed by a 5-sec delay. In a third context-delayed condition, target sentences were followed by presentation of the context cues only after a 5-sec delay interval.

The no-context and context-within conditions can be seen as similar to the no-context and context-before conditions in the balloon study; the contextual cues in the context-within sentences provided appropriate contextual referents that would usually be expected to facilitate comprehension and memory for the target sentences. In fact, the results for these two conditions resembled the results found in the balloon study (Auble, *et al.*, 1979). No-context sentences were difficult to comprehend and were poorly recalled. Context-within sentences were relatively easy to understand and showed enhanced recall. These findings thus support the general conclusions of Bransford and Johnson.

However, for the context-delayed condition, the results differed from those found in Bransford and Johnson. Recall that Bransford and Johnson found that providing the context after the target passage had little effect on comprehension and recall. In the Auble and Franks (1978) work, the context-delayed condition resulted in comprehension equal to the context-within condition. Even more interesting, the context-delayed condition resulted in greater recall than the context-within condition. This result indicates that the relationship between comprehension and recall involves more than just activation of appropriate contextual referents. Auble *et al.* (1979) hypothesized that the difference in results was due to a reorganizational process, which they termed an "aha" effect. Their hypothesis was that encoding of the context-delayed sentences involved two phases: first, an initial encoding of the target sentences that lacked contextual referents and, second, a reorganization of the initial encoding to form a representation including contextual referents when the context words were presented. They argued that this reorganization, or "aha" process, was responsible for the later enhanced recall for context-delayed sentences.

Note that alternative interpretations of the preceding data might be possible. For example, it seems plausible that, when presented with a sentence followed by a 5-sec interval, subjects will think about the sentence. This additional processing may well serve to elaborate the initial encoding of the sentence; later recall may be facilitated by this elaborative processing. The actual experiments included a number of control conditions to assess this elaboration alternative. For example, Auble and Franks compared two context-within conditions, one with a 5-sec delay following each sentence and the other with a 0-sec delay following each sentence. They found equivalent recall in these two cases, indicating that providing a 5-sec interval for elaboration was not effective in itself for enhancing recall performance. Auble *et al.* (1979) not only provided delay intervals in which elaboration could occur but also modified the nature of the sentences used in order to vary potential elaborative processes. (See Auble *et al.* [1979] for details of these manipulations.) Overall, the results of these studies supported the "aha" hypothesis and provided little evidence for the elaboration hypothesis.

It should be mentioned that arguing against an elaboration hypothesis on the basis of a lack of recall differences between 0- and 5-sec delay intervals alone is rather weak methodologically. Such an argument would be strengthened by experiments that explicitly manipulated the amount of thinking about the sentence (i.e., elaboration) that occurred prior to receiving the context cue. The next section of this chapter examines research in which quantitative and qualitative aspects of elaborative processing are manipulated and their effects on memory assessed. Incorporating such manipulations into the Auble and Franks paradigm could clarify the effects of elaborative processing and the reorganizational "aha" process on remembering. In Auble and Franks there is no explicit evidence that subjects do in fact elaborate in the interval between the sentence and the cue.

Two methodological points are illustrated by the Auble and Franks study and the comparison of this study with the balloon study. First, manipulations of the sequencing of targets and contexts is an important methodological tool for the precise investigation of the processes involved in comprehension and remembering. Second, the effects of manipulating target–context sequences interact with the different kinds of target and contextual materials that may be used. Using a complex passage and picture, Bransford and Johnson found that providing the context after the target did not aid recall compared to memory for the target without a context. Auble and Franks used less complex sentence targets and word contexts and found greatly enhanced recall in context-after conditions when compared to no-context conditions. Presumably, the simpler materials used by Auble and Franks allowed subjects to form initial encodings of the sentences that could be maintained until the context word was presented, thereby allowing a comprehensible recoding of the sentence. In contrast, the balloon study involved presentation of a whole set of relatively incomprehensible sentences prior to receiving the context picture; it was probably beyond the capacity of subjects to maintain noncomprehended encodings of this whole set of sentences while waiting for the context.

Extending this point a bit, it is not only the time delay between targets and contexts that is methodologically important but also what occurs in the delay interval. In the balloon study, for example, a number of additional incomprehensible sentences occurred in the interval between the first sentence, *If the balloons popped . . .* , and the context-after picture that rendered this sentence comprehensible. In Auble and Franks, the contexts followed the targets without intervening materials. What would happen if the contexts were delayed so that one or two sentences intervened between a target sentence and its appropriate word context? Or what if subjects were presented with a whole list of context words only after receiving the whole list of target sentences? Although these conditions have not been tested, it seems intuitively clear that such interval manipulations will have important effects on results.

NATURE OF CRITERIAL TASK

Finally, consider the fourth major design component involved in investigations of comprehension and memory—the criterial task that measures memory. In the balloon study, an aspect of Bransford and Johnson's claim is that enhanced comprehension results in enhanced memory. The criterial task was recall and they scored for gist accuracy. The question here is whether the relationships demonstrated for the recall measure are generalizable to a whole range of other possible memory measures (e.g., cued recall, recognition, verbatim scoring of recall). Different memory measures involve different cognitive processes, so it is by no means definite that a particular pattern of results will hold for all memory measures. In the present case, Bransford and Johnson were more interested in comprehension processes involving relations between target and context information, so they did not use other criterial tasks. More generally, the pragmatics of experimentation often necessitate leaving out potentially interesting conditions—the possible variations just become too numerous. However, two additional points should be made.

Of theoretical interest, later work by Nyberg (cf. Bransford & Johnson, 1973) did in fact examine the Bransford and Johnson finding using a cued-recall task. The original effect held up. Of methodological interest, there are many cases in the literature where the conclusions drawn about a relationship between comprehension and memory can be radically affected by the choice of memory measures. The importance of the criterial task can be illustrated by comparing the results of an experiment by Franks, Plybon and Auble (in press) with the Auble and Franks (1978) study previously discussed. Franks *et al.* used the same targets and contexts as Auble and Franks and also included two conditions comparable to the no-context and context-within conditions. However, instead of using free recall as a criterial task, Franks *et al.* used a perceptual recognition test to examine memory for sentences. That is, subjects were presented with a list of target sentences under no-context and context-within conditions just as in Auble and Franks. Following this acquisition, subjects were then presented the target sentences masked by white noise and asked to identify (i.e., repeat) the sentences. Identification performance was compared with a baseline condition in which subjects were asked to identify masked sentences without having received the target sentences during a prior acquisition phase. Using this perceptual recognition test as a criterial task, Franks *et al.* found that both the no-context and context-within condition showed greatly enhanced identification of the target sentences they had previously heard during acquisition. Furthermore, the no-context and context-within conditions were just about equivalent in identification performance. These results can be contrasted with those obtained by Auble and Franks where, on a free-recall measure, the no-context condition showed very poor memory performance, and where there was a large difference in recall between the no-context and context-within conditions.

The important methodological point is that choice of criterial task is a critical aspect in the design of experiments investigating the relationships between comprehension and memory. Different tests for memory involve different processes and these different processes may be differentially affected by various aspects of comprehension (see also Bransford, Franks, Morris, & Stein, 1979). Such potential differences require two methodological concerns. First, the experimenter must be aware of the extent to which the criterial task that is chosen will be sensitive to the comprehension manipulation. Second, whether the comprehension manipulation will have the same effect on other criterial tasks must be kept in mind. In other words, what is the generalizability of the results obtained with one task to other measures? The first concern involves whether the design will be able to show any relationship at all between comprehension and memory. The second concern involves the nature and generality of any such relation that is found.

STUDIES OF ELABORATION

A second line of research dealing with the relationships between prior knowledge and memory has been concerned with elaborative processes (e.g., Anderson & Reder, 1979; Craik & Tulving, 1975; Rohwer, 1966). The basic hypothesis underlying this work is that memory for targets will be enhanced to the extent that more contextual information is encoded with each target. For example, the target information *watch* could be presented with one of two contexts: (*a*) *He dropped the* (*watch*); or (*b*) *The old man hobbled across the room and picked up the valuable* (*watch*) *from the mahogany table.* By the elaboration hypothesis, it would be expected that a person would better remember the target *watch* given prior exposure to (*b*) versus (*a*).

For present purposes, we will concentrate on two methodological concerns that contrast these studies with experiments described in the previous section. The first major shift involves the nature of the targets. In contrast with the previous work, which utilized relatively incomprehensible targets, the materials in studies in the present section all involve readily comprehensible targets. Thus, the major focus is on the effects of elaboration given comprehended encodings. The second contrast with the previously described work involves quality versus quantity of contextual information. In the previous section, the concern was with the qualitative nature of contextual information that was necessary for achieving comprehension and enhancing memory. One of the major concerns of the studies of elaboration involves how the quantity of contextual information that is comprehended with a target affects remembering.

An experiment by Craik and Tulving (1975, Experiment 7) is illustrative of the kind of target and context manipulations that are relevant to the elaboration hypothesis. In this study, the to-be-remembered targets were 60 common words (e.g., *eagle*). Contexts consisted of sentence frames (e.g., _____ *has feathers.*). Three levels of context complexity were utilized; simple, medium, and complex. The previous two sentences about the watch illustrate simple and complex sentence frame contexts, respectively.

During an acquisition phase, subjects were presented with a sentence frame context followed by a target word (e.g., _____ *has feathers: eagle*). The target word either fit meaningfully into the sentence (*congruous context*) or did not fit in the sentence (*incongruous context*). An example of an incongruous context would be _____ *is a fruit: eagle*. The subjects' task was to respond as quickly as possible with "yes" for congruous contexts or "no" for targets in incongruous contexts. Following acquisition, two memory tests were given. Subjects first free recalled the targets. They were then given a cued-recall task in which the sentence frames were employed as cues.

The results for congruous contexts supported the elaboration hypotheses. For both free recall and cued recall, greater complexity of sentence frame contexts resulted in greater recall. In terms of methodological components, the results with the two different criterial tasks showed similar effects, although the magnitude of the difference with complexity was greater for the cued recall test. Given these results, one could argue that greater quantities of elaborative context do lead to more effective remembering of targets. However, the results for incongruous contexts question the generality of this conclusion. For incongruous contexts, no differences in recall were found for increasing degrees of complexity of the contexts. Theoretically, this means that increasing the quantity of elaborative context only results in better memory if the target makes sense within that context (is congruous). This result suggests that increasing the quantity of context may not be effective in enhancing memory for incomprehensible targets like those discussed in the previous section, but this research has yet to be carried out.

Methodologically, the results just described reemphasize the importance of including control contexts in the experimental design. The incongruous contexts were comparable to congruous contexts in terms of complexity of elaboration, thus, they were equally good operationalizations of the variable involving quantity of the elaborations. They differed, however, in the quality of the elaborations. The results demonstrate that quantity of context does seem to be an important variable but only when the context bears certain qualitative relationships with the targets. The important methodological point is that manipulations of the quantity of context generally, if not always, also involve manipulations of the qualitative nature of context.

The importance of interrelationships between quantitative and qualitative aspects of contexts can be further illustrated by a series of experiments on elaborative processes conducted by Stein and his colleagues (Stein, Morris, & Bransford, 1978; Stein & Bransford, 1979). A natural conclusion to be drawn from the Craik and Tulving (1975) findings would be that increasing amounts of contextual elaboration result in better memory for target words when the contexts and targets can be comprehended as a coherent, integrated unit. The implication is that, if a context–target combination is comprehensible, increases in the quantity of elaborative contexts should lead to better target memory. The studies by Stein *et al.* (1978) and Stein and Bransford (1979) suggest that even this conclusion is too broad. Their designs, once again, point out the importance of the possible interactions of quantitative and qualitative aspects of contextual information. During the acquisition phase of their experiment, Stein *et al.* (1978) presented three different groups of subjects with sentences like the following: (*a*) *The tall man purchased the crackers*; (*b*) *The tall man purchased the crackers that were on sale*; (*c*) *The tall man purchased the crackers that were on the top shelf.* Following presentation of the acquisition sentences, subjects were presented with cues like, *Which man purchased the crackers?* Subjects were asked to recall the adjectives that were associated with the various men.

The targets in the Stein *et al.* (1978) study were the adjectives to-be-recalled. The sentences in which the adjectives occurred during acquisition formed the contextual information. Note two things about these context manipulations. First, unlike the Craik and Tulving (1975) study, all the target–context combination sentences were readily comprehensible. Second, as in the Craik and Tulving study, the context sentences provided different quantities of elaborative contexts. The contexts involved two degrees of elaborative complexity with sentences like (*b*) and (*c*) providing an additional clause or phrase of information when compared to sentence (*a*).

Since all sentences were comprehensible, the elaboration hypothesis would predict that the target adjective would be better recalled given (*b*) and (*c*) as contexts in comparison to (*a*) as a context. However, Stein *et al.* designed the (*b*) and (*c*) type sentences with a somewhat different hypothesis in mind. They argued that even if comprehension takes place, the qualitative nature of the relationship between targets and contexts can modify any effects attributable to quantitative aspects of the elaborations. Their hypothesis was that effective elaboration involves activation of information that clarifies the significance or relevance of concepts (e.g., *tall man*) relative to the events in which they occur. They designed sentences like (*c*) to have *precise elaborations* while sentences like (*b*) were designed to have *imprecise elaborations*. Sentences like (*a*) were termed *base sentences*. As hypothesized, the results showed that, whereas both the precise and imprecise sentences involved a greater quantity of elaborations than the base sentences, only precise elaborative contexts led to enhanced recall of the target adjectives. Targets from imprecise contexts were recalled no better than targets from base contexts.

The Stein *et al.* (1978) and Stein and Bransford (1979) studies also involved a number of other control contexts designed to examine alternative interpretations for their findings (see also Bransford, Stein, Shelton, & Owings, 1981). However, for present purposes, the methodological point is that quantitative aspects of contexts can be important, but one must always ask "Quantity of what?" The qualitative nature of the elaborative contexts places constraints on the effectiveness of such quantitative manipulations.

Interestingly, at the time of this writing, no studies have appeared that simultaneously manipulate varying degrees of both the amount of elaborative context and the qualitative aspects of the elaborations such as their precision. For example, it would be interesting to examine the effects of simple, medium, and complex contexts, like those in the Craik and Tulving study, and systematically vary elaborations in their degree of "precision," as did Stein *et al.* (1978). It should also be noted that the present discussion of elaborative processes has concentrated on the nature of targets and contexts. To date there has been little work in this area that is concerned with the other two major methodological components: target–context sequencing and criterial task. As in other areas of research examining the relation between comprehension and memory, manipulations of these latter two components could permit further clarification of the nature and effects of elaborative processing.

EFFECTS OF CONTEXT ON SIGNIFICANCE

In this section, we examine how memory for targets is influenced by contextual information that alters the meaning or significance of the target. Intuitively it seems obvious that the context in which a message occurs can change the meaning of that message and thus also the memory for that message. For example, the statement *it looks awful* implies one thing if your mechanic tells you this when you have just taken your car in for repair. Your memory for this statement may emphasize expense and the generally poor condition of the car. On the other hand, if someone says *it looks awful* at an art gallery, your memory may emphasize the aesthetic qualities of the art being viewed. Thus, identical statements can take on different significances as a function of context.

The significant features of target material have been manipulated in the research literature by changing the contextual perspective from which the material is to be understood. For example, Pichert and Anderson (1977) presented the following passage to subjects. One group of subjects was told to read the passage from the perspective of a potential burglar.

> The two boys ran until they came to the driveway. "See, I told you today was good for skipping school," said Mark. "Mom is never home on Thursday," he added. Tall hedges hid the house from the road so the pair strolled across the finely landscaped yard. "I never knew your place was so big," said Pete. "Yeah, but it's nicer now than it used to be since Dad had the new stone siding put on and added the fireplace."
>
> There were front and back doors and a side door which led to the garage which was empty except for three parked 10-speed bikes. They went to the side door, Mark explaining that it was always open in case his younger sisters got home earlier than their mother.
>
> Pete wanted to see the house so Mark started with the living room. It, like the rest of the downstairs, was newly painted. Mark turned on the stereo, the noise of which worried Pete. "Don't worry, the nearest house is a quarter of a mile away," Mark shouted. Pete felt more comfortable observing that no houses could be seen in any direction beyond the huge yard.
>
> The dining room, with all the china, silver and cut glass, was no place to play so the boys moved into the kitchen where they made sandwiches. Mark said they wouldn't go to the basement because it had been damp and musty ever since the new plumbing had been installed.
>
> "This is where my Dad keeps his famous paintings and his coin collection," Mark said as they peered into the den. Mark bragged that he could get spending money whenever he needed it since he'd discovered that his Dad kept a lot in the desk drawer.
>
> There were three upstairs bedrooms. Mark showed Pete his mother's closet which was filled with furs and the locked box which held her jewels. His sisters' room was uninteresting except for the color TV which Mark carried to his room. Mark bragged that the bathroom in the hall was his since one had been added to his sisters' room for their use. The big highlight in his room, though, was a leak in the ceiling where the old roof had finally rotted [Pichert & Anderson, 1977, p. 310].

Pichert and Anderson also asked another group of subjects to read the same passage from the perspective of a home buyer. A third group was asked to read the passage with no directed perspective. All subjects then rated the idea units in the passage on a 5-point scale as to whether they were essential to the passage or could be eliminated because they were unimportant to the theme of the passage. A low correlation was obtained (.11) between the rankings for the three groups, suggesting that idea units that were important from one perspective were unimportant from the other perspectives. Intuitively, this appears obvious: burglars are interested in movable items in a house; home buyers are interested in more permanent features.

Pichert and Anderson then asked three new groups of subjects to read the passage from the three perspectives. Subjects recalled the passages immediately after reading them and recalled them again one week later. It was found that ideas significant for the perspective from which the story had been read were recalled better than idea units rated as low in significance. This was true both for immediate and delayed recall results. From these data, Pichert and Anderson concluded that recall of the target passage is a function of the significance of an idea to a particular contextual perspective.

Pichert and Anderson's work investigated whether different idea units would assume differential importance as a function of overall context. Other research has attempted to examine whether identical information will be understood differently when presented in different contexts. For instance, Barclay, Bransford, Franks, McCarrell, and Nitsch (1974) reported results from a study in which the meaning of words ordinarily considered to have only one meaning (e.g., *piano*) were changed as a function of context. They employed pairs of acquisition sentences such as *The man lifted the piano* or *The man tuned the piano*. Note that in the first sentence, the significant feature of the piano is its heaviness; in the second sentence the piano's sound is most significant. Barclay *et al.* presented subjects with targets consisting of one member of each pair of acquisition sentences and then tested the effectiveness of different retrieval cues. For subjects who had heard *The man lifted the piano*, it was found that a cue such as *Do you remember hearing about something heavy?* was more effective than a cue like *Do you remember hearing about something that makes nice sounds?* The opposite effect was obtained when subjects had heard *The man tuned the piano*. This pattern of results suggests that context affects not only the words (or ideas) selected as important but also affects the significant target features that are encoded.

Note that in this study, a no-context, or control condition, was not employed. In all cases, the target was presented during acquisition within a particular context (e.g., *piano* always occurred in a sentence.) This can present some difficulty in unambiguously interpreting the results. Without a no-context condition, it is unclear whether recall improves at time of test when the context is appropriate or whether recall is hindered when the context is inappropriate. For example, consider the case where one group received *The man lifted the piano,* whereas a second group received *piano* during acquisition. Would recall for *piano,* given the cue *something heavy,* be better in the context condition than in the no-context condition? Would recall for *piano,* given the cue *something that makes nice sounds,* be worse in the context than in the no-context condition? An alternate possibility is that subjects who received target words (e.g., *piano*) without any context would exhibit excellent retention for either type of retrieval cue.

Barclay *et al.,* investigated the just mentioned issue by conducting a second study that included a no-context condition in addition to the context conditions. Results indicated that, relative to the no-context condition, recall was improved when the context matched acquisition and was debilitated when context was shifted between acquisition and test.

Up until this point, the significance of an item has been manipulated by changes in *meaning.* In other words, varying the context has, to some degree, altered the meaning or importance of a word or idea. It has been tacitly assumed in all of the research discussed that the semantic features of an item are the ones receiving attention. This assumption is correct in most situations. However, in some tasks, meaning is not the critical variable to which attention is directed. For instance, Craik and Tulving (1975) compared recognition memory for words in two conditions. In one condition, subjects were asked whether the target word rhymed with another word (e.g., *Say yes or no;* _____ *rhymes with regal*; *eagle*). Note that in this condition, the meaning of the target word is deemphasized; subjects must notice acoustic features of the target in order to perform well on the task. Craik and Tulving compared recognition memory for this condition with a second condition in which the task involved focusing on the meaning of the target (e.g., *Say yes or no;* __ *has feathers*; *eagle*). They found that performance in the rhyme context was poorer than that in the meaningful context. Craik and Tulving concluded that encoding words at a meaningful level was inherently better for memory than encoding words in terms of their acoustic features.

Morris, Bransford, and Franks (1977) questioned Craik and Tulving's (1975) conclusion that memory is superior when the item is encoded meaningfully during acquisition. They assumed that the rhyme context and the meaning context focus subjects' attention on different types of significant features about the word. In one case meaning, is significant; in the other case, the acoustic properties of the word are important. From this perspective, later memory for that word will be dependent on whether the memory test activates the relevant significant features (or reinstates the appropriate context). In a study discussed earlier, for example, we noted that if *piano* was encoded in the context of *The man lifted the piano,* memory was relatively poor when subjects were cued with *something that makes nice sounds.* Similarly, if a word is encoded primarily in terms of acoustic features, a test that taps semantic information may not elicit optimal memory performance, and if a word has been encoded at a meaningful level, a test that taps knowledge of acoustic features of that word may not be optimal. Morris *et al.* (1977) further argued that tasks requiring subjects to identify particular words on a recognition test implicitly tap semantic information. If the acquisition context has been to encode only acoustic features, then particular words may not be remembered. Instead, it may only be possible to recall what the word ''sounds like''; the exact acquisition target may be confused with other words which sound similar to it. Thus it may be that a test that taps acoustic information might be more appropriate for words initially encoded in the context of the rhyming task.

To test this hypothesis, Morris *et al.* presented subjects with two types of acquisition tasks. The first task involved deciding whether a target word fit meaningfully into a sentence frame context, (e.g., _____ has ears: *dog*); the second task involved deciding if the target rhymed with another word in a rhyming context, (e.g., _____ *rhymes with log*: *dog*). Furthermore, two types of memory test were given. One was a standard recognition test. The other involved presentation of an entirely new set of words. Subjects were required to decide whether each of these new words *rhymed* with the target words previously presented. This second test was designed to tap primarily acoustic rather than semantic information. Results for the traditional recognition test replicated the results obtained by Craik and Tulving (1975). Target words presented in a meaningful context were remembered better than those presented in an acoustic context. However, this relationship was reversed for the rhyming test. On this test, the acoustic condition was superior to the semantic condition. This pattern of results suggests that awareness of the significant information encoded at acquisition is important in designing a test to tap memory for that information. If cues employed during a memory test do not match the significant features encoded, it will appear that the information has not been retained. In reality, a change to appropriate cues may result in the apparently ''lost'' information being recovered. Thus, in all research on memory, the experimenter must be aware of the context in which acquisition information has been encoded. Optimal memory performance can be achieved only if the experimenter is aware of the significant aspects of the acquisition material and creates an appropriate context to tap this information during test. These results underscore the methodological importance of one's choice of a criterial task (see also Fisher & Craik, 1980; McDaniel, Friedman, & Bourne, 1978; Tulving, 1979).

REORGANIZATION AND
CHANGES IN SIGNIFICANCE

In the preceding studies, the significance of information was manipulated by varying the context in which that information was presented. Sometimes, however, the significance of a message is altered by the presentation of new information *after* the message has been assimilated. An example of this phenomenon often occurs while reading a murder mystery novel. While reading the novel. certain clues and bits of information may stand out; the reader may even have organized the information into patterns suggesting particular characters as the likely murderer. When the end of the novel is reached and the murderer has been discovered, the information which seemed significant beforehand will often be altered (assuming that the reader had not "solved" the crime beforehand). Some of the information which seemed significant before will no longer be of importance, whereas other information previously considered irrelevant will now be seen as important. In short, one's interpretation of previously stored information can sometimes be modified by the presentation of new information.

Investigations of how memory for information is altered by presentation of later contextual information can be viewed as involving manipulations of the sequence of target and context. In the previous section, the significance of the target was varied by presenting it in conjunction with different contextual information. However, investigations of how memory can be altered by new information require the presentation of the target material first; the contextual information is presented afterwards. The effects of this contextual information can then be assessed by comparing memory in the latter condition with conditions receiving different contextual information or no information at all.

Anderson and Pichert (1978) have investigated how memory can be modified by the presentation of new contextual information that alters the significance of previously encoded target information. They used the passage about two boys playing hooky from school that was presented earlier (cf. Pichert & Anderson, 1977). As in the previous study, subjects were instructed to read the passage from the perspective of either a home buyer or a burglar, and then to recall as much of the passage as possible. However, in this study, subjects were also asked to recall the passage a second time. Half of the subjects recalled the story again from the same perspective (no new contextual information) and the other half were now given the other perspective (e.g., if the story had originally been read and recalled from the home buyer perspective, subjects were now told the burglar perspective and asked to try to recall the story from that perspective). As in the previously mentioned work by these investigators, the idea units in the story were divided into units important to each perspective. It was found that the pattern of results from the first recall test replicated those obtained by Pichert and Anderson (1977). Subjects recalled more idea units rated as important to their perspective than units rated as relatively unimportant. On the second recall test, however, subjects who had been given a different perspective tended to recall additional, previously unrecalled information that was important to the new perspective (but unimportant to the perspective from which the story had originally been read). This shift did not occur for subjects who had simply recalled the same story twice from the same perspective. This pattern of results suggests that the presentation of a context that alters the significance of a passage may make different elements of that passage available for recall.

Anderson and Pichert's design illustrates a methodological point made previously in our discussion of the balloon study; namely, that manipulations of target–context sequencing are important for investigating the processes underlying comprehension and remembering. Anderson and Pichert's finding of improved recall on the second test for subjects who received the new context provides evidence that context can affect retrieval processes as well as encoding processes. Without the change in context manipulation and the double test, it would be unclear whether results such as those of Pichert and Anderson were attributable to encoding effects, retrieval effects, or both.

A study by Fass and Schumacher (1981) provides an additional illustration of the importance of target–context sequencing. These investigators were also interested in distinguishing context effects on encoding versus retrieval processes. They used a design and materials similar to Anderson and Pichert's but added an additional target–context sequencing manipulation. In addition to immediate, within-session tests of recall (as used by Anderson & Pichert), they included a 24-hour delayed-recall test. Subjects in the delayed condition read the home buyer/burglar passage from one contextual perspective and then returned a day later and attempted to recall the passage either from the same perspective or from the new perspective. With the 24-hour delay, only the perspective at time of initial encoding was related to the information recalled (that is, subjects who were prompted to change perspective did not show an increase in recall for items relevant to the new perspective). These results indicate that there are important temporal constraints on the effects of context on retrieval processes. Methodologically, the point is that differences in target–context sequencing that involve manipulations of the delay interval between target and context can have a major impact on the results obtained and upon the conclusions that can be drawn concerning the effects of context on encoding and retrieval processes.

The previously discussed studies illustrate how target–context sequencing manipulations can be used to examine encoding versus retrieval processes. Another important area of research uses target–context sequencing manipulations to examine processes involving reorganization in the storage of target information. A study by Spiro (1977) can be used to illustrate the methodological considerations relevant to the investigation of such reorganization processes. His experiment was designed to investigate how the presentation of later contextual information can alter memory of previously encoded information. Unlike Anderson and Pichert, Spiro focused on changes and distortions in memory for old information rather than on whether a new context can result in recall of additional old information that was previously not remembered.

Spiro argued that reorganization or alteration of memory for target information depends upon two factors. First, the target information must be integrated with prior knowledge structures. Formation of such an integrated memory representation will involve some loss in the identity of the specific target information presented. Second, new contextual information must significantly alter the interpretation of this integrated representation. If the new context merely supplements already encoded target information, little reorganization of memory would be expected. Spiro's methodology was designed to manipulate these two factors.

In the experiment, all subjects were first presented with one of two stories about an engaged couple named Bob and Margie. In both stories, Bob tells Margie that he does not want to have children. In one story, Margie has similar views and is relieved; in the other, she is horrified and the couple is arguing vehemently as the story ends. In order to manipulate the integration of the story with previous knowledge, subjects were told either to try to remember the story verbatim or were told that the experiment was concerned with their reactions to situations involving interpersonal interactions. It was expected that subjects in the latter condition would be more likely to integrate the target information with prior knowledge structures. Spiro manipulated the amount of reinterpretation involved in the experiment in the following manner: After the story was presented he mentioned additional contextual information that would either reinforce the interpretation of the stability of Bob and Margie's relationship or change that interpretation. Spiro mentioned either that Bob and Margie were now married and happy (reinforcing the interpretation for the story in which Margie was relieved, and changing the interpretation for the story in which Margie was upset) or that Bob and Margie had broken their engagement (changing the interpretation when Margie was relieved, and reinforcing it when she was upset). The greatest alterations in memory were expected when subjects attempted to integrate the material into their knowledge base and when the later contextual information changed the interpretation of the story. The results of a recall test for the target story confirmed these expectations. Reorganization of memory was assessed by examining errors in the recall of the target information. These errors involved changes or distortions of relationships present in the original target or the addition of relations not present in the original target. The greatest alterations in memory for the story occurred in the integrated, change in interpretation conditions. For instance, one subject who was told that Bob and Margie were happily married after disagreeing about children recalled "they separated, but realized after discussing the matter that their love mattered more." This information had not been presented during acquisition.

Spiro also included an additional measure in his design in order to rule out the alternative interpretation that the observed changes in recall were simply due to a guessing strategy. In other words, it is possible that subjects' memory for the target information only appeared to be altered by context; the changes could actually be due to the fact that subjects were no longer able to remember many aspects of the story and hence resorted to guessing based on what might be expected to occur in such situations in general. In order to evaluate this possibility, Spiro asked subjects to rate how confident they were that the information they recalled was accurate. Two results from the confidence rating task are particularly noteworthy. First, the overall level of confidence was equivalent for integration versus nonintegration conditions and for conditions that received contradictory or confirmatory contextual information. Thus, even though recall was less accurate in the integration condition that received contradictory information, subjects still seemed to believe that they were remembering the material accurately (i.e., subjects did not feel that they were simply employing a guessing strategy). Secondly, there was no difference in confidence level ratings between items that were remembered correctly or incorrectly for the integration–contradictory condition. This result indicates that subjects in this condition were unaware that their "errors" were actually wrong. If a guessing strategy had been employed, it seems reasonable to expect that subjects might have been at least somewhat aware that they were guessing. The use of confidence ratings can therefore provide the experimenter with information that is not available from memory scores per se.

In terms of methodology, Spiro's study involved two different context manipulations. First, the target information was set in the context of a memory experiment versus an experiment concerned with reaction to interpersonal relations. Second, additional context information was provided after the target passage in order to either reinforce or alter initial interpretations of the passage. In general, Spiro's design illustrates how manipulations of context information and target–context sequencing can be used to investigate memory reorganization. The design also illustrates how recall, and, more specifically, errors in recall, can be used as a criterial task to assess such reorganization.

Thus far in this chapter, we have only minimally discussed the choice of criterial tasks. But this choice is important. Studies of reorganization and changes in significance can be used to illustrate some of the important considerations that are involved in choice of criterial tasks. Note, for example, that in Spiro's experiment, as well as in the experiments by Pichert and Anderson that were discussed earlier, free recall was used as the measure of memory and of changes in memory. One advantage of free recall is that it permits the experimenter to observe a wide range of possible changes in memory. Nevertheless, there are also possible disadvantages of free recall as a criterial task. In addition to the fact that it can sometimes be difficult to decide whether a particular response is a paraphrase versus an actual distortion of an original message, free-recall measures may underestimate the amount of distortion or change that actually occurred. For example, subjects may fail to report many kinds of information of which they do not feel reasonably sure (e.g., see Anderson, 1977; Dooling and Christiaansen, 1977a, 1977b). In Spiro's experiment, the confidence rating data indicate that subjects were equally confident for all material that they reported as remembered. However, it is possible that additional changes in memory occurred in the various conditions that did not appear in the recall protocols because subjects felt less confident about that information and curtailed their responding.

One alternative to the use of free recall as a criterial task is to assess recognition memory. Under these conditions, the data of interest for assessing reorganization or changes in significance involve the degree to which subjects falsely recognize various items containing information that was not actually presented during acquisition. False recognition measures have been used by a number of investigators in order to assess inferences or assumptions that may have been made at the time of acquisition or, in some cases, at the time of testing (e.g., Bransford, 1979; Bransford, Barclay, & Franks, 1972; Johnson, Bransford, & Solomon, 1973; Singer, 1980; Snyder & Uranowitz, 1978). For present purposes, we shall focus on a series of studies by Dooling and associates (Dooling & Christiaansen, 1977a, 1977b; Sulin & Dooling, 1974). They used the false recognition paradigm to assess how specific contextual information available at the time of acquisition as well as only at the time of test influence retention.

In several of their studies, Dooling and his colleagues used passages such as the following:

> Gerald Martin strove to undermine the existing government to satisfy his political ambitions. Many of the people of his country supported his efforts. Current political problems made it relatively easy for Martin to take over. Certain groups remained loyal to the old government and caused Martin trouble. He confronted these groups directly and so silenced them. He became a ruthless, uncontrollable dictator. The ultimate effect of his rule was the downfall of his country [Sulin & Dooling, 1974, pp. 256–257].

By informing some subjects that Gerald Martin was actually Adolf Hitler, Dooling and his associates were able to alter the significance of the passage for subjects; the story could now be understood with respect to preexperimental knowledge about Hitler. Dooling and associates also manipulated the time when the contextual information (i.e., Hitler) was provided. For example, it could occur at time of acquisition or at time of test.

In one study, Dooling and Christiaansen (1977a) investigated the effects of several different context and target–context sequencing manipulations. Their design included conditions in which different groups of subjects (a) read the "Gerald Martin" passage and never received the "Hitler" information; (b) were informed that "Gerald Martin" was Hitler before they read the passage; or (c) were told that "Gerald Martin" was actually Hitler approximately one minute before taking the memory test. For each of these conditions, half of the subjects received the test two days after acquisition and the other half received the test one week after acquisition.

The test, which was a recognition test, included seven sentences from the passage plus a set of foil sentences. Some of the foils were related to knowledge about Adolf Hitler; for example, a highly related foil would be, *He hated the Jews particularly and so persecuted them*. The dependent variable was the proportion of time subjects falsely recognized these thematically related foils.

Results indicated that, at the two-day retention interval, subjects who had been told at acquisition that the passage was about Hitler were more likely to falsely recognize high-thematically related foils than were subjects who thought that the passage was about a fictitious Gerald Martin. In contrast, subjects who were told that the passage was about Hitler just prior to the test were no more likely to falsely recognize high-thematically related foils than were subjects who thought that the passage was about a fictitious "Gerald Martin."

The pattern of results differed when the test was delayed for one week. First, there was an even greater difference between the group who had been told about Hitler at acquisition and the one who thought the passage was about Gerald Martin; the "Hitler" group was even more likely to falsely recognize related facts. Second, the subjects who were told that the passage was about Hitler just prior to the memory test were more likely to falsely recognize related foils than were those who still thought the original passage had been about Gerald Martin. With longer delays between acquisition and test (one week as opposed to two days), the context after condition did affect false recognition responses.

Note that, in the study just discussed, Dooling and Christiaansen (1977a) informed one group of their subjects that the passage was about Hitler one minute before they received the memory test. In a second experiment, Dooling and Christiaansen (1977a) added an additional variation to this context after manipulation. One group of subjects received information that the passage was about Hitler right after they had read it. At the one-week retention test (which was the only retention interval used in this particular experiment), subjects in this latter condition (the "immediate" context-after condition) were more likely to recognize thematically related foils than were subjects who received the Hitler context just prior to taking the test. Indeed, subjects in the immediate-context-after condition were more likely to recognize related foils than were subjects in the context-before condition (those who were told about Hitler before reading the passage). Dooling and colleagues note that this latter result was unexpected. One possible reason for the result is that subjects in the context-before condition may, to some extent at least, be able to reflect on what the passage did **not** state about what they already knew about Hitler as well as what it did state. Subjects in the immediate-context-after condition would have had less of an opportunity to make this kind of differentiation.

One possible test of the hypothesis that subjects sometimes encode information about what was **not** said as well as what was said may be as follows: One group of context-before subjects could be asked to decide whether each of the statements in a passage about Hitler seemed true. A second group could be asked to judge the truthfulness of each statement *and* to evaluate whether the passage omitted important facts about Hitler. Given a test one week later, which group would be more likely to falsely recognize thematically related foils, and how would their performance compare to subjects in the immediate-context-after condition? To the best of our knowledge, this question has not yet been put to an experimental test.

Consider one additional issue with respect to using recognition as a criterial task. When experimenters use false-recognition data to make inferences about memory processes, it is imperative that they are able to show that false positives, which are actually errors, stem from the use of previously acquired information as opposed to some indiscriminate tendency on the part of subjects to say "yes" to any foil item. One approach to this problem is to include recognition foils that are unrelated to the information acquired during acquisition (some people call these items *noncases*; e.g., Bransford & Franks, 1971, 1972). If subjects in a particular condition falsely recognize noncases as well as thematically related foils, one would be inclined to conclude that the subjects had not learned adequately or that information they had learned had been forgotten. In the Dooling and colleagues' experiments, subjects in all conditions received "neutral" foil items that were unrelated to the information received at acquisition. All subjects exhibited a strong tendency to reject these foils (i.e., to say they did not recognize them). The use of items such as these therefore constitutes an important control.

Finally, what about subjects' tendencies to correctly recognize items that were actually presented during acquisition? In the Dooling and colleagues experiment, for example, subjects in all experimental conditions exhibited essentially equivalent recognition of items that had actually been presented (old items). Does this mean that, irrespective of experimental condition, subjects' abilities to remember particulars was equivalent? Dooling and Christiaansen (1977a) argue that these data should be interpreted with caution. They note that the old items (those actually experienced during acquisition) in their experiments were congruent with the "famous person" theme (e.g., Hitler). There are, therefore, several reasons why subjects could feel that they recognize these old items. One reason is that subjects may actually be able to retrieve this information from "episodic memory" (cf. Tulving, 1972). Another reason is that subjects may be reconstructing on the basis of general knowledge and, hence, may assume that this old information must have been presented (just as they erroneously assumed that the high-thematically related foils had also been presented). It is important to realize, therefore, that equivalences in memory performance do not necessarily imply equivalences in the processes that produce particular effects.

SUMMARY AND CONCLUSIONS

To summarize, we have discussed a number of studies that investigate how memory is influenced by previously acquired knowledge. There are many additional studies relevant to this issue (see especially Voss, this volume), but our goal was not to provide an exhaustive review of the literature. Instead, we have attempted to highlight some methodological considerations that are important irrespective of the particular study that is done. The essence of our methodological framework is simple: A researcher must pay careful attention to the nature of (a) the target information; (b) the contextual information; (c) the target–context sequencing; and (d) the criterial test. We have tried to illustrate how changes in each of these components can have important effects on the results and on the conclusions one draws.

It is especially important to be mindful of the fact that any particular experiment involves one of many possible instantiations of the four components in our methodological framework. Given certain types of target materials, for example, a context after manipulation may reveal no affect on performance (e.g., Bransford & Johnson; 1972). With other types of targets, however, or with changes in the target context sequencing, context-after effects may appear (Anderson & Pichert, 1977; Auble & Franks, 1978) and then disappear (e.g., Fass & Schumacher, 1981). Similarly, targets and contexts may be kept constant, yet results may vary as a function of changes in criterial tasks (e.g., Morris, Bransford, & Franks, 1977). The challenge for the researcher is to understand why particular effects occur in some conditions but not in others, and to work toward the development of a general theory that accounts for these differences in effects. By remaining mindful of the fact that any particular experiment represents only one of many possible instantiations of the four components in our methodological framework, the researcher reduces the probability of creating a theory that is unduly restricted in its applicability. When evaluating a study, therefore, one needs to ask not only what was done; one needs to consider additional ways in which it could have been conducted as well.

ACKNOWLEDGMENTS

Preparation of this chapter was supported in part by Grant NIE-G-79-0117 by the National Institute of Education. We are indebted to Nancy J. Vye for her helpful comments and criticisms.

REFERENCES

Anderson, J. R., & Reder, L. M. An elaborative processing explanation of depth of processing. In L. S. Cermak & F. I. M. Craik (Eds.), *Levels of processing and human memory*. Hillsdale, N.J.: Lawrence Erlbaum Associates, 1979.

Anderson, R. C. The notion of schemata and the educational enterprise. In R. C. Anderson, R. J. Spiro, & W. E. Montague (Eds.), *Schooling and the acquisition of knowledge*. Hillsdale, N.J.: Lawrence Erlbaum Associates, 1977.

Anderson, R. C., & Pichert, J. W. Recall of previously unrecallable information following a shift in perspective. *Journal of Verbal Learning and Verbal Behavior*, 1978, *17*, 1–12.

Auble, P. M., & Franks, J. J. The effects of effort toward comprehension on recall. *Memory and Cognition*, 1978, *6*, 20–25.

Auble, P. M., Franks, J. J., & Soraci, S. A. Effort toward comprehension: Elaboration or "aha!"? *Memory and Cognition*, 1979, *7*, 426–434.

Barclay, J. R., Bransford, J. D., Franks, J. J., McCarrell, N. S., & Nitsch, K. Comprehension and semantic flexibility. *Journal of Verbal Learning and Verbal Behavior*, 1974, *13*, 471–481.

Bransford, J. D. *Human cognition: Learning, understanding and remembering*. Belmont, Ca.: Wadsworth Publishing Co., 1979.

Bransford, J. D., Barclay, J. R., & Franks, J. J. Sentence memory: A constructive versus interpretive approach. *Cognitive Psychology*, 1972, *3*, 193–209.

Bransford, J. D., & Franks, J. J. The abstraction of linguistic ideas. *Cognitive Psychology*, 1971, *2*, 331–350.

Bransford, J. D., & Franks, J. J. The abstraction of linguistic ideas: A review. *Cognition: An International Journal of Psychology*, 1972, *1*, 211–249.

Bransford, J. D., Franks, J. J., Morris, C. D., & Stein, B. S. Some general constraints on learning and memory research. In L. S. Cermak & F. I. M. Craik (Eds.), *Levels of processing and human memory*. Hillsdale, N.J.: Lawrence Erlbaum Associates, 1979.

Bransford, J. D., & Johnson, M. K. Contextual prerequisites for understanding: Some investigations of comprehension and recall. *Journal of Verbal Learning and Verbal Behavior*, 1972, *11*, 717–726.

Bransford, J. D., & Johnson, M. K. Considerations of some problems of comprehension. In W. G. Chase (Ed.), *Visual information processing*. New York: Academic Press, 1973.

Bransford, J. D., & McCarrell, N. S. A sketch of a cognitive approach to comprehension. In W. Weimer & D. Palermo (Eds.), *Cognition and the symbolic processes*. Hillsdale, N.J.: Lawrence Erlbaum Associates, 1974.

Bransford, J. D., Stein, B. S., Shelton, T. S., & Owings, R. A. Cognition and adaptation: The importance of learning to learn. In J. Harvey (Ed.), *Cognition, social behavior, and the environment*. Hillsdale, N.J.: Lawrence Erlbaum Associates, 1981.

Craik, F. I. M., & Tulving, E. Depth of processing and the retention of words in episodic memory. *Journal of Experimental Psychology: General,* 1975, *104,* 268–294.

Dooling, D. J. & Christiaansen, R. E. Episodic and semantic aspects of memory for prose. *Journal of Experimental Psychology: Human Learning and Memory,* 1977, *3,* 428–436.(a)

Dooling, D. J., & Christiaansen, R. E. Levels of encoding and retention of prose. In G. H. Bower (Ed.), *The psychology of learning and motivation,* (Vol. 11). New York: Academic Press, 1977.(b)

Fass, W., & Schumacher, G. Schema theory and prose retention: Boundary conditions for encoding and retrieval effects. *Discourse Processes,* 1981, *4,* 17–26.

Fisher, R. P., & Craik, F. I. M. The effects of elaboration on recognition memory. *Memory and Cognition,* 1980, *8,* 400–404.

Franks, J. J., Plybon, C. J. and Auble, P. M. Units of episodic memory in perceptual recognition. *Memory and Cognition,* in press.

Johnson, M. K., Bransford, J. D., & Solomon, S. Memory for tacit implications of sentences. *Journal of Experimental Psychology,* 1973, *98,* 203–205.

McDaniel, M. A., Friedman, A., & Bourne, L. E., Jr. Remembering the levels of information in words. *Memory and Cognition,* 1978, *6,* 156–164.

Morris, C. D., Bransford, J. D., & Franks, J. J. Levels of processing versus transfer appropriate processing. *Journal of Verbal Learning and Verbal Behavior,* 1977, *16,* 519–533.

Paivio, A. *Imagery and verbal processes.* New York: Holt, Rinehart, & Winston, 1971.

Pichert, J. W., & Anderson, R. C. Taking different perspectives on a story. *Journal of Educational Psychology,* 1977, *69,* 309–315.

Rohwer, W. D., Jr. Constraints, syntax, and meaning in paired-associate learning. *Journal of Verbal Learning and Verbal Behavior,* 1966, *5,* 541–547.

Singer, M. The role of case-filling inferences in the coherence of brief passages. *Discourse Processes,* 1980, *3,* 185–201.

Snyder, M., & Uranowitz, S. W. Reconstructing the past: Some cognitive consequences of person perception. *Journal of Personality and Social Psychology,* 1978, *36,* 941–950.

Spiro, R. J. Remembering information from text: The "state of schema" approach. In R. C. Anderson, R. J. Spiro, & W. E. Montague (Eds.), *Schooling and the acquisition of knowledge.* Hillsdale, N.J.: Lawrence Erlbaum Associates, 1977.

Stein, B. S., & Bransford, J. D. Constraints on effective elaboration: Effects of precision and subject generation. *Journal of Verbal Learning and Verbal Behavior,* 1979, *18,* 769–777.

Stein, B. S., Morris, C. D., & Bransford, J. D. Constraints on effective elaboration. *Journal of Verbal Learning and Verbal Behavior,* 1978, *17,* 707–714.

Sulin, R. A., & Dooling, D. J. Intrusion of the thematic idea in retention of prose. *Journal of Experimental Psychology,* 1974, *103,* 255–262.

Tulving, E. Episodic and semantic memory. In E. Tulving & W. Donaldson (Eds.), *Organization of memory.* New York: Academic Press, 1972.

Tulving, E. Relation between encoding specificity and levels of processing. In L. S. Cermak & F. I. M. Craik (Eds.), *Levels of processing and human memory.* Hillsdale, N.J.: Lawrence Erlbaum Associates, 1979.

Underwood, B. J., & Schultz, R. W. *Meaningfulness and verbal learning.* Philadelphia: Lippincott, 1960.

CHAPTER **14**

HARRY P. BAHRICK
DEMETRIOS KARIS

Long-Term Ecological Memory

HISTORICAL ASPECTS

The inclusion of a separate chapter on methods used to study memory under real-life conditions suggests that most of the methods discussed in other chapters of this book are not optimal for the study of ecological memory. Why this is so can be appreciated by considering the historical context in which the scientific study of memory began about 100 years ago. To establish psychology as a science within academic institutions, early psychologists adhered closely to the model provided by the physical sciences. This model emphasized the experimental method and laboratory control over critical variables. Relevance of scientific findings to the problems and experiences of everyday life was not necessary in order to gain acceptance for the new science. In fact, psychologists who worked on applied problems were generally awarded lower status among their peers, even in the pragmatically oriented United States.

In this context, memory research could not focus on "remembrance of things past." Only psychoanalysts or psychotherapists who worked predominantly outside of academic institutions were much concerned with individual memories. Experimental psychologists defined the process of forgetting in terms of retrieval decrements of acquired information over time. Since all performance measures had to be obtained under

427

HANDBOOK OF RESEARCH METHODS IN
HUMAN MEMORY AND COGNITION

controlled conditions, the methods of studying memory were limited to those that could be accommodated within the time constraints of longitudinal laboratory work. Standard memory terminology reflects this constraint, and tends to confuse the uninitiated. We speak of memories as "long-term" if the retention interval exceeds 30 sec and the bulk of the published articles on memory deals with intervals of a few seconds or minutes. However, the climate of research has changed during the last decade. Scientists have become more aware of their obligations to be responsive to the problems of society, and the lack of ecological relevance of most memory research has become a matter of explicit concern. Thus, Neisser (1976) is critical of the laboratory tradition and demands a commitment to the study of variables that are ecologically important rather than just those that are easily manageable. A broader view of scientific methodology has also taken hold, and a more sophisticated and secure psychological establishment is now more willing to consider methods that depart from the tradition of laboratory control to facilitate the investigation of problems that can only be studied in an ecological setting. Parallel developments in the biological sciences have given great impetus to ecological research.

The new *zeitgeist* does not signal the abandonment of the lessons of methodology acquired over the past century. These lessons remain the most important legacy of psychology. Rather, the *zeitgeist* has broadened the criteria of evaluating research, so that tradeoffs among criteria are appropriate. It is acceptable to sacrifice some control over critical variables in order to investigate ecologically important phenomena that would otherwise be neglected. The methods discussed in this chapter must be evaluated from this perspective. Kinsey's findings (Kinsey, Pomeroy, & Martin, 1948) concerning human sexual behavior are now generally held to be important contributions to scientific knowledge. This evaluation is not based on the rigor of the methods Kinsey and his associates employed, but on the fact that the findings were the best available information in an area of great interest that did not lend itself to more rigorously controlled research.

MAJOR PARAMETERS OF ECOLOGICAL
MEMORY CONTENT

All classifications of memory content are likely to be somewhat arbitrary, and none are unique to ecological situations. We have chosen to emphasize two dimensions of variation of memory content, because they reveal the magnitude of the content areas neglected by traditional research, and because they provide a convenient frame for discussing methods applicable to ecological memory. These two dimensions are the episodic versus semantic dimension, and the individual versus shared content dimension. The episodic–semantic distinction was introduced by Munsat (1966). It has been discussed in other chapters of this book and is familiar to most readers. Episodic memory refers to content organized in regard to time and place, whereas semantic memory refers to generalized knowledge and meanings not primarily associated with a particular sequence of events in time. It is assumed here that this distinction refers to a continuum, rather than a dichotomy, since generalized knowledge is rooted in episodic experiences. However, the identity of these roots is gradually lost, and eventually most meanings and general knowledge become disassociated from the context in which they were acquired.

Because most semantic knowledge must be accumulated over a long time span, the process of acquiring generalized knowledge is not readily observed or manipulated in the laboratory. As a result, traditional memory research virtually excludes investigations of the acquisition or the loss of semantic memory content and is limited to the study of the acquisition and loss of episodic content.

The second dimension, individual versus shared memory content, refers to the distinction between memories unique to a particular person versus content assumed to be common to several individuals. Again, a dimension of variation, rather than a true dichotomy, is involved, since all experiences can be viewed as unique. We, therefore, must limit the discussion of shared memory content to identical reports of several individuals, or to situations in which identical information is presented to several individuals. Individual memories, sometimes also labeled autobiographical memories, have been of great interest to psychotherapists, biographers, novelists, and so forth, but traditionally they have been ruled out of scientific psychology because of the limited opportunity for replication and verification of content.

These two dimensions of content, episodic-semantic, and individual-shared, are here treated as orthogonal, thus yielding a four-fold classification of memory content: individual- or shared-episodic content, and individual- or shared-semantic content. Of these four types of content, only the shared-episodic content, as presented in a laboratory and tested after brief time intervals, has been the subject of traditional psychological research. Semantic content has been largely omitted because of the time constraints of the laboratory, and individual content because of problems of verification. This chapter will discuss the methods employed in recent years to investigate the neglected content of semantic memory, as well as individual episodic and nonlaboratory, shared-episodic memory. Of course, a given memory content cannot always be assigned exclusively to one cell of the implied four-fold table. A given episodic content may have individual as well as shared components, and autobiographical content may have episodic as well as semantic aspects. Thus, recent investigations of so-called *flashbulb memories* (Brown & Kulik, 1977) focus on prominent events in the news, for example, the assassination of President Kennedy. The details of the event broadcast over the news media represent the shared-episodic content, whereas the specific activities of respondents at the time they learned of the assassination constitute the individual aspects of the flashbulb memory. Childhood memories reported to a psychotherapist may refer in part to specific events, that is, episodic content, and in part to general feelings, beliefs, or attitudes, which represent the semantic, autobiographical content. Such complexities of the stream of consciousness were recognized and discussed long ago by William James. They illustrate that all types of memory content interact in our experience. The suggested classification is useful, nevertheless, because methodological problems that are the principal concern of this chapter, vary depending upon the content categories. Ultimately, the differentiation of methods appropriate to the investigation of various types of content should improve our capability to investigate interactions among various types of content, and this should help us come to grips with the complexity of ecological memory.

CRITERIA FOR THE EVALUATION OF
ECOLOGICAL METHODS

The remainder of this chapter is devoted to a description of the methods used to study ecological memory and to a discussion of the advantages and shortcomings of these methods. Formal evaluation of methods is commonplace in the construction of psychological tests and in other areas of applied psychology, but comparatively rare in experimental psychology. The assessment of psychological tests, for example, routinely includes quantitative data regarding reliability and validity, but the reader will look in vain for these terms in the subject index of most textbooks of experimental psychology. It can be argued that the assessment of validity of a selection test is relatively straightforward, and that the assessment of validity of a method of measuring memory is not. Validity of a method for the experimental psychologist is defined by the relevance of observations to the questions asked in the investigation (Bahrick & Noble, 1966, Melton, 1936), and the degree of relevance cannot be assessed by a simple test–criterion correlation. Notwithstanding this greater challenge, we believe that an explicit consideration of the sensitivity of dependent variables to the phenomena under investigation should routinely be included in psychological research. Because experimental psychologists have been cavalier in investigating the validity of their methods, and have tended to assume, or infer, validity rather than investigate it directly, there is a paucity of formal evaluative data evident here and elsewhere in the methodological literature. A nearly comparable dearth of data concerning the reliability of experimental methods is even less justifiable. Such data are readily obtainable and interpretable, but they are rarely obtained or used. In an earlier publication, Bahrick (1967) has reported major differences in reliability of various indicants of memory, as well as the deplorable fact that the least reliable of several alternative methods continues to be the method of choice for most investigators. The writers hope that the present volume will act as a stimulus toward evaluative research, and toward greater utilization of research data in the selection of methods.

METHODS OF INVESTIGATING SHARED-SEMANTIC MEMORY

Shared-semantic memory covers all of the knowledge common to individuals growing up in the same culture. This includes the meaning of words and the syntax of the common language, information about the natural and synthetic environment, as well as all of the remaining content areas of formal and informal education. Major problems must be overcome to apply memory research effectively to most of that content. The phenomena of primary interest are the losses over time of previously acquired information. If we continue to live in a given environment, we are constantly reexposed to the sources of much of our common knowledge, for example, we continue to hear, read, speak, and write our language. As a result, there is little likelihood of forgetting the relevant information. Individuals rarely forget simple arithmetic, or the meaning of common words. Normative investigations of semantic memory content can establish how much information individuals have, and surveys, quizzes, tests, and so on illustrate this approach. Such normative information does not reveal much concerning the process of forgetting, although it may reveal surprising ignorance concerning information to which we are continuously exposed. Thus Nickerson and Adams (1979) recently demonstrated that most individuals have only very inaccurate knowledge regarding the appearance of a coin they continuously use. This provides interesting evidence regarding our habits of attention, and of processing information in daily life, and it certainly demonstrates important differences between ecological learning and laboratory learning. The findings do not permit inferences regarding the loss of semantic memory content, however, since it is not clear whether the lack of knowledge reflects a forgetting process or a failure to encode the relevant information. The logic of inference regarding the forgetting process is the same for ecological and laboratory situations. Forgetting of semantic memory content can be inferred only on the basis of a comparison of performance over time, and such comparisons are likely to show evidence of forgetting only if exposure to the relevant information diminishes during the retention interval. The research discussed in this chapter will focus on investigations of the loss of information over time. It will exclude much of the recent work on psycholinguistics concerning the organization and retrieval of semantic information (see an excellent review by Kintsch, 1974), but not directly concerned with the forgetting process.

Longitudinal Designs

In longitudinal designs, performance is measured at the beginning of the retention interval and at later points during the interval, so as to yield the necessary comparisons. In developmental psychology, such comparisons always involve the same individuals, who are tested repeatedly, but in traditional memory research, it is more common to select different individuals for the testing at different intervals. Testing the same individuals repeatedly has the advantage of control over individual differences; however, there is the danger that later test performance will be affected by the practice or interference resulting from the earlier tests and will therefore fail to yield an unbiased estimate of the amount of forgetting during the interval. To avoid this problem, laboratory research in memory has primarily used between-subject comparisons. Semantic memory content is generally retained over much longer time intervals than the intervals involved in typical laboratory research, and the problems created by successive testing are likely to be trivial because of the long intervals between successive tests. For that same reason, however, the longitudinal approach becomes cumbersome. Investigators cannot conveniently wait many years to complete a study of memory. In a rapidly developing science, changes of methodology, of the focus of interest, and so forth, would render many investigations obsolete before their completion. In addition, the problems of maintaining contact with a large number of subjects over a long time period are prohibitive in a mobile society. Notwithstanding these problems, the longitudinal approach has been used when the retention interval did not exceed one or two years; such investigations have dealt primarily with the retention of academic subjects by school children. Two recent investigations have tested the retention of foreign languages over a summer recess. It is of interest here that the studies reached opposite conclusions, and that these almost certainly reflect differences in methodology. Cohen (1976) found substantial evidence of forgetting of Spanish during a summer recess. At the end of the summer during which the children did not use the language, their sentences were shorter and they made many more errors. The children were first-graders and the test was an oral-recall test in which children responded to questions regarding pictorial material presented on cards. Smythe, Jutras, Bramwell, and Gardner (1973) found no evidence of forgetting and some evidence of reminiscence in the performance of high school students retested for their knowledge of French either at the end of a summer recess, or at the end of an 8-month period. The test used by Smythe *et al.* was a multiple choice achievement test. Although the two studies differ in regard to the age of the children and other variables, the critical difference is likely to be the fact that Cohen used free- and cued-recall measures, whereas Smythe *et al.* exclusively tested recognition memory. The contrasting results suggest that the recall measure is far more sensitive to the changes that occurred during the retention interval.

Much has been written about differences between recall and recognition measures of retention, and it would not be appropriate to review all of this material. Although it is generally found that recognition performance is superior to recall performance, the important consideration in selecting an indicant of memory is the sensitivity of the indicant to the phenomena of interest. Either recognition or recall may be more sensitive to changes that occur during a particular retention interval, depending upon the degree of original learning, and the length of the interval. With high degrees of original learning and short retention intervals, recognition performance is likely to remain near the ceiling and fail to reveal forgetting, whereas recall measures are more sensitive. With low levels of learning, or very long retention intervals, recall performance may decline to a point where it is no longer sensitive to further retention losses, whereas recognition performance may continue to reflect changes over time. This problem has been discussed elsewhere (Bahrick, 1964; and Nelson, 1978) but it is important to note here that ecological memory investigations that extend over long time periods are likely to require both recall and recognition measures to reflect adequately the changes occurring during the entire retention interval. During the early portion of the interval, recall tests are likely to yield more information, and during later portions, the recognition measures. For highly overlearned semantic material, neither ordinary recall nor recognition measures may demonstrate significant losses of retention, but measures of latency of recall, or recognition tests requiring discrimination among highly similar foils may reflect important changes. An illustration of this will be given later. Because semantic content is generally more complex than the usual material selected for laboratory research in memory, it is particularly important to obtain several indicants of retention and to examine their interrelations at various times during the retention interval.

Cross Sectional Methods

Cross sectional designs involve concurrent testing of various subject groups who acquired the relevant knowledge at various time intervals preceding the test. The great advantage of this type of design is that a study of memory covering very long time periods can be completed in a comparatively short time. This avoids the problems mentioned earlier in regard to longitudinal methods. The primary disadvantage of cross sectional designs is associated with lack of control over the conditions under which the knowledge to be tested was acquired. As a result, performance on retention tests reflects not only losses of information during the retention interval, but also differences in the degree of original learning. Whereas this is true to some extent in all memory research, the problem is minimized in longitudinal investigations in which the experimenter can monitor the acquisition process. Furthermore, there is great likelihood in cross sectional designs that individuals available for testing will differ systematically in other important ways, and that these differences will also affect retention performance. Those individuals who acquired the knowledge long ago may not only have received somewhat different training, they may also differ from other subject groups in their motivation, in the amount of rehearsal of the material, or in their general aptitude for learning. Because of these potential problems, it is desirable to have large numbers participate as subjects in each group, and to assess the relevant characteristics as carefully as possible.

Even if these requirements cannot be met, however, cross sectional research may yield valuable information. Lachman and Mistler-Lachman (1976) report a study of lexical dominance in bilinguals that illustrates this point. They used a picture-naming task, in which their bilingual subjects were required to name each object shown as quickly as possible in the language indicated by the experimenter. The subjects were all

German natives who had changed to an English language environment. The critical variable was the number of years that had elapsed since the language change had occurred. Figure 14.1 shows that response latencies become significantly shorter in the adopted language for those subjects who had changed languages more than 20 years ago. Only six subjects were involved in this study, and many important variables regarding their background, age, verbal aptitude, use of German during the interim, and so on, were not controlled, and yet the study provides important information about long-term semantic memory which cannot be obtained under conditions of laboratory control. The study illustrates quite well the benefits and limitations to be expected from cross sectional, ecological research.

THE METHOD OF CROSS SECTIONAL ADJUSTMENT

This method can be used in semistructured situations in which a very large number of individuals acquired the same information. The time of acquisition should date back from a few months to many years, but both the level of original knowledge and the degree of rehearsal during the retention interval must be estimated with acceptable reliability.

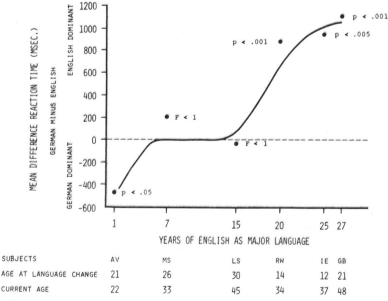

Figure 14.1. Comparison of Picture Naming Latencies in German and English (adapted from Lachman and Mistler-Lachman, 1976, copyright 1976 by the S.I.P.E., reprinted by permission).

The subjects are assigned to time groups based on how long ago they acquired the information, and average retention performance is calculated for each time group. The obtained averages yield an unadjusted cross sectional retention curve. This curve reflects not only retention losses, but also differences among the groups in the degree of original knowledge, as well as the amount or type of rehearsal activity. Since the effects of original learning and rehearsal may be large, it is necessary to correct the obtained results. The corrections or adjustments are made by means of multiple regression based on intercorrelations among uncontrolled rehearsal or original learning variables and dependent retention scores. The adjusted group means then reflect statistical estimates of retention performance adjusted to constant conditions of original learning and rehearsal. The adjusted means are either calculated directly from the multiple regression equations, or indirectly by calculating the adjustments and adding them to the unadjusted means. The logic of this technique of covariance analysis is described by Neter and Wasserman (1974, p. 711) and other standard texts. The adjustments can be calculated to reflect any of a number of assumptions that may be of interest in regard to the degree of original learning or the type and amount of rehearsal.

To illustrate the need for and the effect of such adjustments, data are presented from a study by Bahrick (1979), in which 275 students and 576 alumni of Ohio Wesleyan University were tested for their verbal and spatial memory related to the city of Delaware, Ohio. The attendance of the alumni dated from 1929 to 1979, and they were assigned to one of eight groups in accordance with the interval between their attendance at the college and the time of testing. The characteristics of the eight groups are summarized in Table 14.1. The subjects also filled out a questionnaire. The questionnaire related to conditions influencing the degree of original learning (for example, driving a car while living in Delaware) and to the amount of rehearsal of the material during the retention interval. The most important rehearsal variables are frequency, duration, recency, and distribution of visits to Delaware during the retention interval. Inspection of the questionnaire data in Table 14.1 reveals gross differences among the groups in regard to visits during the retention interval. The frequency and duration of visits per year, for example, is much greater for the extreme groups (1, 2, 7, 8) than for the middle groups (3, 4, 5, 6). The alumni who happened to be available for this study differed systematically between groups, and this gross bias in subject selection across time groups significantly affects retention performance. Figure 14.2 shows an example of retention curves for the recall of the spatial sequence of streets. The curve based on unadjusted means shows a loss of information for about 10 years, and this is followed

Table 14.1

Means and Standard Deviations of Key Independent Variables for the Eight Time Groups

Group	Retention interval (Months)		Frequency of visits (Number per Year)		Recency of visits (Months)		Duration of visits (Days/Year)		Visits with car (Percent)		Car on campus (Months)	
	Mean	SD	Mean	SD	Mean	SD	Mean	SD	Mean	SD	Mean	SD
1	13.66	2.43	2.32	3.24	6.44	4.98	5.22	7.05	63.89	46.35	9.11	10.43
2	44.35	7.39	.90	1.38	25.79	17.19	1.96	3.23	47.41	49.04	9.61	10.13
3	76.46	9.38	.41	.52	30.03	28.04	.57	.77	65.03	45.35	11.53	10.15
4	126.25	15.95	.18	.21	71.67	52.48	.27	.38	54.87	48.87	7.40	9.33
5	179.20	16.52	.18	.36	106.85	67.60	.19	.36	52.73	49.31	7.16	11.15
6	249.20	20.66	.21	.35	112.69	97.68	.32	.55	53.85	45.98	6.22	11.65
7	340.58	49.47	.62	.93	79.45	116.09	.85	1.28	61.22	43.41	3.60	8.15
8	556.42	48.98	1.04	2.11	20.17	49.46	1.32	2.15	83.47	29.01	2.84	6.98

by an apparent gain of information during the remaining years of the 46-year retention interval. Also shown in the figure are the adjusted curves. These provide estimates of the retention, assuming that none of the subjects had visited the city during the retention interval. The adjustments were calculated in two ways. In one case (group-specific adjustments), intercorrelations among independent and dependent variables were calculated separately from the data for each time group. The multiple regression equations for the adjustment of means were then based on partial regression coefficients peculiar to that group. In the second case (pooled adjustments), intercorrelations were calculated for the pooled data from all groups, with indicator variables designating time groups (Neter & Wasserman, 1974, pp. 308–312). This approach yields common partial regression coefficients for the regression equations applicable to all groups. The pooled adjustment approach permits the use of a larger number of observations for the purpose of determining the regression equation. This reduces sampling error, but entails the risk of systematic error if the assumption of homogeneity of regressions across groups is not justified.

It can be seen that, for the data in Figure 14.2, both methods of calculating adjustments lead to similar retention estimates. Table 14.2

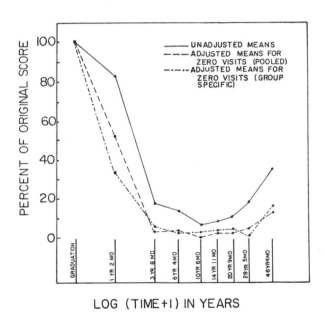

LOG (TIME+1) IN YEARS

Figure 14.2. Retention Curve for Recall of the Spatial Sequence of Streets (adapted from Bahrick, 1979, copyright 1979 by The American Psychological Association, reprinted by permission).

Table 14.2
Partial Regression Coefficients and Multiple Correlations for Calculating Adjustments and Maintenance Predictions

	Frequency of visits	Recency of visits	Duration of visits	Percentage of visits with car	Months of driving car on campus	Distribution of visits	Mult R
Recall of street names	.2163	−.9934	.2646	.0026	.0325	−.7832	.6323
Recall of street sequence	.3892	−1.2373	.9169	.0026	.0735	−1.2619	.6035

439

gives the pooled partial regression coefficients of the independent variables used to calculate adjustments for the dependent variable. It is apparent that the adjusted curves are lower than the unadjusted curve, and this is not surprising. The unadjusted data points reflect not only information acquired by each group during original learning, but also information reacquired on visits during the retention interval. When the reacquired information is discounted, the estimated performance level is lower. More important, the adjusted curves no longer exhibit the strong terminal rise, or the attenuated retention loss during the first year of the retention interval which is characteristic of the unadjusted curve. The regularity of the adjusted curves based on independent calculations documents the viability of the method of adjustment as a way of dealing with systematic differences among subjects available for this investigation. The multiple regression adjustments yield a corrected memory function relatively free of the systematic differences in subjects across time groups.

The method also permits estimates of retention performance as a function of various degrees of original learning or of rehearsal of the material. Figure 14.3 shows predicted contour-retention curves based on changes in one rehearsal variable, with all other conditions assumed constant. The frequency of visits per year is set at 0, 1, 2, 3, and 4, with an assumed duration of 1 day per visit. To obtain the values for these curves, the appropriate multiplier (0, 1, 2, 3, 4) is applied to the partial regression coefficient for frequency of visits shown in Table 14.2. The regression equation is then solved to obtain the appropriate adjustment, and the adjustment is added to the retention predicted on the basis of no visits during the retention interval.

THE TREATMENT OF RETENTION TIME AS AN INDEPENDENT VARIABLE

A different technique was used to generate the values in Figures 14.4 and 14.5. These data are taken from an unpublished study (Bahrick, Note 1) of the retention of Spanish language learned by 733 individuals who had taken one or more courses in Spanish in high school or college. They were assigned to 1 of 9 groups in accordance with their retention-interval, which ranged from 0 to 50 years. Retention measures were obtained from a test that yielded several subscores; the scores from a subtest on reading comprehension are used here for illustration. Figure 14.4 shows predicted contour retention curves for individuals who took one, three, or five courses of Spanish and obtained an average grade of "C," or "passing." Figure 14.5 shows curves for individuals who took

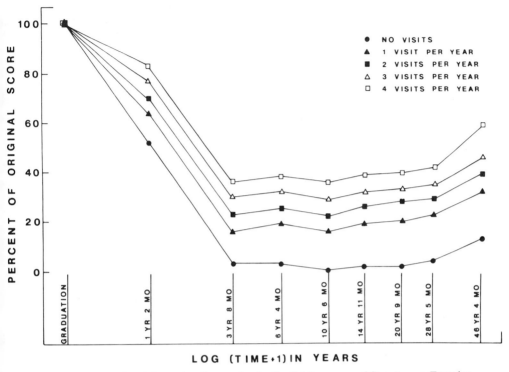

Figure 14.3. Predicted Retention Curves for the Spatial Sequence of Streets as a Function of the Frequency of Visits per Year.

three courses and earned an average grade of "A" ("excellent") or "C," respectively. The multiple regression technique used to obtain these functions differs in two ways from the technique described earlier: (*a*) time is treated as a quantitative variable, rather than as an indicator variable; and (*b*) higher order terms for independent variables are included in the regression equation, whenever this inclusion leads to significant increases in the predictable portion of the variance of the dependent variable. The regression equation used to generate the values for Figures 14.4 and 14.5 is:

$$Y = 6.3 + .94\,X_1 - 6.09X_2 + 2.96X_3 - .41X_4 + 3.88X_5$$
$$- .14X_6 + 5.86X_7 + 1.55X_8 + .15X_9 \quad (1)$$

Where Y = The Reading Comprehension Score
$X_1 = \log(\text{ret.} + 1)$
$X_2 = (\log(\text{ret.} + 1)^2$

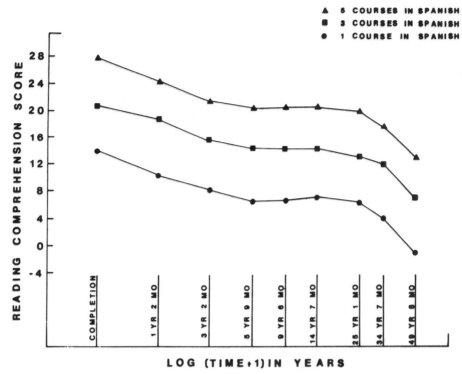

Figure 14.4. Contour Retention Curves for Spanish Reading Comprehension for Individuals Who Took One, Three, or Five Courses of Spanish.

$$X_3 = (\log (\text{ret.} + 1))^3$$
$$X_4 = (\log (\text{ret.} +)^4$$
$$X_5 = \text{Number of Spanish courses taken}$$
$$X_6 = (\text{Number of Spanish courses})^2$$
$$X_7 = (\text{mean grade received})$$
$$X_8 = (\text{mean grade})^2$$
$$X_9 = \text{number of courses in other Romance languages}$$

To generate the values in Figures 14.4 and 14.5, the regression equation (Eq. 1) was solved for the retention interval characteristic of each group.

The inclusion of higher order terms for independent variables in the regression analysis makes it possible to improve the accuracy of prediction whenever the partial regression of a variable is nonlinear in relation to the dependent variable.

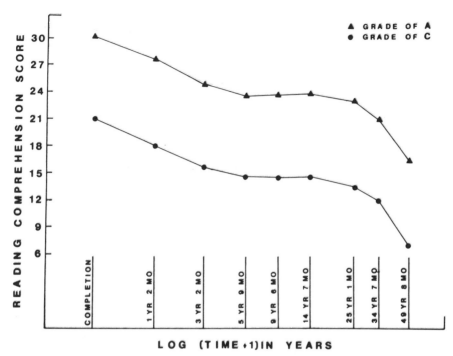

Figure 14.5. Contour Retention Curves for Spanish Reading Comprehension for Individuals with Grades of "A" and "C" in Their Spanish Courses.

The treatment of retention time as a quantitative variable results in a smoothed function in which the adjustment of individual points of the curve is a function of the mean retention values of all of the groups, so as to obtain the best fitting general function. The higher the degree of the polynomial used, the less smoothing is being carried out. In this particular case, the use of an eighth-degree polynomial for retention time, to fit the nine data points, would be equivalent to using the previously described indicator function method. When retention time is treated as an indicator variable, no adjustment is made to the performance of any group on the basis of mean performance of any other group. Adjustments are limited to those needed to control the effects of other independent variables.

The inclusion of retention time as a quantitative variable is particularly advisable if the number of individuals per group is too small to yield dependable group averages, or, if there is reason to believe that retention performance of any group is strongly affected by subject characteristics which could not be assessed or controlled.

LIMITATIONS OF CROSS SECTIONAL METHODS

Cross sectional procedures offer new options for investigating long term memory, but at the same time, these procedures present problems of reliability and validity of measurement which must be considered individually for each investigation. (See Lachman, Lachman, & Taylor, 1981, or Schaie, 1977 for discussions of these problems.) The methods not only make it possible to investigate retention over very long time periods, they also permit estimates of the effects of variables that were uncontrolled and varied over a wide range. Limitations arise from the large number of individuals needed for each study, the difficulty of assessing important variables that may differentiate the subjects of various time groups, and the confounding of developmental and cognitive causes of forgetting.

The need for large numbers of subjects is inherent in the multiple regression approach. Adjustments are valid only to the extent to which correlations on which they are based are reliable, and errors in correlations may be large unless the correlations are based upon a large number of paired observations.

Adjustments based on multiple regression are likely to be inadequate if important variables are not assessed at all, so that no adjustments for inequalities among groups can be made. For the study mentioned earlier, an illustration of this problem would be a systematic change in motivation or intelligence of individuals who learned Spanish fifty years ago versus those who learned more recently. Another possible reason for inadequate adjustments lies in faulty assessment of variables. The fault may reflect systematic changes of measurement in time, such as those produced by grade inflation, or improved methods of teaching Spanish during the last 50 years, or it may reflect unreliability of individual measures. Reliability problems may arise, because the measures are estimates obtained from each subject, based upon his or her own memory. Some estimates are verifiable (e.g., grades obtained in a course, or number of courses taken) but others are not (e.g., number or duration of visits to a city during the retention interval). Most errors of measurement will lead to adjustments that are too small to fully correct the inequalities between groups. Errors of measurement, particularly random errors, diminish correlations of the adjustor variable with the dependent variable, and this attenuation of correlations results in diminished adjustments. Thus, the adjusted curves in Figure 14.2 continue to reflect *some* of the effects of uncontrolled rehearsal variables. Nevertheless, the validity of adjustments is assured by the multiple correlation attained in the regression equation. The situation is analogous to the interpretation of the test–criterion correlation

of a selection test. The correlation assures the indicated validity, in spite
of concerns regarding reliability of test scores or criterion scores.
    A further limitation to interpreting most cross sectional memory data
arises from failure to control for developmental, that is, age-related,
changes of the subjects. Although most memory experiments confound
changes related aging of the individual with changes due to cognitive
effects on the memory trace, the problem is trivial in experiments involving short spans, but significant in investigations covering a span
of several decades.

    Their example, interference, as well as organic processes of
process of information over a long period of time reflects cognitive
deterioration, and the data available from cross sectional investigations
using not permit sorting out of these effects. Only those investigations in which the age of individuals varies greatly at the time of
acquisition permit the comparison of retention functions necessary to estimate the contributions of cognitive versus organic factors.

METHODS OF INVESTIGATING INDIVIDUAL-
SEMANTIC MEMORIES

   Memories that constitute the general knowledge of our personal
history, including attitudes and feelings, fall under the category of individual-semantic memories. Less research has dealt with this type of
content than with the other categories, although much of the discussion
of individual-episodic content applies to semantic content as well.
   A good example of research in this area is the study by Bahrick,
Bahrick, & Wittlinger (1975) on memory for the names and faces of high
school classmates. Using the cross sectional adjustment method described earlier, Bahrick et al., tested almost 400 high school graduates
ranging in age from 17 to 74. Tests were constructed from yearbooks,
and included free recall, picture-cued recall, recognition, and matching
tests using pictures and names. Research that focuses on memory for
information regarding past jobs, addresses, and telephone numbers would
also be relevant here, but very little has been published. Schonfield, as
described by Schonfield and Stones (1979), asked subjects ranging from
age 20 to age 85 to recall the names and gender of all their school
teachers. He then calculated the proportion of possible names recalled
for each of six age groups, and found only a slight decline with age. In
general, verification of such semantic autobiographical material is often
difficult, but more manageable than verification of the episodic content.
It should be noted that the classification of the above content as "

dividual'' is somewhat arbitrary, since the information regarding the
names and faces of classmates, the names of teachers, and so forth is
shared by all of the members of a class. However, the method used
involved the construction of separate tests based the information
pertinent to each individual, and thus the method is ...icable to individual-semantic content.

Memories of general attitudes and feelings also belong this content
category, and they present the greatest difficulty of assessification. Social psychologists have done interesting laborat and ver-
manipulating attitudes and then examining the changes th ork by
subjects' memories of their original attitudes. (See, for example, ir in
& Reckman, 1973). It is still unclear, however, whether those als
would be applicable to measuring memories for attitudes in re
situations over a longer time span.

METHODS OF INVESTIGATING
SHARED-EPISODIC MEMORY

If specific events are experienced by many people, or if information
about such events is widely available, then memory for these events
may be classified as *shared-episodic*. Traditional laboratory methods
generally tapped shared-episodic memory, for all subjects were presented
with identical information to remember. However, material tended to be
unnatural (meaningless letter sequences, lists of words, and paired-associates were often used) and retention intervals were very short. (There
were, however, some exceptions to this latter limitation. See Cofer, 1943;
Smith, 1951; Titchener, 1923; Wickelgren, 1972; and Worchester, 1957.)
Most of this traditional research has little ecological relevance because
the situations and materials that were employed differed radically from
those found in everyday life. For this reason, and because the other
hapters of this book deal with this literature, it will not be reviewed

basic problem with nonlaboratory research in this content area
he as in other areas: there is a lack of control over original
subsequent rehearsal. To limit this problem, it is imperative
opriate material carefully. In studies of individual-episodic
iects usually generate episodes themselves, or are asked
about past events, whereas in studies of individual-
bjects are asked about memories that are not as-
time or place (for example, high school class-
ed-episodic content must focus on information

about events to which many people were exposed—but only for a relatively brief period of time. If the exposure is prolonged, it is difficult to assign the memory content to the episodic-semantic continuum, or to specify memory lapses precisely in regard to time. The evolution of nonlaboratory methods for studying shared-episodic memory reflects the success of investigators in dealing with this problem, although a complete solution is still not at hand, as the following discussion will show.

Nonlaboratory methods of studying shared-episodic memory began with research aimed at assessing long-term memory for significant public events by Warrington & Silberstein (1970) and Warrington & Sanders (1971). Warrington and Sanders (1971) picked nine 2-year periods between 1930 and 1968 and constructed a 12-item questionnaire for each of these 2-year periods. They chose "finite events judged to be the most striking and significant at the time" from the *Times* review of the year. Subjects in four age groups from age 40 to 79 first completed a recall version of these questionnaires and, immediately afterwards, multiple choice versions. Warrington and Sanders, also constructed a test to measure memory for well-known faces. They used photographs of contemporary personalities and of personalities "whose public life was sharply terminated at a finite time in the past" (the late 1940s to the early 60s). There were also both recall and recognition versions of this test. Warrington and Sanders point out a major problem with their questionnaires: it is impossible to ensure that the questions dealing with various time periods are equally difficult. If the questions on the earlier time periods were more difficult, this alone could explain their findings of performance decrements for the older items. In addition, "striking," or "significant" events are likely to appear repeatedly in mass media and books, leading to increased variance of exposure to the information. For these reasons, Squire and Slater (1975) devised memory tests based on single classes of events that occurred repeatedly over many years (1957–1972): the names of television shows running for only one season and the names of winning race horses. Squire and Slater argued that popular exposure to the programs was similar. The percentage of time spent watching television has remained relatively constant, they report, and Neilsen ratings were similar over the time periods. Since they picked only race horses that had won the Kentucky Derby, the Preakness, or the Belmont Stakes, this ensured that exposure to the names of race horses was roughly equivalent. The interpretation of the data in terms of a temporal gradient of memory loss is somewhat clouded, however, by the possibility that subjects may learn of an event, not at the time it occurred, but through later exposure.

To determine the extent to which one could learn the test items after the event, both Warrington and Sanders (1971) and Squire and Slater (1975) used control groups of teenagers who were too young to have experienced the earlier events. Squire and Slater used an additional group of adults who had lived abroad during part of the period covered by the tests. Since the teenagers did poorly on the early events, and adults did poorly on events occurring while they lived abroad, Squire and Slater concluded that little learning occurs after the initial broadcasts of the events.

Here, again, we must emphasize that the distinction between episodic and semantic memory content is not absolute, but refers to a continuum. Warrington and Sanders included a test of well-known faces in their study, whereas Squire and Slater used television programs. The television shows remained on the air for several months, and the exposure to the well-known faces probably occurred over a considerable time period. When questionnaires are used for the purpose of plotting an exact time course of retrograde amnesia (Mair, Warrington, & Weiskrantz, 1979; Sanders & Warrington, 1971; Squire, 1975), or the effects of aging (Squire, 1974; Warrington & Sanders, 1971) it is necessary to choose information that not only was presented at a particular time, but that also disappeared from the news immediately afterwards. (We call such events *comet events*.) Researchers have tried to do this, but no objective measures are now available to validate their selection of questionnaire items. Tests of individuals who were out of the country provide an alternative control that should be pursued; a search for better validation of the time limits applicable to test items should also be pursued.

Refinements of this questionnaire technique will provide a valuable tool for both clinical and experimental studies of long term memory, but problems remain. One problem is the difficulty in assessing the extent of exposure to the events on an individual basis. If an alcoholic who develops Korsakoff's psychosis has not read newspapers or watched television for years, then the use of these questionnaire techniques to assess memory impairment may be misleading. Findings regarding individuals are also difficult to interpret in the absence of information about possible differences associated with sex, age, or cultural factors in original learning.

A variety of materials beyond television programs or public events may serve for tests of shared-episodic memory. Among such materials are the contents of books, plays, and movies. The exact procedures and materials will determine the nature of the memory tested and its position in the episodic–semantic continuum. For example, the memories Neisser and Hupcey (1975) tap in their experiment with members of a Sherlock Holmes society are probably more semantic than episodic, whereas memory for the contents of novels assigned in school probably share more of the characteristics of episodic memory. The books assigned in school are typically read once within a relatively short time period, whereas the members of the Sherlock Holmes Society read, reread, and discussed the exploits of Sherlock Holmes repeatedly over many years. Rubin's (1977) study on "very long term memory for prose and verse" used Hamlet's Soliloquy, the preamble to the Constitution, and the 23rd Psalm, and this material, like the Sherlock Holmes stories, also becomes semantic as a result of rehearsal in a variety of contexts and over an extended time period.

METHODS OF INVESTIGATING INDIVIDUAL-EPISODIC MEMORIES

Individual-episodic memories include all the personal memories of specific events and experiences that we acquire throughout our lives. We will use the term *autobiographical memory* here, although autobiographical memory also includes what we are labeling individual-semantic: our general knowledge of occupations, feelings, or experiences that are not tied to specific incidents. The store of autobiographical memories is almost limitless, or so it seems. The vast extent and complexity of these memories means that here, more than in other areas, the questions we ask will determine the validity of our methods and the nature of the information we collect. An obvious starting point is to ask, "How accurate are our autobiographical memories?" How they are organized and retrieved, and combined and transformed are other questions. And what about early childhood memories, which have fascinated both researchers and the public for years? Is there really childhood amnesia, as Freud proposed. Is there a change in the number or type of memories that can be recalled after age 5? What about individual differences? It would be most surprising if there were not dramatic differences among individuals in all functions of the memory system.

There are many problems in studying autobiographical memory. Some of these are inherent in the study of memory for real life events, such as the lack of control over the conditions of original learning and rehearsal, whereas others are chiefly characteristic of autobiographical memory, such as the problem of verification. Equally problematical and challenging, is the role of personality and motivational variables in the memory system (see, for example, Cantor & Kihlstrom, 1981; Goethals & Reckman, 1973; Kihlstrom, 1980; Markus, 1977; and Snyder & Uranowitz, 1978). The ways in which individuals think about their lives and themselves will affect the organization of autobiographical memories and their change over time. As Kihlstrom writes, "The self is a cognitive structure which guides the processing of information in memory: New information is examined for self-reference and coded accordingly; and the self-schema can interact with the encoded attribute of self-reference (and other more specific attributes) to guide subsequent retrieval attempts [Kihlstrom, 1980, p. 23]." We will not discuss this research here, but will focus instead on techniques designed to provide basic information on autobiographical memory. The complexity of autobiographical memory is reflected in the diversity of these techniques. We shall distinguish among three main categories:

1. Techniques in which the subject recalls memories while in the laboratory (*free recall, prompt-word techniques,* and *flashbulb memories*—here the problem of verification is most severe.
2. Techniques in which existing records are used to check the accuracy of recall, which may have occurred naturally (e.g., during a court trial), or in the laboratory
3. Techniques in which the subject is instructed to keep records of day to day activities, which can then be used to construct memory tests

The two latter techniques are described in the section, "Techniques which Permit Verification."

Free Recall

Free recall has great potential for use in studying autobiographical memory, but there has been little development of appropriate methodologies. Smith (1952) took one approach and recalled "as many incidents as possible" from each of 14 time periods from throughout her life (5 periods through young adulthood, and 9 from age 20 to 61). Time periods were chosen to represent residence in one state or country, and recall continued periodically over several months. Smith recalled over 6,000 memories and did an extensive analysis of the frequency and nature of these memories in each of the time periods. Since she had kept detailed diaries throughout her life and had access to her mother's diaries, she could check the accuracy of many of her memories and also study what types of memories were forgotten. Psychologists in the 1950s, however, were not attentive to this type of nonlaboratory study and gave little notice to it. Waldfogel's (1948) earlier work, on the other hand, became more widely known, in part because of his more conventional methodology and analysis. Waldfogel's research was partially motivated by a desire to investigate Freud's theories of infantile amnesia and "screen" memories, and he used a free-recall technique to collect memories from 124 college students. (See Mosak, 1969, for a discussion of some psychoanalytically-oriented research on early recollections.) Waldfogel's technique was simple: He had subjects write, for 85 minutes, every experience they could remember from before their eighth birthday, date the experience, and then rate each one as very pleasant, neutral, unpleasant, or very unpleasant. Subjects also indicated whether they felt the memory was genuine or whether it stemmed from information they were exposed to at a later date. A little over a month later he unexpectedly requested that subjects repeat this procedure. The reliability coefficients of the two recall scores were .70 for males and .76 for females, indicating a fair amount of variability. This is understandable in light of Waldfogel's finding that almost 50% of the memories from the second recall were new, although the total number of recalled memories had increased by only 10%.

Asking subjects to recall memories and then rate them along various dimensions is certainly an improvement over some of the very early questionnaire studies (see Dudycha & Dudycha, 1941, for a review), but Waldfogel's procedure of exhaustive free recall is limited to early childhood or other brief time periods. Given a long interval most subjects could continue recalling memories for months, as did Smith (1952). The limitations of this technique led to a revival of Galton's (1883) chronometric word association technique and its subsequent modification into what has now become a fairly popular prompt-word technique.

The Prompt-Word Techniques

Galton's (1883) technique, which he tried only on himself, involved choosing 75 "suitable" words and examining them one by one. "So soon as about a couple of ideas in direct association with the word had arisen" Galton released the spring on his chronograph and recorded reaction time and his associations, which he later dated (p. 188). Galton's principal objective, which he met admirably, was "to show that a large class of mental phenomena, that have hitherto been too vague to lay hold of, admit of being caught by the firm grip of genuine statistical inquiry [p. 197]."

When Galton's technique was revived in the 1970s, there was a concern for objective quantification, leading to an emphasis on simple parameters of recall, such as reaction time and the age of memories.

Crovitz and Schiffman (1974), for example, were interested mainly in determining the frequency of memories as a function of their age. They gave subjects 20 concrete nouns and instructed them to "think of a specific memory associated with each word" and then briefly describe it in writing. Afterward, subjects dated these memories. The frequency of memories, Crovitz and Schiffman found, decreased regularly as a function of their age. To compare this *semantic-cuing* technique with Waldfogel's exhaustive free recall, Crovitz and Quina-Holland (1976) changed the instructions and required that each memory originate during childhood. In their first investigation, they requested a childhood memory associated with each of 12 nouns, whereas for the second investigation, each subject was given just one noun and told to write down 10–15 specific childhood memories associated with it. Crovitz and Quina-Holland were interested mainly in comparing their technique with Waldfogel's, but focused on only one variable, the proportion of all childhood memories assigned to each year between age 1 and 7. The correlations among the data from each of Crovitz and Quina-Holland's two studies and Waldfogel's experiment were .995 and .986, indicating satisfactory reliability, and all three experiments showed a steady increase of recall with age. This does not demonstrate the equivalence of the two methods, as Crovitz and Quina-Holland claim, for there may be significant differences in the content of the memories recalled, and the methods were not compared in this respect.

When Robinson (1976) used a prompt-word technique to study autobiographical memories, he collected more information and analyzed the data more thoroughly. He used 3 classes of prompt words, *object words* (16 nouns), *activity words* (16 verbs), and *affect words* (16 adjectives), for he was interested in comparing the following "properties of recollection" as a function of prompt class: response latency (time required to retrieve a memory), the age of the memory, the specificity with which the memory could be dated, and the type of experience the memory represented. Like Crovitz, though, he limited the memories that could be recalled by specifying that they must relate to specific incidents. This may be necessary if the age of the memory is of major importance, because only specific memories can be uniquely dated. It is very common, however, to have general memories of activities that occurred frequently or of feelings that were pervasive during a certain period in one's life. Karis (Note 2) modified Robinson's procedure partly for these reasons and allowed subjects to recall any memory, general or specific. Karis was interested in individual differences in the nature and extent of autobiographical memories. Since he was particularly interested in the recall of early memories he further modified Robinson's procedure and specified, along with each prompt word, one of three time periods from which the memory was to originate: before first grade, during seventh, eighth, or ninth grade, and within the last two years. Afterward subjects reread, dated, and rated their memories on a variety of dimensions, including specificity and imagery.

Prompt-word techniques have also been used to compare the memories of various age groups. Franklin and Holding (1977) were interested in changes in the recall of autobiographical memories as a person ages. They used a cross sectional approach with five groups of adults ranging in age from 25 to over 70 and, like Karis, permitted what they termed "recurrent" events. For example, "My husband does a hundred pushups a day with one hand [p. 531]" would be labelled a recurrent event by Franklin and Holding. Crovitz, Robinson, and others, who demand only specific memories, would not accept such a memory. Fitzgerald (Note 3) used Robinson's technique to study autobiographical memory in seventh graders, ninth graders, and college students. In one study, he followed Robinson's procedure exactly, whereas in another he read to subjects autobiographical memories they had previously recalled when presented with prompt words. The initial memories were to serve as prompts for the recall of additional memories, allowing Fitzgerald to examine the relationship between each pair of memories. As might be expected, the second memories were usually from the same time period as the prompt memories.

Chew (Note 4) also modified Robinson's procedure in several ways to investigate the effects of various types of prompt words. She used low- and high-imagery words in one experiment, whereas in another she used some prompts related to achievement or intimacy motivation (e.g., *success, loneliness*) and subjects whose motivation on these personality dimensions had been previously assessed. In both studies, Chew was interested in examining response latencies as a function of the memories' age. To do this, she requested that memories originate from either the last 4 years (*recent memories*) or from the years before the age of 8 (*remote memories*).

The basic prompt-word technique can be modified in any number of ways. Not only can one specify a time period from which memories are to originate or systematically vary the prompts, but one can also specify the type of memory that is to be recalled. In several brief studies early in this century, Washburn and her colleagues at Vassar presented subjects with a series of words and recorded how long it took to recall a pleasant or unpleasant personal experience (Baxter, Yamanda, & Washburn, 1917), the proportion of pleasant memories recalled (Morgan, Mull, & Washburn, 1919; Washburn, Harding, Simons, & Tomlinson, 1925) or, without any prompt words, the intensity of the emotion produced when recalling an incident involving anger, joy, or fear, with the corresponding speed of recall and remoteness of the incident (Washburn, Giang, Ives, & Pollack, 1925). More recently, Teasdale and Fogarty (1979) investigated the accessibility (as indexed by reaction time) of pleasant and unpleasant memories after inducing either a happy or depressed mood in their subjects. Teasdale and Fogarty used normal subjects whereas Lloyd and Lishman (1975) carried out a similar study, but with clinically depressed patients.

The variety of ways in which the prompt-word technique can be modified provides the flexibility necessary for studying diverse aspects of autobiographical memory. One can focus on the effects of various prompts, on the age or content of the memories recalled, or on the speed of recall. One can also hold a specific aspect of the memory constant (by instructing subjects, for example, to recall a certain type of memory, or a memory from a certain time period), and examine the resulting changes in the other parameters.

Flashbulb Memories

"Flashbulb memories," write Brown and Kulik (1977), "are memories for the circumstances in which one first learned of a very surprising and consequential (or emotionally arousing) event [p. 73]." The assassination of President John F. Kennedy is the prototypical case and has been studied, independently of Brown and Kulik, by Yarmey and Bull (1978). Since the emphasis is on the individual situation in which a respondent found himself or herself at the time of hearing about the event, and not on the event itself, these studies clearly investigate individual-episodic memory content. Brown and Kulik used this method in relation to Kennedy's death, as well as the death, or near death, of eight other political or religious leaders. Subjects were asked, *Do you recall the circumstances in which you first heard that . . . , and if so, would you describe these circumstances in detail.* An almost identical technique was used near the end of the last century by Colgrove (1899). Colgrove asked 179 "middle aged and aged" people, *Do you recall where you were when you heard that Lincoln was shot?* (33 years earlier). One-hundred and twenty-seven answered "yes" and described the situation. This was a lower percentage (71%) than found by the more recent investigators, but in these recent studies, subjects were asked about less remote events (not older than 12 years) and were younger. Subjects used by Yarmey and Bull (1978) ranged in age from those who were only 6 in 1963 (when Kennedy was assassinated) to those who were over 54.

The applicability of the technique just described is obviously limited to a few situations, but should prove useful as one of several techniques to assess developmental changes in episodic memory, especially in early childhood memories. The technique could also be adopted to a questionnaire format similar to those that test memory for public events. This would require identifying events from the different epochs used. The events would need to be surprising and arousing, since these characteristics seem to be important influences in the formation of flashbulb memories. The previously discussed problems of verification of subjective reports would apply to this technique, also.

Techniques That Permit Verification

In the techniques discussed previously, the accuracy of the recalled memories is often in doubt. Even when an autobiographical memory is "basically" correct there may be many small or subtle changes—of emphasis, of certain details, of changes in time or location, and so on. These can provide valuable information about the memory process. To study such changes one must have an exact record of the events or experiences that are recalled, and keeping such a record outside the laboratory without creating an artificial environment is very difficult. Within the last few years, however, several ingenious techniques have emerged. Some, like Linton's (1978) self analysis, or Klinger's (1978) "thought sampling," involve some disruption of normal routines, whereas others take advantage of special situations or populations.

VERIFICATION VIA RECORD-KEEPING

One obvious way to deal with the problem of accuracy is to keep records of day to day events for later testing. With substantial time frames this can become a herculean feat and motivational problems can become severe. Marigold Linton (1975, 1978, 1979a) circumvented this problem by using only herself as a subject. Every day for over six years she recorded the two most important events of the day and rated them along a variety of dimensions. Periodically she tested herself by selecting two events, determining which came first, and then dating them. Forgetting did not follow a time course like that found by Ebbinghaus, (Note 5) in which forgetting is rapid at first and gradually tapers off. Instead, forgetting continued at a "low, fairly steady rate, with the number of forgotten items usually increasing slightly from year to year [Linton, 1979a, p. 85]." The method also permits an analysis of retention as a function of *emotionality* and *importance* (for she rated memories on these dimensions), or as a function of mood at each test session, but the results of these types of analyses have not yet been reported. A more natural, although less rigorous, method is to use as subjects individuals who have kept extensive diaries. This was done by Smith (1952), as mentioned previously, although, as in Linton's study, the only subject was the author herself.

Dworkin (in Goldfinger, Note 6) took another approach, involving record keeping by the subject, that was quite similar to Linton's method. However, since Dworkin was mainly interested in studying the interaction between personality and memory, there were differences in both his rating and his recall procedures. Dworkin gave a group of undergraduate women special forms on which to record, before going to sleep, the most significant event of each day throughout a three week period. They briefly described the event, answered several questions about it, and rated it on a variety of dimensions. They also used a checklist to describe their feelings during the event. Every morning they turned in the form they had completed the previous night. Two weeks after this three week period Dworkin unexpectedly asked the women to remember all the events they had originally written. Dworkin had previously administered a variety of personality tests to these women and had also determined which ones had a "schema" for sociability/friendliness. This made it possible to answer such questions as, "Do those with a schema for friendliness remember interpersonal situations more accurately than others?"

Another similar approach, not yet applied to the study of autobiographical memory, involves "thought sampling," and has been used in the study of daydreams and the "flow of consciousness." In a study by Klinger (1978) subjects carried around with them an alarm device that beeped several times a day at random intervals (with a mean of 40 minutes). When the beeper went off the subject was instructed to fill out a thought sampling questionnaire immediately. Modifying this questionnaire to include questions about ongoing activities would provide a data base with which to check later memories, but it is unclear how disruptive such a technique would be, and how it compares to nightly record keeping (as used by Dworkin, for example). It is certainly the most accurate way of recording events as experienced by an individual, for it eliminates changes that may occur between an event and the recording of it at a later time.

These approaches provide valuable information but can be criticized, because by introducing record keeping they interfere with the normal memory process. There are both advantages and disadvantages to each technique, however. Using Klinger's technique, for example, we get an unbiased sampling of a variety of everyday events, but really important events or experiences may be missed. Instructing some subjects to record various details about important events immediately after they occur, and to turn the records in periodically would be one way of combining techniques.

VERIFICATION WITHOUT RECORD-KEEPING

Sheingold and Tenney (Note 7) and Neisser (1981) both developed techniques in which accuracy can be assessed without the necessity of record keeping. Sheingold and Tenney (1979) recruited college students and children at three age groups (4:6, 8, and 12:6) who had a sibling born when they were 4-years-old. They then asked them 20 questions, such as, *Who told you that your mother was leaving to go to the hospital?*, *Who took care of you while your mother was in the hospital?*, and *Did you get any presents at that time?* There was no difference between the groups of children and the college students, 20-year-old college students recalled as much about a sibling birth that occurred 16 years ago as children of 4:6 recalled about one that occurred 7 months in the past, but accuracy was judged with respect to the mother's recall, which was not verified. When Sheingold and Tenney gave their questionnaires to college students who had ranged in age from 1 to 17 when a sibling was born they found that age 3 was the youngest age at which anything could be remembered about the birth, and that by age 4 a great deal was remembered. This corresponds well to the early memory research (via questionnaire) which found that the earliest memories, on the average, originated between the ages of 3 and 4 (Dudycha & Dudycha, 1941; Waldfogel, 1948).

Neisser (1981) studied autobiographical memory by taking advantage of two interesting and unusual real life situations, the first, "Watergate," the second, an unusual kindergarten teacher. John Dean, special counsel to President Nixon, testified for several days before the Senate "Watergate" Committee in 1973, giving detailed descriptions of conversations, meetings, memos, and all the events leading up to the break-in at the headquarters of the Democratic National Committee. Only later was it revealed that Nixon had taped everything that transpired in his Oval Office, permitting an analysis of the accuracy of Dean's testimony and the ways he had "misremembered." In situations like this we may

have a record of the actual conversations and can thus check the accuracy
of testimony, but we have no way of determining the honesty of the
witness. Neisser argues convincingly that Dean had no reason to lie,
because the transcripts are as damning as his testimony, but it is impossible to determine whether Dean distorted his testimony to present
himself in a more favorable light.

Dean's recall performance cannot be adequately described in terms
of episodic or semantic accuracy because Neisser discovered that Dean
was accurate only in remembering "repeated episodes, rehearsed presentations, or overall impressions [p. 20]." Neisser terms these memories
for a repeated sequence of events *repisodic*. Dean often fails to describe
any single episode correctly, but succeeds in accurately portraying general conclusions drawn from a sequence of such episodes. Dean's repeated episodes of meeting with Nixon can be termed a *repisode,* and
Dean told the truth, Meisser writes, at the repisodic level. His descriptions of specific memories were incorrect, but he was accurate in describing the theme of his many meetings with Nixon: Nixon not only
knew about the cover-up but wanted it to succeed, and was using illegal
strategies. Linton (Note 8), in reviewing the results of her long-term
mnemonic self-analysis, uses the term "semantic" to describe memories
that Neisser would label "repisodic." As previously noted, the episodic-
semantic dimension is not a dichotomy, and Linton's conclusions seem
also to apply to Neisser's analysis of Dean's memory: "Increased experience with any particular event class increased semantic (or general)
knowledge about the event and its context. Increased experience with
such similar events, however, makes specific episodic knowledge increasingly confusable, and ultimately episodes cannot be distinguished
[Linton, 1979b, p. 4]."

In a second investigation, Neisser and Gold (1979) made use of
unusually accurate records kept by a kindergarten teacher. Using these
records, they constructed memory tests and administered them to former
students. Others have made use of school records, but not to study
memory per se. Yarrow, Campbell, and Burton (1970), for example,
studied the retrospective reports of mothers and their children on various
areas relevant to personality development, such as maternal care and
familial environment. The children were between age 8 and age 34 when
their mothers were interviewed, and all had attended a nursery school
that had kept detailed and uniform records for over 30 years. Yarrow
et al. were particularly interested in comparisons between the school
records and the retrospective reports from the mothers and their children
and found that distortions were common in the retrospective accounts.
In another study, Yarrow *et al.* observed the responses of mothers and

children to the initial separation when the children began kindergarten, and then interviewed the mothers 5 to 9 months later about these experiences.

It is clear that there are a variety of opportunities for the verification of autobiographical memory, and that techniques that exploit these opportunities are suitable for establishing the reliability of various types of autobiographical memory reports. The use of trial data, and Dean's case in particular, also brings up interesting questions of metamemory: How good are we at judging the accuracy of our own recall? Is there as much variation here as in other aspects of autobiographical memory? To answer such questions Herrmann and Neisser (1978) developed a questionnaire that asked about memory in a variety of everday situations (e.g., *In the process of telling someone a joke or story you forgot the punchline or ending . . . (a) rarely or never . . . (e) very frequently).* Some of the questions ask about memory in situations that could be assessed objectively in the laboratory, permitting a characterization of the accuracy of an individual's metamemory. It would be easier to test metamemory using the technique of Nelson and Narens (1980a), but this is limited to one aspect of metamemory, "feeling of knowing." Nelson and Narens developed a set of 300 general information questions to tap shared-semantic memory content. When subjects were unable to answer a question, they were requested to give "feeling of knowing" ratings, defined as the likelihood (on a 9-point scale) of being able to recognize the correct answer. Actually presenting answers (and foils) after subjects give ratings permits verification and provides a measure of the accuracy of metamemory (see Nelson & Narens, 1980b).

Techniques Designed to Reveal the Organization of Autobiographical Memory

How do people group the events of their lives in memory? Is the content of autobiographical memory organized in separate chunks—school life, professional life, family life—or is there a more continuous temporal organization? Are generalizations possible, or do some people think of their lives in terms of a sequence of interpersonal relationships, whereas others organize memories around places they have lived or jobs they have held? Do some people have a strong sense of the "flow" of time, with life events specifically "tagged," whereas for others temporal order is unimportant, and events are clustered in other ways? Because so little is known about the answers to these questions, research will have to make use of very unconstrained and open-ended procedures.

This minimizes the danger of biasing the results with the investigators preconceptions. One unstructured method would be to ask individuals, *Tell me about your life,* and record their answers. One could then examine how people organize their replies, and what they include or omit. Modified techniques might impose various time limits: *Tell me about your life. Take about five minutes (or ten, or thirty, or an hour).* The data can then be examined to show the effects of age, sex, occupation, or personality variables. This adds to the complexity of research on the organization and content of personal memories, but is likely to yield greatly expanded knowledge of ecological memory. Gerontologists have been interested in some of these questions and in the functions of reminiscence (Havighurst & Glasser, 1972), but have not usually focused on the general questions raised here. Gerontologists, of course, are interested in aging, and little has been done with young or middle-aged individuals, although Linton (1979b) has done research with children in which she asked such general questions as, *Tell me something that happened today, yesterday, or last Christmas; Tell me about when you got hurt, when you had fun, or when you weren't good.*

Open-ended techniques designed to reveal overall organization may be followed by techniques using prompt-words to elicit memories from various epochs. This approach may also reveal individual differences in the responses to various types of prompts. Certain personality characteristics and organizational structures may facilitate access to autobiographical memories on the basis of certain prompting, whereas for other subjects, a specific context may be necessary for retrieval. Ecological research has both the advantage and disadvantage of blurring the distinctions among psychological processes. This means that studying the organization of autobiographical memory will not be easy, for it will require novel techniques that focus on more than just memory. A wide variety of individuals varying in age, sex, and occupation, and family and cultural backgrounds must be included. The products of such research, however, should be of interest to psychotherapists, sociologists, biographers, jurists, and many others.

CONCLUDING COMMENTS

This chapter has dealt with methods of investigating memory for real life experiences that are often difficult to specify and impossible to control. A four-fold classification into individual and shared episodic and semantic content was used to organize the discussion. This classification does not permit the unambiguous assignment of memory content into one of four categories, but it may provide a useful focus on methodological problems, which tend to differ among content categories. The cross sectional method, for instance, adjusts for the effects of varying degrees of exposure and rehearsal of information during the acquisition and retention intervals. Repeated exposure is likely for semantic, but not for episodic content, since the process of repeated exposure transforms episodic into semantic content. The Squire and Slater (1975) technique of testing for information pertaining to a single type of event, for example, the names of horses who won the Kentucky Derby, assumes approximately equal and brief exposure to the target information. The technique is therefore most appropriate for testing shared-episodic content, while Robinson's (1976) prompting technique is designed to elicit autobiographical content, which varies among individuals.

The various methods differ widely in their degree of departure from laboratory traditions, but all involve a loss of control over the conditions under which memory content is acquired. It seems appropriate, in conclusion, to review two principles that should govern the acceptability of these important methodological changes. One principle was stated at the outset. Control remains a desideratum, but not the only criterion of acceptability, and sacrifice of control is acceptable to the extent to which it yields important information not otherwise obtainable. The second principle has influenced many areas of psychological research during recent years, but has not been made explicit in regard to the evaluation of methods of memory research. Objective verifiability remains a paramount criterion of scientific truth, but it need not apply to the individual datum as long as it applies to the generalizations that are ultimately established by using a given method. Stephenson (1980) in an important recent paper shows that the subjective statements obtained by (Q) methodology from a 4-year-old child are useful scientific data because they can be transformed by explicit procedures into what he has called a *concourse* and ultimately into an objective operant factor structure. This same principle applies to autobiographical memories for which no objective content verification is possible. The immediate data may be unreliable and subjective, but the scientific validity of the method must be determined on the basis of the significance and replicability of generalizations it will yield, and not on the basis of the subjectivity of individual reports. This principle was recognized implicitly at least 100 years ago when psychophysical reports were accepted into psychology, but during the interim undue emphasis was often given to immediate, rather than ultimate verification.

A related, but separate issue involves the distinction between generalizations concerning memory versus generalizations concerning individual's reports about their memory. The methods we have discussed limit conclusions to the latter type of generalizations unless reports about content can be verified. When content is verifiable, it is possible to compare the two types of generalization and to establish generalizations about the relations between them. This provides the basis for the ecological study of metamemory, a rapidly developing area.

REFERENCE NOTES

1. Bahrick, H. P. *Fifty years of retention of knowledge of Spanish acquired in school.* Unpublished manuscript.
2. Karis, G. D. Individual differences in autobiographical memory. Unpublished doctoral dissertation, Cornell University, 1980.
3. Fitzgerald, J. M. Sampling and resampling autobiographical memory in adolescent subjects. Paper presented at the meeting of the American Psychological Association, Toronto, August 1978.
4. Chew, B. R. *Probing for remote and recent autobiographical memories.* Paper presented in a symposium on "Studies of Personal Recollections" at the meeting of the American Psychological Association, New York, September 1979.
5. Ebbinghaus, H. *Memory: A contribution to experimental psychology,* (H. A. Ruger and C. E. Bussenius, trans.). New York: Teachers College, 1913. (Originally published, 1885.)
6. Goldfinger, S. H. Processing bias: *Individual differences in the cognition of situations.* Unpublished doctoral dissertation, Cornell University, 1981.
7. Sheingold, K., & Tenney, Y. J. *Memory for a salient childhood event.* Paper presented at the meeting of the Society for Research in Child Development, March 1979, San Francisco.
8. Linton, M. *Cuing events in adults' and children's autobiographical memory.* Paper presented in a symposium on "Studies of Personal Recollections" at a meeting of the American Psychological Association, New York, September 1979.(b)

REFERENCES

Bahrick, H. P. Retention curves: Facts or artifacts. *Psychological Bulletin,* 1964, *61,* 188–194.
Bahrick, H. P. Relearning and the measurement of retention. *Journal of Verbal Learning and Verbal Behavior,* 1967, *6,* 84–89.
Bahrick, H. P. Maintenance of knowledge: Questions about memory we forgot to ask. *Journal of Experimental Psychology: General,* 1979, *108*(3), 296–308.
Bahrick, H. P., Bahrick, P. O., & Wittlinger, R. P. Fifty years of memories for names and faces: A cross-sectional approach. *Journal of Experimental Psychology: General,* 1975, *104*(1), 54–75.
Bahrick, H. P., & Noble, M. E. Motor Behavior. In J. Sidowski (Ed.), *Experimental Methods and Instrumentation in Psychology.* New York: McGraw–Hill, 1966.
Baxter, M. F., Yamada, K., & Washburn, M. F. Directed recall of pleasant and unpleasant experiences. *The American Journal of Psychology,* 1917, *28,* 155–157.

Brown, R., & Kulik, J. Flashbulb memories. *Cognition*, 1977, *5*, 73–99.

Cantor, N., & Kihlstrom, J. F. Cognitive and social processes in personality: Implications for behavior therapy. In C. M. Franks & G. T. Wilson (Eds.), *Handbook of behavior therapy*. New York: Guilford Press, 1981.

Cofer, C. N. Recall of verbal materials after a four-year interval. *Journal of General Psychology*, 1943, *29*, 155–156.

Cohen, Andrew D. The Culver City Spanish Immersion Program: How does summer recess affect Spanish speaking ability. *Language Learning*, 1976, *24*, No. 1, 55–68.

Colegrove, F. W. Individual memories. *American Journal of Psychology*, 1899, *10*, 228–255.

Crovitz, H. F., & Quina-Holland, K. Proportion of episodic memories from early childhood by years of age. *Bulletin of the Psychonomic Society*, 1976, *7*(1), 61–62.

Crovitz, H. F., & Schiffman, H. Frequency of episodic memories as a function of their age. *Bulletin of the Psychonomic Society*, 1974, *4*, 517–518.

Dudycha, G. J., & Dudycha, M. M. Childhood memories: A review of the literature. *Psychological Bulletin*, 1941, *38*(8), 668–682.

Franklin, H. C., & Holding, D. H. Personal memories at different ages. *Quarterly Journal of Experimental Psychology*, 1977, *29*, 527–532.

Galton, F. *Inquiries into human faculty and its development*. London: Macmillan and Co., 1883.

Goethals, G. R., & Reckman, R. F. The perception of consistency in attitudes. *Journal of Experimental Social Psychology*, 1973, *9*, 491–501.

Havighurst, R. J., & Glasser, R. An exploratory study of reminiscence. *Journal of Gerontology*, 1972, *27*(2), 245–253.

Herrman, D. J., & Neisser, U. An inventory of everyday memory experiences. In M. M. Gruneberg, P. E. Morris, & R. M. Sykes (Eds.), *Practical aspects of memory*. New York: Academic Press, 1978.

Kihlstrom, J. F. On personality and memory. In N. Cantor & J. F. Kihlstrom (Eds.), *Personality, cognition, and social interaction*. Hillsdale, N.J.: Lawrence Erlbaum Associates, 1980.

Kinsey, A. C., Pomeroy, W. B., & Martin, C. E. *Sexual behavior in the human male*. Philadelphia, Saunders, 1948.

Kintsch, W. *The representation of meaning in memory*. Hillsdale, N.J.: Lawrence Erlbaum Associates, 1974.

Klinger, E. Modes of normal conscious flow. In K. S. Pope & J. L. Singer (Eds.), *The stream of consciousness: Scientific investigations into the flow of human experience*. New York: Plenum Press, 1978.

Lachman, R. & Mistler-Lachman, J. Dominance Lexicale ches les bilingues *Bulletin de Psychologie*, 1976, *Special Annuel La Memoire Semantique*, 281–288.

Lachman, J. L., Lachman, R. & Taylor, D. W. Reallocation of Mental Resources Over The Productive Lifespan: Assumptions and Task Analyses. In F. I. M. Craik & S. E. Trehub (Eds.), *Aging and cognitive processes*. New York: Plenum Press, 1981.

Linton, M. Memory for real world events. In D. A. Norman & D. E. Rumelhart (Eds.), *Explorations in cognition*. San Francisco: Freeman, 1975.

Linton, M. Real world memory after six years: An *in vivo* study of very long-term memory. In M. M. Gruneberg, P. E. Morris, & R. N. Sykes (Eds.), *Practical aspects of memory*. New York: Academic Press, 1978.

Linton, M. I remember it well. *Psychology Today*, July, 1979, 81–86.(a)

Lloyd, G. G., & Lishman, W. A. Effect of depression on the speed of recall of pleasant and unpleasant experiences. *Psychological Medicine*, 1975, *5*, 173–180.

Mair, W. G. P., Warrington, E. K., & Weiskrantz, L. Memory disorder in Korsakoff's psychosis. *Brain*, 1979, *102*, 749–783.

Markus, H. Self-schemata and processing information about the self. *Journal of Personality and Social Psychology*, 1977, *35*(2), 63–78.

Melton, A. W. The methodology of experimental studies of human learning and retention. I. The functions of a methodology and the available criteria for evaluating different experimental methods. *Psychological Bulletin*, 1936, *33*, 305–394.

Morgan, E., Mull, H. K., & Washburn, M. F. An attempt to test moods or temperaments of cheerfulness and depression by directed recall of emotionally toned experiences. *The American Journal of Psychology*, 1919, *30*, 302–303.

Mosak, H. H. Early recollections: Evaluation of some recent research. *Journal of Individual Psychology*, 1969, *25*(1), 56–63.

Munsat, S. *The Concept of Memory*. New York: Random House, 1966.

Neisser, U. Cognition and reality: *Principles and implications of cognitive psychology*. San Francisco: Freeman, 1976.

Neisser, U. John Dean's memory: A case study. *Cognition*. 1981, *9*, 1–22.

Neisser, U., & Hupcey, J. A. A Sherlockian Experiment. *Cognition*, 1975, *3*, 307–311.

Neisser, U., & Gold, E. Recollections of Kindergarten. *Quarterly Newsletter of the Laboratory of Comparative Human Cognition*. (In press).

Nelson, T. O. Detecting small amounts of information in memory: Savings for non-recognized items. *Journal of Experimental Psychology: Human Learning and Memory*, 1978, *4*, 453–468.

Nelson, T. O., & Narens, L. Norms of 300 general-information questions: Accuracy of recall, latency of recall, and feeling-of-knowing ratings. *Journal of Verbal Learning and Verbal Behavior*, 1980, *19*, 338–368.(a)

Nelson, T. O., & Narens, L. A new technique for investigating the feeling of knowing *Acta Psychologica*, 1980, *46*, 69–80.(b)

Neter, J., & Wasserman, W. *Applied linear statistical models*. Homewood, Il.: Irwin, 1974.

Nickerson, R. S., & Adams, M. J. Long term memory for a common object. *Cognitive Psychology*, 1979, *11*, 287–307.

Robinson, J. A. Sampling autobiographical memory. *Cognitive Psychology*, 1976, *8*, 578–595.

Rubin, D. C. Very long-term memory for prose and verse. *Journal of Verbal Learning and Verbal Behavior*, 1977, *16*, 611–621.

Sanders, H. I., & Warrington, E. K. Memory for remote events in amnesic patients. *Brain*, 1971, *94*, 661–668.

Schaie, K. W. Quasi-experimental research designs in the psychology of aging. In J. E. Birren & K. W. Schaie (Eds.), *Handbook of the Psychology of Aging*. New York: Van Nostrand Reinhold Company, 1977.

Schonfield, D., & Stones, M. J. Remembering and aging. In J. F. Kihlstrom & F. J. Evans (Eds.), *Functional disorders of memory*. Hillsdale, N.J.: Lawrence Erlbaum Associates, 1979.

Smith, M. E. Delayed recall of previously memorized material after forty years. *Journal of Genetic Psychology*, 1951, *79*, 337–338.

Smith, M. E. Childhood memories compared with those of adult life. *Journal of Genetic Psychology*, 1952, *80*, 151–182.

Smythe, P. C., Jutras, G. C., Bramwell, J. R., & Gardner, R. C. Second language retention over varying intervals. *Modern Language Journal*, 1973, *57*, 400–405.

Snyder, M., & Uranowitz, S. W. Reconstructing the past: Some cognitive consequences of personal perception. *Journal of Personality and Social Psychology*, 1978, *36*(9), 941–951.

Squire, L. R. Remote memory as affected by aging: *Neuropsychologia*, 1974, *12*, 429–435.

Squire, L. R. A stable impairment in remote memory following electroconvulsive therapy. *Neuropsychologia*, 1975, *13*, 51–58.

Squire, L. R., & Slater, P. C. Forgetting in very long-term memory as assessed by an improved questionnaire technique. *Journal of Experimental Psychology: Human Learning and Memory*, 1975, *104*(1), 50–54.

Stephenson, William. Newton's Fifth Rule and Q Methodology: Application to Educational Psychology. *American Psychologist*, 1980, *35*, 882–889.

Teasdale, J. D., & Fogarty, S. J. Differential effects of induced mood on retrieval of pleasant and unpleasant events from episodic memory. *Journal of Abnormal Psychology*, 1979, *88*(3), 248–257.

Titchener, E. B. Relearning after 48 years. *American Journal of Psychology*, 1923, *34*, 468–469.

Waldfogel, S. The frequency and affective character of childhood memories. *Psychological Monographs: General and Applied*, 1948, 62(4) (Whole No. 291).

Warrington, E. K., & Sanders, H. I. The fate of old memories. *Quarterly Journal of Experimental Psychology*, 1971, *23*, 432–442.

Warrington, E. K., & Silberstein, M. A questionnaire technique for investigating very long term memory. *Quarterly Journal of Experimental Psychology*, 1970, *22*, 508–512.

Washburn, M. F., Giang, F., Ives, M., & Pollock, M. Memory revival of emotions as a test of emotional and phlegmatic temperaments. *The American Journal of Psychology*, 1925, *36*, 456–459.

Washburn, M. F., Harding, L., Simons, H., & Tomlinson, D. Further experiments on directed recall as a test of cheerfulness and depressed temperaments. *The American Journal of Psychology*, 1925, *36*, 454–456.

Wickelgren, W. A. Trace resistance and the decay of long-term memory. *Journal of Mathematical Psychology*, 1972, *9*, 418–455.

Worcester, D. A. Learning ability and retention after long periods. *Journal of Educational Psychology*, 1957, *48*, 505–509.

Yarmey, A. D., & Bull, M. P., III. Where were you when President Kennedy was assassinated? *Bulletin of the Psychonomic Society*, 1978, *11*(2), 133–135.

Yarrow, M. R., Campbell, J. D., & Burton, R. V. Recollections of childhood: A study of the retrospective method. *Monographs of the Society for Research in Child Development*, 1970, *35* (5, Serial No. 138).

Subject Index

A

Acoustic similarity, 73–75, 86
Additive factors logic, 15–16, 243–246, 302, 307–308
Adjusted ratio of clustering, 120, 151
Advanced organizers, 363–364
Age of acquisition, 22–23
Aha effect, 404
Allocation of study time, 235–236
Approximation to English, 351–352
Articulation, 87
Associative information, 3–4
Autobigraphical memory, 429–430, 445–446, 449–460
Availability versus accessibility, 175

B

Backward counting, 197
Batch testing, 4
Beta (β)measure, 9–12
Blocked presentation, 104
Brown-Peterson task, 64–66

C

Categorization tasks
  in search, *see* Search
  in semantic memory, *see* Semantic memory
Category size effect, 291–292
Clustering, 99–104, 114–115, 119–124, 131, 144–151, 157–158, 165–166, 333, 379
  blocked versus random input and, 103–104
  category strength and, 102–103
  as confirmatory analysis, 131
  defining operations for, 99–100
  density of, 119
  errors and, 114–115
  hierarchical, 124, 165–166, 333, 379
  measures of, 119–123, 151
  testing explicit hypotheses about, 144–151, 157–158
Comprehension, *see* Knowledge utilization
Concreteness, 320
Concurrent load taks, 87–89
Conditional inference, 132–133, 136–137, 143–144

Confidence judgments, 5–6, 10, 67,
    418–419
Confirmatory analysis, 131–163
Context effects, 177–179, 183–184,
    216–218, 221–223, 289–290,
    301–302, 395–423
    in cued recall, 177–179, 183–184
    in depth of processing, 216–218
    elaborative processing as, 221–223
    in knowledge utilization, 395–423
    in semantic memory, 289–290, 301–302
Continuous-task procedure, 5
Converging operations, 252–253
Convolution, 17, 124
Corneal reflection, 278
Correlative measurement, 235–237
Counterbalancing
    in free recall, 108–112
    Latin squares and 110–111
    in picture memory, 274–275
Cross-sectional
    adjustment method, 435–440, 445–446
    designs, 434–445
Cued recall, 108, 173–193, 216–218, 375,
    406
    availability versus accessibility and, 175
    context effects in, 177–179, 183–184
    depth of processing and, 216–218
    free recall and, 108, 174–175, 191–193
    guessing and, 185–187
    in incidental learning, 216–218
    in knowledge utilization tasks, 406
    orienting tasks in, 182–183
    measures of, 184–191
    multiple-cuing in, 187–190
    paired-associates and, 176–177
    parameters of, 179–184
    in prose memory, 375
    reaction time in, 190–193
    recognition memory and, 191–193

D

d' measure, 6, 9–13, 84
Deadlline method, 19–20
Density of observations, 237
Depth of processing, 207–223
    confounding factors in, 212–216
    context and, 216–218
    cued recall and, 216–218

    encoding specificity and, 216–218
    indices of, 208–210
    processing time and, 209–210
    recognition memory and, 217–218
    retrieval conditions and, 216–218
Developmental issues, 101–106, 231–235,
    375–376
    category strength, 102–103
    list length, 101–102
    modality effects, 105
    in prose recall, 375–376
    rate of presentation, 106
    rehearsal patterns, 231–235
Differential probe task, 79–80
Direct measurement, 234–237
Discourse, *see* Prose comprehension and
    memory
Distractor tasks, 64–66, 107
Dual tasks, 87–89, 325–327, *see also* Sec-
    ondary tasks

E

Ecological memory, 427–462
    autobiographical memories, 429–430,
        445–446, 449–460
    classification framework, 428–430,
        460–462
    content areas of, 431–460
        individual-episodic memories, 449–460
        individual-semantic memories,
            445–446
        shared-episodic memory, 446–449
        shared-semantic memory, 431–445
    criteria for evaluating methods, 430–431
    flashbulb memories, 430, 454–455
    methods in studying, 431–460
        cross sectional, 434–445
        cross sectional adjustment, 435–440
        exhaustive free recall, 450–451
        longitudinal, 432–434
        prompt-word, 451–454
        questionnaire, 447–449
        self-analysis, 455–456
        semantic cuing, 452–454
        techniques that permit verification,
            455–459
        thought sampling, 456
    parameters of content, 427–462
Elaboration of processing, 221–223

Elaborative context, 221–223
Electro-oculography, 278
Encoding specificity, 178–179, 216–218
Episodic versus semantic information, *see*
  Ecological memory
Errors, 31–32, 113–115, 418–419
  in free recall, 113–115
  in knowledge utilization tasks, 418–419
  in visual search, 31–32
Exploratory analysis, 131, 163–166
Eye movements, 47–50, 55–57, 258–259,
  275–280, 379–380
  in picture memory, 258–259
  in prose comprehension, 379–380
  recording methodologies, 275–280
  in visual search, 47–50, 55–57

F

False alarms, 8–13, *see also* False
  recognition
False recognition, 218, 377, 420–423
Feeling of knowing, 459
Final recall test, 72, 82–83
Fixed set procedure, 78
Flashbulb memories, 430, 454–455
Forced choice tests, 4, 272–273, 275
FRAN model, 124
Free association, 176
Free recall, 68–72, 82–87, 99–125, 406,
  416–421, 450–451
  auditory versus visual presentation, 106
  backward counting and, 107
  blocked versus random input in,
    103–105
  category strength and, 102–103
  clustering, *see* Clustering
  counterbalancing in, 108–112
  delayed, 69–70, 416–417, 420–421
  in ecological memory, 450–451
  exhaustive, 450–451
  final recall test, 72, 82–83
  intrusions in, 113–115
  list length and, 101–102
  in knowledge utilization tasks, 406, 419
  modality effects in, 72, 85–87, 105
  numbers of categories and, 103
  organization in, *see* Organization
  priority in, *see* Priority of recall
  scoring of, 112–115

serial position effects in, *see* Serial position effects
seriation of, *see* Seriation
simultaneous presentation in, 105
as a STM task, 68–72
subjective organization in, *see* Subjective organization
rate of presentation, 106
rehearsal in, *see* Rehearsal

G

Gist recall, 374
Graph theory, 353–354

H

Hierarchical clustering, 124, 165–166, 333,
  379
High threshold, 13, 187

I

Iconic image, 280
Idea units, 352
Image detection task, 337–342
Imagery, 315–343, 365, 401
  concreteness, 320
  general issues, 316–319, 342–343
  hierarchical clustering in, 333
  instructions, 321–323, 365
  in knowledge utilization, 401
  memorization paradigms, 319–323
  mental manipulation paradigms, 333–336
    judgment task, 333
    preparation-time task, 333
    mental rotation, 333–336
    mental scanning, 333–336
  multidimensional scaling in, 333
  perceptual analog paradigms, 330–333
    psychophysical judgments in, 330–333
    similarity judgments in, 331–333
  question answering paradigms, 337–342
    mental comparison task, 337–342
    image detection task, 337–342
    image evaluation task, 337–342
  ratings of, 320
  selective interference paradigms,
    323–330
    dual task procedures, 325–327

scanning task, 327–328
signal detection in, 300
Incidental learning, 182–183, 197–225
    cued recall and, 182–183
    depth of processing in, *see* Depth of
        processing
    elaborative processing in, 221–223
    intentional learning and, 197–206
    interactions in, 223–225
    interitem processing in, 204–206, 223
    orienting tasks in, 202–225
    recall versus recognition tests in,
        204–206, 217–218, 222
    rehearsal in, 204–206, 219–222
    repetition effects in, 219–222
    Types I and II paradigms, 199–200
    Types I and II processing, 219–223
Inferential measurement, 231–234,
    236–237
Input-output analyses, 152–153, 157–158,
    see also Seriation
Instructed forgetting
Interference, 64–66, 76–77, 83–85, 366
    decay and, 83–85
    in prose memory, 366
    proactive, 64–66, 76–77
    release from proactive, 76–77
Interitem processing, 204–206, 223
Interword recall latencies, 119
Intrusions, 113–115
Iso performance curve, 18–20
Item information, 3–4

K

Knowledge activation and utilization,
    367–371, 395–423
    aha effect, 404
    content domain familiarity and, 370–371
    context in, 396–423
        after encoding, 415–423
        congruous and incongruous, 408–410
        elaborative information as, 407–410
        qualitative and quantitative, 409–410
        sequencing of target and, 402–405,
            416–423
        target significance and, 410–415
    criterial task choice, 405–407, 419–420
    issues in, 395–396
    methodological framework for, 398–406

perspective taking in, 368, 411–417
prerequisites to comprehension, 396–407
reorganization and, 417–423
schema and, 367–369
scripts and, 369–370
in text processing, 367–371

L

Lag-latency function, 16
Language as fixed effects, 21, 108–109,
    305–306, 336
Latency, *see* Reaction time
Latin squares, 110–111
Leading-edge strategy, 356
Levels of processing, *see* Depth of
    processing
Lexical decision tasks, *see* Semantic
    memory
Longitudinal designs, 432–434

M

Masking, 269–270
Memory span, 72–75
Mental comparison task, 337–342
Mental rotation, 333–336
Metamemory, 459
Micro- and macroprocesses, 356–357
Modality effects, 85–87, 336
Monte Carlo procedures, 139, 149
Multidimensional scaling, 333, 378–379
Multiflash paradigm, 279–280
Multiple regression, 436–444

N

Narrative, *see* Prose comprehension and
    memory
Negative recency effect, 72

O

Order logic, 309–310
Organization, 103–105, 116–124, 129–169
    alphabetical, 144–150
    of autobiographical memory, 459–460
    clustering, *see* Clustering
    conceptual and analytic issues in,
        131–133

conditional inference of, 132–133,
    136–137, 143–144
confirmatory analysis of, 131–163
exploratory analysis of, 131, 163–166
hierarchical clustering, see Hierarchical
    clustering
input, 103–10, 123
input-output analyses, 152–153, 157–158
interword latencies and, 119
item-pair information, 144–159
output-output analyses, see Subjective
    organization
primary, 116–119, see also Serial posi-
    tion effects
priority of recall, 156–157, 168–169,
    378–379
rehearsal and, 123
secondary, 119–123
of semantic memory, 287
seriation, see Seriation
single-item information in, 133–144
subjective organization, see Subjective
    organization
two dimesional (2D) recall and, 124,
    159, 166–167
unconditional inference of, 132–144
Orienting tasks, see Incidental learning

P

Paired-associates, 67–68, 176–177
Parameter estimation, 244–245, 376–377
Pausal units, 352–353
Pause time technique, 235–236
Payoff matrix, 9–10
Perceptual analogs paradigms, 330–333
Perspective taking, 368, 411–417
Picture memory, 257–282
    counterbalancing in, 274–275
    display devices for, 264–267
    eye movement methodologies, 275–280
    issues in, 258–259
    masking in, 269–270
    paradigms in, 260–261
    sample experiment, 280–282
    serial position effects in, 262–263
    stimulus parameters, 261–264
    types of tests in, 270–274
Point-of-regard evaluation, 277–278
Preload tasks, 88–89

Prememorized lists paradigm, 16
Preparation-time task, 333
Primacy effect, 67, 74, 231–233, 361–362
Priming, 45–46, 360
Priority of recall (PRNI), 118, 141–142
Proactive interference, 64–66, 76–77
Proactive interference (PI) release, 76–77
Probe tasks, 66–74, 79–80, 176–177, 232,
    274
    differential, 79–80
    paired-associates, 176–177
    in picture memory, 274
    position, 232
    in recall, 66–74
    in recognition, 77–80
    sequential, 66
Problem solving, see Strategies
Processing, 204–206, 209–210, 219–223,
    357
    depth of, see Depth of processing
    elaboration of, 221–223
    interitem, 204–206, 223
    of text, see Prose comprehension and
        memory
    time, 209–210
    top-down, 357
    Types I and II, 219–223
Proportion of variance accounted for,
    244–245
Propositional representation, 359–360
Prose comprehension and memory,
    144–159, 164, 168–169, 349–382
    definitions, 350–351
    knowledge and text processing, 367–371
        content domain familiarity and,
            370–371
        perspective taking, 368
        schema, 367–369
        scripts, 369–370
    measures of, 371–382
        eye monitoring, 379–380
        organization, 156–157, 168–169,
            378–379
        reading time, 380–381
        recall, 374–377
        recognition, 377–378
    situational variables in text processing,
        363–367
        advanced organizers, 363–364
        imagery instructions, 365

interference effects, 366
learning objectives, 364
modality and rate, 366
text structure specification, 351–363
graph theory and, 353–354
hierarchical structure, 360
idea units, 352
micro- and macroprocesses, 356–357
pausal units, 352–353
propositional representation, 359–360
readability, 363
rewrite rules, 357–358
secondary-task technique, 355
story grammars, 357–359
surface structure, 360–361
text scrambling, 361
why technique, 360
Proximity data analysis, 144–159, 164
Psychophysical judgments, 330–333

Q

Quasi-F statistic, 21, 305-306, 336
Question answering paradigm, 337–342

R

Ratio of repetition, 119
Reaction times, 15–16, 27–59, 190–191,
243–246, 300, 302–308, 336, 381,
451
additive factors logic and, 15–16,
243–246, 302, 307–308
in autobiographic memory, 451
in cued recall, 190–191
for errors, 304–305
in imagery studies, 336
long values of, 302–303
minimizing variability in, 300
in problem solving, 242–246
in prose comprehension, 381
in semantic memory tasks, 302–305
speed-accuracy trade offs, 18–20,
31–32, 44, 304–305
transformation issue, 302, 336
in visual search, 27–59
Readability, 363
Reading time, 380–381
Real-life memory, *see* Ecological memory
Reasoning, *see* Strategies

Recall, 2, 4, 64–77, 204–206, 217–218,
222, 270–271, 374–377, 433–434,
see also Free recall
paradigms in short-term memory, 64–77
in picture memory, 270–271
in prose memory, 374–377
recognition and, 2, 4, 204–206, 217–218,
222, 433–434
Recency effect, 68–74, 105, *see also* Serial position effects
Recency judgments
Recognition memory, 1–23, 31–32, 44, 84,
204–206, 217–218, 222, 272–275,
304–305, 406, 419–423, 433–434,
see also Search
basic processes in, 2
d' measure of, 6, 9–13, 84
false alarms in, 8–13
forced choice tests of, 272–275
guidelines for experiments on, 20–23
in incidental learning, 204–206,
217–218, 222
in knowledge utilization tasks, 406,
419–423
latency measures of, 5–6, 14–20
measures of, 5–20
in picture memory, 272–275
in prose memory, 377–378
recall and, 2, 4, 204–206, 217–218, 222,
433–434
ROC curve, 11–14
signal detection analysis, 6–14
speed accuracy tradeoffs in, 18–20,
31–32, 44, 304–305
stages in, 26, 15
two alternative forced choice (2AFC)
test, 272–273, 275
types of information in, 3
types of procedures in, 5
types of tests in, 4
yes-no tests, 272, 274–275
Reconstruction test, 273
Rehearsal, 81–83, 87–88, 204–206,
213–222, 231–236, 435–444
concurrent load tasks and, 87–88
displaced, 213–216
in ecological memory, 435–444
in incidental learning, 204–206, 213–216,
219–222
maintenance, 82–83

output order and, 81
overt rehearsal technique, 81–82, 235
pause-time technique, 235–236
serial position effects and, 81
sets, 80, 232
strategies, *see* Strategies
Release from PI, 76–77
Relatedness effect, 288, 294
Relatedness ratings, 294, 299
Relational density, 360
Reliability of methods, 431
Repetition effects, 219–222
Repisodic memories, 458
Response-signal method, 19–20
Retrieval conditions, 216–218
Rewrite rules, 357–358
ROC curves, 11–14
Rule assessment, 239–242

S

Scanning, 15–17, 77–79, 327–328,
    333–336, see also Search
  mental, 333–336
  task, 77–79, 327–328
Schema, 367–369
Scrambling of text, 361
Scripts, 369–370
Search, 27–59, *see also* Recognition
    memory
  active control of, 56–58
  categorized stimuli in, 35–47
  categorization tasks in, 28–35
  positional effects in, 58
  semantic factors in, 29, 45–46
  sequential effects in, 52–54
  sorting tasks in, 28–30, 37–38, 48
  speed-accuracy trade offs in, 31–32, 44
  word-superiority effect in, 55–56
Secondary organization, 119–123
Secondary task technique, 355, *see also*
    Dual tasks
Selective interference paradigm, 323–330
Semantic congruity effect, 340–341
Semantic cuing technique, 452–454
Semantic decision task, *see* Semantic
    memory
Semantic knowledge, *see* Semantic
    memory
Semantic memory, 287–310

category size effect, 291–292
context effects in, 289–290, 301–302
controls in, 293–298
errors data in, 301, 304–305
logics in, 307–310
  additive factors, 307–308
  order, 309–310
  substractive, 308–309
organization of, 287
possible confoundings in, 291–293
quasi-F statistic, 305–306
ratings of materials for, 294–295,
    298–300
reaction time measures in, 290–291, 295
relatedness effect in, 288–290, 294
semantic versus lexical decisions,
    287–288
speed-accuracy tradeoffs in, 304–305
typicality effect in, 288–290, 294
word frequency effect in, 290–291, 295
word length effect, 295
Sequential probe task, 66
Serial-order information, 3–4
Serial position effects, 67–74, 81, 85–87,
    105–117, 231–233, 262–263,
    361–363
modality effects and, 86
negative recency effect, 72
in picture memory, 262–263
primacy effect, 67, 74, 231–233
in prose memory, 361–363
recency effect, 68–74
rehearsal and, 81, 231–233
testing explicit hypotheses about,
    133–142
Seriation, 117–118, 134, 139–141, 161–163
Short-term memory, 63–92
acoustic similarity in, 73–75, 86
capacity estimating formulas, 89–92
concurrent load tasks in, 87–89
distractor tasks in, 64–77
dual tasks in, 87–89
interference in, 64–66, 76–77
memory span studies, 72–75
modality effects in, 72, 85–87
preload tasks in, 88–89
probe tasks in, 66–74, 77–80
recall paradigms in, 64–77
rehearsal and, 80–85
release from PI in, 76–77

scanning tasks in, 77–79, *see also* Search
serial position effects in, 67–72, 74, 85–86
serial recall tasks in, 72–75
task comparisons, 75–76
Signal detection, 6–14, 330
Similarity judgments, 331–333, 378–379
Sorting, 379
Speed-accuracy tradeoffs, 31–32, 44, 304–305
Story recall, *see* Prose memory
Strategies, 229–253, 298, 356
  defined, 229–253, 298, 356
  general issues in, 251–253
  leading edge, 356
  in memory, 231–237
    correlative measurement of, 234–237
    direct measurement of, 234–237
    inferential measurement of, 231–234, 236–237
  in problem solving, 237–251
    response latency analysis in, 242–246
    response pattern analysis of, 238–242
    rule assessment and, 239–242
    task analysis of, 237–239
    thinking aloud and, 246–251
    verbal reports of, 246–251
  rehearsal, 231–237
  in semantic tasks, 298
Study-test procedure, 5
Subject-item interaction, 21–22
Subjective organization, 99–100, 104–105, 114–115, 120–123
  defining operations for, 99–100
  errors and, 114–115
  higher-order units of, 159–161
  input order and, 104–105
  measurement issues, 153–161
  measures of, 120–123
  testing explicit hypotheses about, 153–157
Substraction logic, 308–309

Surface structure, 360–361

T

Task analysis, 237–239
Text, *see* Prose comprehension and memory
Thought sampling, 456
Top-down processing, 357
Topic signalling, 361–362
Training-and-transfer paradigm, 36–37
Two-dimensional (2D) recall, 124, 159, 166–167
Types I and II, 119–200, 219–223
  paradigms, 119–200
  processing, 219–223
Typicality, 288–290, 294–295
  effect, 288–290, 294
  ratings, 294–295

U

Unconditional inference, 132–144
Uninhibited free recall, 114

V

Validity of methods, 430–431
Varied set procedure, 78
Verbalizations, 234, 246
Verbal reports, 246–251, 382
Verification tasks, *see* Semantic memory
Very long-term memory, *see* Ecological memory
Vincentizing, 17, 118
Visual search, *see* Search

W

"Why" technique, 360
Word frequency effect, 290–291, 295
Word length effect, 295
Word superiority effect, 55–56

ACADEMIC PRESS
SERIES IN COGNITION AND PERCEPTION

SERIES EDITORS:
Edward C. Carterette
Morton P. Friedman
Department of Psychology
University of California, Los Angeles
Los Angeles, California

Stephen K. Reed: *Psychological Processes in Pattern Recognition*

Earl B. Hunt: *Artificial Intelligence*

James P. Egan: *Signal Detection Theory and ROC Analysis*

Martin F. Kaplan and Steven Schwartz (Eds.): *Human Judgment and Decision Processes*

Myron L. Braunstein: *Depth Perception Through Motion*

R. Plomp: *Aspects of Tone Sensation*

Martin F. Kaplan and Steven Schwartz (Eds.): *Human Judgment and Decision Processes in Applied Settings*

Bikkar S. Randhawa and William E. Coffman: *Visual Learning, Thinking, and Communication*

Robert B. Welch: *Perceptual Modification: Adapting to Altered Sensory Environments*

Lawrence E. Marks: *The Unity of the Senses: Interrelations among the Modalities*

Michele A. Wittig and Anne C. Petersen (Eds.): *Sex-Related Differences in Cognitive Functioning: Developmental Issues*

Douglas Vickers: *Decision Processes in Visual Perception*

Margaret A. Hagen (Ed.): *The Perception of Pictures, Vol. 1: Alberti's Window: The Projective Model of Pictorial Information, Vol. 2 Dürer's Devices: Beyond the Projective Model of Pictures*

Graham Davies, Hadyn Ellis and John Shepherd (Eds.): *Perceiving and Remembering Faces*

Hubert Dolezal: *Living in a World Transformed: Perceptual and Performatory Adaptation to Visual Distortion*

Gerald H. Jacobs: *Comparative Color Vision*

Diana Deutsch (Ed.): *The Psychology of Music*

John A. Swets and Ronald M. Pickett: *Evaluation of Diagnostic Systems: Methods from Signal Detection Theory*

Trygg Engen: *The Perception of Odors*

C. Richard Puff (Ed.): *Handbook of Research Methods in Human Memory and Cognition*